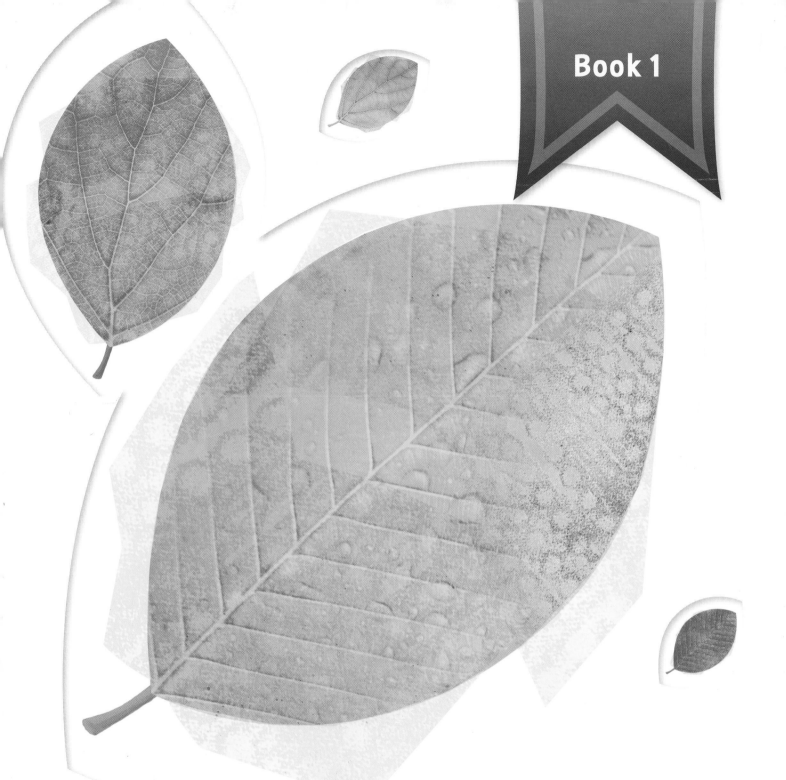

Book 1

Language Arts
Lesson Guide

Book Staff and Contributors

Beth Zemble   *Director, Alternative Learning Strategies; Director, English Language Arts*
Marianne Murphy   *Content Specialist*
Anna Day   *Senior Instructional Designer*
Cheryl Howard, Jenn Marrewa, David Shireman, Frances Suazo   *Instructional Designers*
Mary Beck Desmond   *Senior Text Editor*
Ron Stanley   *Text Editor*
Suzanne Montazer   *Creative Director, Print and ePublishing*
Sasha Blanton   *Senior Print Visual Designer*
David Batchelor, Carol Leigh   *Print Visual Designers*
Stephanie Williams   *Cover Designer*
Amy Eward   *Senior Manager, Writers*
Susan Raley   *Senior Manager, Editors*
Seth Herz   *Director, Program Management Grades K–8*

Maria Szalay   *Senior Vice President for Product Development*
John Holdren   *Senior Vice President for Content and Curriculum*
David Pelizzari   *Vice President, Content and Curriculum*
Kim Barcas   *Vice President, Creative*
Laura Seuschek   *Vice President, Instructional Design and Evaluation & Research*
Aaron Hall   *Vice President, Program Management*

Lisa Dimaio Iekel   *Production Manager*
John Agnone   *Director of Publications*

Credits

About K12 Inc.

K12 Inc., a technology-based education company, is the nation's leading provider of proprietary curriculum and online education programs to students in grades K–12. K^{12} provides its curriculum and academic services to online schools, traditional classrooms, blended school programs, and directly to families. K12 Inc. also operates the K^{12} International Academy, an accredited, diploma-granting online private school serving students worldwide. K^{12}'s mission is to provide any child the curriculum and tools to maximize success in life, regardless of geographic, financial, or demographic circumstances. K12 Inc. is accredited by CITA. More information can be found at www.K12.com.

ISBN-13: 978-1-60153-168--1
ISBN-10: 1-60153-168-0
Printed by RR Donnelley, Roanoke, VA, USA, June 2011, Lot 062011

Contents

Literature & Comprehension

Furry Friends

Flying Friends

Poetry

Classics for All Ages

A Weed is a Flower

Winds and Wings

Rome (A)

Rome (B)

Vocabulary

Writing Skills

Complete Sentences

Write Sentences

Kinds of Sentences

Write Different Types of Sentences

Nouns

Write Steps

Verbs

Sequence Events

Capitalization and Punctuation in a Letter

Write Friendly Letters

Complete and Revise a Paragraph

Semester Review and Checkpoint

Polish and Publish a Paragraph

K¹² Language Arts Orange

General Program Overview and Structure

The K¹² Language Arts Orange program lays a strong foundation for growing readers and novice writers by focusing on comprehension (understanding what you read and uncovering how authors create meaning) and communication (sharing ideas through writing and speaking).

According to the National Reading Panel, a comprehensive reading program includes fluency, text comprehension, spelling, vocabulary, and writing skills. K¹² Language Arts Orange meets these criteria with five independent but related courses:

- ► Literature & Comprehension
- ► Spelling
- ► Vocabulary
- ► Writing Skills
- ► Handwriting

You will spend about two hours each day working with K¹² Language Arts Orange. The following tables describe the courses in the program, the time you can expect to spend on them, and the overarching Big Ideas that are covered.

Course	Daily Lesson Time (approximate)	Online/Offline
K¹² Language Arts Orange Literature & Comprehension	60 minutes	Alternates every other lesson: 60 minutes offline or 10 minutes online, 50 minutes offline
Big Ideas		

- *Guided Reading*   Guided reading teaches students the skills they require to become proficient, independent readers.
- *Fluency*   The ability to decode text quickly, smoothly, and automatically allows readers to focus on comprehension.
- *Comprehension*   Comprehension requires readers to actively think, ask themselves questions, and synthesize information to make meaning from their reading.
- *Analysis*   Readers must pay careful attention to language and literary elements to appreciate the underlying meanings or message of a poet or author's work.
- *Enjoyment*   To develop a lifelong love of reading, new readers should independently read for their own enjoyment.

Course	Daily Lesson Time (approximate)	Online/Offline
K¹² Language Arts Orange Spelling	15 minutes	Each unit: 4 offline lessons, 1 online review
Big Ideas		

- Spelling represents sounds, syllables, and meaningful parts of words.
- The spelling of all English words can be explained by rules or patterns related to word origins.
- Students benefit from spelling instruction that gradually builds on previously mastered concepts of letter-sound relationships.
- Engaging spelling activities help students develop spelling skills needed for both writing and reading.
- Spelling ability correlates to reading comprehension ability.

Course	Daily Lesson Time (approximate)	Online/Offline
K¹² Language Arts Orange Vocabulary	30 minutes	All online
Big Ideas		

- Vocabulary words are words we need to know to communicate and understand.
- A *speaking vocabulary* includes the words we know and can use when speaking.
- A *reading vocabulary* includes the words we know and can read with understanding.
- A *listening vocabulary* includes the words we know and understand when we hear them.
- A *writing vocabulary* includes the words we know and understand when we write.
- The more we read, the more our vocabulary grows.
- Early learners acquire vocabulary through active exposure (by talking and listening, being read to, and receiving explicit instruction).

Course	Daily Lesson Time (approximate)	Online/Offline
K¹² Language Arts Orange Writing Skills	15 minutes	Each unit (approximately): 4 offline lessons, 1 online lesson

Big Ideas

Composition

- Developing writers should study models of good writing.
- Writing can be broken out into a series of steps, or a process, that will help developing writers become more proficient.
- All writers revise, and revision is best performed in discrete tasks.

Grammar, Usage, and Mechanics (GUM)

- Using different kinds of sentences helps writers and speakers express their ideas accurately.
- A noun is a basic part of speech. Understanding nouns gives students a basic vocabulary for building sentences and understanding how language works.
- Recognizing and using action verbs helps writers make their work specific and interesting to readers.
- The use of descriptive adjectives can turn an ordinary piece of writing into one that enables the audience to form clear mental pictures of a scene.
- Using a wide range of adverbs allows a writer to convey specific information about how, when, or where an action occurs.
- Using capital letters correctly draws the reader's attention to important people and places.
- Using commas to separate items in a series makes both reading and understanding the items easier.
- A simple way to give writing a less formal tone is to use contractions.

Course	Daily Lesson Time (approximate)	Online/Offline
K¹² Language Arts Orange Handwriting	10 minutes	All offline

Big Ideas

- Instruction in posture, pencil grip, and letter formation improves students' handwriting skills.
- Proper modeling of letter formation is imperative for developing handwriting skills.
- Students who have formal instruction in handwriting are more engaged in composition writing.

The separation of instruction into the five courses that make up the K[12] Language Arts Orange program offers many benefits for you and students:

- **Focus** – Separate courses allow you to concentrate on one skill at a time. For example, students can develop their reading comprehension skills independent of the skills they need for formal writing. Similarly, they can practice their handwriting outside the writing course, in which they will focus on communicating their ideas in a structured and orderly composition without worrying about penmanship.
- **Self-pacing** – The focused lessons enable you to identify if students understand a skill and whether to move on or work more on that skill. You can decide the pace that works best for students in each course.
- **Organization** – Focused lessons make content easier to find online and in your books. Just use the descriptive titles in the lesson list and table of contents.
- **Visibility** – Progress, mastery, and attendance can be tracked per course, so you can see at a glance how students are progressing in each course.
- **Flexibility** – Separate courses let you take natural breaks. For example, you can work on Language Arts courses at different times of the day, perhaps with Vocabulary before lunch and Writing Skills after dinner. You decide.

Suggested Order of Lessons

We recommend that students complete the Language Arts lessons in the following order each day:

1. Literature & Comprehension

2. Spelling

3. Vocabulary

4. Writing Skills

5. Handwriting

However, a key aspect of K[12] Language Arts Orange is the flexibility it offers students. Following an order that works best for students is vital to their mastery of material. If students benefit from completing the Handwriting lesson first thing in the morning and closing the day with Literature & Comprehension, that is acceptable.

(TIP) After you've completed a unit or two in a course, you'll be familiar with the pattern of the units and lessons, and you'll know exactly where and how to begin. Use these patterns to your advantage if you need to rearrange your day or travel.

How to Work Through a Lesson

Types of Activities

The K[12] Language Arts Orange courses contain offline and online activities as well as assessments.

Offline Activities   Offline activities take place away from the computer. Review the plans in the Lesson Guide, and then work closely with students to complete the activities.

Online Activities   Online activities take place at the computer. At first, you may need to help students learn how to navigate and use the online activities. You may also need to provide support when activities cover new or challenging content. As the course progresses, you will likely find students can complete online activities with minimal support from you. You can then use this time to prepare for the next offline activity or the next course.

Offline Assessments   All assessments in Literature & Comprehension, Spelling, and Writing Skills are done away from the computer, using pencil and paper or oral responses.

- **Literature and Comprehension** assessments, called Semester Checkpoints, will only occur at the end of each semester. In these assessments, students will read short literary selections, and you will assess students' prereading strategies, basic comprehension, and literary analysis through a series of oral questions and written responses. You will also periodically evaluate students' reading fluency.
- **Spelling** features an offline assessment at the end of each unit. Students will complete a Unit Checkpoint covering the spelling of the words from that unit.
- **Writing Skills** has two kinds of assessments, Unit Checkpoint and Write Now, one of which will appear at the end of each unit. The Unit Checkpoint assesses students' mastery of grammar, usage, and mechanics, and the Write Now assessment is a composition assignment. Each semester will end with a Semester Checkpoint that assesses students' mastery of all the grammar, usage, and mechanics from that semester.

For all offline assessments, you will use Answer Keys or rubrics to score students' work. Then enter the results online so that you will have an accurate record of students' knowledge. After you have scored students' work, you will have an opportunity to help students review, revise their work, and even retake the assessment, if necessary.

Online Assessments   Students will complete online assessments, called Unit Checkpoints, in the Vocabulary course. Because these assessments are all online, the computer will score them for you. After students complete the assessment, review with them each exercise that they missed. Students may retake the assessment anytime, though waiting until the next day is recommended.

Where to Begin?

You may begin a lesson in more than one way; either way will get you where you need to go.

Beginning Online (recommended)   We recommend that you begin lessons online. The online lesson screens will walk you through what you need to do, including gathering materials and moving offline. If any materials have been updated, you will have access to them in the online lesson. If the lesson begins with online activities, students will need to come to the computer and complete them. If the lesson begins with offline activities, gather the materials listed and begin the activities described in the lesson plan with students when you're ready.

Beginning Offline   If you do choose to begin a lesson offline, start by checking the lesson overview in the Lesson Guide. The table on the first page of the lesson plan will indicate whether the lesson begins with online or offline activities. If the lesson begins with online activities, students will need to move to the computer and complete them. If the lesson begins with offline activities, gather the materials listed and begin the activities described in the lesson plan with students when you're ready.

How to Use This Book

K¹² Language Arts Lesson Guide contains overviews for the courses in K¹² Language Arts Orange and lesson plans for the Literature & Comprehension, Vocabulary, and Writing Skills courses. Lesson plans for the Spelling and Handwriting courses appear in separate books.

Read and Refer to Course Overviews: Read the course overviews before you begin each course, and refer back to them if you have questions about the courses.

Use the Lesson Plans: Each lesson plan gives you detailed instructions for completing the lesson. The first page of each lesson plan contains some or all of the following elements, depending on the course and lesson . (The example that follows is from a Literature & Comprehension lesson.)

TIP There are a lot of scripted directions and questions in the lesson plans. Why? They are there to ensure that students master the objectives. Follow the plans in the order that they are written and you will help students move through the necessary steps to become a strong and confident reader, communicator, and writer.

Course Name
This banner identifies the section of the book. Each course has its own banner color, so you can easily flip to a section if you know the color.

Lesson Title
The title indicates the lesson topic.

Unit Overview
Content covered in the unit is described in the first lesson of each unit.

Lesson Overview Table
Look here to see an overview of the lesson's activities, their approximate times, and whether they take place online or offline.

Advance Preparation
This section describes what you need to prepare before beginning the lesson.

Big Ideas
These points are the major organizing ideas in Language Arts students will work toward.

Materials
This box lists all materials needed for the lesson and indicates whether they are Supplied or Also Needed.

Story Synopsis
In Literature & Comprehension lessons, read this section for a brief summary of the reading selection.

Keywords
This section lists definitions of teaching terminology specific to the lesson.

Page Number
Each page number is preceded by an abbreviation corresponding to the section of the book you are in.

LC = Literature & Comprehension
VOC = Vocabulary
WS = Writing Skills

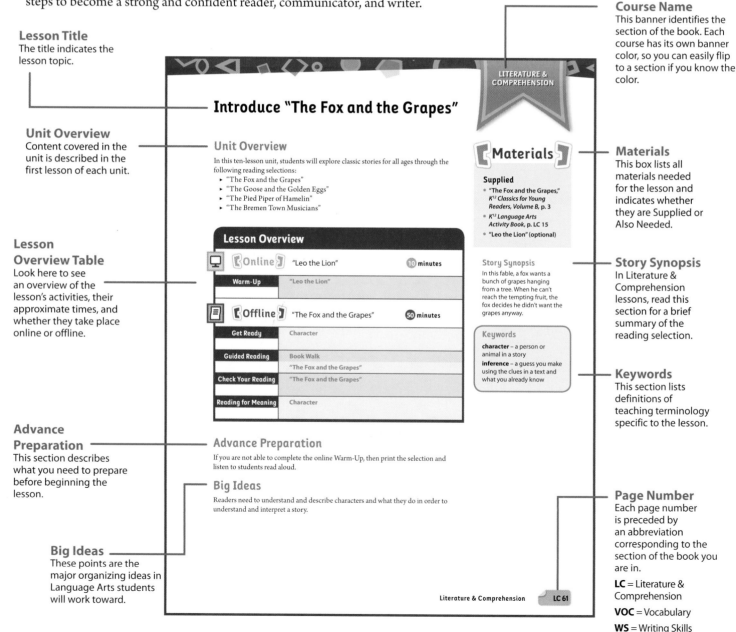

Look for Icons

The lesson plans contain icons to help you quickly see key elements as you work through the lesson. Look for these icons as you use the lesson plans.

Icon	Description
🖥 **⟨Online⟩**	Shows that an activity is online.
📄 **⟨Offline⟩**	Shows that an activity is offline.
TIP	Tips offer additional advice to help you explain the content.
✏	This pencil appears next to activities that provide students with the opportunity to practice their handwriting.
🎖	This blue ribbon indicates that you have reached a milestone that should be rewarded, usually by adding a sticker to the My Accomplishments chart.
⊕ OPTIONAL:	Indicates that an activity is optional.

TIP Schedule time to read over lessons and prepare for each day. Gather your materials in advance, and pay close attention to the Advance Preparation instructions for each lesson.

My Accomplishments Chart

Research shows that rewarding students for quality work and purposeful effort can increase their motivation. To help you reward students, you will receive a My Accomplishments chart for each course in K[12] Language Arts Orange and a sticker sheet. These charts give students a tangible record of their progress and accomplishments throughout the Language Arts program.

The My Accomplishments charts can be found at the front of K[12] *Language Arts Activity Book.*

Throughout the online lessons and the offline materials, look for the reward icon 🏵, which indicates when and where students should place a sticker on the chart.

Encourage students to set goals and watch their stickers accumulate. Praise students to help them understand the connection between their own growing skill set and the My Accomplishments charts. By the end of each course, students should have filled up the charts. (For specific information about how to use the chart in each course, see the My Accomplishments Chart section in the following individual course overviews.)

TIP Help students proudly display and share their accomplishments with others by placing the charts somewhere visible, such as on the refrigerator or wall.

Noodleverse

Do your students have a favorite online activity? Do you wish you could find a favorite activity or practice a skill without hunting through lessons? If so, you and your students will enjoy exploring Noodleverse—K[12]'s fun portal to many of the review and practice activities in the Language Arts program. The online lessons contain links to Noodleverse, where students can create a "buddy" to help them explore, navigate to engaging locations to browse activities, and mark activities as favorites for quick access later. You'll be able to pull up a site map listing every activity, organized by course and topic.

Here are some of the Language Arts items that can be found in Noodleverse:

- Audio recordings of stories and poems from K[12] *Classics for Young Readers, Volume B*
- A book browser for choosing books in Literature & Comprehension
- Spelling practice activities
- Vocabulary practice activities
- Writing Skills practice activities
- Graphic organizers
- Letter Train activities for Handwriting

Student Portfolios

As students work through the K[12] Language Arts Orange program, we recommend keeping a student portfolio as a record of their progress. A simple folder, large envelope, or three-ring binder would work. Students will write on the *K[12] Language Arts Activity Book* pages. If you pull out the pages as students complete them, periodically place the completed pages in the portfolio. The following are examples of the kinds of materials that you should store for each course:

Literature & Comprehension   *K[12] Language Arts Activity Book* pages; your notes from Fluency Check activities

Writing Skills   *K[12] Language Arts Activity Book* pages; any prewriting, drafts, and published compositions; your feedback pages for Write Now assignments

Handwriting   Handwriting samples

(TIP) Look back through the portfolio monthly and at the end of the program with students and celebrate their progress and achievements.

K¹² Language Arts Orange Literature & Comprehension Course Overview

Course	Daily Lesson Time (approximate)	Online/Offline
K¹² Language Arts Orange Literature & Comprehension	60 minutes	Alternates every other lesson: 60 minutes offline *or* 10 minutes online, 50 minutes offline

Course Structure and Materials	
33 Units that vary in length: • 27 units of fiction, nonfiction, and poetry selections • 4 units of Reader's Choice • 2 Semester Checkpoints	**Materials:** • *K12 Language Arts Lesson Guide* • *K12 Language Arts Activity Book* • *K12 Language Arts Assessments* • *K12 Classics for Young Readers, Volume B* • 3 nonfiction magazines: *Wings, Antennae, and Tails*; *All About Ancient Rome*; *Stories of America* • 12 trade books

Course Philosophy

K¹² Language Arts Literature & Comprehension courses for the primary grades includes four effective instructional approaches to reading: read aloud, shared reading, guided reading, and independent reading. Each one contributes to a child's skill level and ability to apply specific reading strategies. K¹² Literature and Comprehension courses for younger students include read aloud and shared reading approaches, as appropriate for early readers. K¹² Language Arts Orange starts with guided reading and throughout the year students progress toward independent reading.

Read Aloud

What Is It?   A proficient reader (in this case, you) reads aloud to students carefully selected texts from various genres. The texts have features that lend themselves to modeling what good readers do. Read aloud is used in K¹² Language Arts Blue and Green.

Shared Reading

What Is It?   In shared reading, students join in reading text while guided by a proficient reader (in this case, you). Shared reading is introduced in K¹² Language Arts Green.

Guided Reading

What Is It?   In guided reading, students read books that have been selected to challenge them and give them problem-solving opportunities. They become familiar with each new book through instruction that supports and enables them to read text themselves.

Why We Do It   Guided reading gives students the chance to use strategies they already know when reading a new text. They will also acquire and practice new reading strategies as they problem-solve and read for meaning. While the Learning Coach provides assistance and modeling, the ultimate goal is for students to read independently. Through shared reading, students learned how print works and how to monitor their understanding of text. Guided reading is the natural next step during which students learn to apply problem-solving strategies when they encounter difficulties decoding and understanding text.

The guided reading scripts for Learning Coaches may seem long, but they are there to help you demonstrate how good readers read. As you work through a guided reading activity, you'll help students apply decoding and comprehension strategies. Students acquire and practice new reading strategies as they listen and ultimately read for themselves. Your role is to follow the script to show students how to work through reading a text. For students to see and hear what you do as you read will enable them to apply known strategies to improve their own comprehension when they come to a difficult word or phrase when they read on their own.

Independent Reading

What Is It?   During independent reading, students need to read books at a level just right for them, or their independent level. The independent reading units in K^{12} Language Arts Orange are based on texts that are at the correct reading level for students.

Why We Do It   Independent reading gives students the opportunity to practice reading for extended blocks of time and independently apply the decoding and comprehension strategies they learned during guided reading. Independent reading both builds fluency and leads to vocabulary development, which has a significant effect on reading achievement. By reading a variety of texts, students are exposed to a variety of topics and information, all of which help them build background knowledge that will contribute to their understanding texts they read in the future.

Reading Approaches in Literature & Comprehension

The Literature & Comprehension course is divided into thirds so that Learning Coaches can model the skills developing readers need. In the first part of the course, you will use guided reading strategies with students. Then, after Unit 10, students will begin to read parts of the selections independently. In the last portion of the course, students will read independently.

Course Section	Reading Approach	Learning Coach Responsibilities
First Third of Course	**Guided Reading**	• Read with students. • Model reading strategies.
Second Third of Course	**Guided Reading** **Independent Reading**	• Read a portion aloud to students while modeling reading strategies; then students finish the reading on their own. • Help students identify and use reading strategies as they read independently.
Last Third of Course	**Independent Reading**	• Have students read on their own, silently or aloud. • Check for comprehension and help students adjust use of reading strategies if necessary.

TIP The literature selections in the course were carefully selected and organized in a manner that complements the reading approaches. We highly recommend that you complete the units in order.

Overview of Literature & Comprehension Lessons

Supplied Materials

The Literature & Comprehension portion of K[12] Language Arts Orange is a blend of fiction, nonfiction, drama, and poetry. Reading selections including classic stories, new favorites, and topics that have been carefully chosen for grade-level readability and interest. Students will read short fiction, plays, poems, nonfiction selections, and longer books.

The following books are supplied for Literature & Comprehension:

K[12] Language Arts Lesson Guide

K[12] Language Arts Activity Book

K[12] Language Arts Assessments

K[12] Classics for Young Readers, Volume B

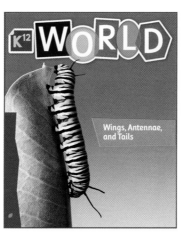

Nonfiction Magazine: Wings, Antennae, and Tails

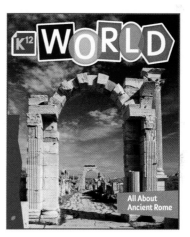

Nonfiction Magazine: All About Ancient Rome

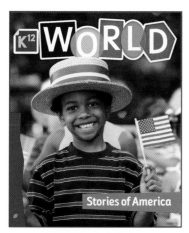

Nonfiction Magazine: Stories of America

The following trade books are also supplied:

- *Buddy: The First Seeing Eye Dog* by Eva Moore
- *Cam Jansen: The Mystery of the Stolen Diamonds* by David A. Adler
- *Clara and the Bookwagon* by Nancy Smiler Levinson
- *Listen, My Children: Poems for Second Graders* edited by Susan Tyler Hitchcock
- *Peter Pan* by J.M. Barrie, adapted by Cathy East Dubowski
- *Sam the Minuteman* by Nathaniel Benchley
- *Surprises!* poems selected by Lee Bennett Hopkins
- *The Bears on Hemlock Mountain* by Alice Dalgliesh
- *The Josefina Story Quilt* by Eleanor Coerr
- *The Long Way Westward* by Joan Sandin
- *Volcanoes! Mountains of Fire* by Eric Arnold
- *A Weed is a Flower: The Life of George Washington Carver* by Aliki

Other Materials

Always have paper and pencils available. You will sometimes also need the following general materials to complete Activity Book pages:

- crayons or colored pencils
- scissors (Safety note: When students are working with scissors, please supervise them to make sure they use their scissors safely and stay seated.)
- glue

Additional materials, ranging from index cards to library books, may be needed for certain lessons.

Four times a year, with your guidance, students will choose a book they want to read from a set list of selections. Selecting their own reading materials motivates students to read more. In turn, they improve their reading ability. You will need to acquire these books on your own from a library or a bookstore. See the Reader's Choice Units section for more details.

How to Use the Materials

Students will write in and tear pages out of the Activity Book and the Assessments book. They will often begin working on a page from the Activity Book in one lesson and then refer back to it or complete it in later lessons. Remember to build students' portfolios with completed Activity Book pages and the occasional assessment.

TIP Look for instructions in Advance Preparation and tips within activities for saving and gathering materials that get used over more than one lesson. Also check the Materials list online or in your Lesson Guide before each lesson to make sure you have all the materials you need.

Lesson Structure

The Literature & Comprehension course consists of 33 units with reading selections from the *Classics* anthology, nonfiction magazines, trade books, and the choice book list. Each lesson should take about 60 minutes to complete.

Lessons occur in a sequence designed to meet new readers' needs and are developmentally appropriate for early readers' growing comprehension abilities. Units vary from 1 to 13 lessons, depending on the length and number of reading selections that they cover. The lessons within a unit follow a basic pattern of activities. Most of your time is spent offline reading and studying the literature selections, as you see in the following table, but every other lesson begins with an online Warm-Up for fluency practice (see Day 2 and Day 4 below). After the last fluency practice in a unit, you will have the option of listening to students' recorded readings and checking for fluency (see Day 4 below). Some lessons will also include activities where students put together many of the ideas from their reading and apply them in a Making Connections activity (see Day 4 below).

This table shows the basic pattern of activities for Literature & Comprehension lessons, but the number of lessons and the actual activities in a unit will vary.

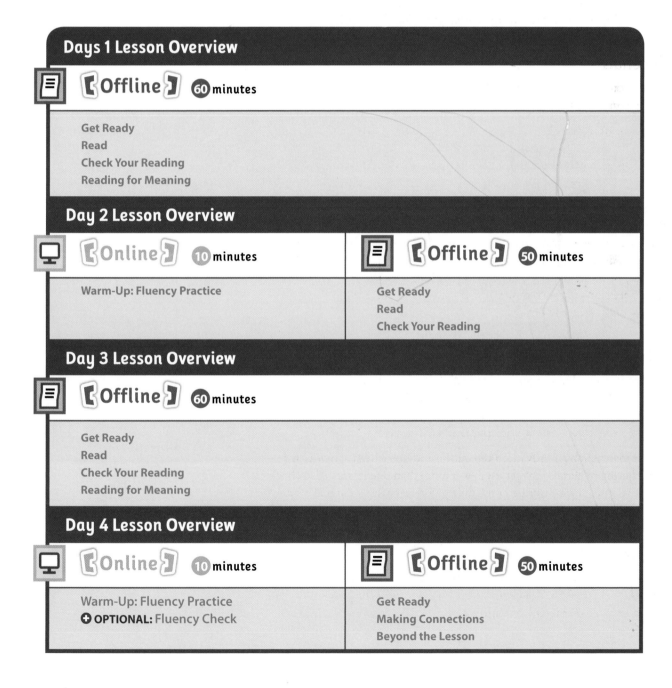

Days 1 Lesson Overview

【Offline】 60 minutes

Get Ready
Read
Check Your Reading
Reading for Meaning

Day 2 Lesson Overview

【Online】 10 minutes

Warm-Up: Fluency Practice

【Offline】 50 minutes

Get Ready
Read
Check Your Reading

Day 3 Lesson Overview

【Offline】 60 minutes

Get Ready
Read
Check Your Reading
Reading for Meaning

Day 4 Lesson Overview

【Online】 10 minutes

Warm-Up: Fluency Practice
➕ OPTIONAL: Fluency Check

【Offline】 50 minutes

Get Ready
Making Connections
Beyond the Lesson

Lesson Activities

Lesson plans in the Literature & Comprehension section of this Lesson Guide include detailed instructions for each activity. Literature & Comprehension lesson plans include the following elements:

Literature & Comprehension activity types:

Activity Type
This label tells you what kind of activity you are working on.

Course Name
This banner identifies the section of the book.

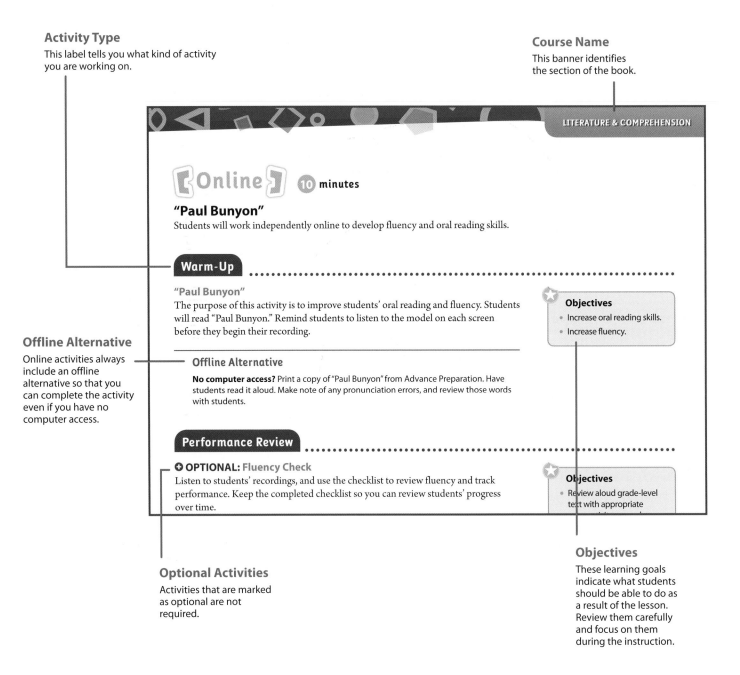

LITERATURE & COMPREHENSION

[Online] **10** minutes

"Paul Bunyon"
Students will work independently online to develop fluency and oral reading skills.

Warm-Up

"Paul Bunyon"
The purpose of this activity is to improve students' oral reading and fluency. Students will read "Paul Bunyon." Remind students to listen to the model on each screen before they begin their recording.

Objectives
- Increase oral reading skills.
- Increase fluency.

Offline Alternative

No computer access? Print a copy of "Paul Bunyon" from Advance Preparation. Have students read it aloud. Make note of any pronunciation errors, and review those words with students.

Performance Review

➕ OPTIONAL: Fluency Check
Listen to students' recordings, and use the checklist to review fluency and track performance. Keep the completed checklist so you can review students' progress over time.

Objectives
- Review aloud grade-level text with appropriate

Offline Alternative
Online activities always include an offline alternative so that you can complete the activity even if you have no computer access.

Optional Activities
Activities that are marked as optional are not required.

Objectives
These learning goals indicate what students should be able to do as a result of the lesson. Review them carefully and focus on them during the instruction.

Handwriting Icon

This icon appears next to the activity title if the activity provides students with the opportunity to practice their handwriting.

Activity Descriptions

These step-by-step instructions help you complete each activity with students. Answers are shown in magenta.

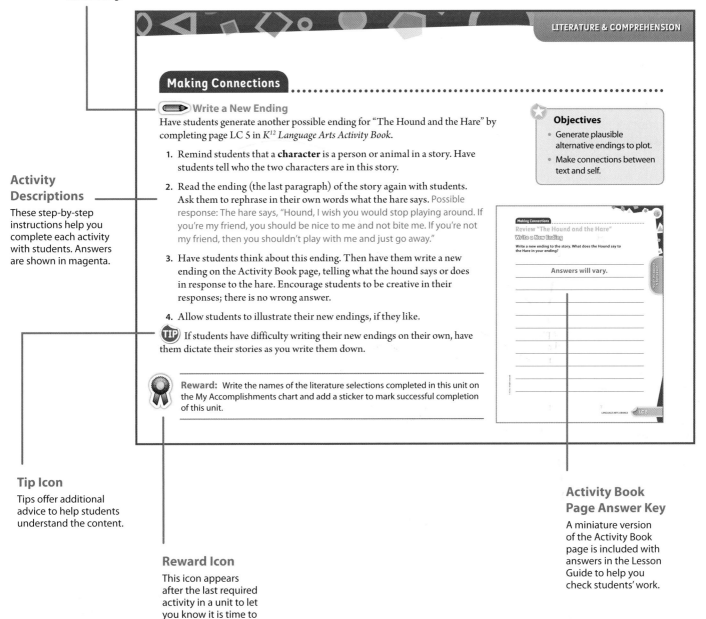

Making Connections

Write a New Ending

Have students generate another possible ending for "The Hound and the Hare" by completing page LC 5 in *K¹² Language Arts Activity Book*.

1. Remind students that a **character** is a person or animal in a story. Have students tell who the two characters are in this story.

2. Read the ending (the last paragraph) of the story again with students. Ask them to rephrase in their own words what the hare says. Possible response: The hare says, "Hound, I wish you would stop playing around. If you're my friend, you should be nice to me and not bite me. If you're not my friend, then you shouldn't play with me and just go away."

3. Have students think about this ending. Then have them write a new ending on the Activity Book page, telling what the hound says or does in response to the hare. Encourage students to be creative in their responses; there is no wrong answer.

4. Allow students to illustrate their new endings, if they like.

TIP If students have difficulty writing their new endings on their own, have them dictate their stories as you write them down.

Reward: Write the names of the literature selections completed in this unit on the My Accomplishments chart and add a sticker to mark successful completion of this unit.

Objectives
- Generate plausible alternative endings to plot.
- Make connections between text and self.

Making Connections
Review "The Hound and the Hare"
Write a New Ending
Write a new ending to the story. What does the Hound say to the Hare in your ending?

Answers will vary.

Tip Icon

Tips offer additional advice to help students understand the content.

Reward Icon

This icon appears after the last required activity in a unit to let you know it is time to add a sticker to the My Accomplishments chart.

Activity Book Page Answer Key

A miniature version of the Activity Book page is included with answers in the Lesson Guide to help you check students' work.

▶ **Warm-Up (Online)**   Every other lesson begins with an online Warm-Up. Students listen to a short reading selection and then record themselves reading the selection. This activity is fluency practice for oral reading. This practice is intended to improve students' ability to read quickly, smoothly, and automatically with rhythm, stress, and intonation. You will be able to access students' recordings at the end of each unit and at the end of each semester so you can give students feedback and record their progress as they gain in fluency.

▶ **Get Ready (Offline)**   The Get Ready includes detailed instructions on how to prepare students for that day's reading selection and lesson. You will provide instruction to help students build background knowledge and strategies needed for comprehension. You will then complete steps for introducing Words to Know, which are words from the selection that students should become familiar with.

▶ **Read (Offline)**   In Read activities, you and students examine and read the selection, focusing on key points related to the lesson's focus.

Begin with a Book Walk. This prereading activity is a structured introduction to the reading selection that familiarizes students with the content and helps them recall related background knowledge and make predictions.

After the Book Walk, you will read the selection using guided reading, independent reading, or a combination of the two, depending on how far through the course you are. At the beginning of the course, you will follow the scripts for guided reading. During the guided/independent reading portion of the course, you will model reading strategies for part of the reading assignment so that students can apply the strategies as they read independently. During the independent-reading portion of the course, students are expected to read independently, but you should monitor students' understanding.

As you complete the reading activities, the scripts and strategies that you model will help you ask questions and highlight key points related to the focus of the lesson. For example, you will be asked to emphasize the Words to Know, and in the first section of the course you will be directed to pause at certain points in the selection and ask students to make predictions. We recommend that you preview the questions you will ask students before reading the selection. You may wish to make notes for yourself and place them on a sticky note in your book so that you can model the appropriate reading strategies for the students.

(Note that audio versions of the stories from the *K¹² Classics for Young Readers, Volume B,* can be found in Noodleverse. If students enjoy a particular reading selection, they might like to later listen to the audio version while following along in the book. Note that the audio versions of stories do not contain models of the necessary reading strategies, so the audio versions can't replace your role.)

TIP As you become more familiar with the approach to guided reading and students develop their comprehension skills, this process will move more comfortably and smoothly. This approach might seem unfamiliar at first, but bear in mind that you are verbalizing what typically occurs internally during reading. It is important for students to hear your approach so that they can model it when they read independently.

- **Check Your Reading (Offline)**   Students will answer questions to show general comprehension of the reading selections. In the first several units of the course, students will answer the questions orally. Later students will answer multiple choice questions. In most cases, these questions require students to know what happened in the selection. As the course progresses, the questions will often require students to make inferences about their reading. The answers to inferential questions cannot be found directly in the selection; they require students to draw conclusions from the text. If students struggle with comprehension questions, you should review the answers and the reading selection before moving forward with Reading for Meaning activities.
- **Reading for Meaning (Offline)**   You will work with students to help them develop a deeper understanding of the reading selection through Reading for Meaning. The ideas examined in these activities will often tie in with instruction presented in the Get Ready. The main focus of Reading for Meaning is comprehension strategies and analysis of the reading selection. For example, you might examine characters or theme in a story or study the literary techniques or figurative language in a poem. Reading for Meaning often has an Activity Book page to complete.
- **Making Connections (Offline)**   Students will apply information and strategies learned from lessons to the reading selection. This activity often involves students making a connection between and among texts or between the text and themselves or the larger world. Making Connections may or may not have a page to complete in the Activity Book.
- **OPTIONAL: Beyond the Lesson (Offline)**   These activities are for students who have extra time and interest in exploring the reading selection further. These activities are not required and can be skipped.
- **Peer Interaction**   In these activities, you will lead a discussion with students about a reading selection. Ideally, students should discuss their reading with their peers, but if necessary you can have the discussion with them.

My Accomplishments Chart

Rewards in Literature & Comprehension are tied to completing units. When students complete a unit, have them add a sticker for that unit to the My Accomplishments chart. Look for the reward icon 🎗 in the Lesson Guide.

Reader's Choice Units

Throughout the Literature & Comprehension course, Planning and Progress in the Online School will alert you to an approaching Reader's Choice unit. These units are designed to give students an opportunity to self-select texts while fine-tuning their comprehension skills. Research indicates that choice enhances performance and motivates early readers. Titles range from classic to contemporary and include fiction, folktales, and nonfiction.

In the four Reader's Choice units spread across the course, you will have a bank of 16 texts to choose from. We suggest you discuss the possible texts with students to ensure they select texts that interest them. To help you choose a text for a Reader's Choice unit, you will have access to a synopsis of the books and information about grade and interest level. These units differ from other units in the course in two important ways:

1. You acquire these texts on your own. Once you and your students have selected a book to read, get a copy through a library or bookstore.

2. You must print the lesson materials. Once you have selected the text, access and print lesson plan and activity pages. They are not provided in *K¹² Language Arts Lesson Guide* or *K¹² Language Arts Activity Book*.

K¹² Language Arts Orange Spelling Course Overview

Course	Daily Lesson Time (approximate)	Online/Offline
K¹² Language Arts Orange Spelling	15 minutes	Each unit: 4 offline lessons, 1 online review
Course Structure and Materials		
36 Units with 5 Lessons	**Materials:** • *K¹² Spelling Handbook*	

K¹² provides the Spelling materials separately from the Language Arts materials, so you will not find Spelling lesson plans or activity pages in *K¹² Language Arts Lesson Guide* or *K¹² Language Arts Activity Book*. Please refer to *K¹² Spelling Handbook* for all materials related to the Spelling course.

K¹² Language Arts Orange Vocabulary Course Overview

Course	Daily Lesson Time (approximate)	Online/Offline
K¹² Language Arts Orange Vocabulary	30 minutes	All online
Course Structure and Materials		
18 Units with 10 Lessons	**Materials:** • *K¹² Language Arts Lesson Guide*	

Course Philosophy

The Vocabulary course of the K[12] Language Arts Orange program is an online course that gives students direct instruction on word meanings through exposure to a wide variety of words. Many of these words are grouped in conceptually related sets, opposites, words with nonliteral meanings, or homophones. Students will be introduced to each set of words and spend time reviewing and practicing the words online.

What Is It? People have various types of vocabulary. We have speaking vocabulary (words we use proficiently when talking with others), listening vocabulary (words we understand well when hearing others speak), reading vocabulary (words we can decode and comprehend), and writing vocabulary (words we can spell and comprehend). Students typically have larger speaking vocabularies than listening, reading, and writing vocabularies. National Reading Panel research shows that students learn most vocabulary indirectly (through daily speaking and listening in the home, listening to stories, reading stories, and so on), but some vocabulary must be learned directly (through instruction on specific words, meanings, and proper uses).

Why We Do It Vocabulary includes the words we need to know to communicate. To write or read something, we must have a strong vocabulary so we can communicate effectively. Students with a strong and varied vocabulary have an easier time comprehending and composing written material. Researchers Margaret McKeown and Isabel Beck concluded that robust vocabulary instruction involving active learning, prior knowledge, and frequent encounters with vocabulary words is powerful and effective.

Overview of Vocabulary Lessons

Materials

The following book is supplied for Vocabulary:

K[12] Language Arts Lesson Guide

You may also need the following general materials to complete the optional flash card activities:

- 3½ x 5-inch index cards
- pen or pencil

Lesson Structure

The K[12] Vocabulary course consists of 18 ten-day units that follow a set, repeated pattern. In each unit, students will work to learn three discrete sets of vocabulary words. The following chart is an overview of how lessons are organized in each unit.

[Online] 15 minutes per day

Day 1 Lesson Overview

| Skills Update (except first unit) | Learn: Introduce Word Set 1 |

Days 2 and 3 Lesson Overview

Practice: Word Set 1

Day 4 Lesson Overview

| Skills Update (except first unit) | Learn: Introduce Word Set 2 |

Days 5 and 6 Lesson Overview

Practice: Word Set 2

Day 7 Lesson Overview

| Skills Update (except first unit) | Learn: Introduce Word Set 3 |

Day 8 Lesson Overview

Practice: Word Set 3

Day 9 Lesson Overview

Unit Review

Day 10 Lesson Overview

Unit Checkpoint

Lesson Activities

Lesson plans in the Vocabulary section of this Lesson Guide include detailed descriptions or instructions for each activity. Please note that the Vocabulary plans are listed unit-by-unit instead of having individual plans for each lesson. Vocabulary lesson plans include the following elements:

Unit Overview
The Unit Overview table lists the activities taking place on each day of the unit. Notice that this overview shows the entire unit instead of just one lesson.

Objectives
These learning goals indicate what students should be able to do as a result of the lessons in this unit.

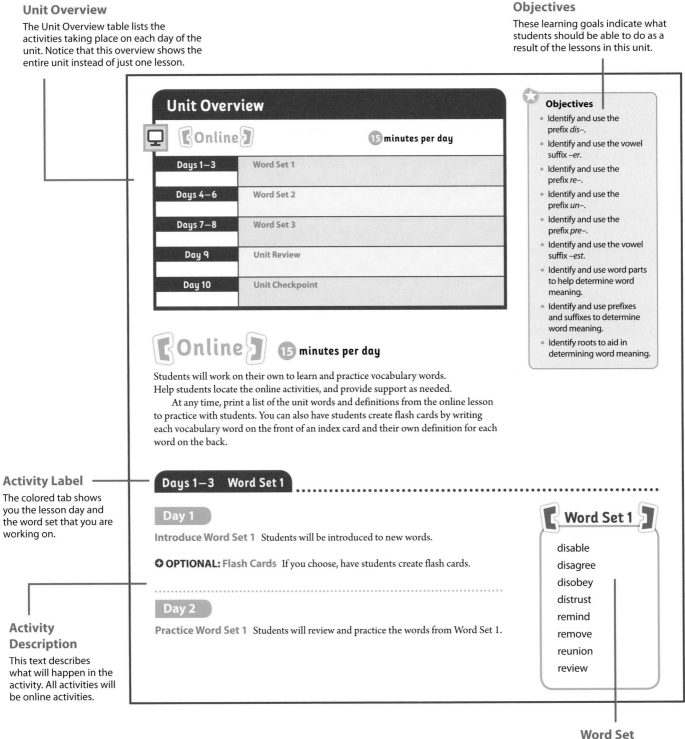

Unit Overview

[Online]   15 minutes per day

Days 1–3	Word Set 1
Days 4–6	Word Set 2
Days 7–8	Word Set 3
Day 9	Unit Review
Day 10	Unit Checkpoint

Objectives
- Identify and use the prefix *dis–*.
- Identify and use the vowel suffix *–er*.
- Identify and use the prefix *re–*.
- Identify and use the prefix *un–*.
- Identify and use the prefix *pre–*.
- Identify and use the vowel suffix *–est*.
- Identify and use word parts to help determine word meaning.
- Identify and use prefixes and suffixes to determine word meaning.
- Identify roots to aid in determining word meaning.

[Online]   15 minutes per day

Students will work on their own to learn and practice vocabulary words. Help students locate the online activities, and provide support as needed.

At any time, print a list of the unit words and definitions from the online lesson to practice with students. You can also have students create flash cards by writing each vocabulary word on the front of an index card and their own definition for each word on the back.

Activity Label
The colored tab shows you the lesson day and the word set that you are working on.

Days 1–3   Word Set 1

Day 1

Introduce Word Set 1 Students will be introduced to new words.

⊕ OPTIONAL: Flash Cards If you choose, have students create flash cards.

Day 2

Practice Word Set 1 Students will review and practice the words from Word Set 1.

Activity Description
This text describes what will happen in the activity. All activities will be online activities.

[Word Set 1]
disable
disagree
disobey
distrust
remind
remove
reunion
review

Word Set
Students will study this list of words during this portion of the unit.

Vocabulary activity types:

- **OPTIONAL Flash Cards (Offline)** This activity is intended for students who have extra time and would benefit from practicing vocabulary words with flash cards. Feel free to skip this activity.

    Gather one index card for each vocabulary word. Have students create flash cards by writing each vocabulary word on the front of each index card and the definition for the word on the back of the index card.

- **Skills Update (Online)** Days 1, 4, and 7 of each unit (after the first unit) contain a Skills Update. Students will refresh their knowledge of vocabulary words from previous units with these online assessments.

- **Learn (Online)** Students will become more familiar with one of three sets of words covered in the unit. The activity typically focuses on each word to give students a definition, a visual cue, and a strong grounding in that word.

- **Practice (Online)** Students will review and practice one of three sets of words covered in the unit. This activity reinforces the meaning and use of the words and focuses on any vocabulary skills particular to the word set being studied, such as identifying prefixes or classifying words.

- **Unit Review (Online)** Students will work independently to review all vocabulary words from the unit in preparation for the Unit Checkpoint. They do the review by playing the online Boat Adventure game.

- **Unit Checkpoint (Online)** Students will work independently to complete an online Unit Checkpoint. This assessment covers all vocabulary words from the unit.

My Accomplishments Chart

Rewards in Vocabulary are tied to completing Unit Checkpoints. Each time students score 80 percent or higher on a Unit Checkpoint, have them add a sticker for that unit to the My Accomplishments chart. If students score lower than 80 percent, review each Checkpoint exercise with them and work with them to correct any exercises they missed. Although students may retake the Unit Checkpoint anytime, we recommend that they wait until the next day.

K¹² Language Arts Orange
Writing Skills Course Overview

Course	Daily Lesson Time (approximate)	Online/Offline
K¹² Language Arts Orange Writing Skills	15 minutes	Each unit (approximately): 4 offline lessons, 1 online lesson

Course Structure and Materials	
36 Units with 5 Lessons: • 18 GUM units • 18 Composition units	**Materials:** • *K¹² Language Arts Lesson Guide* • *K¹² Language Arts Activity Book* • *K¹² Language Arts Assessments*

Course Philosophy

Learning to express one's ideas in writing is a fundamental requirement of an educated person. K¹² Language Arts Orange takes a two-pronged approach to fulfilling this need. Grammar, usage, and mechanics (GUM) lessons teach students the nuts and bolts of communicating in standard written English. Composition lessons teach students how to think about, plan, organize, and write organized communications in a variety of forms. The Writing Skills curriculum includes alternating units of GUM and composition.

Grammar, Usage, and Mechanics (GUM)

What Is It?   The grammar, usage, and mechanics lessons give students practice in learning about sentences and the parts of speech that make up sentences; in using subjects, verbs, and pronouns correctly; and in discovering how capitalization and punctuation marks aid in conveying the message of sentences.

Why We Do It   While it is true that knowing grammar does not make someone a good writer, understanding how grammar works makes writing easier. When students know what a complete sentence is, what kind of punctuation is used within a sentence and at the end of a sentence, or which words need capital letters, students can spend their time focusing on ideas. When the focus is on ideas, not on mechanics, the writing becomes more fluent and expressive.

Composition

What Is It?   In composition lessons, students practice to become more fluent and expressive writers. In these lessons, students learn to write in a variety of forms. They learn to write sentences, structure paragraphs, and finally explore how to put paragraphs together to create short compositions such as a response to literature and a report. They will also learn basic presentation skills.

Why We Do It   Research shows that daily writing practice is essential for the developing writer. The lessons are based on a process-writing model of instruction. Research demonstrates that engaging in a variety of prewriting and planning activities helps novice writers learn to plan and organize their own writing. Throughout each unit, students will practice skills in discrete steps and they will ultimately write a polished piece of writing, ready to be "published" or shared. Students will learn that the writing process is not a straight line forward and that writing always means rewriting for improvement. As you help students through these lessons, encourage them to express their thoughts and ideas. Do not expect perfect form.

Overview of Writing Skills Lessons

Materials

The following books are supplied for Writing Skills:

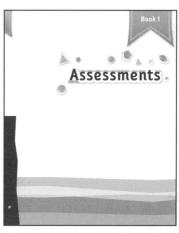

| *K¹² Language Arts Lesson Guide* | *K¹² Language Arts Activity Book* | *K¹² Language Arts Assessments* |

Other Materials

You should always have paper and pencils available for students. You might sometimes also need the following general materials to complete the Activity Book pages:

- ► 3½ x 5-inch index cards
- ► crayons or colored pencils
- ► scissors (Safety note: When students are working with scissors, please supervise students to make sure they use their scissors safely and stay seated.)
- ► glue

How to Use the Materials

Keep in mind that students will write in and tear pages out of the Activity Book, so periodically place some of the Activity Book pages in students' portfolio. In addition, save your students' graphic organizers, drafts, and published compositions in the portfolio to keep track of students' growth as writers. Consult the portfolio regularly with students so that they can see the progress they have made and celebrate it. Remember that student writing is not adult writing. Do not expect perfection, but do look for progress over time and clarity of thought and intent.

The Activity Book also has pages with examples of different types of writing or other kinds of materials that students will refer to over the course of a unit. Look for tips in the Lesson Guide alerting you to store these materials for further use. Be sure to keep these pages in a safe place so you can easily find them and refer to them.

Lesson Structure

The K[12] Writing Skills course consists of 36 units. The units alternate back and forth: odd units are GUM, and even units are Composition.

All units are five lessons long, with each lesson taking about 15 minutes to complete. Although the GUM and Composition units look similar, there are a couple of key differences:

▸ GUM units include an online review lesson on Day 4. Composition units are entirely offline, but include occasional online alternative activities.
▸ GUM units end with a Unit Checkpoint on Day 5. Composition units end with a Write Now activity, which is a writing assignment.

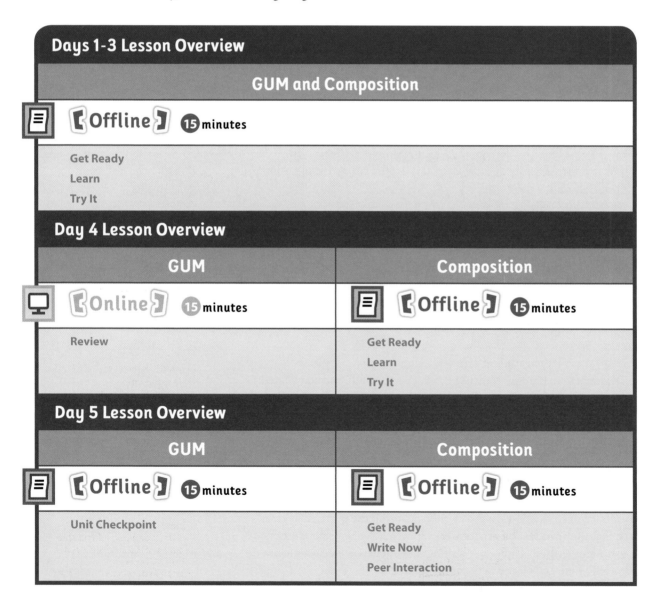

Days 1–3 Lesson Overview

GUM and Composition

【Offline】 15 minutes

Get Ready
Learn
Try It

Day 4 Lesson Overview

GUM	Composition
【Online】 15 minutes	【Offline】 15 minutes
Review	Get Ready
	Learn
	Try It

Day 5 Lesson Overview

GUM	Composition
【Offline】 15 minutes	【Offline】 15 minutes
Unit Checkpoint	Get Ready
	Write Now
	Peer Interaction

Lesson Activities

Lesson plans in the Writing Skills section of this Lesson Guide include detailed descriptions or instructions for each activity. Writing Skills lesson plans include the following elements:

Course Name
This banner identifies the section of the book.

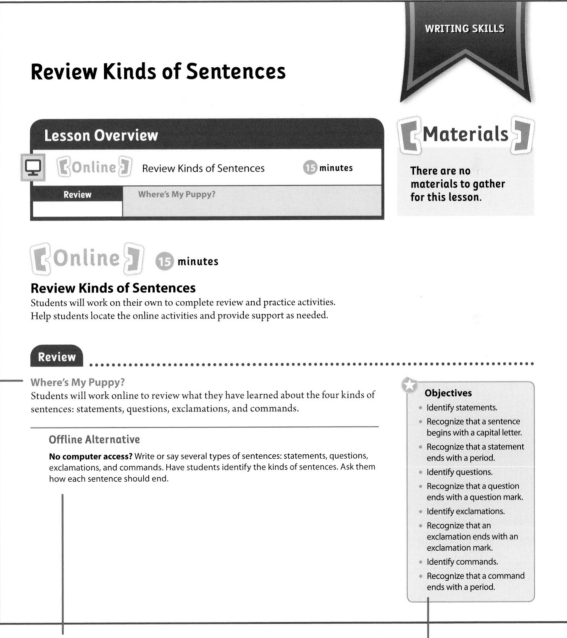

WRITING SKILLS

Review Kinds of Sentences

Lesson Overview

[Online] Review Kinds of Sentences — 15 minutes

| Review | Where's My Puppy? |

Materials

There are no materials to gather for this lesson.

[Online] 15 minutes

Review Kinds of Sentences
Students will work on their own to complete review and practice activities. Help students locate the online activities and provide support as needed.

Review ....

Where's My Puppy?
Students will work online to review what they have learned about the four kinds of sentences: statements, questions, exclamations, and commands.

___

Offline Alternative

No computer access? Write or say several types of sentences: statements, questions, exclamations, and commands. Have students identify the kinds of sentences. Ask them how each sentence should end.

Objectives
- Identify statements.
- Recognize that a sentence begins with a capital letter.
- Recognize that a statement ends with a period.
- Identify questions.
- Recognize that a question ends with a question mark.
- Identify exclamations.
- Recognize that an exclamation ends with an exclamation mark.
- Identify commands.
- Recognize that a command ends with a period.

Activity Description
This text describes what will happen in the activity. For offline activities, it provides step-by-step instructions.

Offline and Online Alternative
An offline alternative is provided for online activities, in case you will not have access to the computer.

An online alternative is offered as an option for some offline activities.

Objectives
These learning goals indicate what students should be able to do as a result of the lesson. Review them carefully and focus on them during the instruction.

Activity Book Page

Activities that have an Activity Book page prompt you to turn to that page at the beginning of the activity.

WRITING SKILLS

Activity Type

This label tells you what kind of activity you are working on.

Learn ··

Revise It and Proofread It

Introduce the concept of proofreading and revising as ways to make writing better. Turn to page WS 9 in *K¹² Language Arts Activity Book*.

1. Explain the difference between proofreading for errors and revising.

   Say: When you look for errors in your writing, you are **proofreading**. Adding capital letters and end marks is an example of proofreading. When you change or rewrite something, you are **revising**. Combining similar sentences into one sentence is an example of revising.

2. Read the rule on the Activity Book page.

3. Read the example sentences. Ask students what errors they see in the sentences. The first letter is not capitalized and the period is missing.

Instructions

The activity instructions will tell you what to say and do. Answers to questions that you ask are shown in magenta.

4. Point to the proofread version of the sentences. Ask students what changes were made to proofread the sentences. The lowercase *j* was crossed out, and an uppercase *J* was added. A period was added to the end of the second sentence.

5. Point to the revised version of the sentences. Ask students what changes were made to revise the sentences. The sentences were combined into one.

6. Have students complete the rest of the Activity Book page. Provide support as necessary.

(TIP) Students can explain the changes needed instead of writing them. You also have the option of having students tell you the changes and your writing them on the Activity Book page.

Objectives

- Combine sentences that have similar elements.
- Use capital letters correctly.
- Punctuate correctly.
- Use a variety of sentence beginnings and lengths.
- Use correct grammar and sentence formation.

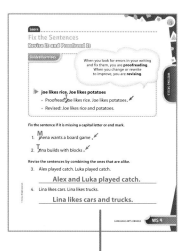

Activity Book Page Answer Key

A miniature version of the Activity Book page is included with answers in the Lesson Guide to help you check students' work.

Write Now

Write to Someone You Know

Help students write a friendly letter. Gather page WS 80 (Use a Graphic Organizer), and turn to page WS 83 in *K¹² Language Arts Activity Book*.

1. Explain that students will use their graphic organizer to write a friendly letter.

2. Have students write their letter on a sheet of paper so they can revise their work and transfer a clean copy to the Activity Book page.

3. Have students write a complete and neat copy of their friendly letter on the Activity Book page. Students can use one or both sides of the paper for their letter. Remind students to start the closing and signature in the center of the page.

4. Use the materials and instructions in the online lesson to evaluate students' finished writing. You will be evaluating their writing for the following:

   ► Purpose and Content: The writing should be a friendly letter that shares news, ideas, feelings, or events. The letter should have a friendly voice. The body of the letter should have a beginning and concluding sentence. The main idea should be supported with a few details. The language should be clear.
   ► Structure and Organization: The letter should have a heading, greeting, body, closing, and signature. They should all be used correctly. The details should be written mostly in time or logical order.
   ► Grammar and Mechanics: All sentences should be complete and punctuated correctly. The greeting and closing should end with a comma.

5. Enter students' scores for each rubric category online.

6. If students scored a 1 in any category, follow the online instructions to help them edit and revise their work.

TIP For an optional activity, have students mail their finished letters. Have them put the letter in the envelope they addressed previously, add a stamp, and mail it. Students can also mail a letter to themselves just for practice. Check the envelope to be sure that it was written correctly. A walk to a mailbox or a visit to the post office will help conclude the experience.

Reward: When students' writing is Level 2 or higher on the grading rubric, add a sticker for this unit on the My Accomplishments chart.

Objectives

- Write a friendly letter.
- Use established conventions for a friendly letter.
- Organize ideas through sequencing.
- Use beginning and concluding statements.
- Use an appropriate organizational pattern in writing.
- Use a voice based on purpose and audience.
- Write a narrative with a beginning, middle, and end.
- Use transition words to signal order.
- Use a graphic organizer to plan.

Handwriting Icon

This icon appears next to the activity title if the activity provides students with the opportunity to practice their handwriting.

Write Now Instructions

The information in the Write Now will show you how to help students complete the writing assignments and explains how to evaluate their writing.

Tip Icon

Tips offer additional advice to help students understand the content.

Reward Icon

This icon appears after the last required activity in a unit to let you know it is time to add a sticker to the My Accomplishments chart.

Writing Skills activity types:

- **Get Ready (Offline)**   The Get Ready is a short activity to prepare students for the new skills that they will learn in the lesson. Often the Get Ready draws on students' previous knowledge or builds background knowledge in preparation for the new skill. Sometimes you will preview examples of different types of writing or other kinds of examples as part of the Get Ready.

- **Learn (Offline)**   In the Learn activity, you will teach students a new skill. Use the examples and tips in the Lesson Guide and the accompanying Activity Book page to explain the new skill. The Activity Book page contains an explanation of the new skill and an example that students can refer back to as they progress through the course.

- **Try It (Offline)**   Students will practice using the new skill that you presented in the Learn by completing a page in the Activity Book.

- **Try It (Online Alternative)**   Some Try It activities have an online alternative that students can complete instead of the Activity Book page or for extra practice.

- **Review (Online)**   Each GUM unit includes an online review activity to provide students with an opportunity to review and practice activities on their own. Students will also have several days to review the GUM skills learned throughout the semester before completing the Semester Checkpoint.

- **Unit and Semester Checkpoint (Offline)**   Each GUM unit ends with an offline Unit Checkpoint, which tests the skills students have learned in the unit. Each semester has an offline Semester Checkpoint that covers the GUM skills learned in the entire semester.

- **Write Now (Offline)**   Each Composition unit ends with a writing assignment. Students complete the writing assignment that they have been planning, drafting, and revising throughout the unit or units. You will evaluate that writing on a three-point scale for purpose and content; structure and organization; and grammar, usage, and mechanics. Sample papers (available online) will help you evaluate students' strengths and weaknesses. You will have access to suggestions for helping students revise writing that does not meet the objectives for the unit.

- **Peer Interaction (Offline)**   Some Composition units include a Peer Interaction activity where students are asked to share their writing with a peer or anyone willing to give feedback. If time allows, students can benefit from this extra practice by then revising their work based on the feedback.

My Accomplishments Chart

Rewards in GUM units of the Writing Skills course are tied to completing Unit Checkpoints. Each time students score 80 percent or higher on a Unit Checkpoint, have them add a sticker for that unit to the My Accomplishments chart. If students score lower than 80 percent, review each Checkpoint exercise with them and work with them to correct any exercises they missed.

Rewards in the Composition units of the Writing Skills course are tied to completing the Write Now assignments in each unit. When students' writing scores score a 2 or higher in each category of the rubric provided for the assignment, have them add a sticker for that unit to the My Accomplishments chart. If students score below a 2 in any category, help them revise their writing so that it meets the requirements for a level 2.

K¹² Language Arts Orange Handwriting Course Overview

Course	Daily Lesson Time (approximate)	Online/Offline
K¹² Language Arts Orange Handwriting	10 minutes	All offline
Course Structure and Materials		
36 Units with 5 Lessons	**Materials:** • *Handwriting Without Tears Second Grade Printing Teacher's Guide* • *Handwriting Without Tears Printing Power* • Lined paper	

Course Philosophy

K¹² supplies the proven Handwriting Without Tears program for students in kindergarten through grade 3. This gentle, multisensory approach focuses on careful practice at a pace that suits students' fine motor skills development.

Overview of Handwriting Lessons

Materials

The following books and materials are supplied for Handwriting:

▶ *Handwriting Without Tears Second Grade Printing Teacher's Guide*
▶ *Handwriting Without Tears Printing Power*
▶ One package of specially lined writing paper for Handwriting Without Tears
  If you need more of this paper, the following options are available:

  ▶ Online lesson openers provide a handwriting sheet that you can print and photocopy.
  ▶ You can order more wide double-lined notebook paper directly from Handwriting Without Tears at http://www.hwtears.com/hwt.

These materials are separate from *K¹² Language Arts Lesson Guide* and *K¹² Language Arts Activity Book*.

Lesson Structure

The K¹² Handwriting program is entirely offline and uses the supplied Handwriting Without Tears materials. Before beginning the program, become familiar with the *Handwriting Without Tears Second Grade Printing Teacher's Guide*. The guide includes a Teaching Guidelines chart to help you plan students' handwriting lessons.

In each lesson, you will work with students for 10 minutes. (You may want to set a timer for 10 minutes; most students enjoy the Handwriting program, so it's easy to lose track of time and do too much in one day.)

Students should complete as many workbook pages as they can, picking up where they left off during the previous Handwriting lesson and continuing from there. They are not expected to complete a set number of pages during a 10-minute lesson. Be sure to monitor students' writing time so you can help them develop good letter formation habits.

Depending on students' pace, the workbook should take 8 to 12 weeks of instruction. Move as quickly or as slowly as students need. When they have completed the workbooks, have students use the packaged lined writing paper from Handwriting Without Tears to practice their handwriting. Also, look for the Handwriting icon throughout the Lesson Guides. This icon indicates that the associated activity provides a perfect opportunity to practice proper handwriting, and if students pay careful attention to their handwriting, this time can also count as Handwriting time.

K¹² Language Arts Orange Keywords

Literature and Comprehension

alliteration – the use of words with the same or close to the same beginning sounds

assonance – a form of alliteration in which vowel sounds are repeated

author – a writer

author's purpose – the reason the author wrote a text: to entertain, to inform, to express an opinion, or to persuade

autobiography – the story of a person's life written by that person

biography – the story of someone's life written by another person

bold type – type that is darker than the surrounding text that draws attention to a word or phrase

brainstorming – an early step in writing that helps a writer come up with as many ideas about a topic as possible

caption – writing under a picture that describes the picture

cause – the reason something happens

character – a person or animal in a story

compare – to explain how two or more things are alike

comprehension – understanding

conclusion – a reasoned decision made about something not stated directly in a text through the consideration of information provided and what is already known

conflict – a problem or issue that a character faces in a story

connection – a link readers make between themselves, information in text, and the world around them

consequence – what happens because of an action or event

consonance – the repetition of consonant sounds, especially at the ends of words

context – the parts of a sentence or passage surrounding a word

context clue – a word or phrase in a text that helps you figure out the meaning of an unknown word

contrast – to explain how two or more things are different

detail – a piece of information in a text

diagram – a drawing or design that shows how pieces of information are related

dialogue – the words that characters say in a written work

draft – an early effort at a piece of writing, not the finished work

drama – another word for play

effect – the result of a cause

fable – a story that teaches a lesson and may contain animal characters

fact – something that can be proven true

fairy tale – a folktale that sometimes has magical elements; sometimes has a happily-ever-after ending

fantasy – a story with characters, settings, or other elements that could not really exist

fiction – make-believe stories

figurative language – words that describe something by comparing it to something completely different
Example: Rain fell in buckets and the streets looked like rivers.

first-person point of view – the telling of a story by a character in that story, using pronouns such as *I*, *me*, and *we*

folktale – a story, which usually teachers a lesson important to a culture, that is passed down through many generations

genre – a category for classifying literary works

glossary – a list of important terms and their meanings that is usually found in the back of a book

graphic organizer – a visual tool used to show relationships between key concepts; formats include webs, diagrams, and charts

heading – a title within the body of a text that tells the reader something important about a section of the text

historical fiction – a type of story that contains facts about real people, places, and events, but also contains fictional elements that add dramatic interest to the story

idiom – an expression that cannot be understood from its literal meaning

illustration – a drawing

illustrator – the person who draws the pictures that go with a story

imagery – language that helps readers imagine how something looks, sounds, smells, feels, or tastes

infer – to use clues and what you already know to make a guess

inference – a guess you make using the clues in a text and what you already know

informational text – text written to explain and give information on a topic

italic – text that slants toward the right

legend – a story that is passed down for many years to teach the values of a culture; a legend may or may not contain some true events or people

line – a row of words in a poem

literal level – a reference to text information that is directly stated

literal recall – the ability to describe information stated directly in a text

literature – made-up stories, true stories, poems, and plays

main character – an important person, animal, or other being who is central to the plot

main idea – the most important idea in a paragraph or text

metaphor – a figure of speech that compares two unlike things, without using the word like or as
Example: The cat's eyes were emeralds shining in the night.

moral – the lesson of a story, particularly a fable

multiple-meaning word – a word that has more than one meaning

myth – a story that explains how something came to be and that usually contains magical figures as characters

narrative – text genre in which a story is told; a narrative text usually includes characters, setting, and plot

narrator – the teller of a story

nonfiction – writings about true things

onomatopoeia – the use of words that show sounds
Example: moo, woof, quack, squash

opinion – something that a person thinks or believes, but which cannot be proven to be true

personification – giving human qualities to something that is not human
Example: The thunder shouted from the clouds.

plot – what happens in a story

poem – a piece of poetry

poetry – writing that is made up of lines that often rhyme and follow a specific rhythm

point of view – the perspective a story is told from

prediction – a guess about what might happen that is based on information in a story and what you already know

K¹² Language Arts Orange Keywords

Literature and Comprehension *continued*

prereading strategy – an activity that prepares students to read a particular text before they begin reading

print features – formatting that draws attention to words in text, such as bold type, underlining, and capital letters

prior knowledge – things you already know from past experience

problem – an issue a character must solve in a story

realistic fiction – a made-up story that has no magical elements

repetition – the use of a word or phrase more than once

resolution – the working out or the end of a conflict in a story

retelling – using your own words to tell a story that you have listened to or read

rhyme – the use of words that end with the same sounds; for example, *cat* and *hat* rhyme

rhythm – a pattern of accented and unaccented syllables; a distinctive beat

scriptal information – things you already know from past experience

self-correct – readers corrections of their own errors without prompting while reading text aloud

self-monitor – the ability of readers to notice if they do or do not understand what they are reading

self-question – to ask questions of yourself as you read to check your understanding

sensory language – language that appeals to the five senses

sequence – order

setting – when and where a story takes place

sidebar – a short text within a larger text that tells something related but not necessary to the main story

simile – a comparison between two things using the word *like* or *as* *Example:* He was as quiet as a mouse.

solution – how a character solves a problem in a story

speaker – the narrator of a poem, the person speaking

stanza – a group of lines in a poem

story events – the things that happen in a story; the plot

story structure elements – components of a story; they include character, setting, plot, problem, and solution

summarize – to tell in order the most important ideas or events of a text

summary – a short retelling that includes only the most important ideas or events of a text

supporting detail – a detail that gives more information about a main idea

table of contents – a list at the start of a book that gives the titles of the book's stories, poems, articles, chapters, or nonfiction pieces and the pages where they can be found

text feature – part of a text that helps a reader locate information and determine what is most important; some examples are the title, table of contents, headings, pictures, and glossary

text structure – the organizational pattern of a text, such as cause and effect, compare and contrast, and chronological order

theme – the author's message or big idea

tone – the author's feelings toward the subject and/or characters of a text

topic – the subject of a text

trait – a quality of a person or other object; what something is like

visual text support – a graphic feature that helps a reader better understand text, such as a picture, chart, or map

---

K¹² Language Arts Orange Keywords

Writing Skills (Composition)

almanac – a book that comes out each year with facts about many topics

atlas – a book of maps

audience – a writer's readers

bibliography card – a note card on which one writes the source of a fact

body (of a friendly letter) – the text of a friendly letter

book review – a piece of writing that gives an opinion about a book and tells about it

brainstorming – before writing, a way for the writer to come up with ideas

business letter – a letter written to an organization or a person at a business

call number – a number given to each item held by a library

card catalog – usually offered online, a record of a library's holdings in alphabetical order by title, author, and subject

cause – an event, object, or situation that makes something else happen

character – a person or animal in a story

chronological order – a way to organize that puts details in time order

citation – a note that says where the author found a specific piece of information

clarity – of writing, the quality of being clear and easy to understand

climax – the turning point in a story

closing (of a friendly letter) – the part of a friendly letter that follows the body *Example:* "Your friend" or "Love"

cluster – a type of graphic organizer in which words and phrases about a topic are jotted down and connected

coherence – of writing, the smooth connection of ideas in a paragraph or essay

command – a kind of sentence that gives an order or makes a request

comparison – a look at how two things are alike

complete sentence – a group of words that tells a complete thought

computer catalog – an online record of a library's holdings; also card catalog

concluding sentence – the last sentence of a paragraph; often summarizes the paragraph

K¹² Language Arts Orange Keywords

Writing Skills (Composition) *continued*

conclusion (in writing) – the final paragraph of a written work

conjunction – a word used to join parts of a sentence, such as and, but, and or

content – the information or ideas in a piece of writing

contrast – a look at how two things are different

declarative sentence – a group of words that makes a statement

definition – a statement that tells what a word means

description – writing that uses words that show how something looks, sounds, feels, tastes, or smells.
Example: The sky is a soft, powdery blue, and the golden sun feels warm on my face.

detail – a fact or description that tells more about a topic

dialogue – the words spoken between people

dictionary – a reference work made up of words with their definitions, in alphabetical order

direct quotation – the exact words of a speaker or writer

domain name – the part of an Internet address stating the website's general type, such as .com, .org, .edu, or .gov.

drafting – of writing, the stage or step in which the writer first writes the piece

effect – something that happens because of another event, object, or situation

encyclopedia – a reference work made up of articles on many topics, usually in alphabetical order

evidence – a specific detail, such as a fact or opinion, that supports a reason

example – a specific instance of something, used to illustrate an idea

exclamation – a kind of sentence that shows strong feeling

exclamatory sentence – a group of words that shows strong feeling

fact – a statement that can be proven true

feedback – information given to help improve a piece of writing

fiction – a story created from the imagination; fiction is not documentation of fact

fictional narrative – a term often used for a short story

figurative language – language that uses devices such as as metaphor, simile, and personification for poetic effect, not precise, factual meaning
Example: "Her eyes are stars" is figurative language to show how shiny and bright her eyes are. In contrast, the literal use of the word *stars* in the sentence "The stars are shining tonight."

first-person point of view – narration of a story by one of the characters, using the first-person pronouns *I* and *me*

focus – the direction or emphasis of a piece of writing; writing with a focus sticks to the main idea and does not include lots of ideas that are unrelated

freewriting – a way for a writer to pick a topic and write as much as possible about it within a set time limit

friendly letter – a kind of letter used to share thoughts, feeling, and news

graphic – a picture, photograph, map, diagram, or other image

graphic organizer – a visual device, such as a diagram or chart, that helps a writer plan a piece of writing

greeting – the part of a letter that begins with the word *Dear* followed by a person's name; also called the salutation

guide words – two words at the top of a dictionary page that show the first and last words on the page

heading – the first part of a letter that has the writer's address and the date

hook – a surprising idea or group of words used to grab the reader's attention, usually at the beginning of a work

how-to paper – a paragraph or essay that explains how to do or make something

imperative sentence – a group of words that gives a command or makes a request

Internet – a global communications system of linked computer networks

interrogative sentence – a group of words that asks a question

introduction – the first paragraph of an essay, identifying the topic and stating the main idea

introductory sentence – the first sentence in a piece of writing

journal – a notebook where a writer regularly records experiences and ideas

logical order – a way to organize that groups details in a way that makes sense

main idea – the most important point of the paragraph

narrative – a kind of writing that tells a story

nonfiction – writing that presents facts and information to explain, describe, or persuade; for example, newspaper articles and biographies are nonfiction

opinion – a statement of belief that cannot be proven true; the opposite of a fact

order of importance – a way to organize that presents details from least to most important, or from most to least important

order words – words that connect ideas, a series of steps, or create a sequence, such as first, next, later, finally

organization – of a piece of writing, the way the ideas are arranged

outline – an organized list of topics in an essay

paragraph – a group of sentences about one topic

paragraph outline – a list of paragraph topics in an essay

paraphrase – to restate information in one's own words

pattern of organization – the order by which details are arranged

personal narrative – an essay about a personal experience of the writer

persuasive essay – an essay in which the writer tries to convince readers to agree with a stand on an issue

plagiarism – using another person's words without giving that person credit as a source

plot – what happens in a story; the sequence of events

point of view – the perspective from which a story is told

presentation – an oral report, usually with visuals

prewriting – the stage or step of writing in which a writer chooses a topic, gathers ideas, and plans what to write

proofreading – the stage or step of the writing process in which the writer checks for errors in grammar, punctuation, capitalization, and spelling

publishing – the stage or step of the writing process in which the writer makes a clean copy of the piece and shares it

purpose – the reason for writing

question – a kind of sentence that asks something

quotation – a report of the exact words spoken or written by a person; usually placed within quotation marks

Writing Skills (Composition) *continued*

reason – a statement that explains why something is or why it should be

reference – a work that contains useful information for a writer, such as an encyclopedia, a dictionary, or a website

research – to find information through study rather than through personal experience

research report – a type of essay based mainly on the author's research

revising – the stage or step of the writing process in which the writer rereads and edits the draft, correcting errors and making changes in content or organization that improve the piece

rubric – the criteria used to evaluate a piece of writing

salutation – the greeting of a letter, which usually says, "Dear (name of recipient)"

search engine – software that searches for websites, usually by keywords

second-person point of view – the telling of a story, or addressing a piece of writing, directly to the audience , using the second-person pronoun *you*

sensory detail – descriptive detail that appeals to any of the five senses—sight, hearing, touch, smell, or taste

sentence – a group of words that tells a complete thought

sentence combining – to join two sentences that have similar parts into one sentence

sequence – the order in which things happen

setting – where and when a literary work takes place

showing language – words used to create pictures in the reader's mind, rather than words that merely tell what happened
Example: "The sun blazed on the street and my bare feet sizzled like a frying egg each time I took a step." [as opposed to] "The sun was hot and my bare feet burned each time I took a step."

signature – the end of a letter where the writer writes his or her name

source – a provider of information; a book, a historical document, online materials, and an interviewee are all sources

spatial order – a way to organize that arranges details by their location

speaker tag – the part of a dialogue that identifies who is speaking

statement – a kind of sentence that tells something

story map – a kind of a graphic organizer that helps a writer plan a story

structure – the way a piece of writing is organized

style – the words the writer chooses and the way the writer arranges the words into sentences

summarize – to restate briefly the main points of a text

supporting details – the sentences that give information about the main idea or topic sentence

supporting paragraphs (body) – a series of paragraphs that give information to support the thesis of an essay

suspense – excitement and uncertainty about what will happen

thank-you note – a kind of friendly letter in which the writer thanks someone for something

theme – the main message that an author wants to communicate to a reader

thesaurus – a reference work that gives synonyms and antonyms for words

thesis – the most important point, or main idea, of an essay

thesis statement – the sentence that states the main idea of an essay

third-person point of view – the telling of a story by someone outside of the action, using the third-person pronouns *he, she,* and *they*

time order – the arrangement of ideas according to when they happened

tone – the writer's attitude toward the topic or subject

topic – the subject of a piece of writing

topic sentence – the sentence that expresses the main idea of the paragraph

transition – a word or phrase that connects ideas

unity – when all sentences in a paragraph or all paragraphs in an essay support the main idea

URL – the Internet address of a website; stands for uniform resource locator

visual – a graphic, picture, or photograph

voice – the way a piece of writing sounds

website – a place on the Internet devoted to a specific organization, group, or individual

Works Cited page – a list of sources cited in the text of a research report

writer's craft – the techniques a writer uses and the decisions a writer makes to develop an essay

writing process – a series of five steps (which can be repeated) to follow during writing: prewriting, drafting, revising, proofreading, and publishing

writing prompt – a sentence, or sentences, that asks for a particular kind of writing

Writing Skills (GUM)

action verb – a word that shows action

adjective – a word that describes a noun or a pronoun

adverb – a word that describes a verb, an adjective, or another adverb

adverb of manner – an adverb that answers the question how

adverb of time – an adverb that answers the question when

article – the adjective *a, an,* or *the*

being verb – a verb that does not show action; for example, *am, is, are, was, were*

closing – the part of a friendly letter that follows the body

collective noun – a word that means a group of things but is usually singular

command – a kind of sentence that gives an order or makes a request

common noun – a word that names any person, place, thing, or idea

complete sentence – a group of words that tells a complete thought

contraction – a shortened word where an apostrophe replaces missing letters

dialogue – the words spoken between two or more people

direct quotation – the exact words of a speaker or writer

exclamation – a kind of sentence that shows strong feeling

friendly letter – a kind of letter used to share thoughts, feelings, and news

K¹² Language Arts Orange Keywords

Writing Skills (GUM) *continued*

future tense – a form of a verb that names an action that will happen later

greeting – the part of a letter that begins with the word *Dear* followed by a person's name; also called the salutation

heading – the first part of a letter that has the writer's address and the date

irregular verb – a verb that does not add *–d* or *–ed* to the present form to make the past and the past participle

noun – a word that names a person, place, thing, or idea

past tense – the form of the verb that tells what already has happened

plural noun – a word that names more than one person, place, thing, or idea

possessive noun – the form of a noun that shows ownership

possessive pronoun – the form of a pronoun that shows ownership

predicate – the verb or verb phrase in a sentence

present tense – the verb form that tells what is happening now

pronoun – a word that takes the place of one or more nouns

proper noun – the name of a particular person, place, thing, or idea; proper nouns begin with a capital letter

question – a kind of sentence that asks something

reflexive pronoun – a word that refers back to another noun or pronoun in the sentence and is necessary to the meaning of the sentence

regular verb – a verb that adds *–d* or *–ed* to the present form to make the past and the past participle

sentence – a group of words that tells a complete thought

singular noun – a word that names one person, place, thing, or idea

speaker tag – the part of dialogue that identifies who is speaking

statement – a kind of sentence that tells something

subject – a word or words that tell whom or what the sentence is about

subject-verb agreement – the way a subject and verb match when both are singular or both are plural

tense – the time that verbs show, such as present, past, or future

verb – a word that shows action or a state of being

Literature & Comprehension

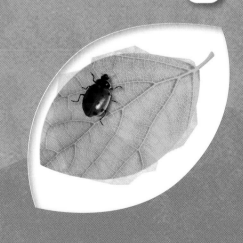

Introduce "The Lion and the Fox"

Unit Overview

In this unit, students will learn about the genre of fiction, identify the elements of fiction, and learn to make a prediction while reading these works:
  ► "The Lion and the Fox"
  ► "The Hound and the Hare"

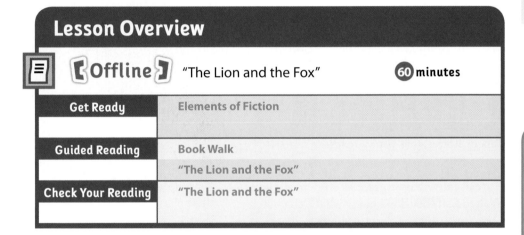

Lesson Overview

Offline	"The Lion and the Fox"	**60 minutes**
Get Ready	Elements of Fiction	
Guided Reading	Book Walk	
	"The Lion and the Fox"	
Check Your Reading	"The Lion and the Fox"	

Big Ideas

  ► Comprehension strategies can be taught through explicit instruction. Active, strong readers use existing knowledge to make predictions before, during, and after reading.
  ► Narrative and expository text differ significantly—for example, in structure, content, and purpose.
  ► Readers should be able to retell the story (or information) in their own words, not repeat verbatim what was written.

[Materials]

Supplied
  ● "The Lion and the Fox," *K¹² Classics for Young Readers, Volume B,* p. 1

Story Synopsis

In this story, a fox outsmarts a lion who lures animals into his den so he can eat them.

Keywords

character – a person or animal in a story
fiction – make-believe stories
plot – what happens in a story
prediction – a guess about what might happen that is based on information in a story and what you already know

 **60 minutes**

"The Lion and the Fox"

Work **together** with students to complete offline Get Ready, Guided Reading, and Check Your Reading activities.

Get Ready

Elements of Fiction

Discuss with students some of the basic elements of fiction to prepare them to read a work of fiction.

1. Tell students that they are going to read a type of writing called **fiction**. Ask students if they know what fiction is and to explain it. If they don't know what fiction is, tell them that fiction is writing that is made up by the author, or writer. The stories are not true.

   ▸ Why do you think we read fiction? for fun, entertainment
   ▸ What are some works of fiction, or stories, that you've read? Answers will vary.

2. Tell students that in fiction, there are usually **characters**. Ask students if they know what a character is and to explain it. If they don't know what a character is, tell them that a character is a person or animal in a story. Have students tell about one or two characters from stories they've read.

3. Explain that fiction also has a **plot**. Plot is what happens in a story. Have students give a brief summary of a story they've read.

 Objectives
- Define fiction.
- Define character.
- Define plot as what happens in a story.
- Set a purpose for reading.

Guided Reading

Book Walk

Prepare students by taking them on a Book Walk of "The Lion and the Fox." Scan the story together and ask students to make predictions about it.

1. Show students *K¹² Classics for Young Readers, Volume B*. Explain that this book contains many of the stories they will read.

   ▸ Make sure students know the difference between the **front and back covers**.
   ▸ Point to the book **title** and read it aloud.
   ▸ Have students look at the pictures on the covers.

2. Tell students that they are going to read a story from the book. Tell them that they can use the **table of contents** to find a story.

   ▸ Explain that a table of contents is a list of the stories in a book and the page numbers where each story can be found.
   ▸ Help students find the table of contents at the front of the book.

3. Help students use the table of contents to find "The Lion and the Fox," and turn to that page.

 Objectives
- Identify genre.
- Define prediction.
- Use text organizational features to locate and comprehend information (table of contents).
- Use an illustration to make a prediction about a reading.
- Read texts for literary experience.
- Identify characters in a story.
- Describe characters and their reactions to major events in the story.

4. Point to and read aloud the **title of the story**.

5. Point to the **illustration**. Remind students that an illustration is a drawing of something from a story. Have students describe what they see in the illustration. Possible answer: a dog, fox, or wolf; a lion; footprints

6. Review the definition of fiction, and then discuss.

   ▶ Do you think this story is fiction? Why or why not? Possible answers: yes, because there are animals in the story; there is an illustration

7. Remind students that a **character** is a person or animal in a story.

   ▶ Who do you think are the characters in the story? a fox, a lion
   ▶ Why do you think these are the characters? Possible answer: because of the title or the picture

8. Explain to students that they have just made a **prediction** about who the characters are. Tell students that a prediction is a guess about what might happen that is based on information in a story and what you already know. Explain that they will be making many predictions when they read.

9. Ask students to make a prediction about what will happen in the story. Model making a prediction about the story.
   Say: When I look at the picture, I see that the lion is lying down inside a cave. The fox looks smart and he looks like he's staying away from the lion. I think that the fox wants to stay away from the lion because the lion might try to hurt him. I think this makes sense because lions eat other animals. Let's read the story together and find out what happens.

TIP Gear this first Book Walk to students' level of experience. If they are already familiar with the text features described and making predictions, have students define the terms and let them point out the features.

"The Lion and the Fox"

Now it's time to read the story. Have students sit next to you so that they can see the pictures and words while you read the story aloud.

1. Read the story aloud all the way through. Track with your finger so students can follow along.

2. Reread the entire story with students, having them chime in and read aloud with you this time. Have them think about the characters and what they do. Tell students that you will pause at certain points in the story to discuss.

3. Begin to reread, pausing to discuss after the phrase, "he caught them and ate them."

   ▶ What character did we meet in this part of the story? the lion
   ▶ What does the lion do? He makes believe that he is very sick; he catches and eats the animals that come near his cave.
   ▶ How would you describe the lion? Possible answers: dishonest, tricky

4. Continue reading. Pause to discuss after the phrase, "he begged the fox to come in and see him."

   ▸ What character did we meet in this part of the story? the fox
   ▸ Do you think the fox will go in? Why or why not? Answers will vary. You may wish to ask students about foxes they know in other stories and what those foxes are like (clever or not clever).

5. Continue reading to the end of the story.

Check Your Reading

"The Lion and the Fox"

Have students retell the story in their own words to develop grammar, vocabulary, comprehension, and fluency skills. When finished, **ask students the following questions** to check comprehension and encourage discussion.

▸ Who are the characters in the story? the lion and the fox
▸ Where does the lion stay? in the cave
▸ Why does the lion pretend he is sick? He is too old and weak to hunt for food.
▸ What does the lion do when the animals come to see him? He eats them.
▸ What does the fox notice? He notices that all the tracks lead into the den, but none come out.
▸ What does the fox do? He stays outside the den and won't go in to see the lion.

Objectives
● Answer questions requiring literal recall of details.
● Identify characters in a story.

Review "The Lion and the Fox"

Lesson Overview

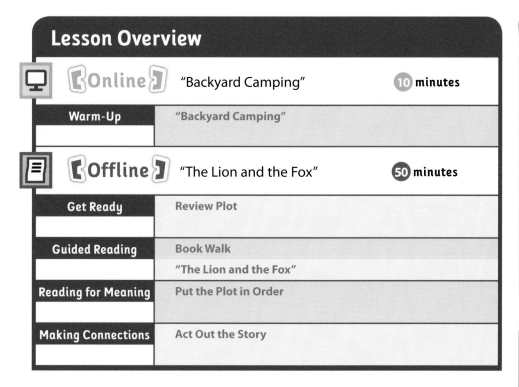

Online "Backyard Camping"		**10** minutes
Warm-Up	"Backyard Camping"	
Offline "The Lion and the Fox"		**50** minutes
Get Ready	Review Plot	
Guided Reading	Book Walk	
	"The Lion and the Fox"	
Reading for Meaning	Put the Plot in Order	
Making Connections	Act Out the Story	

Materials

Supplied
- "The Lion and the Fox," *K¹² Classics for Young Readers, Volume B,* p. 1
- *K¹² Language Arts Activity Book,* pp. LC 1–3

Also Needed
- "Backyard Camping" (optional)
- scissors, round-end safety
- glue stick

Keywords

character – a person or animal in a story
fiction – make-believe stories
plot – what happens in a story

Advance Preparation

If you are not able to complete the online Warm-Up, then print the selection and listen to students read aloud.

Big Ideas

▶ Readers need to be able to sequence and summarize.
▶ Readers should be able to retell the story (or information) in their own words, not repeat what was written.

 **10 minutes**

"Backyard Camping"
Students will work independently online to develop fluency and oral reading skills.

Warm-Up

"Backyard Camping"
The purpose of this activity is to improve students' oral reading and fluency. Students will read "Backyard Camping." Remind students to listen to the model on each screen before they begin their recording.

 Objectives
- Increase oral reading skills.
- Increase fluency.

Offline Alternative

No computer access? Print a copy of "Backyard Camping" from Advance Preparation. Have students read it aloud. Make note of any pronunciation errors, and review those words with students.

 **50 minutes**

"The Lion and the Fox"
Work **together** with students to complete the Get Ready, Guided Reading, Reading for Meaning, and Making Connections activities.

Get Ready

Review Plot
Review with students the elements of a plot.

1. Review with students the definition of **plot** as what happens in a story.

2. Explain to students that a plot has a beginning, middle, and an end, or what happens first, next, and last in a story.

3. Have students describe something that they do every day, such as eating dinner or brushing their teeth, using the words beginning, middle, and end.

 Objectives
- Define plot as what happens in a story.

Guided Reading

Book Walk

Prepare students by taking them on a Book Walk of "The Lion and the Fox." Scan the story together to revisit the characters and events.

1. Have students use the **table of contents** to find "The Lion and the Fox." Ask students to read aloud the title of the story.

2. Have them look at the picture, and then prompt them with these questions.

   ▸ Which characters do you see in the picture? a lion and a fox
   ▸ How does the story begin? Possible response: A lion is too old and weak to hunt.

3. If students do not remember the beginning, model how to recount the beginning of a story.
   Say: I remember the beginning of the story. It said that the lion had gotten old and weak, so he couldn't hunt anymore.

Objectives

- Identify characters in a story.
- Recount or describe key ideas or details from a text read aloud or information presented orally or through other media.
- Read texts for literary experience.
- Describe characters and their reactions to major events in the story.

"The Lion and the Fox"

Now it's time to read the story. Have students sit next to you so that they can see the pictures and words while you read the story aloud.

1. **Say:** Remember, we call the things that happen in a story the **plot**. Today we will focus on the events that happen at the beginning, middle, and end of the story. Chime in and read aloud with me. As we read, we will pause at certain points to talk about the plot, or what is happening.

2. Read the story aloud. Pause to discuss after the phrase, "he caught them and ate them."

   ▸ What did the lion do when he got too old to hunt? He went into his den and pretended he was sick.
   ▸ What happened to the animals that went into his den? The lion ate them.
   Say: If you can answer these questions, then you understand the beginning of the story. Now we'll move on to the middle of the story.

3. Continue reading. Pause to discuss after the phrase, "he begged the fox to come in and see him."

   ▸ What character did we meet in this part of the story? the fox
   ▸ What does the lion want the fox to do? Come in and see him.
   Say: I could retell the middle part of the story with your answers to these questions. I could say, "A fox came along, and the lion wants the fox to come into his den."

4. Continue reading to the end of the story, and then discuss.

   ▸ Did the fox go into the lion's den? Why not? No, he didn't go into the den. He noticed that footprints only went into the den, and he didn't want to be eaten.

Reading for Meaning

Put the Plot in Order

Have students use their knowledge of the plot of "The Lion and the Fox" to help them complete pages LC 1–3 in *K[12] Language Arts Activity Book.*

1. Review with students that stories have plots. A **plot** is what happens in a story.

2. Explain that what happens in a plot happens in an order. Some things happen at the beginning, some things happen in the middle, and some things happen at the end.

3. Review the meanings of the words *beginning, middle,* and *end* by discussing what happened during an event or special time of the day.
   Say: At the beginning of my morning, I woke up and went to the kitchen. In the middle of my morning, I made breakfast for everyone and cleaned up. At the end of my morning, I got dressed. [Or use examples from your own day.]

   ▶ What happened at the beginning, middle, and end of your morning?

4. Explain that students are going to put the parts of the plot from the "The Lion and the Fox" in the order in which they happened.

5. Help students cut out the pictures of events from the story on page LC 1 and glue them in the appropriate spaces on page LC3.

Objectives
- Identify plot elements.
- Describe the overall structure of a story, including describing how the beginning introduces the story and the ending concludes the action.
- Use a graphic organizer to organize information.

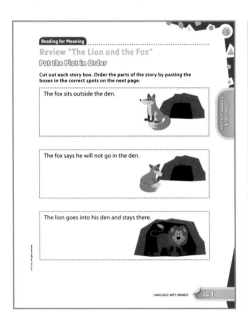

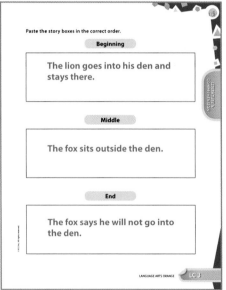

Making Connections

Act Out the Story

Have students act out the story, either by pretending to be the characters or by using stuffed animals, as a response to the text and to reinforce the story's plot.

1. Act out the story. You and students could act out different parts, or students could play all roles. Students may even want to add other animals that enter the lion's den.

2. Allow students to use dialogue from the story or add their own dialogue. Model and encourage students to use different voices for each animal, to reinforce their understanding of characters.

3. As students act out the plot, check to make sure that they are retelling the story in order, with elements from the beginning, middle, and end of the plot. For example, the lion should go into his den and pretend to be sick before animals come to visit him. Other animals should visit the lion in his den and get eaten before the fox stops by. The fox should sit down outside the den and ask about the lion before the lion invites the fox in.

4. If students miss an important point in the plot or retell events out of order, gently interrupt their drama and ask questions about whether the events are in the right order. For example,

   ▸ What did the fox do before he noticed the footprints outside the den?
   ▸ What did the lion say when he saw the fox?

Ask students to continue their story, either from the beginning or from where they left off.

Objectives

- Summarize the plot of a story.
- Recount stories, including fables and folktales from diverse cultures.
- Acknowledge differences in the points of view of characters, including by speaking in a different voice for each character when reading dialogue aloud.
- Speak clearly and at an appropriate pace for the type of communication.

Introduce "The Hound and the Hare"

Lesson Overview

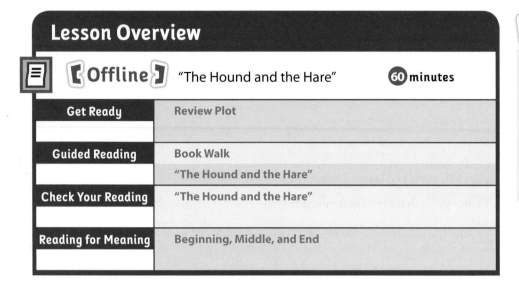

Offline	"The Hound and the Hare"	60 minutes
Get Ready	Review Plot	
Guided Reading	Book Walk	
	"The Hound and the Hare"	
Check Your Reading	"The Hound and the Hare"	
Reading for Meaning	Beginning, Middle, and End	

Big Ideas

▶ Comprehension is the reason for reading.
▶ Comprehension entails having and knowing a purpose for reading
▶ Comprehension entails asking and answering questions about the text.

Materials

Supplied

- "The Hound and the Hare," *K¹² Classics for Young Readers, Volume B*, p. 2
- *K¹² Language Arts Activity Book*, p. LC 4

Story Synopsis

A hound chases a hare, sometimes playfully and sometimes menacingly. The hare wants to know whether the hound is a friend or an enemy.

Keywords

fiction – make-believe stories
character – a person or animal in a story
plot – what happens in a story
prediction – a guess about what might happen that is based on information in a story and what you already know

 **60 minutes**

"The Hound and the Hare"

Work **together** with students to complete offline Get Ready, Guided Reading, Check Your Reading, and Reading for Meaning activities.

Get Ready

Review Plot

Review with students the elements of a plot.

1. Remind students that **plot** is what happens in a story. A plot has a beginning, middle, and an end, or what happens first, next, and last in a story.

2. Have students describe the plot of a story they have read or a movie they've seen using the words *beginning*, *middle*, and *end*.

3. Model the skill. Tell students the plot of the story "The Lion and the Fox."
   Say: At the beginning of the story, a lion was too weak to hunt. He pretended to be sick so animals would visit him in his den, and then he would eat them. In the middle of the story, a fox came to the den but wouldn't go in. The lion asked the fox to come in, but the fox wouldn't. At the end of the story, the fox said he wouldn't go enter because he saw the footprints that led into the den.

Objectives
- Define plot.

Guided Reading

Book Walk

Prepare students by taking them on a Book Walk of "The Hound and the Hare." Scan the story together and ask students to make predictions about it.

1. Tell students that they are going to read a story from *K¹² Classics for Young Readers, Volume B*.

2. Remind students that they can use the **table of contents** to find the story. If necessary, review what a table of contents is. Help students use the table of contents to find "The Hound and the Hare," and turn to that page.

3. Point to and read aloud the **title of the story**.

4. Point to the **illustration**. Remind students that an illustration is a drawing of something from a story. Have students describe what they see in the illustration.

5. Review the definition of **fiction**.

   ▸ Do you think this story is fiction? Why? Answers will vary. Students should express a reason for their opinion about the story's genre. They may cite the pictures or some other reason.

6. Ask students why they are going to read the story.

   ▸ Do you think you're going to read this to get information or for fun? fun

Objectives
- Use text organizational features to locate and comprehend information (table of contents).
- Identify genre.
- Set a purpose for reading.
- Define character.
- Define plot as what happens in a story.
- Use an illustration to make a prediction about a reading.
- Read texts for literary experience.
- Identify characters in a story.
- Describe characters and their reactions to major events in the story.

7. Remind students that a **character** is a person or animal in a story.

   ▸ Who do you think the characters are? Possible answer: I think these are the characters because there are pictures of them.

8. Review the definition of **prediction**. Model making a prediction about the story. Then ask students to make a prediction about what will happen. **Say:** When I look at the picture, I see that the hound looks like he is ready to play. The hare looks like he is talking. I think the hare is saying something to the hound.

   ▸ What do you think will happen? Why? Possible answer: I think the hound will try to play with the hare and the hare won't want to because that's what the picture shows.

"The Hound and the Hare"
Now it's time to read the story. Have students sit next to you so that they can see the pictures and words while you read the story aloud.

1. Read the story aloud all the way through. Track with your finger so students can follow along.

2. Reread the entire story with students, having them chime in and read aloud with you this time. Tell them to think about the characters and what they do. Tell students that you will pause at certain points in the story to discuss.

3. Begin to reread, pausing to discuss after the phrase, "as if playing with another dog."

   ▸ What characters did we meet in this part of the story? a hound and a hare
   ▸ What does the hound do? He startles the hare and plays a game with her.
   ▸ How would you describe the hound? Possible answer: He likes to play games.
   Say: I think that the hound is playing very roughly with the hare and teasing her. He acts like he is playing one moment and then bites the hare the next.

4. Continue reading. Pause to discuss after the phrase, "the hare stopped running."

   ▸ Why did the hare stop running? She didn't know if she would be eaten or be the hound's friend.
   ▸ What do you think the hare will do next? She's going to find out why the hound is acting this way.
   Say: I think the hare is getting upset. I know I get upset when I don't know why someone is acting a certain way. I think that the hare will ask the hound what he is up to.

5. Continue reading to the end of the story.

Check Your Reading

"The Hound and the Hare"
Have students retell the story in their own words to develop grammar, vocabulary, comprehension, and fluency skills. When finished, **ask students the following questions** to check comprehension and encourage discussion.

▶ Who are the main characters in the story? the hound and the hare

▶ What does the hound do after he startles the hare? He begins to chase her.

▶ What is the game that the hound plays with the hare? Sometimes he bites her and sometimes he tumbles her in the grass.

▶ What does the hare do? She stops running.

▶ What does the hare ask the hound? She wants to know whether the hound is her friend or her enemy.

Objectives
- Answer questions requiring literal recall of details.
- Identify characters in a story.

Reading for Meaning

 Beginning, Middle, and End

Review **plot** with students and introduce order words. Turn to page LC 4 in *K¹² Language Arts Activity Book*.

1. Remind students that a story has a **plot**. The plot is what happens in the story. Plots have a beginning, a middle, and an end. Tell students that sometimes we use the words *beginning, middle,* and *end* when we talk about plot, but sometimes we can use other words.
   Say: We can also say **first** for the beginning, **next** for the middle, and **finally** for the end. These are order words that tell the order in which things happened.

2. Give an example of how to use these order words to talk about beginning, middle, and end.
   Say: I can use these order words to tell you about my morning. First, I got out of bed and got dressed. Next, I ate breakfast. Finally, I brushed my teeth.

3. Tell students they will put the parts of "The Hound and the Hare" in order using the words *first, next,* and *finally.*

4. Have students complete the Activity Book page. Have them either write the answers themselves or dictate their answers to you.

5. Review students' answers when they have completed the Activity Book page.

 Brainstorm other order words with students, such as **then**, **second**, and **last**.

Objectives
- Identify plot elements.
- Summarize the plot of a story.
- Describe the overall structure of a story, including describing how the beginning introduces the story and the ending concludes the action.
- Use a graphic organizer to organize information.

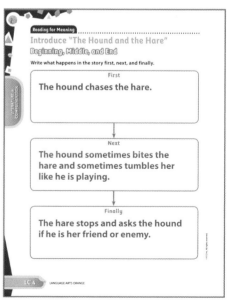

Reading for Meaning

Introduce "The Hound and the Hare"
Beginning, Middle, and End

Write what happens in the story first, next, and finally.

First
The hound chases the hare.

Next
The hound sometimes bites the hare and sometimes tumbles her like he is playing.

Finally
The hare stops and asks the hound if he is her friend or enemy.

LC 4   LANGUAGE ARTS ORANGE

Review "The Hound and the Hare"

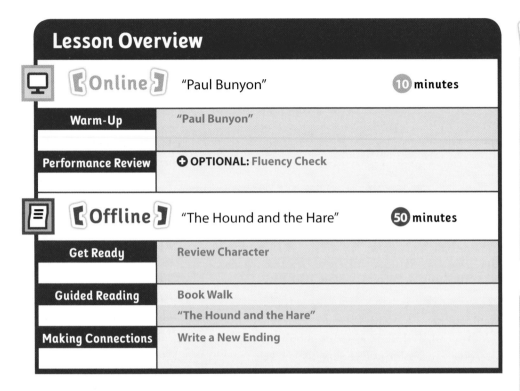

Lesson Overview

Online — "Paul Bunyon" — 10 minutes

Warm-Up	"Paul Bunyon"
Performance Review	⊕ OPTIONAL: Fluency Check

Offline — "The Hound and the Hare" — 50 minutes

Get Ready	Review Character
Guided Reading	Book Walk
	"The Hound and the Hare"
Making Connections	Write a New Ending

Materials

Supplied
- "The Hound and the Hare," *K¹² Classics for Young Readers, Volume B*, p. 2
- *K¹² Language Arts Activity Book*, p. LC 5
- "Paul Bunyon" (optional)
- Fluency Performance Checklist (optional)

Keywords
character – a person or animal in a story
fiction – make-believe stories
plot – what happens in a story

Advance Preparation

If you are not able to complete the online Warm-Up, then print the selection and listen to students read aloud.

Big Ideas

Readers should be able to retell the story (or information) in their own words, not repeat what was written. Active, strong readers employ reading strategies such as making connections between text and self.

 **10 minutes**

"Paul Bunyon"
Students will work independently online to develop fluency and oral reading skills.

Warm-Up

"Paul Bunyon"
The purpose of this activity is to improve students' oral reading and fluency. Students will read "Paul Bunyon." Remind students to listen to the model on each screen before they begin their recording.

> **Objectives**
> - Increase oral reading skills.
> - Increase fluency.

Offline Alternative
No computer access? Print a copy of "Paul Bunyon" from Advance Preparation. Have students read it aloud. Make note of any pronunciation errors, and review those words with students.

Performance Review

✚ OPTIONAL: Fluency Check
Listen to students' recordings, and use the checklist to review fluency and track performance. Keep the completed checklist so you can review students' progress over time.

> **Objectives**
> - Review aloud grade-level text with appropriate automaticity, prosody, accuracy, and rate.

 **50 minutes**

"The Hound and the Hare"
Work **together** with students to complete Get Ready, Guided Reading, and Making Connections activities.

Get Ready

Review Character
Discuss characters in fiction stories.

> **Objectives**
> - Define character.

1. Review with students that a **character** is a person or animal in a story.

2. Have students name some characters they have read about in other stories and tell something about them.

3. Tell students that as they read, they should focus on the characters in the story.

Guided Reading

Book Walk

Prepare students by taking them on a Book Walk of "The Hound and the Hare." Scan the story together to revisit the characters and events.

1. Have students use the **table of contents** to find the story. Ask them to read aloud the title.

2. Have students look at the picture.

   ► Which characters do you see in the picture? a hound and a hare
   ► How does the story begin? Possible answer: A hound startles a hare and chases her.
   ► If students do not remember the beginning, model how to recount the beginning of a story.
   Say: I remember what happens first. A hound startles a hare and begins to chase her.

"The Hound and the Hare"

Now it's time to read the story. Have students sit next to you so that they can see the pictures and words while you read the story aloud.

1. **Say:** We call the things that happen in a story the **plot**. Today we will focus on the events that happen at the beginning, middle, and end of the story. Chime in and read aloud with me. As we read, we will pause at certain points to talk about the plot, or what is happening.

2. Pause to discuss after the phrase, "as if playing with another dog."

   ► Who are the characters in the story? a hound and a hare
   ► What was the game that the hound played with the hare? Sometimes he would bite her and sometimes he would play with her like another dog.
   Say: If you can answer these questions, then you understand the beginning of the story or what happens first. Now we'll move on to the middle of the story, or what happens next.

3. Continue reading. Pause to discuss after the phrase, "the hare stopped running."

   ► What did the hare do after a while? She stopped running.
   ► Why did she do this? She didn't know if she would be eaten or be the hound's friend.
   Say: I could retell the middle part of the story with your answers to these questions. I could say, "After a while, the hare stopped running because she didn't know if she would be eaten or be the hound's friend."

4. Continue reading to the end of the story, and then discuss.

   ► What does the hare tell the hound? She wishes he would act truthfully.
   ► What does the hare want to know? if the hound is her friend or her enemy

TIP If students are capable, have them retell the story in their own words, in order from beginning to middle to end. Make sure they have included the answers to every question above. If they miss one of these plot points, ask them the question and then have them begin retelling again. Prompt them to use the words *first*, *next*, and *finally*.

Objectives

- Use text organizational features to locate and comprehend information (table of contents).
- Identify characters in a story.
- Recount or describe key ideas or details from a text read aloud or information presented orally or through other media.
- Read texts for literary experience.
- Describe characters and their reactions to major events in the story.
- Recount stories, including fables and folktales from diverse cultures.

Making Connections

 Write a New Ending

Have students generate another possible ending for "The Hound and the Hare" by completing page LC 5 in *K¹² Language Arts Activity Book*.

1. Remind students that a **character** is a person or animal in a story. Have students tell who the two characters are in this story.

2. Read the ending (the last paragraph) of the story again with students. Ask them to rephrase in their own words what the hare says. Possible response: The hare says, "Hound, I wish you would stop playing around. If you're my friend, you should be nice to me and not bite me. If you're not my friend, then you shouldn't play with me and just go away."

3. Have students think about this ending. Then have them write a new ending on the Activity Book page, telling what the hound says or does in response to the hare. Encourage students to be creative in their responses; there is no wrong answer.

4. Allow students to illustrate their new endings, if they like.

TIP If students have difficulty writing their new endings on their own, have them dictate their stories as you write them down.

 Reward: Write the names of the literature selections completed in this unit on the My Accomplishments chart and add a sticker to mark successful completion of this unit.

Objectives
- Generate plausible alternative endings to plot.
- Make connections between text and self.

Making Connections
Review "The Hound and the Hare"
Write a New Ending

Write a new ending to the story. What does the Hound say to the Hare in your ending?

Answers will vary.

LANGUAGE ARTS ORANGE — LC 5

Introduce "The Life of a Butterfly"

Unit Overview

In this unit, students will focus on the genre of nonfiction by exploring informational articles on the butterfly and the honeybee. They will then shift their attention to reading poetry about insects. Students will read the following selections:

- ► "The Life of a Butterfly"
- ► "I See a Honeybee"
- ► "Caterpillars"
- ► "Bee Song"
- ► "Bees"
- ► "Wasps"
- ► "Bugs"

Lesson Overview

〖 Offline 〗 "The Life of a Butterfly," Part 1	60 minutes
Get Ready	What Is Nonfiction?
	Words to Know
Guided Reading	Book Walk
	"The Life of a Butterfly," Part 1
Check Your Reading	"The Life of a Butterfly," Part 1
Reading for Meaning	Main Idea and Supporting Details

Big Ideas

- ► Nonfiction texts differ from fiction texts in that they describe real or true things in life, rather than things made up by the author.
- ► To understand important information in a text, readers must be familiar with text features and their purposes.
- ► Readers need to be able to sequence, summarize, and articulate the main idea.
- ► Verbalizing your thoughts while modeling a reading strategy allows students to see what goes on inside the head of an effective reader; it makes visible the normally hidden process of comprehending text.
- ► Comprehension entails an understanding of the organizational patterns of text.

〖 Materials 〗

Supplied

- "The Life of a Butterfly," *Wings, Antennae, and Tails*, pp. 2–9
- *K¹² Language Arts Activity Book*, p. LC 7

Article Synopsis

This article tells about the life cycle of the butterfly. Butterflies start life as an egg, then hatch into a hungry caterpillar. After molting four or five times, the caterpillar sheds its skin a final time and a makes a hard shell called a chrysalis. Inside the shell, the caterpillar, now called a pupa, transforms into a butterfly. After hatching, the butterfly must wait for its wings to dry before it searches for nectar to eat.

Keywords

bold type – type that is darker than the surrounding text that draws attention to a word or phrase

caption – writing under a picture that describes the picture

detail – a piece of information in a text

heading – a title within the body of a text that tells the reader something important about a section of the text

main idea – the most important idea in a paragraph or text

supporting detail – a detail that gives more information about a main idea

topic – the subject of a text

 **Offline** **60** minutes

"The Life of a Butterfly," Part 1

Work **together** with students to complete offline Get Ready, Guided Reading, Check Your Reading, and Reading for Meaning activities.

Get Ready

What Is Nonfiction?

Introduce students to the genre of nonfiction by describing its purpose and what it contains.

1. Ask students if they know what **nonfiction** is. If students don't know, explain that nonfiction is writing about true information or real things. Nonfiction is different from fiction, which is made up from the author's imagination.

   ▶ Why would you read nonfiction? to learn something; for information; for fun

2. Tell students that authors have a purpose, or reason, for writing. Explain that the **purpose** could be to entertain, to inform, to express an opinion, or to persuade readers about something.

3. Tell students that when authors write to inform, they need to include **facts** in their writing. Explain that a fact is something that can be proven true. So you could find the fact in a book with true information, such as an encyclopedia or a dictionary, if you went to look for it.

4. Give students an example of a fact, such as, "We have five fingers on each hand." Then have students give examples of facts.

Objectives
- Define nonfiction.
- Define the author's purpose.
- Define fact.
- Increase concept and content vocabulary.

Words to Know

Before reading "The Life of a Butterfly," Part 1, go over Words to Know with students.

1. Have students say each word aloud.

2. Ask students if they know what each word means.

   ▶ If students know a word's meaning, have them define it and use it in a sentence.
   ▶ If students don't know a word's meaning, read them the definition and discuss the word with them.

antennae – sensors
larva – a young caterpillar
molt – to shed old skin

Guided Reading

Book Walk

Prepare students by taking them on a Book Walk of the magazine *Wings, Antennae, and Tails*. Scan the magazine together and ask students to make predictions about "The Life of a Butterfly."

1. Tell students that they are going to begin reading, in a magazine, a nonfiction article that contains facts.

2. Show students the **front cover** and **back cover** of the magazine. Point to and read aloud the **magazine's title**.

3. Locate the **table of contents** inside the magazine. Explain that this magazine is a collection of **nonfiction** articles on different subjects. Review the definition of nonfiction and have students tell why they will read these articles.

4. Point to "The Life of a Butterfly" in the table of contents and read the title aloud. Have students use the table of contents to find the selection and turn to that page.

5. Point to and read the title of the article. Model how to make predictions about an article using the title and prior knowledge.
   Say: I can make a prediction, or a guess, about what this article is going to be about. The title is "The Life of a Butterfly," so I think this is going to be about butterflies and how they live.

6. Look through the first four pages of the article with students. Have them describe what they see. Answers to questions will vary.

   ▸ What do you see that looks familiar to you?
   ▸ What do you see that is new to you?

7. Model how to make predictions using the pictures.
   Say: This photograph shows a picture of butterfly eggs. I can make a prediction that butterflies must lay eggs. I think the article is going to tell us about butterflies laying eggs.

8. Have students make a prediction using another picture in the first three pages of the article. If students have trouble repeating the model, prompt them with a question.

   ▸ What kinds of information do you think you'll find in this article?

Objectives
- Use text organizational features to locate and comprehend information (table of contents).
- Use an illustration to make a prediction about a reading.
- Use title of the selection to make a prediction.
- Define text features: table of contents, title, heading, caption, glossary, index, and bold text.

"The Life of a Butterfly," Part 1

Now it's time to read the article. Have students sit next to you so that they can see the pictures and words while you read the article aloud.

1. Read pages 2–5 (the first four pages of the article) aloud all the way through. Stop at the end of the page 5, after the sentence, "Then, they are ready for their next big change." As you read, track with your finger so students can follow along. Read the body of the article first. Then point to the photograph on each page and read the caption.

2. Reread pages 2–5 with students, having them chime in and read aloud with you this time. Tell them to look for special words that are different from the rest of the text. Tell students that you will pause at certain points in the article to discuss.

3. Begin to reread and pause to discuss at the end page 2, after the sentence, "The eggs look like tiny beads." Model how to summarize what you have just read as a way to help reading comprehension.
Say: I want to make sure that I understand what I've just read. I can do this by retelling the information in the paragraph in my own words. This paragraph says that all butterflies start out life as eggs.

4. Point to the photograph and caption on page 2. Explain to students what these text features are.
Say: This picture is a photograph. It shows something real. It's not a drawing. It did not come from an illustrator's imagination. The words under the photograph are called a **caption**. A caption explains what's in a photograph or other picture.

 ▶ What does the caption tell us is in the photograph? butterfly eggs

5. Read on and pause to discuss at the end of page 3, after the phrase, "yellow or red spots." Point to the word *larva*. Explain how the word is different from the rest of the text.
Say: This word *larva* looks different from the other words near it. It's darker than the other words. That's called **bold type**. Bold text lets us know that this is an important word. Sometimes words in bold type are words that may be new and have a definition nearby. The word *caterpillar* right before larva is the definition of larva. I know this because the word *or* tells me that *caterpillar* is the definition, or another word for larva.

6. Read to the end of page 5.

Check Your Reading

"The Life of a Butterfly," Part 1
Have students retell "The Life of a Butterfly" in their own words to develop grammar, vocabulary, comprehension, and fluency skills. When finished, **ask students the following questions** to check comprehension and encourage discussion.

 ▶ How many big changes does a butterfly go through? three
 ▶ How do butterflies start their lives? as eggs
 ▶ What is the first big change that butterflies go through? They hatch from the eggs.
 ▶ What is the name of what hatches from the egg? Use the name in bold text in the article. a larva
 ▶ What does a larva eat? Use the photograph on page 3 to help you. lots of leaves
 ▶ What word do we use to describe what happens as the larva grows bigger? What does the word mean? It molts, or sheds its old skin.

Objectives
- Use graphics and visuals to comprehend meaning and answer questions (diagrams, charts, captions).
- Use text features to comprehend text meaning (bold, italic, headers).
- Answer questions requiring literal recall of details.

Reading for Meaning

Main Idea and Supporting Details

Teach students to distinguish the topic of a nonfiction selection from the main idea, identify supporting details, and help them identify examples in "The Life of a Butterfly." Turn to page LC 7 of *K¹² Language Arts Activity Book*.

1. Explain to students that what the article is about is the **topic**. The topic is the subject of a text. You can usually say the topic in one or a few words. The topic of this text is the life cycle of the butterfly.

2. Tell students that the topic of an article is sometimes given in the **title**.

   ▶ Does the title provide the topic for this article ? yes

3. Tell students that the most important idea about a topic is called the **main idea**, which is the idea that the text is mostly about. Explain that there can be a main idea of a whole article or a main idea of part of a reading, such as a paragraph. The main idea is sometimes stated in a complete sentence.

4. Tell students that authors also give smaller pieces of information in nonfiction texts, which are called **details**. Details that give more information about main ideas are called **supporting details**.

5. Tell students you will help them find the main idea and supporting details for a paragraph in "The Life of a Butterfly."

6. Turn to the first paragraph on page 2 (the first page of the article). Tell students that sometimes the main idea is given in one of the sentences in the paragraph.

7. Point to the first sentence. Explain that this sentence is the main idea of this paragraph.
   Say: Let's look at this paragraph. Each sentence in this paragraph tells us about the different ways that you change. I think that the first sentence tells us the main idea because it says that you change in many ways.

8. Explain how the other sentences in the first paragraph are supporting details.
   Say: The other sentences are supporting details. Each sentence tells about one way that you change. For example, the second sentence says, "You get taller." This can't be the main idea, because the other sentences tell about other ways you change. But this can be a supporting detail because it is one of the many ways that you change.

9. Demonstrate this same skill with the second paragraph, showing students that the first sentence of the second paragraph is the main idea and the others are supporting details. Tell students that the main idea of a paragraph does not have to be the first sentence and sometimes the main idea is not stated.

Objectives

- Define topic.
- Identify the topic.
- Define main idea.
- Distinguish the main idea from the topic.
- Define supporting details.
- Identify the main idea and supporting details in a text.
- Use a graphic organizer to organize information.

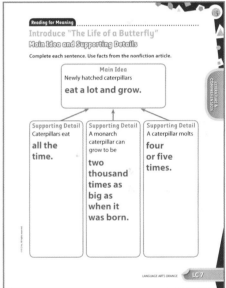

10. Have students point out the main idea (first sentence) and a supporting detail (second sentence) of the third paragraph.

11. Turn to page 3. Explain that there can be main ideas of parts of articles, too.

12. Reread page 3. Have students find the main idea and supporting details of the second page by asking questions.

> ▸ In a word or two, what is this page about? larva
> ▸ What is the most important, or main, idea about larva? The first big change for a butterfly is from egg to larva.
> ▸ What are some details that support this main idea? Butterflies lay their eggs on plants. Larva hatch from the eggs. Not all larva look the same.

13. Have students complete the Activity Book page.

14. Review students' Activity Book page and discuss any changes they need to make.

TIP If students have difficulty completing the Activity Book page, help them fill in the boxes by asking the same questions as those in Step 12.

Review "The Life of a Butterfly"

Lesson Overview

🖥 **[Online]** "Soap Box Derby"	**10** minutes
Warm-Up	"Soap Box Derby"

📄 **[Offline]** "The Life of a Butterfly," Part 2	**50** minutes
Get Ready	Retell Main Ideas
	Words to Know
Guided Reading	Book Walk
	"The Life of a Butterfly," Part 2
Check Your Reading	"The Life of a Butterfly," Part 2
Reading for Meaning	Main Idea and Supporting Details
Making Connections	Main Idea of an Article
Beyond the Lesson	➕ **OPTIONAL:** Make a Butterfly Book

Materials

Supplied

- "The Life of a Butterfly," *Wings, Antennae, and Tails*, pp. 2–9
- *K¹² Language Arts Activity Book*, p. LC 8
- "Soap Box Derby" (optional)

Also Needed

- paper, construction (optional)
- stapler (optional)

Keywords

bold type – type that is darker than the surrounding text that draws attention to a word or phrase

caption – writing under a picture that describes the picture

diagram – a drawing or design that shows how pieces of information are related

heading – a title within the body of a text that tells the reader something important about a section of the text

main idea – the most important idea in a paragraph or text

supporting detail – a detail that gives more information about a main idea

topic – the subject of a text

Advance Preparation

If you are not able to complete the online Warm-Up, then print the selection and listen to students read aloud.

Big Ideas

- ▸ Nonfiction texts differ from fiction texts in that they describe real or true things in life, rather than things made up by the author.
- ▸ To understand important information in a text, readers must be familiar with text features and their purposes.
- ▸ Readers need to be able to sequence, summarize, and articulate the main idea.
- ▸ Verbalizing your thoughts while modeling a reading strategy allows students to see what goes on inside the head of an effective reader; it makes visible the normally hidden process of comprehending text.

 **10 minutes**

"Soap Box Derby"

Students will work independently online to develop fluency and oral reading skills.

Warm-Up

"Soap Box Derby"

The purpose of this activity is to improve students' oral reading and fluency. Students will read "Soap Box Derby." Remind students to listen to the model on each screen before they begin their recording.

Objectives
- Increase oral reading skills.
- Increase fluency.

Offline Alternative

No computer access? Print a copy of "Soap Box Derby" from Advance Preparation. Have students read it aloud. Make note of any pronunciation errors, and review those words with students.

 **50 minutes**

"The Life of a Butterfly," Part 2

Work **together** with students to complete offline Get Ready, Guided Reading, Check Your Reading, Reading for Meaning, Making Connections, and Beyond the Lesson activities.

Get Ready

Retell Main Ideas

Tell students that they are going to continue reading "The Life of a Butterfly." Ask them to use some of the main ideas from the first part of the article to tell about what they read on pages 2–5.

Objectives
- Identify the main idea and supporting details in a text.
- Increase concept and content vocabulary.

Words to Know

Before reading "The Life of a Butterfly," Part 2, go over Words to Know with students.

1. Ask students to define the following words from Part 1 and use them in a sentence:

   antennae   **larva**   **molt**

2. Correct any incorrect or vague definitions.

3. Have students say the words below, which they will encounter in Part 2.

4. Ask students if they know what the word means.

   ▶ If students know the word's meaning, have them define it and use it in a sentence.
   ▶ If students don't know the word's meaning, read them the definition and discuss the word with them.

chrysalis – the hard shell a caterpillar makes the last time it molts

nectar – sweet liquid from flowers

proboscis – the part of a butterfly's life cycle body that works like a straw to drink nectar

pupa – the stage of a butterfly's life cycle when it is inside the chrysalis

Guided Reading

Book Walk

Prepare students by taking them on a Book Walk of the magazine *Wings, Antennae, and Tails*. Scan the magazine together and ask students to make predictions about the article.

1. Read the **title** of the magazine aloud.

2. Have students use the **table of contents** to find "The Life of a Butterfly" and turn to that page.

3. Look through pages 6–9 (last four pages of the article). Model for students how to make predictions using the pictures.
   Say: We've been reading about the big changes that butterflies go through. So far we've read about eggs and caterpillars. I think today we are going to learn about how caterpillars become butterflies, because in this picture I see a butterfly on a flower.

Objectives
- Use text organizational features to locate and comprehend information (table of contents).
- Use an illustration to make a prediction about a reading.
- Identify features of a nonfiction text.
- Use graphics and visuals to comprehend meaning and answer questions (diagrams, charts, captions).

"The Life of a Butterfly," Part 2

Now it's time to read the rest of "The Life of a Butterfly." Have students sit next to you so that they can see the pictures and words while you read the article aloud.

1. Remind students of where the first part of the article finished, to refresh their memory of what happened at the end of the first part.
   Say: Now, what did we read last time? I'm going to go back to the last paragraph we read in the first part of the article. I want to look at it so that I can remember what we read. The article says that caterpillars molt four or five times. Then they are ready for their next big change. So I guess this part of the article will be about the next change.

2. Read pages 6–9 aloud all the way through. Start on page 6 with the phrase, "The last time the caterpillar molts." Track with your finger so students can follow along. Read the body of the article first. Then point to the photographs on each page and read the captions.

3. Reread page 6–9 with students, having them chime in and read aloud with you this time. Tell them to look for facts about butterflies. Tell students you will pause at certain points in the article to discuss.

4. Begin to reread and pause to discuss at the end of page 7, after the sentence, "It

is a butterfly with beautiful colored wings!" Model how to retell what you just read to help comprehension.

Say: We just read that a caterpillar goes into a chrysalis. Then the caterpillar changes again. It comes out of the chrysalis as a butterfly.

5. Read to the end of the article. Pause at the end. Point to the photograph and **caption**. Have students tell the name of these text features. Have them point to the word in **bold text**. Have them tell why the word is in bold and what the word means.

6. Point to the diagram on the last page. Explain what this text feature is and discuss what it shows.

Say: This picture is called a **diagram**. A diagram is a drawing that shows how pieces of information are related. This diagram shows us the different changes in the life of a butterfly.

Check Your Reading

"The Life of a Butterfly," Part 2

Have students retell "The Life of a Butterfly" in their own words to develop grammar, vocabulary, comprehension, and fluency skills. When finished, **ask students the following questions** to check comprehension and encourage discussion.

▶ What is the name of the hard shell that a caterpillar makes? chrysalis
▶ What does the caterpillar become inside the chrysalis? a pupa
▶ When a butterfly comes out of the chrysalis, why doesn't it fly away? Its wings are still wet and need to dry.
▶ What kind of food do butterflies eat? nectar
▶ What part of their bodies do butterflies use to eat nectar? the proboscis
▶ What does the diagram on the last page of the article show? the stages in the life cycle of a butterfly

Objectives
- Use graphics and visuals to comprehend meaning and answer questions (diagrams, charts, captions).
- Use text features to comprehend text meaning. (bold, italic, headers).
- Answer questions requiring literal recall of details.

Reading for Meaning

Main Idea and Supporting Details
Have students identify main ideas and supporting details from the second part of "The Life of a Butterfly" to help them identify the main idea of the entire article. Turn to page LC 8 of *K¹² Language Arts Activity Book*.

1. Review the definition of main idea and how the main idea is different from the topic.

2. Remind students that there can be a main idea of a paragraph, a passage, or an entire article.

3. Review the definition of supporting details and how they relate to the main idea.

4. Tell students that you are going to review with them how to find the main idea and supporting details for a paragraph in today's reading.

5. Reread the first paragraph on page 6. Remind students that sometimes the

Objectives
- Define main idea.
- Distinguish the main idea from the topic.
- Define details.
- Define supporting details.
- Identify the main idea and supporting details in a text.
- Use a graphic organizer to organize information.

main idea of a paragraph is given in one of the sentences, and the other sentences are supporting details. Explain how to identify the main idea and supporting details of this paragraph.

► This paragraph is about what happens the last time the caterpillar molts.
► The first sentence is the main idea. It tells that something different happens.
► The other sentences are supporting details. Each sentence tells a piece of information about what happens the last time the caterpillar molts.

6. Have students demonstrate the skill with the second paragraph. **Say:** Now find the main idea and supporting details of the second paragraph by answering these questions.

► In a word or two, what is this paragraph about? the caterpillar in the chrysalis
► What is the most important, or main, idea? The caterpillar changes again inside the chrysalis.
► What are some details that support this main idea? The caterpillar becomes a pupa.

7. Have students identify the main idea and supporting details for page 8 of the article. Reread the whole page if necessary.

8. Turn to page 9 (last page of the article). Tell students that they are going to find the main idea and supporting details for the last page of the article.

9. Have students complete the Activity Book page.

10. Review the Activity Book page and discuss any changes students should make.

 If students have difficulty completing the Activity Book page on their own, help them fill in the boxes by asking them guiding questions about the article.

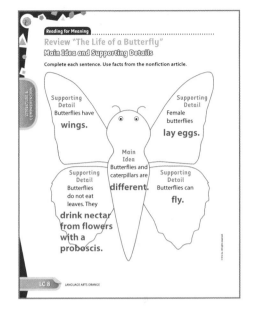

Making Connections

Main Idea of an Article

Help students identify the main idea and some supporting details for "The Life of a Butterfly."

1. Remind students that the purpose of nonfiction articles is to tell important information about a topic.

2. Explain that there is usually a main idea for an article—the most important thing the author wants us to know about the topic.

3. Tell students that they can use the nonfiction text features as clues to the main idea. Discuss the text features that are in this article—headings, a sidebar, bold text, photographs, captions, and a diagram.

4. Look back through the article and talk about what kind of information is

Objectives
• Use text features to comprehend text meaning (bold, italics, headers).
• Identify main idea.

presented in the text features—information about butterflies and their life cycle.

5. Have students suggest a main idea for this article. Guide students to think about the title of the article. Butterflies go through three changes in their life cycle.

6. If students provide a detail, explain why it's a supporting detail and not the main idea. The detail may tell us a piece of information about butterflies, but there are many other small pieces of information, too.

TIP If students continue to have difficulty, review some of the main ideas in the passages that students discussed and wrote about on Activity Book page LC 8.

Beyond the Lesson

✚ OPTIONAL: Make a Butterfly Book
This activity is OPTIONAL. It is intended for students who have extra time, or who would benefit from more work with the life cycle of a butterfly. Feel free to skip this activity.

Objectives
• Identify facts in informational text.

1. Have students label four sheets of construction paper with the four stages in butterfly development (see the diagram in "The Life of a Butterfly" for the titles of the stages).

2. Have students write one fact from "The Life of a Butterfly" article that shows what happens at each stage.

3. Tell students to draw an illustration of each stage of the life cycle on each page of the book. They may use the photographs in the article as a reference.

4. Have students create a title page for their book. Make sure they use a different title than the one for the article.

5. Have students staple the pages together to create a butterfly book.

Introduce "I See a Honeybee"

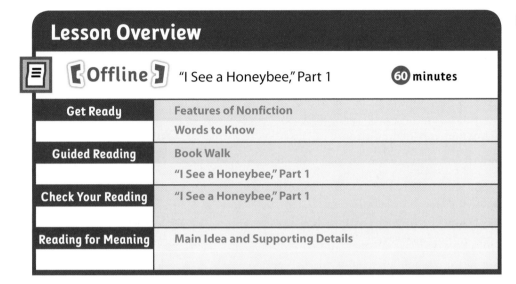

Lesson Overview

Offline "I See a Honeybee," Part 1   **60** minutes

Get Ready	Features of Nonfiction
	Words to Know
Guided Reading	Book Walk
	"I See a Honeybee," Part 1
Check Your Reading	"I See a Honeybee," Part 1
Reading for Meaning	Main Idea and Supporting Details

Big Ideas

▸ Readers need to be able to sequence, summarize, and articulate the main idea.
▸ Readers must understand the relationship between main idea and supporting details.
▸ Guided reading allows students to read a variety of texts and genres with support.
▸ Guided reading provides students with a model of fluent reading.

Materials

Supplied
- "I See a Honeybee," *Wings, Antennae, and Tails,* pp. 10–19
- *K¹² Language Arts Activity Book,* p. LC 9

Keywords

bold type – type that is darker than the surrounding text that draws attention to a word or phrase

caption – writing under a picture that describes the picture

detail – a piece of information in a text

fact – something that can be proven true

heading – a title within the body of a text that tells the reader something important about a section of the text

main idea – the most important idea in a paragraph or text

nonfiction – writings about true things

purpose – the reason for writing

supporting detail – a detail that gives more information about the main idea

topic – the subject of a text

 **60 minutes**

"I See a Honeybee," Part 1

Work **together** with students to complete offline Get Ready, Guided Reading, Check Your Reading, and Reading for Meaning activities.

Get Ready

Features of Nonfiction

Review with students the characteristics of the genre of nonfiction.

1. Have students recall any nonfiction they may have read. Answers will vary.

2. Brainstorm with students a list of everything they know about nonfiction. Make sure students include the following features of nonfiction.

   ▶ It is about true information.
   ▶ It contains facts.
   ▶ It contains text features such as headings, bold text, photographs, captions, and diagrams.
   ▶ It is about a topic.
   ▶ There are main ideas and supporting details.
   ▶ The author's purpose in writing nonfiction is to inform and possibly to entertain.

3. List the features that students miss and review any definitions as necessary.

Objectives
- Define nonfiction.
- Increase concept and content vocabulary.

Words to Know

Before reading "I See a Honeybee," Part 1, go over Words to Know with students.

1. Have students say each word aloud.

2. Ask students if they know what each word means.

   ▶ If students know a word's meaning, have them define it and use it in a sentence.
   ▶ If students don't know a word's meaning, read them the definition and discuss the word with them.

cells – sections of a hive used for storage or raising larvae
drones – worker bees
hive – honeybee home
larvae – young bees

Guided Reading

Book Walk

Prepare students by taking them on a Book Walk of the magazine *Wings, Antennae, and Tails*. Scan the magazine together and ask students to make predictions about "I See a Honeybee."

1. Show students the **front cover** and **back cover** of the magazine. Point to the **magazine title** and read it aloud.

2. Locate the **table of contents** inside the magazine. Review that the magazine is a collection of **nonfiction** articles on different subjects. Have students tell why they read nonfiction articles.

3. Point to "I See a Honeybee" in the table of contents and read the title aloud. Have students use the table of contents to find the article and turn to that page.

4. Point to and read aloud the title of the article. Have students make predictions about the article. Answers to questions may vary.

   ▸ What do you think this article is about?
   ▸ What do you already know about honeybees?

5. Look through pages 10–15 with students. Have them describe what they see. Point to the **photographs** and have students make predictions using the pictures. Answers to questions may vary.

   ▸ What do you see that looks familiar to you?
   ▸ What do you see that is new to you?
   ▸ What kinds of information do you think you'll find in this article?

Objectives

- Identify genre.
- Identify purpose for reading.
- Use text organizational features to locate and comprehend information (table of contents).
- Use an illustration to make a prediction about a reading.
- Use title of the selection to make a prediction.
- Apply information read to answer questions.
- Define text features: illustration, graph, chart, text box, diagram, time line, map.
- Define text features: table of contents, title, heading, caption, glossary, index, bold text.

"I See a Honeybee," Part 1

Now it's time to read "I See a Honeybee." Have students sit next to you so that they can see the pictures and words while you read the article aloud.

1. Read page 10–15 (first six pages of the article) aloud all the way through. Stop at the end of page 15. Track with your finger so students can follow along. Read the body of the article first. Then point to the photograph on each page and read its caption.

2. Reread pages 10–15 with students, having them chime in and read aloud with you this time. Tell students to look for special words that are different from the rest of the text. Tell them you will pause at certain points in the article to discuss.

3. Begin to reread, pausing to discuss at the end of page 10 after the phrase, "twenty thousand more bees." Have students tell about what they read.

   ▸ What did we learn about honeybees on this page? They live in hives of ten or twenty thousand bees.

4. Point to the photograph and caption. Have students tell what these text features are. Identify them if necessary.
   Say: This picture is a **photograph**. The words under the photograph are called a **caption**. A caption is text that explains what's in a photograph or other picture.

5. Point to the word *hive* on the first page. Have students identify this text feature as **bold type**. Identify it for them if necessary.
   Say: This word *hive* is in **bold type**, which is darker than the rest of the text. Bold type tells us a word is important. A bold type word may be new and the meaning of the word might be nearby. The definition is sometimes separated by a comma and the word *or*. What word is the definition of the word *hive*? home.

6. Read on and pause to discuss at the end of page 12, which has the heading "Queen Bees and All the Rest." Have students identify this text feature as a **heading**.

   ▶ What is the purpose of a heading? It's the title of a section of text. It tells us something important about the information that is in the section of text that follows.

7. Read to the end of page 15.

Check Your Reading

"I See a Honeybee," Part 1

Have students retell "I See a Honeybee" in their own words to develop grammar, vocabulary, comprehension, and fluency skills. When finished, **ask students the following questions** to check comprehension and encourage discussion.

Objectives
• Answer questions requiring literal recall of details.

   ▶ Where do honeybees live? in a hive
   ▶ How many honeybees live in a hive? ten or twenty thousand
   ▶ What are drones? male bees
   ▶ What is the important job of the queen bee? She lays eggs.
   ▶ What is one way that worker bees help in the hive? Possible responses: They build the hive; they store food in the cells; they take care of the larvae.
   ▶ What do worker bees do when their queen becomes sick or dies? They choose one of the female larvae to become the new queen.

Reading for Meaning

Main Idea and Supporting Details

Help students review the difference between the topic of a nonfiction selection and the main idea and identify supporting details that give more information about main ideas. Turn to LC 9 of *K¹² Language Arts Activity Book*.

1. Review that what an article is about is called the **topic**. The topic is the subject of a text. You can usually say the topic in one or a few words. Have students identify the topic in "I See a Honeybee." honeybees

2. Point out that the topic of an article is sometimes given in the **title** of the article or text. Have students tell whether or not this is true with this article. Yes

3. Review that the most important idea about a topic is called the **main idea**. Remind students that there can be a main idea of an article or a part of a reading, such as a paragraph. The main idea is usually stated in a complete sentence.

4. Review that smaller pieces of information in nonfiction texts are called **details**. Details that give more information about main ideas are called **supporting details**.

5. Tell students you are going to help them find the main idea and supporting details for a paragraph in "I See a Honeybee."

6. Reread the first paragraph of page 12, which has the heading "Queen Bees and All the Rest." Remind students that sometimes the main idea is given in one of the sentences in the paragraph. Point to the first sentence. Explain that this sentence is the main idea of this paragraph.
   Say: This paragraph talks about the different kinds of honeybees. I think that the first sentence is the main idea because it says there are three types of bees.

7. Explain to students how the other sentences in the first paragraph are supporting details.

   ▸ The other sentences are supporting details. Each sentence tells about the different types of bees.
   ▸ For example, the second sentence says, "There are female worker bees and male drones."
   ▸ This can be a supporting detail because it tells about two kinds of bees.
   ▸ It can't be the main idea, though, because the rest of the paragraph talks about another type of bee, the queen.

8. Identify the main idea and supporting details in the second paragraph, showing students that the first sentence of the second paragraph is the main idea and the others are supporting details.

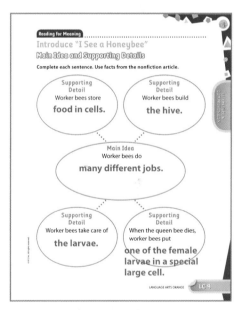

9. Guide students to locate the main idea (second sentence) and supporting details of the third paragraph. Remind them that the main idea of a paragraph does not have to be the first sentence and model how to find the main idea in another sentence.

   ▶ Sometimes the first sentence of a paragraph is not the main idea of a paragraph.
   ▶ The first sentence in this paragraph is not the main idea.
   ▶ It tells about drones, but the rest of the paragraph is about worker bees.
   ▶ The main idea is in the second sentence.
   ▶ That sentence says that most of the eggs become worker bees, and that's what this paragraph is mostly about.
   ▶ The next two sentences are supporting details about worker bees.

10. Tell students that you will help them find the main idea of pages 12–13. Explain that **headings**, like the one on page 12, give a clue to the main idea for the text that follows. Read the heading with students. Then help students find the main idea and supporting details pages 12–13 by asking questions.

    ▶ In a word or two, what is this page about? the types of honeybees
    ▶ What is the most important, or main, idea about honeybees? There are three types of honeybees.
    ▶ What are some details that support this main idea? There are queen bees who lay eggs. There are male drones. There are female worker bees who build the hive and take care of the larvae.

11. Have students complete the Activity Book page. Remind them to use the heading on the page to help them identify the main idea.

12. Review the Activity Book page and discuss any changes they need to make.

(TIP) If students have difficulty completing the Activity Book page, help them fill in the boxes by asking guiding questions as you did for the first two pages of the article.

Review "I See a Honeybee"

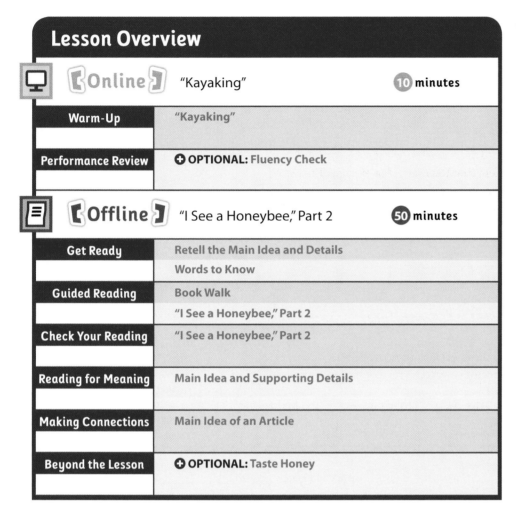

Lesson Overview

🖥 【Online】 "Kayaking" ⑩ minutes

Warm-Up	"Kayaking"
Performance Review	➕ OPTIONAL: Fluency Check

📄 【Offline】 "I See a Honeybee," Part 2 ㊿ minutes

Get Ready	Retell the Main Idea and Details
	Words to Know
Guided Reading	Book Walk
	"I See a Honeybee," Part 2
Check Your Reading	"I See a Honeybee," Part 2
Reading for Meaning	Main Idea and Supporting Details
Making Connections	Main Idea of an Article
Beyond the Lesson	➕ OPTIONAL: Taste Honey

【Materials】

Supplied
- "I See a Honeybee," *Wings, Antennae, and Tails*, pp. 10–19
- *K¹² Language Arts Activity Book*, pp. LC 9–10
- "Kayaking" (optional)
- Fluency Performance Checklist (optional)

Keywords

bold type – type that is darker than the surrounding text that draws attention to a word or phrase

caption – writing under a picture that describes the picture

detail – a piece of information in a text

diagram – a drawing or design that shows how pieces of information are related

heading – a title within the body of a text that tells the reader something important about a section of the text

main idea – the most important idea in a paragraph or text

purpose – the reason for writing

sidebar – a short text within a larger text that tells something related but not necessary to the main story

supporting detail – a detail that gives more information about the main idea

topic – the subject of a text

Advance Preparation

If you are not able to complete the online Warm-Up, then print the selection and listen to students read aloud. Gather page LC 9 in *K¹² Language Arts Activity Book* (Main Idea and Supporting Details).

Big Ideas

- ▶ Readers need to be able to sequence, summarize, and articulate the main idea.
- ▶ Readers must understand the relationship between main idea and supporting details.
- ▶ Verbalizing your thoughts while modeling a reading strategy allows students to see what goes on inside the head of an effective reader; it makes visible the normally hidden process of comprehending text.

 **10 minutes**

"Kayaking"

Students will work independently online to develop fluency and oral reading skills.

Warm-Up

"Kayaking"

The purpose of this activity is to improve students' oral reading and fluency. Students will read "Kayaking." Remind students to listen to the model on each screen before they begin their recording.

Objectives
- Increase oral reading skills.
- Increase fluency.

Offline Alternative

No computer access? Print a copy of "Kayaking" from Advance Preparation. Have students read it aloud. Make note of any pronunciation errors, and review those words with students.

Performance Review

⊕ OPTIONAL: Fluency Check

Listen to students' recordings, and use the checklist to review fluency and track performance. Keep the completed checklist so you can review students' progress over time.

Objectives
- Read aloud grade-level text with appropriate automaticity, prosody, accuracy, and rate.

 **50 minutes**

"I See a Honeybee," Part 2

Work **together** with students to complete offline Get Ready, Guided Reading, Check Your Reading, Reading for Meaning, Making Connections, and Beyond the Lesson activities.

Get Ready

Retell Main Ideas and Details

Tell students that they are going to continue reading "I See a Honeybee." Ask them to use some of the main ideas from the first part of the article to tell about what they read on pages 10–12.

Objectives
- Identify the main idea and supporting details in a text.
- Increase concept and content vocabulary.

Words to Know

Before reading "I See a Honeybee," Part 2, go over Words to Know with students.

1. Ask students to define the following words from Part 1 and use them in a sentence:

cells	**hive**
drones	**larvae**

2. Correct any incorrect or vague definitions.

3. Have students say the words below, which they will encounter in Part 2.

4. Ask students if they know what the word means.

   ▸ If students know the word's meaning, have them define it and use it in a sentence.
   ▸ If students don't know the word's meaning, read them the definition and discuss the word with them.

nectar – sweet liquid from flowers
pollen – a yellowish powder on flowers that helps the flowers make seeds

---

Guided Reading

Book Walk

Prepare students by taking them on a Book Walk of the magazine *Wings, Antennae, and Tails*. Scan the magazine together and ask students to make predictions about the article.

1. Read the **title** of the magazine aloud.

2. Have students use the **table of contents** to find "I See a Honeybee" and turn to that page.

3. Tell students that you are going to read the second part of the article.

4. Look through pages 16–19 (last four pages of the article). Have students describe what they see. Point out the photographs and the **diagram**. Have students make predictions using the pictures. Answers to questions may vary.

   ▸ What do you see that looks familiar to you?
   ▸ What do you see that is new to you?
   ▸ What kinds of information do you think we'll learn in this part of the article?

Objectives

- Identify genre.
- Use text organizational features to locate and comprehend information (table of contents).
- Use an illustration to make a prediction about a reading.
- Define text features: table of contents, title, heading, caption, glossary, index, bold text.
- Define text features: illustration, graph, chart, text box, diagram, time line, map.

"I See a Honeybee," Part 2

Now it's time to read the article. Have students sit next to you so that they can see the pictures and words while you read the article aloud.

1. Remind students of where the first part of the article finished, to refresh their memory of what happened at the end of the first part.

   ▸ Now, what did we read last time?
   ▸ I'm going to go back to the last paragraph we read in the first part of the article. I want to look at it so that I can remember what we read.
   ▸ The last paragraph we read in the first part of the article says, "When their queen becomes weak or dies, worker bees put one of the female larvae in a special, large cell."
   ▸ So, we when we finished reading, we had learned how the bees choose their new queen.

2. Read pages 16–19 aloud all the way through. Start on page 16, which has the heading "Finding Food." Track with your finger so students can follow along. Read the body of the article first. Then point to any photographs or diagrams and read the captions and the accompanying sidebar, Pollen Movers.

3. Reread pages 16–19 with students, having them chime in and read aloud with you this time. Have students look for facts about a special kind of worker bee. Tell them you will pause at certain points in the article to discuss.

4. Begin to reread and pause to discuss at the end of page 16. Point to the heading on this page and have students name the feature and tell what it does. heading; tells us something important about the text that follows

5. Point to the words *pollen* and *nectar*. Have students tell the name of this feature and why it's used. bold text; to tell us that these are important words

6. Model how to retell what was read to help with reading comprehension.
   Say: We just read that another important job of the workers bees is gathering pollen and nectar. We also learned that the name of the worker bee who finds nectar is the scout.

7. Read page 17 of the article.

8. Pause at the end of the page. Point to the **sidebar** and tell students that this is a sidebar. Then read the sidebar and explain its purpose.
   Say: A sidebar contains information that is interesting, but it isn't necessary for understanding the main ideas of the article. This sidebar talks about why flowers need bees to carry pollen. The article is about honeybees, not flowers. So, we don't need the information in the sidebar to understand the article.

9. Read the pages 18–19 and pause. Point to the **diagram** on page 18. Have students tell what this text feature is and explain what it shows.

Check Your Reading

"I See a Honeybee," Part 2

Have students retell "I See a Honeybee" in their own words to develop grammar, vocabulary, comprehension, and fluency skills. When finished, **ask students the following questions** to check comprehension and encourage discussion.

▸ Why do honeybees need nectar? to make honey

▸ When do bees make honey? in the spring and summer

▸ When do bees eat honey? in the winter

▸ What does the scout do? finds nectar and tells the other bees in the hive where it is

▸ How does the scout tell the other bees where to find nectar? She does a dance.

▸ Show how a scout dances to tell other bees where to find nectar. Students should "dance" by wiggling their stomachs and turning in a circle or figure eight to imitate the scout's dance.

Objectives

- Use graphics and visuals to comprehend meaning and answer questions (diagrams, charts, captions).
- Use text features to comprehend text meaning. (bold, italic, headers).
- Answer questions requiring literal recall of details.

Reading for Meaning

Main Idea and Supporting Details

Help students identify main ideas and supporting details from "I See a Honeybee" to help them identify the main idea of the entire article. Gather page LC 10 of *K¹² Language Arts Activity Book*.

1. Review the definition of main idea. Have students explain again how the main idea is different from the topic.

2. Remind students that there can be a main idea of a paragraph, a passage, or an entire article.

3. Review the definition of supporting details and how they relate to the main idea.

4. Tell students that you are going to review with them how to find the main idea and supporting details for a paragraph in today's reading.

5. Reread the first paragraph on page 16, with the heading "Finding Food."

6. Remind students that sometimes the main idea of a paragraph is given in one of the sentences, and the other sentences are supporting details. Explain how to identify the main idea and supporting details of this paragraph.
   Say: This paragraph is about another job of worker bees. I think that the first sentence is the main idea. It says that worker bees have one more important job. The other sentences are supporting details. Each sentence tells a piece of information about this job.

7. Have students demonstrate this skill with the second paragraph. Have them find the main idea and supporting details of the second paragraph by asking them these questions.

   ▸ In a word or two, what is this paragraph about? making honey

   ▸ What is the most important, or main, idea? Worker bees make honey all spring and summer.

   ▸ What are some details that support this main idea? They store the honey in cells. The bees in the hive use the honey for food in winter.

Objectives

- Define main idea.
- Distinguish the main idea from the topic.
- Define details.
- Define supporting details.
- Identify the main idea and supporting details in a text.
- Use a graphic organizer to organize information.

8. Have students identify the main idea and supporting details for pages 16–17 of the article, rereading as necessary.

   ▸ What are these pages about? The pages are about finding food.
   ▸ What is the main idea? Worker bees must find pollen and nectar.
   ▸ What are the supporting details? Bees must gather nectar to make honey. The bees eat honey all winter. A special worker bee called a scout finds the nectar.

9. Turn to pages 18–19. Tell students that they are going to find the main idea and supporting details for these pages.

10. Have students complete the Activity Book page.

11. Review the Activity Book page and discuss any changes students need to make.

TIP If students have difficulty completing the Activity Book page, help them fill in the boxes by asking guiding questions as you did for the first parts of the article.

Making Connections

Main Idea of an Article

Help students identify the main idea of the whole article and some of the supporting details. Gather pages LC 9 and 10 of *K¹² Language Arts Activity Book* that students completed.

Objectives
- Use text features to comprehend text meaning. (bold, italic, headers).
- Identify main idea.

1. Remind students that the purpose of nonfiction articles is to tell important information about a topic.

2. Remind students that there is usually a main idea for an article—the most important thing the author wants us to know about the topic.

3. Review that nonfiction text features are often clues to the main idea. Discuss text the features that are in this article—headings, a sidebar, bold text, photographs, captions, and a diagram.

4. Look back through the article and talk about what kind of information is presented in the text features—information about the different types of honeybees and their jobs. Prompt students with questions.

   ▸ What are the headings about? queen bees; worker bees; finding food; the dance of the honey bees
   ▸ What do we see in the pictures? different kinds of honeybees; what the bees do

5. Discuss some of the main ideas of different parts of the article using the graphic organizers on the Activity Book pages students completed.

   ▸ You completed graphic organizers to find the main ideas of parts of the article. The first one was about worker bees. What was the main idea? Worker bees do many different jobs.
   ▸ The other graphic organizer was about scouts. What was the main idea? Scouts tell the other honeybees where to find nectar by doing a dance.
   ▸ What were some of the other main ideas on other pages in the article? There are three types of honeybees. Worker bees must find pollen and nectar to make honey.

6. Tell students that the sidebar should not be used to find the main idea because the purpose of a sidebar is to give extra information that is not essential to the topic.

7. Have students suggest a main idea for this article. Guide them to think about the title of the article. There are three different types of honeybees, and each type has important jobs to do.

8. If students provide a detail, explain why it's a supporting detail and not the main idea. The detail may tell us a piece of information about honeybees, but there are many other small pieces of information, too.

TIP If students continue to have difficulty, review some of the main ideas in the passages that students discussed and wrote about on their Activity Book pages.

Beyond the Lesson
. . . .

➊ OPTIONAL: Taste Honey

This activity is OPTIONAL. It is intended for students who have extra time and would enjoy sampling honey. Feel free to skip this activity.

Have students taste some different kinds of honey. Check to see if it is safe for students to sample honey.

1. If students have tried basic clover honey, try to find other varieties in the store.

2. Have students taste the honey by itself and on different foods—bread, bananas, and so forth.

3. Ask students to describe the honey using their senses and describing words. For example, have students complete these sentences.

  ▸ I think honey tastes like . . .
  ▸ I think honey smells like . . .
  ▸ I think honey looks like . . .
  ▸ I think honey feels like . . .

Objectives
- Make connections between text and self.
- Make connections between text and the world.
- Use descriptive phrases.

Introduce Creepy-Crawly Poems

Lesson Overview

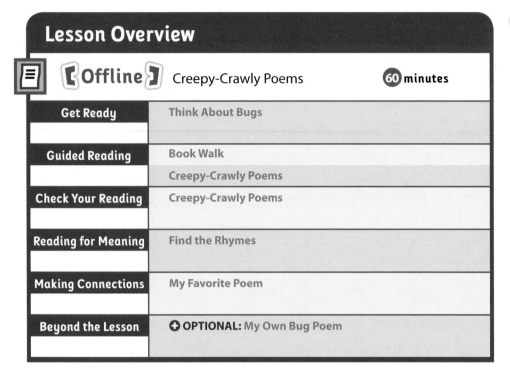

Offline Creepy-Crawly Poems   **60** minutes

Get Ready	Think About Bugs
Guided Reading	Book Walk
	Creepy-Crawly Poems
Check Your Reading	Creepy-Crawly Poems
Reading for Meaning	Find the Rhymes
Making Connections	My Favorite Poem
Beyond the Lesson	⊕ OPTIONAL: My Own Bug Poem

Materials

Supplied
- *Surprises*, pp. 18–23
- *K¹² Language Arts Activity Book*, p. LC 11

Keywords
line – a row of words in a poem
poem – a piece of poetry
poetry– writing that is made up of lines that often rhyme and follow a specific rhythm
repetition – the use of a word or phrase more than once
rhyme – the use of words that end with the same sounds; for example, *cat* and *hat* rhyme
speaker – the narrator of a poem, the person speaking

Big Ideas

▸ Poems are different from prose in structure and content. They are generally organized in lines and often contain rhymes.
▸ Guided reading provides support to early readers as they practice and apply the reading strategies of proficient readers.

 **60 minutes**

Creepy-Crawly Poems

Work **together** with students to complete offline Get Ready, Guided Reading, Check Your Reading, Reading for Meaning, Making Connections, and Beyond the Lesson activities.

Get Ready

Think About Bugs

Prepare students to read poems about insects by thinking of their own feelings about insects.

1. Have students think about some bugs: ones they like, ones they dislike, ones they know, and so forth. Answers will Vary.

2. Ask students to describe these bugs and what they do (for example, they crawl, fly, buzz, and sting).

3. Tell students that they are going to read **poetry** about bugs. Explain that poetry is a special kind of writing that is different from fiction and nonfiction.

4. Have students tell what they know about poetry.

Objectives
- Connect text to prior knowledge.
- Define poetry as a genre.

Guided Reading

Book Walk

Prepare students by taking them on a Book Walk of *Surprises*. Scan the book together, and ask students to make predictions about the poems. For all questions in the Book Walk, answers will vary.

1. Read aloud the **title** and **subtitle** of the book. Tell students that this is a collection of **poetry** by different poets, or people who write poetry.

2. Point out how the **poems** in the book look different from stories and articles they have read.
   Say: These poems look different from the stories we've read. They don't have paragraphs. There are short lines instead. The lines aren't always complete sentences. Sometimes there are only a few words on a line.

3. Tell students that poems are an arrangement of words, usually in **lines**. Lines are short rows of text that may be a complete sentence, part of a sentence, or just a word or two.

4. Tell students that sometimes the words in a poem **rhyme**. When words rhyme, they end with the same sounds. For example, *cat* and *hat* rhyme.

Objectives
- Define poem.
- Differentiate among literary genres.
- Identify characteristics of different genres.
- Define rhyme.
- Set a purpose for reading.
- Define speaker.
- Use text organizational features to locate and comprehend information.
- Use an illustration to make a prediction about a reading.
- Read texts for literary experience.

5. Explain that poems are a way for poets to share feelings or experiences with others. Poets choose their words very carefully. Ask students why they think they might read poetry.

   ▸ Do you read poetry for fun or information? fun
   ▸ How do you feel when you read poetry? Answers will vary.

6. Explain that a poem has a **speaker** who is the narrator of the poem or the person "talking" to the reader.

7. Turn to the **index** of authors and titles. Help students find "Caterpillars" and turn to that page.

8. Point to and read aloud the title of the poem.

9. Have students study the **pictures** and make a prediction.

   ▸ What do you think the poem is about?

10. Have students make predictions for the poems "Bee Song," "Bees," "Wasps," and "Bugs."

Creepy-Crawly Poems

Now it's time to read "Caterpillars." Have students sit next to you so that they can see the pictures and words while you read the poem aloud.

1. Read the poem aloud. Track with your finger so students can follow along.

2. Reread the poem with students, having them chime in and read aloud with you this time. Tell them to think about what feelings and ideas the poet is describing.
   Say: It's a good idea to read a poem twice. I like to read the poem once just to hear the words aloud and enjoy the sounds of the words. I might also listen for rhymes as I read the first time. The second time I read a poem, I think more about what feelings or ideas the poet is trying to tell me about. I try to see what the poet is describing.

3. Read the poems "Bee Song," "Bees," "Wasps," and "Bugs." Read each poem twice.

TIP In "Bee Song," students may not be familiar with the word *drone* or may confuse it with a type of honeybee. If students are unfamiliar with this word, tell them that drone in this poem means "hum" or "buzz."

Check Your Reading ••

Creepy-Crawly Poems

Have students retell "Caterpillars," "Bee Song," "Bees," "Wasps," and "Bugs" in their own words to develop grammar, vocabulary, comprehension, and fluency skills. When finished, **ask students the following questions** to check comprehension and encourage discussion.

   ▸ Which words and phrases repeat in the poem "Caterpillars"? chew, What do caterpillars, Nothing much but
   ▸ In the poem "Bee Song," what do the words *yellow moons* and *black velvet* describe? the bee's body

Objectives
• Answer questions requiring literal recall of details.

▶ Why does the speaker in the poem "Bees" think honeybees are tricky? because the sticky honey doesn't stick to honeybees

▶ Which words in the poem "Wasps" rhyme? tea, me

▶ What do you think happens to the speaker? A wasp chases, sits on, or stings the speaker.

▶ In the poem, "Bugs," what does the speaker do with bugs? kisses them and gives them hugs

Reading for Meaning

Find the Rhymes
Help students identify rhymes in poems. Turn to page LC 11 in *K¹² Language Arts Activity Book.*

1. Review the definition of rhyme.

2. Give students some examples of pairs of words that rhyme—for example *sat/bat, star/car, go/slow.*

3. Give students a single word and have them say a word that rhymes. Provide simple words that have more than one rhyming word, such as *bag, pot,* or *sad.*

4. Have students think of pairs of words that rhyme.

5. Turn to the poems "Bees" on page 21 and "Bugs" on page 23 in *Surprises.*

6. Reread each poem and have students identify the words that rhyme.

7. Have students complete the Activity Book page.

 TIP Students may try to rhyme by matching the sounds at the beginning of words instead of at the ends. If students have difficulty with rhymes, remind them that rhymes are matching sounds at the ends of words. Say pairs of simple rhyming words, such as *say/hay, bug/rug,* or *book/look.* Emphasize the sounds at the ends of the words.

Objectives
- Define rhyme.
- Identify rhyming words.

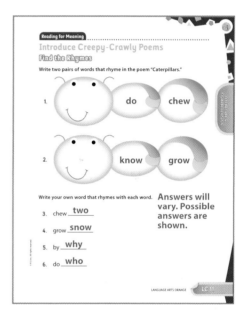

Making Connections

My Favorite Poem
Help students evaluate the poetry they have read by discussing their reactions to and opinions of the poems.

1. Have students talk about their reactions to "Caterpillars," "Bee Song," "Bees," "Wasps," and "Bugs."

2. Have them tell which poem is their favorite and why or describe something they like about each poem. Encourage students to talk about the sounds and structures of the poems, as well as the feelings and ideas described in each poem.

Objectives
- Answer evaluative questions.
- Make connections between text and self.

Beyond the Lesson

⊕ OPTIONAL: My Own Bug Poem

This activity is OPTIONAL. It is intended for students who have extra time and would enjoy and benefit from writing a poem of their own. Feel free to skip this activity.

Have students write their own insect poem.

1. Review poems about insects that students have read.

2. Have students choose an insect to write about.

3. Encourage students to use rhyme in their poem.

Objectives
- Make connections between text and self.
- Write a poem.

Introduce Poems About Feelings

Unit Overview

In this unit, students will learn how poetry can express feelings by reading and exploring the following selections:

- ► "Last Laugh," "At the Top of My Voice," "Keepsakes"
- ► "Ice Skating," "Hope," "Everybody Says"

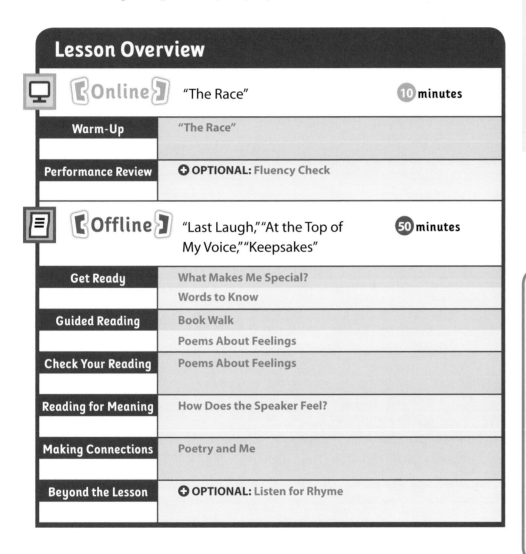

Lesson Overview

🖥️	**⟨Online⟩** "The Race"	🔟 minutes
Warm-Up	"The Race"	
Performance Review	➕ OPTIONAL: Fluency Check	

🗒️	**⟨Offline⟩** "Last Laugh," "At the Top of My Voice," "Keepsakes"	5️⃣0️⃣ minutes
Get Ready	What Makes Me Special?	
	Words to Know	
Guided Reading	Book Walk	
	Poems About Feelings	
Check Your Reading	Poems About Feelings	
Reading for Meaning	How Does the Speaker Feel?	
Making Connections	Poetry and Me	
Beyond the Lesson	➕ OPTIONAL: Listen for Rhyme	

⟦ Materials ⟧

Supplied

- *Surprises*, pp. 26–29
- *K¹² Language Arts Activity Book*, p. LC 13
- "The Race" (optional)
- Fluency Performance Checklist (optional)

Also Needed

- whiteboard (optional)

Poem Synopses

In these three short poems, the speakers describe something special about themselves.

Keywords

first-person point of view – the telling of a story by a character in that story, using pronouns such as *I, me,* and *we*

poem – a piece of poetry

poetry – writing that is made up of lines that often rhyme and follow a specific rhythm

point of view – the perspective a story is told from

prediction – a guess about what might happen that is based on information in a story and what you already know

speaker – the narrator of a poem, the person speaking

Advance Preparation

If you are not able to complete the online Warm-Up, then print the selection and listen to students read aloud. Before beginning Guided Reading, read the poems to identify Words to Know in the text. Preview Reading for Meaning and prepare the graphic organizer shown on a whiteboard or sheet of paper.

Big Ideas

Poems differ from prose in structure and content. They are generally organized in lines and often contain rhymes.

 **Online** **10** minutes

"The Race"

Students will work independently online to develop fluency and oral reading skills.

Warm-Up

"The Race"

The purpose of this activity is to improve students' oral reading and fluency. Students will read "The Race." Remind students to listen to the model on each screen before they begin their recording.

 Objectives
- Increase oral reading skills.
- Increase fluency.

Offline Alternative

No computer access? Print a copy of "The Race" from Advance Preparation. Have students read it aloud. Make note of any pronunciation errors, and review those words with students.

Performance Review

⊕ OPTIONAL: Fluency Check

Listen to students' recordings, and use the checklist to review fluency and track performance. Keep the completed checklist so you can review students' progress over time.

 Objectives
- Read aloud grade-level text with appropriate automaticity, prosody, accuracy, and rate.

 **Offline** **50** minutes

"Last Laugh," "At the Top of My Voice," "Keepsakes"

Work **together** with students to complete offline Get Ready, Guided Reading, Check Your Reading, Reading for Meaning, Making Connections, and Beyond the Lesson activities.

Get Ready

What Makes Me Special?

One reason poets write poetry is to convey feelings. Poets choose their words carefully to express feelings in a concise way. When we read poetry, we want to not only enjoy the sound, but to understand the emotions and ideas the poet is expressing. Help students understand poetry.

 Objectives
- Connect text to prior knowledge.
- Increase concept and content vocabulary.

1. Have students tell something special about themselves: something they can do or a special trait. Give an example if necessary—for example, "I'm very good at knitting."

2. Tell students that some poems are about what makes some people special.

3. Have students tell what they know about poetry. Answers will vary and may include that poems are written in lines, may rhyme, and tell about feelings.

Words to Know

Before reading poems about feelings, go over Words to Know with students.

1. Have students say the word aloud.

2. Ask students if they know what the word means.

   ▸ If students know the word's meaning, have them define it and use it in a sentence.
   ▸ If students don't know the word's meaning, read them the definition and discuss the word with them.

keepsake – something kept to remember something special

(TIP) If students have difficulty understanding the word, talk about keepsakes that you or students have (a photograph of someone special or a memento of an important event, for example) and why you keep them.

Guided Reading

Book Walk

Prepare students by taking them on a Book Walk of *Surprises*. Scan the book together, and ask students to make predictions about the poems. For all questions in the Book Walk, answers will vary.

1. Read aloud the **title** and **subtitle** of the book. Remind students that it's a collection of poetry by different poets, or people who write poetry.

2. Have students describe how the **poems** in the book look different from stories or nonfiction they have read.

3. Review with students that poems are an arrangement of words, usually in **lines**. Lines are short rows of text that may be a complete sentence, part of a sentence, or just a word or two. Sometimes, the words in a poem rhyme, or have similar ending sounds.

4. Review with students that poems are a way for poets to share feelings or experiences with others, and that poets choose their words very carefully.

5. Ask students why they think they read poetry.

   ▸ Do you read poetry for fun or information?
   ▸ What do you think poets are trying to describe in their poems?

6. Explain that a poem has a **speaker** who is the narrator of the poem or the person "talking" to the reader.

7. Tell students that in many poems, the speaker uses the **first-person point of view**. This means that the speaker uses the words *I, me,* and *my.* When a speaker (or narrator) talks about himself, we get his feelings and ideas about the world.

Objectives

- Define poetry as a genre.
- Differentiate among literary genres.
- Set a purpose for reading.
- Define first-person point of view.
- Use text organizational features to locate and comprehend information (table of contents, index).
- Use an illustration to make a prediction about a reading.
- Use the title of the selection to make a prediction.
- Read texts for literary experience.

8. Turn to the **index of authors** and **titles**. Help students find the poem "Last Laugh" and turn to that page.

9. Point to and read aloud the title of the poem.

10. Have students study the **pictures** and make a **prediction**.

    ▶ What do you think the poem is about?

11. Have students make predictions for the poems "At the Top of My Voice" and "Keepsakes."

Poems About Feelings

Now it's time to read the poems. Have students sit next to you so that they can see the pictures and words while you read each poem aloud.

1. Read the poem "Last Laugh" aloud. Track with your finger so students can follow along.

2. Reread the poem with students, having them chime in and read aloud with you this time. Tell them to think about what the speaker is saying and what the speaker says that is special about herself.

3. Read the poems "At the Top of My Voice" and "Keepsakes." Read each poem twice.

Check Your Reading

Poems About Feelings

Have students retell each poem in their own words to develop grammar, vocabulary, comprehension, and fluency skills. When finished, **ask students the following questions** to check comprehension and encourage discussion.

▶ Is the speaker in the poem "Last Laugh" a boy or a girl? How do you know? a girl; She says she wants to be a woman in space.

▶ What three things would the speaker in "Last Laugh" like to do in the future? be an astronaut, visit Mars, and be on TV

▶ What three things does the speaker in "At the Top of My Voice" talk about doing in the poem? stamping, shouting, singing

▶ Name two things the speaker in "Keepsakes" keeps. Possible responses: bottle caps, strings, keys, corks

▶ What do other people think of the speaker's keepsakes? They don't think the keepsakes are valuable or worthwhile.

▶ What does the speaker plan to do with the keepsakes? The speaker isn't sure yet.

Objectives
• Answer questions requiring literal recall of details.

Reading for Meaning

How Does the Speaker Feel?

Encourage students to use their own knowledge in combination with what the speakers in the poems say to make inferences. Turn to page LC 13 in *K¹² Language Arts Activity Book*.

1. Review of the concept of the **speaker** in a poem. Remind students that in "Last Laugh," "At the Top of My Voice," and "Keepsakes" the speakers use the **first-person point of view**, meaning they tell about their own ideas and feelings.

2. Read each of the poems with students, and help them find clue words that show the speaker is using the first-person point of view (*I, me,* and *my*).

3. Tell students that they are going to think about what feelings are in the poems.

4. Explain to students that they can learn about how speakers are feeling by looking at the words they use. Then they can think about what these words remind them of and imagine the speakers' feelings.

5. Turn to the poem "At the Top of My Voice." Explain that students can use a chart like the one in the Activity Book to figure out the speaker's feelings.

6. Gather the chart you prepared. Label each of the boxes and write the title of the poem "At the Top of My Voice" above it. Walk students through the chart, discussing the kind of information that belongs in each box. Write answers in each of the boxes. Answers will vary, but possible responses are shown in Step 9.

7. Point to the box labeled What the Speaker Says.
   Say: What does the speaker in "At the Top of My Voice" talk about? This is what the speaker says.

8. Point to the box labeled What the Speaker Feels.
   Say: How do you think the speaker feels? Think about the words the speaker uses and the way he describes things. These will tell you how the speaker feels.

Objectives
- Make inferences from text.
- Make connections between text and self.

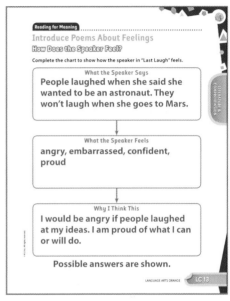

Literature & Comprehension **LC 53**

9. Point to the box labeled Why I Think This.

   Say: What do you know about what the speaker is saying? Does what the speaker says remind you of anything that you have done or felt? This is what you think.

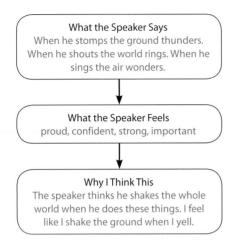

> **What the Speaker Says**
> When he stomps the ground thunders. When he shouts the world rings. When he sings the air wonders.

> **What the Speaker Feels**
> proud, confident, strong, important

> **Why I Think This**
> The speaker thinks he shakes the whole world when he does these things. I feel like I shake the ground when I yell.

10. Have students complete—in their own words—the chart on the Activity Book page using the poem "Last Laugh."

Making Connections

Poetry and Me

Help students connect to the poems by choosing a poem they most identify with and discussing the feelings described in that poem.

1. Have students tell which poem best describes feelings that they understand or have experienced themselves.

2. Have students explain why they understand the feelings that the speaker describes and, if possible, give an example of a time when they felt the same way as the speaker. If students are eager to discuss the poem and do not have difficulty expressing themselves, allow them to talk freely about the poem they choose.

3. Encourage students to address each of the following in their discussion. If necessary, prompt students to complete each of these sentences.

   ▸ The poem that talks about feelings I understand best is . . .
   ▸ The speaker in this poem feels . . .
   ▸ The speaker's feelings remind me of the time when I . . .

Objectives
- Make connections between text and self.

Beyond the Lesson

....

⊕ OPTIONAL: Listen for Rhyme

This activity is OPTIONAL. It is intended for students who have extra time and would enjoy finding the rhyming words in today's poems. Feel free to skip this activity.

Help students identify rhymes in poems.

Objectives
- Define rhyme.
- Identify rhyming words.

1. Tell students that poems often have rhymes at the end of lines. Rhymes help readers enjoy the way poetry sounds.

2. Ask students if they know what a **rhyme** is. If they don't, define rhymes as words that sound the same at the end.

3. Give some examples of simple rhymes (*car/star*, *big/pig*, *jump/thump*). Remind students that the rhyme is at the ends of the words, not at the beginnings.

4. Give students some words (for example, *cat, ball, me*). Ask students to say words that rhyme with each word you give.

5. Tell students that many poems have rhymes.

6. Reread "Last Laugh" with students sitting beside you. Emphasize the last word of each line. Have students listen for words that rhyme.

7. Ask students to look at the last word of each line and point to words that rhyme. *be, free, me, see*

8. Repeat this activity with "At the Top of My Voice" and "Keepsakes."

Introduce More Poems About Feelings

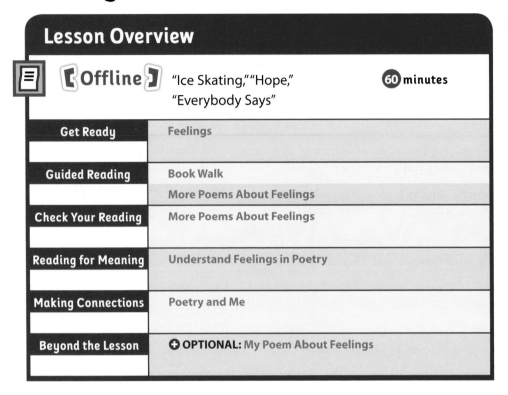

Lesson Overview

Offline — "Ice Skating," "Hope," "Everybody Says" — **60 minutes**

Get Ready	Feelings
Guided Reading	Book Walk
	More Poems About Feelings
Check Your Reading	More Poems About Feelings
Reading for Meaning	Understand Feelings in Poetry
Making Connections	Poetry and Me
Beyond the Lesson	⊕ OPTIONAL: My Poem About Feelings

Materials

Supplied
- *Surprises*, pp. 30–32
- *K¹² Language Arts Activity Book*, p. LC 14

Also Needed
- whiteboard (optional)

Poem Synopses

In these three poems, written from the first-person point of view, the speakers describe their feelings about ice skating, being lonely, and being compared to relatives.

Keywords

first-person point of view – the telling of a story by a character in that story, using pronouns such as *I, me,* and *we*

poem – a piece of poetry

poetry – writing that is made up of lines that often rhyme and follow a specific rhythm

point of view – the perspective a story is told from

speaker – the narrator of a poem, the person speaking

Advance Preparation

Before beginning Guided Reading, read the poems to become familiar with them. Preview Reading for Meaning and prepare a sample graphic organizer on a whiteboard or a sheet of paper to demonstrate how to make inferences about a speaker's feelings.

Content Background

- ▶ Literary point of view means the perspective from which a story or poem is told. Texts can be told from first-, second-, or third-person points of view. While literary point of view differs from the colloquial use of *point of view*, which means opinion or viewpoint, we do learn the narrator's or speaker's feelings in stories told from the first-person point of view.
- ▶ The speaker in a poem is different from the poet. A speaker is like a narrator, or character, telling the poem.

Big Ideas

- ▶ Interpretation occurs between reader and text, as the reader attempts to discover the unstated and to communicate about the text's meaning.
- ▶ By making the effort to understand texts, we can come to understand ourselves.

 **Offline** **60** minutes

"Ice Skating," "Hope," "Everybody Says"

Work **together** with students to complete offline Get Ready, Guided Reading, Check Your Reading, Reading for Meaning, Making Connections, and Beyond the Lesson activities.

Get Ready

Feelings

One reason poets write poetry is to convey feelings. Poets choose their words carefully to express feelings in a concise way. Remind students that good readers stop and think about the feelings a poet is trying to describe.

1. Brainstorm with students a list of different feelings, such as anger, happiness, fear, and frustration. Ask students when or in what types of situations they might feel these emotions.

2. Tell students that often the speakers in poems describe different feelings.

3. Review that poets sometimes write poetry to tell about feelings.

Objectives
- Connect text to prior knowledge.
- Identify the author's purpose.

Guided Reading

Book Walk

Prepare students by taking them on a Book Walk of *Surprises*. Scan the book together, and ask students to make predictions about the poems. For all questions in the Book Walk, answers will vary.

1. Read aloud the **title** and **subtitle** of the book. Review that it's a collection of poetry by different poets, or people who write poetry.

2. Review with students that poems are an arrangement of words, usually in **lines**. Have students explain what lines are and tell other characteristics of poetry that they know.

3. Review that a poem has a **speaker** who is the narrator of the poem or the person "talking" to the reader.

4. Review that in many poems, the speaker uses the **first-person point of view**. When a speaker (or narrator) talks about himself, we get his feelings and ideas about the world.

5. Have students tell the clue words that let us know the speaker is using the first person (*I*, *me*, and *my*). Provide these words if students don't remember them.

6. Turn to the **index of authors** and **titles**. Help students find the poem "Ice Skating" and turn to that page.

7. Point to and read aloud the title of the poem

8. Have students study the picture and make a prediction.

   ▶ What do you think the poem is about?

9. Repeat Steps 6–8 for the poems "Hope" and "Everybody Says."

Objectives
- Identify characteristics of different genres.
- Define first-person point of view.
- Use text organizational features to locate and comprehend information (table of contents, index).
- Use an illustration to make a prediction about a reading.
- Read texts for literary experience.

More Poems About Feelings

Now it's time to read the poems. Have students sit next to you so that they can see the pictures and words while you read the poems aloud.

1. Read the poem "Ice Skating" aloud. Track with your finger so students can follow along.

2. Reread the poem with students, having them chime in and read aloud with you this time. Ask them to think about what the speaker is feeling.

3. Draw students' attention to the speaker's comparison of ice skating to flying. Point out some of the words that refer to flying: *higher, glide in the sky, star, float, soar.*

   ▸ What do you think the speaker is saying that ice skating feels like?

4. Read the poems "Hope" and "Everybody Says." Read each poem twice.

Check Your Reading

More Poems About Feelings

Have students retell each poem in their own words to develop grammar, vocabulary, comprehension, and fluency skills. When finished, **ask students the following questions** to check comprehension and encourage discussion.

▸ What is the speaker in the poem "Ice Skating" doing in the poem? ice skating

▸ What words does the speaker use to compare ice skating to flying? higher and higher, glide in the sky, star in each eye, wind, float, soar

▸ How does the speaker in the poem "Hope" feel in the first line of the poem? lonely

▸ What does the speaker say about this feeling? Possible answer: He doesn't think he will be lonely after a while.

▸ What does everybody say about the speaker in the poem "Everybody Says"? that the speaker looks like different relatives

▸ Who does the speaker want to look like? herself

Objectives
- Answer questions requiring literal recall of details.

Reading for Meaning

Understand Feelings in Poetry

Help students use what the speakers in the poems say and their own knowledge to make inferences. Turn to page LC 14 in *K¹² Language Arts Activity Book.*

1. Review that the speakers in today's poems use the **first-person point of view.** Have students tell what this means. If they cannot define the term, define it for them.

2. Have students tell the clue words that let them know that the speaker is using the first-person point of view, or remind them what the words are (*I, me,* and *my*). Then have students find these clue words in "Ice Skating," "Hope," and "Everybody Says."

Objectives
- Make inferences from text.
- Make connection between text and self.

3. Review with students that poems often convey the feelings of the speaker. Tell students that they are going to think about what feelings are in the poems.

4. Remind students that they can use what a speaker says in a poem and what they know from their own experiences to understand the feelings a speaker is talking about.

5. Turn to the poem "Ice Skating." Explain that students can use a chart like the one in the Activity Book to figure out the speaker's feelings.

6. Gather the chart you prepared. Label each of the boxes and write the title of the poem "Ice Skating" above it. Walk students through the chart, discussing the kind of information that belongs in each box. Write answers in the boxes. Answers will vary, but possible responses are shown in Step 10.

7. Point to the box labeled What the Speaker Says.
Say: What are some words the speaker in the poem "Ice Skating" uses to describe ice skating? This is what the speaker says.

8. Point to the box labeled What I Know.
Say: Have you done or felt anything like what the speaker is describing? This is what you know.

9. Encourage students to think of something similar that they have done or felt; it doesn't have to be ice skating. For example, it could be, "I once went down a giant waterslide and felt really excited and nervous. I felt like I was flying."

10. Point to the box labeled How the Speaker Feels.
Say: How do you think the speaker feels about ice skating? This is how the speaker feels.

What the Speaker Says		What I Know		How the Speaker Feels
I glide in the sky. I can float, I can soar. The earth cannot hold me in place anymore.	+	I once went down a Waterslide and I felt like I was flying. It made me feel excited and proud.	=	The speaker is feeling fast, strong, excited, proud.

11. Have students complete—in their own words—the chart on the Activity Book page using the poem "Hope."

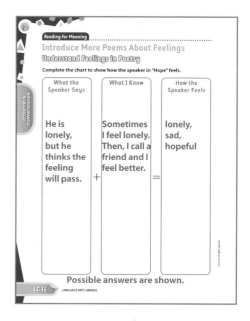

Making Connections

My Feelings in Words

Help students connect to the poems they read by generating words and phrases that describe their feelings about a topic of their choice.

1. Have students tell a list of feelings. Then have them choose one that they would like to talk about.

2. Have students brainstorm a list of words and phrases related to this feeling. Prompt them with questions to help them think of ideas.

   ▶ When have you felt this feeling? Tell me about times when you felt this way.
   ▶ What did you do when you felt this way? How did you act?
   ▶ What did you think when you felt this way?

3. Write down the list of words and phrases on a sheet of paper. Read them together with students when they have finished creating their list.

 If students enjoy writing, have them create an idea web out of their list. Have them put the feeling in the center of the web and write the words and phrases they brainstormed in the outer circles of the web. Have them illustrate their web if they like.

 Reward: Write the names of the literature selections completed in this unit on the My Accomplishments chart and add a sticker to mark successful completion of this unit.

 Objectives
- Make connections between text and self.
- Read and respond to works from various genres.

Beyond the Lesson

✚ OPTIONAL: My Poem About Feelings

This activity is OPTIONAL. It is intended for students who have extra time and would enjoy writing an original poem. Feel free to skip this activity.
   Have students write an original poem.

1. Brainstorm a list of words and phrases related to a feeling.

2. If you wish, have students refer to a poem that they have read to use as a model.

3. Allow students to rhyme their poem or not. If students are interested, allow them to illustrate their poem.

Objectives
- Make connections between text and self.

Introduce "The Fox and the Grapes"

Unit Overview

In this ten-lesson unit, students will explore classic stories for all ages through the following reading selections:
- ▸ "The Fox and the Grapes"
- ▸ "The Goose and the Golden Eggs"
- ▸ "The Pied Piper of Hamelin"
- ▸ "The Bremen Town Musicians"

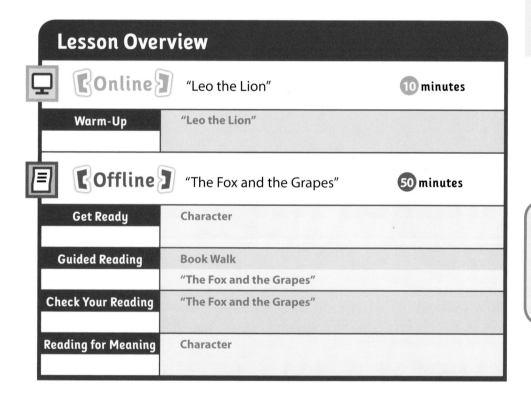

Lesson Overview

🖥	**【Online】** "Leo the Lion"		**10** minutes
Warm-Up	"Leo the Lion"		
📄	**【Offline】** "The Fox and the Grapes"		**50** minutes
Get Ready	Character		
Guided Reading	Book Walk		
	"The Fox and the Grapes"		
Check Your Reading	"The Fox and the Grapes"		
Reading for Meaning	Character		

Advance Preparation

If you are not able to complete the online Warm-Up, then print the selection and listen to students read aloud.

Big Ideas

Readers need to understand and describe characters and what they do in order to understand and interpret a story.

【Materials】

Supplied
- "The Fox and the Grapes," *K¹² Classics for Young Readers, Volume B*, p. 3
- *K¹² Language Arts Activity Book*, p. LC 15
- "Leo the Lion" (optional)

Story Synopsis
In this fable, a fox wants a bunch of grapes hanging from a tree. When he can't reach the tempting fruit, the fox decides he didn't want the grapes anyway.

Keywords
character – a person or animal in a story
inference – a guess you make using the clues in a text and what you already know

 **10 minutes**

"Leo the Lion"

Students will work independently online to develop fluency and oral reading skills.

 **Warm-Up**

"Leo the Lion"

The purpose of this activity is to improve students' oral reading and fluency. Students will read "Leo the Lion." Remind students to listen to the model on each screen before they begin their recording.

 Objectives
- Increase oral reading skills.
- Increase fluency.

Offline Alternative

No computer access? Print a copy of "Leo the Lion." Have students read it aloud. Make note of any pronunciation errors, and review those words with students.

Offline 50 minutes

"The Fox and the Grapes"

Work **together** with students to complete offline Get Ready, Guided Reading, Check Your Reading, and Reading for Meaning activities.

Get Ready

Character

Examining characters helps readers connect with literature. Review literary characters with students.

 Objectives
- Define character.

1. Ask students if they remember what a **character** is. a person or animal who takes part in a story

2. Have students name one or two characters from stories they've read in the past, such as the Lion in "The Lion and the Fox." Consider follow-up questions or discussion about why they remember those characters and what they remember about them.

Guided Reading

Book Walk

Prepare students by taking them on a Book Walk of "The Fox and the Grapes." Scan the story together and ask students to make predictions about it. For all questions in the Book Walk, answers will vary.

1. Tell students that they are going to read a story with an interesting animal character.

2. Have students use the **table of contents** in *K*[12] *Classics for Young Readers, Volume B*, to find "The Fox and the Grapes" and turn to that page.

3. Point to and read aloud the **title of the story**.

4. Have students study the **illustration** and make **predictions** about the story based on the illustration.

   ▸ Who do you think is a **character** in the story?
   ▸ What do you think the story is about?

5. Ask students why they think they are going to read this story.

   ▸ Do you think we're going to read this story for true information? Why or why not?

Objectives
- Identify characters.
- Use text organizational features to locate and comprehend information (table of contents, index).
- Use an illustration to make a prediction about a reading.
- Set a purpose for reading.
- Read texts for literary experience.

"The Fox and the Grapes"

Now it's time to read "The Fox and the Grapes." Have students sit next to you so that they can see the picture and words while you read the story aloud.

1. Read the story aloud all the way through. Track with your finger so students can follow along.

2. Reread the entire story with students, having them chime in and read aloud with you this time. Tell them to think about the character and what he does. Tell students that you will pause at certain points in the story to discuss.

3. Begin to reread, pausing to discuss after the first paragraph.

   ▸ What character have we met? fox
   ▸ How does he feel? How can you tell? hungry; It says so right in the first line.

4. Continue reading. Pause to discuss after the second paragraph.

   ▸ What does the fox want? grapes
   ▸ How does he try to get them? He tries jumping and climbing to reach them.
   ▸ What do you think he will do next? Answers will vary.

5. Continue reading to the end of the story.

Check Your Reading

"The Fox and the Grapes"

Have students retell "The Fox and the Grapes" in their own words to develop grammar, vocabulary, comprehension, and fluency skills. When finished, **ask students the following questions** to check comprehension and encourage discussion.

▶ What does the fox think of the grapes when he first sees them? He thinks they would be good for lunch.

▶ How does the fox try to get the grapes? He tries to jump up, climb the vine, and knock them down with a stick.

▶ What does the fox say when he cannot reach the grapes? He says they must be sour.

▶ What does the fox do at the end of the story? He marches off in a huff.

Objectives

- Answer questions requiring literal recall of details.
- Describe characters and their reactions to major events in the story.

Reading for Meaning

 Character

Help students complete this activity to check comprehension and focus on describing characters. Gather page LC 15 of *K¹² Language Arts Activity Book*

1. Review the definition of **character**.

2. Tell students we learn about characters in a story in three ways: through what they say, what they do, and what others say about them, including what the author or narrator says. These three ways of learning about characters are called **character clues**.

3. Tell students that authors do not always use all of these clues to describe characters. Our job as readers is to look for clues as we read so we can learn about the characters.

4. Tell students they are going to learn about the fox's character by looking at what he says and does.

5. Have students complete Exercises 1–4 on the Activity Book page. If necessary, read the directions and the questions to students. **Reread parts of the story** if they have trouble answering a question.

6. Stop after students have completed the first four exercises and ask the following questions:

   ▶ Do you think the grapes were really sour? Why or why not?
   ▶ Why does the fox say the grapes are sour and walk away? What character clues in the story make you think this?

7. Have students complete Exercises 5 and 6 on the Activity Book page.

TIP If students have difficulty writing their answers, have them dictate their answers to you and you can write them on the Activity Book page.

Objectives

- Make inferences about characters using evidence from the text.
- Describe characters and their reactions to major events in the story.
- Describe characters by what they do, what they say, or what others say about them.

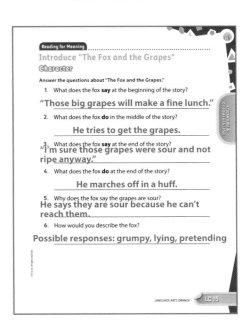

Reading for Meaning

Introduce "The Fox and the Grapes"

Character

Answer the questions about "The Fox and the Grapes."

1. What does the fox **say** at the beginning of the story?

"Those big grapes will make a fine lunch."

2. What does the fox **do** in the middle of the story?

He tries to get the grapes.

3. What does the fox **say** at the end of the story?

"I'm sure those grapes were sour and not ripe anyway."

4. What does the fox **do** at the end of the story?

He marches off in a huff.

5. Why does the fox say the grapes are sour?

He says they are sour because he can't reach them.

6. How would you describe the fox?

Possible responses: grumpy, lying, pretending

LANGUAGE ARTS ORANGE   LC 15

Review "The Fox and the Grapes"

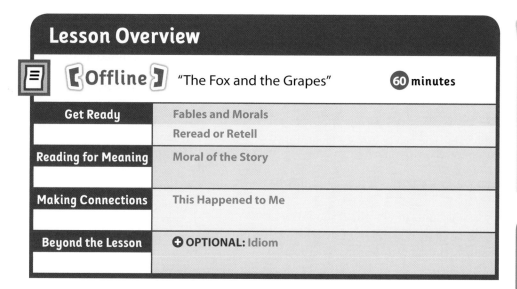

Lesson Overview

Offline "The Fox and the Grapes"   **60** minutes

Get Ready	Fables and Morals
	Reread or Retell
Reading for Meaning	Moral of the Story
Making Connections	This Happened to Me
Beyond the Lesson	⊕ OPTIONAL: Idiom

Big Ideas

To appreciate an author's message, good readers need to recognize the traits of characters.

Materials

Supplied

- "The Fox and the Grapes," *K¹² Classics for Young Readers, Volume B*, p. 3
- *K¹² Language Arts Activity Book*, p. LC 16

Keywords

character – a person or animal in a story

inference – a guess you make using the clues in a text and what you already know

fable – a story that teaches a lesson and may contain animal characters

moral – the lesson of a story, particularly a fable

 **60** minutes

"The Fox and the Grapes"

Work **together** with students to complete offline Get Ready, Reading for Meaning, Making Connections, and Beyond the Lesson activities.

Get Ready

Fables and Morals

Prepare students for reading a fable. Explain the characteristics of a fable and its moral.

1. Explain that some stories teach a lesson. Ask students if they can think of any lessons that they know. Give an example.
   Say: One lesson I learned from my mother and father is that I should treat other people the way that I would like to be treated. If I want people to be nice to me, I should be nice to them. Can you think of any lessons like this that you've learned?

2. Tell students that a **fable** is a story that teaches a lesson called a **moral.**

 Objectives
- Identify characteristics of different genres.
- Recount or describe key ideas or details from a text read aloud or information presented orally or through other media.

Reread or Retell

If you'd like to, reread the story to students. Otherwise, have students retell the story using the pictures as a guide, and then move on to the next activity.

Reading for Meaning

Moral of the Story

Ask students the following questions to check comprehension and focus on fables. **Reread parts of "The Fox and the Grapes"** if they have trouble answering a question.

1. Review the definition of fable with students.

2. Have students describe the fox, thinking about what he says and what he does.

   ▶ Why does the fox want the grapes? He thinks they will be good for lunch.
   ▶ How has the fox tried to get the grapes? He has tried jumping, climbing, and using a stick to knock them down.
   ▶ How do you think the fox feels? Why? He feels angry and frustrated because he can't reach the grapes.
   ▶ What do we learn? The fox acts like he didn't want the grapes, even though he did at the beginning of the story.

3. Discuss the character of the fox with students.

   ▶ Would you want to be like the fox? Why or why not? Answers will vary.

 Objectives
- Identify genre.
- Identify a lesson learned based on a character's actions.
- Identify the author's purpose.
- Identify the moral or lesson of a text.

4. Explain that even though we may not want to be like the fox, we can still learn a lesson from him.

5. Remind students that this story is a **fable** with a **moral**, or a lesson to teach us.

6. Explain that authors teach the moral of a fable through the actions and words of the characters or what happens to the characters.

7. Ask students what they think the moral, or lesson, is that they can learn from the fox. "It is easy to dislike what you cannot have."

8. If students have trouble thinking of the lesson of the story, prompt them with the following additional questions:

   ▶ Do you think the fox still wanted the grapes at the end of the story? Why or why not?

   ▶ What do you think about people who say they don't want something that they really do want?

   ▶ Do you think it's hard or easy to say you don't want something that you really do want? Why?

Making Connections

✏️ This Happened to Me

Help students understand the moral of the story "The Fox and the Grapes." Turn to page LC 16 of *K¹² Language Arts Activity Book*.

1. Ask students if there was ever a time when they wanted something they couldn't have.

2. Have students think about how they felt when that happened.

3. Have students complete the Activity Book page.

TIP If students have difficulty writing their stories, have them dictate the events as you write.

Objectives
* Make connections between text and self.

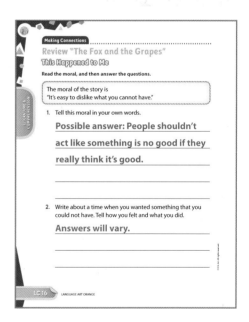

Beyond the Lesson

⊕ OPTIONAL: Idiom

This activity is OPTIONAL. It is intended for students who have extra time and would benefit from learning about idioms and the idiom associated with "The Fox and the Grapes." Feel free to skip this activity.

Objectives
- Identify and use idioms.

1. Review the moral of "The Fox and the Grapes" *"It is easy to dislike what you cannot have."*

2. Explain that this idea of disliking something that you can't have is called *sour grapes*. Ask students if they can guess why this behavior is called sour grapes. It comes from this fable.

3. Explain that the phrase *sour grapes* is an **idiom**. An idiom is a phrase in which the words together have a different meaning than the words alone. The only way to understand an idiom is to learn what it means. It is very difficult to figure out the meaning of an idiom by understanding each word in the phrase.

4. Give examples of other idioms (for example, *lend me a hand, eye on the ball, actions speak louder than words*).

5. Go to the website Idioms by Kids (www.idiomsbykids.com). On this site, children from around the world have illustrated some common idioms.

6. Have students choose one of the idioms from the site that hasn't been illustrated. Have them draw their own silly picture of what their chosen idiom would mean if we took it literally, or simply by the meaning of each individual word.

7. If you have time and interest, allow students to upload their illustration to the website.

(TIP) If you do not want students to visit the Idioms by Kids website with you, use the site on your own for other idiom ideas. Write down a few idioms and have students choose and illustrate one from your list.

Introduce "The Goose and the Golden Eggs"

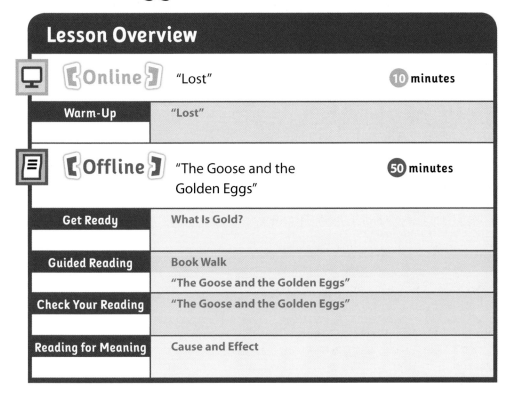

Lesson Overview

🖥	**〖Online〗** "Lost"	**10** minutes
Warm-Up	"Lost"	
📄	**〖Offline〗** "The Goose and the Golden Eggs"	**50** minutes
Get Ready	What Is Gold?	
Guided Reading	Book Walk	
	"The Goose and the Golden Eggs"	
Check Your Reading	"The Goose and the Golden Eggs"	
Reading for Meaning	Cause and Effect	

Advance Preparation

If you are not able to complete the online Warm-Up, then print the selection and listen to students read aloud.

Big Ideas

Identifying cause-and-effect relationships aids in literal and inferential reading comprehension.

〖Materials〗

Supplied

- **"The Goose and the Golden Eggs,"** *K¹² Classics for Young Readers, Volume B,* pp. 4–5
- *K¹² Language Arts Activity Book,* p. LC 17
- **"Lost"** (optional)

Story Synopsis

In this story, a farmer kills his goose that daily lays a golden egg so he can have the riches all at once. His greed costs him his most valuable possession.

Keywords

cause – the reason something happens

character – a person, animal, or other thing that acts like a person in a story, drama, or book

effect – the result of a cause

prediction – a guess about what might happen that is based on information in a story and what you already know

 **minutes**

"Lost"

Students will work independently online to develop fluency and oral reading skills.

Warm-Up ••

"Lost"

The purpose of this activity is to improve students' oral reading and fluency. Students will read "Lost." Remind students to listen to the model on each screen before they begin their recording.

 Objectives
- Increase oral reading skills.
- Increase fluency.

Offline Alternative

No computer access? Print a copy of "Lost." Have students read it aloud. Make note of any pronunciation errors, and review those words with students.

 **minutes**

"The Goose and the Golden Eggs"

Work **together** with students to complete offline Get Ready, Guided Reading, Check Your Reading, and Reading for Meaning activities.

Get Ready •••

What Is Gold?

Help students prepare for "The Goose and the Golden Eggs" by discussing some background information that will help them understand the reading.

 Objectives
- Build background knowledge.

1. Explain to students that they will be reading a story about a goose and golden eggs.

2. Ask students if they know what gold is, and have them tell you what they know about it. Tell students that gold is a metal that can be worth a lot of money.

3. Ask students to describe how they would feel if they were given a piece of gold every day. Ask students to explain why they would feel this way.

4. Tell students to think about this feeling as they read "The Goose and the Golden Eggs."

Guided Reading

Book Walk

Prepare students by taking them on a Book Walk of "The Goose and the Golden Eggs." Scan the story together and ask students to make predictions about it. For all questions in the Book Walk, answers will vary.

1. Have students use the **table of contents** in *K¹² Classics for Young Readers, Volume B,* to find "The Goose and the Golden Eggs" and turn to that page. Point to and read aloud the **title of the story**.

2. Have students study the **illustration** and make **predictions** about the story based on the illustration.

   ▸ Who do you think is a **character** in the story?
   ▸ What do you think the story is about?

3. Ask students why they think they are going to read this story.

   ▸ Do you think we're going to read this story for information? Why or why not?

"The Goose and the Golden Eggs"

Now it's time to read "The Goose and the Golden Eggs." Have students sit next to you so that they can see the pictures and words while you read the story aloud.

1. Read the story aloud all the way through. Track with your finger so students can follow along.

2. Reread the entire story with students, having them chime in and read aloud with you this time. Tell them to think about the character and what he does. Tell students that you will pause at certain points in the story to discuss.

3. Begin to reread, pausing after the second paragraph.

   ▸ What characters have we met? a man and a goose
   ▸ What does the goose do every day? lays a big, golden egg
   ▸ What does the man do with the eggs? sells them at the market

4. Continue reading. Pause after the third paragraph.

   ▸ What does the man think about the goose? The man says that the goose must have many eggs inside her, otherwise she wouldn't be able to lay golden eggs.
   ▸ What does he decide to do? kill his goose
   ▸ What do you think will happen next? Answers will vary.

5. Continue reading to the end of the story.

Objectives

- Use text organizational features to locate and comprehend information (table of contents).
- Use an illustration to make a prediction about a reading.
- Identify characters.
- Apply information read to answer questions.
- Read texts for literary experience.

Check Your Reading

"The Goose and the Golden Eggs"

Have students retell "The Goose and the Golden Eggs" in their own words to develop grammar, vocabulary, comprehension, and fluency skills. When finished, **ask students the following questions** to check comprehension and encourage discussion.

▶ How often does the goose lay her golden eggs? every day
▶ What does the man do with the golden eggs from his goose? He sells them at the market.
▶ What does the man do with the money he makes from selling the eggs? He saves it and slowly becomes rich.
▶ What does the man wish? He wishes he could be very rich.
▶ Why does the man kill the goose? He wants the golden eggs all at once.
▶ What has the man lost at the end of the story, and how does the loss affect him? He has lost the goose, so he won't get any more eggs.

Reading for Meaning

 Cause and Effect

Help students identify cause and effect in "The Goose and the Golden Eggs" by completing a graphic organizer. Turn to page LC 17 of *K¹² Language Arts Activity Book*.

Objectives
- Define cause and effect.
- Identify cause-and-effect relationships in text either stated or inferred.
- Use a graphic organizer to organize information.

1. Ask students if they know the meanings of the words **cause** and **effect**. Tell them that a *cause* is why something happens and an *effect* is what happens because of a cause.

2. Give examples of cause and effect.
   Say: Here is an example of cause and effect. When it rains, I get wet. The rain is the cause since it makes me wet. Getting wet is the effect. It's what happens to me when it rains!

3. Have students give examples of causes and their effects.

4. Tell students that they are going to think about cause and effect in the story they just read.

5. Direct students' attention to the Activity Book page. Read the directions with them. Help students by thinking aloud and talking through ways to find the connections.
   Say: The first cause is that the man sells the golden eggs. This is the reason why something else happens. What happens when the man sells the eggs? He makes money. So this is the effect, or what happens because of the cause. That goes in the Effect column. Let's try the next one together.

6. Have students complete the Activity Book page. If necessary, read the text together with them.

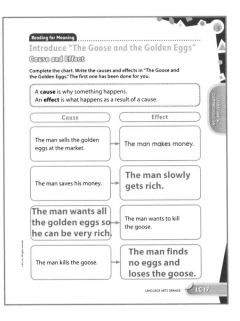

Review "The Goose and the Golden Eggs"

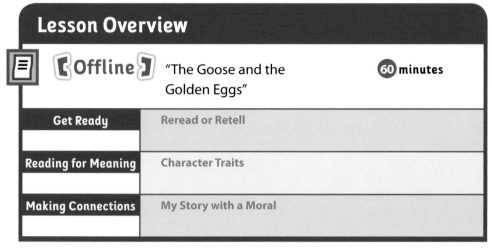

Lesson Overview

Offline	"The Goose and the Golden Eggs"	60 minutes
Get Ready	Reread or Retell	
Reading for Meaning	Character Traits	
Making Connections	My Story with a Moral	

Big Ideas

Good readers recognize and understand the traits of characters so they can appreciate the author's message.

Materials

Supplied

- "The Goose and the Golden Eggs," *K¹² Classics for Young Readers, Volume B*, pp. 4–5
- *K¹² Language Arts Activity Book*, p. LC 18

Also Needed

- crayons

Keywords

character – a person or animal in a story

moral – the lesson of a story, particularly a fable

trait – a quality of a person or other object; what something is like

 **Offline** 60 minutes

"The Goose and the Golden Eggs"

Work **together** with students to complete offline Get Ready, Reading for Meaning, and Making Connections activities.

Get Ready

Reread or Retell
If you'd like to, reread the story to students. Otherwise, have students retell the story using the illustrations as a guide, and then move on to the next activity.

 Objectives
- Recount or describe key ideas or details from a text read aloud or information presented orally or through other media.

Reading for Meaning

 Character Traits
Help students complete this activity to check comprehension and focus on describing character traits. Students will describe character traits by completing a chart. **Reread parts of the story** if they have trouble answering a question. Turn to page LC 18 of *K¹² Language Arts Activity Book*.

1. Tell students that a **trait** is a word that describes what a person is like or how she behaves. Describe your own traits (such as kind, caring, helpful, intelligent, and so on) as an example.

2. Tell students that traits are adjectives, or describing words. They tell how a person is special and describe the way someone looks, thinks, and acts.

3. Have students tell some of their own traits. Give them a sentence starter, such as *I am* _____ . Make sure students use adjectives.

4. Explain that traits are not feelings, like happiness or sadness. Traits generally do not change, like feelings do. They are qualities that are the same in a person all the time.

5. Remind students that we learn about characters in a story in three ways: through what they say, what they do, and what others say about them, including what the narrator says. These are called **character clues**. We use clues to learn about a character's traits.

 Objectives
- Describe character feelings.
- Describe character motivations.
- Describe characters and their reactions to major events in the story.
- Describe characters by what they do, what they say, or what others say about them.
- Make inferences about characters using evidence from the text.
- Support inferences with evidence from text and prior knowledge.

6. Explain that sometimes an author specifically tells us a character's trait. Other times we have to use the clues in a story and think of the trait ourselves.

7. Tell students that they are going to use the clues in today's story to describe the man's character trait.

8. Direct students' attention to the Activity Book page and read the directions with them.

9. Have students complete the Activity Book page. Help by prompting them with questions about what the man's actions and words tell us about him.

   ▶ When someone saves up money for something they want, what does that tell you about the person? Answers will vary.

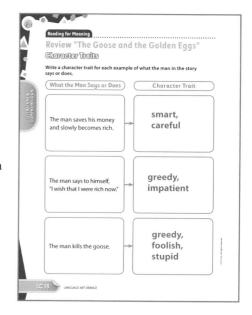

Making Connections

My Story with a Moral

Students will identify the moral of "The Goose and the Golden Eggs." Gather the completed Character Traits page.

1. Have students retell what happens in "The Goose and the Golden Eggs."

2. Have them describe the traits of the man in the story, using the Activity Book page.

3. Remind students that some stories have morals, or lessons. Ask them to tell the moral of a story they have read. For example, "Don't be like people who say they don't like something they can't have" from "The Fox and the Grapes."

4. Explain that authors often tell the moral of a story through what the characters do.

5. To help students come up with the moral for "The Goose and the Golden Eggs," ask the following questions:

   ▶ What does the man do with the money he makes selling the goose's eggs? saves it

   ▶ What happens because the man saves the money? He slowly becomes rich.

   ▶ What does the man think will happen if he kills the goose? He thinks he will find all of her golden eggs inside.

   ▶ Why does he want to find all the eggs at once? so he can be rich right away

   ▶ Why is the man foolish? He didn't know he wouldn't find all the eggs inside the goose. Now that he's killed the goose, he won't get any more eggs.

6. Have students tell what they think the moral of this story is. Possible answer: Don't be greedy.

7. Have students make up a story or tell a true one that illustrates this moral. Students can either tell you their story or write it. If they write it, have them also illustrate it. If students dictate their story, write it down, and then have students illustrate it.

Objectives

- Identify a lesson learned based on a character's actions.
- Identify the author's purpose.
- Identify the moral or lesson of a text.
- Make connections between text and self.

Introduce "The Pied Piper of Hamelin" (A)

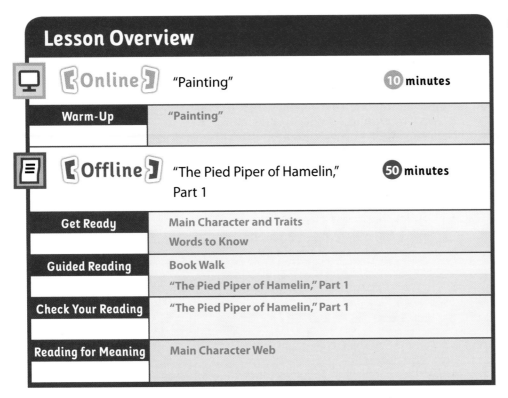

Lesson Overview

🖥	**Online**	"Painting"	🔟 minutes
	Warm-Up	"Painting"	

📄	**Offline**	"The Pied Piper of Hamelin," Part 1	🕔 minutes
	Get Ready	Main Character and Traits	
		Words to Know	
	Guided Reading	Book Walk	
		"The Pied Piper of Hamelin," Part 1	
	Check Your Reading	"The Pied Piper of Hamelin," Part 1	
	Reading for Meaning	Main Character Web	

Advance Preparation

If you are not able to complete the online Warm-Up, then print the selection and listen to students read aloud. Read pages 6–9 of "The Pied Piper of Hamelin" (Part 1) before the Guided Reading to locate the Words to Know in the text. Preview the Reading for Meaning and create a sample graphic organizer on a whiteboard or a sheet of paper to prepare students to complete the Activity Book page on their own.

Big Ideas

To understand the author's message, good readers must recognize the traits of characters.

Materials

Supplied

- "The Pied Piper of Hamelin," *K¹² Classics for Young Readers, Volume B,* pp. 6–13
- *K¹² Language Arts Activity Book,* p. LC 19
- "Painting" (optional)

Also Needed

- whiteboard (optional)

Story Synopsis

In the first part of this story, the town of Hamelin cannot rid itself of the fierce rats that have invaded it. Then a strange man, the Pied Piper, promises to drive away the rats for a price. The Pied Piper plays his pipe, and the rats follow him to their deaths in the river.

Keywords

main character – an important person, animal, or other being who is central to the plot

trait – a quality of a person or other object; what something is like

 **10 minutes**

"Painting"
Students will work independently online to develop fluency and oral reading skills.

Warm-Up

"Painting"
The purpose of this activity is to improve students' oral reading and fluency. Students will read "Painting." Remind students to listen to the model on each screen before they begin their recording.

 Objectives
- Increase oral reading skills.
- Increase fluency.

Offline Alternative
No computer access? Print a copy of "Painting." Have students read it aloud. Make note of any pronunciation errors, and review those words with students.

 **50 minutes**

"The Pied Piper of Hamelin," Part 1
Work **together** with students to complete offline Get Ready, Guided Reading, Check Your Reading, and Reading for Meaning activities.

Get Ready

Main Character and Traits
In stories with many characters, students need to be able to identify the main characters or the most important and central characters to the story.

 Objectives
- Define main character.
- Define character traits.
- Increase concept and content vocabulary.

1. Review the definition of character.

2. Explain to students that a **main character** is one that is very important to the story. A main character is a key part of much or all of the action in the story. Main characters may also do all or most of the talking.

3. Ask students to identify main characters in other stories they've read (for example, the man with the goose from "The Goose and the Golden Eggs").

   ▶ How do you know these are the main characters? Possible answers: The character takes part in all of the action. It is the only character. It is the only character that speaks.

4. Review the definition of **trait** as a character's quality, or what a character is like. Have students describe some of the traits of the characters they named.

5. Have students tell how readers learn about character's traits. what they do, what they say, what others say about them

Words to Know

Review the following words with students before reading the first part of "The Pied Piper of Hamelin."

1. Have students say each word aloud.

2. Ask students if they know what each word means.

   ▸ If students know a word's meaning, have them define it and use it in a sentence.
   ▸ If students don't know a word's meaning, read them the definition and discuss the word with them.

pied – wearing clothing with patches of many different colors
pipe – a long, thin instrument that you blow into to make music
piper – a person who plays a pipe
tawny – a brownish-yellow color like tan

Guided Reading

Book Walk
Prepare students by taking them on a Book Walk of "The Pied Piper of Hamelin." Scan the story together and ask students to make predictions about it. For all questions in the Book Walk, answers will vary.

1. Have students use the **table of contents** in *K¹² Classics for Young Readers, Volume B*, to find "The Pied Piper of Hamelin" and turn to that page.

2. Point to and read aloud the **title of the story**.

3. Have students study the **illustrations** and make **predictions** about the story based on the illustrations.

   ▸ Who do you think is the **main character** in the story?
   ▸ What do you think the story is about?

4. Ask students what type of story they think this will be.

   ▸ Do you think this story is real or made up out of the imagination of the author? Why do you think this?

Objectives
- Use text organizational features to locate and comprehend information (table of contents).
- Use an illustration to make a prediction about a reading.
- Identify characters.
- Read texts for literary experience.

"The Pied Piper of Hamelin," Part 1
Now it's time to read the first part of "The Pied Piper of Hamelin." Have students sit next to you so that they can see the pictures and words while you read the story aloud.

1. Read the story aloud all the way through to the middle of page 9, ending with the sentence, "They rang the bells and shouted for joy." Track with your finger so students can follow along.

2. Reread Part 1 of the story with students, having them chime in and read aloud with you this time. Tell them think about who the main characters are and what they do. Tell students that you will pause at certain points in the story to discuss.

3. Begin rereading Part 1 of the story, pausing to discuss after the fourth paragraph.

   ▸ What main character have we met? the Mayor
   ▸ What does he wish for? for a trap big enough to catch all the rats
   ▸ What would he do to get his wish? give all his gold

4. Continue reading. Pause to discuss on page 7 after the phrase, "I can drive the rats out of the town."

   ▸ What other main character have we met? the Pied Piper
   ▸ What is he like? strange

   Say: In the story, it says the Pied Piper is a very strange man. No one has ever seen him before.

   ▸ What else does the story say about him? tall and thin, with bright blue eyes and light hair
   ▸ What does he say he will do? drive the rats out of town
   ▸ What do you think will happen next? Answers will vary.

5. Continue reading. Pause to discuss at the top of page 8 after the phrase, "and a thousand it shall be."

   ▸ What does the Pied Piper want? a thousand pieces of gold

6. Continue reading until the end of Part 1 on page 9.

Check Your Reading

"The Pied Piper of Hamelin," Part 1

Have students retell Part 1 of "The Pied Piper of Hamelin" in their own words to develop grammar, vocabulary, comprehension, and fluency skills. When finished, **ask students the following questions** to check comprehension and encourage discussion.

▸ What is the problem in the town of Hamelin at the beginning of the story? There are rats everywhere that won't go away.
▸ Describe the Pied Piper. He is a stranger. He is tall and thin, has bright blue eyes and light hair, and wears a long coat of red and yellow.
▸ What does the Pied Piper say he can do? He says he can drive the rats out of the town.
▸ What does the Mayor agree to give the Pied Piper to do this? a thousand pieces of gold
▸ How does the Pied Piper get rid of the rats? He plays his pipe and the rats follow him to the river, where they dance in and drown.
▸ What do you think will happen next? Answers will vary.

Objectives
- Answer questions requiring literal recall of details.
- Describe characters and their reactions to major events in the story.
- Describe characters and their traits.
- Use text to make a prediction.

Reading for Meaning

✏️ **Main Character Web**

Help students begin a character web. Students will complete this page over two lessons. Turn to page LC 19 of *K¹² Language Arts Activity Book*.

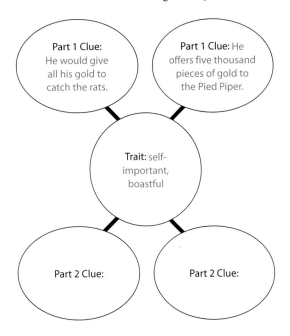

1. Have students identify all of the characters in the story. the Pied Piper, the Mayor, the Wise Men, the children and the people in the town

2. Have students name the two main characters in the story. the Pied Piper, the Mayor

3. Explain that these are the main characters because the story is named after the Pied Piper, and the Mayor is the one who makes the promise to pay the Pied Piper. These two characters take part in most of the action of the story.

4. Tell students that you are going to complete a character web to tell what the Mayor is like.
   Say: To do this, we will examine what the Mayor says, what he does, and what others say about him in this part of the story.

5. Draw a character web on a whiteboard or a sheet of paper. Tell students that you are going to write a character trait for the Mayor in the center of the web. In the outer circles, you are going to write parts of the story that show this trait.
   Say: First I will write what he says or does. Later, after I finish the story, I will decide what character trait all of the things he says or does shows me.

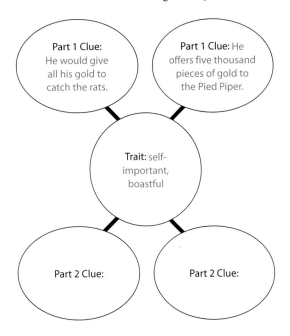

Part 1 Clue: He would give all his gold to catch the rats.

Part 1 Clue: He offers five thousand pieces of gold to the Pied Piper.

Trait: self-important, boastful

Part 2 Clue:

Part 2 Clue:

6. Show students how to write the examples from the story that show what the Mayor says or does. Write "He would give all his gold to catch the rats" in a Part 1 circle. Write "He offers five thousand pieces of gold to the Pied Piper" in another.

Objectives

- Describe characters and their traits.
- Describe characters and their reactions to major events in the story.
- Describe characters by what they do, what they say, or what others say about them.
- Make inferences about characters using evidence from the text.
- Support inferences with evidence from text and prior knowledge.

7. Explain to students that you will fill in the rest of the web after you read Part 2 of the story. At that time, you will also be able to tell what the different things the Mayor says and does tell about his character. You will fill in the center trait then.

8. Tell students that they will now start a character web for the Pied Piper. They will include clues from Part 1. They should write what the Pied Piper says or does, or what other says about him. Later they will choose what character trait the Pied Piper shows.

9. Have students complete the Part 1 circles on Activity Book page. As students complete the character web, make sure they are using clues from the text: what the character looks like, says, does, or what others say about him.

10. **Reread parts of the story** if students have trouble completing the web.

11. Keep the sample character web and the Activity Book page in a safe place so you can add to them after reading the rest of the story.

Introduce "The Pied Piper of Hamelin" (B)

Lesson Overview

☰	[Offline]	"The Pied Piper of Hamelin," Part 2	60 minutes

Get Ready	Cause and Effect
	Words to Know
Guided Reading	Book Walk
	"The Pied Piper of Hamelin," Part 2
Check Your Reading	"The Pied Piper of Hamelin," Part 2
Reading for Meaning	Main Character Web
Beyond the Lesson	⊕ OPTIONAL: Draw a Picture

Advance Preparation

Have students gather the partially completed page LC 19 in *K¹² Language Arts Activity Book* (Main Character Web). Also gather the web you created for the Mayor.

Big Ideas

▸ To understand the author's message, good readers must recognize the traits of characters.
▸ Identifying cause and effect relationships aids in literal and inferential reading comprehension.

[Materials]

Supplied

- "The Pied Piper of Hamelin," *K¹² Classics for Young Readers, Volume B*, pp. 6–13
- *K¹² Language Arts Activity Book*, p. LC 19

Also Needed

- crayons (optional)

Story Synopsis

In the second part of "The Pied Piper of Hamelin," the Pied Piper asks the Mayor for the money he was promised for ridding Hamelin of its rats. When the mayor of Hamelin refuses to pay the agreed upon price for this service, the Pied Piper lures all the children of Hamelin away from the town, and they are never seen again.

Keywords

cause – the reason something happens
effect – the result of a cause
main character – an important person, animal, or other being who is central to the plot
trait – a quality of a person or other object; what something is like

 **60 minutes**

"The Pied Piper of Hamelin," Part 2

Work **together** with students to complete offline Get Ready, Guided Reading, Check Your Reading, and Reading for Meaning, and Beyond the Lesson activities.

Get Ready

Cause and Effect

Good readers can recognize cause-and-effect relationships in stories. Teach students to identify the causes and effects in stories to help them understand the plot.

Objectives
- Define cause and effect.
- Increase concept and content vocabulary.

1. Review with students the definitions of **cause** and **effect**. Have students give an example of a cause-and-effect relationship. (For example, if I don't brush my teeth, I may get cavities.)

2. Tell students that sometimes an effect can become the cause of something else. Give an example.
   Say: If it's raining outside, I put up my umbrella. The rain is the cause and putting up my umbrella is the effect. If I put up my umbrella, then I stay dry. Now putting up my umbrella is the cause and staying dry is the effect.

3. Have students come up with their own examples.

4. Explain that students will look for cause-and-effect relationships like these as they read.

Words to Know

Before reading "The Pied Piper of Hamelin," Part 2, review Words to Know with students.

1. Have students say each word aloud.

2. Ask students if they know what each word means.

   ▶ If students know a word's meaning, have them define it and use it in a sentence.

   ▶ If students don't know a word's meaning, read them the definition and discuss the word with them.

pied –wearing clothing with patches of many different colors
pipe– a long, thin instrument that you blow into to make music
piper – a person who plays a pipe
tawny – a brownish-yellow color like tan

Guided Reading

Book Walk

Prepare students by taking them on a Book Walk of "The Pied Piper of Hamelin."
Scan the story together to revisit the characters and events. For all questions in the
Book Walk, students' will vary.

1. Have students use the **table of contents** in *K¹² Classics for Young Readers,
   Volume B*, to find "The Pied Piper of Hamelin." Ask students to read aloud the
   title of the story.

2. Have students tell what happens at the beginning of the story. If students do
   not remember the beginning, model retelling the beginning of a story.
   Say: I remember the beginning of the story. The town of Hamelin has a problem
   because there are rats everywhere, and the town cannot get rid of them. Do you
   remember what happens next?

3. Have students tell who the main characters are in the story.

   ▸ What are some of the traits of these characters?

4. Have students make predictions about the story.

   ▸ What do you think will happen now that the rats are gone?

"The Pied Piper of Hamelin," Part 2

Now it's time to read Part 2 of "The Pied Piper of Hamelin." Have students sit next to
you so that they can see the pictures and words while you read the story aloud.

1. Read Part 2 of the story aloud all the way through, beginning in the middle of
   page 9 with the phrase, "Then the Pied Piper said to the Mayor," Track with
   your finger so students can follow along.

2. Reread Part 2 the story with students, having them chime in and read aloud
   with you this time. Tell them think about some of the causes and effects in the
   story. Tell students that you will pause at certain points in the story to discuss.

3. Begin to reread, pausing to discuss after the sentence on page 10, "You cannot
   bring them back."

   ▸ What does the Mayor tell the Pied Piper? He will only pay fifty gold pieces
     instead of one thousand.

   ▸ What do you think will happen next? Answers will vary.

Objectives

- Use text organizational
  features to locate and
  comprehend information
  (table of contents).
- Read texts for literary
  experience.
- Identify main character(s).
- Describe characters and
  their traits.

4. Continue reading. Pause to discuss on page 12 after the phrase, "and I could not find the door."

> ▸ What happened to the children of Hamelin? The Pied Piper played music, and they followed him away.

> ▸ Why do you think the Pied Piper did this?
> **Say:** In the story, when the Mayor refuses to pay the Pied Piper's full amount, the Pied Piper says the Mayor will be sorry. I think this has something to do with what the Pied Piper did with the children. What do you think?

5. Continue reading until the end of Part 2, which is the end of the story.

Check Your Reading

"The Pied Piper of Hamelin," Part 2
Have students retell Part 2 of "The Pied Piper of Hamelin" in their own words to develop grammar, vocabulary, comprehension, and fluency skills. When finished, **ask students the following questions** to check comprehension and encourage discussion.

> ▸ What does the Mayor do when the Pied Piper asks for his money? He refuses to pay the thousand pieces of gold and offers fifty instead.

> ▸ What does the Pied Piper do after that? He plays his pipe, and all the children of the town follow him through a door.

> ▸ Why does the little lame boy cry? He cannot keep up to go with the other children.

> ▸ What happens to the children of Hamelin? They disappear and are never seen again.

> ▸ Why is there no music in Hamelin anymore? No one is allowed to sing or play music on the street where the Pied Piper played and made the children disappear.

Objectives
- Answer questions requiring literal recall of details.
- Describe characters and their reactions to major events in the story.
- Describe characters and their traits.

Reading for Meaning

✎ Main Character Web

Help students complete page LC 19 in *K¹² Language Arts Activity Book*.

1. Review the main characters in the story.

2. Review that we learn about character traits by what characters say and do, and what others say about them.

3. Take out the main character web you created for the Mayor. Tell students you are going to complete the web by filling in two more examples from the second part of the story.

4. Read the two examples that you wrote on the web from the first part of the story.

5. Look back at Part 2 of the story with students. Have them point out two examples of what the Mayor says or does or point them out for students. Two examples from the story.

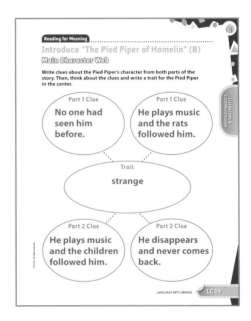

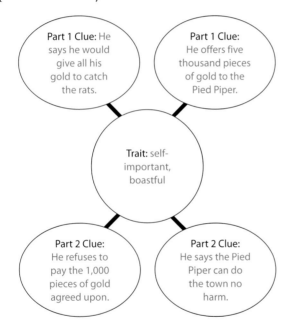

6. Tell students that now that you have gathered all your clues, you can review them and choose a character trait that describes the Mayor. Reread all four clues to students, or have them read them with you.
   Say: What trait descibes the Mayor? The first two clues show me that the Mayor seems to care about the rats, but the second two show me that he is not really honest and doesn't keep his promises. I think the Mayor was just full of himself at the beginning of the story when he said he would pay anything, and he shows that trait again later when he won't pay the money and thinks the Piper can't harm the town. He was self-important, or boastful.
   Write those traits in the center circle.

7. Tell students they are now going to complete their main character web on the Pied Piper.

8. Direct students' attention to the Activity Book page they started after reading Part 1. Review what students have already written about the Pied Piper.

9. Have students complete the Activity Book page for Part 2 of the story. Remind them that they are looking for clues in the text that show what the Pied Piper says or does. They should then review all of their clues and decide what character trait the clues show about the Piper. Students should write that trait in the center.

Beyond the Lesson

⊕ OPTIONAL: Draw a Picture

This activity is OPTIONAL. It is intended for students who have extra time and would benefit from comparing themselves to a character in "The Pied Piper of Hamelin" through drawing. Feel free to skip this activity.

1. Ask students to think about the Pied Piper's character trait and what he is like.

2. Have students draw a picture showing how they are similar to or different from the Pied Piper. Encourage them to add words or sentences that explain the picture.

 TIP Students may choose a character other than the Pied Piper, but they should construct a new character web first, to help them think about the character's trait before they draw.

Objectives
- Make connections between text and self.

Review "The Pied Piper of Hamelin"

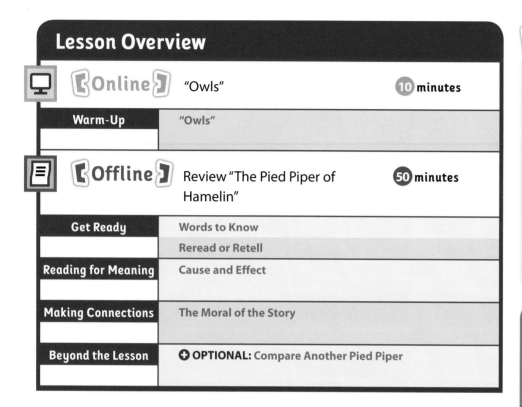

Lesson Overview

🖥️ **[Online]** "Owls"		⑩ minutes
Warm-Up	"Owls"	

📄 **[Offline]** Review "The Pied Piper of Hamelin"		㊿ minutes
Get Ready	Words to Know	
	Reread or Retell	
Reading for Meaning	Cause and Effect	
Making Connections	The Moral of the Story	
Beyond the Lesson	➕ OPTIONAL: Compare Another Pied Piper	

Advance Preparation

If you are not able to complete the online Warm-Up, then print the selection and listen to students read aloud.

Big Ideas

Identifying cause-and-effect relationships aids in literal and inferential reading comprehension.

[Materials]

Supplied

- "The Pied Piper of Hamelin," *K¹² Classics for Young Readers, Volume B*, pp. 6–13
- *K¹² Language Arts Activity Book*, p. LC 20
- "Owls" (optional)

Also Needed

- crayons

Keywords

cause – the reason something happens

effect – the result of a cause

folktale – a story, which usually teaches a lesson important to a culture, that is passed down through many generations

moral – the lesson of a story, particularly a fable

 **10 minutes**

"Owls"

Students will work independently online to develop fluency and oral reading skills.

Warm-Up ·

"Owls"

The purpose of this activity is to improve students' oral reading and fluency. Students will read "Owls." Remind students to listen to the model on each screen before they begin their recording.

Objectives
- Increase oral reading skills.
- Increase fluency.

Offline Alternative

No computer access? Print a copy of "Owls." Have students read it aloud. Make note of any pronunciation errors, and review those words with students.

 **50 minutes**

"The Pied Piper of Hamelin"

Work **together** with students to complete offline Get Ready, Reading for Meaning, Making Connections, and Beyond the Lesson activities.

Get Ready ·

Words to Know

Go over Words to Know with students.

1. Ask students to define the following words and use them in a sentence:

pied	**piper**
pipe	**tawny**

2. Correct any incorrect or vague definitions.

Objectives
- Recount stories, including fables and folktales from diverse cultures.
- Increase concept and content vocabulary.

Reread or Retell

If you'd like to, reread the story to students. Otherwise, have students retell the story using the pictures as a guide.

Reading for Meaning

 Cause and Effect

Help students identify examples of cause and effect from "The Pied Piper of Hamelin." Turn to page LC 20 in *K¹² Language Arts Activity Book*.

1. Remind students that good readers can recognize cause-and-effect relationships in stories.

2. Review with students the definitions of **cause** and **effect**.

3. Have students give an example of a cause-and-effect relationship. (For example, if I don't brush my teeth, I may get cavities.)

4. Have students come up with their own examples.

5. Remind students that sometimes an effect can become a cause. For example, forgetting to brush your teeth can cause your teeth to be dirty. But the effect—dirty teeth—can cause another effect, cavities.

6. Tell students they are going to find examples of causes and effects in the story.

7. Have students complete the Activity Book page. Show them the way the chart works. Trace the arrows between the boxes with your finger, and show students that each effect becomes the cause for another effect.

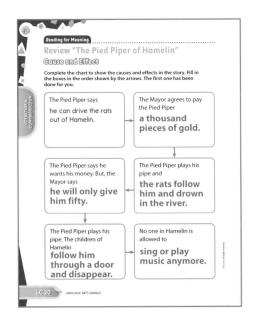

Objectives

- Identify cause-and-effect relationships in text either stated or inferred.

Making Connections

The Moral of the Story

"The Pied Piper of Hamelin" is a folktale and teaches a lesson, or moral. The causes and effects in the story lead to the moral. Help students identify the moral by guiding them to think about the cause-and-effect relationships in the tale. Gather the completed Cause and Effect page.

1. Explain that this story is a **folktale**. Tell students what makes a story a folktale. **Say:** A folktale is a story that is passed down through generations. That means that parents tell their children, and then the children grow up and someday tell the story to their own children and so on. Usually a story is passed down because it tells about something that is important to that group of people. What is important may be the **moral** of the folktale. Remember that a moral is a lesson in a story.

2. Tell students that they are going to think about the moral of "The Pied Piper of Hamelin." Direct students' attention to the Cause and Effect page.

3. Have students reread the causes and effects in their chart.

4. Have them tell what they think the Mayor and townspeople learned from their experiences with the Pied Piper. Possible answer: Keep your promises.

Objectives

- Identify genre.
- Identify characteristics of different genres.
- Identify a lesson learned based on a character's actions.
- Identify the author's purpose.
- Identify the moral or lesson of a text.

5. Explain that this is the moral of the story.

6. If students are having difficulty determining the moral of the story, ask the following questions:

   ▸ What does the Pied Piper say he will do? Does he do it? get rid of the rats; Yes

   ▸ What does the Mayor say he will do? Does he do it? pay the Pied Piper a thousand pieces of gold; No

   ▸ What happens when the Mayor doesn't keep his promise? The Pied Piper leads the children away.

   ▸ What lesson do you think the Mayor learns? Answers will vary.

7. Have students describe a real experience or tell a made-up story that shows this same moral.

8. If desired, have students illustrate their version of the moral through a drawing or a comic strip.

Beyond the Lesson

⊕ **OPTIONAL: Compare Another Pied Piper**
This activity is OPTIONAL. It is intended for students who have extra time and would benefit from reading another version of the story and comparing it to today's selection. Feel free to skip this activity.

If students are interested, they can read Robert Browning's poem, *The Pied Piper of Hamelin*. An excerpt of this poem is included in *K¹² Classics for Young Readers, Volume B*. The poem may be found on the Internet at http://www.poetry-online.org/browning_robert_pied_piper_of_hamelin.htm. Copies of the poem may also be found in libraries in books such as the following: *The Pied Piper of Hamelin*, Robert Browning. New York: Harcourt Brace Jovanovich, 1988.

1. Read the poem aloud to students, and stop to define any unfamiliar words.

2. Discuss with students how the version in *K¹² Classics for Young Readers, Volume B.* and this version are the same or different. Encourage students to consider form, language, and content.

Objectives
• Compare and contrast different versions of the same story.

Introduce "The Bremen Town Musicians" (A)

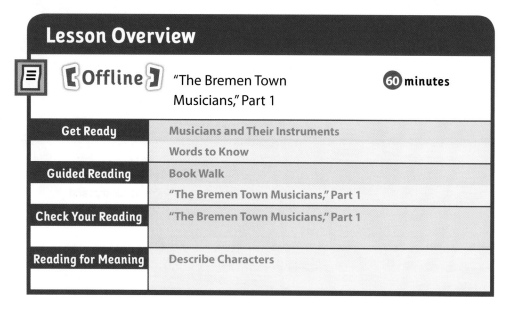

Lesson Overview

| **Offline** | "The Bremen Town Musicians," Part 1 | **60** minutes |

Get Ready	Musicians and Their Instruments
	Words to Know
Guided Reading	Book Walk
	"The Bremen Town Musicians," Part 1
Check Your Reading	"The Bremen Town Musicians," Part 1
Reading for Meaning	Describe Characters

Materials

Supplied

- "The Bremen Town Musicians," *K¹² Classics for Younger Readers, Volume B*, pp. 14–21
- *K¹² Language Arts Activity Book*, p. LC 21

Also Needed

- whiteboard (optional)
- household items – musical instruments (optional)

Advance Preparation

You may want to gather musical instruments to prepare for the Get Ready, in which students will talk about musicians and the benefits of playing music together. Read through page 16 of "The Bremen Town Musicians" (Part 1) before the Guided Reading to locate the Words to Know in the text. Preview the Reading for Meaning and create a sample graphic organizer on a whiteboard or a sheet of paper to prepare students to complete the Activity Book page on their own.

Big Ideas

Guided reading provides students with reading-for-meaning strategies.

Story Synopsis

In the first part of "The Bremen Town Musicians," four animals—a Donkey, a Dog, a Cat, and a Cock—run away from their masters, who intend to kill them because they are no longer useful. These friends decide to go to the town of Bremen and join the band. Readers may want to note that some of the animals refer to their owners as "master" and "mistress."

Keywords

prediction – a guess about what might happen that is based on information in a story and what you already know

character – a person or animal in a story

folktale – a story, which usually teaches a lesson important to a culture, that is passed down through many generations

 **60 minutes**

"The Bremen Town Musicians," Part 1

Work **together** with students to complete offline Get Ready, Guided Reading, Check Your Reading, and Reading for Meaning activities.

Get Ready

Musicians and Their Instruments

In "The Bremen Town Musicians," four animal friends flee their owners and decide to join a band together. To help students connect to the plot of the story, guide them to think about music and the benefits of playing instruments together.

1. Have students name some instruments they know.

2. Have students describe how one or more of these instruments sound.

3. Have students describe what instruments sound like when they are played by a group of musicians, such as a band. Answers will vary.

   ▸ How is the sound of a band different from the sound of one instrument being played?
   ▸ Why do you think people like to play music in bands or listen to bands?

4. Tell students that they are going to read a story about some friends who decide to join a band.

TIP If you have musical instruments, have students play them and describe the sounds. Play an instrument while students play another. Discuss how the experience of playing together is different from playing alone.

> **Objectives**
> • Connect text to prior knowledge.
> • Increase concept and content vocabulary.

Words to Know

Before reading "The Bremen Town Musicians," go over Words to Know with students.

1. Have students say each word aloud.

2. Ask students if they know what each word means.

   ▸ If students know a word's meaning, have them define it and use it in a sentence.
   ▸ If students don't know a word's meaning, read them the definition and discuss the word with them.

cock – a male chicken
master – a male owner of property
mistress – a female owner of property, used in times past

Guided Reading

Book Walk

Prepare students by taking them on a Book Walk of "The Bremen Town Musicians."
Scan the story together and ask students to make predictions about it. For all
questions in the Book Walk, answers will vary.

1. Have students use the **table of contents** in *K¹² Classics for Young Readers,
   Volume B*, to find "The Bremen Town Musicians" and turn to that page.

2. Point to and read aloud the **title of the story**.

3. Have students study the **illustrations** and make **predictions** about the story
   based on the illustrations.

   ▸ Who do you think are the **characters** in the story?
   ▸ What do you think the story is about?

4. Ask students what type of story they think this will be.

   ▸ Do you think this story is real or made up out of the imagination of the
   author? Tell why you think this. Why?

Objectives

- Use text organizational features to locate and comprehend information (table of contents).
- Use an illustration to make a prediction about a reading.
- Identify characters.
- Read texts for literary experience.

"The Bremen Town Musicians," Part 1

Now it's time to read the first part of "The Bremen Town Musicians." You will read
through page 16. Have students sit next to you so that they can see the pictures and
words while you read the story aloud.

1. Read the first part of the story aloud. Stop on page 16, after the sentence, "So
   they all went on together." Track with your finger so students can follow along.

2. Reread the first part of the story with students, having them chime in and read
   aloud with you this time. Tell them to think about who the characters are and
   what they do. Tell students that you will pause at certain points in the story to
   discuss.

3. Begin to reread, pausing to discuss after the sentence about midway on
   page 14, "'I'll run away.'"

   ▸ What character have we met? a Donkey
   ▸ Why is the Donkey running away? In the story, it says that the Donkey had
   become old and useless. Then his master says that the Donkey must be
   killed. The Donkey decides that he's not going to stay and wait to be killed,
   so he runs away.

4. Continue reading. Pause to discuss after the first paragraph on page 15, which ends with "and I can beat the drum."

   ▸ Who is the next character we have met? the Dog
   ▸ Why is he on the road? He is running away from his master, who wants to kill him because he is too old.
   ▸ What does the Donkey suggest that he and Dog do? He wants them to go to Bremen town to play in the band.

5. Continue reading to the end of page 16, pausing to discuss after the sentence "So they all went on together."

   ▸ What other characters have we met? a Cat and a Cock
   ▸ What is each animal going to do in the Bremen town band? The Donkey is going to play the drum, the Dog is going to play the flute, and the Cat and Cock are going to sing.

Check Your Reading

"The Bremen Town Musicians," Part 1

Have students retell the first part of the story in their own words to develop grammar, vocabulary, comprehension, and fluency skills. When finished, **ask students the following questions** to check comprehension and encourage discussion.

▸ Name the four animals in the order that they joined the group. Donkey, Dog, Cat, Cock
▸ What do the owners of the animals plan to do with their animals? kill them
▸ Why do the owners want to do this? because they think the animals are no longer useful
▸ What do the animals do when they learn what the owners are planning? They run away.
▸ What are the animals going to do together? They are going to the town of Bremen to play in the band.
▸ What do you think will happen next? Answers will vary.

Objectives
- Answer questions requiring literal recall of details.
- Identify characters.
- Describe characters and their reactions to major events in the story.
- Use text to make a prediction.

Reading for Meaning

 Describe Characters

Help students begin page LC 21 in *K¹² Language Arts Activity Book*. Students will complete this page over two lessons.

1. Have students identify all of the characters in the story. Donkey, Dog, Cat, Cock

2. Review how we learn about characters in a story: what the characters do and say or what others say about them. Remind students that "others" includes the narrator of the story.

3. Tell students that they are going to think about one of the characters in the story. Show them how to complete a character chart. Examine what the Dog says, what he does, and what others say about him in this part of the story.

Objectives
- Describe characters and their reactions to major events in the story.
- Describe characters by what they do, what they say, or what others say about them.

4. Draw a blank character chart on a whiteboard or a sheet of paper to demonstrate.

5. Tell students that you are going to write clues from the story that tell what the Dog says, what he does, and what other characters say about him.

6. Discuss the Dog with students. Have them think of something the Dog says. For example, the Dog says, "I have run away," on the first page of the story. Write your answer in the first box of the chart.

> What the character says: I will not stay to be killed.

> What the character does: Runs away with the donkey and the other animals.

> What other characters say about the character: Donkey says, "my good friend."

7. Complete your chart with students, having them make suggestions for the other two boxes.

8. Explain to students that you will add more to the chart after you read Part 2 of the story.

9. Tell students that they will now start a character chart of their own for the Donkey. Have students complete the Activity Book page for Part 1 of the story. They will complete the chart after they finish reading Part 2.

10. Keep the sample character chart and the Activity Book page in a safe place so you can add to them after reading the rest of the story.

Introduce "The Bremen Town Musicians" (B)

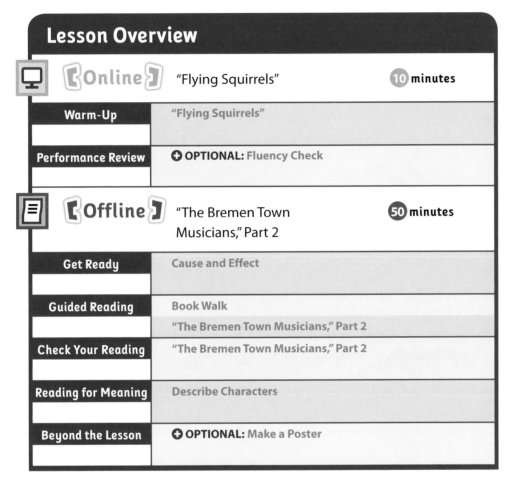

Lesson Overview

Online	"Flying Squirrels"	**10** minutes	
Warm-Up	"Flying Squirrels"		
Performance Review	**⊕ OPTIONAL:** Fluency Check		

Offline	"The Bremen Town Musicians," Part 2	**50** minutes	
Get Ready	Cause and Effect		
Guided Reading	Book Walk		
	"The Bremen Town Musicians," Part 2		
Check Your Reading	"The Bremen Town Musicians," Part 2		
Reading for Meaning	Describe Characters		
Beyond the Lesson	**⊕ OPTIONAL:** Make a Poster		

Materials

Supplied

- "The Bremen Town Musicians," *K¹² Classics for Younger Readers, Volume B*, pp. 14–21
- *K¹² Language Arts Activity Book*, p. LC 21
- "Flying Squirrels" (optional)
- Fluency Performance Checklist (optional)

Also Needed

- crayons (optional)

Keywords

cause – the reason something happens
character – a person or animal in a story
effect – the result of a cause
trait – a quality of a person or other object; what something is like

Advance Preparation

If you are not able to complete the online Warm-Up, then print the selection and listen to students read aloud. Have students gather the partially completed page LC 21 in *K¹² Language Arts Activity Book* (Describe Characters). Also gather the web you created for the Dog.

Big Ideas

- ▶ To understand the author's message, good readers must recognize the traits of characters.
- ▶ Identifying cause-and-effect relationships aids in literal and inferential reading comprehension.
- ▶ Guided reading provides students with reading-for-meaning strategies.

 **10 minutes**

"Flying Squirrels"
Students will work independently online to develop fluency and oral reading skills.

Warm-Up

"Flying Squirrels"
The purpose of this activity is to improve students' oral reading and fluency. Students will read "Flying Squirrels." Remind students to listen to the model on each screen before they begin their recording.

Objectives
- Increase oral reading skills.
- Increase fluency.

Offline Alternative

No computer access? Print a copy of "Flying Squirrels." Have students read it aloud. Make note of any pronunciation errors, and review those words with students.

Performance Review

⊕ **OPTIONAL: Fluency Check**
Listen to students' recordings and use the checklist to review fluency and track performance. Keep the completed checklist so you can review students' progress over time.

Objectives
- Read aloud grade-level text with appropriate automaticity, prosody, accuracy, and rate.

 **50 minutes**

"The Bremen Town Musicians," Part 2
Work **together** with students to complete offline Get Ready, Guided Reading, Check Your Reading, Reading for Meaning, and Beyond the Lesson activities.

Get Ready

Cause and Effect
Good readers can recognize cause-and-effect relationships in stories. Teach students to identify the causes and effects to help them understand the plot.

Objectives
- Define cause and effect.

1. Review with students the definitions of **cause** and **effect**. Have students give an example of a cause and effect relationship. (For example, if I leave milk outside the refrigerator for too long, it will spoil. If it spoils, I can't drink it.)

2. Explain that students will look for cause-and-effect relationships like these as they read.

Guided Reading

Book Walk

Prepare students by taking them on a Book Walk of "The Bremen Town Musicians." Scan the story together to revisit the characters and events.

1. Have students use the **table of contents** in *K¹² Classics for Young Readers, Volume B,* to find "The Bremen Town Musicians." Ask students to read aloud the title of the story.

2. Ask students what happens at the beginning of the story. Four animals run away from their masters. The masters wanted to kill the animals because they were too old and useless.

3. Have students tell who the characters are in the story. Donkey, Dog, Cat, Cock

4. Have students make predictions about the story.

   ▸ What do you think will happen next? Answers will vary.

Objectives

- Use text organizational features to locate and comprehend information (table of contents).
- Use text to make a prediction.
- Read texts for literary experience.
- Identify main character(s).

"The Bremen Town Musicians," Part 2

Now it's time to read the second part of the story. Have students sit next to you so that they can see the pictures and words while you read the story aloud.

1. Beginning on page 17, read the story through to the end. Track with your finger so students can follow along.

2. Reread Part 2 of the story with students, having them chime in and read aloud with you this time. Tell them to think about some of the causes and effects in the story. Tell students that you will pause at certain points in the story to discuss.

3. Begin to reread, pausing to discuss on page 19 after the phrase, "'a way to get that supper.'"

   ▸ What have the animals found? a house with robbers inside eating supper
   ▸ What do the animals want? to get the supper
   ▸ What do you think will happen next? Answers will vary.

4. Continue reading. Pause to discuss after the first paragraph on page 20, which ends with "they soon fell fast asleep."

   ▸ What did the animals do? They climbed on each other and made a lot of noise.
   ▸ What happened because of what the animals did? The animals made noise and scared away the robbers. The animals got the dinner they wanted.

5. Continue reading until the end of the story.

Check Your Reading

"The Bremen Town Musicians," Part 2

Have students retell the second part of "The Bremen Town Musicians" in their own words to develop grammar, vocabulary, comprehension, and fluency skills. When finished, **ask students the following questions** to check comprehension and encourage discussion.

Objectives
- Answer questions requiring literal recall of details.

▶ What do the animals find in the night? a house in which four robbers are eating supper

▶ What do the animals do to frighten off the robbers? They stand on each others' backs and make their loudest music.

▶ What do the animals do when one of the robbers comes back? The Cat scratches him, the Dog bites him, the Donkey kicks him, and the Cock cries out.

▶ What does the robber think happened to him? He thinks a witch scratched him, a man stabbed him, a giant kicked him, and someone called, "Kill the robber, do!"

▶ What happens at the end of the story? The robbers go far away and the animals stay in the house.

Reading for Meaning

Describe Characters

Help students complete page LC 21 of *K¹² Language Arts Activity Book* for Part 2 of the story.

Objectives
- Describe characters and their reactions to major events in the story.
- Describe characters by what they do, what they say, or what others say about them.
- Make inferences about characters using evidence from the text.
- Support inferences with evidence from text and prior knowledge.

1. Tell students that they have learned more about the animals and what they can do in the second part of the story.

2. Take out the character chart you created for the Dog. Tell students you are going to complete the chart by filling in more examples from Part 2 of the story.

3. Review your examples from the first part of the story.

4. Look back at Part 2 of the story with students. Have students point out examples of what the Dog says, what he does, and what others say about him. Write the answers in the chart.

> **What the character says:** "We will think of a way to get that supper."

> **What the character does:** The Dog barked and bit the robber in the leg.

> **What other characters say about the character:** The robber said the Dog was a man who stabbed him in the leg.

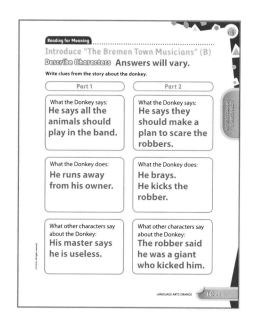

5. Have students turn to the character chart on the Activity Book page. Tell them that they are going to complete their chart by adding more information about the Donkey from the second part of the story.

6. Review with students what they've already written about the Donkey.

7. Have students complete the Activity Book page for Part 2. Remind students that they are looking for clues in the text that tell what the Donkey does, says, and what others say about him.

Beyond the Lesson

⊕ OPTIONAL: Make a Poster

This activity is OPTIONAL. It is intended for students who have extra time and would enjoy creating a poster advertising the Bremen Town Musicians. Feel free to skip this activity.

If students like to draw, have them create a poster advertising the Bremen Town Musicians. Their poster should show all four of the animal characters in the story and what part they play in the band. Tell students to refer to the text to decide what should go on the poster.

> **Objectives**
> - Describe characters by what they do, what they say, or what others say about them.

Review "The Bremen Town Musicians"

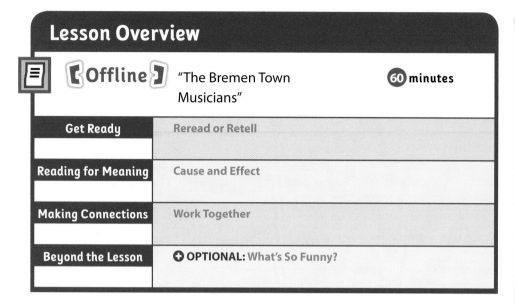

Lesson Overview

☰ **[Offline]**	"The Bremen Town Musicians"	**60** minutes

Get Ready	Reread or Retell
Reading for Meaning	Cause and Effect
Making Connections	Work Together
Beyond the Lesson	⊕ OPTIONAL: What's So Funny?

Big Ideas

Identifying cause-and-effect relationships aids in literal and inferential reading comprehension.

[Materials]

Supplied

- "The Bremen Town Musicians," *K¹² Classics for Young Readers, Volume B, pp. 14–21*
- *K¹² Language Arts Activity Book, p. LC 22*

Keywords

cause – why something happens

effect – what happens because of a cause

folktale – a story, which usually teaches a lesson important to a culture, that is passed down through many generations

moral – the lesson of a story, particularly a fable

 **60 minutes**

"The Bremen Town Musicians"

Work **together** with students to complete offline Get Ready, Reading for Meaning, Making Connections, and Beyond the Lesson activities.

Get Ready

Reread or Retell

If you'd like to, reread the story to students. Otherwise, have students retell the story using the pictures as a guide.

> **Objectives**
> - Recount stories, including fables and folktales from diverse cultures.

Reading for Meaning

 Cause and Effect

Have students build on their understanding of cause and effect by finding the cause-and-effect relationships in "The Bremen Town Musicians." Turn to page LC 22 in *K¹² Language Arts Activity Book.*

1. Remind students that good readers can recognize cause-and-effect relationships in stories so they can understand what happened and why it happened.

2. Review with students the definitions of **cause** and **effect**. Have students give an example of a cause and effect relationship. (For example, if I don't brush my teeth, I may get cavities.)

3. Have students come up with their own examples.

4. Tell students that they are going to find examples of causes and effects in the story.

5. Have students complete the Activity Book page. If necessary, read the instructions and provide guidance.

(TIP) If students have difficulty thinking of causes and effects, give them a cause, such as being in the sun for a long time without sunscreen, and ask for the effect. Or, give an effect, such as flowers and trees growing, and ask for the cause.

> **Objectives**
> - Define cause and effect.
> - Identify cause-and-effect relationships in text either stated or inferred.

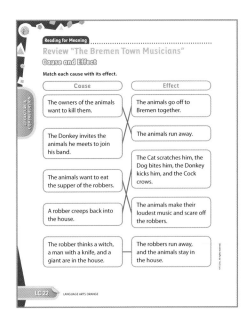

Making Connections

Work Together

"The Bremen Town Musicians" is a folktale and teaches a lesson, or moral. The causes and effects in the story can help us see the moral. Help students identify the moral by guiding them to think about the cause-and-effect relationships in the tale. Gather the completed Cause and Effect page.

1. Explain that this story is a **folktale**. Have students tell the characteristics of a folktale.

2. Explain that some folktales have animals as characters, as well as people. Have students name all of the characters. Make sure they include the robbers.

3. Tell students that they are going to think about the **moral** of the story. Direct students' attention to their completed Activity Book page.

4. Have students reread the causes and effects in their chart.

5. Discuss with students the actions that the animals take.

   ▸ Every time the animals do something, how do they do it? together
   ▸ Why is it important that the animals work together? By working together, they get the robbers' dinner and their house.
   ▸ How do you think the animals feel at the beginning of the story? How do you think they feel at the end? At the beginning they're scared, and at the end they're happy.

6. Have students state a moral, or lesson, that can be learned from the way the animals act in the story. Working together can help you get something done that you couldn't do alone.

7. Have students write a story about a time when they worked together with someone else to achieve something.

TIP You may have students dictate their story as you write it down.

Reward: Write the names of the literature selections completed in this unit on the My Accomplishments Chart and add a sticker to mark successful completion of this unit.

Objectives

- Identify genre.
- Identify characteristics of different genres.
- Identify a lesson learned based on a character's actions.
- Identify the author's purpose.
- Identify the moral or lesson of a text.
- Make connections between text and self.

Beyond the Lesson •

⊕ **OPTIONAL:** What's So Funny?

This activity is OPTIONAL. It is intended for students who have extra time and would enjoy looking at the humor in today's selection. Feel free to skip this activity.

Objectives
- Make connections between text and self.

1. Explain to students that there are some funny parts in "The Bremen Town Musicians." Most of the humor is at the expense of the robbers.

2. Discuss the humor with students.

   ► What are some of the funny parts in the story?
   ► Why are these parts funny?
   ► What do you think of the robbers?
   ► Do you think the animals or the robbers are smarter? Why? Why is this funny?

3. Have students act out the parts of the robbers. Have them show how the robbers might have left their dinner, or how the robber who returned might have behaved in the house or how he might have acted while telling his story to his friends.

Introduce *A Weed is a Flower*

Unit Overview

In this three-lesson unit, students will read *A Weed is a Flower*. Students will explore the following:

▶ The genre of biography
▶ The difference between a topic and a main idea
▶ How writers use details to support the main idea
▶ Context clues as a means for defining unfamiliar words
▶ Creating a summary of the most important ideas in a text

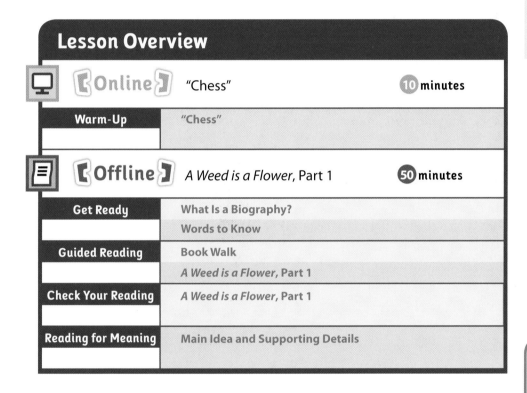

Lesson Overview

〔Online〕	"Chess"	**10** minutes
Warm-Up	"Chess"	
〔Offline〕	*A Weed is a Flower*, Part 1	**50** minutes
Get Ready	What Is a Biography?	
	Words to Know	
Guided Reading	Book Walk	
	A Weed is a Flower, Part 1	
Check Your Reading	*A Weed is a Flower*, Part 1	
Reading for Meaning	Main Idea and Supporting Details	

Advance Preparation

If you are not able to complete the online Warm-Up, then print the selection and listen to students read aloud. Read the book before beginning the Guided Reading to identify Words to Know in the text. Preview the Reading for Meaning and copy the graphic organizer to a whiteboard or a sheet of paper.

Big Ideas

▶ Biographies are a type of nonfiction meant to inform readers about a person's life.
▶ Readers must understand the relationship between main idea and supporting details.

Materials

Supplied

- *A Weed is a Flower* by Aliki
- *K¹² Language Arts Activity Book* p. LC 23
- "Chess" (optional)

Also Needed

- whiteboard (optional)

Story Synopsis

This book is a biography of George Washington Carver, a man born into slavery who became a leading expert on agriculture and taught others during his tenure as a professor at Tuskegee Institute for African Americans. The first part of the story is about Carver's early life. Readers may want to note that the story discusses slavery and describes Carver's abduction as a baby by kidnappers.

Keywords

biography – the story of someone's life written by another person

main idea – the most important idea in a paragraph or text

purpose – the reason for writing

supporting detail – a detail that gives more information about a main idea

topic – the subject of a text

 **Online** **10 minutes**

"Chess"
Students will work independently online to develop fluency and oral reading skills.

Warm-Up •

"Chess"
The purpose of this activity is to improve students' oral reading and fluency. Students will read "Chess." Remind students to listen to the model on each screen before they begin their recording.

Offline Alternative

No computer access? Print a copy of "Chess." Have students read it aloud. Make note of any pronunciation errors, and review those words with students.

Objectives
- Increase oral reading skills.
- Increase fluency.

 **Offline** **50 minutes**

A Weed is a Flower
Work **together** with students to complete offline Get Ready, Guided Reading, Check Your Reading, and Reading for Meaning activities.

Get Ready •

What Is a Biography?
Introduce students to the genre of biography.

1. Tell students that a **biography** is a story about someone's life that's written by another person.

2. Explain that a biography is **nonfiction**. Review that nonfiction is writing about true things and contains **facts**. Tell students that the facts included in a biography are the important events in a person's life or what the person accomplished.

3. Have students describe any biographies they may have read.

4. Have students explain why someone might read a biography. to learn about someone famous, important, or interesting

5. Have students explain why someone might write a biography. reasons similar to above

Objectives
- Identify characteristics of different genres.
- Connect text to prior knowledge.
- Identify purpose for reading.
- Identify the author's purpose.
- Increase concept and content vocabulary.

6. Tell students that the reason an author writes is called the **purpose**. Remind students that author's usually write with one of these purposes: to entertain, to inform, to express an opinion, or to persuade or convince the reader of something. Sometimes an author may write with more than one of these purposes.

7. Have students tell which of these purposes they think applies to biographies. inform, entertain, maybe to persuade the reader that the person in the biography is important or memorable

8. Have students describe some events that would go into their own biographies.

Words to Know

Before reading *A Weed is a Flower*, go over Words to Know with students.

1. Have students say each word aloud.

2. Ask students if they know what each word means.

   ▸ If students know a word's meaning, have them define it and use it in a sentence.
   ▸ If students don't know a word's meaning, read them the definition and discuss the word with them.

slave – a person who is owned by another person
yearned – wanted something very badly

TIP If students are unfamiliar with the concept of slavery, explain as many details as you deem appropriate. For the purposes of this story, students need to know that when the United States was just beginning, people owned slaves who originally came from Africa. Most slaves remained in slavery their entire lives.

Guided Reading ···

Book Walk

Prepare students by taking them on a Book Walk of *A Weed is a Flower*. Scan the book together and ask students to make predictions about the story. For all questions in the Book Walk, answers will vary.

1. Show students the **front cover** of the book. Point to and read aloud the **book title** and the **subtitle**.

2. Tell students that the subtitle lets us know that this book is about George Washington Carver's life. Ask students what kind of book is about a person's life. biography

3. Read the name of the **author** and **illustrator**. Remind students what it means to be an illustrator.

4. Have students look at the illustrations on the **front cover** and **back cover** of the book. Have students make a prediction about what the story will be about.

   ▸ What do you think we might learn about George Washington Carver?

Objectives

- Identify genre.
- Identify purpose for reading.
- Use an illustration to make a prediction about a reading.
- Use the title of the selection to make a prediction.
- Apply information read to answer questions.
- Read a variety of texts for information and pleasure.

5. Turn to the **title page**. Explain that the title page repeats the book title, author's name, and illustrator's name.

6. Ask students to tell you what they think the book might be about.

   ▸ Does the title provide a clue?

7. Look through the book. Have students describe what they see in the **illustrations.**

   ▸ Where do you think the story takes place?
   ▸ When do you think the story takes place, in the present or sometime in the past?
   ▸ What do you think might happen in the story?
   ▸ Have you ever read a story about a person who was born a slave? What was the person's life like?

TIP If students are curious about how the author of *A Weed is a Flower* knows what Carver said or felt, you might explain that authors of biographies written for children sometimes add some fictional details based on the facts of the person's life.

A Weed is a Flower, **Part 1**

Now it's time to read the first part of *A Weed is a Flower*. Have students sit next to you so that they can see the pictures and words while you read the story aloud.

1. Read the first part of the story aloud all the way through. Stop reading on the page with the illustration of George Washington Carver mending a sock, after the sentence, "They, too, loved this quiet boy who was so willing to help." Track with your finger so students can follow along.

2. Reread the first part of the story with students, having them chime in and read aloud with you this time. Tell them to think about the characters and what they do. Tell students you will pause at certain points in the story to discuss.

3. Begin to reread, pausing to discuss on the first page of text after the sentence, "This is his story." Have students tell about what they read.

   ▸ How did George Washington Carver start out in life? as a slave who was sick and had no father
   ▸ What do you think we will learn about him in this book? how he became someone special and important; how he helped people

4. Continue reading and pause to discuss after the sentence, "He asked questions the Carvers couldn't answer." Have students tell about what they read.

   ▸ What happened to George as a baby? He was kidnapped or stolen.
   ▸ Who took care of George when he was returned? his owners, the Carvers

5. Read on and pause to discuss after the phrase, "and soon he was known as the Plant Doctor." Have students tell about what they read.

   ▸ What is George called as a young boy? the Plant Doctor
   ▸ Why do you think people called him this? Answers will vary. Students might say that people called him the Plant Doctor because he was good at taking care of plants, like a doctor is good at taking care of people.

6. Continue to read, and then pause to discuss after the phrase, "and went off to find the answers to his questions." Have students make a prediction.

   ▶ Why did Carver leave his farm? He wanted to go to school and find the answers to his questions.
   ▶ What do you think will happen next? Answers will vary.

7. Read to the end of the sections, stopping after the sentence, "They, too, loved this quiet boy who was so willing to help."

Check Your Reading

A Weed is a Flower, Part 1

Have students retell the first part of *A Weed is a Flower* in their own words to develop grammar, vocabulary, comprehension, and fluency skills. When finished, **ask students the following questions** to check comprehension and encourage discussion.

Objectives
- Answer questions requiring literal recall of details.

   ▶ Why did Moses and Susan Carver take care of George? George's mother was stolen and his father was dead, and George was the Carvers' slave.
   ▶ Why did Moses and Susan think that George was an unusual child? He wanted to know about everything and asked questions the Carvers couldn't answer.
   ▶ What was George good at? taking care of plants
   ▶ Why couldn't George go to school near the Carvers' farm? The schools near the farm were not open to blacks.
   ▶ Name two things that George did so he could go to school. He moved to wherever there are schools. He stayed with different people near schools. He did chores to earn his keep. He worked hard and does his chores well.

Reading for Meaning

Main Idea and Supporting Details
Help students understand the ways in which the topic, main idea, and supporting details differ. Then identify examples from *A Weed is a Flower*. Turn to page LC 23 in *K¹² Language Arts Activity Book*.

Objectives
- Define topic.
- Identify the topic.
- Define main idea.
- Define supporting details.
- Distinguish the main idea from the topic.
- Identify the main idea.
- Identify supporting details.

1. Tell students that they've read a lot of information about George Washington Carver's life. There's a lot to remember. Explain to students that they're going to do an activity to help them focus on the most important things the author has told us so far.

2. Review the concept of **topic**, which is the subject of a text or what a book is about. You can usually state the topic in a word or two. Have students tell what the topic of this book is. Carver's life

3. Review the concept of **main idea** as the most important idea in a text. Point out that there can be a main idea in a paragraph, a part of a text, or in a whole book. A main idea is stated in a complete sentence.

4. Explain that a topic and a main idea are different. Give an example. For instance, a paragraph could be about ice cream, which is the topic. The main idea could be that ice cream comes in many different flavors.

5. Review the concept of **detail**, which is a piece of information in a text.

6. Review that a **supporting detail** is a piece of information that tells more about the main idea. Supporting details are complete sentences. For instance, if the main idea of a paragraph is that ice cream comes in many different flavors, then a supporting detail might be that ice cream can come in more flavors than just chocolate, vanilla, and strawberry.

7. Explain to students that they are going to think about the main idea and supporting details in the first part of the book.

8. Use the first paragraph of the story to review with students how to think about main idea and supporting details. Reread the paragraph. Have students tell the main idea of the paragraph.

9. If students have difficulty, point to the first sentence and tell students that the main idea is stated here: *George Washington Carver had many things against him.* Explain that an author sometimes states a main idea in the text. Other times, students will have to put the main idea in their own words.

10. Have students identify three supporting details for the main idea of the paragraph. He was a sick baby. His father had died. He was a slave.

11. Direct students' attention to the Activity Book page. Explain that they are to fill in a main idea and the supporting details for the first part of the story.

12. Help students understand how to complete the chart by walking through an example.

13. Tell students that today's reading was about George's life as a boy. There are two main ideas for this section. Tell students that **one** main idea of today's reading is *George liked to help others.* Write this in the Main Ideas box.

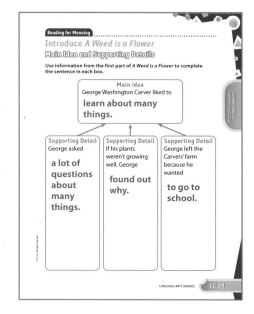

14. Tell students that there are three supporting details for this main idea. He gave people advice about their plants. He helped people where he lived with their chores. People loved George because he was so willing to help.
Write these in the Supporting Detail boxes.

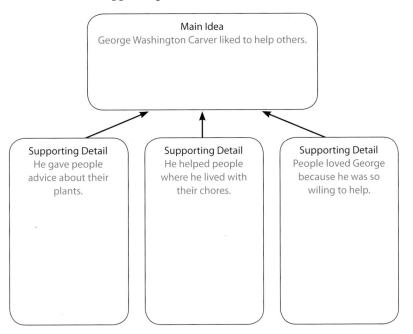

15. Ask students to think about the other main idea of the selected reading and complete the sentence in the Main Idea box on the Activity Book page. If students think of something that is a supporting detail, guide them to fill in their idea in one of the Supporting Detail boxes. Then have them think about the main idea again.

16. Have students think about three supporting details that tell more about this main idea to complete the page. Many students have difficulty distinguishing topic, main idea, and detail. If students need more practice with these concepts, use other paragraphs from the beginning of the story and work through Steps 7–9.

17. Keep the Activity Book page in a safe place so that students can use it to write a summary later.

Explore *A Weed is a Flower*

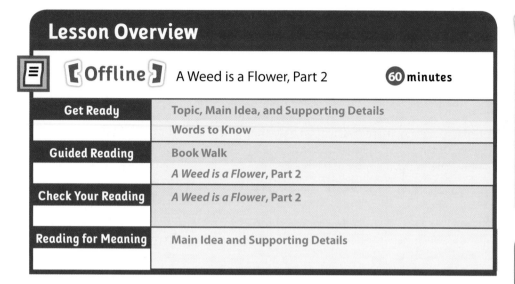

Lesson Overview

[Offline] A Weed is a Flower, Part 2   **60** minutes

Get Ready	Topic, Main Idea, and Supporting Details
	Words to Know
Guided Reading	Book Walk
	A Weed is a Flower, Part 2
Check Your Reading	*A Weed is a Flower*, Part 2
Reading for Meaning	Main Idea and Supporting Details

Advance Preparation

Read the book before beginning the Guided Reading to identify Words to Know in the text. Preview the Reading for Meaning and copy the graphic organizer to a whiteboard or a sheet of paper.

Big Ideas

▶ Biographies are a type of nonfiction meant to inform the reader about a person's life.
▶ Readers must understand the relationship between main idea and supporting details.

Materials

Supplied
- *A Weed is a Flower* by Aliki
- *K¹² Language Arts Activity Book*, p. LC 24

Also Needed
- whiteboard (optional)

Keywords

biography – the story of someone's life written by another person

main idea – the most important idea in a paragraph or text

purpose – the reason for writing

supporting detail – a detail that gives more information about a main idea

topic – the subject of a text

[Offline] 🕐 **minutes**

A Weed is a Flower

Work **together** with students to complete offline Get Ready, Guided Reading, Check Your Reading, and Reading for Meaning activities.

Get Ready

Topic, Main Idea, and Supporting Details

Students need to be able to distinguish the topic of a nonfiction selection from the main idea. Help students review these concepts by having them retell the topic of *A Weed is a Flower* and some of the main ideas from the first part of the book.

1. Ask students what a **topic** is. A topic is what a text is about and can usually be stated in a few words.

2. Ask students what a **main idea** is. The main idea is the most important idea in a text and should be stated in a complete sentence.

3. Remind students that the main idea and topic are different. The topic is the subject of the writing, while the main idea tells something important about that subject.

4. Remind students that they have read the first part of a **biography**. Have students tell what the topic of the book is. George Washington Carver's life

5. Tell students that you are going to pick up the book where you left off and continue reading the next part of the story.
   Say: We read part of *A Weed is a Flower* earlier. Before we begin reading again, it's a good idea to think about what we've already read. That way we have a good idea about where the next part of the story begins. Let's look back at the last page where we stopped reading. It's about how George lived with different people so he could go to school. He helped out the people he lived with by doing chores.

6. Have students review what they read in the first part of the book by retelling the main idea from the first part of the book and some **supporting details**. Remind them that supporting details are pieces of information about a main idea. Main idea: George liked to help others. Supporting details: He helped people with their plants. He did chores for people where he lived.

7. If students provide **supporting details** as the main idea, guide them to think about the main idea and supporting details they wrote on their Activity Book page.

Objectives

- Define topic.
- Identify the topic.
- Define main idea.
- Define supporting details.
- Distinguish the main idea from the topic.
- Identify main idea.
- Identify supporting details.
- Increase concept and content vocabulary.

Words to Know

Before reading *A Weed is a Flower*, go over Words to Know with students.

1. Ask students to define these words from the first part of the story and use them in a sentence:

   slave   **yearned**

2. Correct any incorrect or vague definitions.

3. Teach the Words to Know for the second part of the story. Have students say each word aloud.

4. Ask students if they know what each word means.

   ▶ If students know a word's meaning, have them define it and use it in a sentence.
   ▶ If students don't know a word's meaning, read them the definition and discuss the word with them.

linoleum – a floor covering that is nailed or glued into place
Tuskegee Institute – a college in Alabama started in 1881 for freed African American slaves

Guided Reading

Book Walk

Prepare students by taking them on a Book Walk of *A Weed is a Flower*. Scan the book together and ask students to make predictions about the story.

1. Turn to the second part of the story, beginning with the page that starts with the phrase, "George worked hard for many years," accompanied by an illustration of a grown George painting.

2. Have students make predictions based on the **illustrations.** Answers to questions may vary.

   ▶ What do you think will happen in the next part of the story?
   ▶ Do you know what college is? Why do people go to college?

Objectives

- Use an illustration to make a prediction about a reading.
- Apply information read to answer questions.
- Generate questions during reading.
- Read a variety of texts for information and pleasure.
- Use context clues to determine word meanings.

A Weed is a Flower, Part 2

Now it's time to read the second part of *A Weed is a Flower*. Have students sit next to you so that they can see the pictures and words while you read the story aloud.

1. Read the second part of the story aloud all the way through, beginning on the page with the phrase, "George worked hard for many years." Stop after the sentence, "Before they knew it these became two of the most important crops in Alabama." Track with your finger so students can follow along.

2. Reread the second part of the story with students, having them chime in and read aloud with you this time. Tell them to think about the characters and what they do. Tell students you will pause at certain points in the story to discuss.

3. Begin to reread, pausing to discuss after the sentence, "He experimented with his own plants, and found secrets no one else knew." Have students tell about what they read.

   ▸ Why did Carver want to study agriculture, or farming, and plants? Possible answer: I think Carver wanted to study agriculture because he always liked plants, and he wanted to help people.

   ▸ What do you think will happen next? Answers will vary.

4. Tell students that you are wondering how Carver will help people with his knowledge about plants.
   Say: I wonder how Carver will use his knowledge about plants to help people. One way that I can find out more about something is to read on. This is a good strategy to use when I have a question about a reading selection. I'm going to read on to find out how Carver uses his knowledge to help people.

5. Read on, and pause to discuss after the phrase, "how to make their crops grow better." Mention that the book has answered your question from the earlier section.
   Say: Do you remember my question from the last section? I wanted to know how Carver was going to help people. This section answers my question. The text says that he teaches his students and farmers how to grow their crops better.

6. Before reading on, model how to determine the meaning of an unfamiliar word using context clues.
   Say: I don't know what this word *livelihood* means. I can look at the rest of the words in the sentence and use them to try to figure out the meaning. I see the word *earned*. I know that people can earn money. Carver worked with farmers who earned from the soil. That means they earned money from crops. So, maybe *livelihood* means money.

7. Continue reading, and pause to discuss after the sentence, "They were sure that no one would buy them." Have students ask a question about what they've just read. If students have difficulty, model asking and answering another question about a part of the story, and then have students ask and answer their own question about the same part.

   ▸ What question do you have about what we've just read? Possible answer: How is Carver going to get the farmers to listen to him?

8. Tell students that you will read on to find the answer to their question.

9. Read to the end of the selection, stopping after the sentence, "Before they knew it these became two of the most important crops in Alabama." Have students tell the answer to their question.

   ▸ What is the answer to your question? Possible answer: Carver showed the farmers how many things could be made from sweet potatoes and peanuts.

Check Your Reading

A Weed is a Flower, Part 2

Have students retell the second part of *A Weed is a Flower* in their own words to develop grammar, vocabulary, comprehension, and fluency skills. When finished, **ask students the following questions** to check comprehension and encourage discussion.

Objectives
- Answer questions requiring literal recall of details.

- How did Carver pay for college? He worked and saved money.
- Why did Carver choose to study agriculture? He loved plants and wanted to help people.
- What did Carver try to tell farmers when he was at Tuskegee Institute? He told them to plant things other than cotton, such as sweet potatoes and peanuts.
- What was the reason for Carver's advice to the farmers? He said that sweet potatoes and peanuts were good crops, and it would be better for the soil to grow them.
- Why didn't the farmers listen at first? They were afraid no one would buy sweet potatoes and peanuts.
- What happened when the farmers followed Carver's advice? Sweet potatoes and peanuts became two of the most important crops in Alabama.

Reading for Meaning

Main Idea and Supporting Details

Continue to help students understand topic, main idea, and details by identifying examples from today's reading. Gather page LC 24 of *K¹² Language Arts Activity Book*.

Objectives
- Identify the topic.
- Distinguish the main idea from the topic.
- Identify main idea.
- Identify supporting details.

1. Review with students the definition of **topic** and have students tell the topic of the book.

2. Review the concepts of **main idea** and **supporting details**.

3. Tell students that you are going to help them think about the main idea and supporting details in the second part of the book.

4. Have students complete the Activity Book page. Remind them that they should think about the main idea and supporting details of the second part of the book they just read.

5. If students continue to have difficulty distinguishing main idea and supporting detail, choose a paragraph from early in the selected reading. Reread the paragraph and point out the main idea and supporting details of that paragraph. Then have students try the same activity with a different paragraph.

6. Keep the Activity Book page in a safe place so that students can use it to write a summary later.

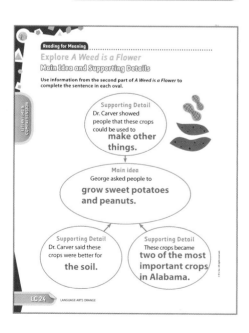

Review *A Weed is a Flower*

Lesson Overview

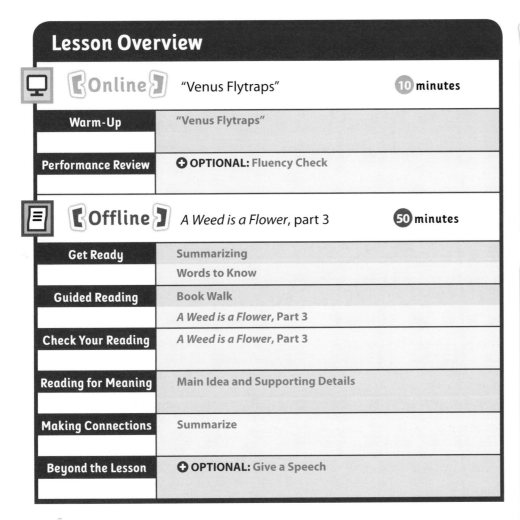

🖥 〔Online〕 "Venus Flytraps" — 🕙 minutes

Warm-Up	"Venus Flytraps"
Performance Review	➕ OPTIONAL: Fluency Check

📄 〔Offline〕 *A Weed is a Flower*, part 3 — 🕔 minutes

Get Ready	Summarizing
	Words to Know
Guided Reading	Book Walk
	A Weed is a Flower, Part 3
Check Your Reading	*A Weed is a Flower*, Part 3
Reading for Meaning	Main Idea and Supporting Details
Making Connections	Summarize
Beyond the Lesson	➕ OPTIONAL: Give a Speech

Materials

Supplied
- *A Weed is a Flower* by Aliki
- *K¹² Language Arts Activity Book*, pp. LC 23–26
- "Venus Flytraps" (optional)
- Fluency Performance Checklist (optional)

Keywords

biography – the story of someone's life written by another person

main idea – the most important idea in a paragraph or text

purpose – the reason for writing

summarize – to tell in order the most important ideas or events of a text

summary – a short retelling that includes only the most important ideas or events of a text

supporting detail – a detail that gives more information about a main idea

topic – the subject of a text

Advance Preparation

If you are not able to complete the online Warm-Up, then print the selection and listen to students read aloud. Have students gather the completed pages LC 23 and 24 in *K¹² Language Arts Activity Book* (Main Idea and Supporting Details).

Big Ideas

Readers need to be able to sequence, summarize, and articulate the main idea.

 **10 minutes**

"Venus Flytraps"
Students will work independently online to develop fluency and oral reading skills.

Warm-Up

"Venus Flytraps"
The purpose of this activity is to improve students' oral reading and fluency. Students will read "Venus Flytraps." Remind students to listen to the model on each screen before they begin their recording.

Objectives
- Increase oral reading skills.
- Increase fluency.

Offline Alternative

No computer access? Print a copy of "Venus Flytraps." Have students read it aloud. Make note of any pronunciation errors, and review those words with students.

Performance Review

⊕ OPTIONAL: Fluency Check
Listen to students' recordings and use the checklist to review fluency and track performance. Keep the completed checklist so you can review students' progress over time.

Objectives
- Read aloud grade-level text with appropriate automaticity, prosody, accuracy, and rate.

 **50 minutes**

A Weed is a Flower
Work **together** with students to complete offline Get Ready, Guided Reading, Check Your Reading, Reading for Meaning, Making Connections, and Beyond the Lesson activities.

Get Ready

Summarizing
Introduce students to the concept of summarizing by having them retell what they've read so far in *A Weed is a Flower*. Gather the completed Main Idea and Supporting Details pages.

1. Tell students that you're going to finish reading *A Weed is a Flower*. Mention that you are going to begin reading where you left off.

Objectives
- Define summary.
- Summarize the plot of a story.
- Increase concept and content vocabulary.

2. Tell students that it's a good idea to review what they've read in the book before reading on. Have them tell what has happened in the book so far, using the activity pages as a guide. Remind them to focus on the **main ideas**, and review this term if necessary.
Say: What you have just done is give a **summary** of what you read. A **summary** is a short retelling that includes only the most important ideas in a text.

3. Explain that when **summarizing** a text, we retell the most important ideas or events in order. Explain that when we summarize a biography, it makes sense to summarize the ideas and events in the order that they happened in the person's life. This is called time order, or chronological order.

Words to Know

Before reading *A Weed is a Flower*, go over Words to Know with students.

1. Ask students to define the following words and use them in a sentence:

linoleum	**Tuskegee Institute**
slave	**yearned**

2. Correct any incorrect or vague definitions.

Guided Reading

Book Walk

Prepare students by taking them on a Book Walk of *A Weed is a Flower*. Scan the book together and ask students to make predictions about the story.

1. Turn to the last part of the story, the page that begins with the phrase, "Soon the whole country knew about Dr. Carver."

2. Have students make predictions based on the **illustrations.**

   ▶ What part of Carver's life do you think this last section of the story will be about? Why? Answers may vary.

Objectives

- Use an illustration to make a prediction about a reading.
- Apply information read to answer questions.
- Generate questions during reading.
- Read a variety of texts for information and pleasure.
- Use context clues to determine word meanings.

A Weed is a Flower, Part 3

Now it's time to read the last part of *A Weed is a Flower*. Have students sit next to you so that they can see the pictures and words while you read the story aloud.

1. Read the last part of the story aloud all the way through, beginning on the page that starts with the phrase, "Soon the whole country knew about Dr. Carver." Read to the end. Track with your finger so students can follow along.

2. Reread the third part of the story with students, having them chime in and read aloud with you this time. Tell them to think about the characters and what they do. Tell students you will pause at certain points in the story to discuss.

3. Begin to reread, pausing to discuss after the sentence, "He used the soap he made and ate the food he grew."

   ▸ What question do you have about what you just read? Possible answer: Why didn't Dr. Carver want to take money for his work?

   If students have difficulty asking and answering their question, model asking and answering another question about a part of the story, and then have students ask and answer their own questions about the same part.

4. Have students explain how they can find the answer to their question. **Say:** There are different ways to answer your question. One strategy is to look back through what you just read to find an answer. If the answer isn't there, another strategy is to read on. Which strategy would work best for your question? Answers will vary.

5. Read to the end of the book.

   ▸ Did you find an answer to your question? What is it? Answers will vary.

Check Your Reading

A Weed is a Flower, Part 3
Have students retell the last part of *A Weed is a Flower* in their own words to develop grammar, vocabulary, comprehension, and fluency skills. When finished, **ask students the following questions** to check comprehension and encourage discussion.

Objectives
- Answer questions requiring literal recall of details.

▸ What part of Dr. Carver's life is this section about? when he was older
▸ How did Dr. Carver take care of himself? He washed and patched his clothes, grew his own food, and made his own soap.
▸ What kind of work did Dr. Carver do even when he was older? He sometimes gave speeches. He worked in his greenhouse and his laboratory. He discovered dyes made from plants.

Reading for Meaning

 Main Idea and Supporting Details

Continue to help students understand topic, main idea, and details by identifying examples from the final pages of *A Weed is a Flower*. Turn to page LC 25 in *K¹² Language Arts Activity Book*.

1. Review the concepts of **topic**, **main idea** and **supporting details**. Have students explain how each of these concepts is different and supports the others.

2. Review the topic of the book.

3. Tell students that you are going to help them think about the main idea and supporting details in the last part of the book.

4. Have students complete the Activity Book page. Remind them that they should think about the main idea and supporting details of the part of the book they just read.

5. Review and discuss students' answers with them.

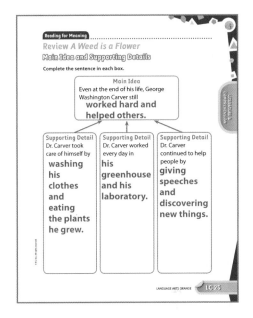

Making Connections

 Summarize

Have students use their completed Activity Book pages to create a summary of the life of George Washington Carver. Gather all the Main Idea and Supporting Details pages, and turn to page LC 26 in *K¹² Language Arts Activity Book*.

1. Review with students the definitions of **summary** and **summarize**.

2. Reread with students the main ideas from all of the pages.

3. Remind students that a summary includes only the most important information from a text.

4. Have students write the main ideas from the Main Idea and Supporting Details pages on the Summarize page.

5. Remind students that a summary of a biography should list important information in the order in which it happened in the person's life. Students should write the main ideas on the Activity Book page in the order in which they occurred during Carver's life.

6. Have students read their completed summary aloud.

(TIP) If students have difficulty writing their summary, have them point to the main ideas in the order in which they would like to include them or number each of the main ideas on the Activity Book pages. Then write the summary for them.

 Reward: Write the names of the literature selections completed in this unit on the My Accomplishments chart and add a sticker to mark successful completion of this unit.

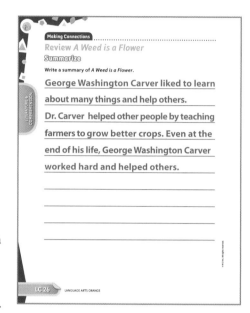

Objectives
- Summarize text and maintain accurate sequence.

Beyond the Lesson

✚ OPTIONAL: Give a Speech

This activity is OPTIONAL. It is intended for students who have extra time and would enjoy speaking in front of others. Feel free to skip this activity.

Have students imagine they are introducing George Washington Carver to speak to a group of students.

1. Have students write a speech about the important events and achievements in Carver's life.

   ▸ Students should start with a summary of Carver's biography.
   ▸ They may want to add supporting details to their speeches.
   ▸ They should focus on only the most important events and retell them in the order in which they happened in Carver's life.

2. Tell students that when they give a speech, they should not read directly from their paper. They should try to look up at their audience. To practice this skill, students should try reading in front of a mirror and looking up at themselves.

3. The speech should not be longer than about 3 minutes.

4. Have students deliver their speech to you or others.

Objectives
- Identify main idea.
- Identify supporting details.
- Restate facts and supporting details of informational text in sequential order.
- Speak clearly and at an appropriate pace for the type of communication.

Introduce "Bee! I'm Expecting You!"

Unit Overview

In this four-lesson unit, students will explore sensory language and imagery in these poems:

- ► "Bee! I'm Expecting You!"
- ► "Something Told the Wild Geese"
- ► "Who Has Seen the Wind?"
- ► "Windy Nights"

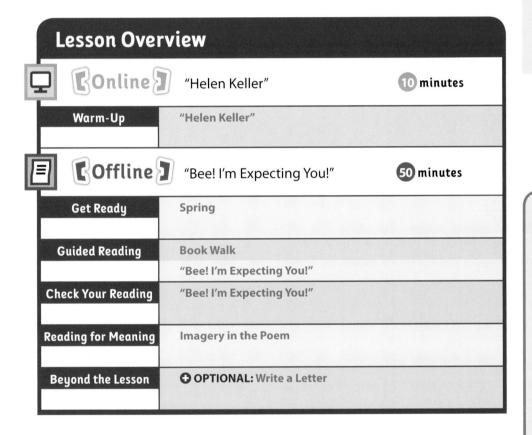

Lesson Overview

🖥	**【Online】** "Helen Keller"	**10** minutes
Warm-Up	"Helen Keller"	

📄	**【Offline】** "Bee! I'm Expecting You!"	**50** minutes
Get Ready	Spring	
Guided Reading	Book Walk	
	"Bee! I'm Expecting You!"	
Check Your Reading	"Bee! I'm Expecting You!"	
Reading for Meaning	Imagery in the Poem	
Beyond the Lesson	✚ OPTIONAL: Write a Letter	

Advance Preparation

If you are not able to complete the online Warm-Up, then print the selection and listen to students read aloud.

Big Ideas

The use of imagery and sensory language creates detailed pictures in the reader's mind, so the reader can understand and appreciate the ideas and feelings the writer conveys.

Materials

Supplied
- "Bee! I'm Expecting You!," *Listen, My Children*, p. 11
- "Helen Keller" (optional)

Also Needed
- crayons
- paper, drawing

Poem Synopsis

In this poem, a fly writes a letter to a bee describing the coming of spring and asking when the bee will arrive.

Keywords

first-person point of view – the telling of a story by a character in that story, using pronouns such as *I*, *me*, and *we*

imagery – language that helps readers imagine how something looks, sounds, smells, feels, or tastes

poem – a piece of poetry

point of view – the perspective a story is told from

rhyme – the use of words that end with the same sounds; for example, *cat* and *hat* rhyme

speaker – the narrator of a poem

stanza – a group of lines in a poem

 **10 minutes**

"Helen Keller"
Students will work independently online to develop fluency and oral reading skills.

Warm-Up

"Helen Keller"
The purpose of this activity is to improve students' oral reading and fluency. Students will read "Helen Keller." Remind students to listen to the model on each screen before they begin their recording.

 Objectives
- Increase oral reading skills.
- Increase fluency.

Offline Alternative

No computer access? Print a copy of "Helen Keller." Have students read it aloud. Make note of any pronunciation errors, and review those words with students.

 **50 minutes**

"Bee! I'm Expecting You!"
Work **together** with students to complete offline Get Ready, Guided Reading, Check Your Reading, Reading for Meaning, and Beyond the Lesson activities.

Get Ready

Spring
Poets choose their language carefully to convey images and feelings with few words. In "Bee! I'm Expecting You!" the poet expresses signs of spring in a poetic letter from a fly to a bee. Prepare students by helping them think about images of spring. Answers will vary for all questions.

 Objectives
- Connect text to prior knowledge.

1. Ask students what they think about when they think of spring.

   ▶ What do you imagine?
   ▶ How do you know when it's spring?
   ▶ What do you see, smell, hear, and feel during spring?

2. Have students tell what creatures they think of when they think about spring, such as birds, flowers, baby animals, and maybe insects.

3. Tell students that their descriptions have helped create a picture in your mind of what spring is like.

4. Explain that you are going to read a poem, and students should think about what season the poet describes.

Guided Reading

Book Walk

Prepare students by taking them on a Book Walk of *Listen, My Children*. Scan the book together, and ask students to make predictions about the poems. For all questions in the Book Walk, answers will vary.

1. Read aloud the **title** of the book. Tell students that it's a collection of poetry by different poets, or people who write poetry.

2. Review with students that **poems** are a way for poets to share feelings or experiences with others, and that poets choose their words very carefully.

3. Ask students why they think they read poetry.

   ▶ What do you think poets are trying to describe in their poems?

4. Scan the book together. Review how the poems in the book look different from stories students have read. Poems are an arrangement of words, usually in **lines**. Sometimes, the words in a poem rhyme, or have similar ending sounds.

5. Explain that a poem has a **speaker** who is the narrator of the poem or the person "talking" to the reader.

6. Tell students that in many poems, the speaker uses the **first-person point of view**. The speaker tells about how he or she sees the world and thinks about it.

7. Tell students that there are clue words that let us know the speaker is using the first person: *I*, *me*, and *my*.

8. Turn to the **table of contents**. Help students find the poem "Bee! I'm Expecting You!" and turn to that page.

9. Point to and read aloud the title of the poem.

10. Point out that the lines in this poem are in **stanzas**. A stanza is a group of lines in a poem. Ask students to tell how many stanzas are in this poem. three

11. Have students study the picture and make a prediction.

    ▶ What do you think the poem is about?

Objectives

- Differentiate among literary genres.
- Set a purpose for reading.
- Define first-person point of view.
- Use text organizational features to locate and comprehend information (table of contents, index).
- Use an illustration to make a prediction about a reading.
- Read texts for literary experience.

"Bee! I'm Expecting You!"

Now it's time to read the poem. Have students sit next to you so they can see the pictures and words while you read the poem aloud.

1. Read the poem aloud. Track with your finger so students can follow along.

2. Ask students if the poem reminds them of another kind of writing. letter

3. If students don't recognize the letter format, show it to them. Focus on the last stanza and the words "letter," "reply," "yours." Point to the last line and explain that this is a way to close a letter, like writing "Sincerely" and your name.

4. Reread the poem with students. Ask them to chime in and read aloud with you. Tell them to think about what the speaker is saying.

Check Your Reading

"Bee! I'm Expecting You!"
Have students retell the poem in their own words to develop grammar, vocabulary, comprehension, and fluency skills. When finished, **ask students the following questions** to check comprehension and encourage discussion.

▶ Who is the speaker in the poem? a fly
▶ To whom is the speaker talking? a bee
▶ What other animals does the speaker talk about? frogs, birds
▶ What words does the speaker use to describe the clover? warm and thick

Objectives
• Answer questions requiring literal recall of details.

Reading for Meaning

Imagery in the Poem
Help students complete this activity to further check their comprehension and focus on the author's use of imagery. Reread parts of the poem if students have trouble identifying the author's use of imagery. Gather the crayons and drawing paper.

Objectives
• Define imagery.
• Identify the author's use of imagery.

1. Ask students to use words to describe spring. Possible answers: warm, flowers

2. Tell them that their words helped you make a picture of spring in your mind.

3. Explain that using words to create a picture in the reader's mind is called **imagery**.

4. Point out that poets use imagery all the time. In "Bee! I'm Expecting You!" the poet uses imagery to create a mental picture of a season. Have students identify the season the poet describes. spring

5. Ask students to point to the words and phrases that create this image in their mind. fly, bee, frogs got home, birds mostly back, clover warm and thick
   If students have trouble recognizing the signs of the season, point them out, and then ask how each sign in the poem describes spring. Remind students of what they think about when they think of spring.

6. Tell students that the poet also creates another image. Ask the following questions to help students imagine the fly writing a letter to the bee:

   ▶ What is happening in the poem?
   ▶ Who is writing?
   ▶ What do you see in your mind when you think of this image?
   ▶ How does this image make you feel?

7. Have students draw an image that the poem makes them think about. The image could be related to the signs of spring or to the fly writing a letter to the bee.

Beyond the Lesson ....

⊕ OPTIONAL: Write a Letter

This activity is OPTIONAL. It is intended for students who have extra time and would benefit from more writing. Feel free to skip this activity.

Objectives
- Make connections between text and oneself.
- Write a letter.

1. After reading "Bee! I'm Expecting You!" have students write a letter back from the bee to the fly.

2. If students need help with the structure of a letter, start them off. Tell them to write "Dear Fly," on one line and then continue with the body of the letter. Remind students to close the letter by writing something like, "Yours truly, Bee."

3. Have students use their own images of spring in the letter. If students have difficulty thinking of what to say, suggest some opening sentences.

   ▸ I got your letter. I'm coming soon. I know it's time for me to come back because _____.

4. If they wish, students can illustrate their letter.

Introduce "Something Told the Wild Geese"

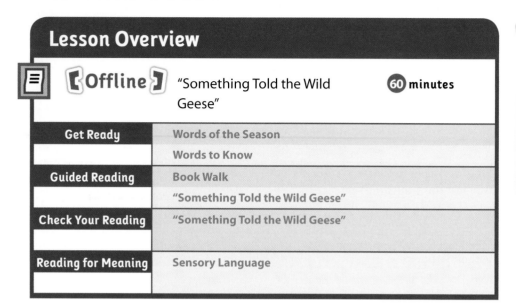

Lesson Overview

	[Offline] "Something Told the Wild Geese"	**60** minutes
Get Ready	Words of the Season	
	Words to Know	
Guided Reading	Book Walk	
	"Something Told the Wild Geese"	
Check Your Reading	"Something Told the Wild Geese"	
Reading for Meaning	Sensory Language	

Big Ideas

The use of imagery and sensory language creates detailed pictures in the reader's mind, so the reader can understand and appreciate the ideas and feelings the writer conveys.

[Materials]

Supplied

- "Something Told the Wild Geese," *Listen, My Children*, p. 9
- *K¹² Language Arts Activity Book*, p. LC 27

Poem Synopsis

This poem describes the signs of late summer, when the wild geese sense the onset of autumn and the coming of winter, and decide it is time to leave for warmer places.

Keywords

poetry – writing that is made up of lines that often rhyme and follow a specific rhythm

repetition – repeating words or phrases

sensory language – language that appeals to the five senses

 **60 minutes**

"Something Told the Wild Geese"

Work **together** with students to complete offline Get Ready, Guided Reading, Check Your Reading, and Reading for Meaning activities.

Get Ready ....

Words of the Season

Poets use sensory language, or words that appeal to the five senses, to help them create a mental image of an object, an idea, or a feeling. Help students begin to understand sensory language by having them use sensory language to describe the season.

 Objectives
- Define sensory language.
- Increase concept and content vocabulary.

1. Have students tell what their five senses are. If students don't know, tell them the five senses are sight, hearing, smell, taste, and touch (or feeling).

2. Have students tell what season they are in right now.

3. Have students tell how they know it's this season using their five senses. Prompt students with sentence starters, such as, *I know it's this season because I can see _____. I can hear _____. I can smell _____.*

4. Explain that the language they used to describe the season is called **sensory language**. Sensory language describes things we can see, hear, smell, taste, and feel or touch.

Words to Know

Before reading "Something Told the Wild Geese," go over Words to Know with students.

1. Have students say the word aloud.

2. Ask students if they know what the word means.

   ▸ If students know the word's meaning, have them define it and use it in a sentence.
   ▸ If students don't know the word's meaning, read them the definition and discuss the word with them.

luster-glossed – smooth, shiny look

TIP Help students think of objects that might be described as luster-glossed, such as a new car, dress shoes, or silverware.

Guided Reading

Book Walk

Prepare students by taking them on a Book Walk of *Listen, My Children*. Scan the book together, and ask students to make predictions about the poem. For all questions in the Book Walk, answers will vary.

1. Read aloud the **title** of the book. Review that the book is a collection of poetry by different poets, or people who write poetry.

2. Turn to the **table of contents**. Help students find "Something Told the Wild Geese" and turn to that page.

3. Point to and read aloud the title of the poem. Ask students what they think the title means.

4. Have students study the picture and make a prediction.

   ▸ What bird is this?
   ▸ What do you think the poem is about?

5. Explain that many wild geese migrate in the fall to warmer places and return to colder places in the spring.

6. Have students define *migrate* if possible and try to give an example of another animal that migrates, such as other birds or salmon.

7. If students don't know what *migrate* means, tell them it's when animals move from one location to another depending on the seasons. When it's cold, the animals move to warmer places, and when it's warm they move back again.

8. Tell students that they are going to read a poem that uses **sensory language** to describe two seasons. As they read, have students think about what the seasons might be.

"Something Told the Wild Geese"

Now it's time to read the poem. Have students sit next to you so they can see the pictures and words while you read the poem aloud.

1. Read the poem aloud. Track with your finger so students can follow along.

2. Ask students if there are any words that they don't understand and define those words for them.

3. Have students tell what seasons they think the poet is describing and explain why they think this.

4. Reread the poem with students. Ask them to chime in and read aloud with you. Tell them to think about what the speaker is saying.

Objectives

- Use text organizational features to locate and comprehend information (table of contents).
- Use an illustration to make a prediction about a reading.
- Use title of the selection to make a prediction.
- Read texts for literary experience.

Check Your Reading

"Something Told the Wild Geese"

Have students retell the poem in their own words to develop grammar, vocabulary, comprehension, and fluency skills. When finished, **ask students the following questions** to check comprehension and encourage discussion.

- What words or phrases are repeated in the poem? something, something told the wild geese
- What word does the poet use to describe the fields? golden
- What color are the leaves? green
- What words have quotation marks around them? snow, frost
- What season is mentioned in the next to last line? summer
- What season is in the cry of the geese in the last line? winter

Objectives
- Answer questions requiring literal recall of details.
- Identify the use of repetition in poetry.

Reading for Meaning

Sensory Language

Have students further check comprehension and focus on sensory language. They will identify the author's use of sensory language by completing a chart. Turn to page LC 27 in *K¹² Language Arts Activity Book*.

1. Ask students if they remember the definition of sensory language. Sensory language is the use of words that appeal to our senses to create a description.

2. Explain that the poet uses sensory language to describe two seasons. Have students identify the two seasons described in the poem.

3. If students have difficulty identifying the seasons, point to the last two lines of the poem, reread the lines, and tell students that the seasons are summer and winter.

4. Show examples of sensory language in the poem that describe late summer. For example, the "sagging orchards" are trees that would be filled with apples in the late summer in places such as Canada or the northern United States.

5. Tell students that they are going to complete an activity that will help them identify the sensory language that describes these two seasons. Then you and students will talk more about the poem.

6. Have students complete the Activity Book page.

Objectives
- Define sensory language.
- Identify how sensory details and figurative language enhance poetry.
- Identify the use of repetition in poetry.

Reading for Meaning
Introduce "Something Told the Wild Geese"
Sensory Language

Write words from the poem that describe things you can see, hear, taste, smell, or feel. Write words for late summer in the first column. Write words for winter in the second column.

Late Summer	Winter
fields lay golden	snow
leaves were green	frost
berries, luster-glossed	ice
warm feathers	
sagging orchards	

LANGUAGE ARTS ORANGE   LC 27

7. Ask the following questions to determine why the poet describes these two seasons:

- ► The poet describes the signs of summer and its end, but what season are the geese thinking about? winter
- ► Let's look back at the poem. What are the geese "told" to do? go, fly
- ► Think back to our conversation before we read the poem. What do wild geese do? migrate
- ► Why do the geese need to "go"? Winter is coming and they need to migrate.
- ► The word "something" is repeated in the poem. How is the repetition in the poem like the seasons and what the geese do every winter? Seasons repeat every year, and the geese migrate every time winter comes.
- ► What do you think the "something" is that tells the geese to go? instinct, nature, the weather, memory

TIP If students find the language in the poem challenging, help them identify examples of sensory language and explain the language to them.

Introduce "Who Has Seen the Wind?"

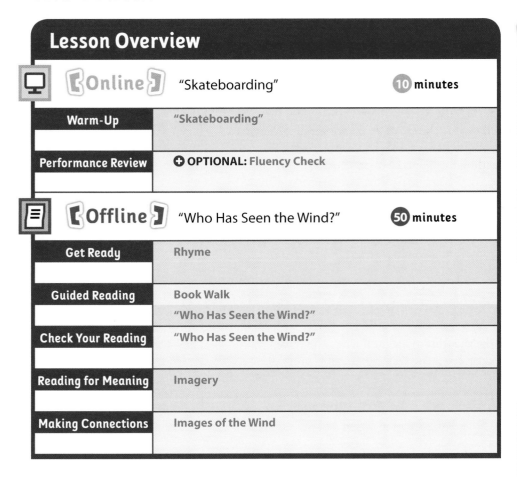

Lesson Overview

🖥️ **[Online]**	"Skateboarding"	🔟 minutes
Warm-Up	"Skateboarding"	
Performance Review	⊕ **OPTIONAL:** Fluency Check	

📄 **[Offline]**	"Who Has Seen the Wind?"	🗓️ minutes
Get Ready	Rhyme	
Guided Reading	Book Walk	
	"Who Has Seen the Wind?"	
Check Your Reading	"Who Has Seen the Wind?"	
Reading for Meaning	Imagery	
Making Connections	Images of the Wind	

Advance Preparation

If you are not able to complete the online Warm-Up, then print the selection and listen to students read aloud.

Big Ideas

The use of imagery and sensory language creates detailed pictures in the reader's mind, so the reader can understand and appreciate the ideas and feelings the writer conveys.

[Materials]

Supplied

- "Who Has Seen the Wind?," *Listen, My Children*, p. 7
- *K¹² Language Arts Activity Book*, p. LC 28
- "Skateboarding" (optional)
- Fluency Performance Checklist (optional)

Poem Synopsis

The poet describes some of the signs that the wind is passing through, even though no one has ever seen the wind.

Keywords

imagery – language that helps readers create a picture in their minds

personification – giving human qualities to something that is not human *Example:* The thunder shouted from the clouds.

poem – a piece of poetry

poetry – writing that is made up of lines that often rhyme and follow a specific rhythm

repetition – repeating words or phrases

rhyme – the use of words that end with the same sounds; for example, *cat* and *hat* rhyme

 **10 minutes**

"Skateboarding"
Students will work independently online to develop fluency and oral reading skills.

Warm-Up

"Skateboarding"
The purpose of this activity is to improve students' oral reading and fluency. Students will read "Skateboarding." Remind students to listen to the model on each screen before they begin their recording.

Objectives
- Increase oral reading skills.
- Increase fluency.

Offline Alternative

No computer access? Print a copy of "Skateboarding." Have students read it aloud. Make note of any pronunciation errors, and review those words with students.

Performance Review

⊕ OPTIONAL: Fluency Check
Listen to students' recordings and use the checklist to review fluency and track performance. Keep the completed checklist so you can review students' progress over time.

Objectives
- Read aloud grade-level text with appropriate automaticity, prosody, accuracy, and rate.

 **50 minutes**

"Who Has Seen the Wind?"
Work **together** with students to complete offline Get Ready, Guided Reading, Check Your Reading, Reading for Meaning, and Making Connections activities.

Get Ready

Rhyme
Many poets use rhyme to make their poetry more enjoyable and memorable for the reader. Help students prepare to read "Who Has Seen the Wind?" by thinking of rhyming words.

Objectives
- Define rhyme.
- Identify rhyming words.

1. Tell students that they are going to read a poem.

2. Review with students that poems are often written in lines and sometimes express feelings.

3. Remind students that sometimes poems **rhyme**. Have them tell what a rhyme is, or define the word for them. Explain that in poems the rhyming words come at the ends of the lines.

4. Tell students that you're going to play a rhyming game. Have them say a word, and you say as many words as you can that rhyme.

5. Switch roles. You give students a word, and they give words that rhyme. Give simple words, such as *cat*, *ball*, and *me*.

TIP If students have difficulty providing rhyming words, tell them that it's the sounds at the ends of words that rhyme, not the sounds at the beginnings. Emphasize the ending sounds of some simple rhyming pairs, such as *cat/sat*, *me/bee*, and *ball/tall*.

Guided Reading

Book Walk

Prepare students by taking them on a Book Walk of *Listen, My Children*. Scan the book together, and ask students to make predictions about the poem.

1. Read aloud the **title** of the book. Review that it's a collection of poetry by different poets, or people who write poetry.

2. Turn to the **table of contents**. Help students find "Who Has Seen the Wind?" and turn to that page.

3. Point to and read aloud the title of the poem.

4. Have students study the picture and make a prediction.

   ▸ What do you think the poem is about? Answers will vary.

5. Point out that the lines in this poem are in **stanzas**. Review that a stanza is a group of lines in a poem. Ask students to tell how many stanzas are in this poem. two

6. Tell students to listen for the rhymes in "Who Has Seen the Wind?"

Objectives

- Use text organizational features to locate and comprehend information (table of contents).
- Use an illustration to make a prediction about a reading.
- Read texts for literary experience.
- Identify rhyme in a literary selection.
- Define stanza.
- Identify stanzas in poetry.

"Who Has Seen the Wind?"

Now it's time to read "Who Has Seen the Wind?" Have students sit next to you so they can see the pictures and words while you read the poem aloud.

1. Read the poem aloud. Track with your finger so students can follow along.

2. Ask students if there are any words that they don't understand and define those words for them.

3. Have students point to and say words that they hear that rhyme. Remind students that the rhymes in poems come at the ends of the lines.
   you/through, I/by

4. Reread the poem with students. Ask them to chime in and read aloud with you. Tell them to listen for the rhymes at the ends of the lines.

TIP If students cannot identify the rhymes, point to the rhyming words and say them slowly so students can hear the sounds.

Check Your Reading

"Who Has Seen the Wind?"

Have students retell the poem in their own words to develop grammar, vocabulary, comprehension, and fluency skills. When finished, **ask students the following questions** to check comprehension and encourage discussion.

- ▶ The speaker asks the question, "Who has seen the wind?" What is the answer in the poem? neither I nor you
- ▶ What does this answer to the speaker's question mean? No one has seen the wind.
- ▶ In the first stanza, how does the speaker say you can tell the wind is passing through? You can see the leaves trembling.
- ▶ In the second stanza, what do the leaves do? bow down their heads
- ▶ What line in the poem repeats? Who has seen the wind?

Objectives

- Answer questions requiring literal recall of details.
- Identify the use of repetition in poetry.

Reading for Meaning

Imagery

Discuss "Who Has Seen the Wind?" with students to further check their comprehension and focus on imagery. Help students look back at the poem to answer questions.

1. Discuss what the poet is trying to tell the reader.

- ▶ What is the question is in the poem? Who has seen the wind?
- ▶ How does the speaker answer this question? Neither you nor I; no one has seen the wind.
- ▶ How does the speaker say you can tell the wind is passing? by looking at the leaves

Objectives

- Define imagery.
- Identify the author's use of imagery.
- Identify how sensory details and figurative language enhance poetry.
- Define personification.
- Identify personification.

2. Ask students for the definition of imagery. words that create a picture in your mind

3. Explain that the poet uses imagery to describe the wind.

4. Ask students to identify the two images of the leaves that the poet uses to tell us the wind is passing. the leaves trembling and bowing their heads

5. Discuss these images with students.

- ▶ Are the leaves actually trembling and bowing their heads? Why or why not? The leaves are not actually doing these things because they aren't human. They can't tremble, and they don't have heads.
- ▶ What are the leaves really doing? moving in the wind
- ▶ Why do you think the poet describes the leaves like they are human? Why doesn't she just say they are shaking or bending? Answers will vary.

6. Tell students that when poets describe something that is not human as though it were human, it is called **personification**. We can say *The river is singing* to mean that the water is making noise as it trickles over the stones. But the river does not actually sing.

Making Connections •

 Images of the Wind

Encourage students to create sensory language. Turn to page LC 28 in *K¹² Language Arts Activity Book.*

1. Tell students that in this poem, the poet uses sensory language to create an image of the wind. The image she creates is visual. It appeals to the sense of sight.

2. Read the two examples of visual imagery from the poem given on the Activity Book page.

3. Have students think of other ways they are able to tell when the wind is passing through. Encourage them to create images that rely on senses other than sight. Have them describe how the wind sounds, smells, or feels, for example.

4. Have students complete the Activity Book page.

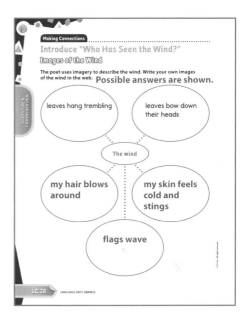

Introduce "Windy Nights"

Lesson Overview

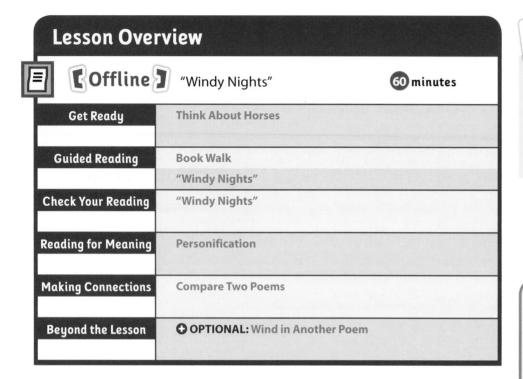

Offline "Windy Nights" **60** minutes

Get Ready	Think About Horses
Guided Reading	Book Walk
	"Windy Nights"
Check Your Reading	"Windy Nights"
Reading for Meaning	Personification
Making Connections	Compare Two Poems
Beyond the Lesson	⊕ OPTIONAL: Wind in Another Poem

Big Ideas

Personification is a common device in poetry and similar to imagery. The poet creates an image of an object by giving it human traits, so the reader can better understand what the poet is trying to describe.

Materials

Supplied

- "Windy Nights," *Listen, My Children*, p. 8
- *K¹² Language Arts Activity Book*, p. LC 29

Poem Synopsis

The poet uses personification to describe the wind as a man on a galloping horse.

Keywords

personification – giving human qualities to something that is not human
Example: The thunder shouted from the clouds.

poem – a piece of poetry

poetry – writing that is made up of lines that often rhyme and follow a specific rhythm

repetition – repeating words or phrases

 **60 minutes**

"Windy Nights"

Work **together** with students to complete offline Get Ready, Guided Reading, Check Your Reading, Reading for Meaning, Making Connections, and Beyond the Lesson activities.

Get Ready

Think About Horses

In this poem, the poet uses personification and describes the wind as a man galloping on a horse. Talk with students about their knowledge of horses to help them understand the descriptions in the poem.

1. Discuss with students what they know about horses. Have them describe how horses move. In particular, have them describe galloping and demonstrate it by galloping around the room.

2. Have students tell what it's like (or what they think it's like) when a horse gallops by. Have them describe how it might look, sound, and feel: noisy, heavy, or fast, for example.

3. Tell students that they are going to read a poem called "Windy Nights" that mentions a galloping horse. Tell them to keep the picture of the galloping horse in their mind as you read.

TIP The image of a man on a galloping horse would have been familiar to readers when this poem was written in the late 1800s. If students are unfamiliar with horses, help them understand what a galloping horse is like by describing it for them. Also, have students think of more familiar examples of things that would cause the same effects as a galloping horse: a large, fast truck rumbling by or a subway train passing underground, for example.

Objectives
- Connect text to prior knowledge.
- Build background knowledge.

Guided Reading

Book Walk

Prepare students by taking them on a Book Walk of *Listen, My Children*. Scan the book together, and ask students to make predictions about the poem.

1. Read aloud the **title** of the book. Review that it's a collection of poetry by different poets, or people who write poetry.

2. Turn to the **table of contents**. Help students find "Windy Nights" and turn to that page.

3. Point to and read aloud the title of the poem.

Objectives
- Use text organizational features to locate and comprehend information (table of contents).
- Use an illustration to make a prediction about a reading.
- Read texts for literary experience.
- Identify rhyme in a literary selection.
- Define stanza.
- Identify stanzas in poetry.

4. Have students study the **picture** and make a prediction.

   ▸ What do you think the poem is about? Answers will vary.

5. Point out that the lines in this poem are in **stanzas**. Review that a stanza is a group of lines in a poem. Ask students to tell how many stanzas are in this poem. two

6. Review the definition of **rhyme**. Have students give examples of words that rhyme. Point out that many poems have rhymes at the ends of the lines.

"Windy Nights"

Now it's time to read the poem. Have students sit next to you so they can see the pictures and words while you read "Windy Nights" aloud.

1. Read the poem aloud. Track with your finger so students can follow along.

2. Ask students if there are any words that they don't understand and define those words for them.

3. Have students point to and say words they hear that rhyme. Remind students that the rhymes in poems come at the ends of the lines. you/through, I/by

4. Reread the poem with students, having them chime in and read aloud with you. Tell them to listen for the rhymes at the ends of the lines.

TIP If students cannot identify the rhymes, point to the rhyming words and say them slowly, emphasizing the final sounds, so students can hear them.

Check Your Reading

"Windy Nights"

Have students retell the poem in their own words to develop grammar, vocabulary, comprehension, and fluency skills. When finished, **ask students the following questions** to check comprehension and encourage discussion.

▸ What words repeat in the poem? whenever, by, gallop
▸ What time of day is it in the first stanza? How do you know? night; The moon and stars are out and it's dark. The poet says it's late at night.
▸ How does the poet describe the wind in the second line? What does this mean? The wind is high; it's blowing a lot.
▸ What happens to trees in the poem when the wind blows? What does this mean? They cry aloud; they're making a lot of noise.
▸ Who do you think is the galloping man in the poem? the wind

Objectives

- Answer questions requiring literal recall of details.
- Identify the use of repetition in poetry.
- Make inferences using evidence from the text.

Reading for Meaning

Personification

Personification is a common poetic device but may be difficult for students to understand. Help students understand how the poet personifies the wind in the poem "Windy Nights."

Objectives
- Define personification.
- Identify personification.

1. Have students think about a tree.

2. Have students explain how they are different from a tree: Answers will vary.

   ▸ What makes you human?
   ▸ What traits do you have that a tree doesn't?
   ▸ What can you do that a tree can't?

3. Have them describe how a tree is like them, such as tall, straight, strong, or beautiful.

4. Explain personification.
   Say: Sometimes a poet wants to describe for a reader something that isn't human, like a tree. The poet describes this object as though it's human, so the reader can understand the object better. This is called **personification**. Personification is when a poet gives human traits to something that isn't human. For example, saying that leaves are "trembling" and "bowing their heads" is an example of personification.

5. Ask students what "Windy Nights" is about. the wind

6. Explain that the poet uses personification to describe the wind. The poet describes the wind as though it were a person. Have students tell how the poet describes the wind as though it's human. He describes the wind as a man on a galloping horse.

7. Discuss why the poet uses this personification.

   ▸ What is the wind like? What does it sound, look and feel like? Possible answer: The wind moves quickly and sounds like a whistle or a fast moving animal going by. It feels like being a fast moving rollercoaster.
   ▸ What would a man on a galloping horse be like? What does he sound, look, and feel like? Possible answer: A man on a galloping horse moves quickly. He sounds noisy. He looks like a blur as he goes by. He feels like he is moving right through the air.
   ▸ How are the wind and a man on a galloping horse similar? Possible answer: The wind and the man on a galloping horse are similar because they move so quickly they are a blur to people watching. They make noise as they rush by.
   ▸ Why do you think the poet describes the wind as a galloping man? Possible answer: Maybe the poet describes the wind this way because we can't really see the wind, but it moves with such swiftness and we can feel it rush by, just like a man on a galloping horse.

TIP If students have trouble understanding the image of a galloping horse, remind them of familiar examples, such as a rumbling truck or a subway train. Use this familiar image in your discussion of personification. Explain that when the poet wrote this poem, a man on a galloping horse was familiar to readers.

Making Connections

✏️ **Compare Two Poems**

Help students see the connections between poems in this unit by having them complete an activity comparing two poems. Turn to LC 29 in *K¹² Language Arts Activity Book*.

1. Have students choose two of the poems from the unit, either the wings poems or the wind poems: "Bee! I'm Expecting You!" and "Something Told the Wild Geese," or "Who Has Seen the Wind?" and "Windy Nights."

2. Tell students that they will compare and contrast the two poems they chose. That means they are going to tell how the poems are similar and how they are different.

3. Direct students' attention to the Activity Book page.

4. Explain how a Venn diagram works. Tell students that they put the title of one poem over the left side of the diagram and the other title over the right side. In the center of the diagram, they write what is the same about both poems. In the oval on each side, they write what is different about the two poems.

5. Give an example for the chosen poems of how the poems are similar (they are both poems) and how they are different (they are written by different poets).

6. Encourage students to think about many ways they can compare the poems. For example, they might think about the structures of the poems (rhymes, stanzas, length), the subjects of the poems (seasons, wind), or the word choices (sensory language, personification, imagery).

7. Have students complete the Activity Book page.

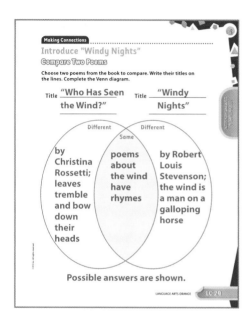

 Reward: Write the names of the literature selections completed in this unit on the My Accomplishments chart and add a sticker to mark successful completion of this unit.

Beyond the Lesson

➕ **OPTIONAL: Wind in Another Poem**

This activity is OPTIONAL. It is intended for students who have extra time, would enjoy reading another poem, and would benefit from more work with personification. Feel free to skip this activity.

1. Read with students Robert Louis Stevenson's poem "The Wind" on page 28 in *Listen, My Children*.

2. Discuss with students the similarities and differences between "The Wind" and "Windy Nights." (For example, they're both written by the same poet and they both talk about the wind.)

Objectives

- Identify personification.
- Make connections between texts.

3. Discuss with students how the poet uses personification in "The Wind." Prompt them with discussion questions.

   ▸ What kind of person does the poet describe? Possible answer: He describes someone who is powerful and strong but invisible.

   ▸ What does the person in the poem do? pushes kites, birds, and people around; makes a rustling sound; sings a loud song

   ▸ Why do you think the poet describes the wind as this kind of person? Possible answer: The person in this poem is strong and makes a lot of noise, but you can't see it. The wind can be the same way. It can be noisy and blow things around, but you don't actually see it.

4. Tell students that the poet personifies the wind in both poems. Have students compare the use of personification in the two poems. Prompt them with discussion questions.

   ▸ How are the people described in the two poems similar? Possible answers: They're both invisible; they both make noise; it's strong enough to throw things around.

   ▸ How are they different? In "Windy Nights" the wind is described as a man on a galloping horse; in the other poem, the wind is like a big, strong person. In "Windy Nights" the sound of the wind is like galloping; in "The Wind" the sound is like a loud song.

   ▸ Which example of personification do you like better? Why? Answers will vary.

Introduce "Living with Latin"

Unit Overview

In this eleven-lesson unit, students will explore Roman myths and investigate aspects of life in ancient Rome while developing the skills of citing evidence, making inferences, and drawing conclusions. They will read the following selections:

- "Living with Latin"
- "Gods and Spirits of Ancient Rome"
- "Clytie"
- "Pandora's Box"
- "Echo"

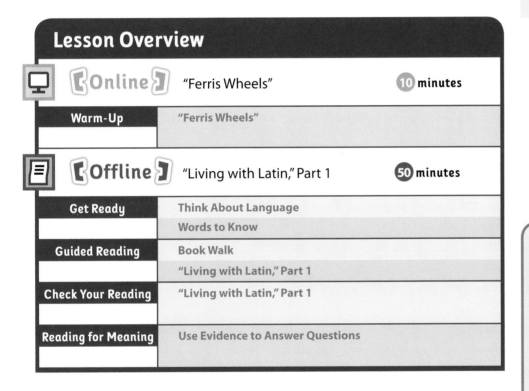

Lesson Overview

Online	"Ferris Wheels"	10 minutes
Warm-Up	"Ferris Wheels"	
Offline	"Living with Latin," Part 1	50 minutes
Get Ready	Think About Language	
	Words to Know	
Guided Reading	Book Walk	
	"Living with Latin," Part 1	
Check Your Reading	"Living with Latin," Part 1	
Reading for Meaning	Use Evidence to Answer Questions	

Advance Preparation

If you are not able to complete the online Warm-Up, then print the selection and listen to students read aloud. Read pages 2–5 of "Living with Latin" before the Guided Reading to locate the Words to Know in the text.

Big Ideas

- Nonfiction texts differ from fiction texts in that they describe real or true things in life, rather than things made up by the author.
- Readers should be able to find and cite evidence from a text in support of their answers to comprehension questions.

Materials

Supplied

- "Living with Latin," *All About Ancient Rome*, pp. 2–9
- *K[12] Language Arts Activity Book*, p. LC 31
- "Ferris Wheels" (optional)

Article Synopsis

This nonfiction article explains the influence of Latin, the language of the ancient Romans, on modern English. By providing examples of some common English words that have Latin roots, the article demonstrates the connection between the two languages.

Keywords

bold type – type that is darker than the surrounding text that draws attention to a word or phrase

caption –writing under a picture that describes that picture

fact – something that can be proven true

heading – a title within the body of a text that tells the reader something important about a section of the text

illustration – a drawing

nonfiction – writings about true things

sidebar – a short text within a larger text that tells something related but not essential to the main story

 **10 minutes**

"Ferris Wheels"

Students will work independently online to develop fluency and oral reading skills.

Warm-Up

"Ferris Wheels"

The purpose of this activity is to improve students' oral reading and fluency. Students will read "Ferris Wheels." Remind students to listen to the model on each screen before they begin their recording.

Objectives
- Increase oral reading skills.
- Increase fluency.

Offline Alternative

No computer access? Print a copy of "Ferris Wheels." Have students read it aloud. Make note of any pronunciation errors, and review those words with students.

 **50 minutes**

"Living with Latin," Part 1

Work **together** with students to complete offline Get Ready, Guided Reading, Check Your Reading, and Reading for Meaning activities.

Get Ready

Think About Language

Help students begin thinking about words and language by building their background knowledge of the manner in which languages influence each other.

Objectives
- Build background knowledge.
- Increase concept and content vocabulary.

1. Explain to students that in different parts of the world, people speak different languages. For example, people speak English in the United States; in Mexico, people speak Spanish; and in China, people speak Chinese.

2. Ask students if they know any other languages and the countries where they are spoken.

3. Tell students that many languages use words that were "borrowed" from other languages. For example, the word *bouquet* is a French word that we use in English. *Kindergarten* is a German word that English speakers use. *Alligator* came from Spanish.

Words to Know

Before reading "Living with Latin," Part 1, go over Words to Know with students.

1. Have students say each word and phrase aloud.

2. Ask students if they know what each word and phrase means.

   ▸ If students know a word's meaning, have them define it and use it in a sentence.
   ▸ If students don't know a word's meaning, read them the definition and discuss the word with them.

Romance languages – modern languages that came from Latin, the language of ancient Rome

root – the part of a word from which other words are formed; for example, *octagon* and *octopus* come for the root *oct* which means "eight"

Guided Reading

Book Walk

Prepare students by taking them on a Book Walk of *All About Ancient Rome*. Scan the magazine together and ask students to make predictions about the article. For all questions in the Book Walk, answers will vary.

1. Show students the **front cover** and **back cover** of the magazine. Point to and read aloud the **magazine title**.

2. Locate the **table of contents** inside the magazine. Remind students that the magazine is a collection of **nonfiction** articles.

3. Point to "Living with Latin" in the table of contents and read the title aloud.

4. Find the article in the magazine using the table of contents and turn to that page.

   ▸ Do you know what Latin is?
   ▸ What do you think this article is about?

5. Look through pages 2–5 of the article. Have students describe what they see. Have students point to and identify the following text features: **bold type**, **illustration**, **photograph**, **caption**, **sidebar**, and **heading**.

6. Have students look at the photographs and illustrations and make predictions about the article.

   ▸ What do you recognize?
   ▸ What looks unfamiliar?
   ▸ What do you think we might learn about in this part of the article?

Objectives

- Identify features of a nonfiction text.
- Use an illustration to make a prediction about a reading.
- Use text features to comprehend text meaning (bold, italic, headers).
- Use text organizational features to locate and comprehend information (table of contents, glossary, chapter, index, title, author, illustrator, caption).
- Read texts to gain information.

"Living with Latin," Part 1

Now it's time to read pages 2–5 of "Living with Latin" (Part 1). Have students sit next to you so that they can see the pictures and words while you read the article aloud.

1. Read pages 2–5 of the article aloud all the way through. Stop at the end of page 5 after the sentence, "So a vacation is when you have free time." Track with your finger so students can follow along. Read the body of the article first. Then point to the photograph or illustration on each page and read the caption. Read the sidebar after reading the main body of the text on that page.

2. Explain to students that you will read the article again. Ask them to chime in and read aloud with you. Tell them to look for the most important ideas in the article. Tell students that you will pause at certain points in the story to discuss.

3. Begin to reread, and pause to discuss at the end of the page 2 after the sentence, "Now, I need to go to the library and catch up on my homework." Have students tell about what they read.

   ▸ Who wrote the journal we just read? a boy
   ▸ Is this boy real or made up by the author? How do you know? made up by the author; The article says "imagine a boy who has just returned from vacation."
   ▸ What is the boy's journal about? what he did on vacation

4. Read on and pause to discuss at the end of page 4 after the phrase, "some words with Latin roots."

   ▸ What have we just learned about English words? Many English words come from Latin, the language of the ancient Romans.

5. Read to the end of page 5.

Check Your Reading

"Living with Latin," Part 1

Have students retell the first part of "Living with Latin" in their own words to develop grammar, vocabulary, comprehension, and fluency skills. When finished, **ask students the following questions** to check comprehension and encourage discussion.

▸ What is Latin? the language of the ancient Romans
▸ How is Latin part of some modern languages? Some modern languages came from Latin.
▸ What does it mean that many English words have "Latin roots"? The words came from Latin.
▸ How are words in English related to their Latin roots? The meanings of the words are related, or similar.

Objectives
• Answer questions requiring literal recall of details.

Reading for Meaning

Use Evidence to Answer Questions

Have students identify evidence in "Living with Latin" that supports their answers to questions. Turn to page LC 31 in *K¹² Language Arts Activity Book*.

1. Review the definition of fact.

2. Remind students that nonfiction texts contain facts.

3. Explain to students that sometimes they will have to answer questions about a nonfiction reading and explain where they found their answer in the reading. The facts from the text support their answer.

4. Ask students a question about the text.

   ▶ What was the language of the ancient Romans? Latin

5. Show students the sentence on page 3 of "Living with Latin" that supports the answer. "Latin is the language the ancient Romans spoke."

6. Have students complete the Activity Book page.

Objectives
- Define fact.
- Define nonfiction.
- Identify and use evidence from the text to support answers.
- Identify concrete answers to questions.

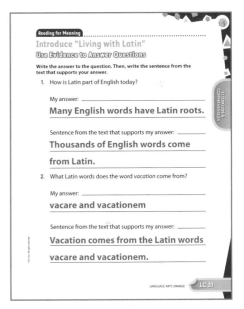

Reading for Meaning
Introduce "Living with Latin"
Use Evidence to Answer Questions

Write the answer to the question. Then, write the sentence from the text that supports your answer.

1. How is Latin part of English today?

My answer: _____
Many English words have Latin roots.

Sentence from the text that supports my answer: _____
Thousands of English words come from Latin.

2. What Latin words does the word *vacation* come from?

My answer: _____
vacare and vacationem

Sentence from the text that supports my answer: _____
Vacation comes from the Latin words vacare and vacationem.

LANGUAGE ARTS ORANGE LC 31

Review "Living with Latin"

Lesson Overview

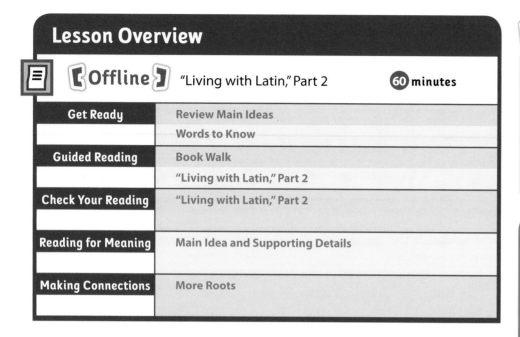

Offline	"Living with Latin," Part 2	60 minutes
Get Ready	Review Main Ideas	
	Words to Know	
Guided Reading	Book Walk	
	"Living with Latin," Part 2	
Check Your Reading	"Living with Latin," Part 2	
Reading for Meaning	Main Idea and Supporting Details	
Making Connections	More Roots	

Advance Preparation

Read pages 6–9 of "Living with Latin" before the Guided Reading to locate the Words to Know in the text. Have students gather the completed page LC 31 in *K¹² Language Arts Activity Book* (Use Evidence to Answer Questions).

Big Ideas

Readers must understand the relationship between main idea and supporting details.

Materials

Supplied

- "Living with Latin," *All About Ancient Rome*, pp. 2–9
- *K¹² Language Arts Activity Book*, pp. LC 31–32

Keywords

bold type – type that is darker than the surrounding text that draws attention to a word or phrase

caption – writing under a picture that describes that picture

fact – something that can be proven true

heading – a title within the body of a text that tells the reader something important about a section of the text

illustration – a drawing

main idea – the most important idea in a paragraph or text

nonfiction – writings about true things

supporting detail – a detail that gives more information about a main idea

 **60 minutes**

"Living with Latin," Part 2

Work **together** with students to complete offline Get Ready, Guided Reading, Check Your Reading, Reading for Meaning, and Making Connections activities.

Get Ready

Retell Main Ideas

Tell students that they will begin reading "Living with Latin" where they stopped reading. Ask them to use some of the main ideas from the first part of the article to tell about what they read in Part 1.

 Objectives
- Identify main idea.
- Increase concept and content vocabulary.

Words to Know

Go over Words to Know with students.

1. Ask students to define the following words and use them in a sentence:

   root   **Romance languages**

2. Correct any incorrect or vague definitions.

Guided Reading

Book Walk

Prepare students by taking them on a Book Walk of *All About Ancient Rome*. Scan the magazine together and ask students to make predictions about the article.

1. Read the **title** of the magazine aloud.

2. Have students use the **table of contents** in *All About Ancient Rome* to find "Living with Latin" and turn to that page.

3. Have students read the title of the article aloud.

4. Tell students that you are going to read the second part of the article.

5. Look through pages 6–9 of the article. Have students describe what they see. Point to the **photographs** and **illustrations** and have students make predictions using the pictures. Answers may vary.

   ▸ What kinds of things do you see in these pictures?
   ▸ What do you think we'll read about in this part of the article?

 Objectives
- Identify features of a nonfiction text.
- Use an illustration to make a prediction about a reading.
- Use text features to comprehend text meaning. (bold, italic, headers).
- Use text organizational features to locate and comprehend information (table of contents, glossary, chapter, index, title, author, illustrator, caption).
- Read texts to gain information.
- Identify main idea.

"Living with Latin," Part 2

Now it's time to read the remainder of "Living with Latin." Have students sit next to you so that they can see the pictures and words while you read the article aloud.

1. Remind students of where the first part of the article finished. Reread the last paragraph on page 5 to refresh students' memory of what happened at the end of the first part.

2. Read pages 6–9 of the article (Part 2) aloud all the way through. Stop at the end of the article. Track with your finger so students can follow along. Read the body of the article first. Then point to the photographs or illustrations and read the captions.

3. Explain to students that you will read the last half of the article again. Ask them to chime in and read aloud with you. Tell them to look for the most important ideas in the article. Tell students that you will pause at certain points in the story to discuss

4. Begin to reread and pause at the end of page 7. Point to the three text boxes on the page.
   Say: I see that there are three boxes of words on this page. The words *stadium, famous,* and *athlete* are all in bold type. They must be important. Inside the boxes there are more words that look different. *Stade, fama,* and *athleta* are all in **italic type**. Authors use italic type to highlight special words they want readers to notice.

5. Have students tell about what they read on the page 7.

   ▸ What was the main idea of the page we just read? The words *stadium, famous,* and *athlete* came from Latin.

6. Read on and pause to discuss at the end of page 8 after the phrase, "a box that held books."

   ▸ What was the main idea of this page? The words *aquarium* and *library* came from Latin.

7. Read to the end of the article.

Check Your Reading

"Living with Latin," Part 2

Have students retell the second part of "Living with Latin" in their own words to develop grammar, vocabulary, comprehension, and fluency skills. When finished, **ask students the following questions** to check comprehension and encourage discussion.

▸ What English word comes from the Latin word *stade*? stadium

▸ What does the Latin word *stade* mean? A stade was a place in ancient Rome where races were held.

▸ How is a stadium different from a stade? Today we can watch lots of different events in a stadium, not just races.

▸ What English word comes from the Latin words *libri* and *librarium*? library

▸ Point to the sentence in the text that supports your answer. "Library comes from two Latin words, *libri* and *librarium*."

▸ How is a library different from a librarium? A library is a building, but a librarium was a box.

Objectives
- Answer questions requiring literal recall of details.
- Identify and use evidence from the text to support answers.

Reading for Meaning

Main Idea and Supporting Details

Have students gather the Use Evidence to Answer Questions page. They will use this page to help them identify the main idea and supporting details for "Living with Latin." Turn to page LC 32 in *K¹² Language Arts Activity Book*.

1. Ask students what a topic, main idea, and supporting details are. If they don't remember, review the definitions.

2. Remind students about the difference between the topic and the main idea: The **topic** is what the article is about, and the **main idea** is the most important idea about that topic. The topic may be stated in one or a few words. The main idea is stated in a sentence.

3. Have students identify the topic of the article. Latin roots in English

4. Have students look back over the article and review the questions and their answers on the completed Use Evidence to Answer Questions page. Doing so should help them think of the article's main idea. Many words in English have Latin roots.

5. Have students give a main idea for the article. If they have trouble, try starting the sentence for them so that they can fill in the blanks.

6. Have students tell one **supporting detail** from the article. Remind students that a supporting detail is a small piece of information that supports the main idea. Possible answer: The word *famous* comes from the Latin word *fama*.

7. Have students complete the Main Idea and Supporting Details page. Tell them to write the main idea in their own words and then find three additional supporting details.

TIP If students wish to add more supporting details, add more boxes to the graphic organizer and connect them to the main idea.

Objectives
- Define main idea.
- Define supporting details.
- Define topic.
- Distinguish the main idea from the topic.
- Identify the topic.
- Identify main idea.
- Identify supporting details.

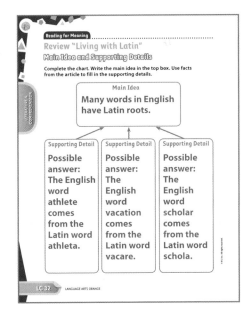

Making Connections

More Roots

Have students work with more Latin roots of modern English words to help them fully understand the relationship between the two languages.

1. Tell students that Latin roots are in many other words in English.

2. Give students two or three of the following Latin roots and their definitions. Have students see if they can think of English words that come from these roots.

   ▸ *audire*, to hear audio, auditorium
   ▸ *cavus*, hollow cavity, cave
   ▸ *octo*, eight octopus, octagon
   ▸ *quartus*, fourth quart, quarter
   ▸ *silere*, quiet or still silence

Objectives
- Identify and apply content and academic vocabulary.

Introduce "Gods and Spirits of Ancient Rome"

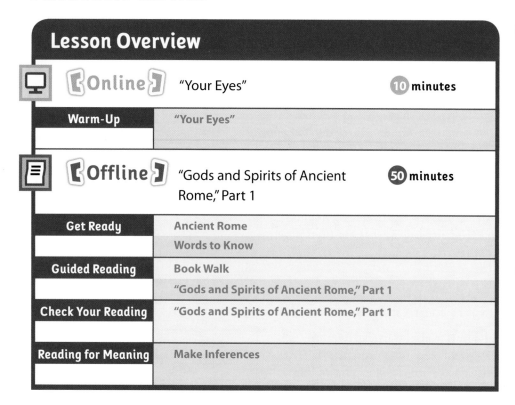

Lesson Overview

Online — "Your Eyes" — 10 minutes

Warm-Up	"Your Eyes"

Offline — "Gods and Spirits of Ancient Rome," Part 1 — 50 minutes

Get Ready	Ancient Rome
	Words to Know
Guided Reading	Book Walk
	"Gods and Spirits of Ancient Rome," Part 1
Check Your Reading	"Gods and Spirits of Ancient Rome," Part 1
Reading for Meaning	Make Inferences

Advance Preparation

If you are not able to complete the online Warm-Up, then print the selection and listen to students read aloud. Read pages 10–14 of "Gods and Spirits of Ancient Rome" before the Guided Reading to locate the Words to Know in the text. Preview the Reading for Meaning and prepare a sample graphic organizer on a whiteboard or a sheet of paper to demonstrate how to make inferences from the text.

Big Ideas

▶ Active strong, readers make inferences during and after reading to increase comprehension.
▶ Guided reading provides support to early readers as they practice and apply the reading strategies of proficient readers.

Materials

Supplied
- "Gods and Spirits of Ancient Rome," *All About Ancient Rome*, pp. 10–17
- *K¹² Language Arts Activity Book*, p. LC 33
- "Your Eyes" (optional)

Also Needed
- map – Europe, Asia, Africa
- whiteboard (optional)

Article Synopsis
This nonfiction article explains the ancient Roman belief in gods, goddesses, and spirits. It discusses the three main gods and how the Romans paid tribute to their gods and spirits.

Keywords

bold type – type that is darker than the surrounding text that draws attention to a word or phrase

caption – writing under a picture that describes that picture

context clue – a word or phrase in a text that helps you figure out the meaning of an unknown word

fact – something that can be proven true

heading – a title within the body of a text that tells the reader something important about a section of the text

nonfiction – writings about true things

sidebar – a short text within a larger text that tells something related but not essential to the main story

 **10 minutes**

"Your Eyes"

Students will work independently online to develop fluency and oral reading skills.

Warm-Up •

"Your Eyes"

The purpose of this activity is to improve students' oral reading and fluency. Students will read "Your Eyes." Remind students to listen to the model on each screen before they begin their recording.

Objectives
- Increase oral reading skills.
- Increase fluency.

Offline Alternative

No computer access? Print a copy of "Your Eyes." Have students read it aloud. Make note of any pronunciation errors, and review those words with students.

 **50 minutes**

"Gods and Spirits of Ancient Rome," Part 1

Work **together** with students to complete offline Get Ready, Guided Reading, Check Your Reading, and Reading for Meaning activities.

Get Ready •

Ancient Rome

Help students prepare for reading "Gods and Spirits of Ancient Rome" by giving them some background information on ancient Rome. Gather the map of Europe, Asia, and Africa.

Objectives
- Build background knowledge.
- Increase concept and content vocabulary.

1. Have students tell what they know about Rome.

2. Tell students that modern Rome is a city in the country of Italy. Show students Italy and Rome on the map.

3. Discuss with students what they know about ancient Rome.

   ▶ What does the word *ancient* mean? Possible answers: old; a long time ago
   ▶ What do you know about ancient Rome? Answers will vary.

4. Tell students about ancient Rome, depending on their prior knowledge.

   ▸ Thousands of years ago, the people who lived in ancient Rome, called Romans, ruled many different parts of the world. They controlled lands in Europe, Asia, and Africa. [Show students these places on the map.]
   ▸ The area that the Romans ruled was called an empire.
   ▸ In ancient Rome, the Romans had their own culture, or a way that they lived. They had their own language, beliefs, laws, and ways of living their everyday lives.

Words to Know

Before reading "Gods and Spirits of Ancient Rome," Part 1, go over Words to Know with students.

1. Review the Words to Know to become familiar with their meanings. You will use context clues to define the words as you read the article.

2. Read the words to students, but do not teach their meanings.

3. Tell students that they will learn more about what these words mean as they read the article.

ancient – very old; from times very long ago
myth – a story that explains how something came to be and that usually contains magical figures as characters
priest – a religious leader in ancient times that acted as the link between people and gods
spirit – a special being, similar to a ghost, that ancient people believed lived in their homes and in nature
temple – a building used to worship a god or gods

Guided Reading

Book Walk

Prepare students by taking them on a Book Walk of *All About Ancient Rome*. Scan the magazine together and ask students to make predictions about the article. For all questions in the Book Walk, answers will vary.

1. Point to and read aloud the **magazine title**.

2. Locate the **table of contents** inside the magazine. Explain that the selection is a **nonfiction** article from the magazine.

3. Point to "Gods and Spirits of Ancient Rome" in the table of contents and read the title aloud. Find the article in the magazine using the table of contents and turn to that page.

   ▸ What do you think this article is about?
   ▸ What do you already know about gods and spirits?

4. Look through the article. Have students describe what they see. Have them point to and identify the following text features: **bold type**, **illustration**, **photograph**, **caption**, **sidebar**, and **heading**.

Objectives

- Use text organizational features to locate and comprehend information (table of contents, glossary, chapter, index, title, author, illustrator, caption).
- Use title of the selection to make a prediction.
- Use an illustration to make a prediction about a reading.
- Read texts to gain information.
- Identify features of a nonfiction text.
- Use text features to comprehend text meaning (bold, italic, headers).
- Define context clues.
- Use context clues to determine word meanings.

5. Point to and read aloud each heading. Explain that headings are titles inside the article. They help us understand what is in each section of the article "Gods and Spirits in Ancient Rome."

6. Have students look at the photographs and illustrations and make predictions about the article.

   ▸ What do you see in this illustration on pages 10 and 11? Why do you think this is an illustration and not a photograph?
   ▸ What do you see in the photographs on pages 12 and 13? Do these things look old or new?
   ▸ Why do you think these are photographs and not illustrations like the one on pages 10 and 11?

"Gods and Spirits of Ancient Rome," Part 1

Now it's time to read pages 10–14 of "Gods and Spirits of Ancient Rome" (Part 1). Have students sit next to you so that they can see the pictures and words while you read the article aloud.

1. Read pages 10–14 of the article aloud all the way through. Stop at the end of page 14, which has the heading "Gifts for the Gods." Point to the heading as you read it. Track with your finger so students can follow along. Read the body of the article first. Then point to the photograph or illustration on each page and read the caption. Read the sidebar after reading the main body of the text on that page.

2. Explain to students that you will read the article again. Ask them to chime in and read aloud with you. Tell them to look for the words in bold type. Tell students that you will pause at certain points in the article to discuss.

3. Begin to reread and at the end of page 10 point to the words in bold type: *ancient*, *myths* and *spirits*. Explain to students that these are important words that may be unfamiliar to them.

4. Tell students that they can often find the meaning of a word in a nonfiction article by using **context clues**, or other words in a text that can help them understand the meaning of an unfamiliar word.

5. Describe, and show students, how to use context clues to define the word *ancient*.

   ▸ I can look for a context clue for the word *ancient* in the words nearby.
   ▸ At the beginning of the sentence, I see the words *Long ago*. I know the Romans lived a long time ago, so I think *ancient* means long ago.
   ▸ This kind of context clue is called a synonym, or a word that means the same thing.

6. Describe, and show students, how to use context clues to define the word *myths*.

   ▸ I can look for a context clue for the word *myths* in the words nearby.
   ▸ In the sentence before, I see the word *stories*, which I think may be a synonym.
   ▸ In the same sentence, it says the Romans wrote myths. So I think *myths* are a kind of story. That's called an explanation of a word.

7. Describe, and show students, how to use context clues to define the word *spirits*.

   ▸ I can look for a context clue for the word *spirits* in the words nearby.
   ▸ The sentence before talks about special beings that lived in people's homes and nature. The article says these beings were called *spirits*.
   ▸ I think *spirits* were special beings that the Romans believed in. This kind of context clue is called a definition, because it tells the meaning of the word.

8. Read on and pause to discuss after the body of page 12, which has the heading "Three Top Gods." Have students identify the heading.

   ▸ What were the three top gods? Jupiter, Juno, Minerva
   ▸ What was each one the god of? Jupiter was king of all gods; Juno looked after women and babies; Minerva was the goddess of learning

9. Read the sidebar on page 13.

   ▸ What is the sidebar about? Greek and Roman names

10. Read page 14, which has the heading "Gifts for the Gods." Help students use context clues to define *temples*.
    Say: Let's look for context clues for the word *temples*. I see that people built special buildings to keep the gods happy.

    ▸ What context clues do you see? Temples were like the gods' homes.
    ▸ What do you think is the definition of *temples*? Possible answer: Temples are buildings where people keep their gods happy.

11. Help students use context clues to define the word *priests*.
    Say: Let's look for context clues for the word *priests*. I see that people took care of the temples.

    ▸ What context clues do you see? Priests made sure everyone did everything right in the temples.
    ▸ What do you think is the definition of *priests*? Possible answer: people who took care of the temples and what people did in them

Check Your Reading

"Gods and Spirits of Ancient Rome," Part 1
Have students retell "Gods and Spirits of Ancient Rome" in their own words to develop grammar, vocabulary, comprehension, and fluency skills. When finished, **ask students the following questions** to check comprehension and encourage discussion.

Objectives
• Answer questions requiring literal recall of details.

▸ Who were the three top Roman gods? Jupiter, Juno, Minerva
▸ Why was Jupiter most important? He was the king of the gods.
▸ What did Juno look after and protect? women, babies, the city of Rome
▸ What was Minerva the goddess of? learning
▸ What were some of the gifts that Romans gave to their gods? food, money, animals, flowers
▸ Why did priests make sure that people presented their gifts correctly in the temples? The Romans thought that the gods would get angry if the gifts were presented in the wrong way.

Reading for Meaning

Make Inferences

Guide students to use the information in a text and their own experiences to make inferences. Turn to page LC 33 in *K¹² Language Arts Activity Book*.

1. Have students recount what they have learned in "Gods and Spirits of Ancient Rome."
   Say: I've learned that the ancient Romans believed in gods and spirits. They wrote stories about them and believed that they were real. What do you remember?

2. Tell students that they are going to make **inferences** about what they've read. To make inferences, you use facts that you have read and your own ideas and experiences to figure out more about what you read, particularly something that is written down.

3. Tell students that they make inferences all the time. Describe a situation for students and guide them to make inferences.

   ▸ Imagine you see a young boy crying and looking at a broken toy on the ground. What do you think may have happened? Answers will vary. Students may say that a toy the child likes has broken.

   ▸ You've just made an inference based on the facts I gave you and what you already know about children and toys.

   ▸ Sometimes you can make more than one inference. What other inference could you make about this scene? Answers will vary. Students may say that the boy is very sad.

4. Tell students that they can learn more about the ancient Romans by making inferences about the article "Gods and Spirits of Ancient Rome."

5. Turn to page 12 with the heading "Three Top Gods." Tell students that you are going to show them how to make inferences about the Roman gods.

6. Reread the first paragraph.

   ▸ What does the article say about Jupiter? He was king of the sky. The Romans wanted him on their side.

   ▸ What do you think about these facts? A king is powerful. I would want someone powerful on my side.

   ▸ Why would the Romans want Jupiter on their side? Possible answers: because he could protect them and help them in war; because power was important to the Romans

7. Tell students that they have just made an inference using the facts and what they know to tell something about the ancient Romans that isn't written in the article.

8. Draw a chart with three boxes on a whiteboard or a sheet of paper. Tell students that you are going to make an inference about the god Juno.

9. Label the first box "What I Read." Write the sample answer below and read it to students.

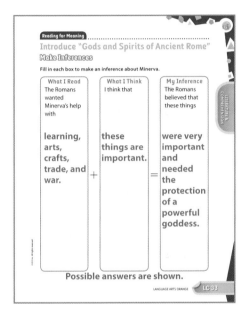

Objectives

- Define inference.
- Make inferences using text and prior knowledge.
- Support inferences with evidence from text and prior knowledge.

10. Label the second box "What I Think." Write the sample response below and read it to students.

11. Label the third box "My Inference." Write the sample response below and read it to students.

What I Read		What I Think		My Inference
Juno was the queen of the gods and looked after women, babies, and Rome.	+	I think that moms, babies, and the town where I live are important and special. I would want someone to look out for them and protect them.	=	The Romans thought these things were important and needed help and protection.

12. Explain that more than one inference may be drawn from these facts. Ask students if they have another inference about Juno. Possible answer: Rome got attacked a lot and the Romans wanted the help of a goddess.

13. Have students complete the Activity Book page.

Review "Gods and Spirits of Ancient Rome"

Lesson Overview

☰	**Offline**	"Gods and Spirits of Ancient Rome," Part 2	**60** minutes

Get Ready	Review Making Inferences
	Words to Know
Guided Reading	Book Walk
	"Gods and Spirits of Ancient Rome," Part 2
Check Your Reading	"Gods and Spirits of Ancient Rome," Part 2
Reading for Meaning	Make Inferences
Making Connections	Draw Conclusions

[Materials]

Supplied
- "Gods and Spirits of Ancient Rome," *All About Ancient Rome*, pp. 10–17
- *K¹² Language Arts Activity Book*, pp. LC 33–34

Also Needed
- whiteboard (optional)

Keywords

bold type – type that is darker than the surrounding text that draws attention to a word or phrase

caption – writing under a picture that describes that picture

conclusion – a reasoned decision made about something not stated directly in a text through the consideration of information provided and what is already known

context clue – a word or phrase in a text that helps you figure out the meaning of an unknown word

fact – something that can be proven true

heading – a title within the body of a text that tells the reader something important about a section of the text

illustration – a drawing

inference – a guess you make using the clues in a text and what you already know

nonfiction – writings about true things

Advance Preparation

Read pages 15–17 of "Gods and Spirits of Ancient Rome" before the Guided Reading to locate the Words to Know in the text. For the Get Ready, write the following sentences on a whiteboard or a sheet of paper: *A young girl sat in the park. It was a sunny day. She was reading about the weather.* Have students gather the completed page LC 33 in *K¹² Language Arts Activity Book* (Make Inferences).

Big Ideas

▶ Comprehension skills can be taught through explicit instruction.
▶ When we draw conclusions, we use the information in a text and our inferences to make a decision about what we've read.

 **Offline** 60 minutes

"Gods and Spirits of Ancient Rome," Part 2

Work **together** with students to complete offline Get Ready, Guided Reading, Check Your Reading, Reading for Meaning, and Making Connections activities.

Get Ready

Review Making Inferences

Review with students how to make an inference about a text.

1. Review with students that an **inference** is a decision that readers make after thinking about the facts in a text and what they already know.

2. Write the following sentences on a whiteboard or a sheet of paper: *A young girl sat in the park. It was a sunny day. She was reading about the weather.*

3. Have students read the sentences and make an inference about what is happening. The student is reading the book for a project, or the student likes learning about weather.

Objectives
- Define inference.
- Make inferences using text and prior knowledge.
- Increase concept and content vocabulary.

Words to Know

Before reading "Gods and Spirits of Ancient Rome," Part 2, go over Words to Know with students.

1. Ask students to define the following words and use them in sentences:

ancient	spirit
myths	temple
priest	

2. Correct any incorrect or vague definitions.

3. Review the words in the list below to become familiar with their meanings. You will use context clues to define the words as you read the article.

4. Read the words to students, but do not teach their meanings.

5. Tell students that they will learn more about what these words mean as they read the article.

numina – spirits that ancient Romans identified with objects and places
victory – a win or success

Guided Reading

Book Walk

Prepare students by taking them on a Book Walk of *All About Ancient Rome*. Scan the magazine together and ask students to make predictions about the article.

1. Read the **title** of the magazine aloud.

2. Have students use the **table of contents** to find "Gods and Spirits of Ancient Rome" and turn to that page.

3. Have students read the title of the article aloud.

4. Tell students that you are going to read the second part of the article.

5. Look through pages 15–17 of the article. Have students describe what they see. Point out the **photographs** and **illustration** and have students make predictions using the pictures. Answers to questions may vary.

   ▸ What kinds of things do you see in these pictures?
   ▸ What do you think we'll read about in this part of the article?

"Gods and Spirits of Ancient Rome," Part 2

Now it's time to read pages 15–17 of "Gods and Spirits of Ancient Rome" (Part 2). Have students sit next to you so that they can see the pictures and words while you read the article aloud.

1. Ask students to summarize what they read in the first part of the article. As needed, remind students of where the first part of the article finished. Reread the last paragraph on page 14 to refresh students' memory of what happened at the end of the first part.

2. Read pages 15–17 aloud all the way through. Stop at the end of the article. Track with your finger so students can follow along. Read the body of the article first. Then point to the photographs or illustrations and read the caption.

3. Explain to students that you will read this part of the article again. Ask them to chime in and read aloud with you. Tell them to look for special words that are different from the rest of the text. Tell students that you will pause at certain points in the article to discuss

4. Begin to reread and pause at the end of page 15, which has the heading "One Big Temple." Point to the heading and have students identify the feature. Then have them tell what the page is about.

5. Point to the word *victory* on the same page. Ask students what type of text feature this is. bold type

Objectives

- Use text organizational features to locate and comprehend information (table of contents, glossary, chapter, index, title, author, illustrator, caption).
- Use an illustration to make a prediction about a reading.
- Read texts to gain information.
- Identify features of a nonfiction text.
- Use text features to comprehend text meaning (bold, italic, headers).
- Define context clues.
- Use context clues to determine word meanings.

6. Review with students the meaning of context clues: words in the text that can help them define an unfamiliar word. Show students how to use context clues to define victory.
   Say: In the sentence before the word *victory*, it says that a general won a big battle. Then he thanked the gods for his victory. I think *victory* means a big win.

7. Read page 16 with the heading "All Kinds of Spirits." Have students point to the heading.

8. Point to the word *numina*. Explain that this unfamiliar word has a definition nearby. It's separated by a comma and the word *or*.

9. Have students point to the definition. spirits

10. Read to the end of the article.

Check Your Reading

"Gods and Spirits of Ancient Rome," Part 2
Have students retell the second part of "Gods and Spirits of Ancient Rome" in their own words to develop grammar, vocabulary, comprehension, and fluency skills. When finished, **ask students the following questions** to check comprehension and encourage discussion.

Objectives
- Answer questions requiring literal recall of details.

► Why was the temple of Jupiter, Juno, and Minerva the grandest of all?
  They were the most important Roman gods.
► Describe the temple. It was on top of a hill. It had white marble columns from floor to ceiling. The roof was covered in gold.
► Why did the ancient Romans think they needed to keep spirits happy?
  They believed that spirits could harm people.
► What kinds of gifts did the ancient Romans give to spirits in their homes?
  milk, wine, oil, food

Reading for Meaning

Make Inferences

Review with students how to make inferences by using the information from the article "Gods and Spirits of Ancient Rome" and their own experiences. Turn to page LC 34 in *K¹² Language Arts Activity Book.*

1. Have students recount what they learned in the second part of the article. Prompt them with a model retelling.
   Say: I've learned that the ancient Romans built a giant temple to their three most important gods. They put this temple on a big hill. What do you remember?

2. Tell students that they are going to make inferences about what they've read.

3. Review how to make inferences. When you make an inference, you make a decision about what you've read using facts from the reading and what you already know.

4. Have students complete the Activity Book page using page 17 from the article, which has the heading "Spirits at Home."

Objectives
- Define inference.
- Make inferences using text and prior knowledge.
- Support inferences with evidence from text and prior knowledge.

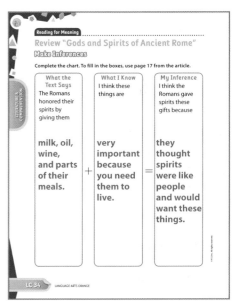

Making Connections

Draw Conclusions

Teach students how to draw conclusions about "Gods and Spirits of Ancient Rome." Have them gather the completed Make Inferences pages.

Objectives

- Define conclusion.
- Draw conclusions using evidence from text.
- Draw conclusions using prior knowledge.
- Support conclusions with evidence from text and prior knowledge.

1. Explain to students that sometimes after they read they may need to answer questions.

2. Tell students that they can use their inferences and the information from the text to answer some questions.

3. Explain that a special kind of inference is called a **conclusion**. A conclusion is a decision that readers make after looking at all of the facts in an article and thinking about the inferences they have made as well as what they know.

4. Tell students that you are going to help them use the text and their inferences to make some conclusions about the whole article they read.

5. Ask students the following questions to help them draw conclusions about the article. Have them look at the Make Inferences page to help them think of ideas.

   ▶ Why do you think the Romans believed that gifts like food and money would make their gods and spirits happy? Possible answer: The Romans thought their gods and spirits were like people and would like the same things people do.
   ▶ What did you read in the article that makes you think this? Possible answers: The Roman gods were men and women; their gods and spirits lived in places like houses and temples.
   ▶ What do you know from your own life that makes you think this? Possible answers: People like presents; I've read other myths, and the gods are always like people.

6. Ask students the following questions. After each question, ask the same two follow-up questions: What did you read that makes you think this? What do you know that makes you think this? Answers to questions will vary.

   ▶ Why do you think the Romans wrote stories about their gods and goddesses?
   ▶ Why do you think there were both male and female gods?
   ▶ Why do you think the Romans believed that gods and spirits could harm people?

Introduce "Clytie"

Lesson Overview

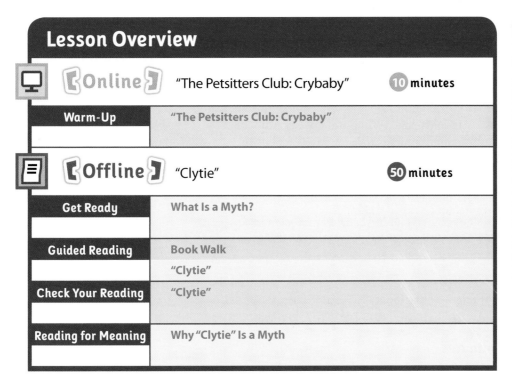

🖥️ **Online**	"The Petsitters Club: Crybaby"	**10** minutes
Warm-Up	"The Petsitters Club: Crybaby"	
📄 **Offline**	"Clytie"	**50** minutes
Get Ready	What Is a Myth?	
Guided Reading	Book Walk	
	"Clytie"	
Check Your Reading	"Clytie"	
Reading for Meaning	Why "Clytie" Is a Myth	

Materials

Supplied

- "Clytie," *K¹² Classics for Young Readers, Volume B*, pp. 22–23
- *K¹² Language Arts Activity Book*, p. LC 35
- "The Petsitters Club: Crybaby" (optional)

Also Needed

- crayons (optional)

Story Synopsis

In this Roman myth, the goddess Clytie waits, with her neck craned and face tilted to the sun, so that she may watch the god Apollo cross the sky. She stands so long that the other gods turn her into a sunflower.

Keywords

myth – a story that explains how something came to be and that usually contains magical figures as characters

Advance Preparation

If you are not able to complete the online Warm-Up, then print the selection and listen to students read aloud.

Big Ideas

- ▶ Myths are part of the foundation of Western literature and have contributed themes and archetypal characters that are part of our culture even today.
- ▶ Through reading a diverse array of classic and contemporary literature as well as challenging informational texts in a range of subjects, students are expected to build knowledge, gain insights, explore possibilities, and broaden their perspective.
- ▶ Guided reading provides students with a model of fluent reading.

 **10** minutes

"The Petsitters Club: Crybaby"
Students will work independently online to develop fluency and oral reading skills.

Warm-Up

"The Pettsitters Club: Crybaby"
The purpose of this activity is to improve students' oral reading and fluency. Students will read "The Petsitters Club: Crybaby." Remind students to listen to the model on each screen before they begin their recording.

 Objectives
- Increase oral reading skills.
- Increase fluency.

Offline Alternative

No computer access? Print a copy of "The Petsitters Club: Crybaby." Have students read it aloud. Make note of any pronunciation errors, and review those words with students.

 **50** minutes

"Clytie"
Work **together** with students to complete offline Get Ready, Guided Reading, Check Your Reading, and Reading for Meaning activities.

Get Ready

What Is a Myth?
Introduce students to the genre of myth.

1. Explain that a **myth** is a special kind of story that comes from long ago. Myths explain how something came to be, and they usually have magical characters.

2. Explain that the ancient Romans used myths to explain things that happened in the world around them.

   ▸ Why do you think we read myths today? Possible answers: They're fun to read. They have interesting characters. They help us learn about the ancient Romans.

3. Tell students that many myths included the Roman gods and goddesses. Review with students what gods and goddesses are.

4. Tell students that an important Roman god was Apollo, the god of the sun.

 Objectives
- Define myth.
- Identify genre.
- Identify characteristics of different genres.
- Identify purpose for reading.

Guided Reading

Book Walk

Prepare students by taking them on a Book Walk of "Clytie." Scan the story together and ask students to make predictions about it.

1. Have students use the **table of contents** of K^{12} *Classics for Young Readers, Volume B* to find "Clytie" and turn to that page.

2. Point to and read aloud the **title of the story**.

3. Have students study the **illustrations** and make **predictions** about the story based on the illustrations.

   ▸ Who do you think these people are in the pictures? Clytie, Apollo, gods, goddesses

   ▸ Do you see anything unusual or special in these pictures? A man is flying through the sky in some kind of carriage. The flower has a face.

   ▸ What do you think might happen in the story? Answers will vary.

Objectives

- Use an illustration to make a prediction about a reading.
- Use text organizational features to locate and comprehend information (table of contents, illustrations).
- Read texts for literary experience.
- Read and discuss texts from different cultures, traditions, and time periods.

"Clytie"

Now it's time to read the story. Have students sit next to you so that they can see the pictures and words while you read the story aloud.

1. Read the story aloud all the way through. Track with your finger so students can follow along.

2. Explain to students that you will read the story again. Ask them to chime in and read aloud with you. Tell them to think about myths and what we read in them. Tell students that you will pause at certain points in the story to discuss.

3. Begin to reread and pause to discuss at the end of the second paragraph, after the phrase "the chariot of the sun."

   ▸ What is Clytie? Where does she live? a water goddess; in a river
   ▸ Who does Clytie love? the sun god Apollo

4. Read on and pause to discuss at the end of the fourth paragraph, after the phrase "more pale and thin." Model how to make an inference about Clytie's feelings.
   Say: I wonder why Clytie eats nothing but dewdrops? I know that the story says she loved Apollo. I know when I'm really excited about something, it changes my appetite and what I want to eat. Maybe Clytie is so in love with Apollo that she isn't hungry for real food.

5. Continue reading to the end of the story.

Check Your Reading

"Clytie"

Have students retell "Clytie" in their own words to develop grammar, vocabulary, comprehension, and fluency skills. When finished, **ask students the following questions** to check comprehension and encourage discussion.

▶ Where does Clytie stand to watch Apollo? on the banks of her river home
▶ What does Apollo do every day? He drives his chariot across the sky.
▶ How long does Clytie stand and watch for Apollo? nine days
▶ What happens to Clytie when she only eats dewdrops? She becomes pale and thin.
▶ What does it mean that the "gods took pity on her"? They felt sorry for her.
▶ What do the gods change Clytie into? a sunflower

Objectives
• Answer questions requiring literal recall of details.

Reading for Meaning

Why "Clytie" Is a Myth

Guide students to identify the elements of a myth in "Clytie." Turn to page LC 35 in *K¹² Language Arts Activity Book*.

1. Remind students that a myth explains how something came to be and includes magical characters.

2. Have students complete the Activity Book page.

Objectives
• Identify genre.
• Identify characteristics of different genres.

Review "Clytie"

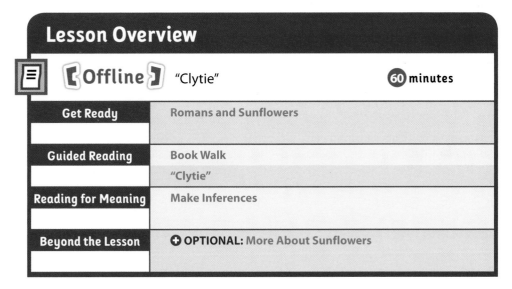

Lesson Overview

[Offline] "Clytie" — **60** minutes

Get Ready	Romans and Sunflowers
Guided Reading	Book Walk
	"Clytie"
Reading for Meaning	Make Inferences
Beyond the Lesson	⊕ OPTIONAL: More About Sunflowers

Materials

Supplied
- "Clytie," *K¹² Classics for Young Readers, Volume B*, pp. 22–23
- *K¹² Language Arts Activity Book*, p. LC 36

Also Needed
- crayons (optional)
- paper, poster (optional)

Keywords

inference – a guess you make using the clues in a text and what you already know

myth – a story that explains how something came to be and that usually contains magical figures as characters

Big Ideas

▸ Readers make inferences about characters and their feelings and motivations to better understand an author's message or central idea.

▸ Interpretation occurs between reader and text, as the reader attempts to discover the unstated and to communicate about the text's meaning.

 60 minutes

"Clytie"

Work **together** with students to complete offline Get Ready, Guided Reading, Reading for Meaning, and Beyond the Lesson activities.

Get Ready

Romans and Sunflowers

Ask students why they think the Romans wrote a myth about sunflowers. Answers will vary. You may wish to remind students that myths are written to explain where something came from.

 Objectives
- Define myth.

Guided Reading

Book Walk

Prepare students by taking them on a Book Walk of "Clytie." Scan the story together and ask students to recall what they remember about it.

1. Have students use the **table of contents** in *K¹² Classics for Young Readers, Volume B*, to locate "Clytie" and turn to that page.

2. Have students read the title of the story aloud.

3. Have students tell how the story begins. If students have trouble remembering, prompt them.
   Say: I remember how the story begins. There's a beautiful water goddess named Clytie who lives in a river. Do you remember anything else about the beginning?

 Objectives
- Use text organizational features to locate and comprehend information (table of contents).
- Read texts for literary experience.
- Read and discuss texts from different cultures, traditions, and time periods.

"Clytie"

Now it's time to reread the story. Have students sit next to you so that they can see the pictures and words while you read the story aloud.

1. Explain to students that you will focus on making inferences about what happens in the story. Ask them to chime in and read aloud with you. Tell students that you will pause at certain points in the story to talk about what Clytie and the other gods do.

2. Begin to reread and pause to discuss at the end of the third paragraph, after the phrase "she stood looking after him."
   ▸ How does Clytie feel about Apollo? She loves him.

3. Read to the end of the story.

Reading for Meaning

 Make Inferences

Model for students how to make inferences about the motivations of the characters in the myth. Students will make their own inferences about what happens in the story by completing page LC 36 in *K¹² Language Arts Activity Book*.

1. Review that an **inference** is a guess that you make using clues and your own prior knowledge.

2. Remind students that they make inferences all the time in daily life and that they can do it in their reading, too.

3. Explain that when they make inferences while reading, they can understand why something happens.

4. Tell students that they are going to make inferences about characters in a myth.

5. Model how to make an inference about Clytie to answer questions about the text.
   Say: For example, I might want to know the answer to this question: Why did Clytie stand for nine days and eat nothing but dewdrops? I know from the story that she loved Apollo. I know that when I love something and really look forward to it, I think about it all the time. Sometimes I have trouble thinking about anything else.

6. Model how to make an inference to answer the question.
   Say: I think Clytie stands for nine days and eats nothing but dewdrops because she loves Apollo so much that she forgets about everything else.

7. Have students complete the Activity Book page.

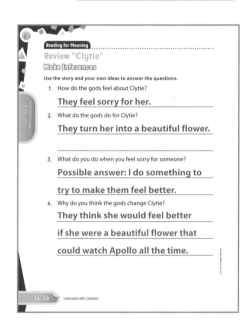

Beyond the Lesson

 ⊕ **OPTIONAL: More about Sunflowers**

This activity is OPTIONAL. It is intended for students who have extra time, enjoy being artistic, and would be interested in learning more about sunflowers. Feel free to skip this activity.

1. Have students learn more about sunflowers. They may use books from the library or information on the Internet.

2. Have students make a sunflower poster with a drawing of the flower and facts about the plant.

Introduce "Pandora's Box"

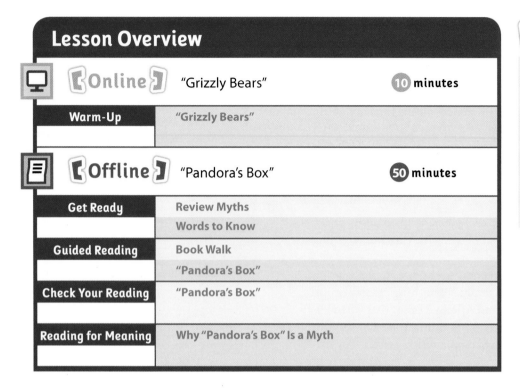

Lesson Overview

Online	"Grizzly Bears"	10 minutes
Warm-Up	"Grizzly Bears"	

Offline	"Pandora's Box"	50 minutes
Get Ready	Review Myths	
	Words to Know	
Guided Reading	Book Walk	
	"Pandora's Box"	
Check Your Reading	"Pandora's Box"	
Reading for Meaning	Why "Pandora's Box" Is a Myth	

Advance Preparation

If you are not able to complete the online Warm-Up, then print the selection and listen to students read aloud.

Content Background

The Pandora story is a myth of Greek origin, but elements of the story are related by Roman mythographer Hyginus in the *Fabulae*.

Big Ideas

Myths are part of the foundation of Western literature and have contributed themes and archetypal characters that are part of our culture even today.

Materials

Supplied

- "Pandora's Box," *K¹² Classics for Young Readers, Volume B,* pp. 24–27
- *K¹² Language Arts Activity Book,* p. LC 37
- "Grizzly Bears" (optional)

Story Synopsis

In this myth, the young maiden Pandora wants desperately to open a box given to her by the king of the gods, but he has told her never to open it. Pandora finally gives in to her curiosity and opens the box. Consequently, she releases pain and sorrow that the world has never seen. In the box, however, there is also Hope that brings comfort to all who suffer.

Keywords

myth – a story that explains how something came to be and that usually contains magical figures as characters

 **10 minutes**

"Grizzly Bears"

Students will work independently online to develop fluency and oral reading skills.

"Grizzly Bears"

The purpose of this activity is to improve students' oral reading and fluency. Students will read "Grizzly Bears." Remind students to listen to the model on each screen before they begin their recording.

 Objectives

- Increase oral reading skills.
- Increase fluency.

Offline Alternative

No computer access? Print a copy of "Grizzly Bears." Have students read it aloud. Make note of any pronunciation errors, and review those words with students.

Offline **50 minutes**

"Pandora's Box"

Work **together** with students to complete offline Get Ready, Guided Reading, Check Your Reading, and Reading for Meaning activities.

Get Ready

Review Myths

Review with students the characteristics of myths.

1. Ask students to tell you what a myth is. Review the characteristics of myths.

2. Have students tell about other myths they have read, such as "Clytie." Have them tell what that myth explains and what magical characters were in the story.

3. Review with students that many myths came from ancient Rome. Discuss what they know about this culture.

 Objectives

- Identify genre.
- Identify characteristics of different genres.
- Increase concept and content vocabulary.

Words to Know

Before reading "Pandora's Box," go over Words to Know with students.

1. Have students say the word aloud.

2. Ask students if they know the word means.

   ▸ If students know the word's meaning, have them define it and use it in a sentence.
   ▸ If students don't know the word's meaning, read them the definition and discuss the word with them.

maiden – an old-fashioned word for a young woman

Guided Reading

Book Walk

Prepare students by taking them on a Book Walk of "Pandora's Box." Scan the story together and ask students to make predictions about it.

1. Have students use the **table of contents** in *K*¹² *Classics for Young Readers, Volume B,* to find "Pandora's Box," and turn to that page.

2. Point to and read aloud the **title of the story**.

3. Have students study the **illustrations** and make **predictions** about the story based on the illustrations.

   ▸ Who do you think the young woman in the pictures is? Pandora
   ▸ What do you think the creatures are? scary, terrible things; a fairy or a goddess
   ▸ What do you think might happen in the story? Answers will vary.

Objectives

- Use an illustration to make a prediction about a reading.
- Use text organizational features to locate and comprehend information (table of contents, illustrations).
- Read texts for literary experience.
- Read and discuss texts from different cultures, traditions, and time periods.
- Answer inferential questions.

"Pandora's Box"

Now it's time to read "Pandora's Box." Have students sit next to you so that they can see the pictures and words while you read the story aloud.

1. Read the story aloud all the way through. Track with your finger so students can follow along.

2. Explain to students that you will read the story again. Ask them to chime in and read aloud with you. Tell them to think about myths and what we read in them. Tell students that you will pause at certain points in the story to discuss.

3. Begin to reread and pause to discuss on page 24 after the phrase, "that a maiden could wish."

   ▸ How would you describe Pandora? pretty, smart, lucky

4. Read on and pause at the end of the sixth paragraph, on page 25 after the phrase, "remembered and stopped."

   ▸ What does Pandora want to do that she is not supposed to do? open the box that the king of the gods gave her
   ▸ What do you think will happen next? Answers will vary.

5. Continue reading to the end of the story. Ask students to make inferences.

   ▶ How would you describe the way pain and sorrow look?
   scary, ugly, dangerous
   ▶ How does hope look? pretty, sweet, kind
   ▶ Do you think that these are good illustrations of these feelings? Why or why not? Yes. Pain and sorrow are bad feelings, and hope is a good feeling.

Check Your Reading

"Pandora's Box"
Have students retell "Pandora's Box" in their own words to develop grammar, vocabulary, comprehension, and fluency skills. When finished, **ask students the following questions** to check comprehension and encourage discussion.

Objectives
- Answer questions requiring literal recall of details.

   ▶ What does the king of the gods give to Pandora? a box
   ▶ What happens when Pandora looks inside the box? Pain and sorrow come out.
   ▶ What else comes out of the box? Hope
   ▶ Where does Hope go? everywhere that there is pain and sorrow

Reading for Meaning

Why "Pandora's Box" Is a Myth
Have students identify the elements of a myth in "Pandora's Box." Turn to page LC 37 in *K¹² Language Arts Activity Book*.

Objectives
- Identify genre.
- Identify characteristics of different genres.

1. Remind students that a myth explains how something came to be and includes magical characters.

2. Have students complete the Activity Book page.

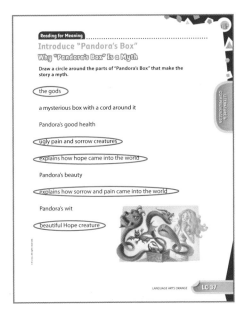

Explore "Pandora's Box"

Lesson Overview

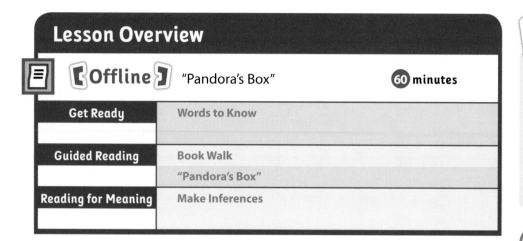

Offline	"Pandora's Box"	**60** minutes
Get Ready	Words to Know	
Guided Reading	Book Walk	
	"Pandora's Box"	
Reading for Meaning	Make Inferences	

Big Ideas

Readers make inferences about characters and their feelings and motivations to better understand an author's message or central idea.

Materials

Supplied
- "Pandora's Box," *K¹² Classics for Young Readers, Volume B,* pp. 24–27
- *K¹² Language Arts Activity Book,* p. LC 38

Keywords

inference – a guess you make using the clues in a text and what you already know

myth – a story that explains how something came to be and that usually contains magical figures as characters

[Offline] 60 minutes

"Pandora's Box"

Work **together** with students to complete offline Get Ready, Guided Reading, and Reading for Meaning activities.

Get Ready

Words to Know

Go over Words to Know with students.

1. Ask students to define the following word and use it in a sentence:

   maiden

2. Correct any incorrect or vague definitions.

Objectives
- Increase concept and content vocabulary.

Guided Reading

Book Walk

Prepare students by taking them on a Book Walk of "Pandora's Box." Scan the story together and ask students to revisit the characters and events.

1. Have students use the **table of contents** in *K¹² Classics for Young Readers, Volume B,* to locate "Pandora's Box" and turn to that page.

2. Have students read aloud the title of the story.

3. Have students look at the **pictures** of the story.

   ▸ Who are the characters in these pictures? Pandora, pain and sorrow, Hope

Objectives
- Use text organizational features to locate and comprehend information (table of contents, illustrations).
- Read texts for literary experience.
- Read and discuss texts from different cultures, traditions, and time periods.

"Pandora's Box"

Now it's time to reread "Pandora's Box." Have students sit next to you so that they can see the pictures and words while you read the story aloud.

1. Explain to students that you will focus on making inferences about what happens in the story. Ask them to chime in and read aloud with you. Tell students that you will pause at certain points in the story to talk about what Pandora does.

2. Begin to reread and pause on page 25 after the phrase, "wondering what could be inside it."

   ▸ How does Pandora feel about the box? She really wants to open it to find out what's inside.

3. Read on and pause after the sentence, "Then she suddenly remembered and stopped."

   ▸ Why do you think Pandora doesn't open the box? The king of the gods told her not to, and she wants to do what he told her.

4. Read to the end of the story.

Reading for Meaning

Make Inferences

Help students make inferences about "Pandora's Box." Turn to page LC 38 in *K¹² Language Arts Activity Book*.

1. Review the definition of **inference** as a guess made using clues in the text and prior knowledge.

2. Tell students that they can make inferences to answer questions about a story.

3. Model how to make an inference about Pandora to answer questions about the text.
   Say: For example, I might want to know the answer to this question: Why does Pandora want to open the box, even though the king of the gods has told her not to? I know from the story that Pandora wonders every day what is inside the box. She wonders what good it does to have a box when you don't know what's inside. I know that when someone gives me a gift, I'm very curious to find out what's inside, and I can hardly wait to open it because there might be something really good inside.

4. Model how to make an inference to answer the question.
   Say: I think Pandora is very curious about what is inside the box because she thinks there might be something really good inside.

5. Direct student's attention to the activity page. Read the directions to them. Explain that they will be answering multiple choice questions.
   Say: To answer a multiple choice question, you need to read the question carefully. Then read each choice below it. Pick the choice that best answers the question.

6. Have students complete the Activity Book page.

Objectives

- Make inferences about characters using evidence from the text.
- Support inferences with evidence from text and prior knowledge.

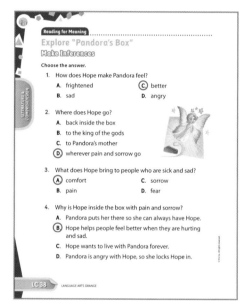

Reading for Meaning

Explore "Pandora's Box"
Make Inferences

Choose the answer.

1. How does Hope make Pandora feel?
   A. frightened   C. better
   B. sad   D. angry

2. Where does Hope go?
   A. back inside the box
   B. to the king of the gods
   C. to Pandora's mother
   D. wherever pain and sorrow go

3. What does Hope bring to people who are sick and sad?
   A. comfort   C. sorrow
   B. pain   D. fear

4. Why is Hope inside the box with pain and sorrow?
   A. Pandora puts her there so she can always have Hope.
   B. Hope helps people feel better when they are hurting and sad.
   C. Hope wants to live with Pandora forever.
   D. Pandora is angry with Hope, so she locks Hope in.

LC 38   LANGUAGE ARTS ORANGE

Review "Pandora's Box"

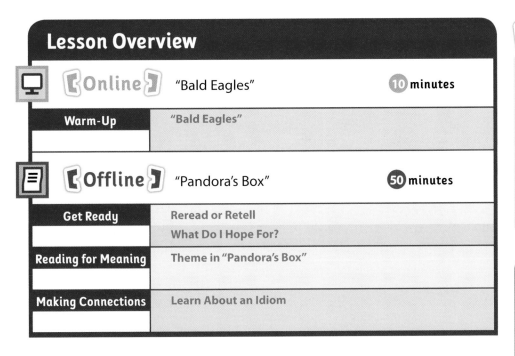

Lesson Overview

Online	"Bald Eagles"		**10** minutes
Warm-Up	"Bald Eagles"		
Offline	"Pandora's Box"		**50** minutes
Get Ready	Reread or Retell		
	What Do I Hope For?		
Reading for Meaning	Theme in "Pandora's Box"		
Making Connections	Learn About an Idiom		

Materials

Supplied
- "Pandora's Box,"
  *K¹² Classics for Young
  Readers, Volume B,*
  pp. 24–27
- *K¹² Language Arts Activity
  Book,* p. LC 39
- "Bald Eagles" (optional)

Keywords
myth – a story that explains
how something came to be
and that usually contains
magical figures as characters
theme – the author's
message or big idea

Advance Preparation

If you are not able to complete the online Warm-Up, then print the selection and
listen to students read aloud.

Big Ideas

- ▶ Readers need to recognize themes so they can identify why an author is
  writing, or the central message of a piece of literature.
- ▶ Interpretation occurs between reader and text, as the reader attempts to
  discover the unstated and to communicate about the text's meaning.

Online **10** minutes

"Bald Eagles"
Students will work independently online to develop fluency and oral reading skills.

Warm-Up

"Bald Eagles"
The purpose of this activity is to improve students' oral reading and fluency. Students
will read "Bald Eagles." Remind students to listen to the model on each screen before
they begin their recording.

Objectives
- Increase oral reading skills.
- Increase fluency.

Offline Alternative

No computer access? Print a copy of "Bald Eagles." Have students read it aloud. Make note of any pronunciation errors, and review those words with students.

 **Offline** **50** minutes

"Pandora's Box"

Work **together** with students to complete offline Get Ready, Reading for Meaning, and Making Connections activities.

Get Ready

Reread or Retell

If you'd like to, reread "Pandora's Box" to students. Otherwise, have students retell the story using the pictures as a guide. Make sure students tell the events in sequential order.

What Do I Hope For?

Help students prepare to identify theme by talking about the big ideas in "Pandora's Box."

1. Describe a time when you felt sad, lonely, or upset.

2. Have students describe a similar situation.

3. Describe how thinking about fixing the situation or thinking about something that made you feel happy made you feel better.

4. Ask students what they wished for when they felt sad or upset. Have them tell whether wishing for this thing made them feel better.

5. Tell students that sometimes hoping that things will get better can make a bad situation feel a little better.

Objectives
- Make connections between text and oneself.
- Recount stories, including fables and folktales from diverse cultures.
- Summarize the plot of a story.

Reading for Meaning

 Theme in "Pandora's Box"

Define theme for students. They will think more about the theme in "Pandora's Box" as they complete the activity. Turn to page LC 39 in *K¹² Language Arts Activity Book*.

1. Explain that stories often have a message, or a "big idea," that the author is trying to tell the reader. This is called a **theme**.

2. Tell students we learn about the theme through the plot of a story and how the characters think and feel about what happens.

Objectives
- Define theme.
- Identify theme.
- Make connections between text and self.

3. Explain that a theme is different from what a story is about. You can usually tell what a story is about using one or a few words. A theme is a whole sentence that explains what the author wants us to learn about people and life.

4. Remind students that "Pandora's Box" is a myth, so it explains how something came to be. Ask students what things the myth explains. pain, sorrow, and hope

5. Explain that pain, sorrow, and hope are what the story is about. Now you are going to help them think about a theme for this story.

   ► When you read this story, what did you learn about hope, sorrow, and pain? Possible answer: Wherever pain and sorrow go, hope is there too to make people feel better.

6. Tell students that sometimes a theme is stated in the story. Reread the last two paragraphs of the story with students. Have them paraphrase what these paragraphs say. Wherever there is pain and sorrow, hope can bring people comfort.

7. Have students complete the Activity Book page.

TIP If students have difficulty understanding theme, explain that a theme is like advice that the author is giving to the reader. Provide an example of advice that you might give to students to help them in life: If you work hard, you will be rewarded. Ask students to tell advice they might give to a younger relative or friend. Remind them to give their advice in a complete sentence.

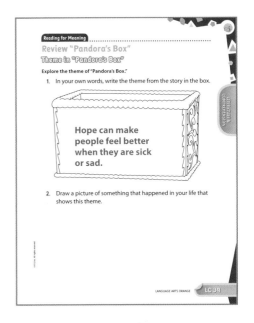

Making Connections

Learn About an Idiom
Help students understand the idioms that we use today that come from the myth.

1. Explain to students that the phrase "Pandora's box" is an **idiom**. An idiom is a phrase where the words don't mean literally what they say.

2. Tell students that today we use the phrase Pandora's box to mean something that will lead to a lot of trouble or problems.

3. Give a sentence as an example: *I'm worried that letting you eat dessert before dinner will open a Pandora's box for every meal.*

4. Ask students to explain what kinds of problems or troubles might come if they were allowed to eat dessert before dinner. Possible responses: They might not want to eat the healthy part of the m eal; they might want to eat dessert before dinner every night; they might want to eat dessert before every meal.

5. Have students make up a sentence using the idiom and tell it to you. Answers will vary.

> **Objectives**
> - Define idiom.
> - Identify and use idioms.
> - Make connections between text and the world.

Introduce "Echo"

Lesson Overview

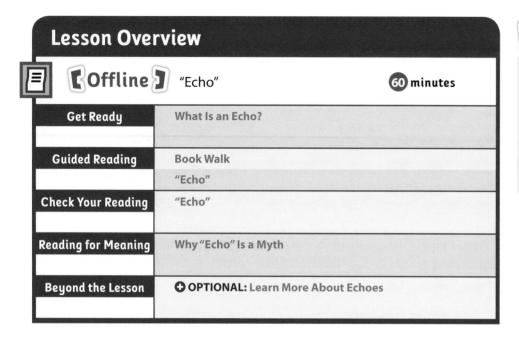

Offline	"Echo"	60 minutes
Get Ready	What Is an Echo?	
Guided Reading	Book Walk	
	"Echo"	
Check Your Reading	"Echo"	
Reading for Meaning	Why "Echo" Is a Myth	
Beyond the Lesson	➕ OPTIONAL: Learn More About Echoes	

Big Ideas

Myths are part of the foundation of Western literature and have contributed themes and archetypal characters that are part of our culture even today.

Materials

Supplied

- "Echo," *K¹² Classics for Young Readers, Volume B,* pp. 28–29
- *K¹² Language Arts Activity Book,* p. 40

Story Synopsis

In this Roman myth, the young girl Echo teases too much and angers Juno, the queen of the gods. Juno punishes the young girl by making sure she is never able to speak first but only answer when called. The young girl fades until she is nothing but a voice.

Keywords

myth – a story that explains how something came to be and that usually contains magical figures as characters

 **60 minutes**

"Echo"

Work **together** with students to complete offline Get Ready, Guided Reading, Check Your Reading, Reading for Meaning, and Beyond the Lesson activities.

Get Ready

What Is an Echo?

Prepare students to read the myth "Echo" by talking about echoes.

1. Have students tell what an echo is.

2. Have students show how to make an echo. They can yell outside in a woody area, against large buildings, or even into a small tunnel such as an air duct. If there isn't a good place to make an actual echo, have students try to imitate the sound of an echo.

3. Remind students that myths explain how something came to be.

4. Have students guess how echoes came to be.

Objectives
- Connect to prior knowledge.
- Identify characteristics of different genres.

Guided Reading

Book Walk

Prepare students by taking them on a Book Walk of "Echo." Scan the story together and ask students to make predictions about it. For all questions in the Book Walk, answers will vary.

1. Have students use the **table of contents** in *K¹² Classics for Young Readers, Volume B*, to find "Echo" and turn to that page.

2. Point to and read aloud the **title of the story**.

3. Have students study the **illustration** and make **predictions** about the story based on the illustration.

   ▸ Who do you think the people are in the picture?
   ▸ Where are they?
   ▸ What do you think might happen in the story?

Objectives
- Use an illustration to make a prediction about a reading.
- Use text organizational features to locate and comprehend information (table of contents, illustrations).
- Read texts for literary experience.
- Read and discuss texts from different cultures, traditions, and time periods.

"Echo"

Now it's time to read "Echo." Have students sit next to you so that they can see the pictures and words while you read the story aloud.

1. Read the story aloud all the way through. Track with your finger so students can follow along.

2. Explain to students that you will read the story again. Ask them to chime in and read aloud with you. Tell them to think about myths and what we read in them. Tell students that you will pause at certain points in the story to discuss

3. Begin to reread and pause at the end of the second paragraph, after the phrase, "very naughty, too."

   ▸ What character have we met? Echo
   ▸ What do we learn about her? She is smart and pretty but she loves to tease and play tricks.

4. Read on, pausing at the end of the fifth paragraph, after the sentence, "Queen Juno was very angry."

   ▸ What new character have we met? Queen Juno
   ▸ What is she queen of? the gods
   ▸ What do you think will happen next? Answers will vary.

5. Continue reading to the end of the story.

Check Your Reading

"Echo"

Have students retell "Echo" in their own words to develop grammar, vocabulary, comprehension, and fluency skills. When finished, **ask students the following questions** to check comprehension and encourage discussion.

▸ Whom does Echo like to tease? all the people she knows
▸ How does Queen Juno punish Echo? She says that Echo can never speak first again, but only repeat what others say to her.
▸ What happens to Echo over time? She fades away until she is just a voice.
▸ How can you hear Echo? If you call to her, she'll answer you back.

Objectives
• Answer questions requiring literal recall of details.

Reading for Meaning

Why "Echo" Is a Myth

Have students identify how "Echo" fits the genre of mythology. Turn to page LC 40 in *K¹² Language Arts Activity Book*.

1. Remind students that a myth explains how something came to be and includes magical characters.

2. Have students answer questions to determine how the story is a myth.

3. Have students complete the Activity Book page.

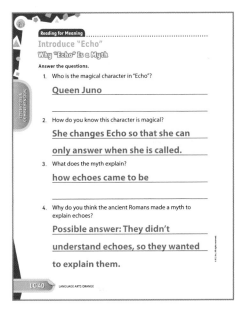

Beyond the Lesson

⊕ OPTIONAL: Learn More About Echoes

This activity is OPTIONAL. This activity is intended for students who have extra time and would enjoy learning more about echoes. Feel free to skip this activity.

1. Have students use the library or the Internet to learn more about how echoes work. Here are two websites that have information on echoes:

   ▶ *What Causes an Echo?* (www.worsleyschool.net/science/files/echo/echo.html)
   ▶ *How Does an Echo Work?* (www.whyzz.com/how-does-an-echo-work)

2. Have students try to create echoes in different locations, such as at home, near city buildings, and in natural areas such as woods.

Review "Echo"

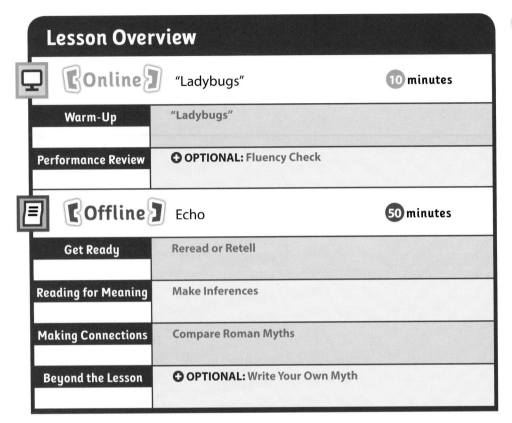

Lesson Overview

🖥 【Online】 "Ladybugs"　　　⑩ minutes

Warm-Up	"Ladybugs"
Performance Review	➕ OPTIONAL: Fluency Check

📄 【Offline】 Echo　　　㊿ minutes

Get Ready	Reread or Retell
Reading for Meaning	Make Inferences
Making Connections	Compare Roman Myths
Beyond the Lesson	➕ OPTIONAL: Write Your Own Myth

【Materials】

Supplied

- "Echo," *K¹² Classics for Young Readers, Volume B,* pp. 28–29
- *K¹² Language Arts Activity Book,* p. LC 41
- "Ladybugs" (optional)
- Fluency Performance Checklist (optional)

Also Needed

- crayons (optional)

Keywords

inference – a guess you make using the clues in a text and what you already know

myth – a story that explains how something came to be and that usually contains magical figures as characters

Advance Preparation

If you are not able to complete the online Warm-Up, then print the selection and listen to students read aloud.

Big Ideas

Readers make inferences about characters and their feelings and motivations to better understand an author's message or central idea.

 **10** minutes

"Ladybugs"

Students will work independently online to develop fluency and oral reading skills.

 Warm-Up ....

"Ladybugs"

The purpose of this activity is to improve students' oral reading and fluency. Students will read "Ladybugs." Remind students to listen to the model on each screen before they begin their recordings.

Objectives
- Increase oral reading skills.
- Increase fluency.

Offline Alternative

No computer access? Print a copy of "Ladybugs." Have students read it aloud. Make note of any pronunciation errors, and review those words with students.

 **Performance Review** ....

⊕ OPTIONAL: Fluency Check

Listen to students' recordings and use the checklist to review fluency and track performance. Keep the completed checklist so you can review students' progress over time.

Objectives
- Read aloud grade-level text with appropriate automaticity, prosody, accuracy, and rate.

 50 minutes

"Echo"

Work **together** with students to complete offline Get Ready, Reading for Meaning, Making Connections, and Beyond the Lesson activities.

Get Ready ....

Reread or Retell

If you'd like to, reread "Echo" to students. Otherwise, have students retell the story using the pictures as a guide. Make sure students tell the events in sequential order. Then move on to the next activity.

Objectives
- Recount stories, including fables and folktales from diverse cultures.

Reading for Meaning

Make Inferences

Model for students how to make inferences about "Echo." Then have students make their own inferences about what happens in the story.

1. Review the definition of **inference**.

2. Tell students that they can make inferences to answer questions about a story.

3. Model how to make an inference about Echo:

   ▸ I wonder why Echo likes to tease so much? In the story it says she laughs when she teases.
   ▸ I know that sometimes people think it's funny when they tease and play tricks on other people. It makes them feel like they're better than others.
   ▸ I think Echo thought it was funny to tease and it probably made her feel better than other people.

4. Model how to make an inference about Juno:

   ▸ I wonder why Juno gets angry when Echo plays a trick her?
   ▸ I know I get angry sometimes when people play tricks on me because I don't always like people laughing at me and making fun of me.
   ▸ I think Juno gets angry because she doesn't want Echo making fun of her.

5. Ask questions to lead students to make inferences about the characters in the text.

   ▸ What does Juno do to punish Echo? Juno fixes it so that Echo can never speak first, but can only answer when called.
   ▸ What do you think should happen to people who tease others a lot? Answers will vary.
   ▸ Why do you think Juno picked this punishment for Echo? Juno doesn't want Echo to be able to tease anyone ever again.

Making Connections

 Compare Roman Myths

Have students make connections between the myths read in this unit by choosing two myths to compare. Turn to page LC 41 in *K¹² Language Arts Activity Book*.

1. Review with students the titles of the three myths they read in this unit.

   ▸ "Clytie"
   ▸ "Pandora's Box"
   ▸ "Echo"

2. Tell students to choose two of the myths that they would like to compare and contrast.

3. Explain that students are going to complete the Venn diagram on the Activity Book page to compare and contrast the two myths.
   Say: When we compare two things, we say how they are alike. When we contrast two things, we say how they are different. You are going to compare and contrast two myths by explaining how they are alike and different. This diagram is a good tool to show how things are alike and different.

4. Have students complete the Activity Book page.

   ▶ They will write the title of one myth at the top of the left side of the diagram and the title of the other myth at the top of the right.

   ▶ On the left, they will write characteristics that are only in their first myth. On the right, they will write characteristics that are only in their second myth. In the middle, students will write characteristics that the two myths share.

5. Ask students which myth they liked best and why.

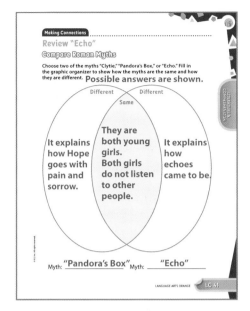

Making Connections
Review "Echo"
Compare Roman Myths

Choose two of the myths "Clytie," "Pandora's Box," or "Echo." Fill in the graphic organizer to show how the myths are the same and how they are different. **Possible answers are shown.**

Different   Different

Same

It explains how Hope goes with pain and sorrow.

They are both young girls. Both girls do not listen to other people.

It explains how echoes came to be.

Myth: "Pandora's Box"   Myth: "Echo"

LANGUAGE ARTS ORANGE   LC 41

Beyond the Lesson

⊕ OPTIONAL: Write Your Own Myth

This activity is OPTIONAL. This activity is intended for students who have extra time and enjoy creative writing and mythology. Feel free to skip this activity.

1. Tell students that they are going to write their own myth.

2. Start by having students think of something in the world that they would like to explain.

3. Have students brainstorm the characters for their myth. Make sure they include at least one of the Roman gods they've learned about.

4. Have students brainstorm the central plot: How will they explain this phenomenon?

5. Have students write their own myth. They can illustrate their story if they like.

Objectives
- Make connections between text and the world.
- Make connections between text and self.

Introduce "A Day in Ancient Rome" (A)

Unit Overview

In this eleven-lesson unit, students will learn more about the culture of ancient Rome by reading fiction and nonfiction. They will identify facts, recognize character traits, and explore a literary theme while reading the following selections:

- ▸ "A Day in Ancient Rome"
- ▸ "Androcles and the Lion"
- ▸ "Pliny Saw It All"
- ▸ *Volcanoes!*

Lesson Overview

☰	[Offline] "A Day in Ancient Rome," Part 1	60 minutes

Get Ready	What Is a Fact?
	Words to Know
Guided Reading	Book Walk
	"A Day in Ancient Rome," Part 1
Check Your Reading	"A Day in Ancient Rome," Part 1
Reading for Meaning	Find the Facts
Making Connections	What I Want to Know

Advance Preparation

Read pages 18–21 of "A Day in Ancient Rome," before beginning the Guided Reading to identify Words to Know in the text.

Big Ideas

- ▸ Narrative text and expository text differ significantly—for example, in structure, content, and purpose.
- ▸ Comprehension is facilitated by an understanding of physical presentation (headings, subheads, graphics, and other features).
- ▸ Nonfiction texts differ from fiction texts in that they describe real or true things in life, rather than things made up by the author.

[Materials]

Supplied

- ● "A Day in Ancient Rome," *All About Ancient Rome,* pp. 18–25
- ● *K¹² Language Arts Activity Book,* p. LC 43

Article Synopsis

This article is an example of narrative nonfiction. The text describes a day in the life of a fictitious young girl who lives in ancient Rome. Though the character is fictional, the information about life in ancient Rome is factual. The first part of the article discusses the first part of the young girl's day, as she eats breakfast, goes to school, learns domestic skills, and plays at home.

Keywords

fact – something that can be proven true

fiction – make-believe stories

inference – a guess you make using the clues in a text and what you already know

nonfiction – writings about true things

opinion – something that a person thinks or believes, but which cannot be proven to be true

sidebar – a short text within a larger text that tells something related but not essential to the main story

 **60 minutes**

"A Day in Ancient Rome," Part 1

Work **together** with students to complete offline Get Ready, Guided Reading, Check Your Reading, Reading for Meaning, and Making Connections activities.

Get Ready

What Is a Fact?

Review with students what facts are, how to identify them, and how to differentiate them from opinions.

1. Have students tell a **fact** they know. If students have trouble thinking of a fact, give them examples, such as *The sun is hot, The earth is round,* or *Today it is cloudy.*

2. Review the definition of a fact as something that can be proven true.

3. List some resources where someone could look for facts: nonfiction books, encyclopedias, Internet sites, atlases, almanacs, and so forth.

4. Ask students if they could find proof of their fact by looking in sources such as the ones you listed.

5. Explain that when judging whether something is a fact, students don't actually have to look up the fact. They just need to know whether they could find the fact in a resource if they wanted to.

6. Ask students if they know what an **opinion** is. something that a person thinks or believes, but which cannot be proven to be true

7. Have students tell an opinion about the fact they gave earlier. Tell students that there can be many different opinions about a fact.
   Examples: Sunny days are the best. Rainy days are boring.

8. Review that nonfiction texts contain facts.

Objectives

- Define fact.
- Define opinion.
- Distinguish between fact and opinion.
- Define nonfiction.
- Increase concept and content vocabulary.

Words to Know

Before reading "A Day in Ancient Rome," Part 1, go over Words to Know with students.

1. Have students say each word aloud.

2. Ask students if they know what each word means.

   ▸ If students know a word's meaning, have them define it and use it in a sentence.
   ▸ If students don't know a word's meaning, read them the definition and discuss the word with them.

ancient – very old; from times very long ago

bargaining – discussing the price of something before buying it

chariot – a two-wheeled cart pulled by horses that was used in battle or races in ancient times

rhetoric – public speaking

spin – to make thread from tiny, thin strands of a fiber such as wool

tunic – a loose piece of clothing that hangs to the knees and was worn in ancient times

tutor – a teacher who gives private lessons to a student

weave – to make something by passing strands of material over and under each other

Guided Reading

Book Walk

Prepare students by taking them on a Book Walk of *All About Ancient Rome*. Scan the magazine together and ask students to make predictions about the article. For all questions in the Book Walk, answers will vary.

1. Show students the **front cover** and **back cover** of the magazine. Point to the **magazine title** and read it aloud. Review that the magazine is a collection of nonfiction articles.

2. Locate the **table of contents** inside the magazine.

3. Point to "A Day in Ancient Rome" in the table of contents and read the title aloud. Find the article in the magazine using the table of contents and turn to that page.

4. Point to and read the title of the article.

   ▶ What do you think this article is about?
   ▶ What do you already know about ancient Rome?

5. Look through pages 18–21 of the article with students. Have students describe what they see. Point out the **photographs** and **illustrations** and have students make predictions about the article by asking them the following questions.

   ▶ What kinds of people do you see in the illustrations?
   ▶ Why do you think these are illustrations and not photographs?
   ▶ What do you see that reminds you of your life? What do you see that is different from your life?

Objectives

- Use text organizational features to locate and comprehend information (table of contents, illustrations, captions, photographs).
- Use an illustration to make a prediction about a reading.
- Use title of the selection to make a prediction.
- Distinguish between fiction and nonfiction.
- Read texts to gain information.
- Use context clues to determine word meanings.
- Make inferences using text and prior knowledge.

"A Day in Ancient Rome," Part 1

Now it's time to read pages 18–21 of "A Day in Ancient Rome" (Part 1). Have students sit next to you so that they can see the pictures and words while you read the article aloud.

1. Read pages 18–21 aloud all the way through. Stop at the end of the page 21, after the phrase, "and he brought her a toy camel." Track with your finger so students can follow along. Read the body of the article first. Then point to the illustration on each page and read the caption. Read the sidebar after reading the main body of the text on that page.

2. Explain to students that you will read the article again and that this time they are to chime in and read aloud with you. Tell students to think about the girl in the story and what she does and that you will pause at certain points in the story to discuss.

3. Reread pages 18–19 of the article and then discuss with students the special type of nonfiction that they are reading.

   ▸ Is Julia real or a fictional character made up by the author? fictional Why do you think this? Possible answer: to make the article more interesting

   ▸ Explain that this article is a special kind of nonfiction that combines factual information with characters like those found in **fiction**. Review the definition of fiction. Sometimes authors of nonfiction add fictional details, such as characters, to make the story more interesting. In this article, the character Julia and her friends and family are fictional. What they feel and think is fictional. But the things they do in ancient Rome are real and factual.

   ▸ On page 19, point to parts of the first paragraph that are facts: Shops sell things like sandals and glass. The character Julia eats bread for breakfast. Explain that what the shops sell and the kind of food available are facts because you can look in a resource to prove what ancient Romans sold in shops and ate for breakfast.

   ▸ Point to parts of the text that are fictional: It will be a beautiful day (page 18) and Julia's favorite shop is the bakery (page 19). Explain that these are not facts because these are the fictional character Julia's feelings about the day and bakeries, and they can't be proven.

   ▸ Tell students that as they read the rest of the article, they should think about which parts of the story are factual and which parts are fictional.

4. Reread to the middle of page 20, pausing after the sentence, "Doing lessons all morning made her hungry." Remind students that they can use context clues to unlock the meaning of unfamiliar words. Have students point to the context clue that defines **rhetoric**. public speaking

5. Have students make an inference about the teaching of rhetoric in ancient Rome.

   ▸ Why do you think only boys in ancient Rome learned rhetoric? Only boys will have the need for public speaking skills; only boys are in government.

6. Read to the end of page 21. Have students make an inference about Julia's life.

   ▸ What else does Julia learn besides what she learns in school? She learns to do things around her house.

   ▸ Why does Julia only go to school for half the day and learn skills around the house for the other half? Julia and girls need to learn how to run households. That will be their job in the future.

Check Your Reading

"A Day in Ancient Rome," Part 1

Have students retell the first part of the article in their own words to develop grammar, vocabulary, comprehension, and fluency skills. When finished, **ask students the following questions** to check comprehension and encourage discussion.

Objectives
- Answer questions requiring literal recall of details.

▶ What kinds of goods were sold in ancient Roman shops? leather sandals, wine, glass, pottery, baked goods

▶ Where did the teachers in ancient Rome come from? Greece

▶ What subjects were taught to girls in ancient Roman schools? To boys? Girls learned to read, write, and do math. Boys learned rhetoric.

▶ What was a girl in ancient Rome expected to do when she was about 14? She was expected to get married and move into her husband's home.

▶ What were toys in ancient Rome made of? Use the sidebar to find the answer. clay, metal

Reading for Meaning

Find the Facts

Help students distinguish between fact and fiction in the article by modeling how to identify facts.

Objectives
- Define fact.
- Distinguish between fiction and nonfiction.
- Identify facts.

1. Remind students that "A Day in Ancient Rome" is a nonfiction article that has some fictional elements.

2. Explain that Julia is a fictional character.
   Say: We know that Julia is a fictional character and not an actual person. We cannot find information about this particular girl in a reference book. But her character is based on what real children in ancient Rome were like. The author has made up Julia's thoughts and feelings, but what she does in her daily life is what many Roman children would have done.

3. Explain to students that you will help them figure out what parts of the article are facts and what parts are fiction.

4. Reread the first page and a half of the article, pausing after the sentence, "She buys a thick slice of brad for breakfast." To identify the facts in the article, model for students how to ask questions.
   Say: When I read a passage about what Julia does, I first take out her name. Then I think about whether girl in ancient Rome would do things like go to school early in the morning, pass by shops that sell the goods described, and eat bread for breakfast. I ask myself, "Could I find out from a book or the Internet whether a girl in ancient Rome would do these things?" The answer is yes. I could look up whether Roman girls went to school, and what Romans sold in shops and ate for breakfast. So these pieces of information must be facts.

5. Point out the fictional elements on the first page and a half, such as Julia's feelings about the day and her favorite store.

6. Read on to the middle of page 20 and pause after the sentence, "Doing lessons all morning made her hungry." Have students point out the factual and fictional elements. Help students identify these elements if they have difficulty.

   ▶ **Facts:** People bargained for goods; teachers came from Greece; girls learned reading, writing, and math but not rhetoric; ancient Romans ate foods such as bread, eggs, cheese, and salad; some Roman men were soldiers and went to Egypt.
   ▶ **Fictions:** Julia tries hard to pay attention in school; Julia looks forward to lunch.

7. Read to the end of page 21 and pause. Have students point out the facts and the fictitious elements on this page.

   ▶ **Facts:** Girls learned skills such as spinning, weaving, and cooking; girls married at around 14 and moved in with their husbands; children played with toys such as animals and chariots made of metal and clay.
   ▶ **Fictions:** Julia likes to play with her sister and their toys; Julia has an uncle.

Making Connections

 What I Want to Know

Help students ask questions as they read, as well as think about the answers in the text, by having them start a Know-Wonder-Learn (KWL) chart on page LC 43 in *K¹² Language Arts Activity Book*.

1. Have students fill in the Know column of the chart with at least three facts from pages 18–21 of "A Day in Ancient Rome."

2. Tell students that while they now know some facts about life for children in ancient Rome, there must be more.

3. Tell students that good readers ask questions as they read and then look to find the answers. Explain the six ways to start a question about what they are reading: *Who, What, Where, When, Why,* and *How.* These are called the 5Ws and H questions.
   Say: You have written down some facts you already know. What are some questions that you have about life in ancient Rome? What do you wonder?

4. Have students complete the Wonder column of the chart with at least three questions that begin with one of the 5Ws and H. Their questions may be on any topic about daily life in ancient Rome. Students' questions need not align with the facts they entered in the Know column, because students may wonder about completely different subjects related to daily life in ancient Rome. Possible answers:

   ▶ **Know:** Ancient Romans had bakeries. Roman girls went to school. Roman girls also learned how to spin and weave.
   ▶ **Wonder:** What did ancient Roman houses look like? Why did Roman girls get married at 14? What other toys did Roman children have?

5. Explain that students will fill in the Learn column after they finish reading the article.

6. Keep the Activity Book page in a safe place so students can add to it after reading the rest of the article.

 Objectives
- Generate questions before reading.
- Identify important questions that need to be answered (5Ws and H).
- Make connections between text and self.

Introduce "A Day in Ancient Rome" (B)

Lesson Overview

💻 **【Online】**	"The Great Wall of China"	**10** minutes
Warm-Up	"The Great Wall of China"	
📄 **【Offline】**	"A Day in Ancient Rome," Part 2	**50** minutes
Get Ready	Recall the Facts	
	Words to Know	
Guided Reading	Book Walk	
	"A Day in Ancient Rome," Part 2	
Check Your Reading	"A Day in Ancient Rome," Part 2	
Reading for Meaning	What I Learned	
Making Connections	Life Today and Long Ago	
Beyond the Lesson	⊕ OPTIONAL: Learn More About Daily Life in Ancient Rome	

【Materials】

Supplied

- "A Day in Ancient Rome," *All About Rome*, pp. 18–25
- *K¹² Language Arts Activity Book*, p. LC 43
- "The Great Wall of China" (optional)

Article Synopsis

The second part of this article about a fictitious girl in ancient Rome discusses the Roman baths and the evening meal of a Roman family.

Keywords

bold type – type that is darker than the surrounding text that draws attention to a word or phrase

caption – writing under a picture that describes the picture

fact – something that can be proven true

fiction – make-believe stories

inference – a guess you make using the clues in a text and what you already know

narrative – text genre in which a story is told; a narrative text usually includes characters, setting, and plot

nonfiction – writings about true things

Advance Preparation

If you are not able to complete the online Warm-Up, then print the selection and listen to students read aloud. Read pages 22–25 of "A Day in Ancient Rome" before beginning the Guided Reading to identify Words to Know in the text. Have students gather the partially completed KWL chart on page LC 43 in *K¹² Language Arts Activity Book*.

Big Ideas

Active, strong readers employ these reading strategies:

▸ Use existing knowledge to make sense of texts.
▸ Ask questions before, during, and after reading.
▸ Make connections between text and self.

 **10 minutes**

"The Great Wall of China"

Students will work independently online to develop fluency and oral reading skills.

Warm-Up

"The Great Wall of China"

The purpose of this activity is to improve students' oral reading and fluency. Students will read "The Great Wall of China." Remind students to listen to the model on each screen before they begin their recording.

 Objectives
- Increase oral reading skills.
- Increase fluency.

Offline Alternative

No computer access? Print a copy of "The Great Wall of China." Have students read it aloud. Make note of any pronunciation errors, and review those words with students.

 **50 minutes**

"A Day in Ancient Rome," Part 2

Work **together** with students to complete offline Get Ready, Guided Reading, Check Your Reading, Reading for Meaning, Making Connections, and Beyond the Lesson activities.

Get Ready

Recall the Facts

Review what students read in the first part of "A Day in Ancient Rome" to reinforce their comprehension of the text and help identify facts.

 Objectives
- Identify facts.
- Increase concept and content vocabulary.

1. Review with students that the article featured a fictitious girl named Julia. Remind students that Julia is made up by the author, but she represents a typical girl in ancient Rome.

2. Have students recall some of the facts in the article about daily life in ancient Rome. Possible answers: There were shops that sold items like glass and pottery. Students learned from Greek teachers. Girls went to school and learned things like reading, writing, and math. Only boys learned rhetoric.

TIP If students retell fictional elements of Julia's life, such as her feelings about an activity, review with students the difference between fact and fiction. Then give them one or two facts from the article before having them identify other facts themselves.

Words to Know

Before reading the second half of "A Day in Ancient Rome" go over Words to Know from Part 1 of the article with students.

1. Ask students to define the following words and use them in sentences:

   ancient   spin
   bargaining   tutor
   chariot   weave
   rhetoric

2. Correct any incorrect or vague definitions.

3. Have students say the word below, which they will read in Part 2.

4. Ask students if they know what the word means.

   ▸ If students know the word's meaning, have them define it and use it in
     a sentence.
   ▸ If students don't know the word's meaning, read them the definition and
     discuss the word with them.

steam – water in the form of hot gas

Guided Reading

Book Walk

Prepare students by taking them on a Book Walk of *All About Ancient Rome*. Scan the magazine together and ask students to make predictions about the article.

1. Read the **title** of the magazine aloud.

2. Have students use the **table of contents** to find "A Day in Ancient Rome" and turn to that page.

3. Have students read the title of the article aloud.

4. Tell students that you are going to read the second part of the article.

5. Look through pages 22–25 of the article. Have students describe what they see. Point to the **photographs** and **illustrations** and have them make predictions using the pictures, asking them the following questions.

   ▸ What do you see in the photos on page 22 of the reading selection?
     Roman baths
   ▸ What do you see in the photo on page 23 of the text? the remains of a
     Roman bath Why do you think this is a photo of the remains and not
     a photo of Julia and Flavia at the baths? Answers will vary. Students
     should recognize that the baths are real, but Julia and Flavia are fictional
     characters. We don't have photos of them.
   ▸ What looks unusual in the last picture in the article? Answers will vary.
     Possible answers: I didn't expect Julia and Flavia to look like this; Julia and
     Flavia look like they are made of stone.

Objectives

- Use text organizational features to locate and comprehend information (table of contents, glossary, chapter, index, title, author, illustrations, caption).
- Use an illustration to make a prediction about a reading.
- Read texts to gain information.
- Make inferences using text prior knowledge.

"A Day in Ancient Rome," Part 2

Now it's time to read pages 22–25 of "A Day in Ancient Rome" (Part 2). Have students sit next to you so that they can see the pictures and words while you read the article aloud.

1. Remind students of where the first part of the article finished. Reread page 21 to refresh students' memory of what happened at the end of the first part.

2. Read pages 22–25 of the article aloud all the way through. Stop at the end of the article. Track with your finger so students can follow along. Read the body of the article first. Then point to the photograph and illustrations and read the captions.

3. Explain to students that you will read the story again and that this time they are to chime in and read aloud with you. Tell students to look for new facts about life in ancient Rome and that you will pause at certain points in the story to discuss.

4. Reread page 22 and pause after the sentence, "The girls jump right out again." Have students make inferences and predictions about what they read by asking them these questions:

   ▸ Where does Julia go? Why? to the baths; to get clean
   ▸ Why do you think ancient Romans went to bath houses instead of having baths in their houses? Possible answers: They couldn't afford baths in their houses. There was no way to keep a bath in a house. They wanted to bathe with their friends.
   ▸ What do you think will happen next? Possible answers: They will do other things at the baths or go to the stores.

5. Reread page 23 and pause after the phrase, "quick dip in the cold water." Have students recall what they just read.

   ▸ Say: What are the steps in the girls bathing routine? They jump in a pool of cold water; they go in a pool of warm water; they go to the steam room where servants scrape dirt off their skin; they go back in the warm water; they finish with a quick dip in the cold water.

6. Read to the end of the article. Have students make inferences about Julia's family by asking them these questions:

   ▸ Why do Julia and her family have servants? Possible answers: They're rich. Everyone in ancient Rome had servants.
   ▸ Why do Julia and her family lie down when they eat? Possible answers: Her family was rich, and rich people liked to relax while they ate. The ancient Romans thought that was the best way to eat.

Check Your Reading

"A Day in Ancient Rome," Part 2
Have students retell the second part of the article in their own words to develop grammar, vocabulary, comprehension, and fluency skills. When finished, **ask students the following questions** to check comprehension and encourage discussion.

▶ What is a fact about the ancient Roman bath houses? Possible answers: Neighbors go to the baths together. There are pools of hot and cold water and steam rooms. Servants scrape the dirt off people in the baths.

▶ Describe something from today's reading that is fictional. Possible answers: Julia likes going to the baths. She sees her friend Flavia at the baths. Julia's favorite food is pork.

▶ How did the ancient Romans eat dinner? lying on couches on their left sides

▶ Name one food that the ancient Romans ate for dinner. Possible answers: vegetables, pork, figs, grapes, lettuce

Objectives
• Answer questions requiring literal recall of details.

Reading for Meaning

 What I Learned

Have students complete the KWL chart on page LC 43 in *K¹² Language Arts Activity Book*.

1. Review with students what they wrote in the first two columns of their KWL chart.

2. Tell students that in this half of the article, they learned more facts about life for children in ancient Rome.

3. Ask students to recall some facts from the article.

4. Have students complete the Learn column of the chart with facts they learned in the second part of the article.

5. After they have finished, ask students if all of their questions from the Know column were answered. If not, have students tell where they might find the answers, such as the Internet, nonfiction books, or an encyclopedia.

Objectives
• Distinguish between fiction and nonfiction.
• Identify facts.
• Apply information read to answer questions.

Making Connections

Life Today and Long Ago

Help students make a connection to life in ancient Rome by thinking about how their own daily lives are similar to and different from the life of the character Julia in "A Day in Ancient Rome."

Objectives
- Make connections between text and self.

1. Have students retell the parts of daily life in ancient Rome that they read about in the article, including eating, going to school, playing, and bathing.

2. Have students describe some of these routines in their own daily lives. They could describe how and what they eat for breakfast or dinner, how they clean themselves, and what learning is like for them.

3. Have students compare and contrast their lives with the life of Julia from the article. Answers will vary.

   ▶ How was life for Julia and the ancient Romans like yours?
   ▶ How was life for Julia and the ancient Romans different from yours?

Beyond the Lesson

⊕ OPTIONAL: Learn More About Daily Life in Ancient Rome

This activity is OPTIONAL. This activity is intended for students who have extra time and would enjoy learning more about ancient Roman culture. Feel free to skip this activity.

Objectives
- Make connections between text and the world.
- Answer who, what, where, when, why, and how questions.

Allow students to find answers to the unanswered questions in their KWL chart. If they're interested, have them conduct more research on ancient Rome. They may want to start with some of the following books and websites:

▶ *Growing Up in Ancient Rome*, Mike Corbishley. Mahwah, N.J.: Troll Associates, 1994
▶ *Daily Life in Ancient Rome*, http://rome.mrdonn.org/
▶ BBC's *Primary History: Romans*, http://www.bbc.co.uk/schools/primaryhistory/romans/

Introduce "Androcles and the Lion"

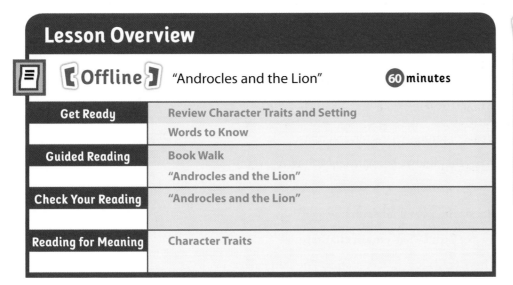

Lesson Overview

Offline	"Androcles and the Lion"	60 minutes

Get Ready	Review Character Traits and Setting
	Words to Know
Guided Reading	Book Walk
	"Androcles and the Lion"
Check Your Reading	"Androcles and the Lion"
Reading for Meaning	Character Traits

Advance Preparation

Read "Androcles and the Lion" before beginning the Guided Reading activity to identify Words to Know in the text.

Big Ideas

To understand and interpret a story, readers need to understand and describe characters and what they do.

Materials

Supplied

- "Androcles and the Lion," *K¹² Classics for Young Readers, Volume B*, pp. 30–35
- *K¹² Language Arts Activity Book*, p. LC 44

Story Synopsis

In this story, set in ancient Rome, the runaway slave Androcles removes a painful thorn from the paw of a lion. Androcles and the lion become friends. Androcles is then recaptured by the Romans and forced to face a hungry lion before a crowd in an arena. The lion turns out to be the same lion Androcles saved, and the amazed crowd calls for their release. Readers may want to note that Androcles is a slave with a cruel master.

Keywords

character – a person or animal in a story

main character – an important person, animal or other being who is central to the plot

setting – when and where a story takes place

trait – a quality of a person or other object; what something is like

 **60 minutes**

"Androcles and the Lion"

Work **together** with students to complete offline Get Ready, Guided Reading, Check Your Reading, and Reading for Meaning activities.

Get Ready

Review Character Traits and Setting

Review with students the literary elements of setting, character, and traits.

1. Have students tell some of the things they know about ancient Rome.

2. Review the definition of **setting**: when and where a story takes place.

3. Review with students that fictional stories have **characters**.

4. Have students define what a character is and what a **main character** is.

5. Remind students that characters have **traits**, or characteristics. The traits may include the character's physical appearance and how the character behaves.

6. Have students describe some of their own traits.

7. Have students tell how we learn about characters' traits in stories. through what they do, what they say, what they think, and what others say about them
If students have difficulty remembering how to learn about characters' traits, prompt them with the following model:
Say: I remember that one way to learn about a character's traits is by looking at what they say in a story. Can you remember another way we learn about characters and their traits?

Objectives
- Define setting.
- Define character.
- Define main character.
- Define character traits.

Words to Know

Before reading "Androcles and the Lion," go over Words to Know with students.

1. Have students say the word aloud.

2. Ask students if they know what the word means.

   ▸ If students know the word's meaning, have them define it and use it in a sentence.
   ▸ If students don't know the word's meaning, read them the definition and discuss the word with them.

game – wild animals, birds, or fish that are hunted for food or sport

Guided Reading

Book Walk

Prepare students by taking them on a Book Walk of "Androcles and the Lion." Scan the story together and ask students to make predictions about it. For all questions in the Book Walk, answers will vary.

1. Have students use the **table of contents** of *K¹² Classics for Young Readers, Volume B,* to find "Androcles and the Lion," and turn to that page.

2. Point to the **title of the story** and read it aloud.

3. Have students study the **illustrations** and make **predictions** about the story based on the illustrations, asking them the following questions:

   ▸ How would you describe the lion in the illustrations?
   ▸ How does the lion look compared to other lions you have seen?
   ▸ What can you predict about the relationship between Androcles and the lion?

"Androcles and the Lion"

Now it's time to read the story. Have students sit next to you so that they can see the pictures and words while you read the story aloud.

1. Read the story aloud all the way through. Track with your finger so students can follow along.

2. Explain to students that you will read the story again and that this time they are to chime in and read aloud with you. Tell students to think about the characters of Androcles and the lion and that you will pause at certain points in the story to discuss.

3. Reread the first two paragraphs of the story on page 30, ending with the phrase, "than his master had been," and then pause to discuss.

   ▸ What character have we met? Androcles
   ▸ What did he do? run away from his master
   ▸ What do you think will happen next? Answers will vary.

4. Continue to read, pausing on page 31 after the phrase, "soft part of his paw."

   ▸ What other character have we met? the lion
   ▸ What problem does the lion have? It has a thorn stuck in its paw.
   ▸ What does the lion want? It wants Androcles to take out the thorn.
   ▸ What do you think will happen next? Answers will vary.

5. Continue reading and pause to discuss at the top of page 32 after the sentence, "They lived together in the cave and became good friends."

   ▸ Why did the lion stay with Androcles and hunt for him? The lion was happy and thankful that Androcles had helped him.

6. Read on, pausing to discuss midway through page 33 after the phrase, "fight for his life with a hungry lion."

   ▸ Where is Androcles? in prison
   ▸ What does he have to do? fight with a lion to save his own life
   ▸ What do you think will happen next? Answers will vary.

7. Read to the end of the story.

Check Your Reading

"Androcles and the Lion"

Have students retell the story in their own words to develop grammar, vocabulary, comprehension, and fluency skills. When finished, **ask students the following questions** to check comprehension and encourage discussion.

   ▸ What is the setting of the story? ancient Rome
   ▸ Who are the two main characters in the story? Androcles, the lion
   ▸ Why does Androcles run away from his master? His master is cruel and Androcles doesn't have enough food. He also has to work very hard.
   ▸ What happens to the lion and Androcles after Androcles removes the thorn? They become friends.
   ▸ What does Androcles do when the lion charges him in the circus? He stands still and waits.
   ▸ What happens when the people see that Androcles and the lion are friends? Androcles and the lion are set free.

Objectives
- Answer questions requiring literal recall of details.
- Identify setting.
- Identify main characters.

Reading for Meaning

Character Traits

Guide students to analyze Androcles and his character traits to prepare to understand the plot and theme of the story. Turn to page LC 44 in *K¹² Language Arts Activity Book*.

1. Model for students how to identify a character's traits and evidence in the text that supports your idea:

   ▸ I think that one trait of Androcles is that he is brave. There is support in the story for my idea.
   ▸ For example, Androcles runs away from the cruel master in Rome and he runs to the forest where there are wild animals. I think that's brave because he could have been caught by his master or attacked by an animal.

Objectives
- Describe characters and their traits.
- Describe characters by what they do, what they say, or what others say about them.
- Describe the characters in the story using evidence from the text.

▶ Then, the author says on the second page of the story that Androcles was a brave man. Also Androcles took the thorn out of the lion's paw, even though the lion could have hurt him.

▶ Finally on the fourth page of the story, it says that Androcles stands still in the circus and waits for the lion. He doesn't try to run. I think all of these examples show that Androcles is brave.

2. Have students complete the Activity Book page. Have them write a trait (different from your example of bravery) for Androcles in the center of the diagram and around it sentences that support that trait.

3. If students have difficulty thinking of another character trait Androcles exhibits, prompt them.
   Say: Androcles helps the lion because he sees the lion is suffering. What does this act show about Androcles? He is kind or caring.

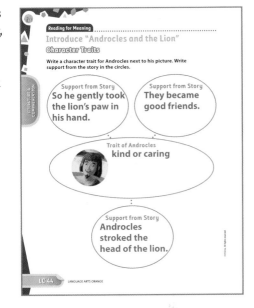

Explore "Androcles and the Lion"

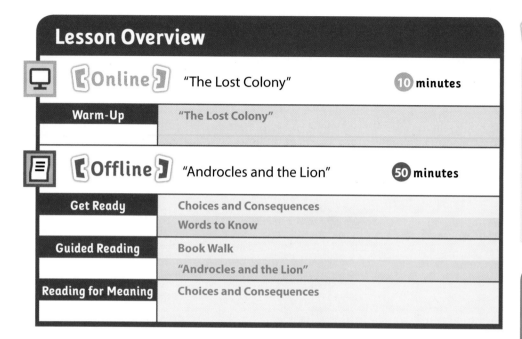

Lesson Overview

🖥 **〔Online〕** "The Lost Colony"	**10** minutes
Warm-Up	"The Lost Colony"

📄 **〔Offline〕** "Androcles and the Lion"	**50** minutes
Get Ready	Choices and Consequences
	Words to Know
Guided Reading	Book Walk
	"Androcles and the Lion"
Reading for Meaning	Choices and Consequences

〔Materials〕

Supplied
- "Androcles and the Lion," *K¹² Classics for Young Readers, Volume B,* pp. 30–35
- *K¹² Language Arts Activity Book,* p. LC 45
- "The Lost Colony" (optional)

Keywords

character – a person or animal in a story

consequence – what happens because of an action or event

Advance Preparation

If you are not able to complete the online Warm-Up, then print the selection and listen to students read aloud.

Big Ideas

- ▶ To understand and interpret a story, readers need to understand and describe characters and what they do.
- ▶ Identifying choices and consequences helps readers to understand characters and the central message in a story.

 **Online** **10** minutes

"The Lost Colony"

Students will work independently online to develop fluency and oral reading skills.

 **Warm-Up** ··

"The Lost Colony"

The purpose of this activity is to improve students' oral reading and fluency. Students will read "The Lost Colony." Remind students to listen to the model on each screen before they begin their recordings.

Objectives
- Increase oral reading skills.
- Increase fluency.

Offline Alternative

No computer access? Print a copy of "The Lost Colony." Have students read it aloud several times. Make note of any pronunciation errors, and review those words with students.

Offline **50** minutes

"Androcles and the Lion"

Work **together** with students to complete offline Get Ready, Guided Reading, and Reading for Meaning activities.

Get Ready ··

Choices and Consequences

Discuss with students that characters in stories often have to make choices and experience the consequences of their choices.

 Objectives
- Define consequence.
- Increase concept and content vocabulary.

1. Have students describe a choice they made today. Have them tell the options they had to choose from and which choice they made.
   Example: I had to choose between wearing my new, tight party shoes or my old, comfortable sneakers.

2. Explain to students that their choices have **consequences**, or things that happen because of what they do. The consequences are different depending on their choices. Have students describe the consequence of the choice they described.
   Example: I wore my new party shoes and now my feet hurt.

3. Explain that characters in stories often have to make choices, too. Sometimes the choices are difficult or serious, and the choices also have consequences.

4. Tell students that the choices characters make and the consequences of those choices tell us about the characters and their traits.

(TIP) If students have difficulty giving an example of a choice and consequence, provide an example. For instance, you could talk about trying to decide whether to do a chore or take a break. Describe the consequence of your choice—you had to wait to take your break, or you still had to do you chore.

Words to Know

Go over Words to Know with students.

1. Ask students to define the following word and use it in a sentence:

   game

2. Correct any incorrect or vague definitions.

Guided Reading

Book Walk

Prepare students by taking them on a Book Walk of "Androcles and the Lion." Scan the story together and ask students to revisit the characters and events. For all questions in the Book Walk, answers will vary.

1. Have students use the **table of contents** of *K¹² Classics for Young Readers, Volume B,* to locate "Androcles and the Lion" and turn to that page.

2. Have students read the title of the story aloud.

3. Have them look through the **illustrations** and tell how the story begins. If students have trouble remembering, prompt them.
   Say: I remember how the story begins. There's a slave named Androcles, and he has a very cruel master. Androcles decides to run away one night. What do you remember about the beginning?

> **Objectives**
> - Use text organizational features to locate and comprehend information (table of contents, illustrations).
> - Read texts for literary experience.
> - Read and discuss texts from different cultures, traditions, and time periods.

"Androcles and the Lion"

Now it's time to reread "Androcles and the Lion." Have students sit next to you so that they can see the pictures and words while you read the story aloud.

1. Explain to students that they will focus on the choices Androcles makes as you read. Ask them to chime in and read aloud with you. Tell students that you will pause at certain points in the story to talk about what happens.

2. Begin to reread the story, pausing at the start of the second paragraph on page 30 after the phrase, "Androcles ran away."
   Say: What choice does Androcles make? to run away from his master

3. Read on, pausing to discuss after the third paragraph on page 31, which ends with the phrase, "in his joy."

   ▶ What does Androcles decide to do for the lion? pull out the thorn
   ▶ Do you think that this is a hard decision to make? Why or why not? Answers will vary.

4. Continue reading, pausing to discuss on page 33 after the sentence, "Androcles was frightened, but he did not move."

   ▶ Why do you think Androcles stood still when the lion came rushing out of the cage? Answers will vary.

Reading for Meaning

 Choices and Consequences

Guide students to identify Androcles's choices and their consequences. Turn to page LC 45 in *K¹² Language Arts Activity Book*.

1. Explain to students that when we look closely at the choices a character makes and the consequences of his actions, we learn something about the character.

2. Model for students how to identify Androcles's choices and their consequences. Reread the first two paragraphs of the story and remind students of the first decision that Androcles makes: to run away from his master.

3. Explain that Androcles had a choice: He could stay with his master or run away. Discuss the consequences of each choice.
   Say: If Androcles stayed with his master, he would have suffered and been a slave. If he ran away, he might suffer in the forest, but he would be free. He knew what would happen if he stayed, but he didn't know what might happen if he ran away. Androcles made the choice to run away because he decided that the animals in the forest would not be any more cruel than his master, and at least he would be free.

4. Have students tell what happens because Androcles chooses to run away. He is free, and he meets the lion.
   Explain that this is the consequence of his choice.

5. Have students complete the Activity Book page.

> **Objectives**
> • Identify choices that a character makes and their consequences.

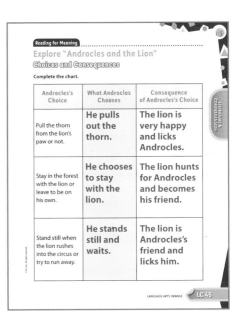

Reading for Meaning
Explore "Androcles and the Lion"
Choices and Consequences
Complete the chart.

Androcles's Choice	What Androcles Chooses	Consequence of Androcles's Choice
Pull the thorn from the lion's paw or not.	He pulls out the thorn.	The lion is very happy and licks Androcles.
Stay in the forest with the lion or leave to be on his own.	He chooses to stay with the lion.	The lion hunts for Androcles and becomes his friend.
Stand still when the lion rushes into the circus or try to run away.	He stands still and waits.	The lion is Androcles's friend and licks him.

LANGUAGE ARTS ORANGE   LC 45

Review "Androcles and the Lion"

Lesson Overview

[Offline] "Androcles and the Lion"   **60** minutes

Get Ready	Reread or Retell
Reading for Meaning	Problem and Solution
Making Connections	Theme in "Androcles and the Lion"

Materials

Supplied
- "Androcles and the Lion," *K¹² Classics for Younger Readers, Volume B,* pp. 30–35
- *K¹² Language Arts Activity Book,* pp. LC 44–46

Keywords

consequence – what happens because of an action or event

problem – an issue a character must solve in a story

solution – how a character solves a problem in a story

theme – the author's message or big idea

Advance Preparation

Have students gather the completed pages LC 44 and 45 in *K¹² Language Arts Activity Book* (Character Traits page and Choices and Consequences page).

Big Ideas

▸ Readers need to synthesize, draw conclusions, and interpret what they have read.

▸ To understand and interpret a story, readers need to understand and describe characters and what they do.

▸ The problems characters face is a central element of fiction. To solve their problems, characters must make choices. Understanding those choices and their consequences is key to understanding characters and the central message of the story.

 **60 minutes**

"Androcles and the Lion"

Work **together** with students to complete offline Get Ready, Reading for Meaning, and Making Connections activities.

Get Ready ....

Reread or Retell

If you'd like to, reread "Androcles and the Lion" to students. Otherwise, have students retell the story using the pictures as a guide. Make sure students tell the events in sequential order. Then move on to the next activity.

Objectives
- Recount stories, including fables and folktales from diverse cultures.

Reading for Meaning ....

Problem and Solution

Help students identify Androcles's problems, the choices he makes to solve his problems, and the consequences of those choices. Turn to page LC 46 in *K¹² Language Arts Activity Book*.

1. Explain that we have to make choices all the time to solve problems.

2. Give an example: You might not have enough money at the grocery store to make a purchase.

3. Identify your choices: You could choose not to purchase the item, buy a less expensive item, or go back to the store later when you have enough money.

4. Discuss the **consequences** of each choice. You may not be able to get what you need or you may have to spend more time coming back later.

5. Have students describe a problem they have faced. Guide them to identify the choices and consequences they needed to consider and describe how they solved the problem.

6. Explain that in stories, characters are faced with problems that need solutions. Define **problem** and **solution** as we use them in fiction (see Keywords).

7. Model for students how to identify a problem Androcles faces, the steps he takes to solve the problem (which may involve choices), and how he ends up solving the problem:

   ▸ Problem: Androcles is a slave to a cruel master.
   ▸ Steps he takes: He chooses to run away. He creeps along city walls. He runs until he's tired.
   ▸ Consequences of his choices: He finds food in the forest. He finds a cave and chooses to stay in it.
   ▸ Solution to the problem: Androcles escapes and lives in the forest.

8. Have students complete Exercises 1–4 on the Activity Book page to identify another problem that Androcles faces and the choices he makes to reach a solution. (They will complete Exercise 5 in the next activity.)

Objectives
- Define problem.
- Define solution.
- Identify the problem a character faces.
- Identify the solution to a problem a character faces.
- Identify choices that a character makes and their consequences.

Making Connections

Theme in "Androcles and the Lion"

Teach students how to recognize the theme by analyzing the problems and solutions in the story. Have students gather their completed Character Traits page and Choices and Consequences page, and turn to page LC 46 in *K¹² Language Arts Activity Book.*

1. Remind students that stories often have a big idea, or **theme** that the author is trying to tell the reader. Review the definition of theme. **Say:** We often learn about the theme through what happens to the characters in the story.

2. Remind students that a theme is expressed in a complete sentence that tells us something about people or life.

3. Tell students that you are going to help them think about a theme for this story.

4. Review what students learned about Androcles and his traits, choices, and solutions to problems by using the Character Traits page and the Choices and Consequences page.

5. Discuss with students what the theme might be for this story.

   ▶ What does Androcles decide to do for the lion even though he is afraid? help the lion by removing a thorn from his paw.

   ▶ What happens when Androcles removes the thorn? The lion is thankful and becomes Androcles's friend.

   ▶ What happens in the arena when the lion meets with Androcles? He is happy to see Androcles and doesn't hurt him.

   ▶ What do the people do when they hear Androcles's story? They let Androcles and the lion go free.

   ▶ What message is the author trying to tell us about people and how we should behave? Possible answers: Treat others kindly and they will be kind to you. A smaller creature can help a mighty creature. Help and friendship come in all sizes.

6. Have students complete Exercise 5 on the Theme in "Androcles and the Lion" page.

Objectives
- Define theme.
- Identify theme.

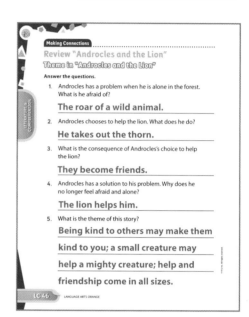

Introduce "Pliny Saw It All" (A)

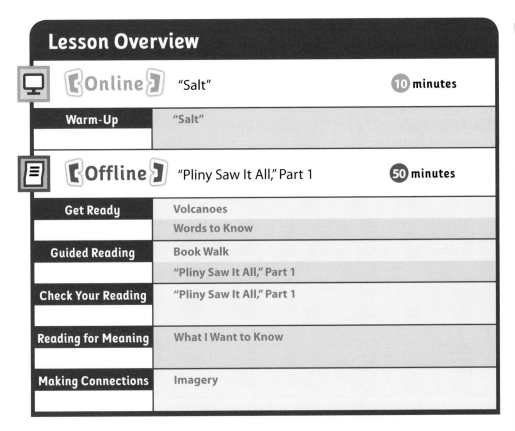

Lesson Overview

🖥 **【Online】**	"Salt"	**10** minutes
Warm-Up	"Salt"	

🗐 **【Offline】**	"Pliny Saw It All," Part 1	**50** minutes
Get Ready	Volcanoes	
	Words to Know	
Guided Reading	Book Walk	
	"Pliny Saw It All," Part 1	
Check Your Reading	"Pliny Saw It All," Part 1	
Reading for Meaning	What I Want to Know	
Making Connections	Imagery	

Materials

Supplied

- "Pliny Saw It All," *All About Ancient Rome*, pp. 26–35
- *K¹² Language Arts Activity Book*, p. LC 47
- "Salt" (optional)

Story Synopsis

In A.D. 79, Pliny the Younger was a witness to the eruption of the volcano Mount Vesuvius. He wrote his observations in letters that provide a record for history. The first part of this nonfiction article describes Pliny's accounts of what he saw.

Keywords

bold type – type that is darker than the surrounding text that draws attention to a word or phrase

fact – something that can be proven true

illustration – a drawing

imagery – language that helps readers create a picture in their minds

nonfiction – writings about true things

Advance Preparation

If you are not able to complete the online Warm-Up, then print the selection and listen to students read aloud. Read pages 26–29 of "Pliny Saw It All" before beginning the Guided Reading to identify Words to Know in the text.

Big Ideas

- ▶ Active, strong readers employ these reading strategies: using existing knowledge to make sense of texts; asking questions before, during, and after reading; and making connections between text and self.
- ▶ The use of imagery and sensory language creates detailed pictures in the reader's mind, so the reader can understand and appreciate the ideas and feelings the writer conveys.
- ▶ Readers who visualize, or form mental pictures, when they read have better recall of text than those who do not.

 **Online** **10 minutes**

"Salt"

Students will work independently online to develop fluency and oral reading skills.

Warm-Up ··

"Salt"

The purpose of this activity is to improve students' oral reading and fluency. Students will read "Salt." Remind students to listen to the model on each screen before they begin their recording.

───────────────────────────────────

Offline Alternative

No computer access? Print a copy of "Salt." Have students read it aloud several times. Make note of any pronunciation errors, and review those words with students.

> **Objectives**
> - Increase oral reading skills.
> - Increase fluency.

 **Offline** **50 minutes**

"Pliny Saw It All," Part 1

Work **together** with students to complete offline Get Ready, Guided Reading, Check Your Reading, Reading for Meaning, and Making Connections activities.

Get Ready ··

Volcanoes

Have students recall their knowledge of volcanoes and provide some new information on volcanoes.

1. Discuss volcanoes with students.

   ► What do volcanoes do? They erupt.
   ► What do volcanoes produce? lava, ash

2. If students are unfamiliar with volcanoes, provide some basic background information: Volcanoes are mountains that sometimes release hot gases, ash, rocks, and lava, which is flowing, melted rock.

3. Tell students that the gas and lava that come out of volcanoes may reach temperatures above 700 degrees Fahrenheit.

> **Objectives**
> - Connect text to prior knowledge.
> - Build background knowledge.
> - Increase concept and content vocabulary.

4. Help provide a context for understanding the heat of a volcano.

▸ What is the hottest day you can remember? Answers will vary. Explain to students that a volcano is much, much hotter than the hottest day they can remember.

▸ Do you know of any specific volcanoes? Answers will vary. If students don't know any volcanoes, give some examples such as Mauna Loa in Hawaii (the largest volcano on earth) and Mount Fuji in Japan, which is often seen in Japanese art.

Words to Know

Before reading "Pliny Saw It All," Part 1, go over Words to Know with students.

1. Have students say each word aloud.

2. Ask students if they know what each word means.

▸ If students know a word's meaning, have them define it and use it in a sentence.

▸ If students don't know a word's meaning, read them the definition and discuss the word with them.

ash – a grayish white powder that is left after something has burned

erupting – pushing out volcanic matter such as lava with great force

volcano – an opening in the surface of the earth through which gases, lava, and ash are forced out

Guided Reading

Book Walk

Prepare students by taking them on a Book Walk of *All About Ancient Rome*. Scan the magazine together and ask students to make predictions about the article. For all questions in the Book Walk, answers will vary.

1. Point to the **magazine title** and read it aloud. Review that the magazine is a collection of nonfiction articles about ancient Rome.

2. Locate the **table of contents** inside the magazine.

3. Point to "Pliny Saw It All" in the table of contents and read the title aloud. Find the article in the magazine using the table of contents.

   ▸ Who do you think Pliny was?
   ▸ What do you think he saw?

4. With students, look through pages 26–29 of the article. Have them describe what they see. Point out the **map** and **illustrations**. Have students make predictions about the article.

   ▸ Look at the map. What place do you think this article is about?
   ▸ What is happening in the illustrations?
   ▸ Why do you think these are illustrations and not photographs?

"Pliny Saw It All," Part 1

Now it's time to read pages 26–29 of "Pliny Saw It All" (Part 1). Have students sit next to you so that they can see the pictures and words while you read the article aloud.

1. Read pages 26–29 of the article all the way through. Stop at the end of the page 29, after the phrase "the volcano had completely buried both cities." Track with your finger so students can follow along.

2. Explain to students that you will read this part of the article again and that this time they are to chime in and read aloud with you. Tell them to think about what Pliny saw and how the volcano looked. Tell students that you will pause at certain points in the story to discuss.

3. Begin to reread. Pause after reading page 27 and point out the map on page 26 and discuss.

   ▸ Read the place names to students.
   ▸ Discuss the key and what it shows. Have students point to an example on the map of each item in the key.
   ▸ Have students locate Vesuvius on the map and use the compass to find the location of other points of interest in relation to Vesuvius.
     If you are at Vesuvius, in what direction is Misenum? west or northwest
     If you are at Vesuvius, in what direction is Pompeii? south or southeast

4. Point to the **bold type** words on the first page. Have students tell what text feature this is and why it's used. bold type; to emphasize important words

Objectives

- Use text organizational features to locate and comprehend information (table of contents).
- Use title of the selection to make a prediction.
- Use an illustration to make a prediction about a reading.
- Identify features of a nonfiction text.
- Read texts to gain information.
- Identify the purpose of and interpret information from features of informational texts: illustrations, graphs, charts, titles, text boxes, diagrams, headings, table of contents, graphic organizers, timelines, and maps.
- Identify the meaning of graphics and symbols: computer icons, map features, chart, and graph features.

5. Continue reading and pause in the middle of page 29, after the phrase, "right next to them."
   Say: What do you think will happen next?

6. Read to the end of page 29.

Check Your Reading
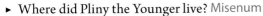

"Pliny Saw It All," Part 1

Have students retell the first part of the article in their own words to develop grammar, vocabulary, comprehension, and fluency skills. When finished, **ask students the following questions** to check comprehension and encourage discussion.

> **Objectives**
> • Answer questions requiring literal recall of details.

- ▶ Where did Pliny the Younger live? Misenum
- ▶ What was the name of the volcano that Pliny saw erupt? Mount Vesuvius
- ▶ How did Pliny describe the cloud of ash that came from the volcano? It looked like the trunk of a tree with small branches of ash shooting from the sides.
- ▶ What did Misenum look like the day after the volcano erupted? There was ash, which looked like snow, covering the ground.
- ▶ What did the volcano do to the cities of Pompeii and Herculaneum? completely buried them in ash and hot rocks

Reading for Meaning

 What I Want to Know

Help students ask questions as they read and think about the answers in the text by having them start a KWL chart on page LC 47 in *K¹² Language Arts Activity Book*.

> **Objectives**
> • Define fact.
> • Identify facts.
> • Generate questions before reading.
> • Identify important questions that need to be answered (5Ws and H).
> • Make connections between text and self.

1. Explain that in this first part of the article, we've read about what Pliny saw. But we also read some facts about the eruption of Mount Vesuvius.

2. Review the definition of **fact**.

3. Have students fill in the Know column of the chart with at least three facts from the article about the eruption of Mount Vesuvius in A.D. 79.

4. Remind students that good readers ask questions as they read and then look to find the answers.

5. Remind students about six ways to start a question about their reading: *Who, What, Where, When, Why,* and *How.* These are called the 5Ws and H questions.

6. Have students complete the Wonder column of the chart with at least three questions that begin with one of the 5Ws and H. Their questions may be on any topic related to Mount Vesuvius or volcanoes in general. Students' questions need not align with the facts they enter in the Know column of the chart, because they may wonder about completely different subjects related to volcanoes and Vesuvius.

7. Explain that students will complete the Learn column after they finish reading the article.

8. Keep the Activity Book page in a safe place so students can add to it after reading the rest of the article.

Making Connections

Imagery

This nonfiction article uses imagery to help the reader envision what Pliny saw. Review imagery with students and discuss how the imagery in the article adds to the reader's understanding of the facts.

1. Discuss with students that this article describes events that happened a long time ago. There are no photographs of the eruption of Mount Vesuvius. Pliny's descriptions are all we have to tell us what that day was like.

2. Explain that the author of the article describes what Pliny saw to help the reader imagine what the eruption was like. The descriptions help us make a mental picture of something we did not see or experience.

3. Review with students that language that helps us to imagine something is called **imagery**. Define imagery for students.

4. Discuss with students the kinds of imagery the author uses.

   ▸ What things does the author say that Pliny saw? The ash cloud looked like a pine tree; ash swept through the air; there were bright flames; the ash made it look as dark as night; the fallen ash looked like snow.

   ▸ What things does the author say that Pliny felt? the ground shake

5. Have students look at the illustrations in the first three pages of the article.

   ▸ Do you think the illustrator did a good job drawing what is described in the article? Why or why not? Answers will vary.

Objectives
- Define imagery.
- Identify the author's use of imagery.
- Answer evaluative questions.

Introduce "Pliny Saw It All" (B)

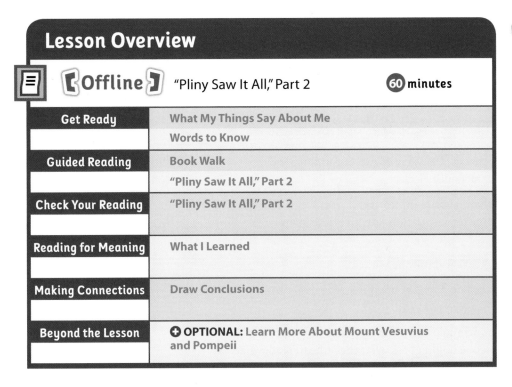

Lesson Overview

[Offline] "Pliny Saw It All," Part 2   **60** minutes

Get Ready	What My Things Say About Me
	Words to Know
Guided Reading	Book Walk
	"Pliny Saw It All," Part 2
Check Your Reading	"Pliny Saw It All," Part 2
Reading for Meaning	What I Learned
Making Connections	Draw Conclusions
Beyond the Lesson	**⊕ OPTIONAL:** Learn More About Mount Vesuvius and Pompeii

Advance Preparation

Read pages 30–35 of "Pliny Saw It All" before beginning the Guided Reading to identify Words to Know in the text. Have students gather the partially completed KWL chart on page LC 47 in *K¹² Language Arts Activity Book*.

Big Ideas

▸ When we draw conclusions, we use the information in a text and our inferences to make a decision about what we've read.

▸ During reading, readers should ask themselves questions about what they read and look for answers in the text.

[**Materials**]

Supplied

● "Pliny Saw It All," *All About Ancient Rome*, pp. 26–35

● *K¹² Language Arts Activity Book*, pp. LC 47–48

Story Synopsis

The second part of this article discusses what archaeologists have discovered from the ruins of Pompeii and Herculaneum, the two cities buried by the ash of Mount Vesuvius when it erupted in A.D. 79.

Keywords

conclusion – a reasoned decision made about something not stated directly in a text through the consideration of information provided and what is already known

context clue – a word or phrase in a text that helps you figure out the meaning of an unknown word

fact – something that can be proven true

inference – a guess you make using the clues in a text and what you already know

nonfiction – writings about true things

 **60 minutes**

"Pliny Saw It All," Part 2

Work **together** with students to complete offline Get Ready, Guided Reading, Check Your Reading, Reading for Meaning, Making Connections, and Beyond the Lesson activities.

Get Ready

What My Things Say About Me

Review what students read in the first part of "Pliny Saw It All" to reinforce their comprehension of the text and help them identify facts.

1. Have students tell what some of their favorite things are. If possible, have students use their bedroom or home for inspiration. Or, give your own examples of your favorite things.

2. Discuss what these favorite things reveal about the students.

   ▶ What do your favorite things tell or show about you? Possible answers: I like animals/sports/clothes/music, and so forth.

3. Discuss with students what someone might learn about them just by looking in their bedroom. For example, someone might guess what they like to read, what their favorite color is, or whether they are a neat or messy person.

4. Tell students that scientists and historians can learn a lot about how people lived a long time ago by studying the things those people left behind.

5. Tell students that they will finish the article about Pliny and Mount Vesuvius and learn about what life was like when the volcano erupted.

 Objectives
- Make connections between text and self.
- Build background knowledge.
- Increase concept and content vocabulary.

Words to Know

Before reading "Pliny Saw It All," Part 2, go over Words to Learn with students.

1. Ask students to define these words from Part 1 and use them in sentences:

   ash   **volcano**
   erupting

2. Correct any incorrect or vague definitions.

3. Have students say each of the words below, which occur in Part 2.

4. Ask students if they know what each word means.

   ▶ If students know a word's meaning, have them define it and use it in a sentence.
   ▶ If students don't know a word's meaning, read them the definition and discuss the word with them.

archaeologists – scientists who dig up and study objects and ruins from long ago
frescoes – art created by painting directly on wet plaster
historian – someone who writes about past events
mosaics – pictures or designs made of small pieces of glass, tile, or stone
ruins – the remains of something destroyed or decayed
ruts – tracks or grooves in the ground made by wheeled vehicles

Guided Reading

Book Walk

Prepare students by taking them on a Book Walk of *All About Ancient Rome*. Scan the magazine together and ask students to make predictions about the article. For all questions in the Book Walk, answers will vary.

1. Have students use the **table of contents** to find "Pliny Saw It All" and turn to that page.

2. Have students read the title of the article aloud.

3. Tell students that you are going to read the second part of the article.

4. Look through pages 30–35 of the article. Have students describe what they see. Point out the **photographs** and **illustration** and have students make predictions using the pictures.

   ▶ What do you see in the photographs? Why do you think these are photographs and not illustrations?

   ▶ What do you see in the illustration? Why do you think this is an illustration and not a photograph?

   ▶ What do you think we'll learn about in this part of the article?

> ### Objectives
> - Use text organizational features to locate and comprehend information (table of contents).
> - Use an illustration to make a prediction about a reading.
> - Read texts to gain information.
> - Define context clues.
> - Use context clues to determine word meanings.

"Pliny Saw It All," Part 2

Now it's time to read pages 30–35 of "Pliney Saw It All" (Part 2). Have students sit next to you so that they can see the pictures and words while you read the article aloud.

1. Remind students of where the first part of the article finished. Reread the last paragraph on page 29 to refresh students' memory of what happened at the end of the first part.

2. Read pages 30–35 of the article aloud all the way through. Stop at the end of the article. Track with your finger so students can follow along. Read the body of the article on each page first. Then point out the photographs and illustrations.

3. Explain to students that you will read this part of the article again and that they are to chime in and read aloud with you. Tell them to look for new facts about life in ancient Pompeii. Tell students that you will pause at certain points in the story to discuss.

4. Reread pages 30–31 and pause to discuss. Review the definition of **context clues**. Point to the word **archaeologists**. Tell students that you see a context clue—a definition—in the sentence. Have students point to the definition: scientists who study objects people left behind long ago.

5. Continue reading and pause at the end of page 33 after the phrase, "lay on the floors." Have students find the context clues for **frescoes** and **mosaics**. huge paintings; pictures made out of tiny stone tiles

6. Have students identify one or two things that archaeologists have learned about ancient Pompeii from the ruins. Possible answers: Shops sold cloth, pottery, and glass. People went to the theater, restaurants, and public baths. People had pets.

7. Read to the end of the article. Have students find the context clue for **historian**. someone who writes about past events

Check Your Reading

"Pliny Saw It All," Part 2
Have students retell the second part of the article in their own words to develop grammar, vocabulary, comprehension, and fluency skills. When finished, **ask students the following questions** to check comprehension and encourage discussion.

▶ How do archaeologists know that Pompeii and Herculaneum were busy cities? There were deep ruts in the roads from many carts and wagons.
▶ Name two facts that archaeologists have learned about how people lived in ancient Pompeii. Possible answers: They liked to go to theaters, restaurants, and public baths; they had pets; they put frescoes and mosaics in their houses if they were rich.
▶ What things from the volcano destroyed Pompeii and Herculaneum? ash and very hot air
▶ Where did Pliny write his description of the eruption? in letters to his friend Tacitus

Objectives
• Answer questions requiring literal recall of details.
• Identify facts.

Reading for Meaning

 What I Learned

Have students complete the KWL chart they began on page LC 47 in *K¹² Language Arts Activity Book* with facts from the article and think about where they could find more information about unanswered questions.

1. Review with students what they wrote in the first two columns of their KWL chart.

2. Remind students that in this part of the article, they learned facts about life in ancient Pompeii and Herculaneum.

3. Ask students to recall some facts from the article.

Objectives
• Identify facts.
• Apply information read to answer questions.

4. Have students complete the Learn column of their chart with facts they learned in the second part of the article.

5. When they have finished, ask students if their questions from the Wonder column were answered. If not, have them tell where they might find the answers, such as the Internet, nonfiction books, or an encyclopedia.

Reading for Meaning
Introduce "Pliny Saw It All" (B)
Know, Wonder, Learn

Complete the chart with what you know, wonder about, and learn from your reading.

Know	Wonder	Learn
Mount Vesuvius erupted in 79 A.D.	Did Pliny see anything else?	Pompeii was a busy city.
Pliny the Younger saw the eruption.	What happened to the people in Pompeii and Herculaneum?	People in Pompeii liked to go to the theater.
The eruption caused ash to fall on Misenum.	Has Vesuvius ever erupted again?	Rich people in Pompeii had frescoes in their houses.

Possible answers are shown.

LANGUAGE ARTS ORANGE   LC 47

Making Connections

Draw Conclusions

Teach students how to use the facts from the second part of the article to draw a conclusion about life in ancient Pompeii. Have students take out the KWL chart. This page will help them complete page LC 48 in *K¹² Language Arts Activity Book*.

1. Review with students that a **conclusion** is a decision that readers make after looking at all of the facts in an article and thinking about what they know.

2. Tell students that you will help them use the text and their own knowledge to make some conclusions about life in Pompeii when Mount Vesuvius erupted.

3. Have students look at their completed KWL chart. Point to one fact on students' chart that archaeologists have learned about life in ancient Pompeii.

4. Have students turn to the Draw Conclusions page and write three facts about what scientists have learned about life in Pompeii. They may use facts from their chart or different ones from the article.

5. Have students think about what these facts tell them and write a conclusion about life in or the people of ancient Pompei on the Activity Book page.

Objectives
- Draw conclusions using evidence from text.
- Draw conclusions using prior knowledge.
- Support conclusions with evidence from text and prior knowledge.

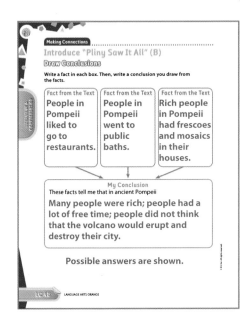

Making Connections
Introduce "Pliny Saw It All" (B)
Draw Conclusions

Write a fact in each box. Then, write a conclusion you draw from the facts.

Fact from the Text	Fact from the Text	Fact from the Text
People in Pompeii liked to go to restaurants.	People in Pompeii went to public baths.	Rich people in Pompeii had frescoes and mosaics in their houses.

My Conclusion
These facts tell me that in ancient Pompeii

Many people were rich; people had a lot of free time; people did not think that the volcano would erupt and destroy their city.

Possible answers are shown.

LC 48   LANGUAGE ARTS ORANGE

Beyond the Lesson

⊕ OPTIONAL: Learn More About Mount Vesuvius and Pompeii

This activity is OPTIONAL. This activity is intended for students who have extra time and would enjoy learning more about Pompeii and its destruction. Feel free to skip this activity.

Preview the titles given here. If you find them suitable, and if students are interested, have students read a book of historical fiction and a nonfiction book about ancient Pompeii, both by Mary Pope Osborne.

▶ *Magic Tree House #13: Vacation under the Volcano.* New York: Random House, 1998.

▶ *Ancient Rome and Pompeii: A nonfiction companion to Vacation under the Volcano.* New York: Random House, 2006.

Objectives
- Make connections between texts.
- Make connections between text and the world.

Introduce *Volcanoes!* (A)

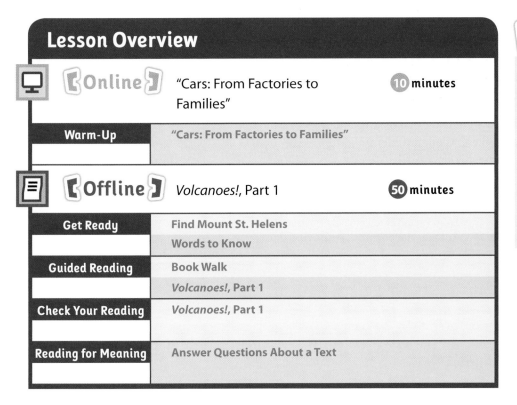

Lesson Overview

【Online】	"Cars: From Factories to Families"	10 minutes
Warm-Up	"Cars: From Factories to Families"	

【Offline】	*Volcanoes!*, Part 1	50 minutes
Get Ready	Find Mount St. Helens	
	Words to Know	
Guided Reading	Book Walk	
	Volcanoes!, Part 1	
Check Your Reading	*Volcanoes!*, Part 1	
Reading for Meaning	Answer Questions About a Text	

【Materials】

Supplied

- *Volcanoes!* by Eric Arnold
- *K¹² Language Arts Activity Book*, p. LC 49
- "Cars: From Factories to Families" (optional)

Also Needed

- map – United States

Story Synopsis

The first two chapters of this nonfiction book describe the eruption of the Mount St. Helens volcano in Washington State in 1980. This section of the book gives details about the eruption itself and its aftermath.

Advance Preparation

If you are not able to complete the online Warm-Up, then print the selection and listen to students read aloud. Read the first two chapters (pp. 4–19) of *Volcanoes!* before beginning the Guided Reading to identify Words to Know in the text.

Big Ideas

- ▶ Active, strong readers determine what is important as they read.
- ▶ Comprehension entails asking and answering questions about the text.

Keywords

fact – something that can be proven true

heading – a title within the body of a text that tells the reader something important about a section of the text

illustration – a drawing

nonfiction – writings about true things

 **10 minutes**

"Cars: From Factories to Families"

Students will work independently online to develop fluency and oral reading skills.

Warm-Up

"Cars: From Factories to Families"

The purpose of this activity is to improve students' oral reading and fluency. Students will read "Cars: From Factories to Families." Remind students to listen to the model on each screen before they begin their recording.

 Objectives
- Increase oral reading skills.
- Increase fluency.

Offline Alternative

No computer access? Print a copy of "Cars: From Factories to Families." Have students read it aloud several times. Make note of any pronunciation errors, and review those words with students.

 **50 minutes**

Volcanoes!, Part 1

Work **together** with students to complete offline Get Ready, Guided Reading, Check Your Reading, and Reading for Meaning activities.

Get Ready

Find Mount St. Helens

To prepare for the reading, have students locate Mount St. Helens on a map.

1. Tell students that they are going to begin reading a book that will tell them about volcanoes.

2. Ask students if they think there are volcanoes in the United States.

3. Tell students that there are, and one of them is Mount St. Helens.

4. Use a map of the United States to locate Washington State and Mount St. Helens. Point out the many cities and towns near the mountain.

5. Tell students that the first part of the book they will read is about Mount St. Helens.

 Objectives
- Build background knowledge.
- Increase concept and content vocabulary.

Words to Know

Before reading *Volcanoes!*, Part 1, go over Words to Know with students.

1. Have students say the word aloud.

2. Ask students if they know what the word means.

   ▶ If students know the word's meaning, have them define it and use it in a sentence.
   ▶ If students don't know the word's meaning, read them the definition and discuss the word with them.

mudflow – a river of thick mud that flows down a mountain or hillside

Guided Reading

Book Walk

Prepare students by taking them on a Book Walk of *Volcanoes!*. Scan the book together and ask students to make predictions about the story.

1. Show students the **front cover** and **back cover** of the book.

2. Point to the **title** and **subtitle**, and the names of the **author** and **illustrator** and read them aloud

3. Point to and read the paragraph on the back cover under "What this book is about . . . ."

4. Tell students that this book is **nonfiction**. Ask them how they can tell. Possible answers: the title, the blurb on the back, the photograph on the cover

5. Have students describe the kinds of **facts** they expect to find in this book.

6. Point to and read the **heading** on page 4. Tell students that this is a chapter book, and this is the title of the first chapter. Have students look through the book and tell how many chapters there are. six

7. With students, look more carefully through the first two chapters. Point to the **illustrations**, **photograph**, and heading for Chapter 2. Have students make predictions about the text. Answers to questions may vary.

   ▶ What do you think happens in Chapter 1?
   ▶ What do you think is described in Chapter 2?

Objectives

- Use an illustration to make a prediction about a reading.
- Use title of the selection to make a prediction.
- Use text features to comprehend text meaning (bold, italic, headers).
- Distinguish between fiction and nonfiction.
- Set a purpose for reading.
- Identify features of a nonfiction text.
- Read texts to gain information.
- Answer scriptal questions.

Volcanoes!, Part 1

Now it's time to read the first two chapters of the book. Have students sit next to you so that they can see the pictures and words while you read the story aloud.

1. Read the first two chapters of the book aloud all the way through. Stop at the end of Chapter 2, on page 19. Track with your finger so students can follow along.

2. Explain to students that you will read these two chapters again and that this time they are to chime in and read aloud with you. Tell them to think about facts about Mount St. Helens. Tell students that you will pause at certain points in the story to discuss.

3. Reread through page 5 and pause to discuss.

   ► What happened on May 18, 1980? It's the day that Mount St. Helens erupted.

4. Continue reading through page 9 and pause to discuss.

   ► What events does the pilot Bruce Judson see? Ash and rock blow through a hole in the side of Mount St. Helens. Then the whole top of the volcano blows off.
   ► Do you think the pilot will get away? Why or why not? Answers will vary. Students should express their opinion and provide a reason for why they think as they do.

5. Read on through page 12 and pause. Point out the **pronunciation guide** for "Yakima" and explain to students that the guide shows how to pronounce the name of the town.

6. Continue reading through page 15 and pause to discuss.

   ► What are some of the things that happen after a volcano erupts? Ash comes down on top of everything; there's thunder and lightning; rocks rain down; the sky becomes pitch black.
   ► What do you think will happen to the family in the cabin? Answer will vary.
   ► Have you ever been afraid of something in nature? What was it like? Answer will vary.

7. Read to the end of Chapter 2.

Check Your Reading

Volcanoes!, **Part 1**

Have students retell the story in their own words to develop grammar, vocabulary, comprehension, and fluency skills. When finished, **ask students the following questions** to check comprehension and encourage discussion.

   ► What state is Mount St. Helens in? Washington
   ► What is the land like around Mount St. Helens? There are forests, rivers, and wildlife.
   ► What is in the ash cloud from the volcano? ash, gas, rocks
   ► What happens in the town of Yakima when the ash cloud covers the sun? The streetlights turn on because it looks like nighttime.
   ► What does the eruption do to the trees on the mountain? It knocks them down and burns them.
   ► Why does the author say that the land around Mount St. Helens "looks like the surface of the moon"? Possible answers: It's bare and dusty like the moon; there are no trees or living things around; there's ash on everything that makes it look like the surface of the moon.

Objectives
- Answer questions requiring literal recall of details.
- Make inferences and draw conclusions.

Reading for Meaning

Answer Questions About a Text

Have students answer questions about what they've read to practice finding information in a nonfiction text. Turn to page LC 49 in *K¹² Language Arts Activity Book*.

1. Remind students that sometimes they will need to answer questions about a nonfiction text.

2. Review the six basic types of questions about reading, the 5 Ws and H: *Who*, *What*, *Where*, *When*, *Why*, and *How*.

3. Tell students that they can find the answers to many questions right in the text. They might need to infer—or figure out—others based on the text and what they already know.

4. Direct students' attention to the Activity Book page.
   Say: Today you are going to answer multiple choice questions.

5. Point to Exercise 1 and read the question aloud.
   Say: This is a multiple choice question. It is a question that you need to answer.

6. Point to the four answer choices in Exercise 1.
   Say: Here are the answer choices that go with the question. Only one of the answer choices is correct. The other three are wrong answers. You are to choose the best answer to the question.

7. Explain to students how to go about answering a multiple choice question.
   Say: To answer a multiple choice question, first read the question and each answer choice. Then decide which choice answers the question.

8. Have students complete the Activity Book page. Remind them to look for the answers in *Volcanoes!*.

Objectives

- Answer who, what, where, when, why, and how questions.

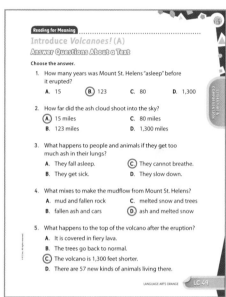

Introduce *Volcanoes!* (B)

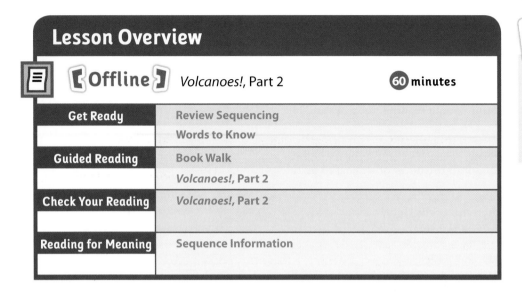

Lesson Overview

[Offline] *Volcanoes!*, Part 2   **60** minutes

Get Ready	Review Sequencing
	Words to Know
Guided Reading	Book Walk
	Volcanoes!, Part 2
Check Your Reading	*Volcanoes!*, Part 2
Reading for Meaning	Sequence Information

Advance Preparation

Read Chapters 3 and 4 (pp. 20–35) of *Volcanoes!* before beginning the Guided Reading to identify Words to Know in the text.

Big Ideas

▶ Readers need to be able to sequence, summarize, and articulate the main idea.
▶ Readers should be able to retell the story (or information) in their own words, not repeat what was written.

Materials

Supplied

- *Volcanoes!* by Eric Arnold
- *K¹² Language Arts Activity Book*, p. LC 50

Story Synopsis

Chapters 3 and 4 of *Volcanoes!* introduce volcanologists, scientists who study volcanoes. The book explains the work that volcanologists do, as well as how volcanoes erupt and grow.

Keywords

fact – something that can be proven true

heading – a title within the body of a text that tells the reader something important about a section of the text

illustration – a drawing

nonfiction – writings about true things

sequence – order

⟦Offline⟧ 🕐 **60 minutes**

Volcanoes!, Part 2

Work **together** with students to complete offline Get Ready, Guided Reading, Check Your Reading, and Reading for Meaning activities.

Get Ready ···

Review Sequencing

Readers need to be able to remember important information from a text in sequence to be able to make sense of the key ideas. Review with students how to sequence information from a text.

1. Remind students that they have read stories in which they put the events in order, or **sequence**.

2. Review with students some of the order words they used to describe the sequence of events: *first, next, then, later, finally, last,* and so forth.

3. Have students practice sequencing by using some of these order words to put in order what they do when they go to bed at night.

Objectives
- Define sequence.
- Increase concept and content vocabulary.

Words to Know

Before reading *Volcanoes!*, Part 2, go over Words to Know with students.

1. Ask students to define this word from Part 1 and use it in a sentence:

   mudflow

2. Correct any incorrect or vague definitions.

3. Have students say each of the words below, which they will encounter in Part 2 (Chapters 3 and 4).

4. Ask students if they know what each word means.

   ▸ If students know a word's meaning, have them define it and use it in a sentence.

   ▸ If students don't know a word's meaning, read them the definition and discuss the word with them.

basalt – lava that cools quickly and turns into rock
fieldwork – work that scientists do at a site instead of at a laboratory
granite – a type of rock that forms when magma cools slowly in cracks beneath the earth's surface
igneous – volcanic
magma – melted rock found beneath the earth's surface
pumice – a lightweight rock made when thick lava cools quickly and forms air bubbles inside
volcanologists – scientists who study volcanoes

Guided Reading

Book Walk

Prepare students by taking them on a Book Walk of *Volcanoes!*. Scan the book together and ask students to make predictions about the story. For all questions in the Book Walk, answers will vary.

1. Have students read aloud the **title** and **subtitle** of the book. Then have them read the names of the **author** and **illustrator**.

2. Remind students that this is a nonfiction chapter book. Have them tell what the book is about.

3. Look through the second part of the book, Chapters 3 and 4. Point to and read the **headings** on pages 20 and 26.

4. Point out the **illustrations** and photographs. Have students make predictions about the text.

   ▸ What do you think happens in Chapter 3?
   ▸ Who do you think the people are in the photographs?
   ▸ What do you think we'll learn about in Chapter 4?

Objectives

- Use an illustration to make a prediction about a reading.
- Use chapter titles to make predictions and comprehend text.
- Identify features of a nonfiction text.
- Read texts to gain information.
- Use context clues to determine word meanings.
- Answer inferential questions.

Volcanoes!, **Part 2**

Now it's time to read the next two chapters of *Volcanoes!*. Have students sit next to you so that they can see the pictures and words while you read the story aloud.

1. Remind students that you are going to continue reading from where the first part of the story finished. Have students tell what happened in the first part.

2. Read Chapters 3 and 4 of the book aloud all the way through. Stop at the end of Chapter 4. Track with your finger so students can follow along.

3. Explain to students that you will read these chapters again and that this time they are to chime in and read aloud with you. Tell them to think about what volcanologists do and how volcanoes work. Tell students that you will pause at certain points in the story to discuss.

4. Begin to reread Chapter 3 and pause at the end of page 21 to discuss.

   ▸ What is the context clue that tells us what a *volcanologist* is on page 20? scientists who study volcanoes
   ▸ What context clue tells us what *magma* is on page 21? melted rock found beneath the earth's surface
   ▸ How did volcanologist Dave Johnston know that Mount St. Helens was going to erupt? It had started to have small eruptions and there was a swelling on the north side.

5. Read to the end of Chapter 3 and pause to discuss.

   ▸ Why did Harry Truman refuse to leave, even though Dave Johnston warned him to go? Possible answers: He had lived there too long; he would rather die than leave his home.

   ▸ Why did Dave Johnston stay on the mountain even though he knew it was dangerous? Possible answers: He believed his job was important; he wanted to help save people who lived nearby; he didn't know how dangerous it was.

6. Begin to reread Chapter 4 and pause at the end of page 31 to discuss.

   ▸ What are some of the tools that volcanologists use? special thermometers, fireproof suits, submarines

   ▸ What are some of the places where volcanologists work? in laboratories, on volcanoes, inside submarines

7. Read to the end of Chapter 4.

Check Your Reading

Volcanoes!, Part 2

Have students retell the story in their own words to develop grammar, vocabulary, comprehension, and fluency skills. When finished, **ask students the following questions** to check comprehension and encourage discussion.

Objectives
- Answer questions requiring literal recall of details.

   ▸ What caused the swelling on the side of Mount St. Helens before it erupted? magma moving up into the volcano

   ▸ Why did volcanologist Dave Johnston want people to leave the area around Mount St. Helens? He knew a big eruption was coming and he wanted them to be safe.

   ▸ Why do volcanologists study volcanoes? to learn about them and predict when they will erupt

   ▸ What happens when plates in the earth's crust bump each other and form a crack? Magma and gas push through the crack.

   ▸ What is magma called once it is outside a volcano? lava

   ▸ How does a volcano grow? when lava and ash build up on the sides

Reading for Meaning

Sequence Information

To help them retain important information from their reading, have students practice putting important facts in sequence. Turn to page LC 50 in *K¹² Language Arts Activity Book*.

1. Review that **sequence** is the order in which things happen.

2. Have students turn to page 32 in *Volcanoes!*.

3. Explain that they are going to sequence the events that happen when a volcano erupts.

4. Reread pages 32–35 with students.

5. Have students complete the Activity Book page.

TIP Remind students to look for the answers in the book.

Objectives

- Sequence important information.
- Describe the connection between a series of historical events, scientific ideas or concepts, or steps in technical procedures in a text.

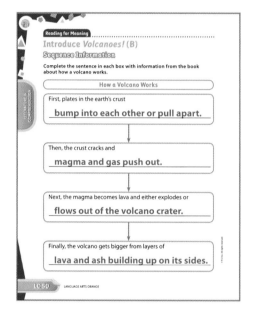

Introduce *Volcanoes!* (C)

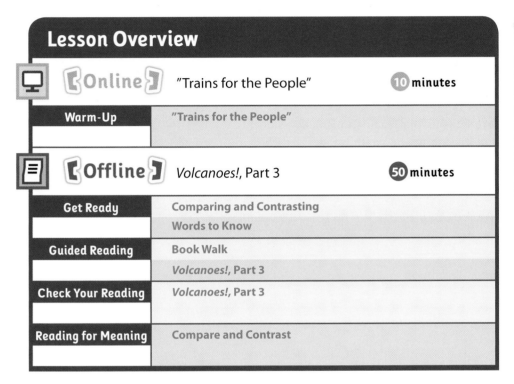

Lesson Overview

Online	"Trains for the People"	10 minutes
Warm-Up	"Trains for the People"	

Offline	*Volcanoes!*, Part 3	50 minutes
Get Ready	Comparing and Contrasting	
	Words to Know	
Guided Reading	Book Walk	
	Volcanoes!, Part 3	
Check Your Reading	*Volcanoes!*, Part 3	
Reading for Meaning	Compare and Contrast	

Advance Preparation

If you are not able to complete the online Warm-Up, then print the selection and listen to students read aloud. Read Chapters 5 and 6, (pp. 36–48) of *Volcanoes!* before beginning the Guided Reading to identify Words to Know in the text.

Big Ideas

Signal words—such as *before, consequently, compare, contrast, therefore*—are a guide to understanding the relationship between and among ideas.

Materials

Supplied
- *Volcanoes!* by Eric Arnold
- *K¹² Language Arts Activity Book*, p. LC 51
- "Trains for the People" (optional)

Story Synopsis

The final two chapters of the book describe the eruption of Mount Vesuvius in A.D. 79 and the myths that Romans told about volcanoes. The book also explains some of the beliefs that Hawaiians held about volcanoes. The conclusion returns to the recent past and describes how people and nature have recovered from the eruption of Mount St. Helens.

Keywords

compare – to explain how two or more things are alike

contrast – to explain how two or more things are different

heading – a title within the body of a text that tells the reader something important about a section of the text

illustration – a drawing

inference – a guess you make using the clues in a text and what you already know

myth – a story that explains how something came to be and that usually contains magical figures as characters

nonfiction – writings about true things

 **10 minutes**

"Trains for the People"

Students will work independently online to develop fluency and oral reading skills.

Warm-Up

"Trains for the People"

The purpose of this activity is to improve students' oral reading and fluency. Students will read "Trains for the People." Remind students to listen to the model on each screen before they begin their recording.

Objectives
- Increase oral reading skills.
- Increase fluency.

Offline Alternative

No computer access? Print a copy of "Trains for the People". Have students read it aloud several times. Make note of any pronunciation errors, and review those words with students.

 **50 minutes**

Volcanoes!, Part 3

Work **together** with students to complete offline Get Ready, Guided Reading, Check Your Reading, and Reading for Meaning activities.

Get Ready

Comparing and Contrasting

Review with students how to compare and contrast.

Objectives
- Define compare.
- Define contrast.
- Increase concept and content vocabulary.

1. Review with students the definitions of **compare** and **contrast**.

2. Remind students that when they compare and contrast, they are looking at how two things are the same and different. They should consider all the qualities of the two things.

3. Have students compare and contrast two familiar objects, such as an apple and an orange or rain and snow.

4. Remind students that they read about a man called Pliny the Younger in an article from the magazine *All About Ancient Rome*. Ask students to tell what Pliny saw and what he did.

Words to Know

Before reading *Volcanoes!*, Part 3, go over Words to Know with students.

1. Ask students to define the following words from Parts 1 and 2 (Chapters 1–4) and use them in sentences:

basalt	**magma**
fieldwork	**mudflow**
granite	**pumice**
igneous	**volcanologists**

2. Correct any incorrect or vague definitions.

3. Then have students say each of the words below, which they will encounter in Part 3 (Chapters 5 and 6).

4. Ask students if they know what each word means.

   ► If students know a word's meaning, have them define it and use it in a sentence.

   ► If students don't know a word's meaning, read them the definition and discuss the word with them.

blacksmith – a person who makes and repairs objects made of iron
moonscape – a landscape that looks empty and gray like the surface of the moon

Guided Reading

Book Walk

Prepare students by taking them on a Book Walk of *Volcanoes!*. Scan the book together and ask students to make predictions about the story. For all questions in the Book Walk, answers will vary.

1. Have students read aloud the **title** and **subtitle** of the book. Then have them read the names of the **author** and **illustrator**.

2. Look through the last part of the book (Chapters 5 and 6). Point to and read the **headings** on pages 36 and 42.

3. Point out the **illustrations**. Have students make predictions about the text.

   ► Do you see anything familiar in the pictures in Chapter 5?

   ► What do you think Chapter 5 will be about?

   ► What do you think we'll learn in Chapter 6?

Objectives

- Use an illustration to make a prediction about a reading.
- Use chapter titles to make predictions and comprehend text.
- Read texts for literary experience.
- Answer inferential questions.

Volcanoes!, Part 3

Now it's time to read the last two chapters of *Volcanoes!*. Have students sit next to you so that they can see the pictures and words while you read the story aloud.

1. Remind students that you are going to continue reading from where you left off last time. Have students describe what they read about in Chapters 3 and 4.

2. Read Chapters 5 and 6 aloud all the way through. Stop at the end of Chapter 6. Track with your finger so students can follow along.

3. Explain to students that you will read these chapters again and that this time they are to chime in and read aloud with you. Tell them to think about the description of Pliny and the ancient Romans and that you will pause at certain points in the story to discuss.

4. Begin to reread Chapter 5 and pause at the end of page 38.

   ▸ Who did the ancient Romans believe caused volcanoes? Vulcan, the god of fire and blacksmith of the gods

5. Read to the end of Chapter 5 and pause to discuss.

   ▸ Who did the Hawaiians believe caused volcanoes? Pele, the goddess of fire
   ▸ Why do you think the Hawaiians believed that Pele had a bad temper? Possible answer: because she caused volcanoes to erupt

6. Read to the end of Chapter 6 and pause to discuss.

   ▸ What were some of the signs that nature was healing after the Mount St. Helens eruption? Plants and trees were growing; birds, insects, and animals returned.
   ▸ Why do you think the McNutts decided to stay near Mount St. Helens? Possible answer: They like it there; they aren't afraid of the volcano; they don't think the volcano will erupt again.

Check Your Reading

Volcanoes!, Part 3

Have students retell the story in their own words to develop grammar, vocabulary, comprehension, and fluency skills. When finished, **ask students the following questions** to check comprehension and encourage discussion.

▶ What is named after Pliny? a type of cloud that bursts from a volcano
▶ What word does the word *volcano* come from? Vulcan, the ancient Roman god of fire
▶ Where did the Hawaiians say that the spirit of Pele went to live? in the volcano Kilauea
▶ Where is the Ring of Fire, where many volcanoes are located? on the shores around the Pacific Ocean
▶ How does volcanic ash help plants grow? It makes the soil rich.

Objectives
• Answer questions requiring literal recall of details.

Reading for Meaning

Compare and Contrast

Help students compare and contrast the ancient Roman and Hawaiian stories about volcanoes. Turn to page LC 51 in *K¹² Language Arts Activity Book*.

1. Review that you have just read about two different cultures—the ancient Romans and the early Hawaiians—and the stories they tell to explain volcanoes.

2. Have students summarize the story that each culture tells about volcanoes. If they have trouble remembering, refer to the book for prompting.

3. Direct student's attention to the Activity Book page. Explain that they are going to compare and contrast the stories told by the ancient Romans and the Hawaiians about the origin of volcanoes.

4. Review with students how to complete a Venn diagram: Place ideas that belong to only one culture in the outer parts of the ovals. Place ideas that are similar to both cultures in the overlapping part of the ovals in the center.

5. Remind students to look for the main ideas and supporting details of each story to help them decide what to put in the diagram.

6. Have students complete the Activity Book page.

Objectives
• Compare and contrast different versions of the same story.
• Compare and contrast the most important points presented by two texts on the same topic.

Review *Volcanoes!*

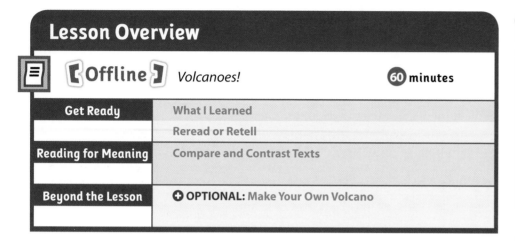

Lesson Overview

[Offline] *Volcanoes!* **60** minutes

Get Ready	What I Learned
	Reread or Retell
Reading for Meaning	Compare and Contrast Texts
Beyond the Lesson	➕ OPTIONAL: Make Your Own Volcano

Big Ideas

▸ Comprehension is facilitated when readers connect new information to information previously learned.

▸ Signal words—such as *before, consequently, compare, contrast, therefore*—are a guide to understanding the relationship between and among ideas.

▸ Comprehension is enhanced when information is presented through more than one learning modality; learning modalities are visual (seeing), auditory (hearing), and kinesthetic (touching).

[Materials]

Supplied

- *Volcanoes!* by Eric Arnold
- "Pliny Saw It All," *All About Ancient Rome,* pp. 26–35
- *K¹² Language Arts Activity Book,* p. LC 52

Keywords

compare – to explain how two or more things are alike

contrast – to explain how two or more things are different

nonfiction – writings about true things

 **60 minutes**

Volcanoes!

Work **together** with students to complete offline Get Ready, Reading for Meaning, and Beyond the Lesson activities.

Get Ready

What I Learned

Help students recall what they've read by discussing what they learned from the book.

1. Discuss with students what they learned from reading *Volcanoes!*.

2. Have students tell whether they would like to visit a volcano or become a volcanologist.

Objectives

- Recount or describe key ideas or details from a text read aloud or information presented orally or through other media.
- Make connections between text and self.

Reread or Retell

If you'd like to, reread the book to students. Otherwise, have students retell it using the pictures as a guide. Make sure students tell the most important information. Give the following prompts to guide them.

▶ Tell what happened when Mount St. Helens erupted.
▶ Tell what volcanologists do.
▶ Tell what happens when a volcano erupts.
▶ Tell how the Romans and Hawaiians explained volcanoes.
▶ Tell what happened a few months after Mount St. Helens erupted.

Reading for Meaning

Compare and Contrast Texts

Have students compare and contrast the story of Pliny in *Volcanoes!* with the magazine article, "Pliny Saw It All" in *All About Ancient Rome*. Turn to page LC 52 in *K¹² Language Arts Activity Book*

1. Remind students that they read an article about Pliny. Have them use the **table of contents** in *All About Ancient Rome* to find "Pliny Saw It All."

2. Have students retell what they read about in the article. Make sure they describe the main ideas from the article. If students have trouble remembering the main ideas of the article, prompt them.

   ▸ What did Pliny see?
   ▸ What happened to Pompeii and Herculaneum?
   ▸ What kinds of things have archaeologists learned from the ruins of Pompeii and Herculaneum?

3. Direct students' attention to the Activity Book page. Explain that they are going to compare and contrast the stories about Pliny in the article and in the book *Volcanoes!* (pages 36–37).

4. Review with students how to complete a Venn diagram: Place main ideas and details that belong to only one text in the outer parts of the circles. Place main ideas and details that are similar to both texts in the overlapping part of the circles in the center.

5. Remind students to look for the main ideas and supporting details of each story to help them decide what to put in the diagram.

6. Have students complete the Activity Book page.

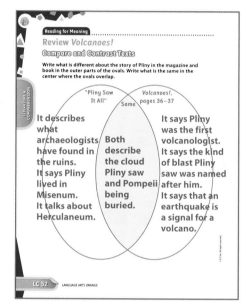

Beyond the Lesson

 OPTIONAL: Make Your Own Volcano

This activity is OPTIONAL. This activity is intended for students who have extra time and would be interested in building their own model volcano. Feel free to skip this activity.

Have students make a homemade volcano from common household items. Use one of these websites for materials and instructions.

▸ Enchanted Learning, *Volcano Craft*, http://www.enchantedlearning.com/crafts/nature/volcano/

▸ *Baking Soda & Vinegar Chemical Volcano*, http://chemistry.about.com/od/chemicalvolcanoes/ss/volcano.htm

Introduce *Peter Pan* (A)

Unit Overview

In this five-lesson unit, students will read *Peter Pan* by J.M. Barrie (adapted by Cathy East Dubowski). Students will focus on the following elements and skills as they read:

▶ The genre of fantasy
▶ The choices characters make and their consequences
▶ The theme of the novel

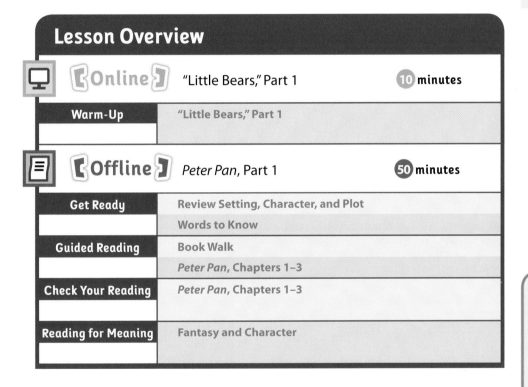

Lesson Overview

🖥	**【Online】** "Little Bears," Part 1	**10** minutes
Warm-Up	"Little Bears," Part 1	

📄	**【Offline】** *Peter Pan*, Part 1	**50** minutes
Get Ready	Review Setting, Character, and Plot	
	Words to Know	
Guided Reading	Book Walk	
	Peter Pan, Chapters 1–3	
Check Your Reading	*Peter Pan*, Chapters 1–3	
Reading for Meaning	Fantasy and Character	

Advance Preparation

If you are not able to complete the online Warm-Up, then print the selection and listen to students read aloud. Read Chapters 1–3 (pp. 5–27) of *Peter Pan* before beginning the Guided Reading to identify Words to Know in the text.

Big Ideas

Verbalizing your thoughts while modeling a reading strategy allows students to see what goes on inside the head of an effective reader; it makes visible the normally hidden process of comprehending text.

【Materials】

- *Peter Pan* by J.M. Barrie (adapted by Cathy East Dubowski)
- "Little Bears," Part 1 (optional)

Story Synopsis

We meet the Darlings of London who have three children and their nursemaid dog Nana. The three children—Wendy, John, and Michael—are left on their own one night and are visited by Peter Pan, a magical boy who can fly and never grows up. Peter convinces the children to fly away with him to Neverland and meet the lost boys, children who have no parents.

Keywords

character – a person or animal in a story

fantasy – a story with characters, settings, or other elements that could not really exist

genre – a category for classifying literary works

plot – what happens in a story

prediction – a guess about what might happen that is based on information in a story and what you already know

setting – when and where a story takes place

 **10 minutes**

"Little Bears," Part 1

Students will work independently online to develop fluency and oral reading skills.

Warm-Up

"Little Bears," Part 1

The purpose of this activity is to improve students' oral reading and fluency. Students will read "Little Bears," Part 1. Remind students to listen to the model on each screen before they begin their recording.

 Objectives
- Increase oral reading skills.
- Increase fluency.

Offline Alternative

No computer access? Print a copy of "Little Bears," Part 1. Have students read it aloud. Make note of any pronunciation errors, and review those words with students.

 **50 minutes**

Peter Pan, Part 1

Work **together** with students to complete offline Get Ready, Guided Reading, Check Your Reading, and Reading for Meaning activities.

Get Ready

Review Setting, Character, and Plot

Before reading *Peter Pan*, review with students how to identify **setting**, **characters** and **plot elements** in a story.

1. Have students define **setting**, **character**, and **plot**. Remind them of the definitions if necessary.

2. Tell students that you are going to begin reading a novel, or a fictional chapter book.

3. As they read, students should focus on identifying the setting, the characters, and the plot of the section of the book that you read.

 Objectives
- Define setting.
- Define character.
- Define plot as what happens in a story.
- Increase concept and content vocabulary.

Words to Know

Before reading Chapters 1–3 of *Peter Pan*, go over Words to Know with students.

1. Have students say the word aloud.

2. Ask students if they know what the word means.

   ▶ If students know the word's meaning, have them define it and use it in a sentence.
   ▶ If students don't know the word's meaning, read them the definition and discuss the word with them.

nurse – a woman who takes care of a young child; a babysitter
thimble – a small plastic or metal cap that you wear on your finger to protect it when you sew

Guided Reading

Book Walk

Prepare students by taking them on a Book Walk of *Peter Pan*. Scan the book together and ask students to make predictions about the story. For all questions in the Book Walk, answers will vary.

1. Show students the **front cover** and **back cover**.

2. Have students point to and read the **title** and **author**. Explain that J.M. Barrie wrote the original book, *Peter Pan*, and Cathy East Dubowski rewrote the book to make it shorter and easier to read.

3. Have students tell if they have ever heard, read, or seen this story before. If they have, have them tell what they know about it.

4. Read the text on the back cover to students. Have them tell whether any of the characters sound familiar.

5. Introduce the genre of **fantasy**. Define fantasy and discuss why someone would read fantasy. Have students predict, from the text on the back cover, what elements of this story might not be real.

6. Read through the **table of contents**. Explain to students that you're going to read Chapters 1 through 3.

7. Look through the chapters and read their titles. Have students look at the **illustrations** and describe what they see.

   ▶ Who do you think are some of the characters in the story?
   ▶ Who is the boy covered in leaves?
   ▶ What do you think will happen in this part of the book?

Objectives
- Define fantasy.
- Use an illustration to make a prediction about a reading.
- Identify setting.
- Identify characters.
- Describe setting.
- Use text to make a prediction.
- Answer who, what, where, when, why, and how questions.

Peter Pan, **Chapters 1–3**

Now it's time to read Chapters 1–3 of *Peter Pan.* Have students sit next to you so that they can see the pictures and words while you read the story aloud.

1. Read Chapters 1–3, including reading the chapter titles, aloud all the way through. Track with your finger so students can follow along.

2. If there is time, continue with Step 3. If not, go on to Check Your Reading.

3. You will reread Chapters 1–3 with students, having them chime in and read aloud with you. Tell them to think about the setting, the characters, and what happens as you read. Pause at certain points in the story to discuss.

4. Begin to reread, pausing at the top of page 6 to ask the following questions.

   ▶ Where does the story take place? Where is that? London; It's a city in England, a country across the Atlantic Ocean.

   ▶ Look at the picture. When do you think this takes place—in modern times or long ago? Why do you think this? long ago; The people are wearing clothing from long ago that I've seen in other stories.

   ▶ What characters have we met? the Darlings, their dog Nana

5. Continue reading and pause at the top of page 7 to discuss the story.

   ▶ What is Neverland? How would you describe it? Possible answers: Neverland is a make-believe place where children can play all the time and pretend. There are people and things there that children like to imagine and dream about.

6. Continue reading and then pause at the top of page 12 to discuss Peter Pan.

   ▶ What is Peter Pan like? Possible answers: He is a boy who never grows up. He can fly. He is magical.

7. Read on and pause at the end of Chapter 1.

   ▶ What do you think will happen next? Answers will vary.

8. Continue reading with Chapter 2 and pause to discuss at the bottom of page 16 after the phrase, "chained her in the yard."

   ▶ Why did Mr. Darling put Nana out in the yard? He was embarrassed and angry that the children felt bad for Nana when she drank Mr. Darling's medicine.

9. Read to the end of Chapter 2 and pause to discuss.

   ▶ What do you think will happen next? Answers will vary.

10. Continue reading and pause to discuss at the bottom of page 18, the first page of Chapter 3, after the phrase, "tinkling of golden bells."

    ▶ Who is Tinker Bell? a fairy; a friend of Peter Pan

11. Read on, and pause to discuss at the end of page 21 after the sentence, "That seemed to please Peter."

    ▶ What does Wendy do for Peter Pan? She sews his shadow back on.

    ▶ What seems strange about Peter? He doesn't know what a kiss is; his shadow can come off.

12. Read to the middle of page 22 and then pause to discuss.

   ▸ Why did Peter run away as a baby and join the fairies? He didn't want to
     grow up.

13. Read to the end of Chapter 3, and discuss.

   ▸ Why does Peter want Wendy to come with him? He wants her to be a
     mother to him and the lost boys and tell them stories.
   ▸ What do you think will happen next? Answers will vary.

Check Your Reading

Peter Pan, **Chapters 1–3**
Have students retell the story in their own words to develop grammar, vocabulary,
comprehension, and fluency skills. When finished, **ask students the following
questions** to check comprehension and encourage discussion.

   ▸ When and where does this part of the story take place? at the Darlings' house in
     London one night when the parents are going out
   ▸ Use one or two words to describe each of these characters: Mrs. Darling,
     Mr. Darling, Wendy, Peter Pan, and Tinker Bell. Possible answers: The mother
     is nice and caring. The father is mean and wants everyone to admire him.
     Wendy seems kind and curious. Peter Pan is magical and doesn't grow up.
     Tinker Bell is angry and jealous of Wendy.
   ▸ Where does Peter Pan take the Darling children? away to meet the lost boys in
     Neverland How to they get there? They fly.
   ▸ What do you think will happen in the next chapters? Possible answer: I think
     we're going to find out what Neverland is like.

Objectives
- Answer questions requiring
  literal recall of details.
- Describe characters and
  their traits.

Reading for Meaning

Fantasy and Character
Students will build a foundation for reading the rest of the novel by discussing the
elements of fantasy in *Peter Pan* and the motivations of the characters. Ask students
the following questions to guide the discussion.

   ▸ Fantasy is a story with characters, settings, or other elements that could not
     really exist. But there are some parts of fantasy stories that could be real. What
     parts of this story could be real? Possible answers: There could be a family with
     three children and a dog that lives in London. The mother and father could go
     to parties. The children might have to take medicine.
   ▸ What parts of the story could not be real? Possible answers: A dog acts as a
     babysitter to children. Peter Pan is a boy who never grows up and he flies.
     Tinker Bell is a small, bright fairy that flies. The children all fly away with Peter.
     Peter gets separated from his shadow.
   ▸ Use three words to describe Wendy. Possible answers: caring, curious, grown
     up, polite, brave, smart
   ▸ Why did Peter run away from his parents? He didn't want to grow up.
   ▸ Why does Peter want Wendy to come with him? He wants her to be a mother
     to him and the lost boys and to tell them stories.

Objectives
- Identify characteristics of
  different genres.
- Describe characters and
  their traits.
- Answer inferential questions.

Introduce *Peter Pan* (B)

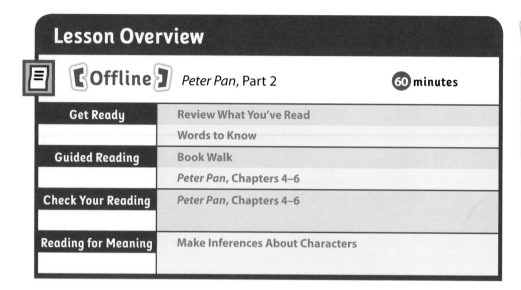

Lesson Overview

[Offline] *Peter Pan*, Part 2 **60 minutes**

Get Ready	Review What You've Read
	Words to Know
Guided Reading	Book Walk
	Peter Pan, Chapters 4–6
Check Your Reading	*Peter Pan*, Chapters 4–6
Reading for Meaning	Make Inferences About Characters

Advance Preparation

Read Chapters 4–6 (pp. 28–41) of *Peter Pan* before beginning the Guided Reading to identify Words to Know in the text.

Big Ideas

▶ Comprehension entails asking and answering questions about the text.
▶ Comprehension strategies can be taught through explicit instruction.

[Materials]

Supplied

- *Peter Pan* by J.M. Barrie (adapted by Cathy East Dubowski)

Story Synopsis

In Chapters 4 through 6, the children fly with Peter Pan and Tinker Bell to the Neverland. As the group flies above the island, Tinker Bell tricks the lost boys into shooting Wendy with an arrow, but she is unharmed. Peter explains that Wendy is to be their new mother, and the boys build Wendy a new house. We also meet Captain Hook, who hates Peter because the boy cut off Hook's hand and fed it to a crocodile that follows Hook wherever he goes.

Keywords

character – a person or animal in a story

context clue – a word or phrase in a text that helps you figure out the meaning of an unknown word

fantasy – a story with characters, settings, or other elements that could not really exist

inference – a guess you make using the clues in a text and what you already know

plot – what happens in a story

setting – when and where a story takes place

summarize – to tell in order the most important ideas or events of a text

 **60 minutes**

Peter Pan, Part 2

Work **together** with students to complete offline Get Ready, Guided Reading, Check Your Reading, and Reading for Meaning activities.

Get Ready

Review What You've Read

Before reading Chapters 4–6 of *Peter Pan*, have students retell what they've read so far in the story.

1. Have students retell the **plot** of Chapters 1–3. Make sure students identify the **setting** as London and describe the **characters**, including all of the Darlings, Peter Pan, and Tinker Bell.

2. Tell students that you will read the next part of the book, beginning with Chapter 4.

3. Remind students that as you read, they should focus on identifying and describing the setting, new characters, and the plot.

> **Objectives**
> - Summarize the plot of a story.
> - Identify setting.
> - Identify characters.
> - Increase concept and content vocabulary.

Words to Know

Before reading *Peter Pan*, Chapters 4–6, go over Words to Know with students.

1. Ask students to define the following word from earlier chapters and use it in a sentence:

   thimble

2. Correct any incorrect or vague definitions.

3. Have students say the word below, which they will encounter in the next chapters.

4. Ask students if they know what the word means.

   ▸ If students know the word's meaning, have them define it and use it in a sentence.
   ▸ If students don't know the word's meaning, read them the definition and discuss the word with them.

nightclothes – pajamas; what you wear to bed

Guided Reading

Book Walk

Prepare students by taking them on a Book Walk of *Peter Pan*. Scan the book together and ask students to make predictions about the story.

1. Show students the **front cover** of the book. Have students read the **title** and the **author**.

2. Have students tell what kind of novel this is. fantasy

3. Have students explain what makes this book a fantasy. There are things in the story that cannot be real.

4. Tell students that you're going to read Chapters 4 through 6. Have students find Chapter 4 in the **table of contents** and turn to that page.

5. Review with students what was happening in the story when you left off. Summarize what has happened and ask students to chime in. Then model the reading strategy by going back and rereading the last two paragraphs of Chapter 3 to review.

6. Look through Chapters 4–6 and read the chapter titles. Have students look at the **illustrations** and describe what they see.

   ▶ What do you think happens in this part of the book? Answers will vary.

Objectives
- Identify characteristics of different genres.
- Use an illustration to make a prediction about a reading.
- Use chapter titles to make predictions and comprehend text.
- Use text to make a prediction.

Peter Pan, Chapters 4–6

Now it's time to read Chapters 4–6 of *Peter Pan*. Have students sit next to you so that they can see the pictures and words while you read the story aloud.

1. Read Chapters 4–6 (pp. 28–41) aloud all the way through, including the chapter titles. Track with your finger so students can follow along.

2. If there is time, continue with Step 3. If not, go on to Check Your Reading.

3. You will reread Chapters 4–6 with students, having them chime in and read aloud with you. Tell them to think about the setting, the characters, and what happens as you read. Pause at certain points in the story to discuss.

4. Begin rereading Chapter 4 and at the end of page 29, pause to discuss the setting and characters and have students make a prediction.

   ▶ Where is this part of the story going to take place? on the island of Neverland
   ▶ Who lives on the island? the lost boys, pirates
   ▶ Make predictions: What do you think will happen next? Answers will vary.

5. Read on and then pause to discuss at the end of the chapter. Have students summarize what they read, prompting them with these questions.

   ▶ What just happened at the end of the chapter? The children were separated, and Wendy is flying alone with Tinker Bell.
   ▶ How does Tinker Bell feel about Wendy? Tinker Bell is jealous of Wendy.

6. Continue reading and pause to discuss at the bottom of page 33 after the sentence, "The lost boys crowded around Wendy."

   ▸ What characters have we met in Chapter 5? the lost boys
   ▸ What does Tinker Bell tell the boys to do to Wendy? shoot her

7. Read on and pause to discuss in the middle of page 35 after the sentence, "But for a whole week!"

   ▸ How does Peter Pan feel about Tinker Bell's behavior? He doesn't like it; he's angry at her.

8. Read to the end of Chapter 5 and pause to discuss, prompting students with these questions.

   ▸ What does Wendy agree to do? be a mother to the lost boys
   ▸ What do you think will happen next? Answers will vary.

9. Continue reading Chapter 6 and pause to discuss at the end of page 39 after the phrase, "gave the croc its taste for me!"

   ▸ What characters have we met in this chapter? Captain Hook, Smee
   ▸ Why does Captain Hook want to kill Peter Pan? He cut off Hook's hand and fed it to a crocodile that now wants to eat Hook.

10. Read to the end of Chapter 6.

Check Your Reading

Peter Pan, Chapters 4–6

Have students retell the story in their own words to develop grammar, vocabulary, comprehension, and fluency skills. When finished, **ask students the following questions** to check comprehension and encourage discussion.

Objectives
• Answer questions requiring literal recall of details.

   ▸ Why does Tinker Bell tell the boys to shoot Wendy? She's jealous of Wendy and wants to hurt her or kill her.
   ▸ What saves Wendy when the boys shoot her? the acorn Peter gave her
   ▸ What do the boys make for Wendy? a house underground
   ▸ How does Captain Hook know that the crocodile is near? It swallowed a clock and it ticks.
   ▸ How does Captain Hook plan to kill the lost boys? by giving them a rich, damp cake that will make them sick

Reading for Meaning

Make Inferences About Characters

Students will build a foundation for reading the rest of the novel by describing the characters and discussing their feelings and motivations. Ask students the following questions to guide the discussion.

► Why does Peter want Wendy to come with him to Neverland? He wants her to be a mother to him and the lost boys and to tell them stories.

► How does Tinker Bell try to hurt Wendy? Tinker Bell tells the lost boys to shoot Wendy.

► Why doesn't Tinker Bell like Wendy? Tinker Bell wants Peter Pan all to herself.

► Why does Wendy agree to be a mother to the lost boys? Possible answers: She wants to play at being a mother; she feels sorry for the boys; she is a responsible and caring person.

► Give two words to describe Captain Hook. Possible answers: mean, scary, angry, hateful, tricky.

Objectives

- Describe characters and their traits.
- Describe character motivations.
- Describe character feelings.
- Answer inferential questions.

Introduce *Peter Pan* (C)

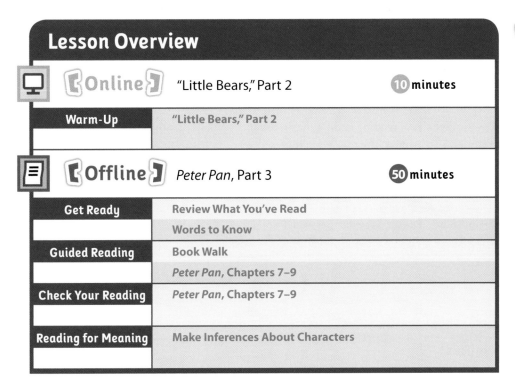

Lesson Overview

🖥️ **[Online]**	"Little Bears," Part 2	**10** minutes
Warm-Up	"Little Bears," Part 2	

📄 **[Offline]**	*Peter Pan*, Part 3	**50** minutes
Get Ready	Review What You've Read	
	Words to Know	
Guided Reading	Book Walk	
	Peter Pan, Chapters 7–9	
Check Your Reading	*Peter Pan*, Chapters 7–9	
Reading for Meaning	Make Inferences About Characters	

Advance Preparation

If you are not able to complete the online Warm-Up, then print the selection and listen to students read aloud. Read Chapters 7–9 (pp. 42–57) of *Peter Pan* before beginning the Guided Reading to become familiar with the story.

Big Ideas

- ▶ Comprehension entails having and knowing a purpose for reading.
- ▶ Comprehension entails actively thinking about what is being read.

Materials

Supplied

- *Peter Pan* by J.M. Barrie (adapted by Cathy East Dubowski)
- "Little Bears," Part 2 (optional)

Story Synopsis

In Chapters 7 through 9, the Darling children make their home underground in Neverland, where Wendy takes care of the lost boys just like her own mother would. At the Mermaids' Lagoon, the pirates have captured the Indian princess Tiger Lily, but Peter Pan tricks them into releasing her. A fight ensues between Peter and Captain Hook, and Hook wins by cheating. Peter is left stranded on a rock in a rising tide until he is saved by the Neverbird.

Keywords

character – a person or animal in a story

context clue – a word or phrase in a text that helps you figure out the meaning of an unknown word

fantasy – a story with characters, settings, or other elements that could not really exist

inference – a guess you make using the clues in a text and what you already know

plot – what happens in a story

setting – when and where a story takes place

summarize – to tell in order the most important ideas or events of a text

 **10 minutes**

"Little Bears," Part 2

Students will work independently online to develop fluency and oral reading skills.

Warm-Up

"Little Bears," Part 2

The purpose of this activity is to improve students' oral reading and fluency. Students will read "Little Bears," Part 2. Remind students to listen to the model on each screen before they begin their recording.

 Objectives
- Increase oral reading skills.
- Increase fluency.

Offline Alternative

No computer access? Print a copy of "Little Bears," Part 2. Have students read it aloud. Make note of any pronunciation errors, and review those words with students.

 **50 minutes**

Peter Pan, Part 3

Work **together** with students to complete offline Get Ready, Guided Reading, Check Your Reading, and Reading for Meaning activities.

Get Ready

Review What You've Read

Before reading Chapters 7–9 of *Peter Pan*, have students retell what they read so far in the story.

 Objectives
- Summarize the plot of a story.
- Identify setting.
- Identify characters.
- Increase concept and content vocabulary.

1. Have students retell the **plot** of Chapters 4–6. Make sure students identify the **setting** as Neverland and describe the new **characters** they've met, including the lost boys, Captain Hook, and Smee.

2. Tell students that you are going to read the next part of the book, beginning with Chapter 7.

3. Remind students to think about identifying and describing the setting, characters, and plot as you read.

Words to Know

Before reading *Peter Pan*, Chapters 7–9, go over Words to Know with students.

1. Ask students to define the following words from earlier chapters and use them in sentences:

   nightclothes   **thimble**

2. Correct any incorrect or vague definitions.

Guided Reading •••

Book Walk

Prepare students by taking them on a Book Walk of *Peter Pan*. Scan the book together and ask students to make predictions about the story.

1. Show students the **front cover** of the book. Have students read the **title** and the **author**.

2. Tell students that you will begin reading at Chapter 7, where you left off. Have students find the chapter in the **table of contents** and turn to that page.

3. Tell students that you're going to review what was happening in the story when you left off. Go back and reread the last two paragraphs of Chapter 6 to review.

4. Look through Chapters 7–9. Read the chapter titles, and have students look at the **illustrations** and describe what they see.

   ▶ What do you think happens in this part of the book? Answers will vary.

> **Objectives**
> * Use an illustration to make a prediction about a reading.
> * Use chapter titles to make predictions and comprehend text.
> * Use text to make a prediction.
> * Use context clues to determine word meanings.

Peter Pan, Chapters 7–9

Now it's time to read Chapters 7–9 of *Peter Pan*. Have students sit next to you so that they can see the pictures and words while you read the story aloud.

1. Read Chapters 7–9 aloud all the way through. Track with your finger so students can follow along.

2. If there is time, continue with Step 3. If not, move on to Check Your Reading.

3. You will reread Chapters 7–9 with students, having them chime in and read aloud with you. Tell them to think about the setting, the characters, and what happens as you read. Pause at certain points in the story to discuss.

4. Begin to reread, pausing to discuss at the end of page 43 to summarize the plot and discuss problems and solutions.

   ▶ What place does this chapter describe? the lost boys' home underground
   ▶ Do you think there's anything strange about what the children eat for meals? Sometimes they don't eat anything because Peter Pan serves pretend food.
   ▶ How do Wendy and the boys solve the problem of the Never tree that grows in the middle of the room? They chop it down to the floor to make more room or put a door on top to make a table out of the stump.

5. Read on to the end of the chapter and pause for students to make inferences and use context clues, prompting them with these questions.

   ► Why are Michael and John forgetting their parents? because they've been away so long

   ► Why do you think Wendy is so happy? Possible answers: She likes pretending to be a mother; she likes taking care of people; she wants to be a mother someday.

   ► What do you think the word *mending* means on page 45? Use context clues to help you. fixing holes in clothes; The story says Wendy is fixing holes in socks, and the illustration shows her doing the same thing.

6. Continue reading with Chapter 8. Pause to discuss at the top of page 46 and have students use context clues.

   ► What do you think a *lagoon* is? a body of water

7. Pause at the end of page 47 to identify a new character.

   ► Who is Tiger Lily? the daughter of the Indian chief; an Indian princess

8. Pause at the end of page 49 to discuss the plot.

   ► How does Peter Pan trick the pirates? He pretends to be Captain Hook and tells the pirates to let Tiger Lily go.

9. Pause to discuss at the end of Chapter 8.

   ► What does Hook do when he hears the crocodile ticking? He flees; he swims away.

10. Read on with Chapter 9. Pause at the end of page 54 to discuss plot.

    ► How does Peter save Wendy? He ties her to a kite that carries her off the rock.

11. Pause to discuss at the top of page 56.

    ► How does the Neverbird help Peter? She gives Peter her nest.

    ► How does Peter help her in return? He gives her Smee's hat for a nest.

Check Your Reading

Peter Pan, Chapters 7–9

Have students retell the story in their own words to develop grammar, vocabulary, comprehension, and fluency skills. When finished, **ask students the following questions** to check comprehension and encourage discussion.

► How is the children's home in Neverland different from homes in the real world? The children live underground; they sit on mushrooms; they eat make-believe food; they have a tree growing in the middle of the house.

► Where do Chapters 8 and 9 take place? at Mermaids' Lagoon

Objectives

• Answer questions requiring literal recall of details.

• Make inferences about characters using evidence from the text.

▶ When Hook hears Peter Pan's voice and thinks it's a ghost, or a spirit, how does Hook feel? scared, nervous   What do the other pirates think of Hook for acting that way? They don't admire him anymore.

▶ Why does Peter help Captain Hook during their fight? He always wants a fair fight.

▶ Why does the Neverbird help Peter? It helps because Peter had once helped the Neverbird.

Reading for Meaning

Make Inferences About Characters

Students will build a foundation for reading the rest of the novel by describing the characters and discussing their feelings and motivations. Ask students the following questions to guide the discussion.

▶ Why does Peter trick the pirates to save Tiger Lily instead of waiting until the pirates leave to help her? Possible answers: He likes to have fun and adventures; pretending to be Hook is more fun; he wants to embarrass Hook or make him angry; he wants to embarrass the pirates and show how foolish they are.

▶ Why does Peter want to fight fairly even though he doesn't like Hook? Possible answers: He's honorable; a fair fight is more fun or challenging than cheating; he wants to embarrass Hook by beating him fair and square.

▶ Why does Hook cheat? Possible answers: He doesn't care about being fair; he's mean and tricky.

▶ Why does Peter save Wendy before he saves himself? Possible answers: He's brave; he really cares about Wendy; he thinks that nothing bad will happen to him anyway.

▶ How do Peter and the Neverbird help each other? Peter once protected the bird's nest when it fell in the water; the Neverbird gives Peter her nest; Peter gives the Neverbird the pirate's hat for her eggs.

Objectives
- Describe characters and their traits.
- Describe character motivations.
- Describe character feelings.
- Answer inferential questions.

Introduce *Peter Pan* (D)

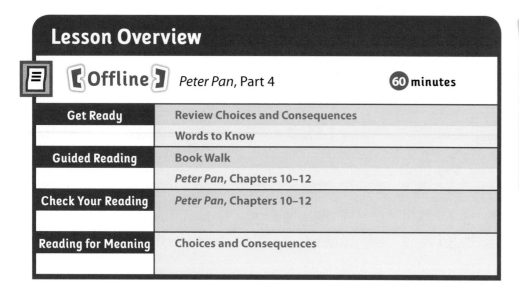

Lesson Overview

〔Offline〕 *Peter Pan*, Part 4		60 minutes
Get Ready	Review Choices and Consequences	
	Words to Know	
Guided Reading	Book Walk	
	Peter Pan, Chapters 10–12	
Check Your Reading	*Peter Pan*, Chapters 10–12	
Reading for Meaning	Choices and Consequences	

Advance Preparation

Read Chapters 10–12 (pp. 58–79) of *Peter Pan* before beginning the Guided Reading to identify Words to Know in the text.

Big Ideas

▸ Comprehension requires an understanding of story structure.
▸ Comprehension entails actively thinking about what is being read.
▸ Identifying choices and consequences helps readers understand characters and the central message in a story.

〔Materials〕

Supplied

● *Peter Pan* by J.M. Barrie (adapted by Cathy East Dubowski)

● *K¹² Language Arts Activity Book*, p. LC 53

Story Synopsis

Wendy describes life in London; her brothers ask to go home. The lost boys also wish to go but Peter Pan refuses. The pirates capture the children, and Hook tries to poison Peter. Tinker Bell drinks the poison but is revived. Peter sneaks aboard the pirate ship to rescue the children and fights Hook. Hook jumps overboard and is eaten by the crocodile. Peter guides all the children home.

Keywords

character – a person or animal in a story

consequence – what happens because of an action or event

context clue – a word or phrase in a text that helps you figure out the meaning of an unknown word

fantasy – a story with characters, settings, or other elements that could not really exist

inference – a guess you make using the clues in a text and what you already know

plot – what happens in a story

setting – when and where a story takes place

summarize – to tell in order the most important ideas or events of a text

 **60** minutes

Peter Pan, Part 4

Work **together** with students to complete offline Get Ready, Guided Reading, Check Your Reading, and Reading for Meaning activities.

Get Ready

Review Choices and Consequences

Review the concepts of choices and consequences.

1. Have students retell the **plot** of Chapters 7–9 of *Peter Pan*. Make sure students identify the **setting**, the **characters** involved in the action, and what happens to them.

2. Review with students that characters in stories, like real people, make choices. Their choices have **consequences**. Have students define consequence.

3. Have students give an example of a choice they made and the outcome, or consequence, of the choice. Discuss their choice. Answers will vary.

   ▸ Why did you make this choice and not another?
   ▸ What might have happened if you had made a different choice?

4. Tell students that you are going to read the next part of the book, Chapters 10–12, beginning with Chapter 10 where you left off.

5. Remind students that as you read, they should think about the choices that Peter Pan and Wendy make and the consequences of their choices.

Objectives
- Summarize the plot of a story.
- Identify setting.
- Identify characters.
- Define consequence.
- Increase concept and content vocabulary.

Words to Know

Before reading Chapters 10–12 of *Peter Pan*, go over Words to Know with students.

1. Ask students to define the following words from earlier chapters and use them in sentences:

   nightclothes   **thimble**

2. Correct any incorrect or vague definitions.

3. Then have students say the word below, which they will encounter in the next chapters.

4. Ask students if they know what the word means.

   ▸ If students know the word's meaning, have them define it and use it in a sentence.
   ▸ If students don't know the word's meaning, read them the definition and discuss the word with them.

aye – yes

Guided Reading

Book Walk

Prepare students by taking them on a Book Walk of *Peter Pan*. Scan the book together and ask students to make predictions about the story.

1. Show students the **front cover** of the book. Have students read the **title** and the **author**.

2. Tell students that you will begin reading at Chapter 10, where you left off. Have students find the chapter in the **table of contents** and turn to that page.

3. Review what you read when you left off by rereading the last three paragraphs of Chapter 9.

4. Look through Chapters 10–12 and read the chapter titles. Have students look at the **illustrations** and describe what they see.

   ▶ What do you think will happen in this part of the book? Answers will vary.

Objectives

- Use an illustration to make a prediction about a reading.
- Use chapter titles to make predictions and comprehend text.
- Use text to make a prediction.

Peter Pan, **Chapters 10–12**

Now it's time to read Chapters 10–12 of *Peter Pan*. Have students sit next to you so that they can see the pictures and words while you read the story aloud.

1. Read Chapters 10–12 aloud all the way through. Track with your finger so students can follow along.

2. If there is time, continue with Step 3. If not, move on to Check Your Reading.

3. You will reread Chapters 10–12 with students, having them chime in and read aloud with you. Tell them to think about the setting, the characters, and what happens as you read. Pause at certain points in the story to discuss.

4. Begin rereading Chapter 10 and pause to discuss at the end of page 60. Have students make inferences.

   ▶ Why does Peter hate Wendy's story about the Darlings? Possible answers: It reminds him that his mother didn't leave the window open for him; he's jealous of Wendy because she has a mother who cares; he doesn't want Wendy to make the lost boys think that a home with parents is better than Neverland.

   ▶ The lost boys are sad that Wendy is leaving. What is her solution to this problem? She offers to take them home with her.

5. Read on, pausing to discuss in the middle of page 62 after the sentence, "There seemed nothing more for Wendy to say." Have students describe Peter Pan's motivation.

   ▶ Why doesn't Peter want to go back home with Wendy and the boys? He wants to be a boy forever and never grow up.

6. Read to the end of the chapter. Pause there to have students retell part of the story.

   ▶ What tricks does Hook play on the Indians and the boys? He surprises the Indians and attacks them in the dark; he beats the Indians' tom-toms so the children think it's safe to come out.

7. Begin rereading Chapter 11. Pause at the top of page 67 to review the plot.

   ▶ How does Hook try to harm Peter? He tries to poison Peter.
   ▶ What happens to Tinker Bell? She drinks the poison instead.

8. Read to the end of Chapter 11, and pause to discuss.

   ▶ How is Tinker Bell saved? Peter asked children to clap if they believe in fairies, and they do, so Tinker Bell lives.
   ▶ What will happen next? Answers will vary.

9. Continue reading with Chapter 12. Pause to discuss at the end of page 73.

   ▶ How does Peter Pan trick Hook? He ticks like the crocodile.

10. Pause to discuss again at the end of page 74.

   ▶ What happens to the pirates who go into the cabin with Peter? They don't come out.

11. Read on, and pause to discuss at the end of page 76.

   ▶ How does Peter Pan trick Hook this time? He dresses up and pretends to be Wendy so Hook will come close to fight him.

12. Read to the end of Chapter 12.

Check Your Reading

Peter Pan, Chapters 10–12
Have students retell the story in their own words to develop grammar, vocabulary, comprehension, and fluency skills. When finished, **ask students the following questions** to check comprehension and encourage discussion.

▶ Where do Chapters 10 and 11 take place? in the lost boys' underground home
▶ Why do you think Hook doesn't like Peter's crowing? Possible answers: He finds it annoying; he is angry that Peter is boastful; he's jealous of Peter.
▶ How does Hook trick the boys into coming out of the house? He plays tom-toms like the Indians, so the boys will think the Indians won the battle against the pirates.
▶ Where does Chapter 12 take place? onboard the pirate ship
▶ Why does Peter strut up and down the deck for a while after Hook is gone? He is proud of defeating Hook. He wants to show off.

Objectives
- Answer questions requiring literal recall of details.
- Make inferences using text and prior knowledge.

Reading for Meaning ∙∙∙

Choices and Consequences

Have students look at some of the choices that Peter Pan and Wendy make and the consequences of their choices by completing page LC 53 in *K¹² Language Arts Activity Book*. This activity will build a foundation for identifying the theme of the novel.

> **Objectives**
> • Identify choices that a character makes and their consequences.

1. Review with students that characters, like people in real life, make choices about their actions. Their choices lead to consequences, or outcomes.

2. Tell students that a character's choices tell us something about the character's traits, or what kind of person the character is.

3. Turn to page 22 in *Peter Pan*. Tell students that this is the part of the story where Peter Pan and Wendy meet for the first time, and Peter explains how he came to be a boy forever.

4. Read page 22, beginning with the sentence, "I ran away the day I was born." Pause after the sentence, "So I ran away to live with the fairies." Discuss Peter's choices and consequences in this passage, prompting students with these questions.

   ▸ What choice does Peter make when he hears his parents talking? He decides to run away.
   ▸ Why does he make this choice? He doesn't want to grow up.
   ▸ What is the consequence of his choice? He lives with the fairies, not his parents, and he will always be a boy.

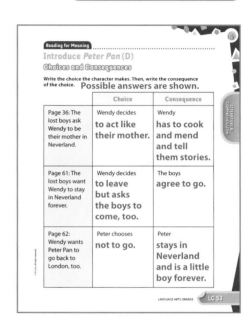

5. Have students complete the Activity Book page. Remind them to go back to the text to get more information if needed.

6. Discuss why the character makes each choice.
   Say: What does this choice tell us about the character? Wendy's choices show us she wants to grow up and that she is responsible and mature. She likes playing house, but she does want to go home and she knows that she will eventually grow up. Peter's choices show us that he doesn't want to grow up and that he would prefer to play and not have any responsibilities.

7. Have students keep the Activity Book page in a safe place so they can refer to it after reading Chapters 13 and 14.

Review *Peter Pan*

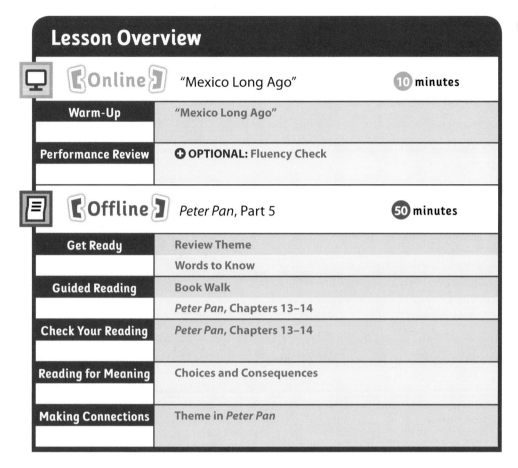

Lesson Overview

Online — "Mexico Long Ago" — 10 minutes

Warm-Up	"Mexico Long Ago"
Performance Review	⊕ OPTIONAL: Fluency Check

Offline — *Peter Pan*, Part 5 — 50 minutes

Get Ready	Review Theme
	Words to Know
Guided Reading	Book Walk
	Peter Pan, Chapters 13–14
Check Your Reading	*Peter Pan*, Chapters 13–14
Reading for Meaning	Choices and Consequences
Making Connections	Theme in *Peter Pan*

Advance Preparation

If you are not able to complete the online Warm-Up, then print the selection and listen to students read aloud. Read Chapter 13 (pp. 80–85) of Peter Pan before beginning the Guided Reading to identify Words to Know in the text. Have students gather the completed page LC 53 in *K¹² Language Arts Activity Book* (Choices and Consequences).

Big Ideas

▸ Reading strategies are conscious plans that readers apply and adapt to make sense of text.
▸ Comprehension requires the reader to self-correct errors made while reading by using a wide variety of strategies.
▸ Identifying choices and consequences helps readers to understand characters and the central message in a story.

〖Materials〗

Supplied

- *Peter Pan* by J.M. Barrie (adapted by Cathy East Dubowski)
- *K¹² Language Arts Activity Book*, pp. LC 53–54
- "Mexico Long Ago" (optional)
- Fluency Performance Checklist (optional)

Story Synopsis

Wendy and the boys return to London and the Darlings adopt the lost boys, but Peter Pan leaves. Mrs. Darling allows Wendy to return to Neverland once a year. Over time, Peter often forgets Wendy, and she ultimately decides she is too old for Neverland. She allows her daughter and later her granddaughter to go.

Keywords

character – a person or animal in a story

consequence – what happens because of an action or event

fantasy – a story with characters, settings, or other elements that could not really exist

inference – a guess you make using the clues in a text and what you already know

plot – what happens in a story

setting – when and where a story takes place

summarize – to tell in order the most important ideas or events of a text

theme – the author's message or big idea

 **10 minutes**

"Mexico Long Ago"

Students will work independently online to develop fluency and oral reading skills.

Warm-Up

"Mexico Long Ago"
The purpose of this activity is to improve students' oral reading and fluency. Students will read "Mexico Long Ago." Remind students to listen to the model on each screen before they begin their recording.

Objectives
- Increase oral reading skills.
- Increase fluency.

Offline Alternative

No computer access? Print a copy of "Mexico Long Ago." Have students read it aloud. Make note of any pronunciation errors, and review those words with students.

Performance Review

⊕ OPTIONAL: Fluency Check
Listen to students' recordings and use the checklist to review fluency and track performance. Keep the completed checklist so you can review students' progress over time.

Objectives
- Read aloud grade-level text with appropriate automaticity, prosody, accuracy, and rate.

 **50 minutes**

Peter Pan, Part 5

Work **together** with students to complete offline Get Ready, Guided Reading, Check Your Reading, Reading for Meaning, and Making Connections activities.

Get Ready

Review Theme
Review theme to prepare students for thinking about the theme of *Peter Pan*.

1. Have students retell the **plot** of Chapters 10–12 of *Peter Pan*. Make sure students identify the **settings**, the **characters** involved in the action, and what happens to them.

2. Review the definition of **theme** in literature.

Objectives
- Summarize the plot of a story.
- Identify setting.
- Identify characters.
- Define theme.
- Increase concept and content vocabulary.

3. Have students retell a theme from a work they have recently read, such as "Androcles and the Lion": When you show others kindness, they will be kind to you in return.

4. Tell students that you are going to finish reading *Peter Pan* and have them think about the theme of the story.

Words to Know

Before reading *Peter Pan*, Chapters 13–14, go over Words to Know with students.

1. Ask students to define the following words from earlier chapters and use them in sentences:

   aye   **nightclothes**   **thimble**

2. Correct any incorrect or vague definitions.

3. Have students say the phrase below, which they will encounter in Chapter 13.

4. Ask students if they know what the phrase means.

   ▸ If students know the meaning, have them define it and use it in a sentence.
   ▸ If students don't know the meaning, read them the definition and discuss the phrase with them.

begged her pardon – apologized; said "sorry"

Guided Reading

Book Walk

Prepare students by taking them on a Book Walk of *Peter Pan*. Scan the book together and ask students to make predictions about the story.

1. Show students the **front cover** of the book. Have students read the **title** and the **author**.

2. Tell students that today you're going to finish reading the book, beginning with Chapter 13, where you left off. Have students find the chapter in the **table of contents** and turn to that page.

3. Tell students that you're going to review what was happening in the story when you left off. Reread the last two paragraphs of Chapter 12 to review.

4. Look through Chapters 13 and 14 and read the chapter titles. Have students look at the **illustrations** and describe what they see.

   ▸ What do you think happens in this part of the book? Answers will vary.

Objectives

- Use an illustration to make a prediction about a reading.
- Use chapter titles to make predictions and comprehend text.
- Use text to make a prediction.
- Answer who, what, where, when, why, and how questions.

Peter Pan, Chapters 13–14

Now it's time to read Chapters 13 and 14. Have students sit next to you so that they can see the pictures and words while you read the story aloud.

1. Read Chapters 13 and 14 aloud all the way through. Track with your finger so students can follow along.

2. If there is time, continue with Step 3. If not, go on to Check Your Reading.

3. You will reread Chapters 13 and 14 with students, having them chime in and read aloud with you. Tell them to think about the setting, the characters, and what happens as you read. Pause at certain points in the story to discuss.

4. Begin rereading and pause at the end of page 81, and have students summarize the plot.

   ▶ How did Mr. Darling react to the children's leaving at the beginning of the story? How did Mrs. Darling react? Mr. Darling punished himself by living in Nana's kennel until the children came home. Mrs. Darling always leaves the window open for the children.

5. Read on and pause at the top of page 83 after the sentence, "We can't both have Wendy." Have the students make inferences.

   ▶ Why does Peter lock the window so Wendy can't get in? He doesn't want Wendy to go home and stay with her parents. He wants her to return to Neverland with him.

6. Read to the end of Chapter 13 and pause to discuss. Look back at page 85, and have students use context clues to define an unfamiliar word.

   ▶ What does the word *reunion* mean? when people get back together after they haven't seen each other for a long time

7. Continue reading with Chapter 14. Pause to discuss in the middle of page 89 after the sentence, "But Peter had already flown away."

   ▶ What does Mrs. Darling allow Wendy to do every spring? go back to Neverland with Peter

8. Pause to discuss again at the end of page 90.

   ▶ Who does Peter forget? He forgets some of the other people from Neverland, such as Captain Hook and Tinker Bell.

9. Pause to discuss at the end of the first paragraph on page 91.

   ▶ What does Peter often forget to do as the years pass? to go back for Wendy

10. Read to the end of the book.

Check Your Reading

Peter Pan, Chapters 13–14

Have students retell the story in their own words to develop grammar, vocabulary, comprehension, and fluency skills. When finished, **ask students the following questions** to check comprehension and encourage discussion.

Objectives
- Answer questions requiring literal recall of details.

▸ Why doesn't Peter want to stay with the Darlings like the other lost boys?
  He wants to be a boy forever and not grow up.

▸ What happens to the lost boys when they stay with the Darlings?
  They grow up.

▸ Why does Peter forget Wendy and many others from Neverland? He has new adventures that crowd out the old ones.

▸ Why can't Wendy fly away with Peter one year? because she's grown up

▸ Who flies away with Peter when Wendy grows up? Wendy's daughter Jane

▸ Who goes when Jane grows up? Jane's daughter Margaret

Reading for Meaning

Choices and Consequences

Students will look at Peter Pan's and Wendy's choices in the last two chapters of the book. Gather the Choices and Consequences page, and turn to page LC 54 in *K¹² Language Arts Activity Book.*

Objectives
- Identify choices that a character makes and their consequences.

1. Have students define **consequences**.

2. Direct student's attention to the completed Choices and Consequences page. Review the choices Wendy and Peter made and the consequences of their choices.

3. Tell students that they are going to identify choices and consequences in Chapters 13 and 14.

4. Have students complete the Activity Book page. Remind them to go back to the text to get more information if needed.

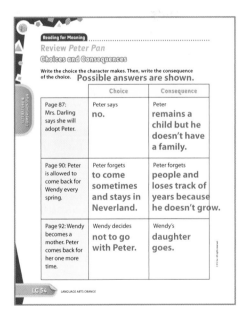

Making Connections

Theme in *Peter Pan*

Have students use both completed Choices and Consequences pages to help them identify the theme in *Peter Pan*.

1. Have students provide the definition of **theme**. Remind students that a theme is a complete sentence that describes what the author wants the reader to know about life or people.

2. Have students review their Choices and Consequences pages.

3. Discuss with students how to use the choices that Peter Pan and Wendy make to think about the theme.

   ▸ What do Wendy's choices tell us about her? What kind of person is she? Wendy wants to grow up. She is responsible and makes choices that will help other people.

   ▸ What does Wendy have in her life at the end of the story? husband, house, daughter

   ▸ Do you think Wendy is happy at the end of the story? Why or why not? Yes, I think she's happy. She gets back to her home and her parents. Then she grows up and has a husband, daughter, and granddaughter of her own.

   ▸ What do Peter's choices tell us about him? Peter doesn't want to grow up. He wants to play and not have any responsibilities forever.

   ▸ What does Peter have in his life at the end of the story? fun and adventure in Neverland; He never has to grow up.

   ▸ What does Wendy have that Peter will never have? a family

   ▸ Do you think Peter is happy at the end of the story? Why or why not? He's sort of happy. He has fun on Neverland. But he's sad that Wendy can't come back. And he doesn't have a family or friends who stay around. He also doesn't remember people.

4. Read the first sentence of the book. Tell students this is part of the theme: All children must grow up. But there's more the author says about this theme. Discuss what the author might be saying about growing up.
   Say: What do you think the author is trying to tell the reader about growing up? Everyone must grow up. There are some things you'll miss when you grow up, like playing and not having responsibilities, but there are good things about becoming an adult, like having a family.

5. If students wish, have them draw a picture of what they want to be when they grow up.

Objectives
- Determine the theme, moral, or lesson of a work of literature.

Reward: Write the names of the literature selections completed in this unit on the My Accomplishments chart and add a sticker to mark successful completion of this unit.

Introduce "The Jackals and the Lion"

Unit Overview

In this unit, students will read "The Jackals and the Lion." In the accompanying lessons, students will focus on

- ► The genre of drama
- ► The elements of a fable in the form of a play
- ► Comprehension strategies used during independent reading

Lesson Overview

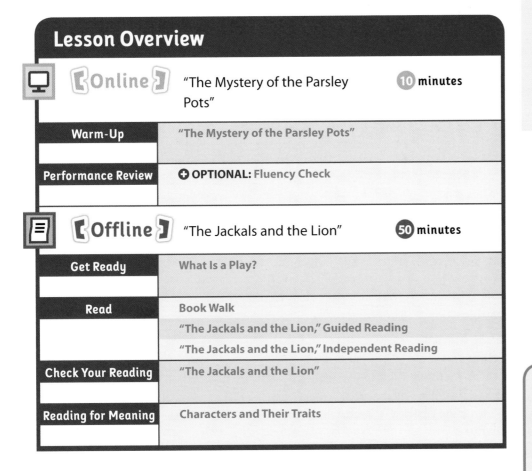

🖥 **[Online]** "The Mystery of the Parsley Pots"		**10** minutes
Warm-Up	"The Mystery of the Parsley Pots"	
Performance Review	⊕ **OPTIONAL:** Fluency Check	

📄 **[Offline]** "The Jackals and the Lion"		**50** minutes
Get Ready	What Is a Play?	
Read	Book Walk	
	"The Jackals and the Lion," Guided Reading	
	"The Jackals and the Lion," Independent Reading	
Check Your Reading	"The Jackals and the Lion"	
Reading for Meaning	Characters and Their Traits	

Advance Preparation

If you are not able to complete the online Warm-Up, then print the selection and listen to students read aloud. Preview the Read and note the parts of the play that you will read aloud and the parts that students will read independently. With this unit, students begin to move toward becoming independent readers. First, they will listen to you read part of a selection. Then they will read the rest of the selection on their own. You will need to monitor their progress during reading, check their comprehension after reading, and review their reading strategies.

Materials

Supplied
- "The Jackals and the Lion," *K¹² Classics for Young Readers, Volume B,* pp. 36–41
- *K¹² Language Arts Activity Book,* pp. LC 55–57
- "The Mystery of the Parsley Pots" (optional)
- Fluency Performance Check (optional)

Story Synopsis

This play tells the story of two jackals who are being chased by a hungry lion. The father jackal tricks the lion by telling him that there is another, bigger lion in the forest. The jackal lures the lion to a well, and when the lion sees his own reflection, he thinks it is the rival lion and jumps in. The jackals have rid themselves of their predator.

Keywords

bold type – type that is darker than the surrounding text that draws attention to a word or phrase

character – a person or animal in a story

drama – another word for play

italic – type that slants toward the right

problem – an issue a character must solve in a story

solution – how a character solves a problem in a story

trait – a quality of a person or other object; what something is like

Online 10 minutes

"The Mystery of the Parsley Pots"

Students will work independently online to develop fluency and oral reading skills.

Warm-Up

"The Mystery of the Parsley Plots"

The purpose of this activity is to improve students' oral reading and fluency. Students will read "The Mystery of the Parsley Pots." Remind students to listen to the model on each screen before they begin their recording.

Objectives
- Increase oral reading skills.
- Increase fluency.

Offline Alternative

No computer access? Print a copy of "The Mystery of the Parsley Pots." Have students read it aloud. Make note of any pronunciation errors, and review those words with students.

Performance Review

⊕ OPTIONAL: Fluency Check

Listen to students' recordings and use the checklist to review fluency and track performance. Keep the completed checklist so you can review students' progress over time.

Objectives
- Read aloud grade-level text with appropriate automaticity, prosody, accuracy, and rate.

 **Offline** 50 minutes

"The Jackals and the Lion"

Work **together** with students to complete offline Get Ready, Read, Check Your Reading, and Reading for Meaning activities.

Get Ready

What Is a Play?

Discuss the elements of drama with students.

1. Ask students the following questions about **drama**. Provide the answers if students are unfamiliar with plays.
   ▸ Have you ever been to a play? Answers will vary.
   ▸ What do you know about plays? Possible answers: Plays are stories told by actors on a stage; there is an audience, and the actors wear costumes; there are also other things on the stage that tell you where the story is happening.

Objectives
- Define drama.
- Answer scriptal questions.
- Connect text to prior knowledge.

▶ What do you expect to see when you go to a play? Possible answers: characters; costumes; sets, props, or things on the stage that tell something about the setting; an audience; a stage; maybe curtains

▶ How is a play similar to television shows or movies? How is it different? Possible answers: Plays and movies are similar because there are actors, a story, and props. They are different because in a movie, the audience is watching something taped or filmed, and the actors aren't live.

2. Tell students that plays are a type of writing called **drama**. Have students tell if they've ever read a play and what the play was about.

3. Explain that drama looks different from poetry, fictional stories, and nonfiction articles and books like ones they've read before.

TIP If students are confused about the difference between a movie and a play, make sure they understand the differences between the two. The audience goes to a theater to see both, but in a movie the actors are not performing live on the stage.

Read ···

Book Walk
Prepare students by taking them on a Book Walk of "The Jackals and the Lion." Scan the play together and ask students to make predictions about the story.

1. Show students the **front cover** and **back cover** of *K¹² Classics for Young Readers, Volume B*. Remind them that the book is a collection of stories.

2. Use the **table of contents** to locate "The Jackals and the Lion." Read the **title** and have students turn to that page.

3. Tell students that "The Jackals and the Lion" is a play.

4. Explain to students that you will read the first two pages of the play aloud, stopping to ask questions as you've done in previous lessons. Students will then read the rest of the play on their own and come back to you to discuss it.

5. Point to the list of characters. Ask students if they know what this is. If they don't, explain that at the beginning of every play, there is a list of characters.

6. Look at the first page of the play. Point out the text in **bold type**, the colon, and the regular text that follows. Ask students if they know why the text looks like this. Explain that in a play, we know which character is speaking by the bold type with a colon after it. The bold type tells us the character's name. The words that follow the colon are what the character says.

7. Point to the text in **italic** on the second page of the play. Tell students that this is italic, or italic type. It is type that slants toward the right and looks different from regular type. Explain that this text is a stage direction. It tells what the characters are doing on stage.

Objectives

- Use text organizational features to locate and comprehend information (table of contents, title, illustrator).
- Identify the structure and elements of drama, including dialogue.
- Use an illustration to make a prediction about a reading.
- Read on-level text with purpose and understanding.
- Identify setting.
- Identify characters.
- Identify the problem a character faces.
- Summarize the plot of a story.
- Use text to make a prediction.
- Self-monitor comprehension by predicting, rereading, checking for sense, drawing on background knowledge, summarizing, clarifying, checking for context clues, and self-questioning.

8. Look at the **illustrations** on the first two pages. Have students describe what they see and make predictions, prompting them with these questions.

  ► Who do you see in the illustrations? children dressed in costumes, people watching

  ► Why are there children in costumes and people watching them? This is a play. The children are actors and the people watching are the audience.

  ► What do you think will happen in the play? Answers will vary.

"The Jackals and the Lion," Guided Reading

Now it's time to read the play. Have students sit next to you so that they can see the pictures and words while you read the play aloud.

1. Read the first two pages aloud all the way through. Read all character names and stage directions. Track with your finger so students can follow along.

2. Explain to students that you will reread the first two pages and that this time they are to chime in and read aloud with you. Tell them to think about the different parts of a play that you talked about during the Book Walk and that you will pause at certain points in the story to discuss.

3. Begin to reread and pause to discuss at the end of the first page. Point to the list of characters and the name of Lion in bold type.
   Say: I am reading the character names aloud because I am showing you how you would read the play silently to yourself.

  ► When a play is performed, no one reads aloud the list of the characters. The actors don't say the name of the character they are playing before they speak.

  ► When a play is performed, the actors only say what the character says— the part after the colon.

  ► We know which character is speaking because there are different actors playing them, or because an actor uses different voices for each character.

4. Pause at the top of the second page after Mother Jackal's lines.

  ► Where does this play take place? in a forest
  ► What problem do the jackals have? A lion is looking for them and wants to eat them.

5. Read the stage directions in a softer voice to differentiate them from the characters' lines. Pause after the stage directions. Explain that you are reading the stage directions aloud because you are showing students how you would read the play silently to yourself. When a play is performed, no one reads the stage directions aloud. The actors simply perform these actions on the stage.

6. Read to the end of the second page, and pause to discuss.

  ► What other characters have we met who are not in the list of characters? little jackals
  ► Why do you think these characters are not in the list? They don't have big parts or speaking parts.
  ► What is Father Jackal's idea for solving their problem? to go talk to the lion
  ► What do you think will happen next? Possible answer: The father will talk to the lion.

"The Jackals and the Lion," Independent Reading

Have students read pages 38–41 of "The Jackals and the Lion" independently using the strategies from the Reading Strategies Guide on page LC 55 in *K¹² Language Arts Activity Book*.

1. Tell students they are going to read the rest of the play on their own.

2. Tell students that as they read, they should use the same strategies you use together in guided reading.

   ▸ Do a book walk of the rest of the play before reading.
   ▸ Predict what will happen.
   ▸ Ask questions while reading to check their understanding.

3. Tell students to pause sometimes in their reading and ask themselves these questions:

   ▸ Where does this part of the story take place?
   ▸ What are the characters like?
   ▸ What just happened in the story?
   ▸ What do I think will happen next?

4. Remind students that if they get to the end of a section of the play or the end of a page, and they are confused about what happened, they should use strategies to repair their understanding. Go over these strategies with students:

   ▸ Summarize: Tell yourself in one or two sentences what just happened.
   ▸ Make inferences: Use your own prior knowledge about something to understand why something happens.
   ▸ Reread: You may want to read a passage again, perhaps a little slower, to make sure you don't miss important information.
   ▸ Read on: If there's a question and you can't find the answer by rereading, the answer may be further on in the text. Read another page and see if the answer is there.
   ▸ Use context clues: When you come across an unfamiliar word, look for nearby clues in the surrounding text to help you define it.

5. Tell students that you will discuss the story and their reading strategies when they have finished.

6. Have students read the remainder of "The Jackals and the Lion," keeping the Reading Strategies Guide handy to refer to as they read independently.

TIP Students should take about 6–10 minutes to read the rest of the play.

Check Your Reading

"The Jackals and the Lion"

Discuss students' reading strategies and have them retell parts of the story to check comprehension.

> **Objectives**
> - Answer questions requiring literal recall of details.
> - Evaluate reading strategies.

1. **Have students retell the story in their own words** to develop grammar, vocabulary, comprehension, and fluency skills. Make sure students have **answered the following questions** in their story summary, or ask them these questions to check comprehension.

   ▸ What does Father Jackal tell the lion? that there is a bigger lion in the forest
   ▸ Where did the Father Jackal take the lion to see the other lion? to a well
   ▸ What does the lion see in the well? his own reflection
   ▸ What does the lion do? He jumps into the well after the other lion he sees.

2. If students have answered all the questions correctly, move on to the next activity or lesson. If students have trouble answering the questions, discuss the reading strategies they used to help their comprehension, prompting them with the following questions. Answers to questions will vary.

   ▸ Did you do a book walk and look through the chapters before you read them?
   ▸ Did you stop sometimes and ask yourself what just happened or what characters you met? When did you do that?
   ▸ Did you stop sometimes and ask yourself what might happen next? When did you do that?
   ▸ Were there times when you were confused about something in the story? When?
   ▸ What did you do when you didn't understand something?

3. If students cannot answer the questions about the text and their reading strategies, or if they seem confused about what they read, have them reread the play aloud beginning with the third page. Prompt them to pause and use the appropriate reading strategies to aid in their comprehension.

4. As students read aloud, count the number of words they struggle to read on any one page. If the number reaches five or more, stop them and read the rest of the play aloud to them.

5. As you read, pause at appropriate points in the story and ask questions about the setting, characters, and plot.

Reading for Meaning

Characters and Their Traits

Have students begin working on page LC 57 in *K¹² Language Arts Activity Book*. Students will complete this page over two lessons. They will recognize character traits by examining how characters solve problems.

1. Have students tell what a character **trait** is.

2. Review with students how we learn about characters and their traits in stories: by what they say, what they do, and by what others say about them.

3. Explain that one way we can learn about a character's traits is what they do to solve a problem.

4. Have students define **problem** and **solution**.

5. Have students tell what problem the jackals have. A lion wants to eat them.

6. Have students describe how Father Jackal solves the problem and tell what they think of his plan. Prompt students with questions if necessary.

   ▸ How does Father Jackal trick the lion? He tells the lion that there's a bigger lion at the bottom of the well. Then the lion jumps in to get the other lion.
   ▸ What do you think of this idea? Possible answer: I think this was smart, because the jackal knew the lion would think that his reflection was another lion.

7. Have students explain how Father Jackal's solution to his problem helps readers learn about his character trait.

   ▸ How would you describe Father Jackal for thinking of this plan? smart, clever

8. Have students complete the chart on the Activity Book page. Tell students to use both the dialogue and the stage directions for evidence. They will complete the exercise that follows the chart when they reread the play.

9. Have students keep the Activity Book in a safe place so they can complete it later.

10. Refer to these for possible answers for the chart:

Character	Trait	Proof from Play
Father Jackal	brave	The jackals go to the lion's den.
Lion	foolish	The lion jumps down into the well.

Objectives
- Identify the problem a character faces.
- Identify the solution to a problem a character faces.
- Describe characters and their traits.
- Describe characters in the story using evidence from the text.

Review "The Jackals and the Lion"

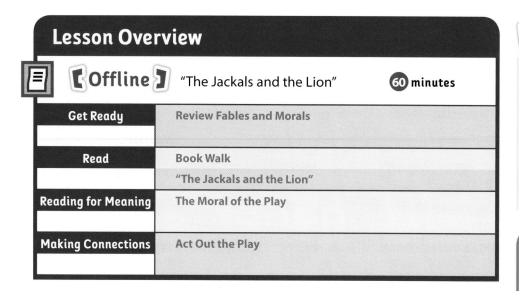

Lesson Overview

[Offline]	"The Jackals and the Lion"	60 minutes
Get Ready	Review Fables and Morals	
Read	Book Walk	
	"The Jackals and the Lion"	
Reading for Meaning	The Moral of the Play	
Making Connections	Act Out the Play	

Materials

Supplied

- "The Jackals and the Lion," *K¹² Classics for Young Readers, Volume B,* pp. 36–41
- *K¹² Language Arts Activity Book,* pp. LC 55–57

Keywords

bold type – type that is darker than the surrounding text that draws attention to a word or phrase

character – a person or animal in a story

drama – another word for play

fable – a story that teaches a lesson and may contain animal characters

italic – type that slants toward the right

moral – the lesson of a story, particularly a fable

trait – a quality of a person or other object; what something is like

Advance Preparation

Have students gather the partially completed page LC 57 in *K¹² Language Arts Activity Book* (The Moral of the Play). Also have students gather the Reading Strategies Guide on page LC 55. If you've misplaced the guide, you can print another copy from the online lesson.

Big Ideas

- ▶ Comprehension is facilitated by an understanding of physical presentation.
- ▶ Comprehension entails an understanding of the organizational patterns of text.
- ▶ Comprehension requires an understanding of story structure.
- ▶ To understand and interpret a story, readers need to understand and describe characters and what they do
- ▶ Reading strategies are conscious plans that readers apply and adapt to make sense of text.

[Offline] 60 minutes

"The Jackals and the Lion"

Work **together** with students to complete offline Get Ready, Read, Reading for Meaning, and Making Connections activities.

Get Ready

Review Fables and Morals

Prepare students to recognize the elements of a fable in the play by discussing fables and morals.

1. Have students tell what a **fable** is.

2. Have students explain what the **moral** of a fable or story is.

3. Have students retell a fable that they've read and tell what the moral of the story is.
   Examples: "The Fox and the Grapes," "The Fox and the Lion"

4. Tell students that they will reread the play "The Jackals and the Lion." They are going to think about how the play is a fable and consider what its moral might be.

Objectives

- Define fable.
- Define moral.
- Recount stories, including fables and folktales from diverse cultures.

Read

Book Walk

Prepare students by taking them on a Book Walk of "The Jackals and the Lion." Scan the play together and ask students to make predictions about the story.

1. Show students the **front cover** of K^{12} *Classics for Young Readers, Volume B*.

2. Have students use the **table of contents** to locate "The Jackals and the Lion" and turn to that page in the book.

3. Have students read the title.

4. Have students use the pictures to tell how the play begins. Some jackals are afraid because a lion wants to eat them.

Objectives

- Use text organizational features to locate and comprehend information (table of contents).
- Retell a story naming plot, setting, character(s), problem, and solution.
- Recount stories, including fables and folktales from diverse cultures.
- Read on-level text with purpose and understanding.
- Self-monitor comprehension by predicting, rereading, checking for sense, drawing on background knowledge, summarizing, clarifying, checking for context clues, and self-questioning.

"The Jackals and the Lion"

Have students reread "The Jackals and the Lion" independently using the strategies from the Reading Strategies Guide.

1. Tell students they are going to reread the play on their own. Remind them to do a Book Walk of the play before they read.

2. Remind students to pause frequently as they read and ask themselves questions, to make sure they understand what they have just read.

3. Remind students to use tools, or strategies, when they don't understand something. Have students review the reading strategies they can use, or prompt them with one or two.

- ▶ Summarize
- ▶ Make inferences
- ▶ Reread
- ▶ Read on
- ▶ Use context clues

4. Remind students to refer to the Reading Strategies Guide as they read.

5. Tell students that when they have finished, you will discuss their understanding of the story and the strategies they used.

6. Have students reread the play. When they have finished reading the play to themselves, have them read it aloud to an adult, a sibling, a peer, or even the family pet.

7. Have students retell the story to you.

 Students should take about 8–12 minutes to read the play.

Reading for Meaning

The Moral of the Play

Have students complete the partially completed page LC 57 in *K¹² Language Arts Activity Book* by recognizing the elements of a fable in the play and identifying the moral.

1. Explain that this play is a **fable** in the form of drama. Have students define fable and **moral**.

2. Have students identify how the play is like a fable: It teaches us a lesson.

3. Discuss with students the characters and how their traits lead us to the moral of the play, prompting them with the following questions.

- ▶ How would you describe the lion in one sentence? He is foolish.
- ▶ How would you describe Father Jackal in one sentence? He is clever.
- ▶ What problem does the lion need to solve? He needs to get something to eat.
- ▶ What problem does the jackal need to solve? He needs to protect his family from the lion.
- ▶ Which character do you think should be able to solve his problem best? Why? Possible answer: The lion should be able to solve his problem best because he is bigger and stronger than the jackals.
- ▶ Which character actually solves his problem? Why is he able to do this? Father Jackal, because he is smarter than the lion
- ▶ What do you think is the moral or lesson of the play? Possible answer: Using your wits can make you stronger than someone more powerful.

Objectives

- Describe characters and their traits.
- Identify the problem a character faces.
- Identify the solution to a problem a character faces.
- Identify the moral or lesson of a text.
- Identify a lesson learned based on a character's actions.
- Compare and contrast characters from different stories.
- Compare and contrast literary elements in two or more literary selections.

4. Have students complete the final exercise on the activity page.

5. Discuss with students how the characters in this play are like characters in other fables. Have students tell about other stories they've read with lions or jackals or similar characters, such as "The Fox and the Lion."

6. Have students describe how these characters in other fables are similar. The fox is smart. The lion is foolish.

7. Explain to students that these types of characters often appear in fables and folktales. Discuss what message these characters tell us: The physically weaker character outsmarts the physically stronger character, which shows us that brains are more important than strength or power.

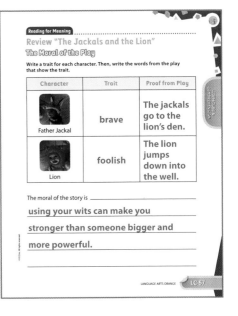

Reading for Meaning
Review "The Jackals and the Lion"
The Moral of the Play
Write a trait for each character. Then, write the words from the play that show the trait.

Character	Trait	Proof from Play
Father Jackal	brave	The jackals go to the lion's den.
Lion	foolish	The lion jumps down into the well.

The moral of the story is _____ using your wits can make you stronger than someone bigger and more powerful.

LANGUAGE ARTS ORANGE LC 57

Making Connections

Act Out the Play
Encourage students to act out the play to reinforce their understanding of the structure of drama and the characters' traits.

1. Tell students that they are going to do a dramatic reading of the play. This is like acting out the play without having to memorize the lines.

2. Have students use either stuffed animals or simple props to indicate which character they're portraying. For example, students may want to wear a hat or scarf around their heads as the lion's mane.

3. Remind students that when they read the different parts aloud, they should not read the names of the characters or the stage directions. They should only read the lines that the characters are saying.

4. Tell students they should use a different voice for each character that reflects that character's traits.

5. Have students practice their reading at least once before performing for you and others.

Objectives
- Read aloud grade-level text with appropriate expression.
- Acknowledge differences among characters, including the use of a different voice for each character when reading dialogue aloud.

Reward: Write the names of the literature selections completed in this unit on the My Accomplishments chart and add a sticker to mark successful completion of this unit.

Introduce *Clara and the Bookwagon*

Unit Overview

In this unit, students will read *Clara and the Bookwagon* by Nancy Smiler Levinson. In the accompanying lessons, students will

- ▸ Identify character traits.
- ▸ Compare and contrast settings.
- ▸ Sequence important events.
- ▸ Develop comprehension strategies during independent reading.

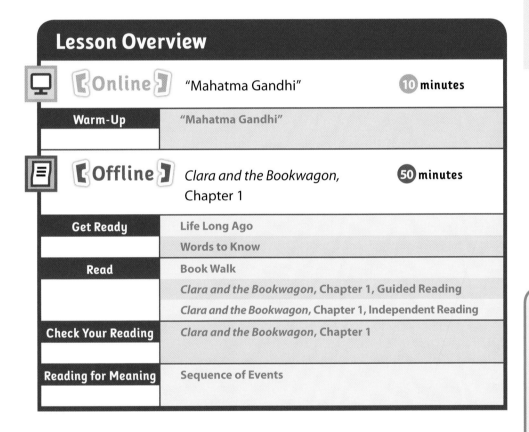

Lesson Overview

🖥	**⟦Online⟧** "Mahatma Gandhi"	**10** minutes
Warm-Up	"Mahatma Gandhi"	

📄	**⟦Offline⟧** *Clara and the Bookwagon,* Chapter 1	**50** minutes
Get Ready	Life Long Ago	
	Words to Know	
Read	Book Walk	
	Clara and the Bookwagon, Chapter 1, Guided Reading	
	Clara and the Bookwagon, Chapter 1, Independent Reading	
Check Your Reading	*Clara and the Bookwagon,* Chapter 1	
Reading for Meaning	Sequence of Events	

Advance Preparation

If you are not able to complete the online Warm-Up, then print the selection and listen to students read aloud. Read Chapter 1 (pp. 4–19) of *Clara and the Bookwagon* before beginning the Read to identify Words to Know in the text. Preview the Read and note the parts of the story that you will read aloud and the parts that students will read independently. Have students gather the Reading Strategies Guide on page LC 55 in *K¹² Language Arts Activity Book.* If you've misplaced the guide, you can print another copy from the online lesson.

⟦Materials⟧

Supplied

- *Clara and the Bookwagon* by Nancy Smiler Levinson
- *K¹² Language Arts Activity Book,* pp. LC 55, 59–60, 62
- "Mahatma Gandhi" (optional)

Story Synopsis

The first chapter of *Clara and the Bookwagon* introduces us to the title character, Clara, who lives on a farm in the early 1900s with her mother, father, and siblings. Clara loves stories and wants to learn to read, but her father has made it clear that there is no time for stories on a busy farm.

Keywords

character – a person or animal in a story

historical fiction – a type of story that contains facts about real people, places, and events, but also contains fictional elements that add dramatic interest to the story

plot – what happens in a story

sequence – order

 **10 minutes**

"Mahatma Gandhi"

Students will work independently online to develop fluency and oral reading skills.

Warm-Up

"Mahatma Gandhi"

The purpose of this activity is to improve students' oral reading and fluency. Students will read "Mahatma Gandhi." Remind students to listen to the model on each screen before they begin their recording.

 Objectives
- Increase oral reading skills.
- Increase fluency.

Offline Alternative

No computer access? Print a copy of "Mahatma Gandhi." Have students read it aloud. Make note of any pronunciation errors, and review those words with students.

 **50 minutes**

Clara and the Bookwagon, Chapter 1

Work **together** with students to complete offline Get Ready, Read, Check Your Reading, and Reading for Meaning activities.

Get Ready

Life Long Ago

Prepare students to read a story set in the early 1900s by thinking about what life was like at the turn of the twentieth century.

1. Help students think about life in 1900. Explain the time as being before a grandparent or other elderly relative or friend was born. However, the early 1900s was later than the days of George Washington, or even Abraham Lincoln.

2. Have students describe what they think life was like in the early 1900s. If students need help generating ideas, ask questions to prompt them. Answers to questions will vary.

   ▸ How do you think people traveled from place to place? Do you think they used cars?
   ▸ What machines do you think they had in their houses? Do you think they had dishwashers and microwaves?
   ▸ What kinds of foods do you think they ate?
   ▸ What do you think people did for fun?
   ▸ How much do you think things cost compared to what they cost today? How much do you think candy cost?

 Objectives
- Connect text to prior knowledge.
- Build background knowledge.
- Increase concept and content vocabulary.

3. When students have given their ideas, provide some background information on life in America in the early twentieth century.

   ▸ Cars had not been invented. People used horses, carriages, and wagons to travel.
   ▸ There was electricity, but no televisions, washing machines, or mircowave ovens. Some people had radios to listen to, but not many because they were expensive. People washed their clothes by hand.
   ▸ People ate a lot of the same foods we eat today, but not prepackaged items. They ate mostly meat, fruits, vegetables, and breads. They made the food themselves. It did not come ready made.
   ▸ For fun at home, people read books, listened to the radio, and played games.
   ▸ Things cost a lot less then than they do today. Some candy cost a penny!

4. Tell students that they are going to begin reading a book about life around the time of 1905–1910.

Words to Know

Before reading *Clara and the Bookwagon*, go over Words to Know with students.

1. Have students say the word aloud.

2. Ask students if they know what the word means.

   ▸ If students know the word's meaning, have them define it and use it in a sentence.
   ▸ If students don't know the word's meaning, read them the definition and discuss the word with them.

bookwagon – a horse-drawn traveling library used in the early 1900s

Read

Book Walk

Prepare students by taking them on a Book Walk of *Clara and the Bookwagon*. Scan the book together and ask students to make predictions about the story.

1. Show students the **front cover** and **back cover**.

2. Point to the **title** and **author** and read them aloud.

3. Review with students what a *bookwagon* is.

4. Read the text on the back cover and discuss what you learn from it.

   ▸ Who are two people we expect to read about in the book? Clara, her father
   ▸ Where do they live? on a farm
   ▸ What do we learn about Clara? She wants to learn to read, but her father won't let her.

5. Tell students that this book is **historical fiction**. Have students tell what **fiction** is. Then explain that in historical fiction, the author combines fictional characters with facts and sometimes real people from a time in history. The characters and what they say, think, and feel are all made up by the author. But the details about their setting and time period are based on facts.

6. Read through the **table of contents**. Locate Chapter 1 and turn to that page.

7. Explain to students that they're going to read Chapter 1. You're going to read the first four pages of the chapter aloud, stopping to ask questions as you've done in previous lessons. Then students are going to read the rest of the chapter on their own and come back to you to discuss.

8. Look through the first four pages of Chapter 1. Read the chapter title. Have students look at the **illustrations** and describe what they see.

   ▸ What people do you see? a family of a girl, a little boy, a baby, a father, and a mother
   ▸ Where do they live? on a farm
   ▸ What are some of them doing? chores on a farm, like cooking and planting
   ▸ How do you know that this story takes place long ago? Possible answers: The characters' clothes are from long ago. For example, the mother and Clara's dresses are long. Also, the father is plowing the field with a horse instead of with a machine. The stove in the kitchen looks old.

Clara and the Bookwagon, Chapter 1, Guided Reading

Now it's time to read the story. Have students sit next to you so that they can see the pictures and words while you read the story aloud.

1. Read pages 4–7 of *Clara and the Bookwagon* aloud all the way through. Track with your finger so students can follow along.

2. Begin to reread pages 4–7 with students, having them chime in and read aloud with you this time. Tell them to think about the setting, the characters, and what happens as you read and that you will pause at certain points in the story to discuss.

Objectives

- Define historical fiction.
- Use an illustration to make a prediction about a reading.
- Read texts for literary experience.
- Use text to make a prediction.
- Identify setting.
- Identify characters.
- Read on-level text with purpose and understanding.
- Self-monitor comprehension by predicting, rereading, checking for sense, drawing on background knowledge, summarizing, clarifying, checking for context clues, and/or self-questioning.
- Repair comprehension using strategies: reread, use prior knowledge, self-question, identify context clues, determine word meaning, and read on.
- Generate questions during reading.

3. Pause at the end of page 5 and check students' comprehension.
   Say: What chores does Clara do on her farm? She helps feed the chickens, helps her mother cook, and helps take care of her younger siblings.

4. Read to the end of page 7. Have students identify characteristics of historical fiction and make a prediction.

   ▸ What part of the story so far do you think is fiction? the characters, their farm
   ▸ What part of the story do you think is historical, or real, about past times? The kinds of chores people did on farms; the fact that Clara and other farm children did not go to school.
   ▸ What do you think is going to happen in the rest of this chapter? Answers will vary.

Clara and the Bookwagon, **Chapter 1, Independent Reading**

Have students read the rest of Chapter 1 of *Clara and the Bookwagon* independently using the strategies from the Reading Strategies Guide.

1. Tell students they are going to read the rest of Chapter 1 on their own. Remind them to do a Book Walk of the rest of the chapter before they read and predict what might happen.

2. Remind students to pause frequently to ask themselves questions about what they have just read, just as you did during the Guided Reading. They should ask questions like the following:

   ▸ Where is this story taking place?
   ▸ What just happened in the story?
   ▸ What characters did I meet? What are they like?
   ▸ What will happen next?

3. Make sure students have the Reading Strategies Guide. Remind students that when they don't understand something they read, they should use the strategies listed to help them improve their understanding.

4. Tell students that when they have finished, you will discuss their understanding of the story and the strategies they used.

TIP Check back with students in about 5 minutes to see if they have completed the reading and if they are having any difficulties.

Check Your Reading

Clara and the Bookwagon, Chapter 1

Have students answer multiple choice questions on pages LC 59–60 of *K¹² Language Arts Activity Book.* They may refer to the story as they answer the questions. If students seem to have difficulty understanding the text, discuss their reading strategies using the Reading Strategies Guide.

Objectives
- Answer questions requiring literal recall of details.
- Describe characters and their traits.
- Answer inferential questions.
- Evaluate reading strategies.

1. Turn to the Activity Book page.
   Say: Today you are going to answer multiple choice questions.

2. Point to Question 1 and read the question aloud.
   Say: This is a multiple choice question. First there is a question that you need to answer.

3. Point to the four answer choices.
   Say: Here are the answer choices that go with Question 1. Only one of these is the right answer. The other three are wrong answers. Choose the best answer to the question.

4. Explain to students how to go about answering a multiple choice question.
   Say: First read the question and each answer choice. Then, decide which answer choice is the best answer to the question.

5. Have students complete the Activity Book page. Remind them to look for the answers in Chapter 1 of *Clara and the Bookwagon.*

6. If students have answered all the questions correctly, move on to the next activity. If students have trouble answering any of the questions, ask them to tell you about the story. Then discuss the reading strategies they used Answers to questions will vary.

   ▸ Did you do a Book Walk and look through the chapters before you read them?
   ▸ Did you stop sometimes and ask yourself what just happened or what characters you met? When did you do that?
   ▸ Did you stop sometimes and ask yourself what might happen next? When did you do that?
   ▸ Were there times when you were confused about something in the story? When?
   ▸ What did you do when you didn't understand something?

7. If students cannot answer the questions about the text and their reading strategies, or if they seem confused about what they read, have them reread Chapter 1 aloud beginning with page 8. Prompt them to stop and use the appropriate reading strategies to aid in their comprehension.

8. Count how many words students struggle to read on any one page. If the number reaches five or more, stop students and tell them that you will read the rest of Chapter 1 aloud to them.

9. If you reread the story aloud, stop at appropriate points in the story and ask questions about the setting, characters, and plot.

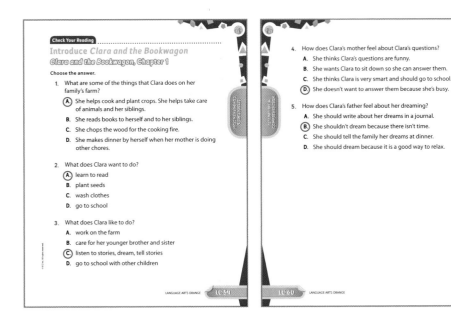

Check Your Reading

Introduce *Clara and the Bookwagon*

Clara and the Bookwagon, **Chapter 1**

Choose the answer.

1. What are some of the things that Clara does on her family's farm?
   - **(A.)** She helps cook and plant crops. She helps take care of animals and her siblings.
   - B. She reads books to herself and to her siblings.
   - C. She chops the wood for the cooking fire.
   - D. She makes dinner by herself when her mother is doing other chores.

2. What does Clara want to do?
   - **(A)** learn to read
   - B. plant seeds
   - C. wash clothes
   - D. go to school

3. What does Clara like to do?
   - A. work on the farm
   - B. care for her younger brother and sister
   - **(C)** listen to stories, dream, tell stories
   - D. go to school with other children

4. How does Clara's mother feel about Clara's questions?
   - A. She thinks Clara's questions are funny.
   - B. She wants Clara to sit down so she can answer them.
   - C. She thinks Clara is very smart and should go to school.
   - **(D)** She doesn't want to answer them because she's busy.

5. How does Clara's father feel about her dreaming?
   - A. She should write about her dreams in a journal.
   - **(B)** She shouldn't dream because there isn't time.
   - C. She should tell the family her dreams at dinner.
   - D. She should dream because it is a good way to relax.

LANGUAGE ARTS ORANGE   LC 59

LC 60   LANGUAGE ARTS ORANGE

Reading for Meaning

Sequence of Events

Students will identify some of the main events in Chapter 1 of the story. Turn to page LC 62 from *K¹² Language Arts Activity Book*.

> **Objectives**
> - Define plot as what happens in a story.
> - Define sequence.
> - Sequence events in a text.
> - Use a graphic organizer to organize information.

1. Have students tell what a **plot** is.

2. Review that events in a plot happen in a **sequence**, or order. Remembering the sequence of events can help readers remember the important things that happen in the story.

3. Remind students that when they think about the sequence of events in a plot, they should include only the main, or most important, events that happen.

4. Tell students that they are going to begin putting the important events from the book into a sequence chart.

5. Have students tell what main events they learned about in Chapter 1.

6. Direct students' attention to the Activity Book page. Explain that in the first box, they should put in something important that they learn about the main character and the setting of the story. Clara lives on a farm a long time ago and wants to learn to read.

7. Have students fill in this event and one more main event from Chapter 1. Possible answer: Clara's father says there is no time on the farm for her to dream.

8. Check students' sequence chart to make sure that they have included a main event and not a less important, or minor, event. Examples of minor events that students should **not** include are that Clara helps her mother cook, or that Clara loves to hear the stories in church.

9. Tell students they will continue to fill in the chart as they read the next chapters of the book.

10. Have students keep the Activity Book page in a safe place so they can continue to add events as they read.

Explore *Clara and the Bookwagon*, Chapter 2

Lesson Overview

[Offline]	*Clara and the Bookwagon,* Chapter 2	**60** minutes

Get Ready	Review Compare and Contrast
	Words to Know
Read	Book Walk
	Clara and the Bookwagon, Chapter 2, Guided Reading
	Clara and the Bookwagon, Chapter 2, Independent Reading
Check Your Reading	*Clara and the Bookwagon,* Chapter 2
Reading for Meaning	Sequence of Events
Making Connections	Compare and Contrast

Advance Preparation

Preview the Read and note the parts of the story that you will read aloud and the parts that students will read independently. Have students gather the partially completed page LC 62 in *K¹² Language Arts Activity Book* (Sequence of Events). Also have students gather the Reading Strategies Guide. If you've misplaced the guide, you can print another copy from the online lesson.

Big Ideas

► Readers need to be able to sequence, summarize, and articulate the main idea.
► Signal words—such as *before, consequently, compare, contrast, therefore*—are a guide to understanding the relationship between and among ideas.
► Comprehension entails asking and answering questions about the text.
► Self-questioning improves comprehension and ensures that reading is an interactive process.
► When reading historical fiction, readers must be able to distinguish between the elements that are historical and the elements that are fictional.
► Comprehension requires the reader to self-monitor understanding.
► Comprehension requires the reader to self-correct errors made while reading by using a wide variety of strategies.

[Materials]

Supplied
- *Clara and the Bookwagon* by Nancy Smiler Levinson
- *K¹² Language Arts Activity Book,* pp. LC 55, 61, 62

Story Synopsis

In the second chapter of *Clara and the Bookwagon* Clara goes with her father to a distant town to buy supplies for the farm. At the general store, Clara sees shelves of books and learns that they may be borrowed. However, Clara's father says that books are for rich people, not farmers, and he refuses to allow Clara to take a book, even though it is free.

Keywords

character – a person or animal in a story

compare – to explain how two or more things are alike

contrast – to explain how two or more things are different

historical fiction – a type of story that contains facts about real people, places, and events, but also contains fictional elements that add dramatic interest to the story

plot – what happens in a story

sequence – order

[Offline] 60 minutes

Clara and the Bookwagon, Chapter 2

Work **together** with students to complete offline Get Ready, Read, Check Your Reading, Reading for Meaning, and Making Connections activities.

Get Ready ....

Review Compare and Contrast

Remind students how to compare and contrast things or ideas.

1. Have students define **compare** and **contrast** and tell what they do when they compare and contrast two things.

2. Have students compare and contrast two of their favorite activities, such as reading a book and playing a game.

3. Have students tell how the two activities are similar and how they are different.

4. Tell students that they are going to continue reading *Clara and the Bookwagon* and think about how two places in the book are similar and different.

> **Objectives**
> - Define compare.
> - Define contrast.
> - Increase concept and content vocabulary.

Words to Know

Before reading *Clara and the Bookwagon*, Chapter 2, go over Words to Know with students.

1. Ask students to define the following word they encountered in Chapter 1 and use it in a sentence:

   bookwagon

2. Correct any incorrect or vague definitions.

Read ....

Book Walk

Prepare students by taking them on a Book Walk of *Clara and the Bookwagon*. Scan the book together and ask students to make predictions about the story.

1. Have students read the **title** and **author**.

2. Have students review what they read in the first chapter by telling the setting, the main characters, and what we learn about Clara and her parents.

3. Use the **table of contents** to locate Chapter 2. Have students read the chapter title.

4. Explain to students that they're going to read Chapter 2. You're going to read the first four pages of the chapter aloud, stopping to ask questions as you've done in previous lessons. Then students are going to read the rest of the chapter on their own and come back to you to discuss.

5. Look through the first four pages of Chapter 2. Have students look at the **illustrations** and describe what they see.

   ‣ What is the setting of the first part of this chapter? Clara's farm
   ‣ What does it look like Clara and her father are doing? going somewhere in their wagon
   ‣ Where do you think they're going? Why? Possible answers: on a trip or errand; they need to get something or see someone

Clara and the Bookwagon, Chapter 2, Guided Reading

Now it's time to read Chapter 2 of *Clara and the Bookwagon*. Have students sit next to you so that they can see the pictures and words while you read aloud.

1. Read pages 20–23 of Chapter 2 aloud all the way through. Track with your finger so students can follow along.

2. Begin to reread pages 20–23 of Chapter 2 with students, having them chime in and read aloud with you this time. Tell them to think about where the story takes place and what happens as you read and that you will pause now and then to discuss.

3. Pause at the end of page 21 and check students' comprehension.

   ‣ Where is Clara going with her father? Why? to town; The family needs corn seed, flour, and sugar.

4. Read to the end of the selection and have students make a prediction.

   ‣ What do you think is going to happen in the rest of this chapter? Answers will vary.

Clara and the Bookwagon, **Chapter 2, Independent Reading**
Have students read the rest of Chapter 2 of *Clara and the Bookwagon* independently using the strategies from the Reading Strategies Guide.

1. Tell students they are going to read the rest of Chapter 2 on their own. Remind them to do a Book Walk of the rest of the chapter before they begin to read and predict what might happen.

2. Remind students to pause frequently to ask themselves questions about what they have just read, just as you did during guided reading. They should ask questions like the following:
   ▸ Where is this story taking place?
   ▸ What just happened in the story?
   ▸ What characters did I meet? What are they like?
   ▸ What will happen next?

3. Make sure students have the Reading Strategies Guide. Remind them to use the strategies listed to help them improve their understanding when they don't understand something they read.

4. Tell students that when they have finished, you will discuss their understanding of the story and the strategies they used.

TIP Check back with students in about 10 minutes to see if they have completed the reading and if they are having any difficulties.

Check Your Reading

Clara and the Bookwagon, **Chapter 2**
Discuss students' reading strategies and have them retell parts of the story to check comprehension.

1. **Have students retell what happened in Chapter 2 in their own words** to develop grammar, vocabulary, comprehension, and fluency skills.

2. **Ask the following questions** to check comprehension.
   ▸ Why do Clara and her father stop on the way to town? to rest and get a drink of water
   ▸ How does the author describe the weather and the place they stop? The sun was warm. The spring air smelled good. There's a stream with clear, cool water.
   ▸ What does Clara see in the store that she wants? books
   ▸ What does the shopkeeper tell her about the books? They can be borrowed for free.
   ▸ Why does Clara's father say she can't have a book? Why do you think he says this? Books are only for rich people. Farmers don't have time to read. He says this because rich people don't have to work all the time, and they can spend some of their time reading.

Objectives
- Answer questions requiring literal recall of details.
- Answer inferential questions.
- Evaluate reading strategies.

3. If students have answered all the questions correctly, move on to the next activity. If students have trouble answering the questions, continue with Step 4.

4. Discuss the reading strategies students used to help their comprehension. Answers to questions will vary.

   ▸ Did you do a Book Walk and look through the chapters before you read them?
   ▸ Did you stop sometimes and ask yourself what just happened or what characters you met? When did you do that?
   ▸ Did you stop sometimes and ask yourself what might happen next? When did you do that?
   ▸ Were there times when you were confused about something in the story? When?
   ▸ What did you do when you didn't understand something?

5. If students cannot answer the questions about the text and their reading strategies, or if they seem confused about what they read, have them reread Chapter 2 aloud beginning with page 24. Prompt them to pause and use the appropriate reading strategies to aid in their comprehension.

6. Count how many words students struggle to read on any one page. If the number reaches five or more, stop students and tell them that you will read the rest of Chapter 2 aloud to them.

7. If you reread the story aloud, stop at appropriate points in the story and ask questions about the characters and plot.

Reading for Meaning

Sequence of Events

Have students identify some of the main events in Chapter 2 of the story. Gather the partially completed Sequence of Events page.

Objectives
- Sequence events in a text.
- Use a graphic organizer to organize information.

1. Have students explain what you do when you retell the plot of a story in sequence. You retell the most important events in the order that they happen.

2. Remind students that when they think about the sequence of events in a plot, they should include only the main, or most important, events that happen.

3. Tell students that they will continue putting important events from the book into a sequence chart.

4. Direct students' attention to the Activity Book page.

5. Have them fill in two of the main, or most important, events from Chapter 2 on the chart. Possible answers: Clara wants to borrow a book from the store in town. Her father says she cannot have a book because books are for rich people.

6. Check students' sequence chart to make sure that they have included main, or important, events and not less important, or minor, events. Examples of minor events that students should **not** include are that the weather is nice and Clara's father buys her a peppermint stick.

7. Tell students they will continue to fill in the chart in the next lesson when they finish the reading the book.

8. Have students keep the Activity Book page in a safe place so they can continue to add events as they read.

Making Connections

Compare and Contrast

Have students practice comparing and contrasting two concepts by thinking about the similarities and differences between rural and town life in the story. Turn to page LC 61 in *K¹² Language Arts Activity Book*.

1. Have students tell the definitions of **compare** and **contrast**.

2. Tell students that they are going to compare and contrast Clara's farm with the town she and her father visit.

3. Direct students' attention to the Activity Book page. Review with students what a Venn diagram is and how to fill in this type of organizer.

4. Have students complete the Activity Book page. Have them use the illustrations as well as the text to help them.

Objectives
- Use a graphic organizer to organize information.
- Draw conclusions using illustrations.
- Compare and contrast plot, setting, and characters of texts by the same author.

Reading for Meaning

Explore *Clara and the Bookwagon*, Chapter 2
Compare and Contrast

Write what farm life is like in the top oval. Write what town life is like in the bottom oval. Write how the places are similar in the middle.

Farm Life
Kids don't wear shoes. There are fields and grass everywhere. There aren't a lot of people around.

Same
People go to stores to buy things. People are friendly.

Town Life
Everyone wears shoes. There are a lot of people around. There are stores with things to buy and books to borrow.

LANGUAGE ARTS ORANGE LC 61

Explore *Clara and the Bookwagon*, Chapters 3 and 4

Lesson Overview

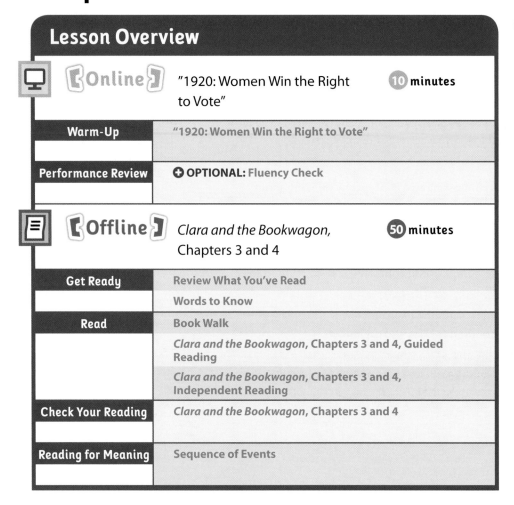

	Online	"1920: Women Win the Right to Vote"	10 minutes
Warm-Up		"1920: Women Win the Right to Vote"	
Performance Review		✚ OPTIONAL: Fluency Check	

	Offline	*Clara and the Bookwagon,* Chapters 3 and 4	50 minutes
Get Ready		Review What You've Read	
		Words to Know	
Read		Book Walk	
		Clara and the Bookwagon, Chapters 3 and 4, Guided Reading	
		Clara and the Bookwagon, Chapters 3 and 4, Independent Reading	
Check Your Reading		*Clara and the Bookwagon,* Chapters 3 and 4	
Reading for Meaning		Sequence of Events	

[Materials]

Supplied

- *Clara and the Bookwagon* by Nancy Smiler Levinson
- *K¹² Language Arts Activity Book,* pp. LC 55, 62
- "1920: Women Win the Right to Vote" (optional)
- Fluency Performance Checklist (optional)

Story Synopsis

In the final two chapters of the book, Miss Mary the librarian comes to Clara's farm in her bookwagon, a carriage with free library books available for borrowing. Clara's father again refuses to let Clara borrow a book, saying she doesn't have time and doesn't know how to read. Miss Mary promises to teach Clara how to read, and Clara promises to finish all her chores before reading each day. Finally her father relents and Clara borrows a book.

Advance Preparation

If you are not able to complete the online Warm-Up, then print the selection and listen to students read aloud. Preview the Read and note the parts of the story that you will read aloud and the parts that students will read independently. Have students gather the partially completed page LC 62 in *K¹² Language Arts Activity Book* (Sequence of Events). Also have students gather the Reading Strategies Guide. If you've misplaced the guide, you can print another copy from the online lesson.

Big Ideas

- ► Readers need to be able to sequence, summarize, and articulate the main idea.
- ► Comprehension requires the reader to self-correct errors made while reading by using a wide variety of strategies.

Keywords

character – a person or animal in a story

historical fiction – a type of story that contains facts about real people, places, and events, but also contains fictional elements that add dramatic interest to the story

plot – what happens in a story

sequence – order

 **Online** 🔟 **minutes**

"1920: Women Win the Right to Vote"

Students will work independently online to develop fluency and oral reading skills.

Warm-Up ●

"1920: Women Win the Right to Vote"

The purpose of this activity is to improve students' oral reading and fluency. Students will read "1920: Women Win the Right to Vote." Remind students to listen to the model on each screen before they begin their recording.

Objectives

- Increase oral reading skills.
- Increase fluency.

Offline Alternative

No computer access? Print a copy of "1920: Women Win the Right to Vote." Have students read it aloud. Make note of any pronunciation errors, and review those words with students.

Performance Review ●

⊕ OPTIONAL: Fluency Check

Listen to students' recordings and use the checklist to review fluency and track performance. Keep the completed checklist so you can review students' progress over time.

Objectives

- Read aloud grade-level text with appropriate automaticity, prosody, accuracy, and rate.

 **50 minutes**

Clara and the Bookwagon, Chapters 3 and 4

Work **together** with students to complete offline as Get Ready, Read, Check Your Reading, and Reading for Meaning activities.

Get Ready

Review What You've Read

Before reading the next part of the book, have students retell what they've read so far.

1. Have students retell the **plot** of Chapters 1 and 2 of *Clara and the Bookwagon*. Make sure students identify the **settings** of the farm and the town and describe the **characters**, particularly Clara and her father.

2. Tell students that they are going to read the rest of the book, beginning with Chapter 3 where they left off.

3. Remind students that as they read, they should focus on identifying and describing new characters and the important events in the plot.

Objectives

- Summarize the plot of a story.
- Identify setting.
- Identify characters.
- Increase concept and content vocabulary.

Words to Know

Before reading *Clara and the Bookwagon*, Chapters 3 and 4, go over Words to Know with students.

1. Ask students to define the following word and use it in a sentence:

   bookwagon

2. Correct any incorrect or vague definitions.

Read

Book Walk

Prepare students by taking them on a Book Walk of *Clara and the Bookwagon*. Scan the book together and ask students to make predictions about the story.

1. Have students read the **title** and **author**.

2. Use the **table of contents** to locate Chapter 3 and have students read the chapter title.

3. Explain to students that they're going to read Chapters 3 and 4. You're going to read the first four pages of Chapter 3 aloud, pausing to ask questions as you've done in previous lessons. Then students are going to read the rest of the book on their own and come back to you to discuss.

4. Look through pages 38–41 of Chapter 3. Have students look at the **illustrations** and describe what they see.

   ▸ What is the setting of this chapter? Clara's farm
   ▸ What does it look like the family is doing? chores on the farm
   ▸ What do you think Clara sees in the distance on pages 40 and 41? Possible answer: a bookwagon
   ▸ What do you think this chapter is going to be about? Answers will vary.

Clara and the Bookwagon, Chapters 3 and 4, Guided Reading

Now it's time to read Chapters 3 and 4 of *Clara and the Bookwagon*. Have students sit next to you so that they can see the pictures and words while you read the story aloud.

1. Read pages 38–41 of Chapter 3 aloud all the way through. Track with your finger so students can follow along.

2. Begin to reread pages 38–41 of Chapter 3 with students, having them chime in and read aloud with you this time. Tell them to think about who they meet in the story as you read and that you will pause now and then to discuss.

3. Pause to discuss at the end of page 39, and have students make inferences.

   ▸ What does Clara's father let her do? stop weeding and pick berries
   ▸ Why do you think he does this? Possible answer: He's nice and he wants to reward Clara for working hard.

4. Read to the end of the page 41, and have students make a prediction.

   ▸ What do you think is in the wagon Clara sees? Possible answer: books
   ▸ What do you think is going to happen in the rest of this book? Answers will vary.

Objectives

- Use an illustration to make a prediction about a reading.
- Use text to make a prediction.
- Identify setting.
- Read on-level text with purpose and understanding.
- Self-monitor comprehension by predicting, rereading, checking for sense, drawing on background knowledge, summarizing, clarifying, checking for context clues, and/or self-questioning.
- Repair comprehension using strategies: reread, use prior knowledge, self-question, identify context clues, determine word meaning, and read on.
- Generate questions during reading.

Clara and the Bookwagon, **Chapters 3 and 4, Independent Reading**
Have students read the rest of Chapters 3 and 4 of *Clara and the Bookwagon* independently using the strategies from the Reading Strategies Guide.

1. Tell students they are going to read the rest of the book on their own. Remind them to do a Book Walk before they read and predict what might happen.

2. Remind students to pause frequently to ask themselves questions about what they have just read, just as you did during guided reading.

3. Make sure students have the Reading Strategies Guide. Remind them that when they don't understand something they read, they should use the strategies listed to help them improve their understanding.

4. Tell students that when they have finished, you will discuss their understanding of the story and the strategies they used.

(TIP) Check back with students in about 10 minutes to see if they have completed the reading and if they are having any difficulties.

Check Your Reading

Clara and the Bookwagon, **Chapters 3 and 4**
Discuss students' reading strategies and have them retell parts of the story to check comprehension.

Objectives
- Answer questions requiring literal recall of details.
- Answer inferential questions.
- Evaluate reading strategies.

1. **Have students retell what happened in Chapters 3 and 4 in their own words** to develop grammar, vocabulary, comprehension, and fluency skills.

2. **Ask the following questions** to check comprehension:

   ▶ Who is Miss Mary, and what does she have? a librarian; books to borrow
   ▶ What does Miss Mary decide to do when Clara says her father won't let her borrow a book? They'll go talk to her father.
   ▶ How do you think Clara feels riding in the wagon with Miss Mary? Possible answers: proud, special, excited, happy
   ▶ What does the word *hearse* mean? What context clues help you understand the word? a wagon for dead people; the words *to pick up the dead*
   ▶ How does Miss Mary try to convince Clara's father to let Clara have a book? She tells him why reading is good and promises to teach Clara how to read.
   ▶ Why does Clara's father finally let her get a book? Possible answers: Clara promises to finish her work every day before reading, and her father knows she keeps her promises. He knows how much Clara wants to read. Miss Mary will teach Clara to read.

3. If students have answered all the questions correctly, move on to the next activity. If students have trouble answering the questions, continue with Step 4.

4. Discuss the reading strategies students used to help their comprehension.
   Answers to questions will vary.

   ▶ Did you do a Book Walk and look through the chapters before you read them?
   ▶ Did you stop sometimes and ask yourself what just happened or what characters you met? When did you do that?
   ▶ Did you stop sometimes and ask yourself what might happen next? When did you do that?
   ▶ Were there times when you were confused about something in the story? When?
   ▶ What did you do when you didn't understand something?

5. If students cannot answer the questions about the text and their reading strategies, or if they seem confused about what they read, have them reread Chapters 3 and 4 aloud beginning with page 42. Prompt them to pause and use the appropriate reading strategies to aid in their comprehension.

6. Count how many words students struggle to read on any one page. If the number reaches five or more, stop students and tell them that you will read the rest of Chapters 3 and 4 aloud to them.

7. If you reread the story aloud, stop at appropriate points in the story and ask questions about the setting, characters, and plot.

Reading for Meaning

Sequence of Events

Have students identify some of the main events in Chapters 3 and 4 to complete the Sequence of Events page.

1. Tell students that they are going to finish their sequence chart by adding main events from Chapters 3 and 4.

2. Direct students' attention to the Activity Book page.

3. Have students fill in two of the main, or most important, events from Chapters 3 and 4 on the sequence chart.

4. Check students' sequence chart to make sure that they have included main, or important, events and not less important, or minor, events. Examples of minor events that students should **not** include are that Miss Mary drives a bookwagon and has books such as *Peter Pan*.

5. Have students keep the completed Activity Book page in a safe place. They will be using the sequence chart to help them write a summary of the book.

Objectives
- Sequence events in a text.
- Use a graphic organizer to organize information.

Reading for Meaning
Explore *Clara and the Bookwagon*, Chapter 3 and 4
Sequence of Events Answers will vary.
Fill in the boxes.

Title, Author, Characters, Setting
Clara and the Bookwagon, Nancy Smiler Levinson, Clara, Miss Mary, Clara's family, a farm long ago

Beginning Main Events
Clara wants to learn to read. Clara's father says there is no time on the farm for her to dream.

Middle Main Events
Clara wants to borrow a book from the store, but her father says no. Miss Mary brings her bookwagon to Clara's farm.

Ending Main Events
Miss Mary says she will teach Clara to read after her work is completed. Clara's father lets her borrow a book.

LC 62   LANGUAGE ARTS ORANGE

Review *Clara and the Bookwagon*

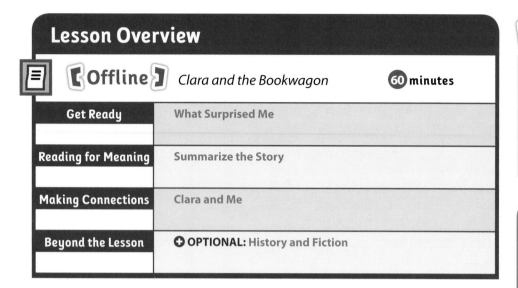

Lesson Overview

[Offline]	*Clara and the Bookwagon*	60 minutes
Get Ready	What Surprised Me	
Reading for Meaning	Summarize the Story	
Making Connections	Clara and Me	
Beyond the Lesson	⊕ OPTIONAL: History and Fiction	

Materials

Supplied

- *Clara and the Bookwagon* by Nancy Smiler Levinson
- *K¹² Language Arts Activity Book*, pp. LC 62, 63

Keywords

character – a person or animal in a story

historical fiction – a type of story that contains facts about real people, places, and events, but also contains fictional elements that add dramatic interest to the story

plot – what happens in a story

sequence – order

summarize – to tell in order the most important ideas or events of a text

summary – a short retelling that includes only the most important ideas or events of a text

Advance Preparation

Have students gather the completed page LC 62 in *K¹² Language Arts Activity Book* (Sequence of Events).

Big Ideas

- ▶ Readers need to be able to summarize a story while maintaining the proper sequence of events.
- ▶ Active, strong readers employ reading strategies such as making connections between the text and themselves.

 **60 minutes**

Clara and the Bookwagon

Work **together** with students to complete offline Get Ready, Reading for Meaning, Making Connections, and Beyond the Lesson activities.

Get Ready

What Surprised Me

Discuss with students what they learned or discovered in *Clara and the Bookwagon* and what elements in the book they found interesting and surprising.

1. Have students tell what they learned about from *Clara and the Bookwagon* that they didn't know before. Possible answers: Not all kids learned to read in the past; there weren't books and libraries for everyone to use; some people had to travel a long way to towns and stores; some people used to think it was a waste of time to read.

2. Have students describe what they learned that they found the most surprising. If necessary, give students the following prompt: *What surprised me the most was _____.* As an example, you may also share something that surprised you.

3. Have students explain why they were surprised by this fact from the story.

Objectives
- Make connections between text and self.
- Evaluate text.

Reading for Meaning

 Summarize the Story

Have students summarize the book. Gather the Sequence of Events page, and turn to page LC 63 in *K¹² Language Arts Activity Book.*

1. Have students tell what a **summary** is.

2. Remind students that when they **summarize** a book or other story, they include only the main events from the story and retell them in the correct **sequence**.

3. Review that a summary is written or told in a person's own words, not copied from the story.

4. Have students tell why they might want to summarize a book. to tell a friend about the book; for a book report; to help them remember the most important events that happened in the book

Objectives
- Define summary.
- Define summarize.
- Summarize text and maintain accurate sequence.
- Use a graphic organizer to organize information.

5. Tell students that they are going to write a summary of *Clara and the Bookwagon*. Remind them that being able to summarize a story is an important skill that helps you remember what you read in a story and tell other people about it. Tell students that they are going to use their sequence chart to help them summarize the book.

6. Have students choose four or five events from the Sequence of Events page that they think are the most important.

7. Direct students' attention to the Summarize the Story page. Show them that the paragraph has been started for them. Point out the title, the indent for the paragraph, and the beginning sentence. Tell students that introducing the title of the book, the name of the author, and the name of the main character is a good way to start a summary of a book.

8. Have students complete the Activity Book page. They should write their summary in time order using complete sentences to complete the paragraph. Students should write a concluding sentence to end the paragraph such as "In the end, Clara is able to borrow a book."

Reading for Meaning ....

Review *Clara and the Bookwagon*

Summarize the Story

Write a summary of *Clara and the Bookwagon*. Possible answer is shown.

In the book *Clara and the Bookwagon* by Nancy Smiler Levinson,

a girl named Clara   lives on a farm a long

time ago and wants to learn to read.

Her father says she cannot have a

book because books are for rich

people. Miss Mary the librarian

brings her bookwagon to Clara's

farm. Miss Mary says she will teach

Clara to read after her work is done.

In the end, Clara's father lets her

borrow a book.

LANGUAGE ARTS ORANGE   LC 63

Making Connections

Clara and Me

Have students compare and contrast Clara's life with their own to help them gain a deeper understanding of the character and her life.

1. Discuss with students how Clara's life is similar to and different from theirs.

2. Tell students to think about what Clara does in her daily life compared to what they do in theirs.

3. Have students evaluate Clara's life and their own. Answers will vary.

> ‣ What parts of Clara's life would you like to experience? Why?
> ‣ What parts of your life do you think are better than Clara's? Why?
> ‣ How is Clara different from you?
> ‣ How is she like you?

Objectives
- Make connections between text and self.

Beyond the Lesson

✚ OPTIONAL: History and Fiction

This activity is OPTIONAL. This activity is intended for students who have extra time and would benefit from learning more about the actual bookwagon that inspired the fictional story. Feel free to skip this activity.

1. Remind students that this book is **historical fiction**. Have students tell what that is, or explain it to them again.

2. Explain that the characters of Clara and her family are make-believe, but the character of Miss Mary is based on a real person.

Objectives
- Make inferences using text and prior knowledge.
- Compare and contrast different versions of the same story.

3. Read aloud the afterword on page 64.

4. Discuss with students what kind of person Miss Mary Titcomb was.

   ▸ Why do you think Miss Mary wanted people who lived far from the cities to have books? Possible answer: She thought everyone should be able to read, even if they were poor or lived on a farm.

   ▸ Do you think it was hard or easy to set up and run the bookwagon in the 1900s? Why do you think this? Possible answer: Yes, because they had to travel everywhere in a horse and wagon, and that probably made travel slow and difficult.

   ▸ Do you think the real Miss Mary would have talked to Clara's father about letting Clara borrow a book? Why or why not? Possible answer: Yes, because the real Miss Mary wanted everyone to be able to read, even on farms.

Reward: Write the names of the literature selections completed in this unit on the My Accomplishments chart and add a sticker to mark successful completion of this unit.

Introduce "The Ugly Duckling"

Unit Overview

In this unit, students will read three classic tales and identify the moral of each story by analyzing story elements such as character and plot. They will read the following selections:

► "The Ugly Duckling"
► "The Grasshopper and the Ant"
► "The Three Wishes"

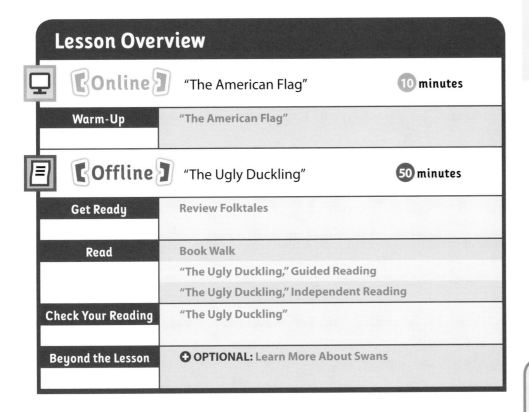

Lesson Overview

🖥	**Online** "The American Flag"	**10 minutes**
Warm-Up	"The American Flag"	

📄	**Offline** "The Ugly Duckling"	**50 minutes**
Get Ready	Review Folktales	
Read	Book Walk	
	"The Ugly Duckling," Guided Reading	
	"The Ugly Duckling," Independent Reading	
Check Your Reading	"The Ugly Duckling"	
Beyond the Lesson	➕ OPTIONAL: Learn More About Swans	

Advance Preparation

If you are not able to complete the online Warm-Up, then print the selection and listen to students read aloud. Preview the Read and note the parts of the story that you will read aloud and the parts that students will read independently. Have students gather the Reading Strategies Guide on page LC 55 in *K¹² Language Arts Activity Book*. If you've misplaced the guide, you can print another copy from the online lesson.

Big Ideas

► Comprehension requires the reader to self-correct errors made while reading by using a wide variety of strategies.
► Reading strategies are conscious plans that readers apply and adapt to make sense of text.
► Self-questioning improves comprehension and ensures that reading is an interactive process.

Materials

Supplied
● **"The Ugly Duckling,"** *K¹² Classics for Young Readers, Volume B,* pp. 42–51
● *K¹² Language Arts Activity Book,* pp. LC 55, 65–66
● **"The American Flag"** (optional)

Story Synopsis

One summer, a young swan hatches in the nest of a mother duck. He is ostracized by the other birds on the farm for being so ugly and different from the other ducklings. The ugly duckling runs away, only to be ridiculed by a cat and a hen. The ugly duckling lives alone through the fall and winter, and in the spring he approaches some swans on a river. He sees his reflection and realizes he is a swan who is now admired for his beauty.

Keywords

fairy tale – a folktale that sometimes has have magical elements; sometimes has a happily-ever-after ending

folktale – a story, which usually teachers a lesson important to a culture, that is passed down through many generations

 **10 minutes**

"The American Flag"

Students will work independently online to develop fluency and oral reading skills.

Warm-Up

"The American Flag"

The purpose of this activity is to improve students' oral reading and fluency. Students will read "The American Flag." Remind students to listen to the model on each screen before they begin their recording.

 Objectives
- Increase oral reading skills.
- Increase fluency.

Offline Alternative

No computer access? Print a copy of "The American Flag." Have students read it aloud. Make note of any pronunciation errors, and review those words with students.

 **50 minutes**

"The Ugly Duckling"

Work **together** with students to complete offline Get Ready, Read, Check Your Reading, and Beyond the Lesson activities.

Get Ready

Review Folktales

Discuss the genre of fairy tales to help students prepare for the lesson.

1. Ask students whether they know any **fairy tales**.

2. Have students tell what fairy tales they remember. Hansel and Gretel, Little Red Riding Hood

3. Explain that a fairy tale is a special kind of folktale. Fairy tales sometimes have magical elements or magical characters. Sometimes they have a happily-ever-after ending. Tell students that we can also find lessons in some fairy tales.

 Objectives
- Define fairy tale.
- Connect text to prior knowledge.

Read

Book Walk

Prepare students by taking them on a Book Walk of "The Ugly Duckling." Scan the story together and ask students to make predictions about the story. For all questions in the Book Walk, answers will vary.

1. Tell students that they are going to read a folktale.

2. Show students the **front cover** and **back cover** of *K¹² Classics for Young Readers, Volume B*. Remind students that the book is a collection of stories.

3. Use the **table of contents** to locate "The Ugly Duckling." Read the **title** and have students turn to that page.

4. Have students read the title.

5. Look through pages 42–43 of the story. Have students look at the **illustrations** and describe what they see, prompting them as follows.

   ▸ What kinds of animals are these?
   ▸ Who is the large bird in this first picture? What is she doing?
   ▸ How does this bird in the second picture compare to the others?

6. Have students use the title and illustrations to make a prediction.

   ▸ What do you think the story will be about?

"The Ugly Duckling," Guided Reading

Now it's time to read "The Ugly Duckling." Have students sit next to you so that they can see the pictures and words while you read the story aloud.

1. Explain to students that you're going to read the first two pages of the story aloud and that they will read the rest of the story on their own.

2. Read pages 42–43 of the story aloud all the way through. Track with your finger so students can follow along.

3. Begin to reread pages 42–43 with students, having them chime in and read aloud with you this time. Tell them to think about the characters they meet as you read and that you will pause at certain points in the story to discuss.

4. Pause at the end of the second paragraph of the story. Have students identify the setting and main characters.

   ▸ Where does the story take place? the country
   ▸ What season is it? summer
   ▸ Who is the story about? a mother duck and her ducklings

5. Pause at the end of the second page, page 43 of the book. Have students describe a character and make predictions.

   ▸ How is the last egg different from the others? it is very large
   ▸ How is the duckling that pops out different from the other chicks? He is very large and ugly.
   ▸ What do you think will happen next? Answers will vary.

Objectives

- Use text organizational features to locate and comprehend information (table of contents, glossary, chapter, index, title, author, illustrator, caption).
- Use an illustration to make a prediction about a reading.
- Read texts for literary experience.
- Identify setting.
- Identify characters.
- Self-monitor comprehension by predicting, rereading, checking for sense, drawing on background knowledge, summarizing, clarifying, checking for context clues, and/or self-questioning.
- Repair comprehension using strategies: reread, use prior knowledge, self-question, identify context clues, determine word meaning, and read on.

"The Ugly Duckling," Independent Reading

Students will read the rest of "The Ugly Duckling" independently using the strategies from the Reading Strategies Guide.

1. Have students read the rest of "The Ugly Duckling" on their own. Remind them to do a Book Walk of the rest of the story before they read and predict what might happen.

2. Remind students to pause frequently to ask themselves questions about what they are reading, just as you did during guided reading. They should ask questions like the following.

   ▶ Where is this story taking place?
   ▶ What just happened in the story?
   ▶ What characters did I meet? What are they like?
   ▶ What will happen next?

3. Have students keep the Reading Strategies Guide handy as they read. Remind them that when they don't understand something, they should use the strategies listed to help them improve their understanding.

4. Tell students that when they have finished, you will discuss their understanding of the story and the strategies they used.

TIP Students should take about 15 minutes to read the rest of "The Ugly Duckling."

Check Your Reading

"The Ugly Duckling"

Discuss students' reading strategies and have them retell parts of the story to check comprehension. Turn to pages LC 65–66 of *K¹² Language Arts Activity Book.*

1. **Have students retell what happened in "The Ugly Duckling" in their own words** to develop grammar, vocabulary, comprehension, and fluency skills.

2. Have students complete the Activity Book page. Remind them how to approach multiple choice questions and to return to their books to look for the answers in "The Ugly Duckling."

3. If students have answered all the questions correctly, move on to the next activity or lesson. If students have trouble answering the questions, continue with Step 4.

4. Discuss the reading strategies students used to help their comprehension, prompting them with the following questions. Answers to questions will vary.

   ▶ Did you do a Book Walk and look through the pages before you read them?
   ▶ Did you stop sometimes and ask yourself what just happened or what characters you met? When did you do that?
   ▶ Did you stop sometimes and ask yourself what might happen next? When did you do that?
   ▶ Were there times when you were confused about something in the story? When?
   ▶ What did you do when you didn't understand something?

Objectives
- Answer questions requiring literal recall of details.
- Describe characters and their traits.
- Answer inferential questions.
- Evaluate reading strategies.

5. If students cannot answer the questions about the text and their reading strategies, or if they seem confused about what they read, have them reread the story aloud beginning with page 44. Prompt them to pause occasionally and use the appropriate reading strategies to aid in their comprehension.

6. Count how many words students struggle to read on any one page. If the number reaches five or more, stop students and tell them that you will read the rest of the story aloud to them.

7. As you read, pause at appropriate points in the story and ask questions about the setting, characters, and plot.

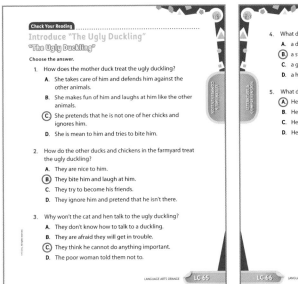
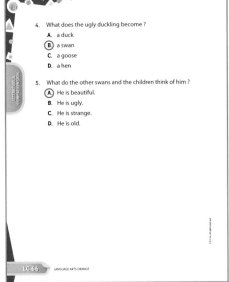

Check Your Reading

Introduce "The Ugly Duckling"
"The Ugly Duckling"

Choose the answer.

1. How does the mother duck treat the ugly duckling?
   A. She takes care of him and defends him against the other animals.
   B. She makes fun of him and laughs at him like the other animals.
   C. She pretends that he is not one of her chicks and ignores him.
   D. She is mean to him and tries to bite him.

2. How do the other ducks and chickens in the farmyard treat the ugly duckling?
   A. They are nice to him.
   B. They bite him and laugh at him.
   C. They try to become his friends.
   D. They ignore him and pretend that he isn't there.

3. Why won't the cat and hen talk to the ugly duckling?
   A. They don't know how to talk to a duckling.
   B. They are afraid they will get in trouble.
   C. They think he cannot do anything important.
   D. The poor woman told them not to.

4. What does the ugly duckling become?
   A. a duck
   B. a swan
   C. a goose
   D. a hen

5. What do the other swans and the children think of him?
   A. He is beautiful.
   B. He is ugly.
   C. He is strange.
   D. He is old.

LC 65   LANGUAGE ARTS ORANGE

LC 66   LANGUAGE ARTS ORANGE

Beyond the Lesson

⊕ OPTIONAL: Learn More About Swans

This activity is OPTIONAL. This activity is intended for students who have extra time and would be interested in learning more about swans. Feel free to skip this activity.

Objectives
- Make connections between text and the world.

1. Find a picture of ducks, ducklings, swans, and cygnets, or baby swans. Pictures may be found online at www.google.com/imghp. Use the search terms "duck," "duckling," "swan," and "cygnet" in the search field.

2. Tell students that the name for a baby swan is *cygnet*.

3. Discuss with students what they see. Answers to questions will vary.

   ▸ How do the different birds (baby swans and baby ducks) look similar? How do the adult ducks and swans looks similar?
   ▸ How do the birds look different?
   ▸ Why might the other animals in "The Ugly Duckling" have thought the baby swan was ugly?
   ▸ Do you think cygnets are ugly? Why or why not?

Explore "The Ugly Duckling"

Materials

Lesson Overview

Offline	"The Ugly Duckling"	**60** minutes

Get Ready	Review Learning About Characters
Read	Book Walk
	"The Ugly Duckling," Independent Reading
Reading for Meaning	Describe the Main Character

Supplied

- "The Ugly Duckling," *K¹² Classics for Young Readers, Volume B,* pp. 42–51
- *K¹² Language Arts Activity Book,* p. LC 67

Keywords

character – a person or animal in a story

fairy tale – a folktale that sometimes has magical elements; sometimes has a happily-ever-after ending

Advance Preparation

Have students gather the Reading Strategies Guide on page LC 55 in *K¹² Language Arts Activity Book.*

Big Ideas

- ▸ Comprehension requires an understanding of story structure.
- ▸ Interpretation occurs between reader and text, as the reader attempts to discover the unstated and to communicate about the text's meaning.
- ▸ To understand and interpret a story, readers need to understand and describe characters and what they do.

"The Ugly Duckling"

Work **together** with students to complete offline Get Ready, Read, and Reading for Meaning activities.

Get Ready

Review Learning About Characters

To prepare students to analyze the main character in "The Ugly Duckling," review with them how to learn about characters.

1. Have students tell what a **character** is in a story.

2. Have students describe how we learn about characters: by what they say, what they do, and what others (including the narrator) say about them.

3. Have students name a character they've read about and describe that character. For example, Father Jackal from "The Jackals and the Lion" is smart and tricky.

Objectives
- Define character.

Read

Book Walk

Prepare students by taking them on a Book Walk of "The Ugly Duckling." Scan the story together and ask students to recall the beginning of the story.

1. Show students the **front cover** of *K¹² Classics for Young Readers, Volume B*.

2. Have them use the **table of contents** to locate the selection and turn to that page.

3. Have students read the title.

4. Have them use the pictures to tell how the story begins. A mother duck has one very large egg, and when it hatches, a huge, ugly duckling comes out.

"The Ugly Duckling," Independent Reading

Have students reread the "The Ugly Duckling" independently using the strategies from the Reading Strategies Guide.

1. Remind students that as they read, they should pause now and then to ask themselves questions. If they get to the end of a section of the story or the end of a page, and they are confused about what happened, they should use strategies to repair their comprehension.

Objectives
- Use text organizational features to locate and comprehend information (table of contents).
- Read texts for literary experience.
- Self-monitor comprehension by predicting, rereading, checking for sense, drawing on background knowledge, summarizing, clarifying, checking for context clues, and/or self-questioning.
- Repair comprehension using strategies: reread, use prior knowledge, self-question, identify context clues, determine word meaning, and read on.
- Generate questions during reading.

2. When students have finished rereading the story to themselves, have them read the story aloud to an adult, a sibling, a peer, or even the family pet.

3. Have students retell the story to you using the pictures as a guide.

TIP Students should take about 15–20 minutes to read the story silently.

Reading for Meaning

Describe the Main Character

Students will describe the character of the ugly duckling in the beginning, middle, and end of the story to help them understand how others view the character, how he views himself, and how he changes. Turn to page LC 67 in *K¹² Language Arts Activity Book*.

1. Tell students that they are going to describe the ugly duckling in the different parts of the story. They should look for parts of the story that tell what other characters say about the ugly duckling, as well as what he says about himself.

2. Look at the story with students. Point out that the story is told in three parts and that a symbol separates the parts. Show students the symbols that separate the parts of the story on pages 46 and 48.

3. Direct students' attention to the Activity Book page. Show them that they are going to describe the ugly duckling in each part of the story. They should choose words that describe the ugly duckling in the beginning, middle, and end of the story. Show them that the first one was done for them as an example.

4. Direct students to find proof from the story to support their description. They should write the language from the book in the second column of the table. Students should think about what others say about the ugly duckling and what he says about himself.

5. Tell students that while the descriptions of the character may be the same in different parts of the story, the support or proof will be different.

6. Have students keep the Activity Book page in a safe place to use it later.

Objectives

- Describe characters by what they do, what they say, or what others say about them.
- Describe the characters in the story using evidence from the text.

Review "The Ugly Duckling"

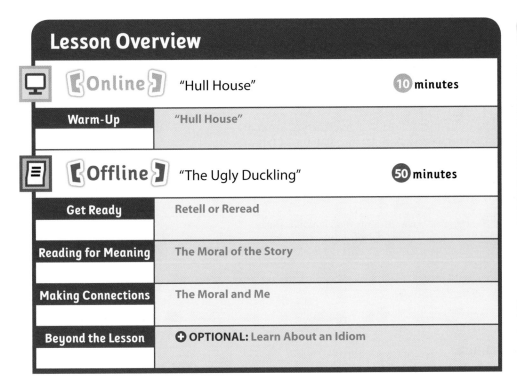

Lesson Overview

【Online】 "Hull House"		**10** minutes
Warm-Up	"Hull House"	
【Offline】 "The Ugly Duckling"		**50** minutes
Get Ready	Retell or Reread	
Reading for Meaning	The Moral of the Story	
Making Connections	The Moral and Me	
Beyond the Lesson	✚ OPTIONAL: Learn About an Idiom	

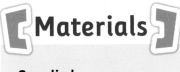

【Materials】

Supplied
- "The Ugly Duckling," *K¹² Classics for Young Readers, Volume B*, pp. 42–51
- *K¹² Language Arts Activity Book*, pp. LC 67–68
- "Hull House" (optional)

Alson Needed
- crayons

Keywords
fairy tale – a folktale that sometimes has magical elements; sometimes has a happily-ever-after ending
moral – the lesson of a story, particularly a fable

Advance Preparation

If you are not able to complete the online Warm-Up, then print the selection and listen to students read aloud. Have students gather the completed page LC 67 in *K¹² Language Arts Activity Book* (Describe the Main Character).

Big Ideas

▸ Readers should be able to retell the story (or information) in their own words, not repeat what was written.
▸ Interpretation occurs between reader and text, as the reader attempts to discover the unstated and to communicate about the text's meaning.
▸ By making the effort to understand texts, we can come to underst and ourselves.

 **Online** **10 minutes**

"Hull House"

Students will work independently online to develop fluency and oral reading skills.

 **Warm-Up** •

"Hull House"

The purpose of this activity is to improve students' oral reading and fluency. Students will read "Hull House." Remind students to listen to the model on each screen before they begin their recording.

Objectives
- Increase oral reading skills.
- Increase fluency.

Offline Alternative

No computer access? Print a copy of "Hull House." Have students read it aloud. Make note of any pronunciation errors, and review those words with students.

 Offline **50 minutes**

"The Ugly Duckling"

Work **together** with students to complete offline Get Ready, Reading for Meaning, Making Connections, and Beyond the Lesson activities.

Get Ready •

Retell or Reread

If you'd like to, have students reread the story to themselves. Otherwise, have students retell the story using the pictures as a guide.

Objectives
- Recount stories, including fables and folktales from diverse cultures.
- Summarize the plot of a story.

Reading for Meaning

The Moral of the Story

Students will think about the character of the ugly duckling to identify the moral of "The Ugly Duckling." Have students use the information on the Describe the Main Character page to help them think about the character of the ugly duckling.

1. Remind students that a **fairy tale** is a type of **folktale**. It is a story that is passed down through generations. Folktales often have a **moral**, or lesson.

2. Have students retell the moral of a folktale or fable that they've read. *Examples:* "The Fox and the Grapes," "The Fox and the Lion"

3. Tell students that they are going to think about the moral of "The Ugly Duckling."

4. Have students review the Describe the Main Character page.

5. Discuss what students learn about the ugly duckling.

   ▶ How do other characters describe the ugly duckling in the first two parts of the story? His mother said he was a good swimmer; other birds said he was ugly and couldn't do anything useful.

   ▶ How does the ugly duckling feel in the first two parts of the story? sad, lonely

   ▶ What does the ugly duckling do when he feels sad and lonely? He leaves to try to find a place where he can fit in.

   ▶ How does the ugly duckling change in the last part of the story? He grows up into a beautiful swan.

   ▶ How do other characters describe the ugly duckling in the last part? The other swans and the children think he is beautiful, too.

   ▶ How does the ugly duckling feel in the last part? happy   Why do you think this? He is beautiful. Others like him. He feels good about himself.

6. Have students think about the character of the ugly duckling and what happens in the story and tell what the moral of the story is. Possible answers: Don't judge people by looks alone; everyone is good at something; sometimes people get better or prettier as they get older; be kind to everyone; don't give up, even when others are mean or unkind; your outside never shows who you are on the inside.

Objectives

- Identify characteristics of different genres.
- Define moral.
- Identify the moral or lesson of a text.

Making Connections

The Moral and Me

Guide students to make a connection between the moral of "The Ugly Duckling" and their own lives. Turn to page LC 68 in *K¹² Language Arts Activity Book*.

1. Direct students' attention to the Activity Book page. For Exercise 1, have students write the lesson of the story in their own words.

2. For Exercise 2, prompt students to tell about a time when they experienced the lesson of this story themselves. Answers will vary.

   ▸ Can you think of a time when you learned this lesson in your own life or when it happened to someone else?
   ▸ What happened? Describe the events for me.

3. Have students complete Exercise 2 on the Activity Book page.

4. For Exercise 3, have students draw a picture that relates to their own story and shows how they experienced the lesson of "The Ugly Duckling."

> **Objectives**
> • Make connections between text and self.

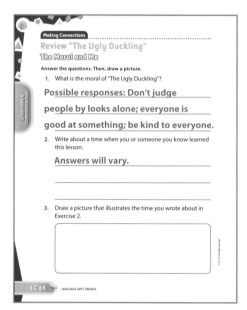

Beyond the Lesson

⊕ OPTIONAL: Learn About an Idiom

This activity is OPTIONAL. This activity is intended for students who have extra time and would benefit from learning about the idiom that we use today that comes from the story. Feel free to skip this activity.

1. Explain to students that the phrase "ugly duckling" is an **idiom**. An idiom is a phrase where the words don't mean exactly what they say.

2. Tell students that today we use the term ugly duckling to mean someone or something that isn't beautiful or good at something when young or new but becomes beautiful or successful later, with age, maturity, and experience.

3. Give a sentence as an example: *The boy was an ugly duckling in the band when he first started, but after a time he became one of the best trumpet players.*

4. Have students make up a sentence using the idiom and tell it to you. Possible answer: The girl felt like an ugly duckling because she couldn't swim well, but after lots of lessons she became a great swimmer.

> **Objectives**
> • Define idiom.
> • Identify and use idioms.
> • Make connections between text and the world.

Introduce "The Grasshopper and the Ant"

Lesson Overview

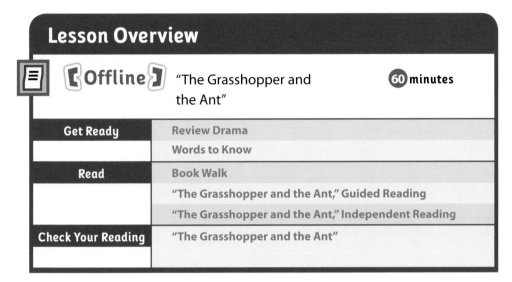

Offline	"The Grasshopper and the Ant" — **60** minutes

Get Ready	Review Drama
	Words to Know
Read	Book Walk
	"The Grasshopper and the Ant," Guided Reading
	"The Grasshopper and the Ant," Independent Reading
Check Your Reading	"The Grasshopper and the Ant"

Advance Preparation

Read "The Grasshopper and the Ant" before beginning the Read to locate Words to Know in the text. Preview the Read and note the parts of the play that you will read aloud and the parts that students will read independently. Have students gather the Reading Strategies Guide on page LC 55 in *K¹² Language Arts Activity Book*.

Big Ideas

▶ Interpretation occurs between reader and text, as the reader attempts to discover the unstated and to communicate about the text's meaning.
▶ Comprehension entails an understanding of the organizational patterns of text.

Materials

Supplied
- "The Grasshopper and the Ant," *K¹² Classics for Younger Readers, Volume B*, pp. 52–59
- *K¹² Language Arts Activity Book*, p. LC 55

Story Synopsis

Grasshopper whiles away the summer months and mocks Ant who toils in preparation for winter. When the cold weather comes, the once carefree Grasshopper must ask the Ant for help, as the Ant has supplies for the winter and the Grasshopper does not.

Keywords

bold type – type that is darker than the surrounding text that draws attention to a word or phrase

character – a person or animal in a story

drama – another word for play

fable – a story that teaches a lesson and may contain animal characters

italic – text that slants toward the right

 **Offline** **60** minutes

"The Grasshopper and the Ant"

Work **together** with students to complete offline Get Ready, Read, and Check Your Reading activities.

Get Ready

Review Drama

Review the elements of drama.

1. Have students tell about a play that they have seen on stage or read, such as "The Jackals and the Lion."

2. Remind students that a play is a type of writing called **drama**.

3. Have students describe some of the ways that drama looks different from other kinds of writing, such as stories and poetry. stage directions, character lists at the beginning, character names, lines that characters say

Objectives
- Define drama.
- Connect to prior knowledge.
- Increase concept and content vocabulary.

Words to Know

Before reading "The Grasshopper and the Ant," go over Words to Know with students.

1. Have students say the word aloud.

2. Ask students if they know what the word means.

   ▸ If students know the word's meaning, have them define it and use it in a sentence.
   ▸ If students don't know the word's meaning, read them the definition and discuss the word with them.

livelong – whole, entire

Read ···

Book Walk

Prepare students by taking them on a Book Walk of "The Grasshopper and the Ant."
Scan the play together and ask students to make predictions about it.

1. Show students the **front cover** and **back cover** of *K¹² Classics for Young Readers, Volume B*. Remind them that the book is a collection of stories.

2. Use the **table of contents** to locate "The Grasshopper and the Ant." Read the **title** and have students turn to that page.

3. Have students read the title.

4. Tell students that they are going to read a play.

5. Look through the first two pages of the play. Have students point to and describe the character list and character names in the text.

6. Point to the heading Scene 1–Summer: A Pleasant Field. Explain that some plays are divided into parts called **scenes**. This heading tells us that this is Scene 1. It also tells us the setting: summer in a field.

7. Have students look at the **illustrations** and describe what they see.

   ▶ What kinds of animals do you see in the pictures? a grasshopper, an ant
   ▶ What does it look like the grasshopper is doing? lying around, singing
   ▶ What is the ant doing? carrying something heavy, working

8. Have students use the title and illustrations to make a prediction.

   ▶ What do you think the play will be about? Answers will vary.

"The Grasshopper and the Ant," Guided Reading

Now it's time to read "The Grasshopper and the Ant." Have students sit next to you so that they can see the pictures and words while you read the play aloud.

1. Explain to students that you're going to read the first two pages of the play aloud. Then they will read the rest of the play on their own.

2. Read pages 52–53 of the play aloud all the way through. Use different voices for the grasshopper and the ant. Track with your finger so students can follow along.

3. Reread pages 52–53 with students, having them chime in and read aloud with you this time. Tell them to think about the characters they meet as you read and that you will pause at certain points in the story to discuss.

4. Begin to reread and pause after the song at the top of page 53. Have students identify the setting and a main character.

   ▶ What character have we met? Grasshopper   What is he doing? Possible answers: relaxing, singing, doing nothing, playing

> **Objectives**
> • Identify characteristics of different genres.
> • Use text organizational features to locate and comprehend information (table of contents).
> • Use the title of the selection to make a prediction.
> • Use an illustration to make a prediction about a reading.
> • Read texts for literary experience.
> • Identify setting.
> • Identify characters.
> • Self-monitor comprehension by predicting, rereading, checking for sense, drawing on background knowledge, summarizing, clarifying, checking for context clues, and/or self-questioning.
> • Repair comprehension using strategies: reread, use prior knowledge, self-question, identify context clues, determine word meaning, and read on.
> • Generate questions during reading.

5. Remind students how to read character names in a play: When they are reading to themselves, they read the name of the character speaking; when the play is performed, the characters' names are not said aloud.

6. Pause at the end of page 53. Point to the stage direction, *An ant comes along*. Review what a stage direction is and how it is different from the text in the same kind of type (italic) above it (the song Grasshopper sings). The stage direction is not spoken; the song is performed aloud.

7. Have students identify another character.

   ▸ What new character do we meet? Ant   What is he doing? working

---

"The Grasshopper and the Ant," Independent Reading

Have students read the rest of "The Grasshopper and the Ant" independently using the strategies from the Reading Strategies Guide.

1. Before students begin, remind them to do a Book Walk of the rest of the play and predict what might happen.

2. Remind students to pause frequently to ask themselves questions, similar to those that follow, about what they are reading, just as you did during guided reading.

   ▸ Where is this story taking place?
   ▸ What just happened in the story?
   ▸ What characters did I meet? What are they like?
   ▸ What will happen next?

3. Students should keep the Reading Strategies Guide handy while reading. Remind them that when they don't understand something, they should use the strategies to help them improve their understanding.

4. Tell students that when they have finished, you will discuss their understanding of the play and the strategies they used.

5. Have students read the rest of the play on their own.

TIP Students should take about 10 minutes to read the rest of "The Grasshopper and the Ant."

Check Your Reading

"The Grasshopper and the Ant"

Discuss students' reading strategies and have them retell parts of the story to check comprehension.

Objectives
- Answer questions requiring literal recall of details.
- Describe characters and their traits.
- Answer inferential questions.
- Evaluate reading strategies.

1. **Have students retell what happened in "The Grasshopper and the Ant" in their own words** to develop grammar, vocabulary, comprehension, and fluency skills.

2. **Ask the following questions** to check comprehension.

   ▸ What activities does Grasshopper think are important? Possible answers: talking with friends, relaxing, having a good time

   ▸ What is Ant doing with his day? gathering food   Why? so he has enough for winter

   ▸ Does Ant ever rest? Yes   What does he do? He sits at home and talks with his friends in the evening.

   ▸ How does Grasshopper look when winter comes? thin, sick

   ▸ What does he want from the ants? food

   ▸ How does Grasshopper feel at the end of the play? Grasshopper is sad and wishes he had worked hard.   How is this different from how he felt at the beginning of the play? At the beginning, he was happy and didn't want to work.

3. If students have answered all the questions correctly, move on to the next activity or lesson. If students have trouble answering the questions, continue with Step 4.

4. Discuss the reading strategies students used to help their comprehension, prompting them with the following questions. Answers to questions will vary.

   ▸ Did you do a Book Walk and look through the pages before you read them?
   ▸ Did you stop sometimes and ask yourself what just happened or what characters you met? When did you do that?
   ▸ Did you stop sometimes and ask yourself what might happen next? When did you do that?
   ▸ Were there times when you were confused about something in the story? When?
   ▸ What did you do when you didn't understand something?

5. If students cannot answer the questions about the text and their reading strategies, or if they seem confused about what they read, have them reread the story aloud beginning with page 54. Prompt them to pause and use the appropriate reading strategies to aid in their comprehension.

6. As they read aloud, count the number of words that students struggle to read on any one page. If the number reaches five or more, stop students and read the rest of the story aloud to them.

7. As you read, pause at appropriate points in the story and ask questions about the setting, characters, and plot.

Explore "The Grasshopper and the Ant"

Lesson Overview

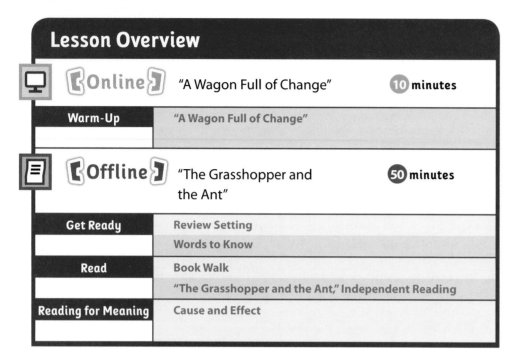

Online	"A Wagon Full of Change"	**10** minutes
Warm-Up	"A Wagon Full of Change"	
Offline	"The Grasshopper and the Ant"	**50** minutes
Get Ready	Review Setting	
	Words to Know	
Read	Book Walk	
	"The Grasshopper and the Ant," Independent Reading	
Reading for Meaning	Cause and Effect	

Materials

Supplied

- "The Grasshopper and the Ant," *K¹² Classics for Young Readers, Volume B,* pp. 52–59
- *K¹² Language Arts Activity Book,* pp. LC 55, 69
- "A Wagon Full of Change" (optional)

Keywords

cause – the reason something happens

character – a person or animal in a story

effect – the result of a cause

setting – when and where a story takes place

Advance Preparation

If you are not able to complete the online Warm-Up, then print the selection and listen to students read aloud. Have students gather the Reading Strategies Guide on page LC 55 in *K¹² Language Arts Activity Book.*

Big Ideas

► Signal words—such as *before, consequently, compare, contrast, therefore*—are a guide to understanding the relationship between and among ideas.
► Interpretation occurs between reader and text, as the reader attempts to discover the unstated and to communicate about the text's meaning.
► Readers need to understand and describe characters and what they do to understand and interpret a story.

 **10 minutes**

"A Wagon Full of Change"
Students will work independently online to develop fluency and oral reading skills.

Warm-Up

"A Wagon Full of Change
The purpose of this activity is to improve students' oral reading and fluency. Students will read "A Wagon Full of Change." Remind students to listen to the model on each screen before they begin their recording.

Objectives
- Increase oral reading skills.
- Increase fluency.

Offline Alternative

No computer access? Print a copy of "A Wagon Full of Change." Have students read it aloud several times. Make note of any pronunciation errors, and review those words with students.

 **50 minutes**

"The Grasshopper and the Ant"
Work **together** with students to complete offline Get Ready, Read, and Reading for Meaning activities.

Get Ready

Review Setting
Review the setting of "The Grasshopper and the Ant" to make sure students understand the change in seasons that is essential to the story.

Objectives
- Define setting.
- Describe setting.
- Increase concept and content vocabulary.

1. Have students tell what a **setting** is: when and where a story takes place.

2. Have students describe the setting in the first scene of "The Grasshopper and the Ant."
   - ▸ Where does the first scene take place? a pleasant field
   - ▸ What season is it in the first scene? summer

3. Have students describe the setting in the second scene of the play.
   - ▸ Where does the second scene take place? in front of Ant's house
   - ▸ What season is it in the second scene? winter

4. Tell students to keep the settings in mind as they reread "The Grasshopper and the Ant."

Words to Know

Before reading "The Grasshopper and the Ant," go over Words to Know with students.

1. Ask students to define the following word and use it in a sentence:

   livelong

2. Correct any incorrect or vague definitions.

Read

Book Walk

Prepare students by taking them on a Book Walk of "The Grasshopper and the Ant." Scan the play together and ask students to recall the beginning.

1. Show students the **front cover** of K^{12} *Classics for Young Readers, Volume B.*

2. Have them use the **table of contents** to locate the selection and turn to that page.

3. Have students read the title.

4. Have them use the pictures to tell how the story begins. Make sure students identify the season. Grasshopper is relaxing in summer.

"The Grasshopper and the Ant," Independent Reading

Students will reread the "The Grasshopper and the Ant" independently using the strategies from the Reading Strategies Guide on page LC 55.

1. Tell students that they will reread the play again to themselves.

2. Remind students that as they read, they should pause sometimes and ask themselves questions.

3. Remind students that if they get to the end of a section of the play or the end of a page, and they are confused about what happened, they should use reading strategies to repair their comprehension. Tell students to keep the Reading Strategies Guide handy as they read.

4. Have students reread the play.

5. When students have finished rereading the play to themselves, have them read it aloud to an adult, a sibling, a peer, or even the family pet.

6. Have students retell the story to you using the pictures as a guide.

TIP Students should take about 10–12 minutes to read the play to themselves.

Objectives

- Use text organizational features to locate and comprehend information (table of contents, glossary, chapter, index, title, author, illustrator, caption).
- Read texts for literary experience.
- Read on-level text with purpose and understanding.
- Read second-grade level text at a rate of 90 words per minute.
- Self-monitor comprehension by predicting, rereading, checking for sense, drawing on background knowledge, summarizing, clarifying, checking for context clues, and/or self-questioning.
- Repair comprehension using strategies: reread, use prior knowledge, self-question, identify context clues, determine word meaning, and read on.
- Generate questions during reading.

Reading for Meaning

Cause and Effect

Students will explore the effects of the actions of the grasshopper and the ant. Turn to page LC 69 in *K¹² Language Arts Activity Book.*

1. Have students define the terms **cause** and **effect**. Have them give an example of a cause-and-effect relationship, such as the hot sun (cause) can give you a sunburn (effect).

2. Tell students that they are going to look at the actions of the Grasshopper and the Ant in the play and think about what effects their actions have.

3. Direct student's attention to the Activity Book page.

   ▸ Explain that they are to write in the Cause box for each character what that character does in the first scene of the play. The first scene takes place during summer.
   ▸ In the Effect boxes, they are to write the consequences of the characters' actions—the effects that happen to both characters in summer and in winter, including things that happen and how the character feels.
   ▸ Remind students that an effect is something that happens because of a cause.

4. Have students complete the Activity Book page.

5. Have students keep this Activity Book page in a safe place to use later.

Objectives

- Define cause and effect.
- Make relevant cause and effect connections between earlier events and later events in a text.

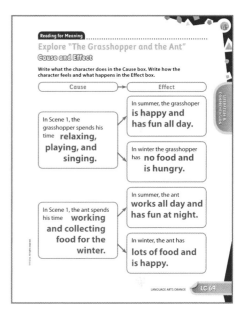

Review "The Grasshopper and the Ant"

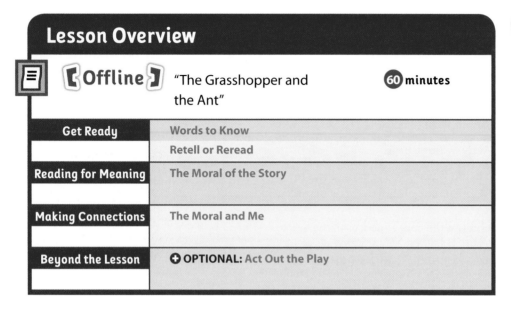

Lesson Overview

☰	**〔Offline〕**	"The Grasshopper and the Ant"	**60** minutes
Get Ready		Words to Know	
		Retell or Reread	
Reading for Meaning		The Moral of the Story	
Making Connections		The Moral and Me	
Beyond the Lesson		➕ **OPTIONAL:** Act Out the Play	

〔 Materials 〕

Supplied
- "The Grasshopper and the Ant," *K¹² Classics for Young Readers, Volume B,* pp. 52–59
- *K¹² Language Arts Activity Book,* pp. LC 69–70

Also Needed
- crayons

Keywords

fable – a story that teaches a lesson and may contain animal characters

moral – the lesson of a story, particularly a fable

Advance Preparation

Have students gather page LC 69 in *K¹² Language Arts Activity Book* (Cause and Effect).

Big Ideas

- ▸ Readers should be able to retell the story (or information) in their own words, not repeat what was written.
- ▸ Active, strong readers employ reading strategies such as making connections between text and themselves.
- ▸ Interpretation occurs between reader and text, as the reader attempts to discover the unstated and to communicate about the text's meaning.
- ▸ By making the effort to understand texts, we can come to understand ourselves.

 **⟦ Offline ⟧** **60** minutes

"The Grasshopper and the Ant"

Work **together** with students to complete offline Get Ready, Reading for Meaning, Making Connections, and Beyond the Lesson activities.

Get Ready

Words to Know

Before rereading or retelling "The Grasshopper and the Ant," go over Words to Know with students.

1. Ask students to define the following word and use it in a sentence:

   livelong

2. Correct any incorrect or vague definitions.

 Objectives

- Increase concept and content vocabulary.
- Recount stories, including fables and folktales from diverse cultures.
- Summarize the plot of a story.

Retell or Reread

If you'd like to, have students reread the play to themselves. Otherwise, have students retell the story using the pictures as a guide.

Reading for Meaning

The Moral of the Story

To identify the moral of the story "The Grasshopper and the Ant," guide students to explore the characters of the Grasshopper and the Ant using the completed Cause and Effect page.

1. Tell students that this play is also **fable**. Have students tell what a fable is and name a fable they've read, such as "The Fox and the Grapes."

2. Remind students that fables have **morals**. Have students tell what a moral is.

3. Tell students that they are going to think about the moral of "The Grasshopper and the Ant."

4. Have students reread the Cause and Effect page to help them think about the characters of the Grasshopper and the Ant.

 Objectives

- Identify characteristics of different genres.
- Define moral.
- Identify the moral or lesson of a text.

5. Discuss what students learn about the Grasshopper and the Ant.

   ▸ What does the Grasshopper do in summer, when there is plenty of food?
   plays, sings, has fun with friends

   ▸ What does the Ant do in summer? works collecting food for the winter

   ▸ Who is better off in the winter, when there is no food to be found?
   the Ant   Why? He stored food in the summer when there was a lot, so he
   has food for the winter.

   ▸ Who do you think is wiser, or smarter, the Grasshopper or the Ant?
   the Ant   Why? The Ant planned for the bad times in the future, instead of
   just playing.

6. Reread with students the last song of the grasshopper.

   ▸ What lesson do you think the Grasshopper learned? Possible answers: It's a
   good idea to plan for the future; don't put off until tomorrow what you can
   do today; it's better to work hard before you play than play all the time.

Making Connections

The Moral and Me
Guide students to make a connection between the moral of "The Grasshopper
and the Ant" and their own lives by creating a comic strip. Turn to page LC 70 in
K¹² Language Arts Activity Book.

1. Have students write the lesson, or moral, of the story in their own words
   on the Activity Book page.

2. Before they continue with the Activity Book page, have students tell
   about a time when they experienced the moral, or lesson, of this story
   themselves. Answers will vary.

   ▸ Can you think of a time when you learned this lesson in your own
   life or when it happened to someone else?

   ▸ What happened? Describe the events for me.

3. On the Activity Book page, have students create a comic strip of the story
   they just told you about their own, or someone else's, experience of this
   lesson. Their strip should include words and pictures that illustrate the
   moral of the story. Tell students to break the comic strip up.

   ▸ In the first box, write the beginning.
   ▸ In the second and third boxes, write the middle.
   ▸ In the fourth box, write the end.

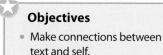

Objectives
• Make connections between
text and self.

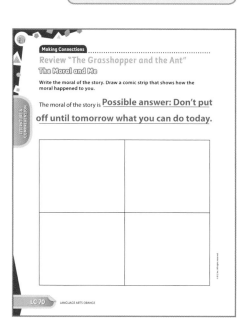

Beyond the Lesson

⊕ OPTIONAL: Act Out the Play

This activity is OPTIONAL. This activity is intended for students who have extra time and would benefit from acting out the play. Feel free to skip this activity.

1. Have students do a dramatic reading of the play. Students may play one role and you play the other, or students can read both parts.

2. Encourage students to use props for each character, such as a toy the Grasshopper is playing with or something heavy the Ant is carrying for work. They may also want to put on something warm, such as a hat or scarf, when the season changes to winter in Scene 2.

3. Remind students that when they say their lines, they should not read the character's name. The names are only there to indicate who is speaking and shouldn't be said aloud during a performance.

4. If students are playing both roles, tell them to use a different voice for each character to indicate which character is speaking.

Objectives

- Make connections between text and the world.
- Acknowledge differences between characters, for example, by using a different voice for each character when reading dialogue aloud.

Introduce "The Three Wishes"

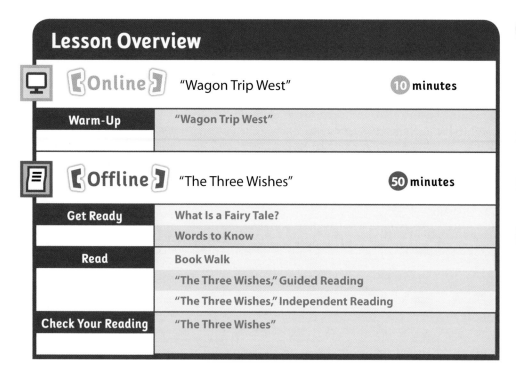

Lesson Overview

Online	"Wagon Trip West"	10 minutes
Warm-Up	"Wagon Trip West"	

Offline	"The Three Wishes"	50 minutes
Get Ready	What Is a Fairy Tale?	
	Words to Know	
Read	Book Walk	
	"The Three Wishes," Guided Reading	
	"The Three Wishes," Independent Reading	
Check Your Reading	"The Three Wishes"	

Materials

Supplied

- "The Three Wishes," *K¹² Classics for Young Readers, Volume B,* pp. 60–63
- *K¹² Language Arts Activity Book,* p. LC 55
- "Wagon Trip West" (optional)

Story Synopsis

A poor woodcutter discovers a magic rabbit caught in a trap in the forest. The rabbit promises to grant three wishes if the woodcutter sets it free. The woodcutter agrees. However, back at home the woodcutter's wife mistakenly wishes for a huge cake, and the wish comes true. In frustration and anger, the woodcutter quickly wastes his remaining two wishes on ridiculous requests.

Keywords

character – a person or animal in a story
fairy tale – a folktale that sometimes has magical elements; sometimes has a happily-ever-after ending

Advance Preparation

Read "The Three Wishes" before beginning the Read to locate Words to Know in the text. Preview the Read and note the parts of the story that you will read aloud and the parts that students will read independently. Have students gather the Reading Strategies Guide on page LC 55 in *K¹² Language Arts Activity Book.*

Big Ideas

▸ Comprehension requires the reader to self-monitor understanding.
▸ Comprehension requires the reader to self-correct errors made while reading by using a wide variety of strategies.
▸ Comprehension entails asking and answering questions about the text.
▸ Comprehension is facilitated when readers connect new information to information previously learned.
▸ Interpretation occurs between reader and text, as the reader attempts to discover the unstated and to communicate about the text's meaning.

 **10 minutes**

"Wagon Trip West"

Students will work independently online to develop fluency and oral reading skills.

"Wagon Trip West"

The purpose of this activity is to improve students' oral reading and fluency. Students will read "Wagon Trip West." Remind students to listen to the model on each screen before they begin their recording.

Objectives
- Increase oral reading skills.
- Increase fluency.

Offline Alternative

No computer access? Print a copy of "Wagon Trip West." Have students read it aloud. Make note of any pronunciation errors, and review those words with students.

[Offline] **50 minutes**

"The Three Wishes"

Work **together** with students to complete offline Get Ready, Read, and Check Your Reading activities.

Get Ready

What Is a Fairy Tale?
Teach students about fairy tales and the common characters in them.

1. Have students tell what a **fairy tale** is.

2. If they do not remember, remind students that a fairy tale is a folktale that sometimes has magic in it, usually a magical character. This character can make things happen that would not happen in real life.

3. Have students describe a fairy tale they've read, such as "Cinderella." Have them tell about the magical characters in the story, such as the Fairy Godmother, and the special things that the character causes to happen (turning a pumpkin into a coach, for example).

4. Remind students that sometimes a fairy tale has a happily-ever-after ending.

Objectives
- Define fairy tale.
- Identify characteristics of different genres.
- Identify recurring characters in folk and fairy tales.
- Increase concept and content vocabulary.

Words to Know

Before reading "The Three Wishes," go over Words to Know with students.

1. Have students say the word aloud.

2. Ask students if they know what the word means.

   ▸ If students know the word's meaning, have them define it and use it in a sentence.
   ▸ If students don't know the word's meaning, read them the definition and discuss the word with them.

woodcutter – a person who chops up wood to sell to people to use in their homes

Read

Book Walk

Prepare students by taking them on a Book Walk of "The Three Wishes." Scan the story together and ask students to make predictions about it.

1. Tell students that they are going to read a fairy tale with a magical character.

2. Show students the **front cover** and **back cover** of *K¹² Classics for Young Readers, Volume B*. Remind students that the book is a collection of stories.

3. Use the **table of contents** to locate "The Three Wishes." Read the **title** and have students turn to that page.

4. Have students read the title.

5. Look at the first page of the story. Have students look at the **illustration** and describe what they see.

   ▸ What kind of animal do you see in the picture? a rabbit
   ▸ What does it look like the rabbit is doing? It looks like it's caught in a trap.

6. Have students use the title and illustrations to make a prediction.

   ▸ What do you think the story will be about? Answers will vary.

"The Three Wishes," Guided Reading

Now it's time to read "The Three Wishes." Have students sit next to you so that they can see the pictures and words while you read the story aloud.

1. Explain to students that you're going to read the first page of the story aloud. Then they will to read the rest of the story on their own.

2. Read page 60 aloud all the way through. Track with your finger so students can follow along.

3. Tell students that you will reread page 60 and this time they are to chime in and read aloud with you. Tell them to think about the characters they meet as you read and that you will pause to discuss.

Objectives

- Use text organizational features to locate and comprehend information (table of contents, glossary, chapter, index, title, author, illustrator, caption).
- Use title of the selection to make a prediction.
- Use an illustration to make a prediction about a reading.
- Read texts for literary experience.
- Identify setting.
- Identify characters.
- Read on-level text with purpose and understanding.
- Read second grade level text at a rate of 90 words per minute.
- Self-monitor comprehension by predicting, rereading, checking for sense, drawing on background knowledge, summarizing, clarifying, checking for context clues, and/or self-questioning.
- Repair comprehension using strategies: reread, use prior knowledge, self-question, identify context clues, determine word meaning, and read on.
- Generate questions during reading.

4. Begin to reread, pausing after the third paragraph, after the sentence, "'No supper for us tonight!'" Have students identify the setting and main character.

   ▸ Where does this story take place? in a forest
   ▸ What character have we met? a woodcutter
   ▸ How would you describe this character? He is poor and has no money for dinner.

5. Pause at the end of the first page. Have students make a prediction.

   ▸ What do you think will happen next? Answers will vary.

"The Three Wishes," Independent Reading

Have students read the rest of "The Three Wishes" independently using the strategies from the Reading Strategies Guide.

1. Tell students they are going to read the rest of "The Three Wishes" on their own. Remind them to do a Book Walk of the rest of the story before they read and predict what might happen.

2. Remind students to pause frequently to ask themselves questions about what they are reading, just as you did during guided reading. They should ask questions like the following:

   ▸ Where is this story taking place?
   ▸ What just happened in the story?
   ▸ What characters did I meet? What are they like?
   ▸ What will happen next?

3. Make sure students have the Reading Strategies Guide handy. Remind them that when they don't understand something they read, they should use strategies to help them improve their understanding.

4. Tell students that when they have finished, you will discuss their understanding of the story and the strategies they used.

5. Have students reread the story on their own.

   TIP Students should take about 5 minutes to read the rest of "The Three Wishes."

Check Your Reading

Objectives
- Answer questions requiring literal recall of details.
- Evaluate reading strategies.

"The Three Wishes"

Discuss students' reading strategies and have them retell parts of the story to check comprehension.

1. **Have students retell what happened in "The Three Wishes" in their own words** to develop grammar, vocabulary, comprehension, and fluency skills.

2. **Ask the following questions** to check comprehension.

   - What is the woodcutter's problem at the beginning of the story? No one bought his sticks, so he has no money for supper.
   - Who is the magical character in this fairy tale? the rabbit   What magic does the rabbit promise to perform? He'll grant the woodcutter three wishes if the woodcutter lets him go.
   - What does the woodcutter give up by letting the rabbit go? food to eat for supper
   - What does the wife do when the woodcutter gets home? wishes for a giant cake
   - What does the woodcutter wish for when this happens? that the cake would stick to his wife's nose
   - What does the woodcutter want to use as his third wish? all the riches in the world   What does he wish for instead? that the cake would fly off his wife's nose and up the chimney

3. If students have answered all the questions correctly, move on to the next activity or lesson. If students have trouble answering the questions, continue with Step 4.

4. Discuss the reading strategies students used to help their comprehension. Check that they used strategies such as a Book Walk, rereading, and asking questions.

5. If students cannot answer the questions about the text and their reading strategies, or if they seem confused about what they read, have them reread the story aloud beginning with page 61. Prompt them to pause and use the appropriate reading strategies to aid in their comprehension.

6. As they read aloud, count of the number of words that students struggle to read on any one page. If the number reaches five or more, stop students and read the rest of the story aloud to them.

7. As you read, stop at appropriate points in the story and ask questions about the setting, characters, and plot.

Explore "The Three Wishes"

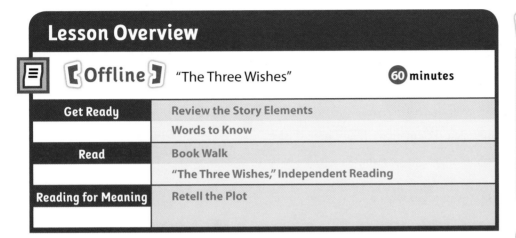

Lesson Overview

☰ [Offline] "The Three Wishes"		60 minutes
Get Ready	Review the Story Elements	
	Words to Know	
Read	Book Walk	
	"The Three Wishes," Independent Reading	
Reading for Meaning	Retell the Plot	

Materials

Supplied

- "The Three Wishes," *K¹² Classics for Young Readers, Volume B,* pp. 60–63
- *K¹² Language Arts Activity Book,* pp. LC 55, 71

Keywords

fairy tale – a folktale that sometimes has magical elements; sometimes has a happily-ever-after ending

plot – what happens in a story

sequence – order

Advance Preparation

Have students gather the Reading Strategies Guide on page LC 55 in *K¹² Language Arts Activity Book.*

Big Ideas

- ▸ Comprehension entails actively thinking about what is being read.
- ▸ Comprehension requires the reader to self-monitor understanding.
- ▸ Interpretation occurs between reader and text, as the reader attempts to discover the unstated and to communicate about the text's meaning.
- ▸ Readers should be able to retell the story (or information) in their own words, not repeat what was written.

 **60 minutes**

"The Three Wishes"

Work **together** with students to complete offline Get Ready, Read, and Reading for Meaning activities.

Get Ready

Review the Story Elements

Review the setting, main characters, and magical element of "The Three Wishes."

1. Have students describe the **setting** of "The Three Wishes."

2. Have students identify the three **main characters** in the story: the rabbit, the woodcutter, and his wife.

3. Remind students that the story is a **fairy tale** and has magical elements. Have students describe the magic in the story.

> **Objectives**
> - Describe setting.
> - Identify main characters.
> - Identify characteristics of different genres.
> - Increase concept and content vocabulary.

Words to Know

Before reading "The Three Wishes," go over Words to Know with students.

1. Ask students to define the following word and use it in a sentence:

   livelong

2. Correct any incorrect or vague definitions.

Read

Book Walk

Prepare students by taking them on a Book Walk of "The Three Wishes." Scan the story together and ask students to recall the beginning.

1. Show students the **front cover** of K^{12} *Classics for Young Readers, Volume B.*

2. Have them use the **table of contents** to locate "The Three Wishes" and turn to that page.

3. Have students read the title.

4. Have them use the pictures to tell how the story begins. A poor woodcutter can't sell his sticks and has no money for supper.

"The Three Wishes," Independent Reading

Have students reread "The Three Wishes" independently using the strategies from the Reading Strategies Guide.

1. Tell students that they will reread the story again to themselves.

2. Remind them that as they read, they should pause sometimes and ask themselves questions.

3. Remind students that if they get to the end of a section of the story or the end of a page, and they are confused about what happened, they should use strategies to repair their comprehension. Tell students to use the strategies from the Reading Strategies Guide.

4. Have students read the story on their own.

5. When they have finished reading the story to themselves, have students read the story aloud to an adult, a sibling, a peer, or even the family pet.

TIP Students should take about 8–10 minutes to read the story to themselves.

Objectives

- Use text organizational features to locate and comprehend information (table of contents).
- Read texts for literary experience.
- Self-monitor comprehension by predicting, rereading, checking for sense, drawing on background knowledge, summarizing, clarifying, checking for context clues, and/or self-questioning.
- Repair comprehension using strategies: reread, use prior knowledge, self-question, identify context clues, determine word meaning, and read on.

Reading for Meaning

Retell the Plot

Guide students to retell the important events in the plot of "The Three Wishes" in sequence, which will prepare them for understanding the moral of the story. Turn to page LC 71 in *K¹² Language Arts Activity Book.*

1. Have students define **plot**: what happens in a story.

2. Remind students that when they retell the plot of a story, they should retell only the most important events.

3. Review that the most important events need to be told in **sequence**, or the order in which the events happened.

4. Review with students some order words that they can use to keep the important events in order: *first, second, next, then, last, finally.*

5. Have students complete the Activity Book page, using the most important events from "The Three Wishes."

6. Have students keep the Activity Book page in a safe place so they can use it to identify the moral of the story.

Objectives

- Sequence events in a text.
- Create and use graphic organizers, diagrams, charts, Venn diagrams, and time lines to demonstrate and support comprehension.

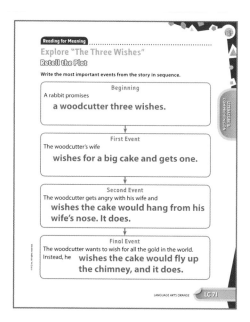

Review "The Three Wishes"

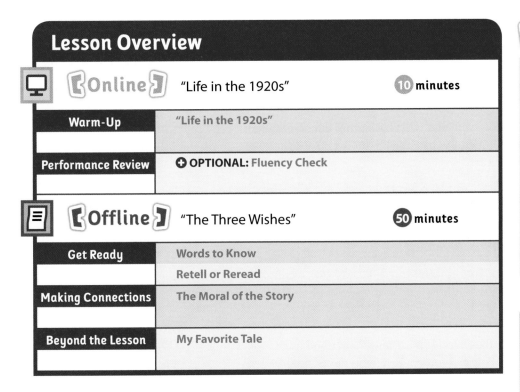

Lesson Overview

🖥 【Online】 "Life in the 1920s" ⑩ minutes

Warm-Up	"Life in the 1920s"
Performance Review	➕ OPTIONAL: Fluency Check

🗎 【Offline】 "The Three Wishes" ㊿ minutes

Get Ready	Words to Know
	Retell or Reread
Making Connections	The Moral of the Story
Beyond the Lesson	My Favorite Tale

【Materials】

Supplied

- "The Three Wishes," *K¹² Classics for Young Readers, Volume B,* pp. 60–63
- *K¹² Language Arts Activity Book,* pp. LC 71–72
- "Life in the 1920s" (optional)
- Fluency Performance Checklist (optional)

Keywords

fairy tale – a folktale that sometimes has magical elements; sometimes has a happily-ever-after ending

moral – the lesson of a story, particularly a fable

Advance Preparation

If you are not able to complete the online Warm-Up, then print the selection and listen to students read aloud. Have students gather the completed page LC 71 in *K¹² Language Arts Activity Book* (Retell the Plot).

Big Ideas

- ▸ Readers should be able to retell the story (or information) in their own words, not repeat what was written.
- ▸ Active, strong readers employ reading strategies such as making connections between text and themselves.
- ▸ Interpretation occurs between reader and text, as the reader attempts to discover the unstated and to communicate about the text's meaning.
- ▸ By making the effort to understand texts, we can come to understand ourselves.

 **10 minutes**

"Life in the 1920s"
Students will work independently online to develop fluency and oral reading skills.

Warm-Up
· ·

"Life in the 1920s"
The purpose of this activity is to improve students' oral reading and fluency. Students will read "Life in the 1920s." Remind students to listen to the model on each screen before they begin their recording.

 Objectives
- Increase oral reading skills.
- Increase fluency.

Offline Alternative

No computer access? Print a copy of "Life in the 1920s." Have students read it aloud. Make note of any pronunciation errors, and review those words with students.

Performance Review
· ·

➕ **OPTIONAL: Fluency Check**
Listen to students' recordings and use the checklist to review fluency and track performance. Keep the completed checklist so you can review students' progress over time.

 Objectives
- Read aloud grade-level text with appropriate automaticity, prosody, accuracy, and rate.

 **50 minutes**

"The Three Wishes"
Work **together** with students to complete offline Get Ready, Making Connections, and Beyond the Lesson activities.

Get Ready
· ·

Words to Know
Before rereading or retelling "The Three Wishes," go over Words to Know with students.

1. Ask students to define the following word and use it in a sentence:

   woodcutter

2. Correct any incorrect or vague definitions.

 Objectives
- Increase concept and content vocabulary.
- Recount stories, including fables and folktales from diverse cultures.
- Summarize the plot of a story.

Retell or Reread

If you'd like to, have students reread the play to themselves. Otherwise, have students retell the story.

Making Connections

 The Moral of the Story

Help students summarize the story, identify the moral, and make a connection between the moral and their own lives, using the completed Retell the Plot page. Turn to page LC 72 in *K¹² Language Arts Activity Book.*

1. Tell students that they are going to think about the moral of "The Three Wishes."

2. Have students reread their sequence of events on the Retell the Plot page.

3. Direct students' attention to the Moral of the Story page. Have them write a summary of the story using their Retell the Plot page. Remind them to use order words such as *first, next, then,* and *finally* to write their summary.

4. Discuss what readers can learn from the behavior of the woodcutter and his wife.

   ▶ What is the wife's wish? a big cake
   ▶ Why does she wish for this? She's hungry and wants something for dinner.
   ▶ Does she make this wish on purpose or by mistake? by mistake because she doesn't know about the three wishes
   ▶ What does the woodcutter wish for the first time? that the cake would hang from his wife's nose   Why does he wish this? He's angry with his wife for wasting their first wish.
   ▶ Do you think the woodcutter should have made the second wish? Why or why not? Possible answer: No, he shouldn't have made the second wish because he wasted it.
   ▶ Do you think the woodcutter should have made the third wish? Why or why not? Possible answer: Yes, he needed to do something to get the cake off his wife's nose.

5. Have students tell what they think the **moral** of the story is and have them write it in their own words in Exercise 2 on the Activity Book page.

6. Have students think about a time when they wished for something they shouldn't have and discuss the consequences, prompting them with the following questions. Answers will vary

   ▶ Did the wish come true?
   ▶ What happened after the wish came true?
   ▶ Was the outcome something you expected? Why or why not?
   ▶ Do you think you should have wished for something else? What?
   ▶ Why should you have made this other wish instead?

7. Have students write about what their experience shows them in Exercise 3 on the Activity Book page.

Objectives

- Summarize the plot of a story.
- Identify the moral or lesson of a text.
- Make connections between text and self.

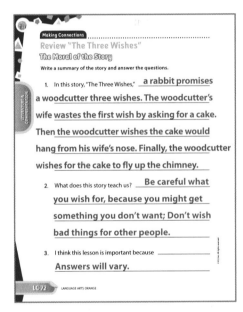

Making Connections
Review "The Three Wishes"
The Moral of the Story
Write a summary of the story and answer the questions.

1. In this story, "The Three Wishes," __a rabbit promises__ a woodcutter three wishes. The woodcutter's wife wastes the first wish by asking for a cake. Then the woodcutter wishes the cake would hang from his wife's nose. Finally, the woodcutter wishes for the cake to fly up the chimney.

2. What does this story teach us? __Be careful what you wish for, because you might get something you don't want; Don't wish bad things for other people.__

3. I think this lesson is important because _____ __Answers will vary.__

LC 72   LANGUAGE ARTS ORANGE

Beyond the Lesson

⊕ OPTIONAL: My Favorite Tale

This activity is OPTIONAL. This activity is intended for students who have extra time and would benefit from comparing and evaluating folktales they've read. Feel free to skip this activity.

1. Have students think about the tales they have read: "The Ugly Duckling," "The Grasshopper and the Ant," and "The Three Wishes." They may also think about other fairy tales, folk tales, or fables they have read that they can remember.

2. Discuss with students what their favorite tale was and why. Ask questions to prompt the discussion. Answers will vary.

   ► Which of the stories you've read was your favorite?
   ► What did you like most about this story? Why?
   ► What was your favorite character in a fairy tale, fable, or folktale you've read? The character may or may not be from your favorite tale.
   ► Why was this character your favorite?

Objectives

- Compare and contrast plot, setting, and characters of texts from different authors.
- Make connections between text and self.
- Evaluate text.

Semester Checkpoint

Unit Overview

In this Semester Checkpoint, students will read "Clouds" (a poem), "The Bear Facts" (a nonfiction article), and "Brother Rabbit Fools Brother Bear" (a folktale) and answer questions to check their progress in the following skills:

▶ Read a grade-level text with the appropriate speed, accuracy, and fluency.

▶ Comprehend the basic elements of a text, including its genre, structure, and literal contents.

▶ Apply reading comprehension skills, such as identifying figurative language, nonfiction features, and story elements, to understand the deeper meaning of a text.

Materials

Supplied

- *K¹² Language Arts Assessments*, pp. LC 1–16
- **Fluency Performance Checklist (optional)**

Lesson Overview

🖥	**〖Online〗 PERFORMANCE REVIEW:** ⊕ **OPTIONAL:** Fluency Check	**20** minutes
🗎	**〖Offline〗 SEMESTER CHECKPOINT:** Reading Comprehension and Analysis	**60** minutes

⭐ Objectives

- Use the title of the selection to make a prediction.
- Use an illustration to make a prediction about a reading.
- Read prose and poetry aloud.
- Read aloud grade-level text with appropriate expression, accuracy, and rate.
- Self-monitor comprehension by predicting, rereading, checking for sense, drawing on background knowledge, summarizing, clarifying, checking for context clues, and self-questioning.
- Repair comprehension using strategies: reread, use prior knowledge, self-question, identify context clues, determine word meaning, and read on.
- Identify genre.
- Identify characteristics of different genres.
- Identify the use of rhythm in poetry.
- Identify the use of repetition in poetry.
- Identify author's use of imagery.

- Distinguish between fiction and nonfiction.
- Identify facts.
- Identify the main idea and supporting details in a text.
- Distinguish between fact and opinion.
- Summarize text and maintain accurate sequence.
- Identify setting.
- Identify choices that a character makes and their consequences.
- Identify the moral or lesson of a text.
- Make inferences using text and prior knowledge.
- Answer questions requiring literal recall of details.
- Answer inferential questions.
- Create and use graphic organizers, diagrams, charts, Venn diagrams, and time lines to demonstrate and support comprehension.

 **20** minutes

PERFORMANCE REVIEW: **Fluency Check**

⊕ **OPTIONAL:** If you have not reviewed students' recordings from this semester, listen to a sampling of them now. Listen to students' recordings and use the checklist to review fluency and track performance. Keep the completed checklist so you can review students' progress over time.

 **60** minutes

SEMESTER CHECKPOINT: **Reading Comprehension and Analysis**

Explain that students are going to show what they have learned this semester.

1. Give students the Semester Checkpoint pages.

2. Read the directions together.

3. Use the Answer Key to score the Checkpoint, and enter the results online.

4. Review each exercise with students. Work with students to correct any exercise they missed.

Clouds

Part 1. Book Walk Have students take you on a Book Walk of "Clouds." Ask the questions and note students' responses.

1. What kind of writing is this? poetry

2. How is this kind of writing different from other kinds? It has lines and stanzas; it may have rhymes.

3. What is the title of this writing? "Clouds"

4. What can you use to make a prediction about this writing? the title, the illustration

5. What prediction can you make based on what you see? It's a poem about clouds.

Part 2. Reading Comprehension Read the poem aloud to students, and then have students read the poem on their own. Ask the questions and note students' responses.

6. Which words rhyme in the poem? hill/still; slow/go

7. Which words or phrases are repeated in the poem? white sheep

8. The speaker uses the words *white sheep* to describe something else. What is it? clouds

9. Why might the poet choose *white sheep* as a description? Clouds look like big, fluffy sheep in the sky.

10. What does the speaker describe when she says, *When the wind stops/You all stand still*? The wind stops blowing and the clouds stop moving.

11. What does the speaker describe when she says, *When the wind blows/You walk away slow*? The wind blows again and the clouds begin moving slowly in the sky.

The Bear Facts

Part 3. Book Walk Have students take you on a Book Walk of "The Bear Facts." Ask the questions and note students' responses.

12. What kind of writing is this? nonfiction

13. How is this kind of writing different from poems and plays? It's in paragraphs, not lines.

14. What is the title? "The Bear Facts"

15. What can you use to make a prediction about this writing? the title, illustration, photographs

16. What prediction can you make based on what you see? Possible answer: It's a nonfiction article about bears.

Part 4. Reading Comprehension Read the first two paragraphs of the story aloud twice. Have students read the rest of the story on their own and answer the multiple choice questions.

Brother Rabbit Fools Brother Bear

Part 5. Book Walk Have students take you on a Book Walk of "Brother Rabbit Fools Brother Bear." Ask the questions and note students' responses.

23. What kind of writing is this? fiction

24. How is this kind of writing different from poems and plays? It's in paragraphs, not lines.

25. What is the title? "Brother Rabbit Fools Brother Bear"

26. What can you use to make a prediction about this writing? the title, the illustration

27. What prediction can you make based on what you see? Possible answer: It's a story about a bear and a rabbit.

Part 6. Reading Comprehension Read the first three paragraphs of the story aloud twice. Have students read the rest of the story to themselves. Ask the questions and note students' responses.

28. Who are the main characters? Brother Bear, Brother Rabbit

29. What is the setting of the story? a day in the woods

30. What is the proper sequence of events in the story? Brother Rabbit pretends to be sleeping on a path. When Brother Bear leaves the fish to collect the rabbits, Brother Rabbit takes the fish and makes a soup.

31. What does Brother Rabbit think of Brother Bear? He thinks Brother Bear is foolish.

32. What happens at the end of the story? Brother Bear scares off Brother Rabbit.

Part 7. Literary Analysis Have students complete the chart and answer the question about the story.

Name _____ Date _____

Semester Checkpoint
Learning Coach Instructions
Reading Comprehension and Analysis

Explain that students are going to show what they have learned this semester.

1. Give students the Semester Checkpoint pages.
2. Read the directions together.
3. Use the Answer Key to score the Checkpoint, and enter the results online.
4. Review each exercise with students. Work with students to correct any exercise they missed.

Clouds
Part 1. Book Walk Have students take you on a Book Walk of "Clouds." Ask the questions and note students' responses.

1. What kind of writing is this?
poetry

2. How is this kind of writing different from other kinds?
It has lines and stanzas; it may have rhymes.

3. What is the title of this writing?
"Clouds"

4. What can you use to make a prediction about this writing?
the title, the illustration

5. What prediction can you make based on what you see?
It's a poem about clouds.

Name _____ Date _____

Part 2. Reading Comprehension Read the poem aloud to students, and then have students read the poem on their own. Ask the questions and note students' responses.

6. Which words rhyme in the poem?
hill/still; slow/go

7. Which words or phrases are repeated in the poem?
white sheep

8. The speaker uses the words *white sheep* to describe something else. What is it?
clouds

9. Why might the poet choose *white sheep* as a description?
Clouds look like big, fluffy sheep in the sky.

10. What does the speaker describe when she says, *When the wind stops/You all stand still?*
The wind stops blowing and the clouds stop moving.

11. What does the speaker describe when she says, *When the wind blows/You walk away slow?*
The wind blows again and the clouds begin moving slowly in the sky.

Name _____ Date _____

The Bear Facts
Part 3. Book Walk Have students take you on a Book Walk of "The Bear Facts." Ask the questions and note students' responses.

12. What kind of writing is this?
nonfiction

13. How is this kind of writing different from poems and plays?
It's in paragraphs, not lines.

14. What is the title?
"The Bear Facts"

15. What can you use to make a prediction about this writing?
the title, illustration, photographs

16. What prediction can you make based on what you see?
Possible answer: It's a nonfiction article about bears.

Part 4. Reading Comprehension Read the first two paragraphs of the story aloud twice. Have students read the rest of the story on their own and answer the multiple choice questions.

Name _____ Date _____

Brother Rabbit Fools Brother Bear
Part 5. Book Walk Have students take you on a Book Walk of "Brother Rabbit Fools Brother Bear." Ask the questions and note students' responses.

23. What kind of writing is this?
fiction

24. How is this kind of writing different from poems and plays?
It's in paragraphs, not lines.

25. What is the title?
"Brother Rabbit Fools Brother Bear"

26. What can you use to make a prediction about this writing?
the title, the illustration

27. What prediction can you make based on what you see?
Possible answer: It's a story about a bear and a rabbit.

Name _____ Date _____

Part 6. Reading Comprehension Read the first three paragraphs of the story aloud twice. Have students read the rest of the story to themselves. Ask the questions and note students' responses.

28. Who are the main characters?
Brother Bear, Brother Rabbit

29. What is the setting of the story?
a day in the woods

30. What is the proper sequence of events in the story?
See below.

31. What does Brother Rabbit think of Brother Bear?
He thinks Brother Bear is foolish.

32. What happens at the end of the story?
Brother Bear scares off Brother Rabbit.

30. **Brother Rabbit pretends to be sleeping on a path. When Brother Bear leaves the fish to collect the rabbits, Brother Rabbit takes the fish and makes a soup.**

Name _____ Date _____

Part 7. Literary Analysis Have students complete the chart and answer the question about the story.

Name _____ Date _____

Semester Checkpoint Answer Key
Reading Comprehension and Analysis

Clouds
Christina Rossetti

White sheep, white sheep,
On a blue hill,
When the wind stops,
You all stand still.

When the wind blows,
You walk away slow.
White sheep, white sheep,
Where do you go?

Name _____ Date _____

Part 1. Book Walk
Do a Book Walk for "Clouds." Listen to the questions and say your answers.

1.–5.

Part 2. Reading Comprehension
Listen to the questions about "Clouds" and say your answers.

6.–11.

Name _____ Date _____

The Bear Facts

Have you ever had a teddy bear to cuddle and snuggle? Have you read books with a bear characters such as Little Bear, Winnie-the-Pooh, or Paddington? How cute and furry they are! How roly-poly!

But, real bears are not so sweet and cuddly. They are wild creatures, and some are very big and very powerful. A grizzly bear can weigh about 900 pounds and stand 8 feet tall. That's about as high as the ceiling in most rooms.

The American black bear, which can grow to 6 feet tall and weigh 600 pounds, is the most common bear in North America. If you and your family go camping, you might see

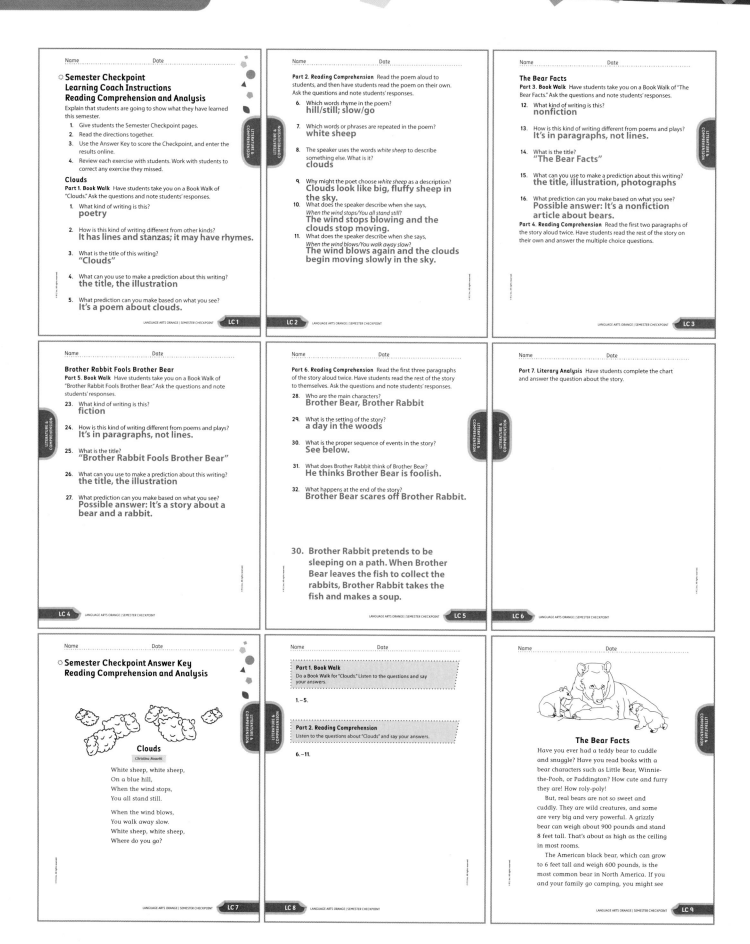

Page LC 10

Name _____ Date _____

one or hear one trying to get at your food. This bear will eat just about anything it gets its paws on, including fish, insects, pine cones, berries, and roots.

A black bear's favorite treat is honey. A black bear can use its sharp claws to rip open a tree with bees in it. The bear reaches in through the hole and pulls out the honeycomb and eats it, bees and all! Bee stings do not bother the bear very much because it has such thick fur.

Baby bears are called cubs. When a mother bear has babies, she usually has one to four cubs. A mother bear takes good care of her cubs. She teaches them how to find food. If she thinks something is a danger to her cubs, she will attack.

So, real bears are not much like teddy bears at all. Real bears are big, strong, wild creatures. They're not for cuddling and snuggling!

Page LC 11

Name _____ Date _____

Part 3. Book Walk
Do a Book Walk for "The Bear Facts." Listen to the questions and say your answers.

12.–16.

Part 4. Reading Comprehension
Read the question about "The Bear Facts" and choose the answer.

17. What kind of writing is "The Bear Facts"?
   A. fiction
   B. nonfiction
   C. poetry
   D. drama

18. What is the topic of "The Bear Facts"?
   A. real bears
   B. teddy bears
   C. mother bears
   D. baby bears

19. What is the main idea of "The Bear Facts"?
   A. Teddy bears are cute and furry.
   B. Black bears will eat just about anything.
   C. Mother bears take good care of their cubs.
   D. Real bears are big, strong, wild creatures.

Page LC 12

Name _____ Date _____

20. Which sentence is a fact from the article?
   A. How roly-poly!
   B. How cute and furry they are!
   C. A black bear's favorite treat is honey.
   D. Have you ever had a teddy bear to cuddle and snuggle?

21. Which sentence is an opinion from the article?
   A. How cute and furry they are!
   B. Baby bears are called cubs.
   C. A grizzly bear can weigh about 900 pounds.
   D. She teaches them how to find food.

22. What might a mother bear do for her cubs?
   A. leave them alone while she looks for food
   B. climb a tree to escape danger that comes near
   C. find the cubs a safe and warm place to sleep
   D. eat all the fish she finds so she can stay strong

Page LC 13

Name _____ Date _____

Brother Rabbit Fools Brother Bear

One day, Brother Bear caught a fish from the stream. As he headed home through the woods, he smacked his big bear lips. He couldn't wait to cook that fish.

Well, sir! Brother Rabbit was hiding in the grass when Brother Bear walked by.

I sure would like to eat some fish, Brother Rabbit thought. So he took a shortcut through the woods, lay down on the path, and closed his eyes.

Brother Bear came along and said, "Oh, my. There's a tired rabbit."

Then, Brother Bear went on his way.

Brother Rabbit ran through the woods again. He threw himself down on the path and closed his eyes. Brother Bear saw him and said, "Oh, dear. There's a second tired rabbit."

Then, Brother Bear kept going.

Brother Rabbit took another shortcut through the woods. Soon, Brother Bear saw him stretched out on the path with his eyes closed.

Page LC 14

Name _____ Date _____

"I'll go get the other two rabbits," Brother Bear said to himself. "I'll take all three home and keep them as servants."

So, Brother Bear laid down his fish. He went back along the path, but he found no rabbits. And, when he came back for his fish, it was gone, too!

Brother Bear looked around. Brother Rabbit was standing in the path with a big cooking spoon. He was stirring soup in an iron pot over a fire.

"I smell fish!" Brother Bear said.

"Naw," said Brother Rabbit. "You smell turnip greens and bacon."

"My nose knows what it knows!" Brother Bear roared. He grabbed the spoon and brought up fish from the bottom of the pot.

Brother Rabbit ran off into the woods. "See you later, Brother Bear!" he called from behind a tree.

Brother Bear chased Brother Rabbit, but he never did catch him. No one ever catches Brother Rabbit. No, sir!

Page LC 15

Name _____ Date _____

Part 5. Book Walk
Do a Book Walk for "Brother Rabbit Fools Brother Bear." Listen to the questions and say your answers.

23.–27.

Part 6. Reading Comprehension
Listen to the questions about "Brother Rabbit Fools Brother Bear" and say your answers.

28.–32.

Page LC 16

Name _____ Date _____

Part 7. Literary Analysis
Complete the chart and answer the question about "Brother Rabbit Fools Brother Bear."

33.

Brother Rabbit's Choice	What Brother Rabbit Chooses	Consequence of This Choice
Whether or not to trick Brother Bear to get the fish	Brother Rabbit decides to **trick Brother Bear and pretend to be different rabbits sleeping in the path.**	Brother Bear **puts down the fish to get the rabbits, and Brother Rabbit gets the fish.**
Whether or not to run away with the fish or trick Brother Bear again	Brother Rabbit decides to **cook fish soup and tell Brother Bear it's turnip greens and bacon.**	Brother Bear **scares off Brother Rabbit and gets to keep the fish soup.**

Page LC 17

Name _____ Date _____

34. What is the moral of the story?

Possible answers: Don't try to trick people because you might get caught; you have to work for what you want, not trick people to get it; it's not right to steal or to trick people.

Literature & Comprehension   **LC 353**

Vocabulary

Vocabulary Words 1

Unit Overview

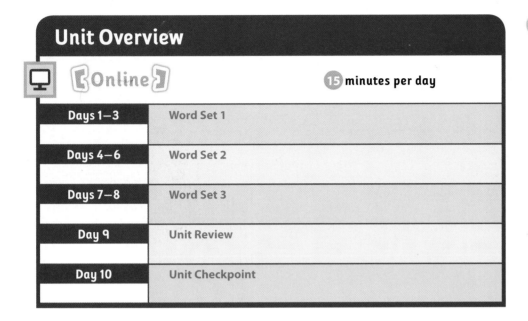

Online   🕐 **15 minutes per day**

Days 1–3	Word Set 1
Days 4–6	Word Set 2
Days 7–8	Word Set 3
Day 9	Unit Review
Day 10	Unit Checkpoint

Objectives

- Identify and use the prefix *dis–*.
- Identify and use the vowel suffix *–er*.
- Identify and use the prefix *re–*.
- Identify and use the prefix *un–*.
- Identify and use the prefix *pre–*.
- Identify and use the vowel suffix *–est*.
- Identify and use word parts to help determine word meaning.
- Identify and use prefixes and suffixes to determine word meaning.
- Identify roots to aid in determining word meaning.

Online   🕐 **15 minutes per day**

Students will work on their own to learn and practice vocabulary words. Help students locate the online activities, and provide support as needed.

At any time, print a list of the unit words and definitions from the online lesson to practice with students. You can also have students create flash cards by writing each vocabulary word on the front of an index card and their own definition for each word on the back.

Days 1–3   Word Set 1

Day 1

Introduce Word Set 1   Students will be introduced to new words.

➕ **OPTIONAL: Flash Cards**   If you choose, have students create flash cards.

Day 2

Practice Word Set 1   Students will review and practice the words from Word Set 1.

Word Set 1

disable
disagree
disobey
distrust
remind
remove
reunion
review

Day 3

Practice Word Set 1 Students will review and practice the words from Word Set 1.

➲ **Learning Coach Check-in** Ask students to tell you the words they've been learning from Word Set 1. See if students can provide the words' meanings.

Days 4–6   Word Set 2

Day 4

Introduce Word Set 2 Students will be introduced to new words.

➕ **OPTIONAL: Flash Cards** If you choose, have students create flash cards.

Word Set 2

precaution
pretest
prevent
preview
unfortunate
unhitch
unpaved
unripe

Day 5

Practice Word Set 2 Students will review and practice the words from Word Set 2.

Day 6

Practice Word Set 2 Students will review and practice the words from Word Set 2.

➲ **Learning Coach Check-in** Ask students to tell you the words they've been learning from Word Set 2. See if students can provide the words' meanings.

Days 7–8   Word Set 3

Day 7

Introduce Word Set 3 Students will be introduced to new words.

➕ **OPTIONAL: Flash Cards** If you choose, have students create flash cards.

Word Set 3

firmer
firmest
plusher
plushest
weaker
weakest

Day 8

Practice Word Set 3 Students will review and practice the words from Word Set 3.

➲ **Learning Coach Check-in** Ask students to tell you the words they've been learning from Word Set 3. See if students can provide the words' meanings.

Day 9   Unit Review

Unit Review Students will play a game to review all words from the unit.

Day 10   Unit Checkpoint

Unit Checkpoint Students will complete an online Unit Checkpoint covering all words from the unit. If necessary, read the directions to students and help them with keyboard or mouse operations.

Rewards:

- If students scored 80 percent or above on the Unit Checkpoint, add a sticker to the Unit 1 box on students' My Accomplishments chart. If students scored under 80 percent, continue to practice the words that they missed and add a sticker to this unit once they have mastered the words.

Vocabulary Words 2

Unit Overview

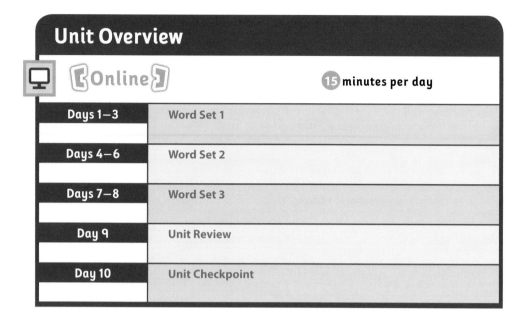

Online 🕐 **minutes per day**

Days 1–3	Word Set 1
Days 4–6	Word Set 2
Days 7–8	Word Set 3
Day 9	Unit Review
Day 10	Unit Checkpoint

Objectives
- Classify and sort common words into categories.
- Identify real-life connections between words and their uses.
- Increase reading vocabulary.

Online 🕐 **minutes per day**

Students will work on their own to learn and practice vocabulary words. Help students locate the online activities, and provide support as needed.

At any time, print a list of the unit words and definitions from the online lesson to practice with students. You can also have students create flash cards by writing each vocabulary word on the front of an index card and their own definition for each word on the back.

Days 1–3 Word Set 1

Day 1

Skills Update Students will review words they've studied previously by answering questions.

Introduce Word Set 1 Students will be introduced to new words.

➕ **OPTIONAL: Flash Cards** If you choose, have students create flash cards.

Word Set 1

comfort
cozy
despair
discouraged
embarrassed
fond
pleasant
sorrow

Day 2

Practice Word Set 1 Students will review and practice the words from Word Set 1.

Day 3

Practice Word Set 1 Students will review and practice the words from Word Set 1.

⮌ **Learning Coach Check-in** Ask students to tell you the words they've been learning from Word Set 1. See if students can provide the words' meanings.

Days 4–6   Word Set 2

Day 4

Skills Update Students will review words they've studied previously by answering questions.

Introduce Word Set 2 Students will be introduced to new words.

✚ **OPTIONAL: Flash Cards** If you choose, have students create flash cards.

Day 5

Practice Word Set 2 Students will review and practice the words from Word Set 2.

Day 6

Practice Word Set 2 Students will review and practice the words from Word Set 2.

⮌ **Learning Coach Check-in** Ask students to tell you the words they've been learning from Word Set 2. See if students can provide the words' meanings.

Word Set 2

expect
gallop
orchard
settle
startle
stiffen
tremble
tumble

Days 7–8 Word Set 3

Day 7

Skills Update Students will review words they've studied previously by answering questions.

Introduce Word Set 3 Students will be introduced to new words.

⊕ OPTIONAL: Flash Cards If you choose, have students create flash cards.

Word Set 3

handsome
huff
lean
spy
trim
vine

Day 8

Practice Word Set 3 Students will review and practice the words from Word Set 3.

➲ Learning Coach Check-in Ask students to tell you the words they've been learning from Word Set 3. See if students can provide the words' meanings.

Day 9 Unit Review

Unit Review Students will play a game to review all words from the unit.

Day 10 Unit Checkpoint

Unit Checkpoint Students will complete an online Unit Checkpoint covering all words from the unit. If necessary, read the directions to students and help them with keyboard or mouse operations.

Rewards:
- If students scored 80 percent or above on the Unit Checkpoint, add a sticker to the Unit 2 box on students' My Accomplishments chart. If students scored under 80 percent, continue to practice the words that they missed and add a sticker to this unit once they have mastered the words.

Vocabulary Words 3

Unit Overview

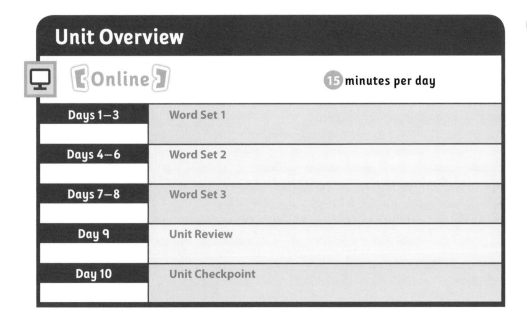

Online		**15** minutes per day
Days 1–3	Word Set 1	
Days 4–6	Word Set 2	
Days 7–8	Word Set 3	
Day 9	Unit Review	
Day 10	Unit Checkpoint	

Objectives
- Increase vocabulary through synonyms.
- Increase vocabulary through antonyms.
- Increase reading vocabulary.

Online   **15** minutes per day

Students will work on their own to learn and practice vocabulary words. Help students locate the online activities, and provide support as needed.

At any time, print a list of the unit words and definitions from the online lesson to practice with students. You can also have students create flash cards by writing each vocabulary word on the front of an index card and their own definition for each word on the back.

Days 1–3   Word Set 1

Day 1

Skills Update Students will review words they've studied previously by answering questions.

Introduce Word Set 1 Students will be introduced to new words.

⊕ OPTIONAL: Flash Cards If you choose, have students create flash cards.

Word Set 1

answer

capture

destroy

remainder

reply

ruin

scrap

seize

Day 2

Practice Word Set 1   Students will review and practice the words from Word Set 1.

Day 3

Practice Word Set 1   Students will review and practice the words from Word Set 1.

➲ **Learning Coach Check-in**   Ask students to tell you the words they've been learning from Word Set 1. See if students can provide the words' meanings.

Days 4–6   Word Set 2

Day 4

Skills Update   Students will review words they've studied previously by answering questions.

Introduce Word Set 2   Students will be introduced to new words.

✚ **OPTIONAL: Flash Cards**   If you choose, have students create flash cards.

Day 5

Practice Word Set 2   Students will review and practice the words from Word Set 2.

Day 6

Practice Word Set 2   Students will review and practice the words from Word Set 2.

➲ **Learning Coach Check-in**   Ask students to tell you the words they've been learning from Word Set 2. See if students can provide the words' meanings.

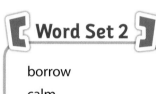

Word Set 2

- borrow
- calm
- collect
- cross
- disperse
- frisky
- joyful
- loan

Days 7–8 Word Set 3

Day 7

Skills Update Students will review words they've studied previously by answering questions.

Introduce Word Set 3 Students will be introduced to new words.

➕ **OPTIONAL: Flash Cards** If you choose, have students create flash cards.

Day 8

Practice Word Set 3 Students will review and practice the words from Word Set 3.

↪ **Learning Coach Check-in** Ask students to tell you the words they've been learning from Word Set 3. See if students can provide the words' meanings.

Word Set 3

ancestor
brawny
goods
modern
scrape
sparkling

Day 9 Unit Review

Unit Review Students will play a game to review all words from the unit.

Day 10 Unit Checkpoint

Unit Checkpoint Students will complete an online Unit Checkpoint covering all words from the unit. If necessary, read the directions to students and help them with keyboard or mouse operations.

Rewards:
- If students scored 80 percent or above on the Unit Checkpoint, add a sticker to the Unit 3 box on students' My Accomplishments chart. If students scored under 80 percent, continue to practice the words that they missed and add a sticker to this unit once they have mastered the words.

Vocabulary Words 4

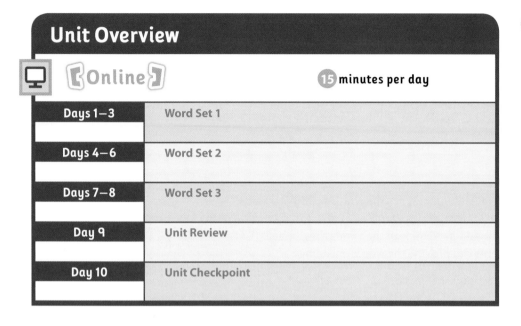

Unit Overview

🖥 **【Online】** ⑮ **minutes per day**

Days 1–3	Word Set 1
Days 4–6	Word Set 2
Days 7–8	Word Set 3
Day 9	Unit Review
Day 10	Unit Checkpoint

Objectives

- Increase vocabulary through compound words.
- Increase vocabulary through contractions.
- Use resources or other tools to determine the meaning of a word.
- Use glossaries, thesauruses, and beginner dictionaries to learn new vocabulary.
- Use knowledge of words to determine the meaning of compound words.

【Online】 ⑮ **minutes per day**

Students will work on their own to learn and practice vocabulary words. Help students locate the online activities, and provide support as needed.

At any time, print a list of the unit words and definitions from the online lesson to practice with students. You can also have students create flash cards by writing each vocabulary word on the front of an index card and their own definition for each word on the back.

Days 1–3   Word Set 1

Day 1

Skills Update Students will review words they've studied previously by answering questions.

Introduce Word Set 1 Students will be introduced to new words.

➕ **OPTIONAL: Flash Cards** If you choose, have students create flash cards.

【 Word Set 1 】

bedspread

countrymen

dewdrop

downpour

ferryboat

patchwork

peppermint

windowpane

Day 2

Practice Word Set 1 Students will review and practice the words from Word Set 1.

Day 3

Practice Word Set 1 Students will review and practice the words from Word Set 1.

⮑ **Learning Coach Check-in** Ask students to tell you the words they've been learning from Word Set 1. See if students can provide the words' meanings.

Days 4–6   Word Set 2

Day 4

Skills Update Students will review words they've studied previously by answering questions.

Introduce Word Set 2 Students will be introduced to new words.

⊕ **OPTIONAL: Flash Cards** If you choose, have students create flash cards.

Day 5

Practice Word Set 2 Students will review and practice the words from Word Set 2.

Day 6

Practice Word Set 2 Students will review and practice the words from Word Set 2.

⮑ **Learning Coach Check-in** Ask students to tell you the words they've been learning from Word Set 2. See if students can provide the words' meanings.

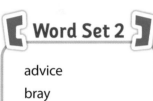

Word Set 2

advice

bray

compete

drone

experiment

fabric

grit

heap

Days 7–8   Word Set 3

Day 7

Skills Update   Students will review words they've studied previously by answering questions.

Introduce Word Set 3   Students will be introduced to new words.

⊕ **OPTIONAL: Flash Cards**   If you choose, have students create flash cards.

Word Set 3

- aren't
- haven't
- they'll
- what'll
- who'll
- wouldn't

Day 8

Practice Word Set 3   Students will review and practice the words from Word Set 3.

⟳ **Learning Coach Check-in**   Ask students to tell you the words they've been learning from Word Set 3. See if students can provide the words' meanings.

Day 9   Unit Review

Unit Review   Students will play a game to review all words from the unit.

Day 10   Unit Checkpoint

Unit Checkpoint   Students will complete an online Unit Checkpoint covering all words from the unit. If necessary, read the directions to students and help them with keyboard or mouse operations.

Rewards:
- If students scored 80 percent or above on the Unit Checkpoint, add a sticker to the Unit 4 box on students' My Accomplishments chart. If students scored under 80 percent, continue to practice the words that they missed and add a sticker to this unit once they have mastered the words.

Vocabulary Words 5

Unit Overview

🖥	⟦Online⟧	🕐 minutes per day
Days 1–3	Word Set 1	
Days 4–6	Word Set 2	
Days 7–8	Word Set 3	
Day 9	Unit Review	
Day 10	Unit Checkpoint	

Objectives
- Identify and define words' and phrases' literal and nonliteral meanings.
- Distinguish between meaning variations in closely related verbs.
- Increase reading vocabulary.

⟦Online⟧ 🕐 **minutes per day**

Students will work on their own to learn and practice vocabulary words. Help students locate the online activities, and provide support as needed.

At any time, print a list of the unit words and definitions from the online lesson to practice with students. You can also have students create flash cards by writing each vocabulary word on the front of an index card and their own definition for each word on the back.

Days 1–3   Word Set 1

Day 1

Skills Update Students will review words they've studied previously by answering questions.

Introduce Word Set 1 Students will be introduced to new words.

➕ **OPTIONAL: Flash Cards** If you choose, have students create flash cards.

⟦ **Word Set 1** ⟧

admire
banjo
hatch
jackal
lame
lemon
stampede
stitch

Day 2

Practice Word Set 1 Students will review and practice the words from Word Set 1.

Day 3

Practice Word Set 1 Students will review and practice the words from Word Set 1.

➲ **Learning Coach Check-in** Ask students to tell you the words they've been learning from Word Set 1. See if students can provide the words' meanings.

Days 4–6   Word Set 2

Day 4

Skills Update Students will review words they've studied previously by answering questions.

Introduce Word Set 2 Students will be introduced to new words.

✚ **OPTIONAL: Flash Cards** If you choose, have students create flash cards.

Day 5

Practice Word Set 2 Students will review and practice the words from Word Set 2.

Day 6

Practice Word Set 2 Students will review and practice the words from Word Set 2.

➲ **Learning Coach Check-in** Ask students to tell you the words they've been learning from Word Set 2. See if students can provide the words' meanings.

Word Set 2

boast
chirp
claim
cleanse
pilot
squawk
steer
tidy

Days 7–8 Word Set 3

Day 7

Skills Update Students will review words they've studied previously by answering questions.

Introduce Word Set 3 Students will be introduced to new words.

⊕ OPTIONAL: Flash Cards If you choose, have students create flash cards.

Day 8

Practice Word Set 3 Students will review and practice the words from Word Set 3.

⊃ Learning Coach Check-in Ask students to tell you the words they've been learning from Word Set 3. See if students can provide the words' meanings.

Day 9 Unit Review

Unit Review Students will play a game to review all words from the unit.

Day 10 Unit Checkpoint

Unit Checkpoint Students will complete an online Unit Checkpoint covering all words from the unit. If necessary, read the directions to students and help them with keyboard or mouse operations.

Rewards:
- **If students scored 80 percent or above on the Unit Checkpoint, add a sticker to the Unit 5 box on students' My Accomplishments chart. If students scored under 80 percent, continue to practice the words that they missed and add a sticker to this unit once they have mastered the words.**

Word Set 3

chariot
creature
echo
harm
temper
wit

Vocabulary Words 6

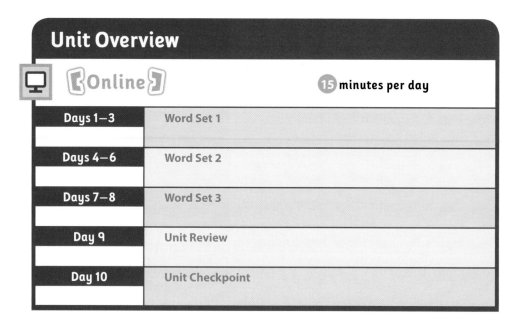

Unit Overview

Online   15 minutes per day

Days 1–3	Word Set 1
Days 4–6	Word Set 2
Days 7–8	Word Set 3
Day 9	Unit Review
Day 10	Unit Checkpoint

Objectives

- Identify and use word parts to help determine word meaning.
- Identify and use prefixes and suffixes to determine word meaning.
- Increase reading vocabulary.

Online   15 minutes per day

Students will work on their own to learn and practice vocabulary words. Help students locate the online activities, and provide support as needed.

At any time, print a list of the unit words and definitions from the online lesson to practice with students. You can also have students create flash cards by writing each vocabulary word on the front of an index card and their own definition for each word on the back.

Days 1–3   Word Set 1

Day 1

Skills Update   Students will review words they've studied previously by answering questions.

Introduce Word Set 1   Students will be introduced to new words.

⊕ **OPTIONAL: Flash Cards**   If you choose, have students create flash cards.

Word Set 1

beautiful
careful
clearly
correctly
fearful
happily
safely
truthful

Day 2

Practice Word Set 1 Students will review and practice the words from Word Set 1.

Day 3

Practice Word Set 1 Students will review and practice the words from Word Set 1.

↻ **Learning Coach Check-in** Ask students to tell you the words they've been learning from Word Set 1. See if students can provide the words' meanings.

Days 4–6 Word Set 2

Day 4

Skills Update Students will review words they've studied previously by answering questions.

Introduce Word Set 2 Students will be introduced to new words.

⊕ **OPTIONAL: Flash Cards** If you choose, have students create flash cards.

Day 5

Practice Word Set 2 Students will review and practice the words from Word Set 2.

Day 6

Practice Word Set 2 Students will review and practice the words from Word Set 2.

↻ **Learning Coach Check-in** Ask students to tell you the words they've been learning from Word Set 2. See if students can provide the words' meanings.

Word Set 2

bound
circus
compliment
confusing
jealous
lagoon
moan
prison

Days 7–8   Word Set 3

Day 7

Skills Update Students will review words they've studied previously by answering questions.

Introduce Word Set 3 Students will be introduced to new words.

✚ **OPTIONAL: Flash Cards** If you choose, have students create flash cards.

Word Set 3

carve
deserve
dough
drain
lunge
ordinary

Day 8

Practice Word Set 3 Students will review and practice the words from Word Set 3.

➦ **Learning Coach Check-in** Ask students to tell you the words they've been learning from Word Set 3. See if students can provide the words' meanings.

Day 9   Unit Review

Unit Review Students will play a game to review all words from the unit.

Day 10   Unit Checkpoint

Unit Checkpoint Students will complete an online Unit Checkpoint covering all words from the unit. If necessary, read the directions to students and help them with keyboard or mouse operations.

Rewards:

• If students scored 80 percent or above on the Unit Checkpoint, add a sticker to the Unit 6 box on students' My Accomplishments chart. If students scored under 80 percent, continue to practice the words that they missed and add a sticker to this unit once they have mastered the words.

Vocabulary Words 7

Unit Overview

🖥 【Online】		🕐 **15** **minutes per day**
Days 1–3	Word Set 1	
Days 4–6	Word Set 2	
Days 7–8	Word Set 3	
Day 9	Unit Review	
Day 10	Unit Checkpoint	

Objectives

- Identify and use word parts to help determine word meaning.
- Identify roots to aid in determining word meaning.
- Increase reading vocabulary.

【**Online**】 🕐 **15 minutes per day**

Students will work on their own to learn and practice vocabulary words. Help students locate the online activities, and provide support as needed.

At any time, print a list of the unit words and definitions from the online lesson to practice with students. You can also have students create flash cards by writing each vocabulary word on the front of an index card and their own definition for each word on the back.

Days 1–3   Word Set 1

Day 1

Skills Update Students will review words they've studied previously by answering questions.

Introduce Word Set 1 Students will be introduced to new words.

➕ **OPTIONAL: Flash Cards** If you choose, have students create flash cards.

【 **Word Set 1** 】

British
glint
layer
pearl
rattle
relax
riot
village

Day 2

Practice Word Set 1 Students will review and practice the words from Word Set 1.

Day 3

Practice Word Set 1 Students will review and practice the words from Word Set 1.

➲ **Learning Coach Check-in** Ask students to tell you the words they've been learning from Word Set 1. See if students can provide the words' meanings.

Days 4–6 Word Set 2

Day 4

Skills Update Students will review words they've studied previously by answering questions.

Introduce Word Set 2 Students will be introduced to new words.

➕ **OPTIONAL: Flash Cards** If you choose, have students create flash cards.

Day 5

Practice Word Set 2 Students will review and practice the words from Word Set 2.

Day 6

Practice Word Set 2 Students will review and practice the words from Word Set 2.

➲ **Learning Coach Check-in** Ask students to tell you the words they've been learning from Word Set 2. See if students can provide the words' meanings.

Word Set 2

captain
capitol
bicycle
recycle
telephone
telescope
television
tricycle

Days 7—8 Word Set 3

Day 7

Skills Update Students will review words they've studied previously by answering questions.

Introduce Word Set 3 Students will be introduced to new words.

⊕ OPTIONAL: Flash Cards If you choose, have students create flash cards.

Day 8

Practice Word Set 3 Students will review and practice the words from Word Set 3.

⮌ Learning Coach Check-in Ask students to tell you the words they've been learning from Word Set 3. See if students can provide the words' meanings.

Word Set 3

autumn

celebrate

design

hearse

quilt

thorn

Day 9 Unit Review

Unit Review Students will play a game to review all words from the unit.

Day 10 Unit Checkpoint

Unit Checkpoint Students will complete an online Unit Checkpoint covering all words from the unit. If necessary, read the directions to students and help them with keyboard or mouse operations.

Rewards:
- If students scored 80 percent or above on the Unit Checkpoint, add a sticker to the Unit 7 box on students' My Accomplishments chart. If students scored under 80 percent, continue to practice the words that they missed and add a sticker to this unit once they have mastered the words.

Vocabulary Words 8

Unit Overview

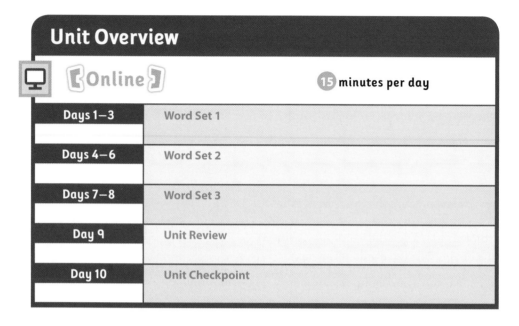

	Online	🕐 15 minutes per day
Days 1–3	Word Set 1	
Days 4–6	Word Set 2	
Days 7–8	Word Set 3	
Day 9	Unit Review	
Day 10	Unit Checkpoint	

Objectives

- Increase vocabulary through homographs.
- Increase vocabulary through homophones.
- Identify real-life connections between words and their uses.
- Increase reading vocabulary.

 🕐 15 minutes per day

Students will work on their own to learn and practice vocabulary words. Help students locate the online activities, and provide support as needed.

At any time, print a list of the unit words and definitions from the online lesson to practice with students. You can also have students create flash cards by writing each vocabulary word on the front of an index card and their own definition for each word on the back.

Days 1–3 Word Set 1

Day 1

Skills Update Students will review words they've studied previously by answering questions.

Introduce Word Set 1 Students will be introduced to new words.

➕ **OPTIONAL: Flash Cards** If you choose, have students create flash cards.

Word Set 1

current
discovery
feature
freckle
funeral
protect
siren
wallet

Day 2

Practice Word Set 1 Students will review and practice the words from Word Set 1.

Day 3

Practice Word Set 1 Students will review and practice the words from Word Set 1.

↻ **Learning Coach Check-in** Ask students to tell you the words they've been learning from Word Set 1. See if students can provide the words' meanings.

Days 4–6   Word Set 2

Day 4

Skills Update Students will review words they've studied previously by answering questions.

Introduce Word Set 2 Students will be introduced to new words.

⊕ **OPTIONAL: Flash Cards** If you choose, have students create flash cards.

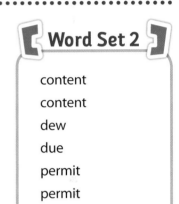

Word Set 2

content
content
dew
due
permit
permit
weak
week

Day 5

Practice Word Set 2 Students will review and practice the words from Word Set 2.

Day 6

Practice Word Set 2 Students will review and practice the words from Word Set 2.

↻ **Learning Coach Check-in** Ask students to tell you the words they've been learning from Word Set 2. See if students can provide the words' meanings.

Days 7–8   Word Set 3

Day 7

Skills Update Students will review words they've studied previously by answering questions.

Introduce Word Set 3 Students will be introduced to new words.

➕ **OPTIONAL: Flash Cards** If you choose, have students create flash cards.

Day 8

Practice Word Set 3 Students will review and practice the words from Word Set 3.

⮑ **Learning Coach Check-in** Ask students to tell you the words they've been learning from Word Set 3. See if students can provide the words' meanings.

Word Set 3

brass
cottage
errand
kettle
miller
pitcher

Day 9   Unit Review

Unit Review Students will play a game to review all words from the unit.

Day 10   Unit Checkpoint

Unit Checkpoint Students will complete an online Unit Checkpoint covering all words from the unit. If necessary, read the directions to students and help them with keyboard or mouse operations.

Rewards:

• If students scored 80 percent or above on the Unit Checkpoint, add a sticker to the Unit 8 box on students' My Accomplishments chart. If students scored under 80 percent, continue to practice the words that they missed and add a sticker to this unit once they have mastered the words.

Vocabulary Words 9

Unit Overview

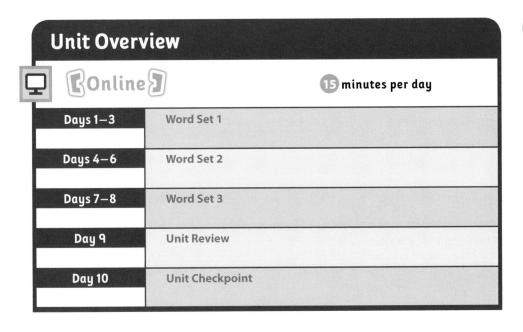

Online	**15** minutes per day
Days 1–3	Word Set 1
Days 4–6	Word Set 2
Days 7–8	Word Set 3
Day 9	Unit Review
Day 10	Unit Checkpoint

Objectives
- Use resources or other tools to determine the meaning of a word.
- Use glossaries, thesauruses, and beginner dictionaries to learn new vocabulary.
- Increase reading vocabulary.

Online **15** minutes per day

Students will work on their own to learn and practice vocabulary words. Help students locate the online activities, and provide support as needed.

At any time, print a list of the unit words and definitions from the online lesson to practice with students. You can also have students create flash cards by writing each vocabulary word on the front of an index card and their own definition for each word on the back.

Days 1–3   Word Set 1

Day 1

Skills Update Students will review words they've studied previously by answering questions.

Introduce Word Set 1 Students will be introduced to new words.

⊕ OPTIONAL: Flash Cards If you choose, have students create flash cards.

Word Set 1

agriculture
bundle
crumble
devote
elevator
fail
gale
harbor

Day 2

Practice Word Set 1 Students will review and practice the words from Word Set 1.

Day 3

Practice Word Set 1 Students will review and practice the words from Word Set 1.

↪ **Learning Coach Check-in** Ask students to tell you the words they've been learning from Word Set 1. See if students can provide the words' meanings.

Days 4–6   Word Set 2

Day 4

Skills Update Students will review words they've studied previously by answering questions.

Introduce Word Set 2 Students will be introduced to new words.

⊕ **OPTIONAL: Flash Cards** If you choose, have students create flash cards.

Day 5

Practice Word Set 2 Students will review and practice the words from Word Set 2.

Day 6

Practice Word Set 2 Students will review and practice the words from Word Set 2.

↪ **Learning Coach Check-in** Ask students to tell you the words they've been learning from Word Set 2. See if students can provide the words' meanings.

Word Set 2

image
jellyfish
kennel
luster
meadow
natural
occasion
pioneer

Days 7–8   Word Set 3

Day 7

Skills Update   Students will review words they've studied previously by answering questions.

Introduce Word Set 3   Students will be introduced to new words.

✚ **OPTIONAL: Flash Cards**   If you choose, have students create flash cards.

Day 8

Practice Word Set 3   Students will review and practice the words from Word Set 3.

➲ **Learning Coach Check-in**   Ask students to tell you the words they've been learning from Word Set 3. See if students can provide the words' meanings.

Day 9   Unit Review

Unit Review   Students will play a game to review all words from the unit.

Day 10   Unit Checkpoint

Unit Checkpoint   Students will complete an online Unit Checkpoint covering all words from the unit. If necessary, read the directions to students and help them with keyboard or mouse operations.

Rewards:
- If students scored 80 percent or above on the Unit Checkpoint, add a sticker to the Unit 9 box on students' My Accomplishments chart. If students scored under 80 percent, continue to practice the words that they missed and add a sticker to this unit once they have mastered the words.

Word Set 3

crumple

desire

rascal

remain

silk

snuggle

Vocabulary Words 10

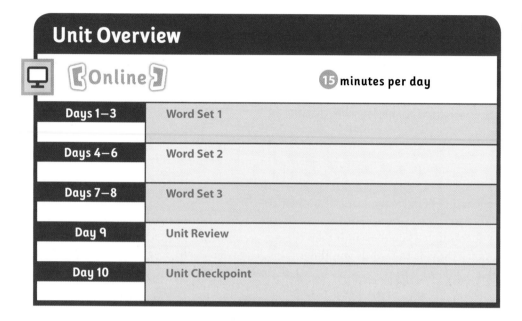

Unit Overview

Online — **15** minutes per day

Days 1–3	Word Set 1
Days 4–6	Word Set 2
Days 7–8	Word Set 3
Day 9	Unit Review
Day 10	Unit Checkpoint

Objectives

- Identify and use the prefix *dis–*.
- Identify and use the vowel suffix *–er*.
- Identify and use the prefix *re–*.
- Identify and use the prefix *un–*.
- Identify and use the prefix *pre–*.
- Identify and use the vowel suffix *–est*.
- Identify and use word parts to help determine word meaning.
- Identify and use prefixes and suffixes to determine word meaning.
- Identify roots to aid in determining word meaning.

Online — **15** minutes per day

Students will work on their own to learn and practice vocabulary words. Help students locate the online activities, and provide support as needed.

At any time, print a list of the unit words and definitions from the online lesson to practice with students. You can also have students create flash cards by writing each vocabulary word on the front of an index card and their own definition for each word on the back.

Days 1–3 Word Set 1

Day 1

Skills Update Students will review words they've studied previously by answering questions.

Introduce Word Set 1 Students will be introduced to new words.

✚ **OPTIONAL: Flash Cards** If you choose, have students create flash cards.

Word Set 1

disappear
disconnect
displace
disuse
reappear
reconnect
replace
reuse

Day 2

Practice Word Set 1 Students will review and practice the words from Word Set 1.

Day 3

Practice Word Set 1 Students will review and practice the words from Word Set 1.

↪ **Learning Coach Check-in** Ask students to tell you the words they've been learning from Word Set 1. See if students can provide the words' meanings.

Days 4–6   Word Set 2

Day 4

Skills Update Students will review words they've studied previously by answering questions.

Introduce Word Set 2 Students will be introduced to new words.

✚ **OPTIONAL: Flash Cards** If you choose, have students create flash cards.

Day 5

Practice Word Set 2 Students will review and practice the words from Word Set 2.

Day 6

Practice Word Set 2 Students will review and practice the words from Word Set 2.

↪ **Learning Coach Check-in** Ask students to tell you the words they've been learning from Word Set 2. See if students can provide the words' meanings.

Word Set 2

prearrange
precook
prepay
preschool
unclear
uncommon
unpaid
unusual

Days 7–8   Word Set 3

Day 7

Skills Update   Students will review words they've studied previously by answering questions.

Introduce Word Set 3   Students will be introduced to new words.

⊕ **OPTIONAL: Flash Cards**   If you choose, have students create flash cards.

Day 8

Practice Word Set 3   Students will review and practice the words from Word Set 3.

⮑ **Learning Coach Check-in**   Ask students to tell you the words they've been learning from Word Set 3. See if students can provide the words' meanings.

Word Set 3

- clearer
- clearest
- fresher
- freshest
- steeper
- steepest

Day 9   Unit Review

Unit Review   Students will play a game to review all words from the unit.

Day 10   Unit Checkpoint

Unit Checkpoint   Students will complete an online Unit Checkpoint covering all words from the unit. If necessary, read the directions to students and help them with keyboard or mouse operations.

Rewards:

- If students scored 80 percent or above on the Unit Checkpoint, add a sticker to the Unit 10 box on students' My Accomplishments chart. If students scored under 80 percent, continue to practice the words that they missed and add a sticker to this unit once they have mastered the words.

Vocabulary Words 11

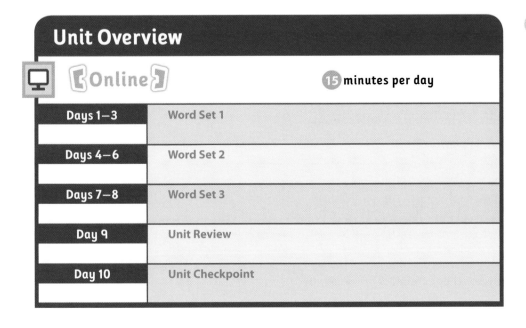

Unit Overview

[Online]   🕐 **minutes per day**

Days 1–3	Word Set 1
Days 4–6	Word Set 2
Days 7–8	Word Set 3
Day 9	Unit Review
Day 10	Unit Checkpoint

Objectives
- Classify and sort common words into categories.
- Increase reading vocabulary.

[Online]   🕐 **minutes per day**

Students will work on their own to learn and practice vocabulary words. Help students locate the online activities, and provide support as needed.

At any time, print a list of the unit words and definitions from the online lesson to practice with students. You can also have students create flash cards by writing each vocabulary word on the front of an index card and their own definition for each word on the back.

Days 1–3   Word Set 1

Day 1

Skills Update   Students will review words they've studied previously by answering questions.

Introduce Word Set 1   Students will be introduced to new words.

➕ **OPTIONAL: Flash Cards**   If you choose, have students create flash cards.

[Word Set 1]

cactus

crane

fern

hamster

hawk

moss

porcupine

turnip

Day 2

Practice Word Set 1   Students will review and practice the words from Word Set 1.

Day 3

Practice Word Set 1   Students will review and practice the words from Word Set 1.

⮕ **Learning Coach Check-in**   Ask students to tell you the words they've been learning from Word Set 1. See if students can provide the words' meanings.

Days 4–6   Word Set 2

Day 4

Skills Update   Students will review words they've studied previously by answering questions.

Introduce Word Set 2   Students will be introduced to new words.

⊕ **OPTIONAL: Flash Cards**   If you choose, have students create flash cards.

Word Set 2

coyote
cricket
dragonfly
duckling
gnat
salamander
swine
tadpole

Day 5

Practice Word Set 2   Students will review and practice the words from Word Set 2.

Day 6

Practice Word Set 2   Students will review and practice the words from Word Set 2.

⮕ **Learning Coach Check-in**   Ask students to tell you the words they've been learning from Word Set 2. See if students can provide the words' meanings.

Days 7–8 Word Set 3

Day 7

Skills Update Students will review words they've studied previously by answering questions.

Introduce Word Set 3 Students will be introduced to new words.

⊕ **OPTIONAL: Flash Cards** If you choose, have students create flash cards.

Day 8

Practice Word Set 3 Students will review and practice the words from Word Set 3.

↻ **Learning Coach Check-in** Ask students to tell you the words they've been learning from Word Set 3. See if students can provide the words' meanings.

> **Word Set 3**
>
> barrier
> briar
> coax
> movement
> musty
> petal

Day 9 Unit Review

Unit Review Students will play a game to review all words from the unit.

Day 10 Unit Checkpoint

Unit Checkpoint Students will complete an online Unit Checkpoint covering all words from the unit. If necessary, read the directions to students and help them with keyboard or mouse operations.

Rewards:
- If students scored 80 percent or above on the Unit Checkpoint, add a sticker to the Unit 11 box on students' My Accomplishments chart. If students scored under 80 percent, continue to practice the words that they missed and add a sticker to this unit once they have mastered the words.

Vocabulary Words 12

Unit Overview

🖥️ 〚Online〛 ⏱️15 **minutes per day**

Days 1–3	Word Set 1
Days 4–6	Word Set 2
Days 7–8	Word Set 3
Day 9	Unit Review
Day 10	Unit Checkpoint

Objectives
- Increase vocabulary through synonyms.
- Increase vocabulary through antonyms.
- Increase reading vocabulary.

〚Online〛 ⏱️15 **minutes per day**

Students will work on their own to learn and practice vocabulary words. Help students locate the online activities, and provide support as needed.

At any time, print a list of the unit words and definitions from the online lesson to practice with students. You can also have students create flash cards by writing each vocabulary word on the front of an index card and their own definition for each word on the back.

Days 1–3 Word Set 1

Day 1

Skills Update Students will review words they've studied previously by answering questions.

Introduce Word Set 1 Students will be introduced to new words.

➕ **OPTIONAL: Flash Cards** If you choose, have students create flash cards.

Word Set 1

boast
brag
cruel
nasty
empty
hollow
ragged
worn

Day 2

Practice Word Set 1 Students will review and practice the words from Word Set 1.

Day 3

Practice Word Set 1 Students will review and practice the words from Word Set 1.

↻ **Learning Coach Check-in** Ask students to tell you the words they've been learning from Word Set 1. See if students can provide the words' meanings.

Days 4–6   Word Set 2

Day 4

Skills Update Students will review words they've studied previously by answering questions.

Introduce Word Set 2 Students will be introduced to new words.

➕ **OPTIONAL: Flash Cards** If you choose, have students create flash cards.

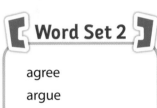

Word Set 2

agree
argue
brave
cowardly
earn
spend
useful
useless

Day 5

Practice Word Set 2 Students will review and practice the words from Word Set 2.

Day 6

Practice Word Set 2 Students will review and practice the words from Word Set 2.

↻ **Learning Coach Check-in** Ask students to tell you the words they've been learning from Word Set 2. See if students can provide the words' meanings.

Days 7–8   Word Set 3

Day 7

Skills Update   Students will review words they've studied previously by answering questions.

Introduce Word Set 3   Students will be introduced to new words.

✚ **OPTIONAL: Flash Cards**   If you choose, have students create flash cards.

Word Set 3

- awfully
- golden
- nonsense
- silvery
- supplies
- tilt

Day 8

Practice Word Set 3   Students will review and practice the words from Word Set 3.

⮑ **Learning Coach Check-in**   Ask students to tell you the words they've been learning from Word Set 3. See if students can provide the words' meanings.

Day 9   Unit Review

Unit Review   Students will play a game to review all words from the unit.

Day 10   Unit Checkpoint

Unit Checkpoint   Students will complete an online Unit Checkpoint covering all words from the unit. If necessary, read the directions to students and help them with keyboard or mouse operations.

Rewards:

- If students scored 80 percent or above on the Unit Checkpoint, add a sticker to the Unit 12 box on students' My Accomplishments chart. If students scored under 80 percent, continue to practice the words that they missed and add a sticker to this unit once they have mastered the words.

Vocabulary Words 13

Unit Overview

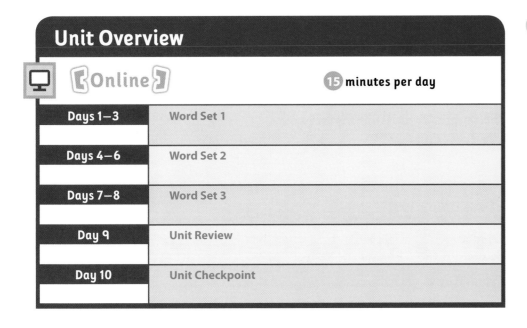

Online 🕐 **15 minutes per day**

Days 1–3	Word Set 1
Days 4–6	Word Set 2
Days 7–8	Word Set 3
Day 9	Unit Review
Day 10	Unit Checkpoint

Objectives
- Increase vocabulary through compound words.
- Increase vocabulary through contractions.
- Use resources or other tools to determine the meaning of a word.
- Use glossaries, thesauruses, and beginner dictionaries to learn new vocabulary.
- Use knowledge of words to determine the meaning of compound words.

Online 🕐 **15 minutes per day**

Students will work on their own to learn and practice vocabulary words. Help students locate the online activities, and provide support as needed.

At any time, print a list of the unit words and definitions from the online lesson to practice with students. You can also have students create flash cards by writing each vocabulary word on the front of an index card and their own definition for each word on the back.

Days 1–3 Word Set 1

Day 1

Skills Update Students will review words they've studied previously by answering questions.

Introduce Word Set 1 Students will be introduced to new words.

➕ **OPTIONAL: Flash Cards** If you c‗‗‗e. have students create flash cards.

Word Set 1

blueberry
daydream
doorway
firewo‗‗
lighth‗‗e
sundo‗‗
sunris‗
tooth‗ ‗te

Day 2

Practice Word Set 1 Students will review and practice the words from Word Set 1.

Day 3

Practice Word Set 1 Students will review and practice the words from Word Set 1.

↪ **Learning Coach Check-in** Ask students to tell you the words they've been learning from Word Set 1. See if students can provide the words' meanings.

Days 4–6   Word Set 2

Day 4

Skills Update Students will review words they've studied previously by answering questions.

Introduce Word Set 2 Students will be introduced to new words.

➕ **OPTIONAL: Flash Cards** If you choose, have students create flash cards.

Day 5

Practice Word Set 2 Students will review and practice the words from Word Set 2.

Day 6

Practice Word Set 2 Students will review and practice the words from Word Set 2.

↪ **Learning Coach Check-in** Ask students to tell you the words they've been learning from Word Set 2. See if students can provide the words' meanings.

Word Set 2

quail
quart
raspberry
steamboat
subway
tear
thread
urge

Days 7–8   Word Set 3

Day 7

Skills Update Students will review words they've studied previously by answering questions.

Introduce Word Set 3 Students will be introduced to new words.

⊕ **OPTIONAL: Flash Cards** If you choose, have students create flash cards.

Day 8

Practice Word Set 3 Students will review and practice the words from Word Set 3.

⮌ **Learning Coach Check-in** Ask students to tell you the words they've been learning from Word Set 3. See if students can provide the words' meanings.

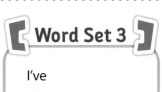

Word Set 3

I've
they're
we're
we've
you're
you've

Day 9   Unit Review

Unit Review Students will play a game to review all words from the unit.

Day 10   Unit Checkpoint

Unit Checkpoint Students will complete an online Unit Checkpoint covering all words from the unit. If necessary, read the directions to students and help them with keyboard or mouse operations.

Rewards:

- If students scored 80 percent or above on the Unit Checkpoint, add a sticker to the Unit 13 box on students' My Accomplishments chart. If students scored under 80 percent, continue to practice the words that they missed and add a sticker to this unit once they have mastered the words.

Vocabulary Words 14

Unit Overview

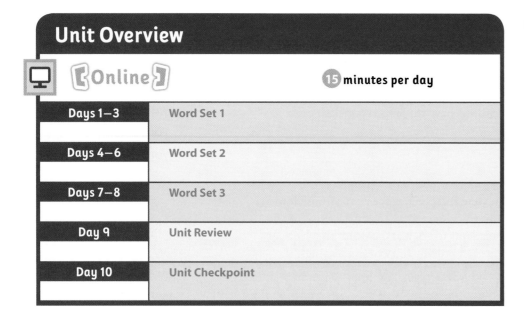

Online · ⏱ 15 minutes per day

Days 1–3	Word Set 1
Days 4–6	Word Set 2
Days 7–8	Word Set 3
Day 9	Unit Review
Day 10	Unit Checkpoint

Objectives

- Identify and define words' and phrases' literal and non-literal meanings, e.g. take steps.
- Distinguish between meaning variations in closely related verbs.
- Increase reading vocabulary.

Online ⏱ 15 minutes per day

Students will work on their own to learn and practice vocabulary words. Help students locate the online activities, and provide support as needed.

At any time, print a list of the unit words and definitions from the online lesson to practice with students. You can also have students create flash cards by writing each vocabulary word on the front of an index card and their own definition for each word on the back.

Days 1–3 Word Set 1

Day 1

Skills Update Students will review words they've studied previously by answering questions.

Introduce Word Set 1 Students will be introduced to new words.

➕ **OPTIONAL: Flash Cards** If you choose, have students create flash cards.

Word Set 1

- ashore
- emigrant
- flood
- hawk
- mushroom
- plague
- snail
- squirt

Day 2

Practice Word Set 1   Students will review and practice the words from Word Set 1.

Day 3

Practice Word Set 1   Students will review and practice the words from Word Set 1.

➲ **Learning Coach Check-in**   Ask students to tell you the words they've been learning from Word Set 1. See if students can provide the words' meanings.

Days 4–6   Word Set 2

Day 4

Skills Update   Students will review words they've studied previously by answering questions.

Introduce Word Set 2   Students will be introduced to new words.

✚ **OPTIONAL: Flash Cards**   If you choose, have students create flash cards.

Word Set 2

command
destroy
frighten
harm
hurl
suggest
terrify
toss

Day 5

Practice Word Set 2   Students will review and practice the words from Word Set 2.

Day 6

Practice Word Set 2   Students will review and practice the words from Word Set 2.

➲ **Learning Coach Check-in**   Ask students to tell you the words they've been learning from Word Set 2. See if students can provide the words' meanings.

Days 7–8   Word Set 3

Day 7

Skills Update   Students will review words they've studied previously by answering questions.

Introduce Word Set 3   Students will be introduced to new words.

➕ **OPTIONAL: Flash Cards**   If you choose, have students create flash cards.

Day 8

Practice Word Set 3   Students will review and practice the words from Word Set 3.

⟳ **Learning Coach Check-in**   Ask students to tell you the words they've been learning from Word Set 3. See if students can provide the words' meanings.

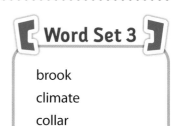

Word Set 3

- brook
- climate
- collar
- express
- handle
- speck

Day 9   Unit Review

Unit Review   Students will play a game to review all words from the unit.

Day 10   Unit Checkpoint

Unit Checkpoint   Students will complete an online Unit Checkpoint covering all words from the unit. If necessary, read the directions to students and help them with keyboard or mouse operations.

Rewards:

- If students scored 80 percent or above on the Unit Checkpoint, add a sticker to the Unit 14 box on students' My Accomplishments chart. If students scored under 80 percent, continue to practice the words that they missed and add a sticker to this unit once they have mastered the words.

Vocabulary Words 15

Unit Overview

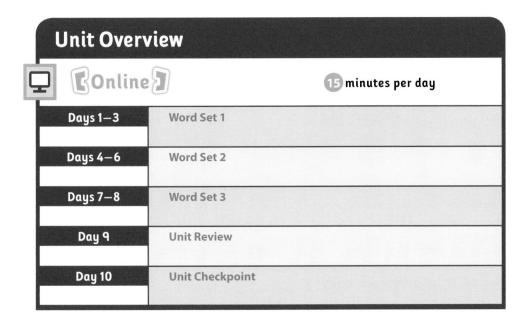

Online ⏱ **minutes per day**

Days 1—3	Word Set 1
Days 4—6	Word Set 2
Days 7—8	Word Set 3
Day 9	Unit Review
Day 10	Unit Checkpoint

⭐ Objectives

- Identify and use pictures and symbols to increase vocabulary.
- Identify and use word parts to help determine word meaning.
- Identify and use prefixes and suffixes to determine word meaning.
- Identify real-life connections between words and their uses.
- Increase reading vocabulary.

Online ⏱ **minutes per day**

Students will work on their own to learn and practice vocabulary words. Help students locate the online activities, and provide support as needed.

At any time, print a list of the unit words and definitions from the online lesson to practice with students. You can also have students create flash cards by writing each vocabulary word on the front of an index card and their own definition for each word on the back.

Days 1—3 Word Set 1

Day 1

Skills Update Students will review words they've studied previously by answering questions.

Introduce Word Set 1 Students will be introduced to new words.

➕ **OPTIONAL: Flash Cards** If you choose, have students create flash cards.

Word Set 1

- ageless
- fearless
- homeless
- mindless
- misplace
- misspell
- mistreat
- misuse

Day 2

Practice Word Set 1 Students will review and practice the words from Word Set 1.

Day 3

Practice Word Set 1 Students will review and practice the words from Word Set 1.

⟳ **Learning Coach Check-in** Ask students to tell you the words they've been learning from Word Set 1. See if students can provide the words' meanings.

Days 4–6   Word Set 2

Day 4

Skills Update Students will review words they've studied previously by answering questions.

Introduce Word Set 2 Students will be introduced to new words.

⊕ **OPTIONAL: Flash Cards** If you choose, have students create flash cards.

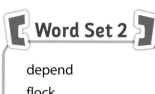

Word Set 2

depend
flock
harness
hospital
pasture
poison
rescue
starve

Day 5

Practice Word Set 2 Students will review and practice the words from Word Set 2.

Day 6

Practice Word Set 2 Students will review and practice the words from Word Set 2.

⟳ **Learning Coach Check-in** Ask students to tell you the words they've been learning from Word Set 2. See if students can provide the words' meanings.

Days 7–8　Word Set 3

Day 7

Skills Update　Students will review words they've studied previously by answering questions.

Introduce Word Set 3　Students will be introduced to new words.

⊕ OPTIONAL: Flash Cards　If you choose, have students create flash cards.

Day 8

Practice Word Set 3　Students will review and practice the words from Word Set 3.

⮌ Learning Coach Check-in　Ask students to tell you the words they've been learning from Word Set 3. See if students can provide the words' meanings.

> **Word Set 3**
>
> companion
> crouch
> innocent
> poultry
> pupil
> slope

Day 9　Unit Review

Unit Review　Students will play a game to review all words from the unit.

Day 10　Unit Checkpoint

Unit Checkpoint　Students will complete an online Unit Checkpoint covering all words from the unit. If necessary, read the directions to students and help them with keyboard or mouse operations.

Rewards:

- If students scored 80 percent or above on the Unit Checkpoint, add a sticker to the Unit 15 box on students' My Accomplishments chart. If students scored under 80 percent, continue to practice the words that they missed and add a sticker to this unit once they have mastered the words.

Vocabulary Words 16

Unit Overview

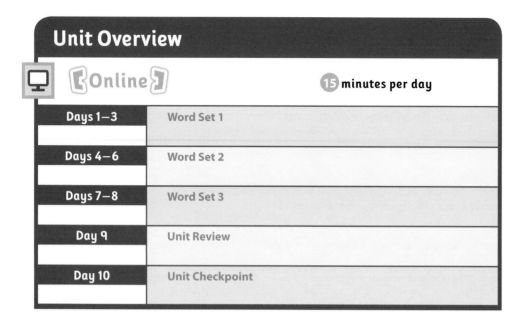

Objectives
- Identify and use word parts to help determine word meaning.
- Identify roots to aid in determining word meaning.
- Increase reading vocabulary.

Online	15 minutes per day
Days 1–3	Word Set 1
Days 4–6	Word Set 2
Days 7–8	Word Set 3
Day 9	Unit Review
Day 10	Unit Checkpoint

Online 15 minutes per day

Students will work on their own to learn and practice vocabulary words. Help students locate the online activities, and provide support as needed.

At any time, print a list of the unit words and definitions from the online lesson to practice with students. You can also have students create flash cards by writing each vocabulary word on the front of an index card and their own definition for each word on the back.

Days 1–3   Word Set 1

Day 1

Skills Update Students will review words they've studied previously by answering questions.

Introduce Word Set 1 Students will be introduced to new words.

⊕ OPTIONAL: Flash Cards If you choose, have students create flash cards.

Word Set 1

bicycle
bilingual
biplane
triangle
tricycle
unicorn
unicycle
unique

Day 2

Practice Word Set 1 Students will review and practice the words from Word Set 1.

Day 3

Practice Word Set 1 Students will review and practice the words from Word Set 1.

⮑ **Learning Coach Check-in** Ask students to tell you the words they've been learning from Word Set 1. See if students can provide the words' meanings.

Days 4–6 Word Set 2

Day 4

Skills Update Students will review words they've studied previously by answering questions.

Introduce Word Set 2 Students will be introduced to new words.

➕ **OPTIONAL: Flash Cards** If you choose, have students create flash cards.

Day 5

Practice Word Set 2 Students will review and practice the words from Word Set 2.

Day 6

Practice Word Set 2 Students will review and practice the words from Word Set 2.

⮑ **Learning Coach Check-in** Ask students to tell you the words they've been learning from Word Set 2. See if students can provide the words' meanings.

Word Set 2

biped
centipede
export
import
pedal
pedestrian
portable
transport

Days 7–8   Word Set 3

Day 7

Skills Update   Students will review words they've studied previously by answering questions.

Introduce Word Set 3   Students will be introduced to new words.

✛ **OPTIONAL: Flash Cards**   If you choose, have students create flash cards.

Day 8

Practice Word Set 3   Students will review and practice the words from Word Set 3.

⟳ **Learning Coach Check-in**   Ask students to tell you the words they've been learning from Word Set 3. See if students can provide the words' meanings.

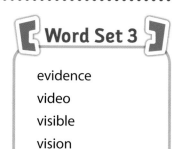

Word Set 3

evidence
video
visible
vision
visit
visitor

Day 9   Unit Review

Unit Review   Students will play a game to review all words from the unit.

Day 10   Unit Checkpoint

Unit Checkpoint   Students will complete an online Unit Checkpoint covering all words from the unit. If necessary, read the directions to students and help them with keyboard or mouse operations.

Rewards:

- If students scored 80 percent or above on the Unit Checkpoint, add a sticker to the Unit 16 box on students' My Accomplishments chart. If students scored under 80 percent, continue to practice the words that they missed and add a sticker to this unit once they have mastered the words.

Vocabulary Words 17

Unit Overview

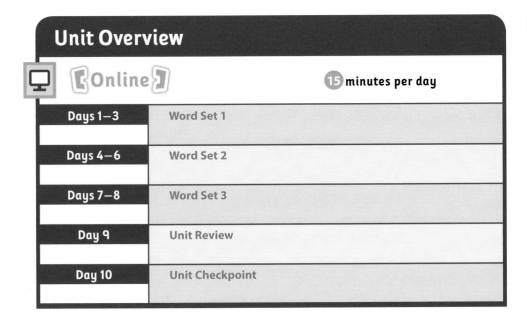

[Online] 🖥 ⑮ minutes per day

Days 1–3	Word Set 1
Days 4–6	Word Set 2
Days 7–8	Word Set 3
Day 9	Unit Review
Day 10	Unit Checkpoint

Objectives

- Increase vocabulary through homographs.
- Increase vocabulary through homophones.
- Increase reading vocabulary.

[Online] ⑮ minutes per day

Students will work on their own to learn and practice vocabulary words. Help students locate the online activities, and provide support as needed.

At any time, print a list of the unit words and definitions from the online lesson to practice with students. You can also have students create flash cards by writing each vocabulary word on the front of an index card and their own definition for each word on the back.

Days 1–3   Word Set 1

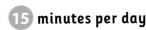

Day 1

Skills Update Students will review words they've studied previously by answering questions.

Introduce Word Set 1 Students will be introduced to new words.

➕ **OPTIONAL: Flash Cards** If you choose, have students create flash cards.

[Word Set 1]

close (klohs)
close (klohz)
hail
hale
object (AHB-jikt)
object (uhb-JEKT)
peak
peek

Day 2

Practice Word Set 1 Students will review and practice the words from Word Set 1.

Day 3

Practice Word Set 1 Students will review and practice the words from Word Set 1.

⟳ **Learning Coach Check-in** Ask students to tell you the words they've been learning from Word Set 1. See if students can provide the words' meanings.

Days 4–6   Word Set 2

Day 4

Skills Update Students will review words they've studied previously by answering questions.

Introduce Word Set 2 Students will be introduced to new words.

⊕ **OPTIONAL: Flash Cards** If you choose, have students create flash cards.

Word Set 2

cabin
canal
channel
craft
deck
dock
harbor
vessel

Day 5

Practice Word Set 2 Students will review and practice the words from Word Set 2.

Day 6

Practice Word Set 2 Students will review and practice the words from Word Set 2.

⟳ **Learning Coach Check-in** Ask students to tell you the words they've been learning from Word Set 2. See if students can provide the words' meanings.

Days 7–8 Word Set 3

Day 7

Skills Update Students will review words they've studied previously by answering questions.

Introduce Word Set 3 Students will be introduced to new words.

✚ **OPTIONAL: Flash Cards** If you choose, have students create flash cards.

Day 8

Practice Word Set 3 Students will review and practice the words from Word Set 3.

➲ **Learning Coach Check-in** Ask students to tell you the words they've been learning from Word Set 3. See if students can provide the words' meanings.

Word Set 3

- conductor
- engineer
- platform
- railroad
- station
- terminal

Day 9 Unit Review

Unit Review Students will play a game to review all words from the unit.

Day 10 Unit Checkpoint

Unit Checkpoint Students will complete an online Unit Checkpoint covering all words from the unit. If necessary, read the directions to students and help them with keyboard or mouse operations.

Rewards:
- If students scored 80 percent or above on the Unit Checkpoint, add a sticker to the Unit 17 box on students' My Accomplishments chart. If students scored under 80 percent, continue to practice the words that they missed and add a sticker to this unit once they have mastered the words.

Vocabulary Words 18

Unit Overview

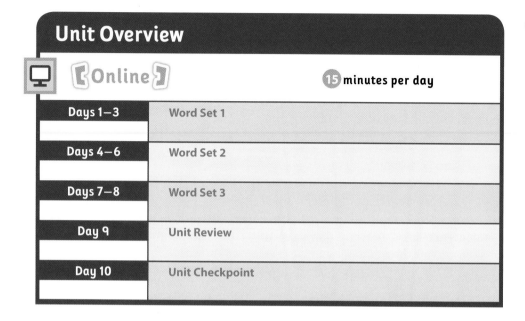

☐ Online   **15** minutes per day

Days 1–3	Word Set 1
Days 4–6	Word Set 2
Days 7–8	Word Set 3
Day 9	Unit Review
Day 10	Unit Checkpoint

Objectives

- Use resources or other tools to determine the meaning of a word.
- Use glossaries, thesauruses, and beginner dictionaries to learn new vocabulary.
- Increase reading vocabulary.

Online   **15** minutes per day

Students will work on their own to learn and practice vocabulary words. Help students locate the online activities, and provide support as needed.

At any time, print a list of the unit words and definitions from the online lesson to practice with students. You can also have students create flash cards by writing each vocabulary word on the front of an index card and their own definition for each word on the back.

Days 1–3 Word Set 1

Day 1

Skills Update   Students will review words they've studied previously by answering questions.

Introduce Word Set 1   Students will be introduced to new words.

⊕ OPTIONAL: Flash Cards   If you choose, have students create flash cards.

Word Set 1

umbrella

uphill

vegetable

violet

wagon

woodpecker

X-ray

xylophone

Day 2

Practice Word Set 1 Students will review and practice the words from Word Set 1.

Day 3

Practice Word Set 1 Students will review and practice the words from Word Set 1.

➲ **Learning Coach Check-in** Ask students to tell you the words they've been learning from Word Set 1. See if students can provide the words' meanings.

Days 4–6   Word Set 2

Day 4

Skills Update Students will review words they've studied previously by answering questions.

Introduce Word Set 2 Students will be introduced to new words.

➕ **OPTIONAL: Flash Cards** If you choose, have students create flash cards.

Word Set 2

aircraft
airport
hangar
jet
landing
pilot
takeoff
wing

Day 5

Practice Word Set 2 Students will review and practice the words from Word Set 2.

Day 6

Practice Word Set 2 Students will review and practice the words from Word Set 2.

➲ **Learning Coach Check-in** Ask students to tell you the words they've been learning from Word Set 2. See if students can provide the words' meanings.

Days 7–8   Word Set 3

Day 7

Skills Update   Students will review words they've studied previously by answering questions.

Introduce Word Set 3   Students will be introduced to new words.

✚ **OPTIONAL: Flash Cards**   If you choose, have students create flash cards.

Day 8

Practice Word Set 3   Students will review and practice the words from Word Set 3.

➲ **Learning Coach Check-in**   Ask students to tell you the words they've been learning from Word Set 3. See if students can provide the words' meanings.

Word Set 3

driver
engine
garage
highway
passenger
tire

Day 9   Unit Review

Unit Review   Students will play a game to review all words from the unit.

Day 10   Unit Checkpoint

Unit Checkpoint   Students will complete an online Unit Checkpoint covering all words from the unit. If necessary, read the directions to students and help them with keyboard or mouse operations.

Rewards:

• If students scored 80 percent or above on the Unit Checkpoint, add a sticker to the Unit 18 box on students' My Accomplishments chart. If students scored under 80 percent, continue to practice the words that they missed and add a sticker to this unit once they have mastered the words.

Writing Skills

What Is a Sentence?

Unit Overview

In this unit, students will
- ▶ Learn what a sentence is.
- ▶ Learn that a sentence begins with a capital letter and ends with a punctuation mark.

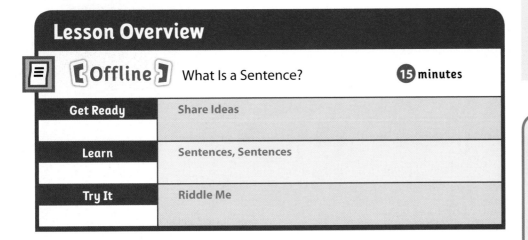

Lesson Overview

[Offline] What Is a Sentence?		15 minutes
Get Ready	Share Ideas	
Learn	Sentences, Sentences	
Try It	Riddle Me	

Content Background

A complete sentence tells a complete thought or complete idea. It has two main parts: the naming part and the action part.
- ▶ The naming part of a sentence is called the subject.
- ▶ The action part of a sentence is called the predicate.

Big Ideas

Sentences are building blocks of paragraphs.

Materials

Supplied
- *K¹² Language Arts Activity Book,* pp. WS 1–2

Also Needed
- whiteboard (optional)
- crayons

Keywords

complete sentence – a group of words that tells a complete thought

predicate – the verb or verb phrase in a sentence

subject – a word or words that tell whom or what the sentence is about

[Offline] 🕙 minutes

What Is a Sentence?

You will work with students to complete Get Ready, Learn, and Try It activities.

Get Ready

Share Ideas

To get students to think about how we express ideas, discuss how to share ideas with others.

▸ If you have an idea, how can you share it with others? Answers may vary.

▸ After getting responses, sum up how to share ideas. Demonstrate to students that they can share an idea by doing it, saying it, or writing it down.

1. Make a funny face.

2. Have students tell what you did: You made a funny face.

   Say: I did it. You said it. Now I am going to write it down.

3. Write a sentence on the whiteboard or a sheet of paper that tells what you did: I made a funny face.

   Say: When we have an idea, we can say it aloud or write it in a sentence. You are going to learn more about using sentences to share ideas.

Objectives

- Share ideas with others.
- Use sentences to share ideas.

Learn

Sentences, Sentences

Introduce the concept of the naming part (the subject) and the action part (the verb) of sentences to students. Turn to page WS 1 in *K¹² Language Skills Activity Book*.

1. **Say:** A **sentence** is a group of words. The words must tell a complete thought.

2. **Say:** A sentence has two parts. The **naming part** tells whom or what the sentence is about.

   Examples: the boy, a tree, some cars

3. **Say:** The **action part** tells what someone or something does.

   Examples: skates, hits the ball, goes fast, grows tall

Objectives

- Recognize word groups that are sentences.
- Recognize that a sentence tells a complete thought.

4. **Say:** Listen to this group of words: *The neighbor's dog.* This sentence doesn't make any sense the way it is. Something is missing. Let's add words to complete the thought.

   ▶ What does the neighbor's dog do? Answers will vary. Possible answers: barks, runs, sits

5. Read the rule on the Activity Book page. Complete the Guided Exercises with students.

6. Have students complete the rest of the Activity Book page. Provide support as necessary.

TIP To help students understand what a complete idea is, tell them that you saw something in the night sky. Draw the top of a star ^ and a complete star ☆. Which one is a complete idea? When we provide complete ideas, people understand us better.

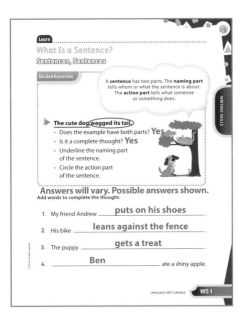

Try It

Riddle Me

Help students remember that a **sentence** is a group of words. The words must tell a complete thought. The sentence must have a naming part and an action part. Turn to page WS 2 in *K¹² Language Skills Activity Book.*

1. Read the instructions to students. Read the riddle together.

2. Read the words in each shape together.

3. Have students complete the Activity Book page. Provide support as necessary.

TIP After students complete the Try It in their Activity Book, have them read the complete sentences aloud. Help them point out the naming part and the action part of each sentence.

Objectives

- Recognize word groups that are sentences.
- Recognize that a sentence tells a complete thought.

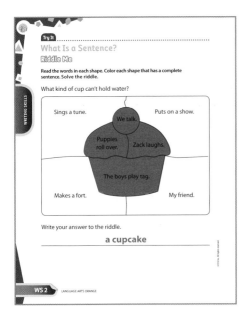

Sentence Beginnings and Endings

Lesson Overview

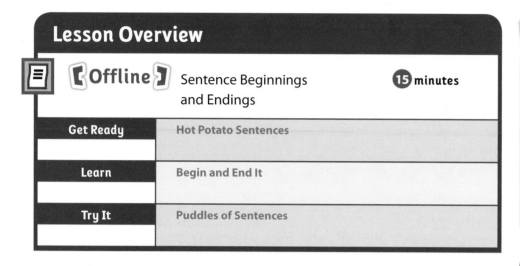

Offline	Sentence Beginnings and Endings	15 minutes
Get Ready	Hot Potato Sentences	
Learn	Begin and End It	
Try It	Puddles of Sentences	

Materials

Supplied
- *K¹² Language Arts Activity Book*, pp. WS 3–4

Also Needed
- household object – small ball, crumpled piece of paper, or other soft object

Keywords

sentence – a group of words that tells a complete thought

Content Background

A complete sentence begins with a capital letter and ends with a mark of punctuation. For a group of words to be a complete sentence, it must also express a complete thought.

 **Offline** 15 minutes

Sentence Beginnings and Endings

You will work with students to complete Get Ready, Learn, and Try It activities.

Get Ready

Hot Potato Sentences

Play a game of Hot Potato with students to review what a sentence is.

1. Remind students that a sentence expresses a complete thought. A complete sentence tells who did what.

Objectives
- Recognize word groups that are sentences.

2. Play a quick game of Hot Potato.

> ► Toss a hot potato (small ball, crumpled piece of paper, or other soft object) to a student.
> ► The student should hold the hot potato and cannot pass it back to you (or to another player, if you are working with more than one student) until you read a complete sentence. The object is to identify complete sentences to get rid of the hot potato as soon as possible.
> ► If the student throws the hot potato on an incomplete sentence, talk about why the sentence is incomplete.

3. After the student has thrown you the hot potato and identified a complete sentence, give the potato back (or to another student) and start again.

4. Begin with these word groups:

> ► A squirrel went up a tree. complete sentence
> ► Rabbits came out of a hole. complete sentence
> ► Spotted deer. incomplete sentence
> ► Birds chirped. complete sentence
> ► The boys heard a bear. complete sentence
> ► Fell on the path. incomplete sentence

Learn

Begin and End It

Emphasize that a sentence begins with a capital letter and ends with a period. Turn to page WS 3 in *K¹² Language Arts Activity Book*.

1. Point to the race car. Explain that the driver begins the race at the green light. She ends the race at the red light. The red light tells the driver to stop.

   Say: A sentence has a beginning and an ending, too. A sentence **begins** with a **capital letter**. It **ends** with an **end mark**. The end mark is often a **period**.

2. Read the rule on the Activity Book page. Complete the Guided Exercises with students.

3. Have students complete the rest of the Activity Book page. Provide support as necessary. If students are struggling, read the sentences aloud.

> ► Bert drove a silver car.
> ► Cars sped around the truck.
> ► The fans stood and cheered.

Hearing the sentences will help students know what capital letter to add if they are unsure.

TIP Emphasize the role of the period by playing Race Cars. Have students move around the room, stopping each time you raise an index card with a bold period printed on it.

Objectives

* Recognize that a sentence begins with a capital letter and ends with an end mark.
* Use a capital letter to begin a sentence and an end mark to end it.

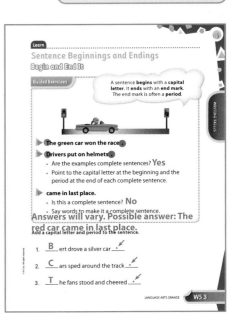

Try It

Puddles of Sentences

Help students recognize how a sentence should begin and how it should end. Turn to page WS 4 in *K¹² Language Arts Activity Book*.

1. Read the first set of directions to students. Read the sentences and word groups together.

2. Have students complete Exercises 1–3. Provide support as necessary.

3. Read the second set of directions to students. Read the sentences together.

   ▸ We jumped in the puddles.
   ▸ Water splashed on us.
   ▸ My boots got muddy and wet.

4. Have students complete Exercises 4–6. Provide support as necessary.

Objectives

• Recognize that a sentence begins with a capital letter and ends with an end mark.

• Use a capital letter to begin a sentence and an end mark to end it.

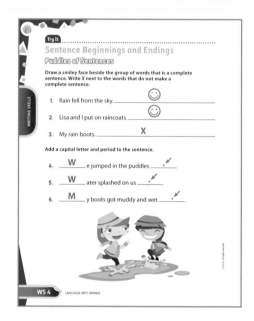

Review Complete and Incomplete Sentences

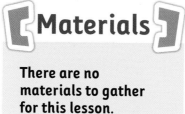

Lesson Overview

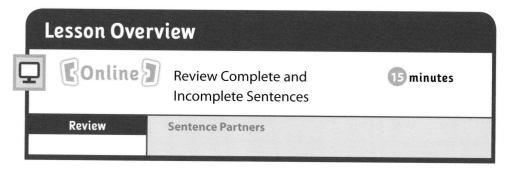

Online	Review Complete and Incomplete Sentences	15 minutes
Review	Sentence Partners	

Materials

There are no materials to gather for this lesson.

Online 15 minutes

Review Complete and Incomplete Sentences

Students will work on their own to complete review and practice activities. Help students locate the online activities and provide support as needed.

Review

Sentence Partners

Students will work online to review what they have learned about complete sentences.

Objectives
- Recognize word groups that are sentences.
- Recognize word groups that are not sentences.

Offline Alternative

No computer access? Write or say several sentences. Make sure some of them are complete sentences and some of them incomplete. Have students identify those that are complete. Ask them to complete those that do not make a complete thought.

Unit Checkpoint

Lesson Overview

 **Offline** Unit Checkpoint **15** minutes

Unit Checkpoint	Complete Sentences

Materials

Supplied
- *K¹² Language Arts Assessments*, pp. WS 1–3

Offline **15** minutes

Unit Checkpoint
You will work with students to complete the Unit Checkpoint.

Unit Checkpoint

Complete Sentences

Explain that students are going to show what they have learned about complete sentences.

1. Give students the Unit Checkpoint pages.

2. Read the directions together. Have students complete the Checkpoint on their own.

3. Use the Answer Key to score the Checkpoint, and then enter the results online.

4. Review each exercise with students. Work with students to correct any exercise that they missed. You may also wish to have them rewrite the sentences in Part 2 so that all three have beginning capital letters and end marks.

 Students who answered one or more questions incorrectly should continue to practice this grammar skill. Read aloud your students' favorite books. Stop from time to time to point out complete sentences. Explain that a complete thought tells who did what.

Example: The clown rides a unicycle.

▸ What does the clown do? He rides a unicycle.
▸ Who (or what) rides the unicycle? The clown does.

Objectives
- Recognize word groups that are sentences.
- Recognize word groups that are not sentences.
- Recognize that a sentence begins with a capital letter and ends with an end mark.
- Use a capital letter to begin a sentence and an end mark to end it.

 Reward: When students answer at 80 percent or above on the Unit Checkpoint, add a sticker for this unit on the My Accomplishments chart.

Name _____ Date _____

☼ Unit Checkpoint Learning Coach Instructions
Complete Sentences

Explain that students are going to show what they have learned about complete sentences.

1. Give students the Unit Checkpoint pages.

2. Read the directions together. Have students complete the Checkpoint on their own.

3. Use the Answer Key to score the Checkpoint, and then enter the results online.

4. Review each exercise with students. Work with students to correct any exercise that they missed.

Name _____ Date _____

☼ Unit Checkpoint Answer Key
Complete Sentences

Part 1. Complete Sentences
Choose the complete sentence.

1. A. likes toads and frogs
   B. Green toads.
   C. Toads hop across the pond.

2. A. A pet hamster.
   B. The cage door opened.
   C. Got loose.

3. A. Ling's happy day.
   B. Glides down the slide at the water park.
   C. Everyone comes to the party.

4. A. Some spiders spin webs
   B. spiders have eight legs.
   C. Most spiders eat bugs.

Name _____ Date _____

5. **A.** Sally walks her dog every day.
   B. Rusty barks at the cats
   C. the cats run up a tree.

6. **A.** We make snack mix.
   B. kim mixes the nuts and fruit.
   C. Adam adds sunflower seeds

Part 2. Sentence Beginnings and Endings
Choose the sentence that begins and ends correctly.

7. A. Bill threw the ball
   B. Sally ran to first base.
   C. the catcher dropped the ball.

8. A. sam wants to play a game.
   B. He looked in the game box
   C. Lori found a good game to play.

Recognize and Fix Sentences

Unit Overview

In this unit, students will
- Review basic sentence structure and punctuation.
- Begin to see the sentence as a basic unit of expression, one that contains a complete thought.
- Recognize that they can build onto a sentence to expand it.
- Make two sentences into one by combining common elements.

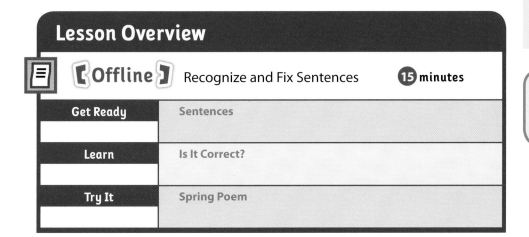

Lesson Overview

[Offline] Recognize and Fix Sentences · **15** minutes

Get Ready	Sentences
Learn	Is It Correct?
Try It	Spring Poem

[Materials]

Supplied
- *K¹² Language Arts Activity Book*, pp. WS 5–6

Also Needed
- whiteboard (optional)
- crayons

Keywords

sentence – a group of words that tells a complete thought

Content Background

A complete sentence tells a complete thought or complete idea. It has two main parts: the naming part and the action part.
- The naming part of a sentence is called the subject.
- The action part of a sentence is called the predicate.

Big Ideas

- Speakers and writers use complete sentences to express their ideas effectively.
- Writers help readers understand ideas by beginning each sentence with a capital letter and ending it with a mark of punctuation.

Offline · 15 minutes

Recognize and Fix Sentences

You will work with students to complete Get Ready, Learn, and Try It activities.

Get Ready

Sentences

Review that a sentence tells a complete thought. It has two parts: a naming part and an action part.

1. Write the word groups listed here.

2. Have students tell you whether each word group is a sentence or not a sentence. If they say that a word group is not a sentence, ask them what part of the sentence is missing.

   ▸ I like the fall. Yes
   ▸ The leaves No; the action part is missing.
   ▸ We pick pumpkins. Yes
   ▸ rakes leaves in the fall. No; the naming part is missing.

 TIP The naming part of a sentence is the subject. The action part is the predicate.

> **Objectives**
> • Distinguish between complete and incomplete sentences.

Learn

Is It Correct?

Explain to students that a sentence begins with a capital letter and ends with an end mark. Turn to page WS 5 in *K¹² Language Arts Activity Book*.

1. Review with students that sentences begin with capital letters and have end marks.

   Say: We can fix sentences that are incorrect by adding capital letters and end marks.

2. Read the rule on the Activity Book page. Complete the Guided Exercises with students.

3. Have students complete the rest of the Activity Book page. Provide support as necessary.

TIP When students point out an error, ask them to explain how the sentence can be fixed. Editing includes finding the error and knowing how to correct it.

> **Objectives**
> • Use capital letters correctly.
> • Punctuate correctly.

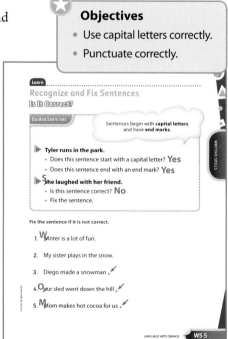

Try It

Spring Poem

Help students edit sentences by making sure each sentence begins with a capital letter and ends with a period. Turn to page WS 6 in *K¹² Language Arts Activity Book*.

1. Read the directions to students. Read the sentences together.

2. Have students complete the Activity Book page. Provide support as necessary.

TIP Students who are having difficulty fixing sentences on paper can explain the changes to you. Write their changes on paper or a whiteboard and have them practice writing editing marks.

Online Alternative

This activity is OPTIONAL. It is intended for students who want extra practice or would prefer to do online practice in place of the offline Try It. Feel free to skip this activity.

Objectives
- Use capital letters correctly.
- Punctuate correctly.

Try It
Recognize and Fix Sentences
Spring Poem

Fix each sentence in the poem. Add a capital letter and period.

1. i am glad spring is here
2. it's the best time of the year
3. leaves are green in the trees
4. flowers bend in the breeze
5. the warm sun shines up high
6. birds play tag in the sky

WS 6   LANGUAGE ARTS ORANGE

Change the Sentence

[Materials]

Supplied
- *K¹² Language Arts Activity Book*, pp. WS 7–8

Also Needed
- index cards (4)

Lesson Overview

	[Offline] Change the Sentence	15 minutes
Get Ready	Complete Sentences	
Learn	Make It Bigger	
Try It	Make Two into One	

Keywords
sentence combining – to join two sentences that have similar parts into one sentence

Big Ideas

Sentence combining—teaching students to construct complex, sophisticated sentences—is an effective instructional strategy and an important element of learning how to write well.

[Offline] 15 minutes

Change the Sentence

You will work with students to complete Get Ready, Learn, and Try It activities.

Get Ready

Complete Sentences

Review complete sentences with students. A complete sentence starts with a capital letter and has an end mark. Gather the index cards.

1. Write the following on the four index cards:

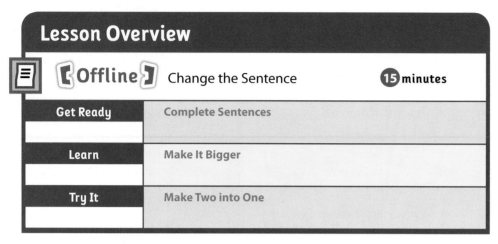

| The | children | play | . |

2. Mix the order of the cards and give them to students. Have students create a complete sentence with the cards.

3. Then ask students to point to the following:

   ▶ Which word goes at the beginning of the sentence and has a capital letter? The
   ▶ Which word is the naming part of the sentence? children or The children
   ▶ Which word is the action part of the sentence? play
   ▶ What is the end mark of the sentence? period (.)

Objectives
- Distinguish between complete and incomplete sentences.
- Recognize that a complete sentence begins with a capital letter and has an end mark.

Learn

Make It Bigger

Review that a sentence has a naming part and an action part. Turn to page WS 7 in *K¹² Language Arts Activity Book*.

1. **Say:** Listen to these sentences: *Lola likes to sing. Lola dances well.*

   ▸ How are the sentences alike? They have the same naming part, *Lola*.

2. **Say:** Listen to these sentences: *Chen runs fast. Evan runs fast.*

   ▸ How are the sentences alike? They have the same action part, *runs fast*.

3. Explain that sentences that have the same naming part or the same action part can be combined into one bigger sentence.

4. Read the rule on the Activity Book page and the first example. Point to the name *Rich* and show students that both sentences have the same naming part. Have students read the combined sentence with you: *Rich likes soccer and baseball.*

5. Complete the rest of the Guided Exercises with students.

6. Have students complete the rest of the Activity Book page. Provide support as necessary.

TIP Read the sentences aloud to help students hear how the sentences are alike. Emphasize the similar words with your voice.

Objectives
- Combine sentences that have similar elements.
- Use a variety of sentence beginnings and lengths.

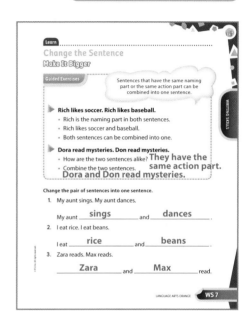

Try It

Make Two into One

Help students recognize that two sentences that have similar parts can be combined into one bigger sentence. Turn to page WS 8 in *K¹² Language Arts Activity Book*.

1. Read the directions to students. Read the sentences together.

2. Have students complete the Activity Book page. Provide support as necessary.

TIP If students have difficulty combining sentences, say the sentence part that the sentences have in common and have students complete the bigger sentence.

Objectives
- Combine sentences that have similar elements.
- Use a variety of sentence beginnings and lengths.

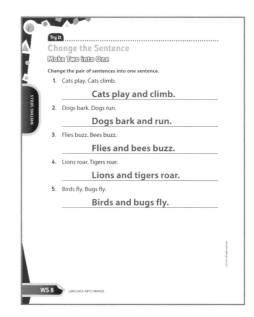

Try It
Change the Sentence
Make Two into One

Change the pair of sentences into one sentence.

1. Cats play. Cats climb.

Cats play and climb.

2. Dogs bark. Dogs run.

Dogs bark and run.

3. Flies buzz. Bees buzz.

Flies and bees buzz.

4. Lions roar. Tigers roar.

Lions and tigers roar.

5. Birds fly. Bugs fly.

Birds and bugs fly.

WS 8   LANGUAGE ARTS ORANGE

Fix the Sentences

Lesson Overview

[Offline] Fix the Sentences		**15** minutes
Get Ready	What Do You Know About Sentences?	
Learn	Revise It and Proofread It	
Try It	Revise and Proofread	

Materials

Supplied
- *K¹² Language Arts Activity Book*, pp. WS 9–10

Content Background

A complete sentence tells a complete thought or complete idea. It has two main parts: the naming part and the action part.
- ▸ The naming part of a sentence is called the subject.
- ▸ The action part of a sentence is called the predicate.

Big Idea

Writing requires rewriting or revision.

[Offline] 15 minutes

Fix the Sentences

You will work with students to complete Get Ready, Learn, and Try It activities.

Get Ready ....

What Do You Know About Sentences?
Review what students know about sentences:

- ▸ A sentence has a naming part and an action or being part.
- ▸ A sentence begins with a capital letter and has an end mark.
- ▸ Two similar sentences can be combined into one bigger sentence.

Tell students that they are going to learn how to improve their writing. Explain that writing means rewriting. All writers, including famous writers and published authors, review, revise, and rewrite their work to make it better.

Objectives
- Distinguish between complete and incomplete sentences.
- Recognize that sentences with common elements can be combined.
- Recognize that a complete sentence begins with a capital letter and has an end mark.

Learn

Revise It and Proofread It

Introduce the concept of proofreading and revising as ways to make writing better. Turn to page WS 9 in *K¹² Language Arts Activity Book*.

1. Explain the difference between proofreading for errors and revising.

    Say: When you look for errors in your writing, you are **proofreading**. Adding capital letters and end marks is an example of proofreading. When you change or rewrite something, you are **revising.** Combining similar sentences into one sentence is an example of revising.

2. Read the rule on the Activity Book page.

3. Read the example sentences. Ask students what errors they see in the sentences. The first letter is not capitalized and the period is missing.

4. Point to the proofread version of the sentences. Ask students what changes were made to proofread the sentences. The lowercase *j* was crossed out, and an uppercase *J* was added. A period was added to the end of the second sentence.

5. Point to the revised version of the sentences. Ask students what changes were made to revise the sentences. The sentences were combined into one.

6. Have students complete the rest of the Activity Book page. Provide support as necessary.

TIP Students can explain the changes needed instead of writing them. You also have the option of having students tell you the changes and your writing them on the Activity Book page.

Objectives
- Combine sentences that have similar elements.
- Use capital letters correctly.
- Punctuate correctly.
- Use a variety of sentence beginnings and lengths.
- Use correct grammar and sentence formation.

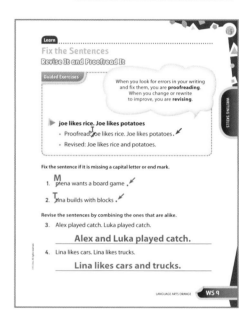

Try It

 Revise and Proofread

Help students recognize how to revise and proofread. Turn to page WS 10 in *K¹² Language Arts Activity Book*.

1. Read the directions to students. Read the sentences together.

2. Have students complete the Activity Book page. Provide support as necessary.

TIP Make sure students work to revise, not just proofread for grammatical errors. Young students who learn to revise at this stage will usually understand better the need to revise as they get older.

Objectives

- Combine sentences that have similar elements.
- Use capital letters correctly.
- Punctuate correctly.
- Use a variety of sentence beginnings and lengths.
- Use correct grammar and sentence formation.

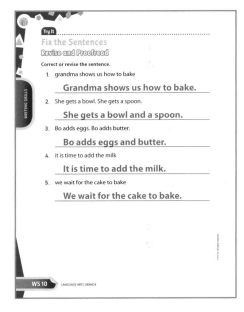

Try It

Fix the Sentences
Revise and Proofread

Correct or revise the sentence.

1. grandma shows us how to bake

   Grandma shows us how to bake.

2. She gets a bowl. She gets a spoon.

   She gets a bowl and a spoon.

3. Bo adds eggs. Bo adds butter.

   Bo adds eggs and butter.

4. it is time to add the milk

   It is time to add the milk.

5. we wait for the cake to bake

   We wait for the cake to bake.

WS 10   LANGUAGE ARTS ORANGE

Write Sentences

Lesson Overview

Offline Write Sentences	**15** minutes
Get Ready	Revise and Proofread
Write Now	Car Wash Sentences

Materials

Supplied
- *K¹² Language Arts Activity Book,* pp. WS 11–12

Offline — 15 minutes

Write Sentences

You will work with students to complete Get Ready and Write Now activities.

Get Ready

Revise and Proofread

Review with students what they have learned about sentences and editing and revising them.

▶ Complete sentences have a naming part and an action or being part.

▶ Similar sentences can be combined into one bigger sentence.

▶ One way to proofread is to add capital letters and end marks.

▶ One way to revise writing is to combine similar sentences into one sentence.

Objectives
- Distinguish between complete and incomplete sentences.
- Combine sentences that have similar elements.
- Use capital letters correctly.
- Punctuate correctly.

Write Now ••

 Car Wash Sentences

In this activity, students will practice writing complete sentences. Turn to page WS 11 in *K¹² Language Arts Activity Book*.

1. **Say:** Good writing is a series of steps. To begin writing about something, let's look at a picture and gather some details about it.

2. Look at the picture on the Activity Book page with students. Have them describe the picture and what is happening in it by answering who, what, how, when, and why questions about what they see.

3. **Say:** Now let's use those details to write three sentences that tell about the picture.

4. Remind students to revise and proofread their sentences.

5. Tell students that they should use good handwriting and leave spaces between words so that others can read what they wrote.

6. When students have completed their writing, use the rubric and the sample writing provided in the online lesson to check their work. You will be evaluating their writing for

   ▸ Purpose and Content: The writing should describe the picture. The sentences should tell about washing the car, and there should be at least two sentences.

   ▸ Structure and Organization: The sentences should be written in a mostly logical order. The word order should make sense.

   ▸ Grammar and Mechanics: At least two sentences should begin with a capital letter and end with a mark of punctuation. Most sentences should contain a complete thought.

7. Enter students' scores for each rubric category online.

8. If students scored a 1 in any category, follow the online instructions to help them edit and revise their work.

 Reward: When students' writing is Level 2 or higher on the grading rubric, add a sticker for this unit on the My Accomplishments chart.

> **Objectives**
> - Use a variety of sentence beginnings and lengths.
> - Use the correct word order in sentences.
> - Spell common, frequently used words correctly.
> - Combine sentences that have similar elements.
> - Write simple sentences.
> - Write sentences that flow.
> - Use correct grammar and sentence formation.

Statements

Unit Overview

In this unit, students will learn about the four different kinds of sentences—statements, questions, exclamations, and commands.

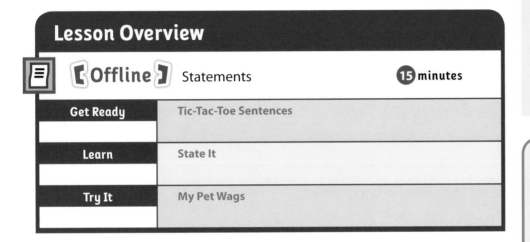

Lesson Overview

	Offline	Statements	15 minutes
Get Ready		Tic-Tac-Toe Sentences	
Learn		State It	
Try It		My Pet Wags	

Content Background

A statement or telling sentence is another name for a declarative sentence.

Big Ideas

Using different kinds of sentences helps writers and speakers express their ideas accurately.

Materials

Supplied
- *K¹² Language Arts Activity Book*, pp. WS 13–14

Also Needed
- whiteboard (optional)
- crayons

Keywords

command – a kind of sentence that gives an order or makes a request

exclamation (eks-kluh-MAY-shuhn) – a kind of sentence that shows strong feeling

question – a kind of sentence that asks something

statement – a kind of sentence that tells something

Offline **15 minutes**

Statements

You will work with students to complete Get Ready, Learn, and Try It activities.

Get Ready

Tic-Tac-Toe Sentences

Review what a complete sentence is while playing Tic-Tac-Toe.

1. Remind students that a sentence is a group of words that tell a complete thought.

2. Draw a Tic-Tac-Toe board on a sheet of paper or a whiteboard.

Objectives
- Recognize word groups that are sentences.

3. Play Tic-Tac-Toe with a student, or have two students play against each other. One player should use X, and the other player should use O.

4. Say a word group to a student. If it is a complete sentence, the student should put an X in the box.

5. Say another word group to the other player (or to yourself). If it is a complete sentence, then the other player (or you) should put an O in the box.

6. Continue taking turns until one player has a complete row of three Xs or Os. That player is the winner.

7. Begin with these examples and add others, if needed:
   ▸ I am sleeping. sentence
   ▸ The rabbit hops away. sentence
   ▸ Reaches the finish line not a sentence
   ▸ All of the bees flew into the hive. sentence
   ▸ Some boys slept in a tent. sentence

Learn

State It
Introduce what a statement is. Turn to page WS 13 in *K¹² Language Arts Activity Book*.

1. Play a game of charades.
   ▸ Pantomime brushing your teeth.
   ▸ Invite students to guess what you are doing. Tell them to use a complete sentence, such as *You are brushing your teeth.*
   ▸ Repeat with other actions.

2. Explain that some sentences tell about someone or something, such as *You are brushing your teeth.* These sentences are called **statements**. A statement begins with a capital letter and ends with a period.

3. Read the rule on the Activity Book page. Complete the Guided Exercises with students.

4. Have students complete the rest of the Activity Book page. Provide support as necessary.

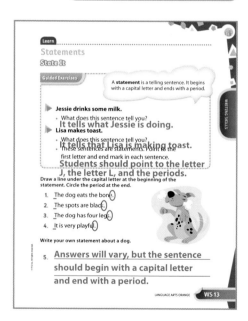

Objectives
- Identify statements.
- Recognize that a sentence begins with a capital letter.
- Recognize that a statement ends with a period.

Try It

My Pet Wags

Help students recognize statements. Turn to page WS 14 in *K¹² Language Arts Activity Book*.

1. Read the first set of directions to students. Read the sentences together. Have students complete Exercises 1–3.

2. Read the second set of directions to students. Read the sentences together. Have students complete the rest of the Activity Book page. Provide support as necessary.

Objectives

- Identify statements.
- Recognize that a sentence begins with a capital letter.
- Recognize that a statement ends with a period.

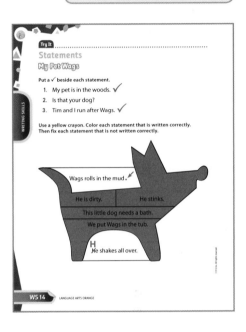

Questions

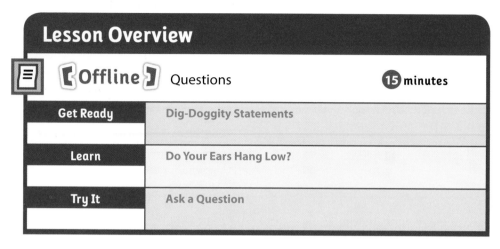

Lesson Overview

Offline Questions — **15** minutes

Get Ready	Dig-Doggity Statements
Learn	Do Your Ears Hang Low?
Try It	Ask a Question

Materials

Supplied

- *K¹² Language Arts Activity Book*, pp. WS 15–16

Keywords

question – a kind of sentence that asks something

Content Background

A question or asking sentence is another name for an interrogative sentence.

Offline — **15** minutes

Questions

You will work with students to complete Get Ready, Learn, and Try It activities.

Get Ready

Dig-Doggity Statements
Review statements.

1. Remind students that statements are telling sentences. They tell about someone or something.

2. Tell students that you are trying to think of a statement that will make a dog wag its tail. Give students this example: *Have.*

   ► Is *Have* a complete statement? No
   ► How could you make this word a complete statement? Answers will vary. Possible answer: Add words to make the sentence *I have supper for you.*

3. Ask students to suggest other statements that might make a dog wag its tail. Give them another statement to get started, such as *You are my favorite pet.*

Objectives
- Recall what a statement is.
- Identify statements.

Learn •

Do Your Ears Hang Low?

Introduce students to questions by singing the song "Do Your Ears Hang Low?" Turn to page WS 15 in *K¹² Language Arts Activity Book.*

1. Sing "Do Your Ears Hang Low?" with students. If you are not familiar with the tune to the song, you can chant the words.

> *Do your ears hang low?*
> *Do they wobble to and fro?*
> *Can you tie them in a knot?*
> *Can you tie them in a bow?*
> *Can you throw them o'er your shoulder*
> *Like a continental soldier?*
> *Do your ears hang low?*

2. **Say:** There are four kinds of sentences. One kind of sentence is a question. A question is an asking sentence.

3. Sing the song again. Help students identify the questions in the song.

4. Read the rule on the Activity Book page and complete the first Guided Exercise with students.

5. For the second Guided Exercise, cover the words *Can you.*

> ▸ Is *tie them in a knot* a question? No
> ▸ Why not? It is not a complete thought. It does not ask a question.

6. Uncover the words and complete the second Guided Exercise with students.

7. Have students complete the rest of the Activity Book page. Provide support as necessary.

Objectives
- Identify questions.
- Recognize that a sentence begins with a capital letter.
- Recognize that a question ends with a question mark.

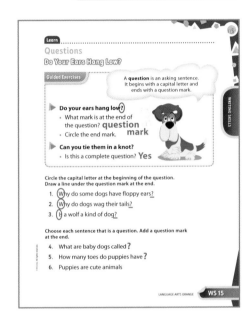

Try It

Ask a Question

Help students recognize how a question should begin and end. Turn to page WS 16 in *K¹² Language Arts Activity Book*.

1. Read the first set of directions to students. Read the sentences together. Have students complete Exercises 1–5.

2. Read the second set of directions to students. Read the sentences together. Have students complete Exercises 6–8. Provide support as necessary.

Objectives

- Identify questions.
- Recognize that a sentence begins with a capital letter.
- Recognize that a question ends with a question mark.

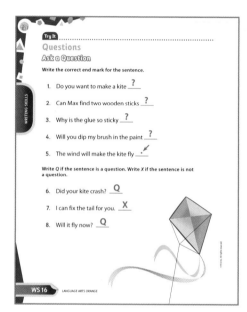

Exclamations and Commands

Lesson Overview

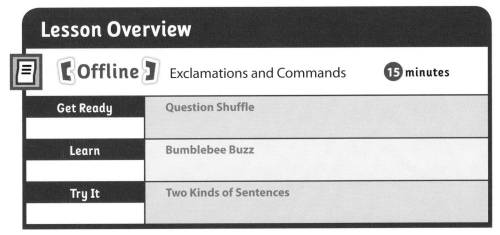

	Offline	Exclamations and Commands	15 minutes
Get Ready		Question Shuffle	
Learn		Bumblebee Buzz	
Try It		Two Kinds of Sentences	

Advance Preparation

For Question Shuffle, write the sentences on a whiteboard or large sheet of paper. If you prefer that students manipulate the sentences, write each word on a separate index card.

Content Background

An exclamation is also called an exclamatory sentence. A command is also known as an imperative sentence.

Materials

Supplied
- *K¹² Language Arts Activity Book*, pp. WS 17–18

Also Needed
- whiteboard (optional)
- index cards (optional)

Keywords

command – a kind of sentence that gives an order or makes a request

exclamation (eks-kluh-MAY-shuhn) – a kind of sentence that shows strong feeling

Offline 15 minutes

Exclamations and Commands

You will work with students to complete Get Ready, Learn, and Try It activities.

Get Ready

Question Shuffle
Play the game Question Shuffle to review statements and questions.

1. Tell students that the object of the game is to change the order of the words in a question to make it a statement.

Objectives
- Rearrange the words in a question to make a statement.
- Create statements aloud.

2. Write this example on the whiteboard or on a large sheet of paper:

   ▶ Question: Do pigs oink?
   ▶ Statement: Pigs do oink.

   Show students how you rearranged the words in the question to make a statement.

3. Read questions or write them on the whiteboard. Have students change the words around in the question to create statements. Have them say their statements aloud.

   ▶ Are we ready for lunch? We are ready for lunch.
   ▶ Is it raining outside? It is raining outside.
   ▶ Can Rosa open the jar? Rosa can open the jar.

TIP For students who need more visual support, you may wish to write the words in each question on separate index cards. Have students rearrange the words to make statements that answer the question.

Learn

Bumblebee Buzz

Introduce two other types of sentences, **exclamations** and **commands**. Turn to page WS 17 in *K¹² Language Arts Activity Book*.

1. Sing or chant the song "Baby Bumblebee."

   I'm bringing home a baby bumblebee.
   Won't my mommy be so proud of me?
   I'm bringing home a baby bumblebee.
   OUCH! It stung me!

2. Ask students how they would probably feel if a bee stung them. Invite them to say the words *It stung me!* using an expressive voice.
   Say: *It stung me!* is a kind of sentence that shows strong feelings. It is called an **exclamation**.

3. Pretend to talk to the bee.
   Say: Go away, bee.
   Explain to students that you are giving the bee an order to go away.
   Say: This kind of sentence is called a **command.**

4. Read the rules on the Activity Book page. Complete the Guided Exercises with students.

5. Have students complete the rest of the Activity Book page. Read the sentences with expression as students complete the page to help them identify the kind of sentence. Provide support as necessary.

   Bees have so many eyes! (Use an excited voice.)
   Stay away from the hive. (Use a demanding voice.)
   Look at the busy bee. (Use a demanding voice.)
   That really hurt! (Use an excited voice.)

TIP Commands are missing the part of the sentence that tells whom or what (the subject). Explain that the naming part is the word *you*, but it is not stated. For example, the command *Hop into bed* means *(You) hop into bed.*

Objectives

- Identify exclamations.
- Recognize that a sentence begins with a capital letter.
- Recognize that an exclamation ends with an exclamation mark.
- Identify commands.
- Recognize that a command ends with a period.

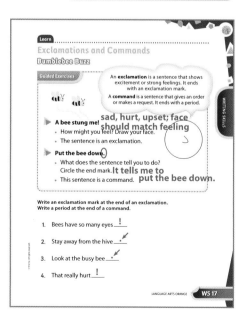

Try It

Two Kinds of Sentences

Help students recognize exclamations and commands and the end punctuation for each kind of sentence. Turn to page WS 18 in *K¹² Language Arts Activity Book*.

1. Read the first set of directions to students. Read the sentences together. Use expression in your voice so that students can more easily identify the kind of sentence. Have students complete Exercises 1–5.

2. Read the second set of directions to students. Read the word groups together. Have students complete Exercises 6–8. Provide support as necessary.

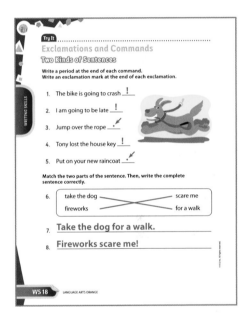

Review Kinds of Sentences

Lesson Overview

Online	Review Kinds of Sentences	15 minutes
Review	**Where's My Puppy?**	

Materials

There are no materials to gather for this lesson.

Online 15 minutes

Review Kinds of Sentences

Students will work on their own to complete review and practice activities. Help students locate the online activities and provide support as needed.

Review

Where's My Puppy?

Students will work online to review what they have learned about the four kinds of sentences: statements, questions, exclamations, and commands.

Offline Alternative

No computer access? Write or say several types of sentences: statements, questions, exclamations, and commands. Have students identify the kinds of sentences. Ask them how each sentence should end.

Objectives

- Identify statements.
- Recognize that a sentence begins with a capital letter.
- Recognize that a statement ends with a period.
- Identify questions.
- Recognize that a question ends with a question mark.
- Identify exclamations.
- Recognize that an exclamation ends with an exclamation mark.
- Identify commands.
- Recognize that a command ends with a period.

Unit Checkpoint

Lesson Overview

☰	**[Offline]** Unit Checkpoint	**15** minutes

Unit Checkpoint	Kinds of Sentences

Materials

Supplied

• *K¹² Language Arts Assessments*, pp. WS 5–8

[Offline] **15** minutes

Unit Checkpoint

You will work with students to complete the Unit Checkpoint.

Unit Checkpoint

Kinds of Sentences

Explain that students are going to show what they have learned about kinds of sentences.

1. Give students the Unit Checkpoint pages.

2. Read the directions together. Have students complete the Checkpoint on their own.

3. Use the Answer Key to score the Checkpoint, and then enter the results online.

4. Review each exercise with students. Work with students to correct any exercise that they missed.

TIP Students who answered one or more questions incorrectly should continue to practice this grammar skill. Read aloud your students' favorite books. Stop from time to time to point out different types of sentences.

 Reward: When students score 80 percent or above on the Unit Checkpoint, add a sticker for this unit on the My Accomplishments chart.

Objectives

• Identify statements.

• Recognize that a sentence begins with a capital letter.

• Recognize that a statement ends with a period.

• Identify questions.

• Recognize that a question ends with a question mark.

• Identify exclamations.

• Recognize that an exclamation ends with an exclamation mark.

• Identify commands.

• Recognize that a command ends with a period.

Name   Date

☼ Unit Checkpoint Learning Coach Instructions
Kinds of Sentences

Explain that students are going to show what they have learned about kinds of sentences.

1. Give students the Unit Checkpoint pages.

2. Read the directions together. Have students complete the Checkpoint on their own.

3. Use the Answer Key to score the Checkpoint, and then enter the results online.

4. Review each exercise with students. Work with students to correct any exercise that they missed.

Name   Date

☼ Unit Checkpoint Answer Key
Kinds of Sentences

Part 1. Kinds of Sentences
Which kind of sentence is the sentence?

1. Today is Tuesday.
   A. statement
   B. question
   C. exclamation
   D. command

2. What day comes next?
   A. statement
   B. question
   C. exclamation
   D. command

3. Put your soccer ball in the bag.
   A. statement
   B. question
   C. exclamation
   D. command

4. I can't wait to play soccer!
   A. statement
   B. question
   C. exclamation
   D. command

Name   Date

Part 2. End Marks
Choose the correct end mark for the sentence.

5. I saw a bird in the bush
   A. .
   B. ?
   C. !

6. Was it a blue bird
   A. .
   B. ?
   C. !

7. That is the biggest nest I've ever seen
   A. .
   B. ?
   C. !

8. Are there eggs in it
   A. .
   B. ?
   C. !

9. When will the babies hatch
   A. .
   B. ?
   C. !

10. Don't touch them
    A. .
    B. ?
    C. !

Name   Date

Part 3. Sentence Beginnings and Endings
Which sentence is written correctly?

11. A. That is a great idea!
    B. you are my best friend.
    C. where is the picture?
    D. Come quickly

12. A. put the box on the table.
    B. What is your answer.
    C. here is my paper.
    D. Did you drop your pencil?

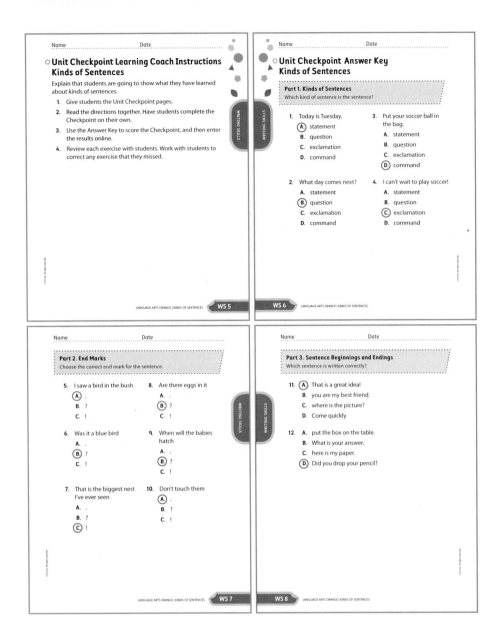

Tell Me About It

Unit Overview

In this unit, students will
- ▶ Recognize and use different types of sentences.
- ▶ Recognize correct and incorrect sentences.
- ▶ Revise sentences for punctuation, fluency, audience, and purpose.
- ▶ Write a variety of sentences with different structures.

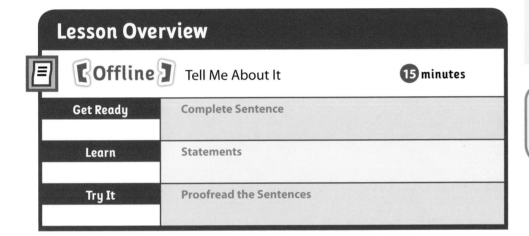

Lesson Overview

〔Offline〕 Tell Me About It		**15** minutes
Get Ready	Complete Sentence	
Learn	Statements	
Try It	Proofread the Sentences	

Content Background

A statement may be called a telling sentence or a declarative sentence.

Big Ideas

To be effective communicators, writers and speakers should recognize and use complete sentences.

〔Materials〕

Supplied
- *K¹² Language Arts Activity Book*, pp. WS 19–20

Also Needed
- whiteboard (optional)
- crayons

Keywords

statement – a kind of sentence that tells something

 **15 minutes**

Tell Me About It

You will work with students to complete Get Ready, Learn, and Try It activities.

Get Ready

Complete Sentence

Review complete sentences.

Objectives
- Identify complete sentences.

1. Review the characteristics of a complete sentence with students.

   ▸ A complete sentence has two parts: a naming part and an action part.
   ▸ A complete sentence tells a complete thought.
   ▸ A complete sentence begins with a capital letter and ends with an end mark.

2. Show students these examples of an incomplete sentence and a complete sentence on a sheet of paper or a whiteboard:

   ▸ about sentences
   ▸ We are learning about sentences.

3. Discuss the examples with students.

   ▸ Which example is a complete sentence? *We are learning about sentences.*
   ▸ Why is the other example not a complete sentence? It doesn't have a naming part; it doesn't tell a complete thought.

Learn

Statements

Introduce statements to students. Turn to page WS 19 in *K¹² Language Arts Activity Book*.

Objectives
- Use statements.

1. Explain that a **statement** is a telling sentence. It is a complete sentence that begins with a capital letter and ends with a period. When spoken, a statement sounds different from a sentence that asks something.

2. **Say:** Listen to these statements:

   ▸ I am standing on my head.
   ▸ You are upside down.

3. Have students listen to the difference between a statement and a question.

   ▸ This is a statement: Pigs roll in mud.
   ▸ This is a question: Do pigs fly?

4. Read the rule on the Activity Book page. Complete the Guided Exercises with students. Be sure they recognize that a statement is another name for a telling sentence.

5. Have students complete the rest of the Activity Book page. Provide support as necessary.

6. After students underline the statements, ask them to point to the capital letter at the beginning of each sentence and the period at the end.

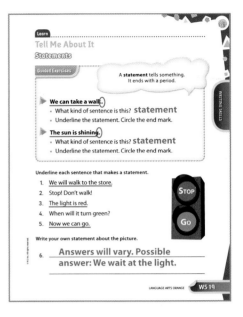

Try It

Proofread the Sentences

Help students to recognize how a statement should begin and end. Turn to page WS 20 in *K¹² Language Arts Activity Book*.

1. Read the first set of directions to students. Read the sentences together. Look at Exercise 1 together to show students how to fix the statement. Then have students complete Exercises 2 and 3.

2. Read the second set of directions to students. Have them complete Exercise 4. Provide support as necessary.

3. When students have finished, review all the answers with them.

   ▸ Make sure that students made the proper edits in the first exercises. If they did not, explain the correct answers.
   ▸ Have students explain to you the statement that they wrote. Be sure that the statement tells something and that it is a complete sentence that begins with a capital letter and ends with a period.

Objectives
- Use statements.
- Recognize that a sentence begins with a capital letter.
- Recognize that a statement ends with a period.

Ask Me About It

Lesson Overview

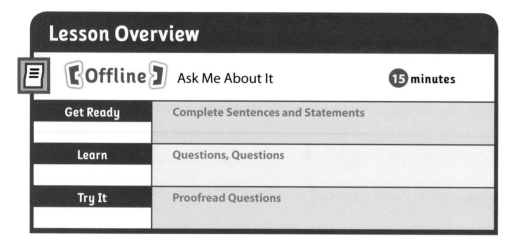

	Offline Ask Me About It	**15** minutes
Get Ready	Complete Sentences and Statements	
Learn	Questions, Questions	
Try It	Proofread Questions	

Materials

Supplied
• *K¹² Language Arts Activity Book*, pp. WS 21–22

Also Needed
• whiteboard (optional)

Keywords

question – a kind of sentence that asks something

statement – a kind of sentence that tells something

Content Background

A statement may be called a telling sentence or declarative sentence. A question may be called an asking sentence or an interrogative sentence.

Big Ideas

To express ideas in a meaningful way that others can easily understand, one needs to understand standard English grammar, usage, and mechanics.

 **Offline** **15** minutes

Ask Me about It

You will work with students to complete Get Ready, Learn, and Try It activities.

Get Ready ....

Complete Sentences and Statements

1. Review the characteristics of a complete sentence with students.

   ▸ A complete sentence has two parts: a naming part and an action part.
   ▸ A complete sentence tells a complete thought.
   ▸ A complete sentence begins with a capital letter and ends with an end mark.

Objectives
• Define a complete sentence.
• Define a statement.
• Use statements.

2. Review the characteristics of a statement or telling sentence with students.

   ▶ A statement tells something.
   ▶ A statement begins with a capital letter and ends with a period.

3. Ask students to give an example of a statement. Answers will vary. Make sure that students give a complete sentence and that it is a statement, not a question.

Learn

Questions, Questions

Introduce questions to students. Turn to page WS 21 in *K¹² Language Arts Activity Book*.

1. Explain that a **question** asks something. It is a complete sentence that begins with a capital letter and ends with a question mark.

2. **Say:** Listen to these questions.

   ▶ Does a dog meow?
   ▶ Does grass grow in the sky?

3. Ask students if the following sentences are questions or statements.

   ▶ How do you feel? question
   ▶ I am fine. statement

4. Explain that sometimes questions begin with special words. These words may start a question: *who, what, where, how, when,* and *why.*

5. Ask students to think of a question that uses one of the question words.

   Examples: Who likes apples? What color is your shirt?

6. Read the rule on the Activity Book page. Complete the Guided Exercises with students. Be sure that they recognize that sentences that ask something are called questions.

7. Have students complete the rest of the Activity Book page. Provide support as necessary.

8. Have students point out the capital letter at the beginning of each sentence and the question mark or period at the end.

Objectives
- Identify questions.
- Use questions.
- Recognize that a sentence begins with a capital letter.
- Recognize that a question ends with a question mark.

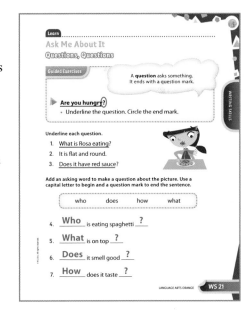

Try It

Proofread Questions

Help students recognize how a question begins and ends. Turn to page WS 22 in *K¹² Language Arts Activity Book*.

1. Read the first set of directions to students. Read the sentences together. Have students complete Exercises 1–5.

2. Read the second set of directions to students. Have them complete Exercise 6. Provide support as necessary.

3. When students have finished, review all the answers with them.

   ▸ Make sure that students made the proper edits in the first exercises.
   ▸ Have students read their edited questions aloud. Be sure students are using the proper expression for asking questions. Remind students that a question does not sound like a statement.
   ▸ Have students read you the question that they wrote. Be sure the question asks something and is a complete sentence with proper punctuation and capitalization.

Objectives
- Use questions.
- Recognize that a sentence begins with a capital letter.
- Recognize that a question ends with a question mark.

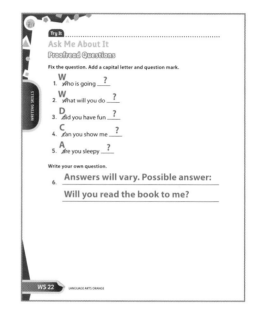

Shout About It

Lesson Overview		
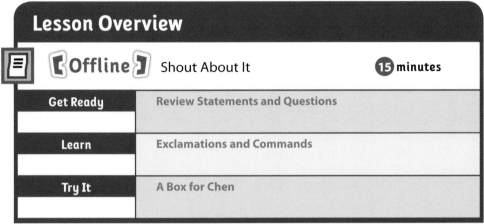 **⟦Offline⟧** Shout About It		**15** minutes
Get Ready	Review Statements and Questions	
Learn	Exclamations and Commands	
Try It	A Box for Chen	

Content Background

An exclamation is also called an exclamatory sentence. A command is also called an imperative sentence.

Big Ideas

To be effective communicators, writers and speakers should recognize and use complete sentences.

Materials

Supplied
- *K¹² Language Arts Activity Book*, pp. WS 23–24

Also Needed
- crayons

Keywords

command – a kind of sentence that gives an order or makes a request
exclamation (eks-kluh-MAY-shuhn) – a kind of sentence that shows strong feeling
question – a kind of sentence that asks something
statement – a kind of sentence that tells something

 **⟦Offline⟧** **15** minutes

Shout About It

You will work with students to complete Get Ready, Learn, and Try It activities.

Get Ready

Review Statements and Questions

1. Review the characteristics of a statement with students.
   - ▶ A statement tells something.
   - ▶ A statement begins with a capital letter and ends with a period.

2. Review the characteristics of a question with students.
   - ▶ A question asks something.
   - ▶ A question begins with a capital letter and ends with a question mark.

 Objectives
- Identify statements.
- Identify questions.

3. Ask students if the following sentences are statements or questions.

   ▶ What time is it? question
   ▶ It is almost noon. statement

Learn •

Exclamations and Commands

Introduce exclamations and commands to students. Turn to page WS 23 in *K¹² Language Arts Activity Book.*

1. Explain that an **exclamation** is a complete sentence that shows excitement and ends with an exclamation mark. A **command** is a complete sentence that tells someone to do something or asks for something. It ends with a period.

2. **Say:** Listen to these exclamations. They show excitement.

   ▶ You are wonderful!
   ▶ That puppy is so cute!

3. **Say:** Listen to these commands. The first one gives an order, and the second one makes a request.

   ▶ Go to your room.
   ▶ Please open it now.

4. Ask students to give an example of an exclamation and a command. Have them explain which end mark goes at the end of each sentence. Answers will vary, but students should recognize that an exclamation mark goes at the end of an exclamation, and a period goes at the end of a command.

5. Read the rules on the Activity Book page. Complete the Guided Exercises with students.

6. Ask students to explain the answers to the Guided Exercises.

   ▶ How do you know the first sentence is an exclamation? It shows excitement.
   ▶ How do you know the second sentence is a command? It tells someone to do something.

7. Have students complete the rest of the Activity Book page. Provide support as necessary.

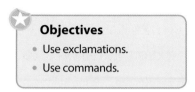 A command can also end with an exclamation point. However, just focus on commands that end with periods. In a command, the subject "you" is understood and is not written in the sentence.

Objectives
- Use exclamations.
- Use commands.

Try It

A Box for Chen

Help students recognize exclamations and commands. Remind them of the punctuation mark that belongs at the end of each kind of sentence. Turn to page WS 24 in *K¹² Language Arts Activity Book*.

1. Read the directions to students. Read the sentences together.

2. Have students complete Exercises 1–6. Provide support as necessary.

3. Check students' work and help them revise any incorrect answers.

TIP Reading aloud the two kinds of sentences in the activity will provide students with practice using appropriate oral expression.

Reward: When students have completed the page correctly, have them read the story aloud, draw a picture of what's inside Chen's box, and write an exclamation to go with the picture.

Objectives

- Use exclamations.
- Recognize that an exclamation ends with an exclamation mark.
- Recognize that a command ends with a period.

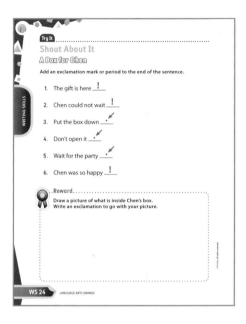

Revise Sentences

Lesson Overview

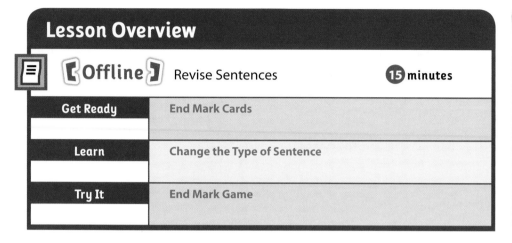	Offline	Revise Sentences	15 minutes
Get Ready		End Mark Cards	
Learn		Change the Type of Sentence	
Try It		End Mark Game	

Materials

Supplied
- *K¹² Language Arts Activity Book*, pp. WS 25–28

Also Needed
- scissors, adult
- whiteboard (optional)
- index cards (optional)

Keywords

command – a kind of sentence that gives an order or makes a request

exclamation (eks-kluh-MAY-shun) – a kind of sentence that shows strong feeling

question – a kind of sentence that asks something

sentence – a group of words that tells a complete thought

statement – a kind of sentence that tells something

Advance Preparation

Cut out the cards from page WS 25 in *K¹² Language Arts Activity Book*.

Big Ideas

To express ideas in a meaningful way that others can easily understand, one needs to understand the conventions of standard English grammar, usage, and mechanics.

 **Offline** 15 minutes

Revise Sentences

You will work with students to complete Get Ready, Learn, and Try It activities.

Get Ready ....

End Mark Cards

Review the four kinds of sentences. Gather the end mark cards.

1. Give students the end mark cards.

2. **Say:** A statement tells something. It begins with a capital letter and ends with a period.

   Have students show the end mark card with the period.

 Objectives
- Identify statements.
- Identify questions.
- Identify exclamations.
- Identify commands.

3. **Say:** A question asks something. It begins with a capital letter and ends with a question mark.

Have students show the card with the question mark.

4. **Say:** An exclamation shows excitement. It begins with a capital letter and ends with an exclamation mark.

Have students show the card with the exclamation mark.

5. **Say:** A command gives an order or makes a request. It begins with a capital letter and ends with a period.

Have students show the card with the period.

6. Ask students to identify the type of sentence and choose the correct end mark card to go with each sentence.

  ▸ I want to go. statement, period end mark card
  ▸ Do you want to go? question, question mark card
  ▸ Let's go! exclamation, exclamation mark card
  ▸ Go now. command, period card

Learn

Change the Type of Sentence

Help students understand how changing the word order changes the type of sentence. Turn to page WS 27 in *K¹² Language Arts Activity Book*.

1. Read the rule on the Activity Book page. Before students begin, have them explain what each of the four kinds of sentences does. Then complete the Guided Exercises with students.

2. Explain that word order is important in sentences. If you say "It is" you are making a statement. If you change the order of the words and say "Is it?" you are asking a question. Give students other examples, such as: "You can do it." "Can you do it?" "You are warm." "Are you warm?"

3. Tell students that to change a sentence they may need to remove or change words, particularly to form a command. For example, *Am I taking out the trash?* is a question, and *Take out the trash* is a command. Have students complete the rest of the Activity Book page. Provide support as necessary.

TIP If students have difficulty stating the purpose of each sentence, write each sentence on an index card or the whiteboard. Ask students to point to the sentence that tells something, asks something, shows excitement, or gives an order.

Objectives

- Use statements.
- Use questions.
- Use exclamations.
- Use commands.
- Use a variety of sentence beginnings and lengths.

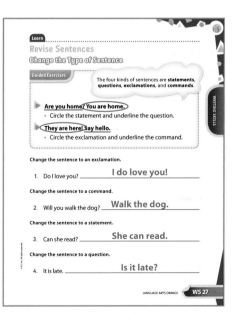

Try It

· ·

End Mark Game

Help students recognize different kinds of sentences and how they should end. Gather the end mark cards and turn to page WS 28 in *K¹² Language Arts Activity Book*.

1. Read the directions to students. Read the sentences together.

2. Give students the end mark cards.

3. Point to a sentence on the game board. Have students select the correct end mark card that goes with the sentence. Have them say the sentence, making sure that they use the proper inflection for the type of sentence.

4. Continue pointing to different sentences until students have selected the correct end mark card for each type of sentence several times in a row.

TIP Students can use the end mark cards for a new game where they make up their own sentences instead of using the game board. They can also play in teams.

Objectives

- Use statements.
- Use questions.
- Use exclamations.
- Use commands.
- Recognize that a statement ends with a period.
- Recognize that a question ends with a question mark.
- Recognize that an exclamation ends with an exclamation mark.
- Recognize that a command ends with a period.

Online Alternative

This activity is OPTIONAL. It is intended for students who want extra practice or would prefer to do online practice in place of the offline Try It. Feel free to skip this activity.

Write Different Types of Sentences

Lesson Overview

Materials

Supplied
- *K¹² Language Arts Activity Book*, pp. WS 29–30

Also Needed
- crayons

[Offline]	Write Different Types of Sentences	⏱ minutes
Get Ready	Four Kinds of Sentences	
Write Now	Write About a Picture	

Big Ideas

Sensory experiences such as visuals, sounds, and other stimuli can help inspire creative thought and written ideas.

[Offline] ⏱ minutes

Write Different Types of Sentences

You will work with students to complete Get Ready and Write Now activities.

Get Ready

Four Kinds of Sentences

Review the four kinds of sentences with students.

- ▶ A statement tells something. It begins with a capital letter and ends with a period. Ask students to say a statement using the correct oral expression.
- ▶ A question asks something. It begins with a capital letter and ends with a question mark. Ask students to ask you a question using the correct oral expression.
- ▶ An exclamation shows excitement. It begins with a capital letter and ends with an exclamation mark. Ask students to give you an exclamation using the correct oral expression.
- ▶ A command gives an order or makes a request. It begins with a capital letter and ends with a period. Ask students to give you an command using the correct oral expression.

Objectives
- Define a statement.
- Define a question.
- Define an exclamation.
- Define a command.
- Use statements.
- Use questions.
- Use exclamations.
- Use commands.

Write Now

 Write About a Picture

Students will practice writing different types of sentences. Turn to pages WS 29–30 in *K*[12] *Language Arts Activity Book*.

1. **Say:** Different kinds of sentences have different purposes. Sentences can make a statement, ask a question, show excitement, or give a command.

2. Look at the picture on the Activity Book page with students. Have them describe the picture using different kinds of sentences.

3. **Say:** Now let's write different types of sentences to describe the picture.

4. Explain that the sentences can be any length. Remind students that all sentences begin with a capital letter but may end with different end marks.

5. Tell students that they should use good handwriting and leave spaces between words so that others can read what they wrote.

6. Have students read their finished sentences to you. Review the sentences together to see if there are four different kinds and that they are written correctly. Have students edit to make corrections.

7. Look for ways to revise the sentences so that they read more fluently. Make sure that the words are written in a logical order. Work with students so that all of the sentences are written correctly.

8. Have students read their sentences aloud. Encourage students to use expression when reading to help distinguish among the four kinds of sentences. For example, a command will sound different from an asking sentence. Model the correct expression if students do not read with the appropriate expression.

9. When students have completed their writing, use the rubric and the sample writing provided in the online lesson to check their work. You will be evaluating their writing for

   ▶ Purpose and Content: The sentences should be about the picture, and most of the sentences should describe well what is happening in the picture.

   ▶ Structure and Organization: There should be examples of most of the sentence types, but one type may have been left out.

   ▶ Grammar and Mechanics: Most sentences should begin with a capital letter and end with the appropriate punctuation.

10. Use the materials and instructions in the online lesson to evaluate students' writing and enter results using the assessment tool.

 Reward: When students complete the activity, allow them to color in the space provided. When students' writing is Level 2 or higher on the grading rubric, add a sticker for this unit on the My Accomplishments chart.

 Objectives

- Use declarative, interrogative, exclamatory, and imperative sentences.
- Make revisions based on audience and purpose.
- Use a variety of sentence structures.
- Use a variety of sentence beginnings and lengths.
- Use the correct word order in sentences.
- Revise by adding or deleting text.
- Revise for logical order.
- Revise for sentence fluency.

What Is a Noun?

Unit Overview

In this unit, students will learn about
- Different kinds of nouns
- Capitalization of proper nouns

[Materials]

Supplied
- *K¹² Language Arts Activity Book*, pp. WS 31–32

Also Needed
- pencils, coloring

Keywords

noun – a word that names a person, place, thing, or idea

Lesson Overview

▤	**[Offline]** What Is a Noun?	**15** minutes
Get Ready	Sentences to Roar About	
Learn	Jungle of Nouns	
Try It	Noun Safari	

Content Background

Nouns are words that name people, places, or things. They are essential elements in most sentences. They form the *who* or *what* (subject) of the sentence.

Big Ideas

A noun is a basic part of speech. Understanding nouns gives students a basic vocabulary for building sentences and understanding how language works.

What Is a Noun?

You will work with students to complete Get Ready, Learn, and Try It activities.

Get Ready •••

Sentences to Roar About

Review what a complete sentence is.

> **Objectives**
> • Recognize word groups that are sentences.

1. Remind students that a **sentence** expresses a complete thought. A sentence tells who did what.

2. Have students pretend that they are in a jungle, surrounded by wild animals.

3. Ask students to roar like a lion for each group of words that is a complete sentence.

   ▸ *Tim and Sue go to the jungle.* roar
   ▸ *The crocodile* do not roar
   ▸ *A big lion roars.* roar
   ▸ *The lion hides in a cave.* roar

4. Repeat the first sentence. Explain that the sentence has two words that name people (*Tim, Sue*) and a word that names a place (*jungle*).

Learn •••

Jungle of Nouns

Introduce nouns to students. Turn to page WS 31 in *K¹² Language Arts Activity Book.*

> **Objectives**
> • Identify nouns.

1. Read the rule on the Activity Book page. Explain that words that name people, places, and things are called **nouns**. Nouns tell whom or what.

2. Read the first example and the first question on the page. Help students locate and underline the noun.
   Say: In the sentence, *Billy* names a person. It is a noun. Words such as *man, grandmother, Doctor Davis, pilot,* and *Rosa* are also nouns that name people.

3. Read the second example. Have students underline the noun that names a place.

4. Cover the word *cave* with your finger. Read the sentence several more times, each time replacing *cave* with another word that name a place, such as *lake, Jungle Store,* or *campground.*
   Say: You can replace a noun that names a place with another noun that also names a place.

5. Read the third example. Help students locate and underline the noun.
   Say: In the sentence, the word *lion* names a thing. *Lion* is a noun.

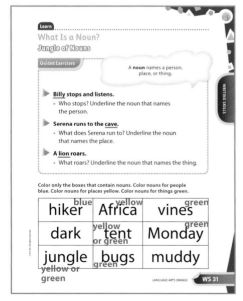

6. Have students name other things that might be in a jungle, such as *trees, monkey, pond, African elephant,* and *flowers.*

7. Have students complete the rest of the Activity Book page. Provide support as necessary. **Note:** Some boxes do not contain nouns, so they will not be colored.

TIP A word that is used as a noun in one instance may be used as another part of speech somewhere else. For example, *bark* may be used to describe the covering on a tree (noun) or to make a noise like a dog (verb).

Try It

Noun Safari

Have students complete page WS 32 in *K¹² Language Arts Activity Book* for more practice identifying nouns.

1. Read the directions to students. Read the sentences together.

2. Have students complete Exercises 1–6. Provide support as necessary.

 Reward: When students complete the Try It, allow them to color in the space provided.

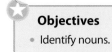

Objectives

• Identify nouns.

Common and Proper Nouns

Lesson Overview

Materials

Supplied
- *K¹² Language Arts Activity Book*, pp. WS 33–34

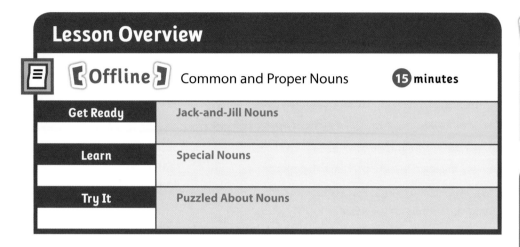

Offline	Common and Proper Nouns	15 minutes
Get Ready	Jack-and-Jill Nouns	
Learn	Special Nouns	
Try It	Puzzled About Nouns	

Keywords

collective noun – a word that means a group of things but is usually singular

common noun – a word that names any person, place, thing, or idea

noun – a word that names a person, place, thing, or idea

proper noun – the name of a particular person, place, thing, or idea; proper nouns begin with a capital letter

Content Background

▶ There are two basic kinds of nouns: common nouns and proper nouns. A common noun names any person, place, or thing. A proper noun names a specific person, place, or thing. A proper noun is always capitalized.

▶ A special kind of common noun is a collective noun. A collective noun names a group, such as *team*, *class*, or *group*.

[Offline] 15 minutes

Common and Proper Nouns

You will work with students to complete Get Ready, Learn, and Try It activities.

Get Ready

Jack-and-Jill Nouns

Review nouns with the rhyme "Jack and Jill went up a hill," which will be familiar to many students.

Objectives
- Identify nouns.

1. Remind students that people have names. Places you visit and things you use have names, too. Words that name people, places, or things are naming words, or **nouns**.

2. Have students listen to this rhyme.

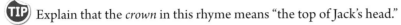

> *Jack and Jill went up a hill,*
> *To fetch a pail of water;*
> *Jack fell down and broke his crown,*
> *And Jill came tumbling after.*

▸ Which nouns in the rhyme name people? Jack, Jill
▸ Which noun names a place? hill
▸ Which nouns name things? pail, water, crown

3. Explain that students will learn about some special nouns for people, places, and things.

TIP Explain that the *crown* in this rhyme means "the top of Jack's head."

Learn

Special Nouns

Introduce proper nouns. Turn to page WS 33 in *K¹² Language Arts Activity Book*.

1. Read this rhyme that uses common nouns.

> *A boy and a girl went up a hill,*
> *To fetch a pail of water;*
> *The boy fell down and broke his crown,*
> *And the girl came tumbling after.*

2. Tell students that *boy* and *girl* could name any two people. Nouns that name any person, place, or thing are called **common nouns**.

3. Give students some examples of common nouns, such as *hill, pail, day, son, month,* or *pet*.

▸ Can you think of other examples of common nouns? Answers will vary.
▸ What are the real, or special, names for the boy and girl in the rhyme? Jack, Jill

4. Explain that nouns that name specific people, places, or things are called **proper nouns**. A proper noun begins with a capital letter.

5. Give students some examples of proper nouns for various categories, such as man, *Mr. Robinson*; boy, *Dylan*; lake, *Lake Michigan*; city, *Los Angeles*; country, *Argentina*; day, *Tuesday*; or month, *August*.

▸ Can you think of other examples of proper nouns for man? for boy? for lake? for city? for country? for day? for month? Answers will vary.

6. Read the rule and examples on the Activity Book page. Complete the Guided Exercises with students.

7. Have students complete the rest of the Activity Book page. Provide support as necessary.

TIP Explain that some nouns are called collective nouns. They name a group of people or things, such as *team, group, class, crowd, flock,* or *herd*. Have students choose a collective noun and use it in a sentence, such as *I saw a flock of sheep at the farm.*

Objectives

- Identify nouns.
- Identify and use proper and common nouns.
- Use a capital letter to begin a proper noun.
- Use collective nouns.

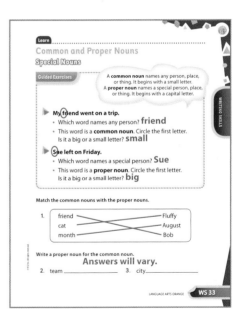

Try It

Puzzled About Nouns

Help students recognize common and proper nouns. Turn to page WS 34 in *K¹² Language Arts Activity Book.*

1. Read the first set of directions to students. Read the words together.

2. Have students complete Exercise 1.

3. Read the second set of directions to students. Read the sentences together.

4. Have students complete Exercises 2–5. Provide support as necessary.

5. Read the third set of directions to students. Have students complete Exercise 6. Provide support as necessary.

TIP Many proper nouns have more than one word in their name, such as *Oak Street, Mullen Park,* or *Brad Jones.* Make sure students circle the entire proper noun in the activities.

Objectives

- Identify nouns.
- Identify and use proper and common nouns.
- Use a capital letter to begin a proper noun.
- Use collective nouns.

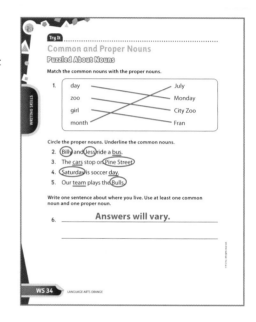

More Nouns

Lesson Overview

Online	More Nouns	15 minutes
Review	Noun Bingo	

Materials

There are no materials to gather for this lesson.

Online 15 minutes

More Nouns

Students will work on their own to complete review and practice activities. Help students locate the online activities and provide support as needed.

Review

Noun Bingo

Students will work online to review what they have learned about common and proper nouns. They will match common nouns with proper nouns that name specific people, places, and things, such as *dentist* and *Dr. Tooth* or *state* and *Texas*.

Objectives
- Identify and use proper and common nouns.

Offline Alternative

No computer access? Write or say several common nouns such as *street*, *park*, *boy*, and *store*. Have students say a proper noun that corresponds to the common nouns you provided (for instance, *Meadow Lane*, *Central Park*, *Brian*, and *Sabrina's Pretzels*).

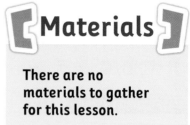

Review Nouns

Lesson Overview

🖥️ **[Online]**	Review Nouns	15 minutes
Review	Mr. McGee's Pet Shop	

[Materials]

There are no materials to gather for this lesson.

[Online] 🕐 minutes

Review Nouns

Students will work on their own to complete review and practice activities. Help students locate the online activities and provide support as needed.

Review

Mr. McGee's Pet Shop

Students will practice identifying nouns to review for the Unit Checkpoint.

Objectives
- Identify nouns.
- Identify and use proper and common nouns.
- Use a capital letter to begin a proper noun.

Offline Alternative

No computer access? Review nouns by writing or saying different kinds of words. Have students identify the common nouns and the proper nouns. You might also give students a common noun and have them give you a proper noun that would go along with it (for instance, *state/Virginia, country/United States, mountain/Mount Everest, river/ Charles River, doctor/Dr. Reid, kitten/Fluffy.*)

Unit Checkpoint

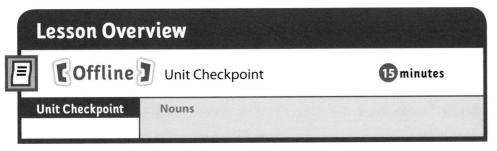

Lesson Overview

	Offline Unit Checkpoint	**15** minutes
Unit Checkpoint	Nouns	

Materials

Supplied

• *K¹² Language Arts Assessments*, pp. WS 9–12

Offline **15** minutes

Unit Checkpoint

You will work with students to complete the Unit Checkpoint.

Unit Checkpoint •

Nouns

Explain that students are going to show what they have learned about nouns.

1. Give students the Unit Checkpoint pages.

2. Read the directions together. Have students complete the Checkpoint on their own.

3. Use the Answer Key to score the Checkpoint, and then enter the results online.

4. Review each exercise with students. Work with students to correct any exercise that they missed.

 Students who answered one or more questions incorrectly should continue to practice this grammar skill. Read aloud students' favorite books. Stop from time to time to point out common and proper nouns.

Objectives
• Identify nouns.
• Identify and use proper and common nouns.
• Use a capital letter to begin a proper noun.

Reward: When students score 80 percent or above on the Unit Checkpoint, add a sticker for this unit on the My Accomplishments chart.

Name _____ Date _____

Unit Checkpoint Learning Coach Instructions
Nouns

Explain that students are going to show what they have learned about nouns.

1. Give students the Unit Checkpoint pages.
2. Read the directions together. Have students complete the Checkpoint on their own.
3. Use the Answer Key to score the Checkpoint, and then enter the results online.
4. Review each exercise with students. Work with students to correct any exercise that they missed.

Name _____ Date _____

Unit Checkpoint Answer Key
Nouns

Part 1. Person, Place, or Thing
Write each noun from the word bank in the correct place on the chart.

| farmer | bike | ocean |
| shoe | Lake Oz | nurse |

Person	Place	Thing
1. farmer	3. ocean	5. bike
2. nurse	4. Lake Oz	6. shoe

Part 2. Nouns
Which word or words in the sentence is a noun?

7. King Kong is scary and huge.
   A. King Kong
   B. scary
   C. huge

8. Go and stand by the fence.
   A. Go
   B. stand
   C. fence

Name _____ Date _____

Part 3. Capital Letters
Which sentence uses capital letters correctly?

9. A. Don swims in bear creek.
   B. Don swims in Bear Creek.
   C. don swims in Bear creek.

10. A. My friend went to Alaska last year.
    B. My friend went to alaska last year.
    C. My friend went to Alaska last Year.

11. A. Our Tulips bloom in March.
    B. Our Tulips Bloom in March.
    C. Our tulips bloom in March.

Name _____ Date _____

Part 4. Common and Proper Nouns
Choose the answer.

12. Which words are common nouns in this sentence?
    We sat by the river and saw Lake Pearl through the trees.
    A. river, Lake, trees
    B. river, saw, trees
    C. river, trees

13. Which words are proper nouns in this sentence?
    Jen picked up the paper at the corner of Main Street.
    A. Jen, Main Street
    B. paper, corner, street
    C. Jen, paper, Main Street

Step-by-Step

Unit Overview

In this unit, students will
- ▶ Recognize that a process is a series of steps.
- ▶ Identify each step or detail required to complete a process.
- ▶ Learn that each step needs to be completed in a specific order.
- ▶ Write a complete set of steps.

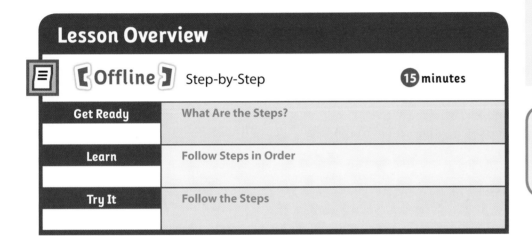

Lesson Overview

Offline Step-by-Step		**15** minutes
Get Ready	What Are the Steps?	
Learn	Follow Steps in Order	
Try It	Follow the Steps	

Advance Preparation

To prepare for the Get Ready, hide the Activity Book under a couch cushion or some other place students can reach. For the Try It, cut a piece of construction paper into a 5-inch square.

Content Background

A set of written steps is also known as a how-to piece of writing. Think of a process of steps as a recipe or set of instructions for learning how to do something.

Big Ideas

Writing is the communication of ideas in a structured, orderly form.

 **15** minutes

Step-by-Step

You will work with students to complete Get Ready, Learn, and Try It activities.

Get Ready

What Are the Steps?

Introduce the idea that we follow steps when we do something. Steps must be followed in a particular order.

1. Tell students that they need to get ready for the lesson. They need to follow these instructions in order to start working. Read the following instructions to students. You may need to alter the instructions depending on where you hid the Activity Book, as noted by the text in brackets.

   ▸ Stand up.
   ▸ Walk to the couch [or to the place you hid the Activity Book].
   ▸ Lift the seat cushion [or perform some other action to reveal the Activity Book].
   ▸ Get the Activity Book.
   ▸ Come back to your seat.

2. When students complete the steps, discuss the meaning of the word *process*. **Say:** You just completed a process. You followed the steps and found the hidden object.

3. Ask students to think about the steps they follow during the day to complete a K¹² lesson. Have students identify the steps in order and explain why they follow this order.

 Objectives
- Identify a process as a series of steps.
- Follow steps in a process.

Learn

Follow Steps in Order

Explore the concept of steps with students. Turn to page WS 35 in *K¹² Language Arts Activity Book*.

1. Tell students that a process is a series of **steps**. The steps have to be followed in order to complete a task or reach a goal. For example, when you wash your hair, you wet it, rub in the shampoo, rinse your hair, and dry it. You cannot rinse out the shampoo or dry your hair before doing the first two steps.

 Objectives
- Organize ideas through sequencing.
- Use transitions to signal order.
- Follow steps in a process.

2. Read the following steps to students. Have students put the steps in the correct order. Ask them to add the words *first*, *next*, and *last* to the steps to make the order clearer.

> ► Dry the clothes.
> ► Wash the clothes.
> ► Put the clothes away.
> First, wash the clothes. Next, dry the clothes. Last, put them away.

3. Ask students to explain what would happen if the steps were followed in a different order. If they are having difficulty, explain that the clothes cannot be dried before they are washed.

4. Read the rule on the Activity Book page. Complete the Guided Exercises with students.

5. Have students complete the rest of the Activity Book page. Provide support as necessary.

6. Keep the Activity Book page in a safe place so students can refer to it later.

TIP Cooking, baking, and following a recipe are great ways to help students learn about steps. Explain that the steps are easy to follow, but they must be done in order.

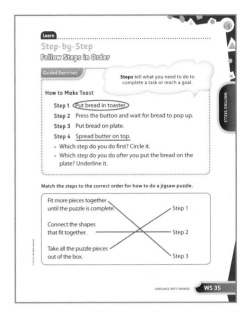

Try It

Follow the Steps

Help students recognize how to put steps in order. Gather the 5-inch square piece of construction paper and turn to page WS 36 in *K¹² Language Arts Activity Book*.

1. Read the directions to students. Read the steps together.

2. Have students complete Steps 1–5. Provide support as necessary.

3. When students are have finished, review the process they went through.

> ► Make sure that students followed each step in order. If they did not, explain the correct steps to them.
> ► Have students explain to you the process they followed to complete their origami house. Check that they have organized their ideas in the correct sequence and that they use transitional words such as *first*, *next*, and *last* to signal order.

4. Keep the Activity Book page in a safe place so students can refer to it later.

Objectives
- Organize ideas through sequencing.
- Follow steps in a process.

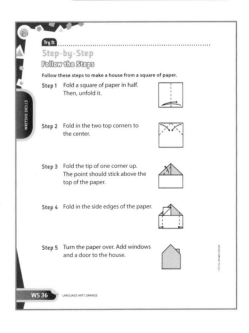

Online Alternative

This activity is OPTIONAL. It is intended for students who want extra practice or who would prefer to do online practice in place of the offline Try It. Feel free to skip this activity.

Details Count

Lesson Overview

[Offline] Details Count   **15** minutes

Get Ready	Review What Steps Are
Learn	Use Details
Try It	Include All the Details

Materials

Supplied
- *K¹² Language Arts Activity Book*, pp. WS 37–38

Also Needed
- whiteboard (optional)

Keywords

detail – a fact or description that gives more information about a topic

---

[Offline] **15** minutes

Details Count
You will work with students to complete Get Ready, Learn, and Try It activities.

Get Ready

Review What Steps Are
Review that steps tell how to do something.

1. Remind students that a process is a series of steps.
   Say: Steps tell what to do to complete a task, follow directions, or reach a goal. Steps are always followed in order.

2. Give students an example of a series of steps for performing a task, such as making hot cocoa.

   ▸ First, put cocoa powder into a cup.
   ▸ Next, add warm milk or water and stir.
   ▸ Last, float marshmallows on the top.

3. Remind students that transition words such as *first*, *next*, and *last* can be used in place of numbers to define the steps in a process. If necessary, go over the steps for making hot cocoa again.

   ▸ What transition words were in the steps for making hot cocoa?
   first, next, last

Objectives
- Organize ideas through sequencing.
- Use transitions to signal order.
- Define process.
- Identify steps in a process.

4. Ask students about some process they are familiar with. You can use a different process than making lemonade if students are not familiar with those steps.

▸ How would you make lemonade? Give as many steps as you can think of and use transition words. Answers will vary, but students should use transition words and put the process in the correct sequence. Possible answer: First, squeeze lemons into a glass. Next, add water and sugar. Last, stir and enjoy.

Learn

Use Details

Introduce details. Turn to page WS 37 in *K¹² Language Arts Activity Book.*

1. Define **details** for students.
Say: Details are additional pieces of information that help a reader understand a piece of writing better.

2. Explain that when we tell about a person, a place, an idea, or an event, we give details so that people will understand what we are telling about. Show students the following examples on a whiteboard or piece of paper:

▸ The dog sat on the steps.
▸ The small, white dog with the pointed ears sat on the steps.

3. Have students read the sentences aloud.
▸ Which sentence gives more information? the second sentence

4. **Say:** Details create a picture. If there are not enough details, we can't understand or see what the writer is telling about.

5. **Say:** Details are also needed in writing about a process. Without enough details, the steps will be unclear, confusing, or hard to follow.

6. Write the following two sets of steps on a whiteboard or piece of paper:

▸ Cut out the shape. Glue it down.
▸ Cut a heart out of red paper. Glue it in the center of a doily.

7. Have students read each set of steps.

▸ Which set of steps has enough details, and which needs more?
The first set needs more details. The second one has enough.

8. Read the following steps to students and ask what detail is missing:

How to Make a Turkey Sandwich
First, place a slice of bread on a plate.
Next, put turkey on the bread.
Then, add lettuce and tomato.
Last, eat your sandwich.

▸ What detail or step is missing? The top slice of bread is missing from the sandwich.

> **Objectives**
> • Identify missing steps in a process.
> • Add details to describe the steps in a process.
> • Follow the directions in a process.

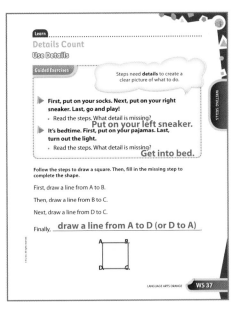

9. Read the rule on the Activity Book page. Complete the Guided Exercises with students.

10. Have students complete the rest of the Activity Book page. Provide support as necessary.

11. Keep the Activity Book page in a safe place so that students can review it later.

(TIP) Have students practice following directions by drawing shapes other than a square. You can have students create a triangle or a rectangle by following similar steps.

Try It

Include All the Details

Remind students that complete processes include many details, or steps. Missing details or steps make it difficult for a reader to complete a process. Turn to page WS 38 in *K¹² Language Arts Activity Book*.

1. Read the directions together.

2. Have students write the steps for planting a seed. Provide support as necessary.

3. When students have finished, review their answers with them.

4. Keep the Activity Book page in a safe place so that students can review it later.

Objectives
- Organize ideas through sequencing.
- Write a logical series of events.
- Identify missing steps in a process.
- Write steps in a process.
- Add details to describe the steps in a process.

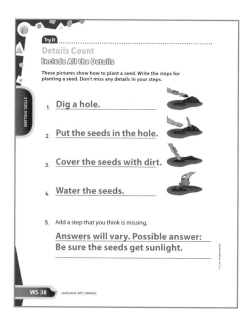

Try It

Details Count

Include All the Details

These pictures show how to plant a seed. Write the steps for planting a seed. Don't miss any details in your steps.

1. Dig a hole.

2. Put the seeds in the hole.

3. Cover the seeds with dirt.

4. Water the seeds.

5. Add a step that you think is missing.

Answers will vary. Possible answer: Be sure the seeds get sunlight.

WS 38   LANGUAGE ARTS ORANGE

Follow Steps

Lesson Overview

 Offline Follow Steps ⏱ **15** minutes

Get Ready	More About Steps
Learn	Fix the Order
Try It	Think of a Process

Materials

Supplied
- *K¹² Language Arts Activity Book*, pp. WS 39–40

Keywords

order words – words that connect ideas, a series of steps, or create a sequence, such as *first, next, later, finally*

 **Offline** ⏱ **15** minutes

Follow Steps

You will work with students to complete Get Ready, Learn, and Try It activities.

Get Ready

More About Steps

Review that a process is a series of steps. Each step tells how to do something, and each step is important to completing the process.

Objectives
- Define process.

1. Remind students that steps can help us do complicated tasks. Ask students to think about something that requires a process or series of steps, such as getting ready for bed.

   ▸ What are the steps to get ready for bed? Answers will vary. Possible answer: I brush my teeth, clean my face, get in my pajamas, say good night.

2. Remind students that in order to get ready for bed, they think of the steps, making sure they include all of the details. They also think of the order of the steps.

Learn

Fix the Order

Introduce the concept of steps in order to students. Turn to page WS 39 in *K¹² Language Arts Activity Book.*

1. Explain that steps are written in a logical **order** or an order that makes sense. Each step must be followed in the order in which it is written. Steps cannot be skipped.

2. **Say:** Steps must be followed in order when you are creating or building something. The order the steps are written in tells you what order to do the steps in. Imagine you were building a house.

   ▸ What would happen if you built the roof before the house or the upstairs before the downstairs? The house would collapse.
   ▸ What would hold the roof up? There would be nothing to hold up the roof.
   ▸ What would happen if you did the last step before the first step? You couldn't do the last step if you didn't do the other steps.
   ▸ What would happen if you tried to put the roof of a car and the tires on before building the body of the car itself? There would be no place to attach the roof and tires.

3. Read the rule on the Activity Book page. Complete the Guided Exercises with students.

4. Have students complete the rest of the Activity Book page. Provide support as necessary.

5. Keep the Activity Book page in a safe place so that students can review it later.

TIP Have students perform simple tasks but give the steps in the wrong order or leave a step out. Encourage students to explain what is wrong with the steps.

Objectives

- Organize ideas through sequencing.
- Identify missing steps in a process.
- Write steps in a process.

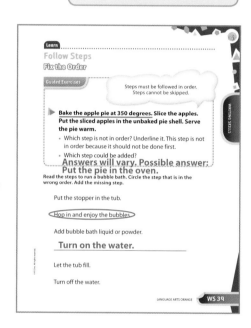

Try It

Think of a Process

Help students think of processes that require steps that must be followed in order. Turn to page WS 40 in *K¹² Language Arts Activity Book*.

1. Read the directions to students.

2. Remind students that when they brainstorm, there are no wrong answers. Students should write down all their ideas.

3. Help students select a process they would like to write directions for. Review the topics with them. Ask students if they know the steps needed to do the process they wrote down.

4. Have students circle the process or topic they would like to write about.

5. Keep the Activity Book page in a safe place so that students can refer to it later when they write about their topic.

Objectives

- Brainstorm and develop possible topics.
- Choose a topic.

Organize Ideas

Lesson Overview

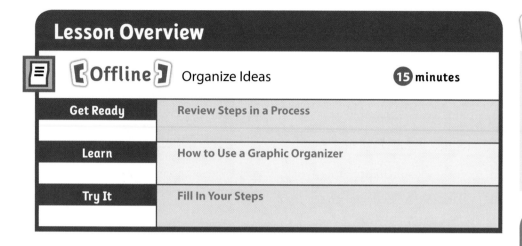

Offline	Organize Ideas	**15** minutes
Get Ready	Review Steps in a Process	
Learn	How to Use a Graphic Organizer	
Try It	Fill In Your Steps	

[Materials]

Supplied
- *K¹² Language Arts Activity Book*, pp. WS 36, 40–44

Also Needed
- crayons

Keywords

graphic organizer – a visual device, such as a diagram or chart, that helps a writer plan a piece of writing

Advance Preparation

Gather page WS 40 in *K¹² Language Arts Activity Book* (Think of a Process), which students used to brainstorm topics, and page WS 36 (Follow the Steps), which they used to create an origami house.

Big Ideas

- Writers use various methods to plan, and novices should use what works for them: freewriting, listing, graphic organizers, or other methods.
- Writing requires thought and planning.

Organize Ideas

You will work with students to complete Get Ready, Learn, and Try It activities.

Get Ready ·

Review Steps in a Process

Review the idea that steps tell how to do something. Gather page WS 36 (Follow the Steps), and turn to page WS 41 in *K¹² Language Arts Activity Book*.

Objectives
- Recognize steps in a process.

1. Explain that we organize ideas by using steps.

2. Show students the Activity Book page instructions they previously used to create an origami house.

   ▸ How did you know what order to do the steps in? The steps were numbered. The steps were in the right order.

   ▸ What is another way you can show someone what order to do steps in? Answers will vary. Possible answer: Words such as *first*, *next*, and *last* keep ideas in order. You can also use arrows.

3. Have students look at the illustration of a robot on Activity Book page WS 41.

   ▸ What are some steps that could have been followed to draw this robot? Answers will vary. Possible answer: Draw a circle for the head. Draw a triangle on top of the circle. Draw the body. Draw rectangles for the arms and legs.

4. Keep both Activity Book pages in a safe place so that students can refer to them later.

5. Tell students that they will learn how to organize steps in preparation for writing their own steps.

Learn

How to Use a Graphic Organizer

Introduce graphic organizers to students. Gather page WS 41 (Review Steps in a Process), and turn to page WS 43 in *K¹² Language Arts Activity Book*.

1. Explain that there are many ways to organize ideas. One way is to make a list of steps. Another way is to use a **graphic organizer** to show the relationship among ideas. In a sequence or process, the graphic organizer shows ideas in order.

2. **Say:** You will be using a graphic organizer that has boxes and arrows. The boxes show the steps. The arrows show how they are connected.

   ▸ One step is written in each box.
   ▸ The steps are written in the correct order.
   ▸ The first step is written in the first box, the second step is written in the second box, and so on.

Objectives

- Organize ideas through sequencing.
- Choose words that convey a clear picture.
- Use an appropriate organizational pattern in writing.
- Write a how-to (directions to complete a task).

3. Read the rule on the Activity Book page.

4. Read the instructions together and have students complete the Activity Book page. Provide support as necessary.

Try It

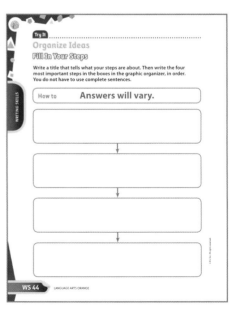

Fill In Your Steps

Help students fill in a graphic organizer for the process they chose to write about. Gather page WS 40 (Think of a Process), and turn to page WS 44 in *K¹² Language Arts Activity Book.*

1. Read the directions to students.

2. Have students complete the graphic organizer. Provide support as necessary.

3. When students have finished, check their work. Students do not need to use complete sentences or include every detail when filling out a graphic organizer, but they should include the most important steps in the process.

TIP Graphic organizers organize information. There are many different kinds of graphic organizers. You can create a graphic organizer for students on almost any topic, including chores, activities, or daily lessons.

Objectives

- Organize ideas through sequencing.
- Choose words that convey a clear picture.
- Write a logical series of events.
- Use an appropriate organizational pattern in writing.
- Write a how-to (directions to complete a task).

Write Steps Using a Graphic Organizer

Lesson Overview

[Offline]	Write Steps Using a Graphic Organizer	**15** minutes
Get Ready	Review Steps in a Process	
Write Now	Write the Steps	

Supplied
- *K¹² Language Arts Activity Book,* pp. WS 36, 40–45

Also Needed
- crayons

Advance Preparation

Gather pages WS 36 and 40–44 in *K¹² Language Arts Activity Book,* which students previously completed.

[Offline] **30** minutes

Write Steps Using a Graphic Organizer
You will work with students to complete Get Ready and Write Now activities.

Get Ready

Review Steps in a Process
Review how to write about a process. Gather pages WS 36, 40, and 41 in *K¹² Language Arts Activity Book.*

1. Spread out the Activity Book pages and give students an opportunity to look at them.

2. Discuss with students what makes a how-to writing easy to follow.

   ▶ What are some of the things you need to remember to do if you are writing a how-to? put steps in the right order; include all steps; include details; use words like *first, next,* and *last* to show order

3. Have students show examples of putting steps in the right order and including necessary steps, details, and transition words in the Activity Book pages.

Objectives
- Recognize steps in a process.

Write Now

Write the Steps

Help students write steps using the ideas in a graphic organizer. Gather page WS 44 (Fill In Your Steps), and turn to page WS 45 in *K¹² Language Arts Activity Book*.

1. Explain that students will use the steps in their graphic organizer to write about a process.

2. Remind students to use transition words such as *first*, *next*, and *last*.

3. Have students write their four steps as complete sentences on a sheet of paper so they can revise their work and transfer a clean copy to the Activity Book page.

4. Follow or have someone else follow students' steps. If someone cannot follow the directions, provide feedback and allow students to revise their directions.

5. Have students write a title for their process and transfer a complete and neat copy of their process on the Activity Book page.

6. Use the materials and instructions in the online lesson to evaluate students' finished writing. You will be looking at students' writing to evaluate the following:

   ▸ Purpose and Content: The writing should tell how to complete the task. There should be four clearly written steps that are mostly easy to understand.

   ▸ Structure and Organization: The steps should be written in a logical order, and they should be numbered correctly.

   ▸ Grammar and Mechanics: Most sentences should be complete and punctuated correctly.

7. Enter students' scores for each rubric category online.

8. If students scored a 1 in any criteria, work with them to proofread and revise their work.

Reward: When students' writing is Level 2 or higher on the grading rubric, add a sticker for this unit on the My Accomplishments chart.

Objectives
- Organize ideas through sequencing.
- Choose words that convey a clear picture.
- Use transitions to signal order.
- Use appropriate organizational pattern in writing.
- Write a how-to (directions to complete a task).

What Is a Verb?

Unit Overview

In this unit, students will
- ▶ Explore verbs that show action.
- ▶ Explore verbs like *was*, *is*, and *am* that do not show action.

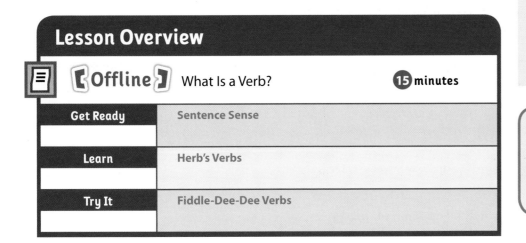

Lesson Overview

[Offline] What Is a Verb?		15 minutes
Get Ready	Sentence Sense	
Learn	Herb's Verbs	
Try It	Fiddle-Dee-Dee Verbs	

Materials

Supplied
- *K¹² Language Arts Activity Book*, pp. WS 47–50

Also Needed
- pencils, coloring

Keywords

action verb – a word that shows action
verb – a word that shows action or a state of being

Advance Preparation

Read the instructions for the Get Ready activity. Cut out the word cards on page WS 47 in *K¹² Language Arts Activity Book* (Sentence Sense).

Content Background

Every sentence needs a verb.

- ▶ The verb is the main word or words in the predicate of a sentence.
- ▶ Verbs often show action.

Big Ideas

Recognizing and using action verbs helps writers make their work specific and interesting to readers.

[Offline] 15 minutes

What Is a Verb?

You will work with students to complete Get Ready, Learn, and Try It activities.

Get Ready

Sentence Sense

Review what a complete sentence is. Gather the word cards from page WS 47 in *K¹² Language Arts Activity Book*.

1. Remind students that a sentence tells a complete thought. A sentence has two main parts:

   ▸ One part names the person or thing.
   ▸ One part tells what the person or thing does.

2. Display the word cards.

3. Have students arrange the word cards to make complete sentences.
   Rabbits hop.
   Balloons pop.
   Bees buzz.
   Cars honk.

4. Have students read and turn face down each card that names a person or thing.
   Rabbits, Balloons, Bees, Cars

5. Read together each word card that is face up, and then have students pantomime the action. hop, pop, buzz, honk

TIP Some students may feel more comfortable repeating the verb while they pantomime the action. Encourage them to do so.

Objectives
- Recognize word groups that are sentences.
- Identify nouns in sentences.

Learn

Herb's Verbs

Introduce verbs to students. Turn to page WS 49 in *K¹² Language Arts Activity Book*.

1. Explain that a **verb** is the action word in a sentence. Verbs are sometimes called doing words.

2. Read the rule on the Activity Book page. Complete the Guided Exercises with students.

Objectives
- Identify verbs in sentences.

3. Read the first example on the page.
   Say: There is a lot of action going on at this barnyard hoedown. In the sentence, *dances* is the verb. It tells us what Herb is doing.

4. Read the second example.
   Say: In the sentence, the words *claps* and *stomps* show more actions.

5. Have students name other actions that might occur at the hoedown.
   Answers will vary. Possible answers: *turn, twist, tap, sing*

6. Invite interested students to act out each action.

7. Have students complete the rest of the Activity Book page. Provide support as necessary.

TIP You may want to start a Verb Word Wall. Begin by posting the verb word cards from Activity Book page 47 on a wall or in a notebook. Encourage students to add index cards with the verbs from Herb's Verbs and other activities.

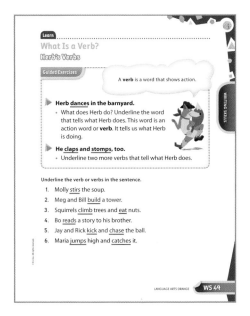

Try It

Fiddle-Dee-Dee Verbs

Help students practice identifying verbs. Turn to page WS 50 in *K¹² Language Arts Activity Book.*

1. Read the directions to students. Read the sentences together.

2. Have students complete Exercises 1–7. Provide support as necessary.

TIP You may want to remind students that a sentence can have more than one verb. If necessary, tell them that Exercise 5 has two verbs.

Objectives
* Identify verbs in sentences.

 Reward: When students complete the Try It, allow them to color in the space provided.

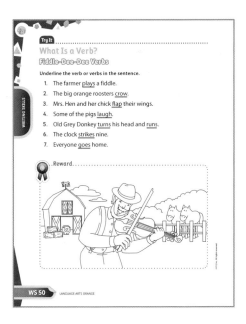

Action Verbs

Lesson Overview

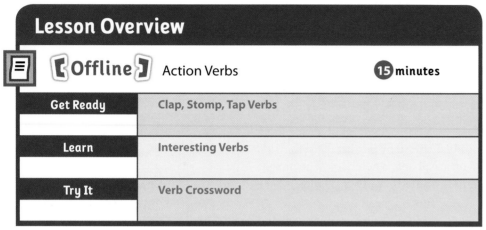

▤	**[Offline]** Action Verbs	**15** minutes
Get Ready	Clap, Stomp, Tap Verbs	
Learn	Interesting Verbs	
Try It	Verb Crossword	

Materials

Supplied

• *K¹² Language Arts Activity Book*, pp. WS 51–52

Keywords

action verb – a word that shows action

Content Background

Action verbs help readers see in their minds what is happening. Using action verbs that are vivid and descriptive makes the sentences students write and speak more interesting to an audience.

[Offline] **15** minutes

Action Verbs

You will work with students to complete Get Ready, Learn, and Try It activities.

Get Ready •

Clap, Stomp, Tap Verbs

Review verbs using the song "If You're Happy and You Know It."

1. Sing or chant the song "If You're Happy and You Know It." Perform the action noted in parentheses.

> *If you're happy and you know it, clap your hands.* (clap, clap)
> *If you're happy and you know it, clap your hands.* (clap, clap)
> *If you're happy and you know it, then your face will surely show it.*
> *If you're happy and you know it, clap your hands.* (clap, clap)

 Objectives

• Identify verbs in sentences.

2. Remind students that *clap* is a verb that shows action.

3. Sing or chant the song with these new verses. Have students name and perform each new action word.

> Verse 2: *If you're happy and you know it, stomp your feet.* stomp
> Verse 3: *If you're happy and you know it, tap your knees.* tap
> Verse 4: *If you're happy and you know it, do all three.* clap, stomp, tap

TIP As a challenge, you may wish to have students make up new verses for the song, adding their own action verbs.

Learn

Interesting Verbs

Review action verbs with students. Turn to page WS 51 in *K¹² Language Arts Activity Book.*

1. Explain that some action verbs are interesting and tell more about the action than others. When we write and talk, it is good to use verbs that are specific and interesting.

2. Read the example on the page.
Say: Both sentences describe how the snake got into the grass. *Goes* and *slithers* are both action verbs, but *slithers* is a more interesting verb. It helps readers see in their mind how the snake moves.

3. To help students better understand what makes a verb interesting, give them pairs of verbs they can act out. The first verb in each pair is general, and the second verb is more specific, vivid, and interesting. Students' actions should show the difference.

> ▸ eat, gobble
> ▸ walk, prance
> ▸ jog, race
> ▸ hold, squeeze

4. Read the rule on the Activity Book page. Complete the Guided Exercises with students.

5. Have students complete the rest of the Activity Book page. Provide support as necessary.

TIP If you are keeping a Verb Word Wall, have students find interesting action verbs in magazines or other print materials. Have them add the words to the Verb Word Wall.

Objectives
- Identify verbs in sentences.
- Use action verbs in sentences.

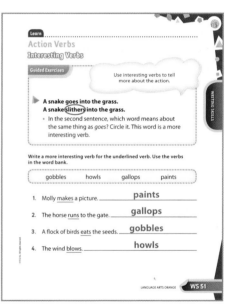

Try It

Verb Crossword

Help students recognize more interesting action verbs. Turn to page WS 52 in
K¹² Language Arts Activity Book.

1. Read the directions to students. Read the clues and the word choices together.

2. Have students complete the crossword puzzle. Provide support as necessary.

TIP Focus on building vocabulary of strong action verbs by suggesting
synonyms, words that mean almost the same thing, for overused verbs, such
as *run* and *take*. Some synonyms for *run* are *gallop*, *trot*, *jog*, and *dash*. Some
synonyms for *take* are *catch*, *grasp*, *grab*, and *capture*.

Objectives
- Identify verbs in sentences.
- Use action verbs in sentences.

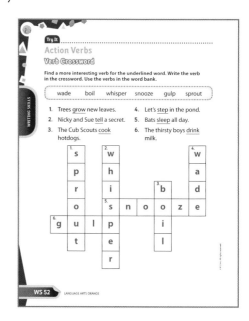

Other Verbs

Lesson Overview

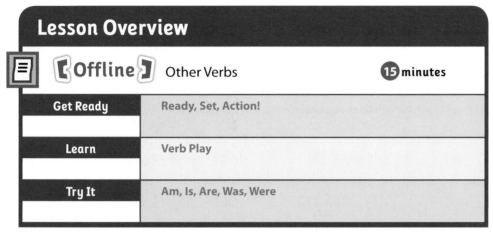

[Offline] Other Verbs		**15** minutes
Get Ready	Ready, Set, Action!	
Learn	Verb Play	
Try It	Am, Is, Are, Was, Were	

Materials

Supplied
- *K¹² Language Arts Activity Book*, pp. WS 53–54

Also Needed
- pencils, coloring

Content Background

The verbs *am*, *is*, *are*, *was*, and *were* are often called "being verbs." They are common in sentences but do not show concrete actions as do most verbs.

[Offline] **15** minutes

Other Verbs

You will work with students to complete Get Ready, Learn, and Try It activities.

Ready, Set, Action!
Review verbs that show action.

1. Remind students that a verb tells what a person or thing does, such as *swim*, *eat*, *sing*, or *drive*.

2. Have students pretend that they are actors in a play of *The Three Little Pigs*.

3. Help students think about the events in the story and the actions taken by the Big Bad Wolf.

4. Have students perform one of the actions from the story after you announce, "Ready, Set, Action!"

Objectives
- Identify verbs in sentences.
- Use action verbs in sentences.

5. Together, create a sentence about the scene, such as *The wolf blows the house down!*

6. Have students name the verb in the sentence.

7. Repeat with other actions.

Learn

Verb Play

Introduce other kinds of verbs. Turn to page WS 53 in *K¹² Language Arts Activity Book.*

1. Explain that most verbs show action. There are a few special verbs that do not show action but still tell what a person or thing does. These words are *am, is, are, was,* and *were.*

2. Read the rule on the Activity Book page.

3. Show students the first example on the page.

   ► Cover the word *are* with your finger.
   ► Replace the word *are* with *feed* as you read the sentence aloud.
   ► Explain that the word *feed* is a verb. It shows action.
   ► Uncover the word *are* and read the sentence.
   ► Explain that *are* is a different kind of verb. It does not show action.

4. Read the second example.

   ► Point to the word *is* and ask if it shows an action. No
     Say: *Is* is a verb, but it does not show action.
   ► Cover the word *is.*
   ► Read the sentence, asking students to replace the word with an action verb. Answers will vary. Possible answers: *plays, scares, chases*

5. Complete the Guided Exercises with students.

6. Have students complete the rest of the Activity Book page. Provide support as necessary.

TIP If you are using a Verb Word Wall, add the verbs *am, is, are, was,* and *were* to the Verb Word Wall.

Objectives

- Identify verbs in sentences.
- Recognize action verbs and being verbs.
- Use action verbs in sentences.

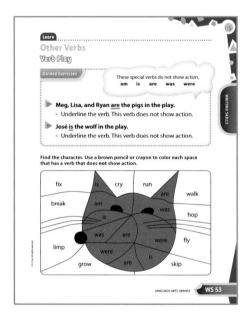

Try It

· ·

Am, Is, Are, Was, Were

Help students recognize and use verbs that do not show action. Turn to page WS 54 in *K¹² Language Arts Activity Book*.

1. Read the first set of directions to students. Read the sentences together. Have students complete Exercises 1–4.

2. Read the second set of directions to students. Have students complete Exercises 5 and 6. Provide Support as necessary.

Objectives

- Identify verbs in sentences.
- Use being verbs in sentences.

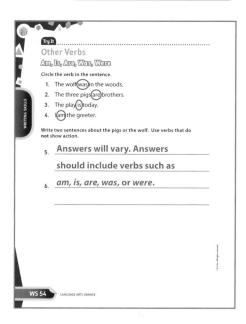

Review Verbs

Lesson Overview

 [Online] Review Verbs   **15** minutes

Review	Web Full of Verbs

[Materials]

There are no materials to gather for this lesson.

[Online] **15** minutes

Review Verbs

Students will work on their own to complete review and practice activities. Help students locate the online activities and provide support as needed.

Review

Web Full of Verbs

Students will work online to review what they have learned about verbs. They will help a spider choose verbs to complete a song.

    Remind students that most verbs tell what someone or something did. Some words, such as *is*, *am*, *are*, *was*, and *were*, are also verbs, but they do not show action.

TIP Three words on each screen are verbs. Any one of the verbs may be chosen.

Objectives
- Identify verbs in sentences.
- Use action verbs in sentences.

Offline Alternative

No computer access? Write or say three verbs and one noun, such as *jump*, *was*, *laughed*, and *chicks*. Have students identify the three verbs and use each one in a sentence.

Unit Checkpoint

Lesson Overview

	Offline	Unit Checkpoint	**15** minutes
Unit Checkpoint	Verbs		

Materials

Supplied

- *K¹² Language Arts Assessments*, pp. WS 13–16

Offline · **15** minutes

Unit Checkpoint

You will work with students to complete the Unit Checkpoint.

Unit Checkpoint

Verbs

Explain that students are going to show what they have learned about verbs.

1. Give students the Unit Checkpoint pages.

2. Read the directions together. Have students complete the Checkpoint on their own.

3. Use the Answer Key to score the Checkpoint, and then enter the results online.

4. Review each exercise with students. Work with students to correct any exercise that they missed.

TIP Students who answered one or more questions incorrectly should continue to practice this grammar skill. Read aloud students' favorite books. Stop from time to time to point out the verbs.

Objectives

- Identify verbs in sentences.
- Use action verbs in sentences.
- Recognize action verbs and being verbs.

Reward: When students score 80 percent or above on the Unit Checkpoint, add a sticker for this unit on the My Accomplishments chart.

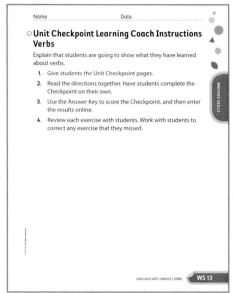

Name _____ Date _____

⚙ Unit Checkpoint Learning Coach Instructions
Verbs

Explain that students are going to show what they have learned about verbs.

1. Give students the Unit Checkpoint pages.
2. Read the directions together. Have students complete the Checkpoint on their own.
3. Use the Answer Key to score the Checkpoint, and then enter the results online.
4. Review each exercise with students. Work with students to correct any exercise that they missed.

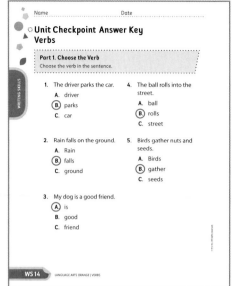

Name _____ Date _____

⚙ Unit Checkpoint Answer Key
Verbs

Part 1. Choose the Verb
Choose the verb in the sentence.

1. The driver parks the car.
   A. driver
   (B) parks
   C. car

2. Rain falls on the ground.
   A. Rain
   (B) falls
   C. ground

3. My dog is a good friend.
   (A) is
   B. good
   C. friend

4. The ball rolls into the street.
   A. ball
   (B) rolls
   C. street

5. Birds gather nuts and seeds.
   A. Birds
   (B) gather
   C. seeds

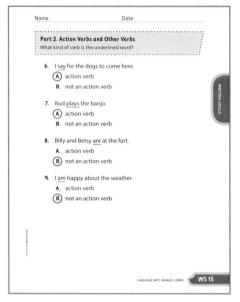

Name _____ Date _____

Part 2. Action Verbs and Other Verbs
What kind of verb is the underlined word?

6. I say for the dogs to come here.
   (A) action verb
   B. not an action verb

7. Bud plays the banjo.
   (A) action verb
   B. not an action verb

8. Billy and Betsy are at the fort.
   A. action verb
   (B) not an action verb

9. I am happy about the weather.
   A. action verb
   (B) not an action verb

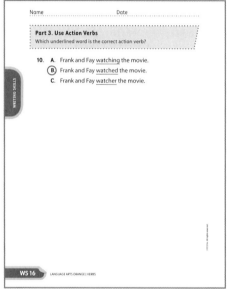

Name _____ Date _____

Part 3. Use Action Verbs
Which underlined word is the correct action verb?

10. A. Frank and Fay watching the movie.
    (B) Frank and Fay watched the movie.
    C. Frank and Fay watcher the movie.

Beginning, Middle, and End

Unit Overview

In this unit, students will
- ▶ Learn to write a sequence.
- ▶ Explore how to use order words.
- ▶ Write a beginning, a middle, and an end.

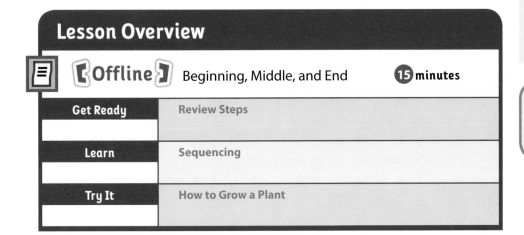

Lesson Overview

Offline Beginning, Middle, and End		**15** minutes
Get Ready	Review Steps	
Learn	Sequencing	
Try It	How to Grow a Plant	

Materials

Supplied
- *K¹² Language Arts Activity Book*, pp. WS 55–56

Also Needed
- crayons

Keywords

sequence – the order in which things happen

Big Ideas

- ▶ Sequencing ideas is the beginning of writing a personal narrative or experience story.
- ▶ Good writers use transitions to help create coherence in written text.

Offline ⏱ **15 minutes**

Beginning, Middle, and End
You will work with students to complete Get Ready, Learn, and Try It activities.

Get Ready

Review Steps

Review the idea that a process is a series of steps. The steps must be followed in a specific order.

1. Ask students for an example of a series of steps. If students have difficulty, provide the following example:

   ▸ First, put cereal into a bowl. Next, slice a banana and add it to the cereal. Then, pour milk in the bowl. Last, get a spoon and eat your breakfast.

2. Read a series of steps in the wrong order and ask students to explain what is wrong.
   Say: Listen to these steps and tell me what is wrong:

   ▸ Run the bathtub.
   ▸ Step into the tub.
   ▸ Get undressed.
   ▸ Get washed.
     You have to get undressed before you step into the tub.
     The steps are out of order.

Objectives
- Identify a process as a series of steps.
- Organize ideas through sequencing.
- Analyze directions for proper sequencing.

Learn

Sequencing

Explore the concept of a sequence with students. Turn to page WS 55 in *K¹² Language Arts Activity Book*.

1. Explain to students that a series of steps is a process or set of directions that can be done in a sequence. A **sequence** is the order in which things happen. Complete sequences have a beginning, a middle, and an end. The beginning always happens first, the middle happens next, and the end happens last.

2. Give students examples of sequences that have a beginning, a middle, and an end, such as the following:

   ▸ Syllables in a word: won-der-ful
   ▸ Parts of a book, story, or song
   ▸ Courses of a meal: appetizer or first course, main course, and dessert

Objectives
- Organize ideas through sequencing.
- Use an appropriate organizational pattern in writing.

3. Describe the following sequence and have students listen for the beginning, middle, and end: Take a slice of bread. Put it in the toaster. When it is done, spread butter on it.

   ▶ What are the beginning, middle, and end of the sequence?
   Beginning: Take the bread. Middle: Toast it. End: Butter it.

4. **Say:** Just as we can divide a set of steps into beginning, middle, and end, we can find the beginning, middle, and end in a story or other set of events. This is called the sequence of events. Just as we can write Step 1, Step 2, and Step 3, we can use beginning, middle, and end.

5. Read the rule and example on the Activity Book page. Complete the Guided Exercises with students.

6. Have students complete the rest of the Activity Book page. Provide support as necessary.

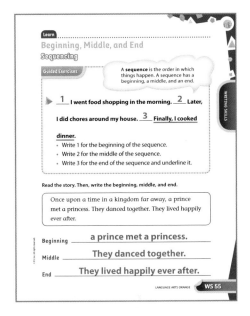

Try It

How to Grow a Plant

Help students recognize that a sequence has a beginning, middle, and an end. Turn to page WS 56 in *K¹² Language Arts Activity Book*.

1. Read the directions to students. Read the sequence together.

2. Tell students that they need to first put the steps in order. Tell them to look for the beginning first. Then they should look for the middle. The remaining event will be the end.

3. Have students complete the Activity Book page. Provide support as necessary.

4. When students have finished, review all the answers with them.

   ▶ Make sure that students put the sequence in the correct order. If they did not, explain the correct order.
   ▶ Have students explain to you the order in which they wrote the sequence. Be sure that in their explanation they break up the sequence into three parts: beginning, middle, and end.

 Reward: When students complete the Activity Book page, allow them to draw in the space provided.

Objectives

- Organize ideas through sequencing.
- Use an appropriate organizational pattern in writing.
- Analyze directions for proper sequencing.

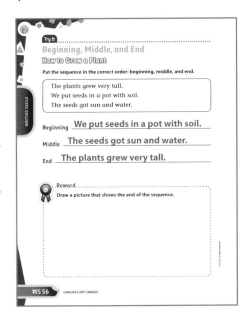

Use Order Words

Lesson Overview

	Offline Use Order Words	**15** minutes
Get Ready	Review Sequences	
Learn	Order Words	
Try It	First, Next, and Finally	

Materials

Supplied
- *K¹² Language Arts Activity Book*, p. WS 57–58

Keywords

order words – words that connect ideas, a series of steps, or create a sequence, such as *first, next, later, finally*

Content Background

Creating a sequence or telling a story using order words is similar to using order words to summarize the plot of a story.

Big Ideas

Good writers use transitions to help create coherence in written text.

Offline **15** minutes

Use Order Words

You will work with students to complete Get Ready, Learn, and Try It activities.

Get Ready

Review Sequences

1. Have students explain what a sequence is. If students have difficulty, remind them that a sequence is a series of steps that has a beginning, middle, and end.

2. Ask students to describe a simple sequence.

   ▶ What is the sequence for brushing your teeth, using *beginning, middle,* and *end* for each step? Answers will vary but should demonstrate three steps with an appropriate beginning, middle, and end. Possible answer: Beginning: Put toothpaste on the toothbrush. Middle: Brush your teeth up and down. End: Rinse your mouth.

Objectives
- Organize ideas through sequencing.
- Use an appropriate organizational pattern in writing.

Learn

Order Words

Introduce order words to students. Turn to page WS 57 in *K¹² Language Arts Activity Book*.

1. Explain to students that **order words** like *first*, *next*, and *finally* can be added to a series of steps, a sequence, or a set of events.

   ▶ When you have a series of steps, you can number them one, two, and three.
   ▶ When you have a sequence, you can talk about the beginning, middle, and end.
   ▶ Order words like *first*, *next*, and *finally* can be used instead of numbers. They can also replace the words *beginning, middle,* and *end.*

2. Tell students that order words keep ideas in order when you want to tell a story or give a series of steps.

   ▶ Read these steps to students: Brush your teeth. Put on your pajamas. Get into bed.
   ▶ Have students repeat these steps, adding order words. First, brush your teeth. Next, put on your pajamas. Finally, get into bed.

3. Read the rule and example on the Activity Book page. Complete the Guided Exercises with students.

4. Have students complete the rest of the Activity Book page. Provide support as necessary.

TIP If students are having difficulty adding order words, you can say the order word and have students complete the sentence.

Objectives

- Organize ideas through sequencing.
- Use transition words to signal order.
- Analyze directions for proper sequencing.

Try It

First, Next, and Finally

Help students recognize how to add order words to organize a series of steps. Turn to page WS 58 in *K¹² Language Arts Activity Book*.

1. Read the first set of directions to students. Read the sentences together. Tell students to think about what order the steps should be in. Then have them complete the first part of the Activity Book page.

2. Read the second set of directions to students. Read the sentences together. Have students complete the rest of the Activity Book page. Provide support as necessary.

Objectives
- Organize ideas through sequencing.
- Use transition words to signal order.
- Analyze directions for proper sequencing.

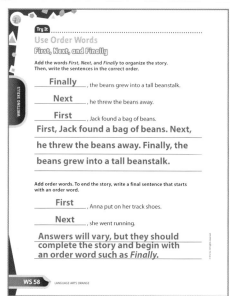

Try It

Use Order Words

First, Next, and Finally

Add the words *First*, *Next*, and *Finally* to organize the story. Then, write the sentences in the correct order.

_____Finally_____, the beans grew into a tall beanstalk.

_____Next_____, he threw the beans away.

_____First_____, Jack found a bag of beans.

First, Jack found a bag of beans. Next, he threw the beans away. Finally, the beans grew into a tall beanstalk.

Add order words. To end the story, write a final sentence that starts with an order word.

_____First_____, Anna put on her track shoes.

_____Next_____, she went running.

Answers will vary, but they should complete the story and begin with an order word such as *Finally*.

WS 58 LANGUAGE ARTS ORANGE

What Happens Next?

Lesson Overview

[Offline] What Happens Next? **15** minutes

Get Ready	Review *First*, *Next*, and *Finally*
Learn	Use Transition Words
Try It	Put It in Order

Materials

Supplied
- *K¹² Language Arts Activity Book*, pp. WS 59–60
- whiteboard (optional)

Keywords

transition – a word or phrase that connects ideas

Advance Preparation

Write the order words *first*, *next*, *then*, *later*, *at last*, and *finally* on a whiteboard or large sheet of paper so that students can refer to them.

Big Ideas

Good writers use transitions to help create coherence in written text.

[Offline] 15 minutes

What Happens Next?

You will work with students to complete Get Ready, Learn, and Try It activities.

Get Ready

Review *First*, *Next*, and *Finally*

Review that order words help tell a story.

1. Encourage students to retell an event or story by prompting them to say what happened first, next, and finally.

2. Remind students that a series of steps or a set of events can be organized as a sequence by adding the words *first*, *next*, and *finally*.

Objectives
- Use transition words to signal order.

3. Write the following sentences on a piece of paper or whiteboard, and have students add order words to organize them into a sequence:

   ▶ Take out your book. First,

   ▶ Read the book. Next,

   ▶ Write about the book. Finally,

Learn

Use Transition Words

Introduce the concept of transition words to students. Turn to page WS 59 in *K¹² Language Arts Activity Book.*

1. **Say:** A sequence or story may have more than three steps or details. Think about the stories you have read. They have more than three events.

   ▶ We can keep these steps, events, or details in a logical order by using **transition words**.

   ▶ Transition words also help sentences make sense because they connect ideas.

2. Show students the words *then, later,* and *at last* on a piece of paper or whiteboard.

3. **Say:** The order words you have learned—*first, next,* and *finally*—are transitions. There are other transitions that show time order or connect ideas in the order in which they happened.

   ▶ *Then, later,* and *at last* are order words. In a sequence or story, these words come before *finally.*

   ▶ The word *finally* is the last or final order word used in a story.

4. Explain that sentences make more sense when order words are added. Write the following sentences, and have students add order words to make the sequence more clear:

   ▶ Ava got on the ride. Evan got on the ride. Jade got on the ride. Ty got on the ride. First, Ava got on the ride. Next, Evan got on the ride. Then, Jade got on the ride. Finally, Ty got on the ride.

5. Tell students that order words like *next* and *then* can be used more than once. For example, we can say, "Ava got on the ride. Then, Evan got on the ride. Then, Jade got on the ride."

6. Explain that *next* and *then* are used in the middle of a sequence, but the order doesn't matter. Both of the following sequences make sense:

   ▶ Next, Bob got on the ride. Then, Sue got on the ride.

   ▶ Then, Bob got on the ride. Next, Sue got on the ride.

Objectives

- Organize ideas through sequencing.
- Use an appropriate organizational pattern in writing.
- Use transition words to signal order.
- Use transitions to connect ideas.

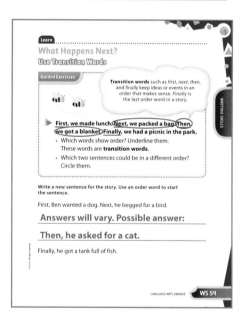

7. Read the following sentences:

   ▶ First, we got in the car. Next, we drove to the pond. Finally, it was time to go home.

8. Have students add details to the story using one of the order words to begin a new sentence. For example, a new third sentence could be added: Later, we fed the ducks.

9. Read the rule and example on the Activity Book page. Complete the Guided Exercises with students.

10. Have students complete the rest of the Activity Book page. Provide support as necessary. If students need assistance, show them a whiteboard or piece of paper with order words to choose from.

TIP Students can add as many details as they like to a sequence or story as long as the word *finally* begins the last sentence.

Try It

Put It in Order

Help students recognize how to add order words to a story so that the events and details are connected in a way that makes sense. Turn to page WS 60 in *K¹² Language Arts Activity Book*.

1. Read the directions to students. Read the order words and sentences together.

2. Have students complete the Activity Book page. Provide support as necessary.

TIP Encourage students to retell stories and events using a variety of order words.

Online Alternative

This activity is OPTIONAL. It is intended for students who want extra practice or who would prefer to do online practice in place of the offline Try It. Feel free to skip this activity.

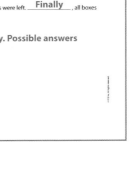

Objectives
- Organize ideas through sequencing.
- Use an appropriate organizational pattern in writing.
- Use transition words to signal order.
- Use transitions to connect ideas.

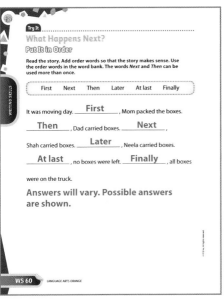

Organize Ideas

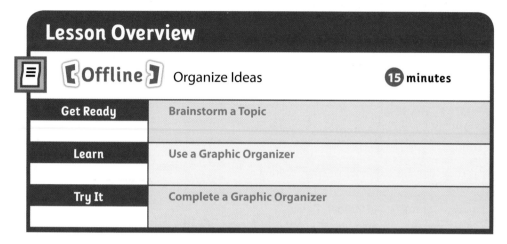

Lesson Overview

 **【Offline】** Organize Ideas   **15** minutes

Get Ready	Brainstorm a Topic
Learn	Use a Graphic Organizer
Try It	Complete a Graphic Organizer

【Materials】

Supplied
- *K¹² Language Arts Activity Book*, pp. WS 61–62

Keywords
graphic organizer – a visual device, such as a diagram or chart, that helps a writer plan a piece of writing

【Offline】 **15** minutes

Organize Ideas
You will work with students to complete Get Ready, Learn, and Try It activities.

Get Ready

Brainstorm a Topic
Review that order words can be used to tell a story and organize a series of steps.

1. Have students brainstorm a topic that they can write as a sequence of events. Their topic should have at least four events in it.

   ▶ Possible topics include doing something students are familiar with, such as playing a favorite game or sport; preparing to do something, such as working on a craft; going somewhere, such as on a camping trip; or participating in a party or special event.

   ▶ Remind students to choose a topic that has events that occur in time order. A topic such as "Why I Like Flowers" is not suitable for this assignment.

2. Help students brainstorm by discussing topics with them and writing the topics in a list. Help them understand which topics are appropriate.

Objectives
- Brainstorm and develop possible topics.
- Choose a topic.

Learn

Use a Graphic Organizer

Introduce graphic organizers to students. Turn to page WS 61 in *K¹² Language Arts Activity Book*.

1. Explain that a **graphic organizer** is a tool for planning. A step-by-step graphic organizer shows steps in the correct order. Since a sequence is a series of events told in time order, the first thing to do is map out the events that occurred in the order in which they happened.

2. Describe the graphic organizer that students will be using: It is a series of boxes connected by arrows.

   ▶ One event is written in each box.
   ▶ The events are written in the correct order.

3. Read the rule on the Activity Book page. Complete the Guided Exercises with students.

4. Have students complete the Activity Book page. Provide support as necessary.

TIP Graphic organizers are useful for planning, and writers can add to them as needed.

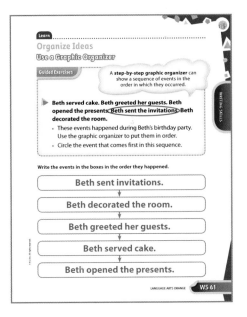

Objectives

- Organize ideas through sequencing.
- Use an appropriate organizational pattern in writing.

Try It

Complete a Graphic Organizer

Help students recognize how to write steps in a graphic organizer. Turn to page WS 62 in *K¹² Language Arts Activity Book*.

1. Read the directions to students. Discuss the activity together. Remind students of the topic they brainstormed in the Get Ready.

2. Tell students that they should have at least four events that go with their topic.

3. Tell students they do not have to write in complete sentences in a graphic organizer. A graphic organizer is a planning tool.

4. Have students complete the graphic organizer, putting their four events in the order in which they occurred. Provide support as necessary.

5. If students would like to include more than four events, add more boxes to the graphic organizer.

6. Keep the graphic organizer in a safe place so students can refer to it when they are ready to write a sequence.

Objectives

- Organize ideas through sequencing.
- Use an appropriate organizational pattern in writing.

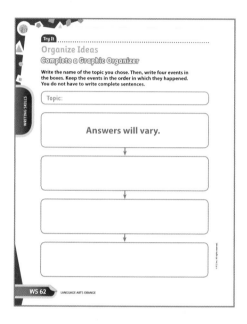

Write a Sequence

Lesson Overview

[Offline] Write a Sequence		**15** minutes
Get Ready	Check the Graphic Organizer	
Write Now	Write Your Sequence	

[Materials]

Supplied

- *K¹² Language Arts Activity Book*, pp. WS 62–63

Advance Preparation

Gather page WS 62 in *K¹² Language Arts Activity Book* (Complete a Graphic Organizer), which students previously completed.

[Offline] **15** minutes

Write a Sequence

You will work with students to complete Get Ready and Write Now activities.

Get Ready

Check the Graphic Organizer

Help students review their graphic organizer. Gather page WS 62 (Complete a Graphic Organizer).

1. Ask students to check that they have at least four events and that the events are written in the order in which they occurred.

2. If they have fewer than four events, have students add events as necessary.

3. If students wish to add more than four events, have them add additional boxes to the graphic organizer.

TIP Remind students that they do not need complete sentences in the graphic organizer, since it is a planning tool.

 Objectives

- Organize ideas through sequencing.
- Use transition words to signal order.
- Use an appropriate organizational pattern in writing.
- Analyze directions for proper sequencing.

Write Now

•••

 Write Your Sequence

Help students write their sequence. Gather page WS 62 (Check the Graphic Organizer), and turn to page WS 63 in *K¹² Language Arts Activity Book*.

1. Explain that students will use the events or steps in their graphic organizers to write a sequence. The sequence will be at least four complete sentences. Each sentence will begin with a transition word.

2. Have students write their four steps as complete sentences on a sheet of paper so they can revise their work and transfer a clean copy to the Activity Book page.

3. Ask students if each sentence begins with an order word and have them add order words if necessary.

4. Ask students if the sentences are in an order that makes sense and have them rearrange the sentences if necessary.

5. Have students write a title for their sequence. The title should tell what they are writing about. For example, if they are writing about a time when they flew a kite, a possible title might be "The Day I Flew a Kite."

6. Remind students that their sentences need details so that their ideas make sense. Ask if they can think of any details to add to the sequence.

7. Have students write a complete and neat copy of their sequence on the Activity Book page.

8. Use the materials and instructions in the online lesson to evaluate students' finished writing. You will be evaluating students' writing for the following:

   ▸ Purpose and Content: The writing should tell what happened, but some of the ideas may not be related.
   ▸ Structure and Organization: The writing should have a beginning, middle, and end, and some transition words should be used.
   ▸ Grammar and Mechanics: Sentences should be written and punctuated correctly, although there may be a minor error or two.

9. Enter students' scores for each rubric category online.

10. If students scored a 1 in any category, follow the online instructions to help them edit and revise their work.

TIP Have students read their sequences aloud. Check that they have used transition words correctly and that the sentences are written in a logical order.

Objectives

- Organize ideas through sequencing.
- Use transition words to signal order.
- Use an appropriate organizational pattern in writing.
- Analyze directions for proper sequencing.
- Use transitions to connect ideas.
- Write a narrative with a beginning, middle, and end.
- Write a title.

Capital Letters in the Heading of a Letter

Unit Overview

In this unit students will
- Learn what to capitalize in the heading, greeting, and closing of a letter.
- Discover where to place commas in the heading, greeting, and closing of a letter.

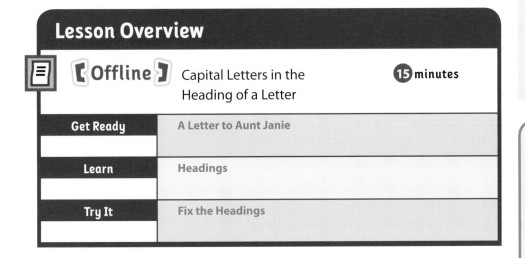

Lesson Overview

Offline	Capital Letters in the Heading of a Letter	**15** minutes
Get Ready	A Letter to Aunt Janie	
Learn	Headings	
Try It	Fix the Headings	

Advance Preparation

- Remove page WS 65 in *K¹² Language Arts Activity Book* (A Letter to Aunt Janie), fold it, and put it in an envelope. Keep the envelope in a safe place so you can refer to it throughout this unit.
- (Optional) Collect samples of real letters that include the five parts: heading, greeting, body, closing, and signature.

Content Background

A friendly letter has five parts: heading, greeting, body, closing, and signature. The heading follows these rules for capitalization:

- In the address, the street name, the city, and the state are all capitalized.
- The month is capitalized.

Big Ideas

When a writer uses the correct letter format, including capitalization and punctuation, the reader can focus on the writer's ideas.

Materials

Supplied
- *K¹² Language Arts Activity Book*, pp. WS 65–68
- whiteboard (optional)

Also Needed
- envelope
- crayons

Keywords

closing (of a friendly letter) – the part of a friendly letter that follows the body Example: *Your friend* or *Love*

greeting – the part of a letter that begins with the word *Dear* followed by a person's name; also called the salutation

heading – the first part of a letter that has the writer's address and the date

 **15** minutes

Capital Letters in the Heading of a Letter

You will work with students to complete Get Ready, Learn, and Try It activities.

Get Ready

A Letter to Aunt Janie

Review proper nouns and introduce the parts of a letter. Gather the envelope containing A Letter to Aunt Janie.

1. Have students open the letter, and read it together. Explain that Ernesto wrote this letter to Aunt Janie.

2. Write the names *Aunt Janie* and *Ernesto* on a whiteboard or sheet of paper.

3. Point to the *A*, *J*, and *E*, and remind students that proper nouns begin with capital letters.

4. Remind students that the names of cities and states are proper nouns, so they also begin with capital letters. Write the names of your city and state, but do not use capital letters. Have students write the capital letters.

5. Explain that Ernesto's letter is a friendly letter. A friendly letter is a way of "talking" to someone through writing. A letter has many proper nouns in it.

6. Tell students that a friendly letter has five parts. Point to each part as you name it.

   ► heading
   ► greeting
   ► body
   ► closing
   ► signature

7. Point to the heading again and read it. Explain that the heading of a letter contains two pieces of information:

   ► The address of the person who wrote the letter
   ► The date the person wrote it

8. Put the letter back in the envelope. Keep the envelope and the letter in a safe place so that students can use it later.

 Objectives

- Use a capital letter to begin a proper noun.
- Use capital letters correctly in the heading of a letter.
- Recognize the parts of a friendly letter.

Learn

Headings

Introduce capital letters in friendly letters. Turn to page WS 67 in *K¹² Language Arts Activity Book*.

1. Read the rule on the Activity Book page. Then read the example together. **Say:** The first line tells the street where Ernesto, the person who wrote the letter, lives. The second line names the city, state, and zip code of the place where he lives.

2. Explain that the specific name for the street, city, and state begin with capital letters.

   ▸ Where is the address? Point to it. Students should point to the first and second line of the heading.

3. **Say:** The third line tells the date. The date includes the month, day, and the year the letter was written. The name of the month is a proper noun, so it begins with a capital letter.

   ▸ Where is the date? Point to it. Students should point to the third line of the heading.

4. Have students complete the rest of the Activity Book page. Provide support as necessary.

TIP Share examples of friendly letters that you have received.

Objectives

- Use capital letters correctly in the heading of a letter.

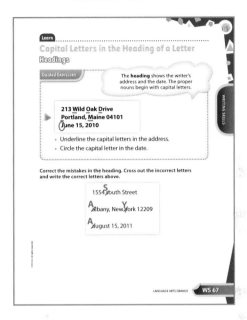

Try It

Fix the Headings

Help students recognize capital letters in the heading of a letter. Turn to page WS 68 in *K¹² Language Arts Activity Book*.

1. Read the first set of directions to students. Have them complete Exercises 1–2.

2. Read the second set of directions to students. Read each line of the heading together.

3. Have students complete Exercise 3. If they have difficulty coming up with the correct letters, you can read the answer to them again. However, students should know without being reminded that the letters should be capitalized.

(TIP) Tell students that when they write out addresses, they can use the full name of the state or the two-letter abbreviation. Use your own state name and its abbreviation as examples.

Objectives

• Use capital letters correctly in the heading of a letter.

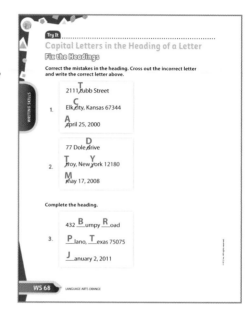

Commas in the Heading of a Letter

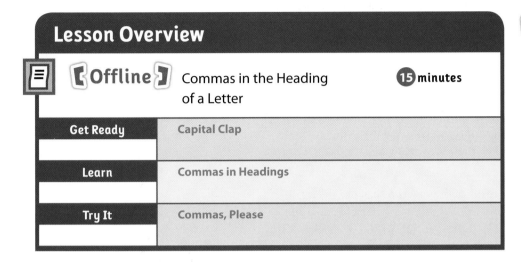

Lesson Overview

【 Offline 】	Commas in the Heading of a Letter	**15** minutes

Get Ready	Capital Clap
Learn	Commas in Headings
Try It	Commas, Please

Materials

Supplied
- *K¹² Language Arts Activity Book,* pp. WS 65, 69–70

Also Needed
- envelope
- crayons

Keywords

closing (of a friendly letter) – the part of a friendly letter that follows the body Example: *Your friend* or *Love*

greeting – the part of a letter that begins with the word *Dear* followed by a person's name; also called the salutation

heading – the first part of a letter that has the writer's address and the date

Advance Preparation

Gather the envelope containing A Letter to Aunt Janie. If you have not prepared the letter, remove page WS 65 in *K¹² Language Arts Activity Book,* fold it, and place it in an envelope.

Content Background

Commas have many uses. In the heading of a letter, a comma

- ▸ Separates the city from the state.
- ▸ Separates the day from the year.

 **Offline** ⏱ **15 minutes**

Commas in the Heading of a Letter

You will work with students to complete Get Ready, Learn, and Try It activities.

Get Ready

Capital Clap

Review words that should be capitalized in the heading of a letter. Have students clap for each kind of word that should begin with a capital letter.

- ► Name of a street clap
- ► Name of a road clap
- ► Name of a city clap
- ► Name of a state clap
- ► Name of a month clap
- ► A number no clap.

 Objectives
- Recognize when to use a capital letter.

Learn

Commas in Headings

Introduce commas in the heading of a friendly letter. Gather the envelope containing A Letter to Aunt Janie, and turn to page WS 69 in the *K¹² Language Arts Activity Book*.

 Objectives
- Use commas correctly in the heading of a letter.

1. Show students the envelope with A Letter to Aunt Janie. Let them open the envelope. Read the letter together.

2. Point to the heading and read it again.

3. Point to the commas. Have students draw a comma in the air by making a dot and then adding a curved tail.

4. Tell students that commas are used to separate words or numbers so that it's easier to read them.

5. Put the letter back in the envelope. Keep the envelope and the letter in a safe place so that students can use it later.

6. Read the letter heading on the Activity Book page together.
   Say: The person who wrote this letter lives in Portland, Maine. *Portland* is the name of the city. *Maine* is the state. Writers put a comma between the city and the state to separate them.

7. Remind students that the third line is the date. A comma is used to separate the number of the day from the number for the year.

8. Read the rule on the Activity Book page. Complete the Guided Exercises with students.

9. Have students complete the rest of the Activity Book page. Provide support as necessary.

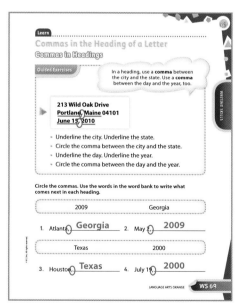

Try It ●

Commas, Please

Have students practice using commas in headings for letters. Turn to page WS 70 in *K¹² Language Arts Activity Book.*

1. Read the first set of directions to students. Read the headings together. Have students complete Exercises 1–4.

2. Read the second set of directions together. Have students complete Exercise 5. Encourage them to use a crayon to complete Exercise 5. Provide support as necessary.

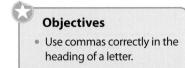

Objectives

- Use commas correctly in the heading of a letter.

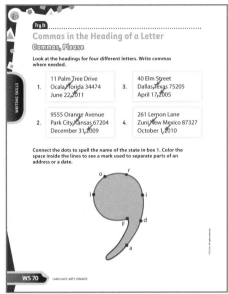

Greeting and Closing of a Letter

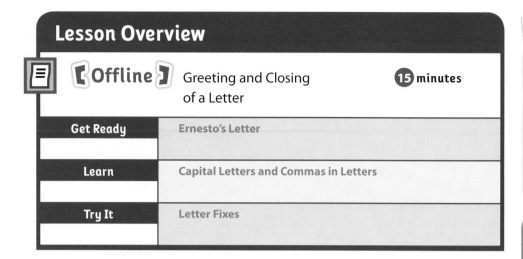

Lesson Overview

☰	**【 Offline 】**	Greeting and Closing of a Letter	**⏱ 15** minutes
Get Ready		Ernesto's Letter	
Learn		Capital Letters and Commas in Letters	
Try It		Letter Fixes	

Materials

Supplied
- *K¹² Language Arts Activity Book,* pp. WS 65, 71–72

Also Needed
- envelope

Keywords

closing (of a friendly letter) – the part of a friendly letter that follows the body Example: *Your friend* or *Love*

greeting – the part of a letter that begins with the word *Dear* followed by a person's name; also called the salutation

heading – the first part of a letter that has the writer's address and the date

Advance Preparation

Gather the envelope containing A Letter to Aunt Janie. If you have not prepared the letter, remove page WS 65 in *K¹² Language Arts Activity Book,* fold it, and place it in an envelope.

Content Background

The greeting and closing of a friendly letter follow specific capitalization and punctuation conventions.

- The greeting begins with a capital letter and ends with a comma.
- The first word of the greeting, such as *Dear,* is usually followed by a person's name, and the person's name also is capitalized.
- The closing begins with a capital letter and ends with a comma.
- When a closing has more than one word, only the first word of the closing is capitalized.

 **15 minutes**

Greeting and Closing of a Letter

You will work with students to complete Get Ready, Learn, and Try It activities.

Get Ready

Ernesto's Letter

Review commas and capitalization in a friendly letter. Gather the envelope containing A Letter to Aunt Janie.

1. Show students the envelope with A Letter to Aunt Janie. Have students take out and look at the letter.

   ▸ Where does Ernesto live and how do you know? 213 Wild Oak Drive, Portland, Maine 04101; he writes his address in the heading of the letter.

2. Have students point to the commas in the heading of the letter. Remind them that the commas separate the city from the state and the day from the year.

3. Have students point to each word in the heading that begins with a capital letter.

   ▸ Why are these words capitalized? They are proper nouns.
   ▸ What is the difference between a common noun and a proper noun? A common noun names any person, place, or thing. A proper noun names a particular person, place, or thing and begins with a capital letter.

4. Put the letter back in the envelope and keep it in a safe place so students can refer to it later.

Objectives

• Recognize proper capitalization and punctuation in the heading of a letter.

Learn

Capital Letters and Commas in Letters

Look at two different parts of a friendly letter—the greeting and the closing. Gather the envelope containing A Letter to Aunt Janie, and turn to page WS 71 in *K¹² Language Arts Activity Book*.

1. Let students open the envelope with A Letter to Aunt Janie and read the letter again.

2. Point to the greeting. Explain that a greeting is a way of saying "hello" to the person you are writing to.

   ▸ What words does Ernesto use to say "hello"? Dear Aunt Janie

3. Point to the closing. Explain that the closing is a way of saying "good-bye" to the person you are writing to.

   ▸ What words does Ernesto use to say "good-bye"? Hugs and kisses

4. Focus students' attention on capital letters in the greeting and closing. Point to the capital letters and tell students that the first word in both the greeting and the closing are always capital letters. The person's name begins with a capital letter, too.

5. Focus on the greeting and closing end marks. Tell students that a comma is placed at the end of the greeting and the closing to separate them from the rest of the letter.

6. Read the rule on page WS 71. Complete the Guided Exercises with students.

7. Have students complete the rest of the Activity Book page. Provide support as needed.

8. Put A Letter to Aunt Janie back in the envelope and keep it in a safe place so students can refer to it later.

Objectives

- Use capital letters in the greeting and closing of a letter.
- Use commas in the greeting and closing of a letter.

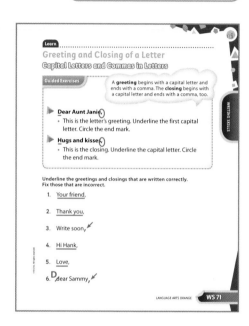

Try It

Letter Fixes

Have students practice using commas and capital letters in friendly letters. Turn to page WS 72 in *K¹² Language Arts Activity Book*.

1. Read the directions to students. Show them that Exercise 1 has been done. Point out that the exclamation mark has been changed to a comma.

2. Read the openings and closings together. Have students complete Exercises 2–10. Provide support as necessary.

TIP If students have difficulty putting the comma above the incorrect punctuation mark, suggest that they put it beside the mark they crossed out.

Objectives

- Use capital letters in the greeting and closing of a letter.
- Use commas in the greeting and closing of a letter.

Try It

Greeting and Closing of a Letter

Letter Fixes

Fix the greetings and the closings. Put a line through each mistake. Write the correct letter or end mark above the mistake. The first one has been done for you.

1. Dear Mr. Jones!
2. H̶i Adam,
3. D̶ear Mimi,
4. H̶ello Dr. Evans,
5. Write soon,
6. Love,
7. Y̶our friend,
8. Goodbye,
9. Thank you,
10. Y̶our cousin,

WS 72   LANGUAGE ARTS ORANGE

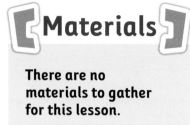

Review Capital Letters and Commas in a Letter

Lesson Overview

〖Online〗	Review Capital Letters and Commas in a Letter	15 minutes
Review	Bunny Letters	

〖Materials〗

There are no materials to gather for this lesson.

〖Online〗 15 minutes

Review Capital Letters and Commas in a Letter

Students will work on their own to complete review and practice activities. Help students locate the online activities and provide support as needed.

Review

Bunny Letters

Students will review the capitalization and punctuation of the heading, greeting, and closing of a letter to prepare for the Unit Checkpoint.

Offline Alternative

No computer access? Write a short letter for students to proofread and revise. Don't put any capital letters or commas in the heading, greeting, or closing of the letter. Put your own address in the heading and the name of a student's friend in the greeting. Have students circle the first letter of all words that must be capitalized and add any missing commas.

Objectives

- Use commas correctly in the heading of a letter.
- Use capital letters correctly in the heading of a letter.
- Use capital letters in the greeting and closing of a letter.
- Use commas in the greeting and closing of a letter.

Unit Checkpoint

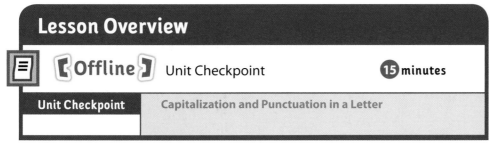

Lesson Overview

 [Offline] Unit Checkpoint	15 minutes
Unit Checkpoint	Capitalization and Punctuation in a Letter

Materials

Supplied

• *K¹² Language Arts Assessments*, pp. WS 17–19

[Offline] 🕐 15 minutes

Unit Checkpoint
You will work with students to complete the Unit Checkpoint.

Unit Checkpoint

Capitalization and Punctuation in a Letter

Explain that students are going to show what they have learned about capitalization and punctuation in a letter.

1. Give students the Unit Checkpoint pages.

2. Read the directions and each letter part together. Have students complete the Checkpoint on their own.

3. Use the Answer Key to score the Checkpoint, and then enter the results online.

4. Review each exercise with students. Work with students to correct any exercise that they missed.

 Reward: When students score 80 percent or above on the Unit Checkpoint, add a sticker for this unit on the My Accomplishments chart.

> **Objectives**
> • Use commas correctly in the heading of a letter.
> • Use capital letters correctly in the heading of a letter.
> • Use capital letters in the greeting and closing of a letter.
> • Use commas in the greeting and closing of a letter.

Name _____ Date _____

⚬ Unit Checkpoint Learning Coach Instructions
Capitalization and Punctuation in a Letter

Explain that students are going to show what they have learned about capitalization and punctuation in a letter.

1. Give students the Unit Checkpoint pages.
2. Read the directions together. Have students complete the Checkpoint on their own.
3. Use the Answer Key to score the Checkpoint, and then enter the results online.
4. Review each exercise with students. Work with students to correct any exercise that they missed.

Name _____ Date _____

⚬ Unit Checkpoint Answer Key
Capitalization and Punctuation in a Letter

Part 1. Headings of Letters
Which heading is written correctly?

1. **(A)** 115 Bay Street
   Clay, New York 13041
   April 6, 2011

   B. 115 Bay Street
   Clay, New York 13041
   April 6 2011

2. **A.** 37 North Elk Street
   Fir Alaska, 67000
   May 27, 2010

   (B.) 37 North Elk Street
   Fir, Alaska 67000
   May 27, 2010

3. **A.** 1216 Forest road
   Orlando Florida 32819
   March 17, 2011

   (B.) 1216 Forest Road
   Orlando, Florida 32819
   March 17, 2011

Name _____ Date _____

Part 2. Greetings and Closings of Letters
Choose the answer.

4. Which greeting is written correctly?
   (A) Dear Steve,
   B. dear Steve,
   C. Dear steve,
   D. Dear Steve

5. Which greeting is written correctly?
   A. Hello Mr. Lee!
   (B.) Hello Mr. Lee,
   C. hello Mr. lee,
   D. Hello Mr. Lee

6. Which greeting is written correctly?
   A. hi Gretel
   B. Hi Gretel
   (C.) Hi Gretel,
   D. Hi gretel,

7. Which closing is written correctly?
   A. Love
   B. love
   (C.) Love,
   D. love,

8. Which closing is written correctly?
   A. Your Friend,
   B. Your friend
   C. Your Friend
   (D.) Your friend,

What Is a Friendly Letter?

Unit Overview

In this unit, students will
- ► Identify the form and purpose of a friendly letter.
- ► Use the established conventions for a friendly letter.
- ► Write a friendly letter.

Lesson Overview

[Offline] What Is a Friendly Letter?		15 minutes
Get Ready	Letter from Rico	
Learn	Purpose, Audience, and Voice	
Try It	To Whom Are You Writing?	

[Materials]

Supplied
- *K¹² Language Arts Activity Book*, pp. WS 73–76

Also Needed
- envelope

Keywords

audience – a writer's readers
friendly letter – a kind of letter used to share thoughts, feelings, and news
purpose – the reason for writing
voice – the way a piece of writing sounds

Advance Preparation

Remove page WS 73 of *K¹² Language Arts Activity Book* (Letter from Rico), fold it, and put it in an envelope. Keep the envelope and the letter in a safe place so you can refer to it throughout this unit.

Content Background

When speaking about writing, *tone* typically refers to an author's attitude toward a subject. Tone can also refer to the style of speaking or writing, as in an informal or formal tone. In this sense, tone helps create voice in a piece of writing.

Big Ideas

Writing varies by purpose and audience. The specific reason for writing and the writer's intended readers (audience) determine the correct form and language to use.

 **15** minutes

What Is a Friendly Letter?

You will work with students to complete Get Ready, Learn, and Try It activities.

Get Ready

Letter from Rico

Help students understand that a friendly letter is a letter between two people who know each other that is used to share thoughts, feelings, or news. Gather the envelope containing the Letter from Rico.

Objectives
- Identify the purpose of a friendly letter.

1. Show students the envelope with the Letter from Rico in it. Let students look at the envelope and open it.

2. Define a **friendly letter** for students.

   ▸ A friendly letter is a letter between two people who know each other.
   ▸ You might write letters to family members, friends, or pen pals.

3. Read the Letter from Rico to students.

   ▸ Who wrote this letter and who did he write to? Rico wrote it to Jamal.

4. Put the Letter from Rico back in the envelope. Keep it in a safe place so that students may refer to it later.

Learn

Purpose, Audience, and Voice

Introduce the ideas of a friendly letter, purpose, audience, and voice to students. Gather the envelope containing the Letter from Rico, and turn to page WS 75 in *K¹² Language Arts Activity Book*.

Objectives
- Identify the purpose of a friendly letter.
- Identify the audience of a friendly letter.

1. Explain that a friendly letter has a **purpose**. The purpose might be one or more of the following:

   ▸ To share news or tell about something that happened
   ▸ To stay in touch with someone or ask about the other person
   ▸ To express feelings or thoughts
   ▸ To invite someone to something

2. Explain that before you can write a letter, you need to know to whom you are writing. The person receiving the letter is the **audience** for the letter.

   ▸ To whom might you write a friendly letter? Answers will vary.

3. Explain that a friendly letter has an informal **voice**. It sounds friendly and natural, as if two people are talking.

   ▶ Words are informal, and they sound the way a person speaks.
   ▶ The voice you use to write to a friend is different from the voice you would use to write to someone you don't know.

4. Read the rule on page WS 75. Then read the Letter from Rico with students. Complete the Guided Exercises with students.

5. Have students complete the rest of the Activity Book page. Provide support as necessary.

6. Keep the envelope with the Letter from Rico in a safe place so that students may refer to it later.

TIP Remind students that the audience determines the voice of a letter. We sometimes say that a friendly letter has an informal tone. But even with an informal tone, the voice the writer adopts will be slightly different in letters to a grandmother and to a friend.

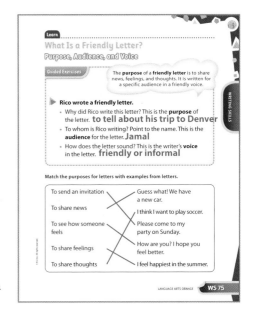

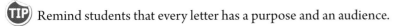

Try It

To Whom Are You Writing?

Help students practice how to plan a letter. Turn to page WS 76 in *K12 Language Arts Activity Book*.

1. Read the directions to students. Read the sentences together.

2. Have students complete the Activity Book page. Provide support as necessary.

3. Discuss the purpose, audience, and voice of a letter with students.

   ▶ Have students think of something they could write about in a letter.
   ▶ Ask students to choose an audience for their letter, such as a friend or grandparent. For example, if you want to tell about a friend's new puppy, you might share this news with your cousin who knows your friend.
   ▶ Ask them to think about the kinds of information or details that they could include in their letter.

TIP Remind students that every letter has a purpose and an audience.

Objectives
• Identify the audience of a friendly letter.

Friendly Letter Format

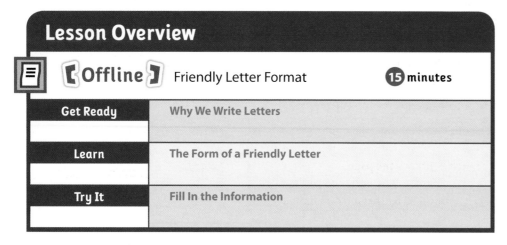

Lesson Overview

☰ **[Offline]** Friendly Letter Format   **15** minutes

Get Ready	Why We Write Letters
Learn	The Form of a Friendly Letter
Try It	Fill In the Information

Advance Preparation

Gather the envelope containing the Letter from Rico. If you have not prepared the letter, remove page WS 73 in *K¹² Language Arts Activity Book*, fold it, and place it in an envelope.

Big Ideas

A friendly letter is written to share thoughts and feelings. It follows a specific form.

 **15** minutes

Friendly Letter Format
You will work with students to complete Get Ready, Learn, and Try It activities.

Get Ready ·

Why We Write Letters
Remind students that letters are written for a reason.

▶ What are some reasons for writing a friendly letter? Answers will vary. Possible answers: sharing thoughts, feelings, or news; telling about something that has happened; sending an invitation; asking a question

Say: You will be writing your own friendly letter. Answers to the following questions will vary.

▶ To whom could you write a friendly letter?
▶ What could you write about?

Materials

Supplied
- *K¹² Language Arts Activity Book*, pp. WS 73, 77–78

Also Needed
- envelope

Keywords

body (of a friendly letter) – the main text of a friendly letter

closing (of a friendly letter) – the part of a friendly letter that follows the body Example: *Your friend* or *Love*

greeting – the part of a letter that begins with the word *Dear* followed by a person's name; also called the salutation

heading – the first part of a letter that has the writer's address and the date

signature – the end of a letter where the writer writes his or her name

Objectives
- Identify the purpose of a friendly letter.

Learn

The Form of a Friendly Letter

Introduce the parts of a letter—heading, greeting, body, closing, and signature—to students. Gather the envelope containing the Letter from Rico, and turn to page WS 77 in *K¹² Language Arts Activity Book*.

1. Explain that a letter has a specific form. There are five parts to a letter: heading, greeting, body, closing, and signature.

2. Describe each part of a friendly letter to students. As you explain each part, point to it on the Letter from Rico:

   ▶ The top part of a letter is the **heading**. The heading has the writer's address and the date. It starts in the center of the page.

   ▶ The **greeting** shows the name of the person who will receive the letter. It starts with the word *Dear,* followed by the person's name, and a comma.

   ▶ The **body** is the main part of the letter. It includes the writer's message or questions. The first line of each paragraph is indented.

   ▶ The **closing** is how the letter ends. It is like saying good-bye. The closing uses words like *Love, Yours truly,* or *Your friend,* followed by a comma.

   ▶ The **signature** is the writer's name. It tells who wrote the letter. It follows the closing on a separate line. Both the closing and the signature start in the center of the page. They line up with the heading at the top of the page.

3. Read the rule on the Activity Book page. Use the Letter from Rico to complete the Guided Exercises with students. Check that students say the correct name of each part and point to it on the letter.

4. Have students complete the rest of the Activity Book page. Provide support as necessary.

5. Put the Letter from Rico back in the envelope and keep it in a safe place so students can refer to it later.

TIP Share a real letter with students and point out the different parts of the letter.

Objectives

- Use established conventions for a friendly letter.
- Recognize the parts of a friendly letter.

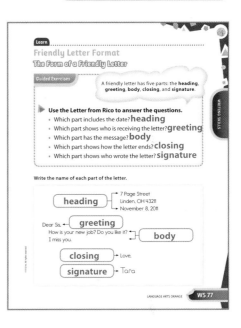

Try It

Fill In the Information

Help students practice with the form of a friendly letter. Turn to page WS 78 in
K¹² Language Arts Activity Book.

1. Read the directions to students.

2. Have students add the missing information. Provide support as necessary.

TIP Assist students if they need help writing their address or today's date.
Have students read the completed letter aloud.

Online Alternative

This activity is OPTIONAL. It is intended for students who want extra practice or
who would prefer to do online practice in place of the offline Try It. Feel free to
skip this activity.

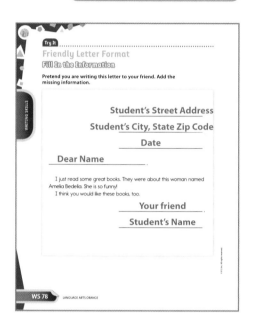

Objectives

- Use established conventions for a friendly letter.
- Recognize the parts of a friendly letter.

Organize a Letter

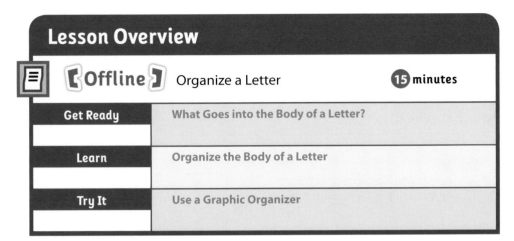

Lesson Overview

	Offline Organize a Letter	**15** minutes
Get Ready	What Goes into the Body of a Letter?	
Learn	Organize the Body of a Letter	
Try It	Use a Graphic Organizer	

Advance Preparation

Gather the envelope with the Letter from Rico. If you have not prepared the letter, remove page WS 73 in *K¹² Language Arts Activity Book,* fold it, and place it in an envelope.

Big Ideas

Friendly letters are written to share news, information, ideas, or feelings.

Materials

Supplied
- *K¹² Language Arts Activity Book,* pp. WS 73, 79–80

Also Needed
- envelope

Keywords

beginning sentence – a sentence that introduces the topic or subject of the writing that follows

concluding sentence – the last sentence of a paragraph; often summarizes the paragraph

graphic organizer – a visual device, such as a diagram or chart, that helps a writer plan a piece of writing

time order – the arrangement of ideas according to when they happened

Offline   **15** minutes

Organize a Letter
You will work with students to complete Get Ready, Learn, and Try It activities.

Get Ready

What Goes into the Body of a Letter?
Explain that the body of a letter tells why the letter was written.

1. **Say:** The **body** of a letter tells why the letter was written.

   ▶ What kinds of things can go in the body of a letter? news, details about something that happened, feelings or thoughts, invitations, questions

Objectives
- Identify the purpose of a friendly letter.

2. **Say:** Pretend I sent you a letter. The body of the letter says, "I would like to invite you to my party. It will be at my house next Friday at 5:00 pm. I hope you can come."

   ▶ What is the purpose of that letter? to invite someone to a party

3. **Say:** Pretend I sent you another letter. The body says, "I went to the zoo last weekend. It was amazing! My favorite part was seeing the lions."

   ▶ What is the purpose of that letter? to share news and feelings

4. **Say:** You will be writing your own letter.

   ▶ Can you think of a purpose for your letter? Answers will vary.

Learn

Organize the Body of a Letter

Introduce beginning sentences, concluding sentences, and time order to students. Gather the envelope containing the Letter from Rico, and turn to page WS 79 in *K¹² Language Arts Activity Book*.

1. Read the rule on the Activity Book page.

2. Explain that a **beginning sentence** introduces a letter and tells what the letter will be about.
   Say: Look at the beginning sentence in the Letter from Rico.

   ▶ What is the letter going to be about? Rico's time he spent in Denver

3. Explain that a **concluding sentence** sums up what has just been written.
   Say: Look at the concluding sentence in the Letter from Rico.

   ▶ How does this sentence sum up the letter? It tells that Rico had a fun time on his trip.

4. Explain that the body of a letter has to be written in an order that makes sense. If the letter is about an event, it makes sense to put the body in **time order**.

   ▶ Is the Letter from Rico written in time order? Yes

5. Explain that a **graphic organizer** helps us see relationships between ideas and order our thoughts. Remind students to write ideas or notes in the graphic organizer. They do not need to write complete sentences. Explain that details and complete sentences are used later when writing a letter.

6. Have students use the Letter from Rico to complete the Activity Book page. Provide support as necessary.

7. Put the Letter from Rico back in the envelope and keep it in a safe place so that students can refer to it later.

Objectives

- Use beginning sentences.
- Use concluding sentences.
- Use a graphic organizer to plan.
- Organize ideas through sequencing.
- Write a narrative with a beginning, middle, and end.
- Use transition words to signal order.

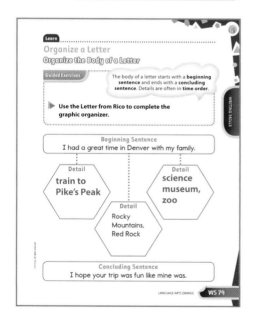

Try It

✏ Use a Graphic Organizer

Help students practice using a graphic organizer to plan their writing. Turn to page WS 80 in *K¹² Language Arts Activity Book*.

1. Read the directions to students. Look over the graphic organizer together.

2. Tell students to use the graphic organizer to plan the body of their friendly letter. Remind them to only write ideas or notes. They will add to their organizer and write complete sentences later.

3. Have students complete the graphic organizer. Provide support as necessary.

4. Keep the Activity Book page in a safe place so that students can use it later.

TIP If the letter is about ideas, and not events, the ideas should flow in the order that makes sense, which might not be time order. Help your student put ideas in a logical order.

Objectives

- Use a graphic organizer to plan.
- Organize ideas through sequencing.

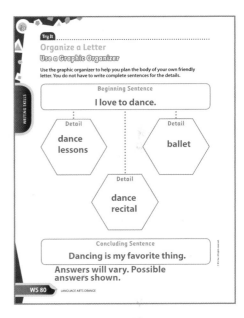

Address an Envelope

Lesson Overview

[Offline] Address an Envelope   **15** minutes

Get Ready	Look at a Letter
Learn	How to Address an Envelope
Try It	Address Your Envelope

[Materials]

Supplied
- *K¹² Language Arts Activity Book*, pp. WS 80–82

Also Needed
- household items – piece of mail
- envelope (2)

Advance Preparation

Gather page WS 80 in *K¹² Language Arts Activity Book* (Use a Graphic Organizer), which students previously completed; two envelopes; and a piece of mail that includes a mailing address, return address, and a canceled stamp.

Big Ideas

Envelopes must be addressed in a precise format for the post office to deliver the mail accurately.

[Offline] ⏱ minutes

Address an Envelope
You will work with students to complete Get Ready, Learn, and Try It activities.

Get Ready ···

Look at a Letter
Introduce mailing an envelope. Gather a piece of mail.

1. **Say:** When you send a letter, several steps need to happen before someone can receive it.

   ▶ What happens between putting a letter in an envelope and having it show up in someone's mailbox? Answers will vary.

2. Explain to students that after you sign a letter, it is placed into an envelope. Then the envelope is sealed and addressed to the person to whom you are sending it, and a stamp is put on it. Mail goes to the post office, where it is sorted by zip codes. Then it goes to the mail carrier who delivers the letter.

3. Show students a piece of mail. Point to the canceled stam p, the mailing address, and the zip code. Tell students that having the correct address and zip code is very important. Each must be written in the correct place. Every letter must also have a stamp, or the post office will not deliver it.

Objectives
- Recognize the importance of properly addressing an envelope.

Learn ···

How to Address an Envelope
Introduce how to address an envelope, including where to put the delivery address, return address, and stamp. Gather a piece of mail and an envelope, and turn to page WS 81 in *K¹² Language Arts Activity Book*.

1. Explain that an envelope has to be addressed correctly and a stamp must be added before a letter can be mailed.

2. Show students a piece of mail. Point to the name and **delivery address**. **Say:** This is the delivery address. It shows where the mail was sent.

3. Point to the **return address**. **Say:** This is the return address. It shows who sent the letter.

4. Point to the **stamp**. **Say:** The stamp is how people pay for the mail. People buy stamps from the post office and put them on envelopes to show they have paid for the post office to deliver the mail.

Objectives
- Address an envelope.

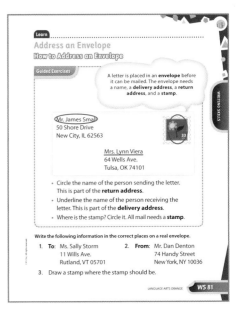

5. Read the rule and show students the sample envelope on the Activity Book page. Complete the Guided Exercises with students.

6. Provide students with a blank envelope. Have them complete the rest of the Activity Book page. Provide support as necessary.

7. Be sure students write the name and address of the recipient, Ms. Sally Storm, in the center of the envelope. The return address, starting with Mr. Dan Denton, should be written in the upper left corner. The stamp belongs on the upper right.

Try It

Address Your Envelope

Help students address an envelope. Gather page WS 80 (Use a Graphic Organizer), and turn to page WS 82 in *K¹² Language Arts Activity Book*.

1. Review the graphic organizer with students. Talk about the person to whom they are writing and what their letter will say.

2. Remind students that they will have to address an envelope before they can send their letter.

3. Read the directions to students. Discuss the activity together.

4. Explain to students that some parts of an address can be abbreviated. The names of states are also abbreviated.

   ▸ Make a list of common abbreviations and show students the abbreviations they need to know to write their own address.
   ▸ Common abbreviations include St., Ave., Blvd, Apt., and directions like N., S., E., and W.
   ▸ Show students the post office abbreviation for their state and the state of the person to whom they are writing.

5. After students practice using the Activity Book page, have students address an actual envelope. Provide support as necessary. Students should write their own address as the return address. Provide them with the address of the person to whom they are writing their letter, but don't write it on the envelope for them.

6. Tell students that when they finish their letter, they will put it in the envelope and send the letter.

7. If they have additional time, have students continue to add details to their graphic organizer to include in the body of their letter.

8. Save students' completed envelope and the graphic organizer for use later in this unit.

(TIP) If students are not mailing letters in the United States, teach them the appropriate conventions for the region in which they are sending mail.

Objectives
• Address an envelope.

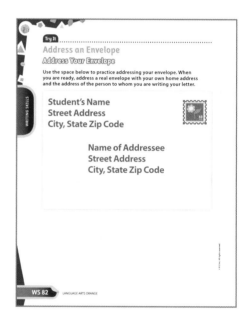

Write a Friendly Letter

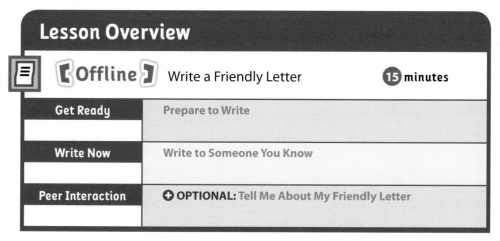

Lesson Overview

Offline — Write a Friendly Letter — **15** minutes

Get Ready	Prepare to Write
Write Now	Write to Someone You Know
Peer Interaction	**+ OPTIONAL:** Tell Me About My Friendly Letter

Materials

Supplied
- *K¹² Language Arts Activity Book*, pp. WS 80, 83–86

Also Needed
- envelope (optional)

Advance Preparation

Have students gather the envelope they addressed and page WS 80 in *K¹² Language Arts Activity Book* (Use a Graphic Organizer), which they previously completed.

Offline **15** minutes

Write a Friendly Letter

You will work with students to complete Get Ready and Write Now activities.

Prepare to Write

Review with students the correct format for a friendly letter.

1. Ask students to describe the parts of a friendly letter.

    ▸ What are the five parts of a friendly letter? heading, greeting, body, closing, signature
    ▸ Where do the heading and the closing start? in the center of the paper

2. Review the body of a friendly letter.

    ▸ What should you do to the first line in each paragraph? Indent it.
    ▸ What are transition words for? They keep ideas in order.
    ▸ What else should you remember about the body of a letter? Answers will vary. There should be a beginning statement and a concluding statement. There should be a beginning, middle, and end. The details should be written in time order or in some other order that makes sense.

> **Objectives**
> - Recognize the parts of a friendly letter.
> - Recall the established conventions of a friendly letter.

Write Now •

Write to Someone You Know

Help students write a friendly letter. Gather page WS 80 (Use a Graphic Organizer), and turn to page WS 83 in *K¹² Language Arts Activity Book*.

1. Explain that students will use their graphic organizer to write a friendly letter.

2. Have students write their letter on a sheet of paper so they can revise their work and transfer a clean copy to the Activity Book page.

3. Have students write a complete and neat copy of their friendly letter on the Activity Book page. Students can use one or both sides of the paper for their letter. Remind students to start the closing and signature in the center of the page.

4. Use the materials and instructions in the online lesson to evaluate students' finished writing. You will be evaluating their writing for the following:

   ► Purpose and Content: The writing should be a friendly letter that shares news, ideas, feelings, or events. The letter should have a friendly voice. The body of the letter should have a beginning and concluding sentence. The main idea should be supported with a few details. The language should be clear.

   ► Structure and Organization: The letter should have a heading, greeting, body, closing, and signature. They should all be used correctly. The details should be written mostly in time or logical order.

   ► Grammar and Mechanics: All sentences should be complete and punctuated correctly. The greeting and closing should end with a comma.

5. Enter students' scores for each rubric category online.

6. If students scored a 1 in any category, follow the online instructions to help them edit and revise their work.

TIP For an optional activity, have students mail their finished letters. Have them put the letter in the envelope they addressed previously, add a stamp, and mail it. Students can also mail a letter to themselves just for practice. Check the envelope to be sure that it was written correctly. A walk to a mailbox or a visit to the post office will help conclude the experience.

Reward: When students' writing is Level 2 or higher on the grading rubric, add a sticker for this unit on the My Accomplishments chart.

Objectives

- Write a friendly letter.
- Use established conventions for a friendly letter.
- Organize ideas through sequencing.
- Use beginning and concluding statements.
- Use an appropriate organizational pattern in writing.
- Use a voice based on purpose and audience.
- Write a narrative with a beginning, middle, and end.
- Use transition words to signal order.
- Use a graphic organizer to plan.

Peer Interaction

⊕ OPTIONAL: Tell Me About My Friendly Letter

This activity is OPTIONAL. It is intended for students who have extra time and would benefit from extra practice. Feel free to skip this activity.

Students can benefit from exchanging letters with someone they know. To complete this optional activity, turn to page WS 85 in *K¹² Language Arts Activity Book*.

1. Send the Activity Book page to someone who is able to complete it, perhaps the recipient of the letter or another student.

2. Have students use the feedback provided from other students to revise their friendly letters.

Objectives

- Use guidance from adults and peers to revise writing.
- Collaborate with peers on writing projects.

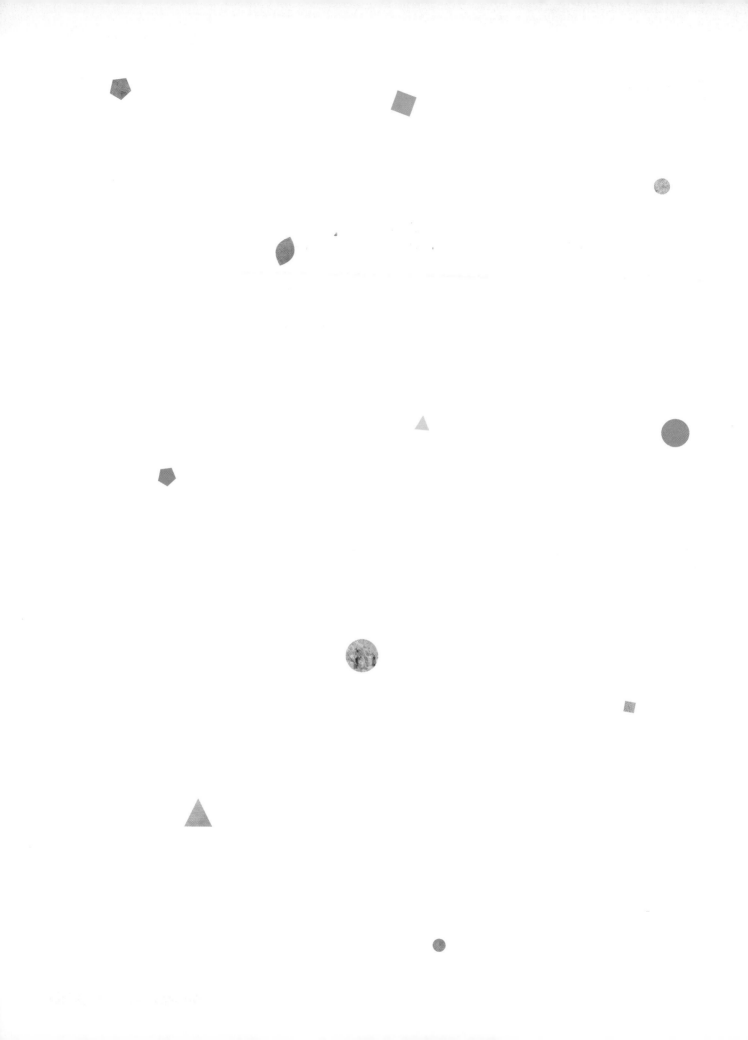

One or Many?

Unit Overview

In this unit, students will
- ► Learn the difference between singular and plural nouns.
- ► Learn to spell the singular and plural forms of nouns.

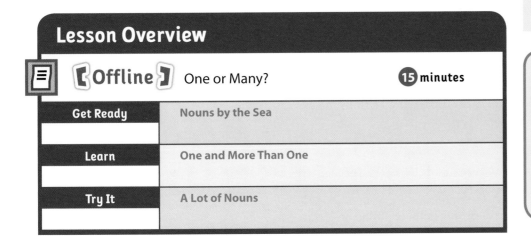

Lesson Overview

	[Offline] One or Many?	**15** minutes
Get Ready	Nouns by the Sea	
Learn	One and More Than One	
Try It	A Lot of Nouns	

[Materials]

Supplied
- *K¹² Language Arts Activity Book*, pp. WS 87–88

Keywords

noun – a word that names a person, place, thing, or idea
plural noun – a word that names more than one person, place, thing, or idea
singular noun – a word that names one person, place, thing, or idea

Content Background

A noun names a person, place, thing, or idea. A noun can be either singular or plural. Most plural nouns are formed by adding –s or –es to the singular form.

Big Ideas

Speakers tend to use the singular and plural forms of nouns correctly. The more challenging aspect of using plural nouns is to spell them correctly.

 **[Offline]** 🕐 **15** minutes

One or Many?
You will work with students to complete Get Ready, Learn, and Try It activities.

Get Ready

Nouns by the Sea
Review nouns with an ocean riddle.

1. Invite students to try to solve the following riddle. Then share the answer with them.

   ▸ Why are fish so smart? because they swim in schools

2. Remind students that the word *fish* is a **noun**. It names a thing. Nouns can also name people or places.

   ▸ What is the noun in the answer to the riddle? schools

3. Challenge students to name other ocean nouns. Answers will vary.
   Possible answers : waves, sand, octopus, shark, shells

4. Explain that a noun can tell about one thing or many things.

 Objectives
- Recall what a noun is.
- Identify nouns.

Learn

One and More Than One
Introduce singular and plural nouns. Turn to page 87 in *K¹² Language Arts Activity Book*.

1. Review the singular and plural of the word *finger*.

   ▸ Hold up one finger and ask students what it is. finger
   ▸ Hold up two fingers and ask students what they are called. fingers

2. Explain the difference between singular and plural.

   ▸ When we talk about one finger, the noun is **singular**.
   ▸ When we talk about more than one finger, we say *fingers*. This noun is **plural**. When we write the plural form of most nouns, we add an –*s* to the end of the noun. Sometimes we have to add –*es* instead.

3. Read the rule on the Activity Book page. Complete the Guided Exercises with students.

4. Have students complete the rest of the Activity Book page. Provide support as necessary.

Objectives
- Identify singular nouns.
- Identify plural nouns.
- Form and use plural nouns.

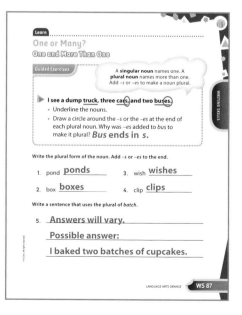

Try It

 A Lot of Nouns

Have students complete page WS 88 in *K¹² Language Arts Activity Book* for more practice with identifying and forming singular and plural nouns.

1. Read the first set of directions to students. Read the words together. Have students complete Exercises 1–8.

2. Read the second set of directions to students. Have students complete Exercise 9. Provide support as necessary.

TIP Make a chore chart together. List chores and responsibilities that students have each week, such as *Feed the cats* and *Read two stories*. Point to each plural noun and talk about how it is spelled.

Objectives
- Identify singular nouns.
- Identify plural nouns.
- Form and use plural nouns.

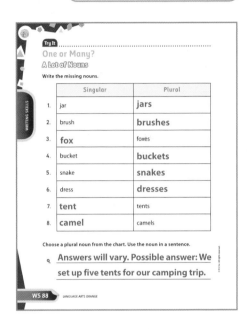

Try It
One or Many?
A Lot of Nouns

Write the missing nouns.

	Singular	Plural
1.	jar	jars
2.	brush	brushes
3.	fox	foxes
4.	bucket	buckets
5.	snake	snakes
6.	dress	dresses
7.	tent	tents
8.	camel	camels

Choose a plural noun from the chart. Use the noun in a sentence.

9. Answers will vary. Possible answer: We set up five tents for our camping trip.

WS 88   LANGUAGE ARTS ORANGE

Focus on Singular and Plural Nouns

Lesson Overview

	Focus on Singular and Plural Nouns	**15** minutes
Review	Planet Noun	

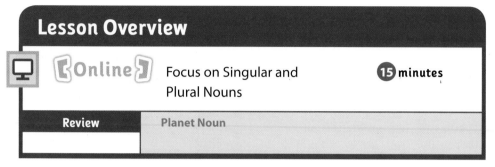

Materials

There are no materials to gather for this lesson.

Online **15** minutes

Focus on Singular and Plural Nouns

Students will work on their own to complete review and practice activities. Help students locate the online activities and provide support as needed.

Review

Planet Noun

Students will work online to practice classifying nouns as singular or plural.

Objectives
- Identify singular nouns.
- Identify plural nouns.
- Form and use plural nouns.

Offline Alternative

No computer access? Write several singular nouns. Have students write the plural of these singular nouns and explain how they formed the plural. Then have students use the plural form in a sentence.

More Plural Nouns

Lesson Overview

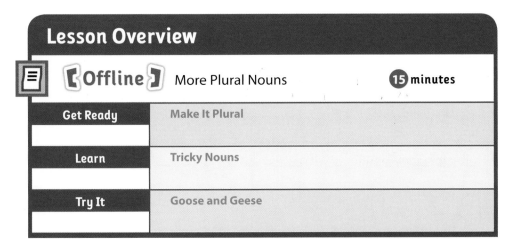

	Offline] More Plural Nouns	15 minutes
Get Ready	Make It Plural	
Learn	Tricky Nouns	
Try It	Goose and Geese	

Materials

Supplied
- *K¹² Language Arts Activity Book*, pp. WS 89–90
- whiteboard (optional)

Keywords
noun – a word that names a person, place, thing, or idea
plural noun – a word that names more than one person, place, thing, or idea
singular noun – a word that names one person, place, thing, or idea

Content Background

Forming the plural of some nouns involves making spelling changes that go beyond simply adding –*s* or –*es* to the singular form. The plurals of these nouns are irregular and must be learned. Common irregular plural nouns are *feet*, *mice*, *geese*, *children*, *men*, *women*, and *teeth*.

 **15** minutes

More Plural Nouns
You will work with students to complete Get Ready, Learn, and Try It activities.

Get Ready

Make It Plural
Review how to form common plural nouns.

1. Write *a*, *b*, and *c* on a whiteboard or a sheet of paper.

2. Have students suggest a singular noun that begins with each letter.

3. Write the following suggested nouns. Then have students add –*s* or –*es* to each word to make it plural. For example,

   ► apple s
   ► box es
   ► cookie s

4. Remind students that most nouns are made plural by adding an –*s* or –*es* to the end of the word. Some nouns, however, are made plural in unusual ways.

Objectives
- Form plural nouns.

Learn

Tricky Nouns

Introduce irregular plural nouns to students. Turn to page WS 89 in *K¹² Language Arts Activity Book*.

1. Explain that some plural nouns do not end in *–s* or *–es*. Some nouns become plural by changing the word in different ways. These plural forms must be learned for each word.

2. Point to your foot.
   Say: My foot has five toes.

3. Point to both of your feet.
   Say: My feet have ten toes.

   ▶ Ask students why the word *foot* changed to *feet. Foot* means one. It is singular. *Feet* means more than one. It is plural.

4. Go over the following pairs with students. Ask them to tell you the plural of each singular word if they know it. Correct students as necessary.

   ▶ tooth teeth
   ▶ mouse mice
   ▶ child children
   ▶ man men
   ▶ woman women
   ▶ goose geese

5. Read the rule on the Activity Book page. Complete the Guided Exercises with students.

6. Have students complete the rest of the Activity Book page. Provide support as necessary. If students are struggling, you may want to provide them with a word bank with the singular form of the irregular plurals they just learned.

TIP Have students choose a pair of nouns on the Activity Book page. Have them draw a picture for each noun in the pair. Have them label the pictures using the correct form for each noun.

Objectives
- Identify singular nouns.
- Identify plural nouns.
- Form and use irregular plural nouns.

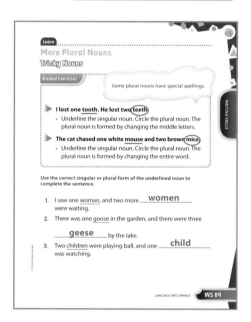

Try It

Goose and Geese

Have students complete page WS 90 in *K¹² Language Arts Activity Book* for more practice with irregular plural nouns.

1. Read the first set of directions to students. Have them complete Exercises 1–5.

2. Read the second set of directions to students. Have them complete Exercise 6. Provide support as necessary.

Objectives
- Identify singular nouns.
- Identify plural nouns.
- Form and use irregular plural nouns.

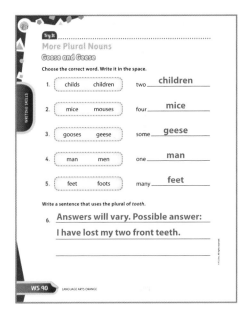

Try It

More Plural Nouns

Goose and Geese

Choose the correct word. Write it in the space.

1. childs / children   two ___children___

2. mice / mouses   four ___mice___

3. gooses / geese   some ___geese___

4. man / men   one ___man___

5. feet / foots   many ___feet___

Write a sentence that uses the plural of *tooth*.

6. **Answers will vary. Possible answer:** I have lost my two front teeth.

WS 90   LANGUAGE ARTS ORANGE

Review Singular and Plural Nouns

Lesson Overview

	Review Singular and Plural Nouns	15 minutes
Review	Noun Sizzle	

Materials

There are no materials to gather for this lesson.

 Online 15 minutes

Review Singular and Plural Nouns

Students will work on their own to complete review and practice activities. Help students locate the online activities and provide support as needed.

Review

Noun Sizzle

Students will work online to review what they have learned about singular and plural nouns.

Offline Alternative

No computer access? Write several singular and plural nouns. For the singular nouns, ask students to tell you the plural noun that matches the noun you provided. Make sure to include nouns that have irregular plural forms. For the plural nouns, ask students to tell you the singular noun that matches the noun you provided. Have students say a couple of sentences using irregular plural nouns.

Objectives
- Identify singular nouns.
- Identify plural nouns.
- Form and use plural nouns.
- Form and use irregular plural nouns.

Unit Checkpoint

Lesson Overview

Offline	Unit Checkpoint	15 minutes
Unit Checkpoint	Singular and Plural Nouns	

Materials

Supplied
- *K¹² Language Arts Assessments*, pp. WS 21–24

Offline 15 minutes

Unit Checkpoint
You will work with students to complete the Unit Checkpoint.

Unit Checkpoint

Singular and Plural Nouns

Explain that students are going to show what they have learned about singular and plural nouns.

1. Give students the Unit Checkpoint pages.

2. Read the directions together. Have students complete the Checkpoint on their own.

3. Use the Answer Key to score the Checkpoint, and then enter the results online.

4. Review each exercise with students. Work with students to correct any exercise that they missed.

TIP Students who answered one or more questions incorrectly should continue to practice this grammar skill. Read aloud students' favorite books. Stop from time to time to point out singular, plural, and irregular plural nouns.

Objectives
- Identify singular nouns.
- Identify plural nouns.
- Form and use plural nouns.
- Form and use irregular plural nouns.

 Reward: When students score 80 percent or above on the Unit Checkpoint, add a sticker for this unit on the My Accomplishments chart.

Name _____ Date _____

⚙ Unit Checkpoint Learning Coach Instructions
Singular and Plural Nouns

Explain that students are going to show what they have learned about singular and plural nouns.

1. Give students the Unit Checkpoint pages.

2. Read the directions together. Have students complete the Checkpoint on their own.

3. Use the Answer Key to score the Checkpoint, and then enter the results online.

4. Review each exercise with students. Work with students to correct any exercise that they missed.

Name _____ Date _____

⚙ Unit Checkpoint Answer Key
Singular and Plural Nouns

Part 1. Identify Singular and Plural Nouns
Choose whether the noun is singular or plural.

1. people
   A. singular
   B. plural *(selected)*

2. axes
   A. singular
   B. plural *(selected)*

3. man
   A. singular *(selected)*
   B. plural

4. geese
   A. singular
   B. plural *(selected)*

5. berries
   A. singular
   B. plural *(selected)*

6. crabs
   A. singular
   B. plural *(selected)*

7. doctors
   A. singular
   B. plural *(selected)*

8. sock
   A. singular *(selected)*
   B. plural

Name _____ Date _____

9. gas
   A. singular *(selected)*
   B. plural

10. stars
    A. singular
    B. plural *(selected)*

11. grape
    A. singular *(selected)*
    B. plural

12. roof
    A. singular *(selected)*
    B. plural

Part 2. Use Singular and Plural Nouns
Which noun belongs in the sentence?

13. Two _____ waved at me.
    A. boy
    B. boys *(selected)*

14. There are six _____ in the sink.
    A. dishs
    B. dishes *(selected)*

15. All of the _____ like cheese.
    A. mouses
    B. mice *(selected)*

16. Mr. Lee cut down four _____.
    A. bushes *(selected)*
    B. bush

17. I folded the _____.
    A. boxes *(selected)*
    B. boxs

18. Lori hung up both of her _____.
    A. dress
    B. dresses *(selected)*

Name _____ Date _____

Part 3. Form Plural Nouns
Choose the correct way to write the plural.

19. What is the correct way to write more than one child?
    A. childs
    B. childrens
    C. children *(selected)*

20. What is the correct way to write more than one foot?
    A. foots
    B. feet *(selected)*
    C. feets

What Is a Thank-You Note?

Unit Overview

In this unit, students will
- ► Identify the form and purpose of a thank-you note.
- ► Write a main idea and supporting details.
- ► Write a thank-you note.

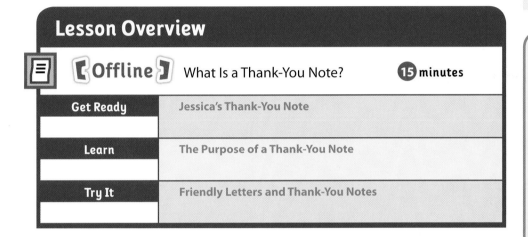

Lesson Overview

[Offline] What Is a Thank-You Note?   **15** minutes

Get Ready	Jessica's Thank-You Note
Learn	The Purpose of a Thank-You Note
Try It	Friendly Letters and Thank-You Notes

Advance Preparation

Pull out page WS 91 in *K¹² Language Arts Activity Book* (Jessica's Thank-You Note).
Keep the page in a safe place so you can refer to it throughout the unit.

Big Ideas

Writing varies by purpose and audience. The specific reason for writing and the
writer's intended readers (audience) determine the correct form and language to use.

Materials

Supplied
- *K¹² Language Arts Activity Book*, pp. WS 91–94

Keywords

audience – a writer's readers
friendly letter – a kind of letter, written between two people who know each other, used to share thoughts, feelings, and news
purpose – the reason for writing
thank-you note – a kind of friendly letter in which the writer thanks someone for something

 **Offline** **15** minutes

What Is a Thank-You Note?

You will work with students to complete Get Ready, Learn, and Try It activities.

Get Ready

Jessica's Thank-You Note

Review a friendly letter with students and introduce thank-you notes. Gather Jessica's Thank-You Note.

1. Remind students that a friendly letter has a purpose: to share thoughts, feelings, and news or ask questions.

2. Remind students that a friendly letter has a voice and an audience. It is written in a friendly or informal tone for a particular reader.

3. Review the five parts of a letter.

   ▶ What are the five parts of a letter? heading, greeting, body, closing, and signature

   Have students point to the five parts of a letter on Jessica's Thank-You Note as they name the parts.

   ▶ Which part explains why the letter was written? the body
   ▶ What order are the ideas in the body? usually time order or logical order

   Have students point to the details in Jessica's Thank-You Note.

4. Explain that a thank-you note is like a friendly letter. It shares the same parts, but it is written for a specific purpose—to say thank you.

5. Read Jessica's Thank-You Note with students.

   ▶ Why did Jessica write this letter? to say thank you for the blanket

6. Keep Jessica's Thank-You Note in a safe place so students can refer to it later.

 Objectives
- Recognize what a friendly letter is.
- Identify the purpose of a friendly letter.
- Recognize the parts of a friendly letter.

Learn

The Purpose of a Thank-You Note

Introduce thank-you notes to students. Gather Jessica's Thank-You Note, and turn to page WS 93 in *K¹² Language Arts Activity Book*.

1. Explain that a **thank-you note** is

   ▶ A thank-you written in a letter, a card, or an e-mail
   ▶ A more formal way to thank people than just telling them thank you

 Objectives
- Identify the purpose of a thank-you note.

2. Discuss the reasons to write a thank-you note.

> ► What are some of the things you can thank someone for? Answers will vary. Possible answers: giving you a gift, coming to your home or a party, doing something for you, inviting you someplace, hosting an event, helping you do something, taking you somewhere

3. Read the rule on the Activity Book page. Then read Jessica's Thank-You Note with students. Complete the Guided Exercises with students.

4. Have students complete the rest of the Activity Book page. Provide support as necessary.

5. Keep Jessica's Thank-You Note in a safe place so students can refer to it later.

TIP If you have cause to write a thank-you note, write and share one with students. If students need to thank someone for a recent gift or kindness, have them write and send a real thank-you note during this unit.

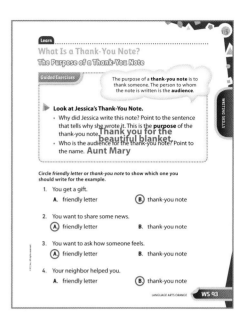

Try It

Friendly Letters and Thank-You Notes

Help students recognize the purposes of a thank-you note and a friendly letter. Turn to page WS 94 in *K¹² Language Arts Activity Book.*

1. Read the directions to students. Read the sentences together.

2. Have students complete the Activity Book pages. Provide support as necessary.

TIP Remind students that friendly letters and thank-you notes have their own purpose and audience.

Objectives
- Identify the purpose of a thank-you note.
- Identify the purpose of a friendly letter.

Online Alternative

This activity is OPTIONAL. It is intended for students who want extra practice or who would prefer to do online practice in place of the offline Try It. Feel free to skip this activity.

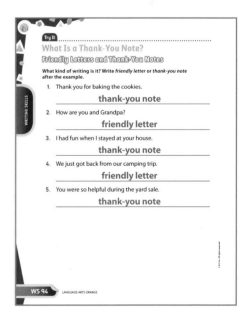

Use the Friendly Letter Format

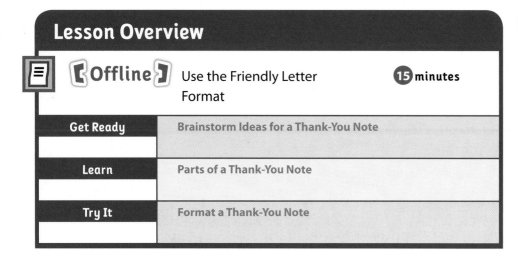

Lesson Overview

Offline	Use the Friendly Letter Format	**15** minutes
Get Ready	Brainstorm Ideas for a Thank-You Note	
Learn	Parts of a Thank-You Note	
Try It	Format a Thank-You Note	

Materials

Supplied
- *K¹² Language Arts Activity Book,* pp. WS 91, 95–96

Keywords

body – the main text of a piece of writing

closing (of a letter) – the part of a letter following the body *Example:* Your friend *or* Sincerely

greeting – the part of a letter that begins with the word *Dear* followed by a person's name; also callled the salutation

heading – the first part of a letter that has the writer's address and the date

signature – the end of a letter or note where the writer writes his or her name

Advance Preparation

Gather Jessica's Thank-You Note. If you have not already done so, remove page WS 91 in *K¹² Language Arts Activity Book.*

Big Ideas

Thank-you notes typically follow the format of a friendly letter.

Offline **15** minutes

Use the Friendly Letter Format

You will work with students to complete Get Ready, Learn, and Try It activities.

Get Ready

Brainstorm Ideas for a Thank-You Note
Review the purpose and audience for a thank-you note and brainstorm ideas.

1. Ask students about the purpose and audience of a thank-you note.

   ▸ What is the purpose of a thank-you note? to thank someone for something
   ▸ Who is the audience for a thank-you note? the person you are thanking

2. Brainstorm ideas for a thank-you note with students. Answers will vary.

   ▸ What are some reasons you could write a thank-you note?
   ▸ Who are some people you could write to?

Objectives
- Brainstorm and develop possible topics.

Learn

Parts of a Thank-You Note

Explore the format of a thank-you note. Gather Jessica's Thank-You Note, and turn to page WS 95 in *K¹² Language Arts Activity Book*.

1. Explain that a **thank-you note** has the same format as a friendly letter.

2. Review each part of a thank-you note with students. If students can name and describe the parts themselves, allow them to do so. Have students point to each part on Jessica's Thank-You Note.

   ▸ The top part of a thank-you note is the **heading**. The heading includes the writer's address and the date. It starts in the center of the page.
   ▸ The **greeting** shows the name of the person who will receive the thank-you note. The greeting includes the word *Dear*, followed by the person's name and a comma.
   ▸ The **body** is the main part of the thank-you note. It includes the message or thank-you, and something positive about the gift, hospitality, or kindness. These are the reasons why the thank-you note is being written.
   ▸ The **closing** is the end of the thank-you note. It uses words such as *Yours truly*, *Your friend*, or *Love*, followed by a comma.
   ▸ The **signature** is the name of the person writing the thank-you note. It follows the closing on a separate line. Both the closing and the signature start in the center of the page. They line up with the heading at the top of the page.

3. Read the rule on the Activity Book page. Use Jessica's Thank-You Note to complete the Guided Exercises with students.

4. Have students use Jessica's Thank-You Note to complete the rest of the Activity Book page. Provide support as necessary.

5. Keep Jessica's Thank-You Note in a safe place so students can refer to it later.

Objectives
● Recognize parts of a friendly letter.

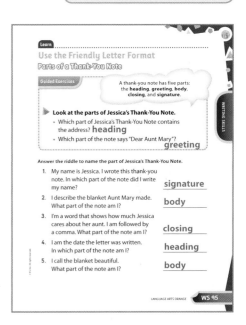

Try It

Format a Thank-You Note

Help students recognize the format of a thank-you note. Turn to page WS 96 in *K¹² Language Arts Activity Book.*

1. Read the directions to students. Read the phrases and sentences in the word bank together.

2. Have students build a thank-you note by writing the parts of the note from the word bank on the lines where they belong in the letter. Provide support as necessary.

TIP Have students read the completed thank-you note aloud.

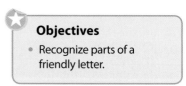

Objectives
- Recognize parts of a friendly letter.

Thank-You Note Plan

Lesson Overview

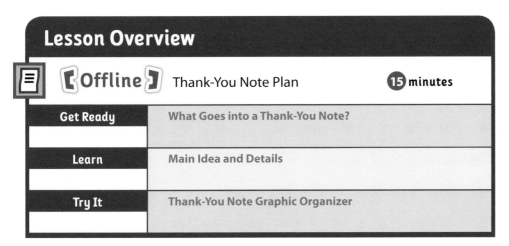

Offline Thank-You Note Plan	**15** minutes

Get Ready	What Goes into a Thank-You Note?
Learn	Main Idea and Details
Try It	Thank-You Note Graphic Organizer

Advance Preparation

Gather Jessica's Thank-You Note. If you have not already done so, remove page WS 91 in *K¹² Language Arts Activity Book*.

Big Ideas

Writers must be able to articulate a main idea and support it with appropriate details.

Materials

Supplied
- *K¹² Language Arts Activity Book*, pp. WS 91, 97–98

Keywords

main idea – the most important point

opinion – a statement of belief that cannot be proven true; the opposite of a fact

supporting details – the sentences that give information about the main idea or topic sentence

Offline **15** minutes

Thank-You Note Plan

You will work with students to complete Get Ready, Learn, and Try It activities.

 **Get Ready**

What Goes into a Thank-You Note?
Review the idea that a thank-you note has a specific format and is written for a specific purpose.

1. Tell students that they need to decide on the purpose of their thank-you note, so they should brainstorm ideas. Ask students the following questions. Answers will vary.

   ▸ Have you received a gift lately?
   ▸ Has someone invited you to a special event or hosted you at their home?
   ▸ Has someone done a particularly kind thing for you?

2. As students consider the answers to these questions, have them jot down their ideas on a piece of paper. Save these ideas for future reference.

 Objectives
- Brainstorm and develop possible topics.

Learn

Main Idea and Details

Show students how to plan the body of a thank-you note. Gather Jessica's Thank-You Note, and turn to page WS 97 in *K¹² Language Arts Activity Book*.

1. Explain that the body of a thank-you note starts with the **main idea** and includes the writer's **opinion**. Then there are reasons or **supporting details** that support the main idea.

2. Explain that writers need to plan what they will say and organize their ideas before writing. Remind students that a graphic organizer is a helpful tool. Writers can think of what they want to say and complete a graphic organizer to plan before they write a thank-you note.

3. Read the rule on the Activity Book page. Complete the Guided Exercises with students.

4. Have students complete the rest of the Activity Book page. Have students use Jessica's Thank-You Note to fill in the rest of the graphic organizer for the note. Provide support as necessary.

5. Keep Jessica's Thank-You Note in a safe place so students can refer to it later.

TIP Remind students that a graphic organizer is used to organize ideas. Students only need to write ideas in the graphic organizer, not complete sentences.

Objectives
- Organize text using main idea and supporting details.
- Use a graphic organizer to plan.

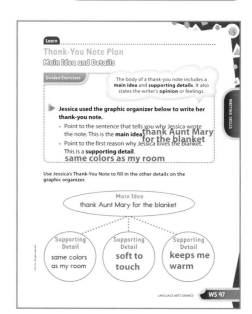

Try It

Thank-You Note Graphic Organizer

Help students plan a thank-you note by filling in a main idea and details in a graphic organizer. If students brainstormed ideas for a thank-you note previously, have them gather their notes. Turn to page WS 98 in *K¹² Language Arts Activity Book*.

1. Read the directions to students. Read the activity together.

2. Have students complete the graphic organizer. Provide support as necessary.

3. Remind students that they only need to write ideas, not complete sentences in the graphic organizer.

4. When students have finished, review the ideas with them. Answers do not need to be complete sentences.

5. Be sure that students have a main idea with details that support the main idea.

6. Make sure students have chosen a topic that is appropriate for a thank-you note.

7. Keep the Thank-You Note Graphic Organizer in a safe place so students can use it to write their thank-you note.

Objectives

- Organize text using main idea and supporting details.
- Use a graphic organizer to plan.

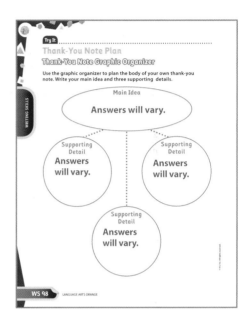

Send a Thank-You Note

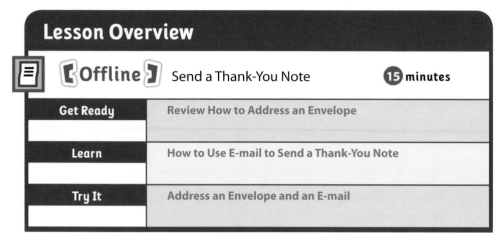

Lesson Overview

≡ [Offline] Send a Thank-You Note · **15** minutes

Get Ready	Review How to Address an Envelope
Learn	How to Use E-mail to Send a Thank-You Note
Try It	Address an Envelope and an E-mail

[Materials]

Supplied
- *K¹² Language Arts Activity Book*, pp. WS 91, 98–100

Also Needed
- household items – piece of mail
- envelope

Keywords

e-mail – electronic message or messages sent and received by computer

Advance Preparation

Gather Jessica's Thank-You Note. If you have not already done so, remove page WS 91 in *K¹² Language Arts Activity Book*. Also gather page WS 98 (Thank-You Note Graphic Organizer), which students previously completed, and a piece of mail that includes a mailing address, return address, and canceled stamp.

Big Ideas

When writing an e-mail, writers should follow the conventions appropriate for the technology, but maintain standard written English.

[Offline] **15** minutes

Send a Thank-You Note

You will work with students to complete Get Ready, Learn, and Try It activities.

 **Get Ready** ....

Review How to Address an Envelope
Review addressing an envelope and introduce students to e-mail. Gather a piece of mail.

1. Show students a piece of mail and have them identify the name and delivery address, the return address, and the stamp.

2. Explain that a letter is placed in an envelope before it can be mailed.

   ▶ How can you send a letter without using an envelope? e-mail

 Objectives
- Identify the parts of an envelope.

Learn

How to Use E-mail to Send a Thank-You Note

Introduce students to the parts of an e-mail, comparing and contrasting them with a written letter. Gather Jessica's Thank-You Note, and turn to page WS 99 in the *K¹² Language Arts Activity Book*.

Objectives
- Identify the purpose of an e-mail.

1. Discuss how regular mail is different from e-mail.

   ▶ What are some of the differences between e-mail and regular mail? Answers will vary. Possible answers: E-mail doesn't need a stamp and is received almost immediately; regular mail takes much longer to arrive. An e-mail is sent from your computer; a letter has to be mailed.

2. Show students Jessica's Thank-You Note. Have students point to the body, heading, greeting, and closing on Jessica's Thank-You Note.
   Say: An e-mail has parts that are kind of like the parts of a letter, but they look a little different.

3. Keep Jessica's Thank-You Note in a safe place so students can refer to it later.

4. Read the rule and example on the Activity Book page.
   Say: The body of an e-mail should have a greeting, a closing, and a signature. It should be written in complete sentences with correct spelling, grammar, and punctuation.

5. **Say:** An e-mail does not have a heading with an address and a date. When you send an e-mail, the date appears automatically.

6. Point to the *To:* line in the example e-mail on the Activity Book page.
   Say: An e-mail has an address line that says "To." The address line is the space where you type the e-mail address of the person to whom you are writing. This is like the delivery address on an envelope.

   ▶ What differences do you notice between the address line on the e-mail and the address line on an envelope? The address line on an envelope has a street address, city, and zip code; the address line on the e-mail only has an e-mail address.

7. Point to the *From:* line in the example e-mail.
   Say: When the person receives the e-mail, he or she will see your e-mail address as well. The address line from the sender says "From." The From line is like the return address on a letter.

8. Point to the *Subject:* line in the example e-mail.
   Say: An e-mail has a subject line. You write the purpose or the main idea of your e-mail in the subject line. For example, you can write the words "Thank you for the gift" in the subject line.

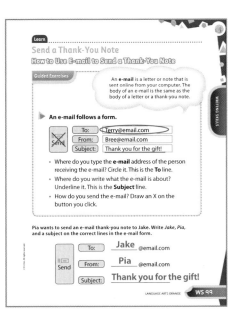

9. **Say:** E-mail programs might look different, but the *To, From,* and *Subject* fields are usually the same.

   ▶ Is there something in a letter that is similar to the *Subject:* line in the e-mail? The beginning and concluding sentences in the letter tell what the letter is about, so they do the same thing as the *Subject:* line in an e-mail.

10. Point to the *Send* button on the example e-mail.
    Say: An e-mail does not require an envelope or a stamp. To send an e-mail, you just click on the word "Send."

11. Complete the Guided Exercises with students.

12. Have students complete the rest of the Activity Book page. Provide support as necessary.

    TIP Show students how to send an e-mail using a real e-mail program.

Try It

Address an Envelope and an E-mail

Help students address an envelope and complete an e-mail form. Gather page WS 98 (Thank-You Note Graphic Organizer), and turn to page WS 100 in *K¹² Language Arts Activity Book.*

> **Objectives**
> * Address an envelope.
> * Identify the purpose of an e-mail.

1. Review students' graphic organizer with them. Ask them who they are writing to and what their letter will say.

2. Remind students that they will have to address an envelope before they can send their letter.

3. Read the first set of directions to students. Discuss the activity together.

4. Have students address the sample envelope. Provide support as necessary. Students should write their own address as the return address. Provide them with the address of the person to whom they are writing their letter, but don't write it on an envelope for them.

5. Tell students that when they finish their letters, they will put the addresses on a real envelope so they can send the letter.

6. Read the second set of directions to students. Discuss the activity together.

7. Have students complete the e-mail form. Provide support as necessary. Students should write their name in the space marked "From." They should enter the name of the person to whom they are writing their letter in the "To" area. The subject line should be what the email is about—"Thank you" or something similar.

8. If they have additional time, students can work on their graphic organizer and continue to add details they will include in the body of their letter.

9. Keep the Thank-You Note Graphic Organizer and the Activity Book page in a safe place so students can refer to it later.

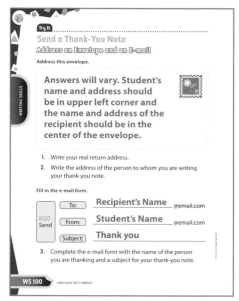

Write a Thank-You Note

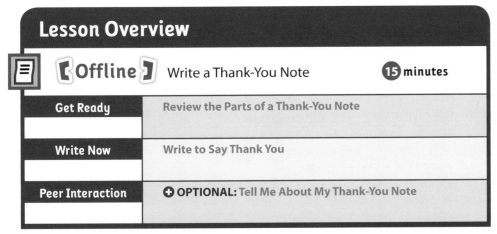

Lesson Overview

	[Offline] Write a Thank-You Note	**15** minutes
Get Ready	Review the Parts of a Thank-You Note	
Write Now	Write to Say Thank You	
Peer Interaction	➕ **OPTIONAL:** Tell Me About My Thank-You Note	

Materials

Supplied
- *K¹² Language Arts Activity Book*, pp. WS 91–104

Also Needed
- envelope

Advance Preparation

Gather Jessica's Thank-You Note. If you have not already done so, remove page WS 91 in *K¹² Language Arts Activity Book*. Also gather page WS 98 (Thank-You Note Graphic Organizer) and the other Activity Book pages students completed in this unit.

Big Ideas

- ▶ Writing varies by purpose and audience. The specific reason for writing and the writer's intended readers (audience) determine the correct form and language to use.
- ▶ When writing an e-mail, writers should follow the conventions appropriate for the technology, but maintain standard written English.
- ▶ Working collaboratively with other students during various stages of the writing process can improve student writing.

 **15 minutes**

Write a Thank-You Note

You will work with students to complete Get Ready and Write Now activities.

Get Ready ···

Review the Parts of a Thank-You Note

Review the parts of a thank-you note. Have students gather Activity Book pages they completed in this unit, including Jessica's Thank-You Note.

1. Spread out the Activity Book pages students have completed in this unit. Give students an opportunity to look at them.

2. Have students reread Jessica's Thank-You Note.

3. Discuss with students the parts of a thank-you note:

   ▸ What are the parts of a thank-you note? heading, greeting, body, closing, signature

4. Point to the heading and closing in the body of the letter.

   ▸ What do you notice about the format of the heading and closing? The heading and the closing start in the center of the paper.

5. Point to the paragraphs in the body of the letter.

   ▸ What do you notice about the paragraphs in the body of the letter? The first line in each paragraph is indented.

6. Review the body of the letter.

   ▸ What should go in the body of a thank-you letter? beginning statement, opinion statement, details, concluding statement

7. **Say:** The beginning sentence should state the main idea. An opinion statement states the writer's opinion or feelings.

   ▸ How many details should be in your letter? at least three
   ▸ Where does the concluding statement go? at the end

8. Have students point out the main idea, an opinion statement, details that support the main idea, and the concluding statement in Jessica's Thank-You Note.

Objectives

- Recognize the established conventions for a thank-you note.

Write Now •

Write to Say Thank You

In this activity, students will practice writing a thank-you note. Turn to page WS 101 in *K¹² Language Arts Activity Book*.

1. Explain that students will use their graphic organizer to write a thank-you note.

2. Have students write their thank-you note on a sheet of paper so they can revise their work and transfer a clean copy to the Activity Book page.

3. Remind students that their thank-you note should include an opinion, details that support the main idea, and a concluding sentence.

4. Remind students to revise and proofread their sentences.

5. Tell students that they should use good handwriting and leave spaces between words so that others can read what they wrote.

6. Have students write a complete and neat copy of their thank-you note on the Activity Book page.

7. Use the materials and instructions in the online lesson to evaluate students' finished writing. You will be looking at students' writing to evaluate the following:

   ▸ Purpose and Content: The purpose of the note should be clear, but it might not be stated in a sentence. The note is appropriate for its audience. The body of the note should have a main idea, an opinion, and details that support the main idea. The order of ideas should make sense. The writer should state an opinion and feelings.

   ▸ Structure and Organization: The note should have a heading, greeting, body, closing, and signature. Each should be written and placed correctly. The writer may have missed a comma in the heading, greeting, or closing. The letter might be written as one paragraph.

   ▸ Grammar and Mechanics: All sentences should be complete. There may be a single error in punctuation.

8. Enter students' scores for each rubric category online.

9. If students scored a 1 in any category, work with them to proofread and revise their work.

TIP Students can use one or both sides of the paper. Remind students to write the closing and signature by starting those lines in the center of the page. Students can mail their finished thank-you note. Have them address an actual envelope, add the stamp, and mail it. Check that they have written the delivery address and return address correctly and in the proper places on the envelope. Students can also mail the note to their Learning Coach.

Objectives

- Use established conventions for a thank-you note.
- Write a thank-you note.
- Organize text using a main idea and supporting details.
- Write an opinion statement.
- Use beginning and concluding statements.
- Write sentences and paragraphs that develop a central idea, consider purpose and audience, and use the writing process.
- Use an appropriate organizational pattern in writing.

Peer Interaction

⊕ **OPTIONAL: Tell Me About My Thank-You Note**

This activity is OPTIONAL. It is intended for students who want feedback on their writing. Feel free to skip this activity. If you choose to do this activity, it should be done **before** Learning Coaches evaluate students' thank-you notes.

Students can benefit from receiving feedback on their thank-you note from someone they know or another student. To complete this optional activity, turn to page WS 103 in K^{12} *Language Arts Activity Book.*

1. Give the Peer Interaction page and the students' completed thank-you note to another person. You may have the person to whom the note is written complete the page, or you may ask another student or adult to read the note and complete the page. You might also have students use the Peer Interaction page to provide others with feedback about their writing.

2. Allow students to read the feedback. Have students revise their notes based on the feedback that they receive.

3. Once students have had a chance to revise their work, use the rubric and the sample writing to evaluate their work.

Objectives

- Use guidance from adults and peers to revise writing.
- Collaborate with peers on writing projects.

Nouns and Verbs

Unit Overview

In this unit, students will
- ▶ Learn to pair singular subjects with singular verbs in sentences.
- ▶ Learn to pair plural subjects with plural verbs in sentences.

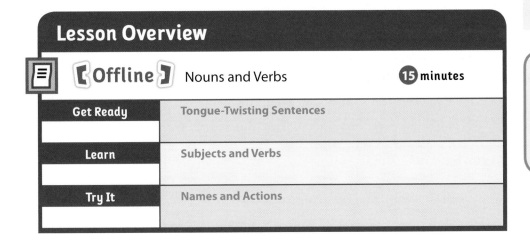

Lesson Overview

[Offline] Nouns and Verbs		15 minutes
Get Ready	**Tongue-Twisting Sentences**	
Learn	**Subjects and Verbs**	
Try It	**Names and Actions**	

Materials

Supplied
- *K¹² Language Arts Activity Book*, pp. WS 105–106

Keywords

subject – a word or words that tell whom or what the sentence is about

verb – a word that shows action or a state of being

Big Ideas

For sentences to flow smoothly, writers must choose subjects and verbs that agree. A singular subject requires a singular verb, and a plural subject requires a plural verb.

[Offline] 15 minutes

Nouns and Verbs

You will work with students to complete Get Ready, Learn, and Try It activities.

Tongue-Twisting Sentences
Review what a complete sentence is with this tongue-twisting activity.

1. Remind students that a sentence is a group of words that tells a complete thought. A complete sentence tells who did what.
   Say: Listen to this sentence: *Kim read a book.* Kim is the who, and *read a book* is what she did, or the action.

Objectives
- Recognize word groups that are sentences.

Say: Listen to this sentence: *The firefighter drives the fire engine. The firefighter* is who, and *drives the fire engine* is what she did, or the action.

2. Read this tongue twister to students. Pause after each line to ask students if the line is a complete sentence.

   ▸ *A skunk sat on a stump.* complete sentence
   ▸ *The skunk stunk.* complete sentence
   ▸ *The stump dumped the stinky skunk.* complete sentence
   ▸ *Stinky with a white stripe.* not a complete sentence

3. Remind students that *Stinky with a white stripe* is not a complete sentence because it does not say what *Stinky with a white stripe* did.

4. Say the tongue twister together, using only the complete sentences. Encourage students to say the lines as fast as they can.

Learn

Subjects and Verbs

Introduce subjects and verbs. Turn to page WS 105 in *K¹² Language Arts Activity Book.*

1. Read the rule and the first example on the Activity Book page. Point to the words *A skunk*.
   Say: The first part of this sentence tells who. It is the naming part, or **subject**.

2. Point to the word *sat*.
   Say: The last part of this sentence tells what the skunk did. This is the **verb** of the sentence.

3. Complete the Guided Exercises with students.

4. Have students complete the rest of the Activity Book page. Provide support as necessary.

Objectives
- Identify the subject of a sentence.
- Identify the verb of a sentence.

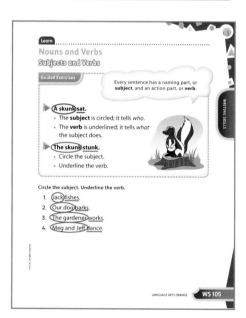

Try It

Names and Actions

Have students complete page WS 106 in *K¹² Language Arts Activity Book* for more practice with recognizing subjects and verbs in sentences.

1. Read the directions to students. Read the words in the word bank together.

2. Have students complete the Activity Book page. Provide support as necessary.

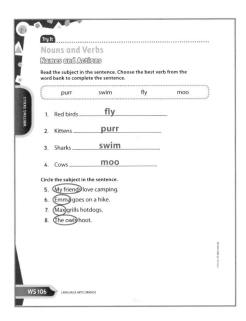

Objectives
- Identify the subject of a sentence.
- Identify the verb of a sentence.

Singular Nouns and Verbs

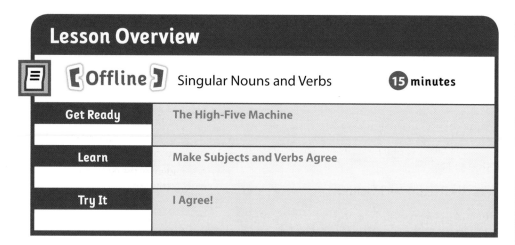

Lesson Overview

Offline Singular Nouns and Verbs **15** minutes

Get Ready	The High-Five Machine
Learn	Make Subjects and Verbs Agree
Try It	I Agree!

Materials

Supplied

- *K¹² Language Arts Activity Book*, pp. WS 107–108

Keywords

subject – a word or words that tell whom or what the sentence is about

subject-verb agreement – the way a subject and verb match when both are singular or both are plural

verb – a word that shows action or a state of being

Content Background

The subject and verb of a sentence must agree. A singular subject needs a singular verb, and a plural subject needs a plural verb.

▸ Example: *The puppy barks at the squirrel.*
  In this sentence, the subject *puppy* is singular, and the verb *barks* is singular.

▸ Example: *The puppies bark at the squirrel.*
  In this sentence, the subject *puppies* is plural, and the verb *bark* is plural.

Common exceptions to the rule are the words *I* and *you*. Both words take the plural form of the verb.

▸ Example: *I pull on my puppy's leash.*
  The singular form of the verb is *pulls*, but the plural form *pull* agrees with the subject *I*.

▸ Example: *You pull on my puppy's leash.*
  The singular form of the verb is *pulls*, but the plural form *pull* agrees with the subject *you*.

 **15 minutes**

Singular Nouns and Verbs

You will work with students to complete Get Ready, Learn, and Try It activities.

Get Ready

The High-Five Machine

Review sentence parts while playing a game called "The High-Five Machine."

Objectives
- Identify the subject of a sentence.
- Identify the verb of a sentence.

1. Remind students that every sentence has two main parts: the subject (the naming part) and the verb (the action part).

2. Stand at one end of the room. You are the High-Five Machine.

3. Have students stand at the opposite end of the room. The object for students is to reach the High-Five Machine and get a high five.

4. Read sentences, one at a time. Have students restate the subject part of the sentence. Players advance one giant step for every correct response.

5. Begin with these sentences:

   ▶ *The lions roar.* The lions
   ▶ *My pets play.* My pets
   ▶ *Three ducks swim and splash.* Three ducks
   ▶ *Maggie cooks.* Maggie
   ▶ *Our doctor talks and smiles.* Our doctor
   ▶ *A branch fell.* A branch

6. Play the game again. Read the same sentences. Have students identify the verb part of the sentence. Players advance one giant step for every correct response.

   ▶ *The lions roar.* roar
   ▶ *My pets play.* play
   ▶ *Three ducks swim and splash.* swim and splash
   ▶ *Maggie cooks.* cooks
   ▶ *Our doctor talks and smiles.* talks and smiles
   ▶ *A branch fell.* fell

Learn

Make Subjects and Verbs Agree

Introduce subject and verb agreement. Turn to page WS 107 in *K¹² Language Arts Activity Book*.

1. Explain that a subject and a verb must agree. They must fit together.
   Say: Look at the puzzle pieces. You can see that they fit together. Subjects and verbs fit together in the same way.

2. Read the rule on the Activity Book page.

3. Read the first example together.

   ▸ Have students identify the subject of the sentence. The cow

4. Explain that this sentence tells about one cow. The subject is singular.
   Say: To make the parts fit together, the verb must be singular, too. An –*s* was added to the verb *moo* to make it singular.

5. Explain that when –*s* is added to a singular noun, the noun becomes plural. However, when –*s* is added to a verb, the verb becomes singular.

6. Read the second example on the page.

   ▸ Have students identify the subject of the sentence. The chick
   Say: This sentence tells about one chick. The subject is singular. To make the verb agree with the subject, an –*s* must be added to the verb *peep* to make it singular.

   ▸ Ask students if the following sentence is correct: *The chick hop.* No

   ▸ Have students say the sentence correctly. The chick hops.

7. Complete the Guided Exercises with students.

8. Have students complete the rest of the Activity Book page. Provide support as necessary.

Objectives

- Use a singular verb to agree with a singular subject.

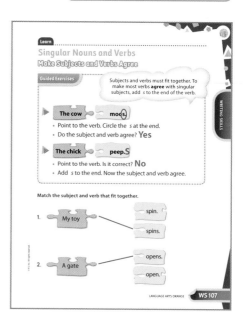

Try It

 **I Agree!**

Have students complete page WS 108 in *K¹² Language Arts Activity Book* for more practice with matching singular subjects and singular verbs.

1. Read the directions to students. Read the words in the word bank together.

2. Have students complete the Activity Book page. Provide support as necessary.

Objectives

- Use a verb that agrees with its subject.
- Use a singular verb to agree with a singular subject.

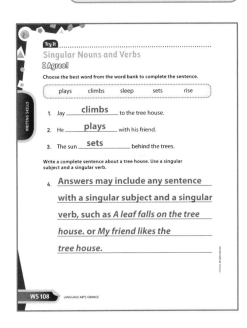

Singular Nouns and Verbs

I Agree!

Choose the best word from the word bank to complete the sentence.

| plays | climbs | sleep | sets | rise |

1. Jay **climbs** to the tree house.

2. He **plays** with his friend.

3. The sun **sets** behind the trees.

Write a complete sentence about a tree house. Use a singular subject and a singular verb.

4. **Answers may include any sentence with a singular subject and a singular verb, such as *A leaf falls on the tree house.* or *My friend likes the tree house.***

WS 108   LANGUAGE ARTS ORANGE

Plural Nouns and Verbs

Lesson Overview

[Offline] Plural Nouns and Verbs **15** minutes

Get Ready	Subject and Verb Dance
Learn	Plural Subjects and Verbs
Try It	Plural Match Up

[Materials]

Supplied

- *K¹² Language Arts Activity Book*, pp. WS 109–110

Keywords

subject – a word or words that tell whom or what the sentence is about

subject-verb agreement – the way a subject and verb match when both are singular or both are plural

verb – a word that shows action or a state of being

[Offline] **15** minutes

Plural Nouns and Verbs

You will work with students to complete Get Ready, Learn, and Try It activities.

Get Ready

Subject and Verb Dance

Review subject-verb agreement.

1. Remind students that a verb must agree with its subject.
   Say: A singular subject must have a singular verb. That means we don't say, "A baby crawl." Instead we say, "A baby crawls." In most cases, a verb is made singular by adding an *–s* to the end. So *crawls* is the correct verb to use.

2. Challenge students to name five singular verbs to complete this sentence:
   - ▸ *The dancer_____.* Answers will vary. Possible answers: leaps, turns, taps, stretches, or bows

Objectives
- Use a verb that agrees with its subject.
- List verbs.

Learn

Plural Subjects and Verbs

Introduce plural subject and verb agreement. Turn to page WS 109 in *K¹² Language Arts Activity Book*.

1. Remind students that a subject and a verb must agree. They must fit together.

2. Read the rule on the Activity Book page.

Objectives
- Use a plural verb to agree with a plural subject.

3. Read the first example together.

   ▶ Have students identify the subject of the sentence. The cows

4. Explain that this sentence tells about more than one cow. The subject is plural. It ends in –s. To make the parts fit together, the verb must be plural, too.
   Say: Remember that a singular verb ends in –s, so a plural verb does not end in –s. Since the verb *moo* has no *s*, it is plural.

   ▶ Have students finish this sentence with the correct form of *eat*:
   The pigs _____. eat
   Say: Because *eat* is plural, it does not end in –s.

5. Complete the Guided Exercises with students.

6. Have students complete the rest of the Activity Book page. Provide support as necessary.

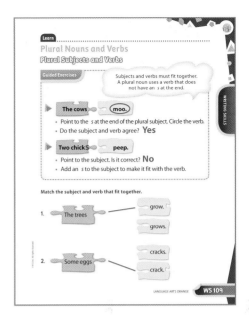

Try It

Plural Match Up
Have students complete page WS 110 in *K¹² Language Arts Activity Book* for more practice matching plural subjects and plural verbs.

1. Read the directions to students. Read the sentences together.

2. Have students complete the Activity Book page. Provide support as necessary.

Objectives
• Use a plural verb to agree with a plural subject.

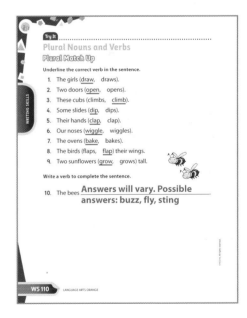

Review Subjects and Verbs

Lesson Overview

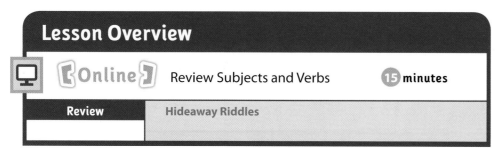

Online	Review Subjects and Verbs	15 minutes
Review	Hideaway Riddles	

Materials

There are no materials to gather for this lesson.

Online — **15** minutes

Review Subjects and Verbs

Students will work on their own to complete review and practice activities. Help students locate the online activities and provide support as needed.

Review

Hideaway Riddles

Students will identify subjects and verbs in sentences, as well as make subjects and verbs agree in sentences as they review for the Unit Checkpoint.

Offline Alternative

No computer access? Give students a subject and two choices for a verb, and have them choose the correct form. Begin with these subjects and verbs: *The dog (barks, bark). The cats (meows, meow). The lions (roars, roar). The monkey (chatters, chatter).*

Objectives

- Identify the subject of a sentence.
- Identify the verb of a sentence.
- Use a verb that agrees with its subject.
- Use a singular verb to agree with a singular subject.
- Use a plural verb to agree with a plural subject.

Unit Checkpoint

Lesson Overview

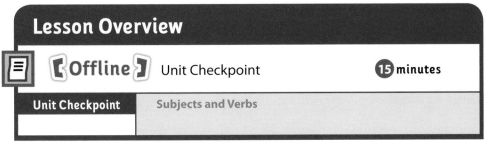

 Offline	Unit Checkpoint	15 minutes
Unit Checkpoint	Subjects and Verbs	

Materials

Supplied

- *K¹² Language Arts Assessments*, pp. WS 25–27

Offline   15 minutes

Unit Checkpoint
You will work with students to complete the Unit Checkpoint.

Unit Checkpoint

Subjects and Verbs

Explain that students are going to show what they have learned about subjects and verbs.

1. Give students the Unit Checkpoint pages.

2. Read the directions together. Have students complete the Checkpoint on their own.

3. Use the Answer Key to score the Checkpoint, and then enter the results online.

4. Review each exercise with students. Work with students to correct any exercise that they missed.

 TIP Students who answered one or more questions incorrectly should continue to practice this grammar skill. Read aloud students' favorite books. Stop from time to time in the middle of a sentence and ask students to provide the correct verb to complete the sentence.

Objectives

- Identify the subject and verb of a sentence.
- Use a verb that agrees with its subject.
- Use a singular verb to agree with a singular subject.
- Use a plural verb to agree with a plural subject.

 Reward: When students score 80 percent or above on the Unit Checkpoint, add a sticker for this unit on the My Accomplishments chart.

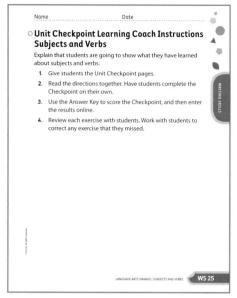

Name _____ Date _____

☼ Unit Checkpoint Learning Coach Instructions
Subjects and Verbs

Explain that students are going to show what they have learned about subjects and verbs.

1. Give students the Unit Checkpoint pages.

2. Read the directions together. Have students complete the Checkpoint on their own.

3. Use the Answer Key to score the Checkpoint, and then enter the results online.

4. Review each exercise with students. Work with students to correct any exercise that they missed.

LANGUAGE ARTS ORANGE | SUBJECTS AND VERBS   **WS 25**

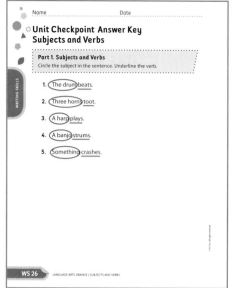

Name _____ Date _____

☼ Unit Checkpoint Answer Key
Subjects and Verbs

Part 1. Subjects and Verbs
Circle the subject in the sentence. Underline the verb.

1. (The drum) beats.

2. (Three horns) toot.

3. (A harp) plays.

4. (A banjo) strums.

5. (Something) crashes.

WS 26   LANGUAGE ARTS ORANGE | SUBJECTS AND VERBS

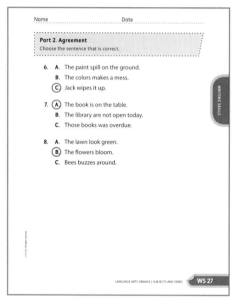

Name _____ Date _____

Part 2. Agreement
Choose the sentence that is correct.

6. A. The paint spill on the ground.
   B. The colors makes a mess.
   (C) Jack wipes it up.

7. (A) The book is on the table.
   B. The library are not open today.
   C. Those books was overdue.

8. A. The lawn look green.
   (B) The flowers bloom.
   C. Bees buzzes around.

LANGUAGE ARTS ORANGE | SUBJECTS AND VERBS   **WS 27**

What Is a Paragraph?

Unit Overview

In this unit, students will
- ▸ Develop paragraphs.
- ▸ Distinguish between a topic and a main idea.
- ▸ Use details to support a main idea.

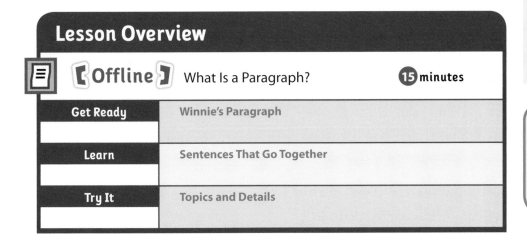

Lesson Overview

☰	**【Offline 】** What Is a Paragraph?	**15** minutes
Get Ready	Winnie's Paragraph	
Learn	Sentences That Go Together	
Try It	Topics and Details	

Advance Preparation

Pull out page WS 111 in K¹² *Language Arts Activity Book* (Winnie's Paragraph). Keep the page in a safe place so you can refer to it throughout the unit.

Big Ideas

- ▸ Complete sentences are the building blocks of paragraphs.
- ▸ Paragraphs are the building blocks of longer works.
- ▸ Paragraphs should have a discrete focus.

【Materials】

Supplied
- K¹² *Language Arts Activity Book*, pp. WS 111–114

Also Needed
- household items – book
- whiteboard (optional)

Keywords

paragraph – a group of sentences about one topic
topic – the subject of a piece of writing

Offline ⏱ **15 minutes**

What Is a Paragraph?

You will work with students to complete Get Ready, Learn, and Try It activities.

Get Ready

Winnie's Paragraph

Explain to students that they can recognize a paragraph when they look at a page of writing. Gather a book that has indented paragraphs and Winnie's Paragraph.

1. Point to Winnie's Paragraph.
   Say: Print has a shape. When you look at a page of writing, you can see small blocks of words on the page. Each block of writing is called a paragraph. A paragraph is a group of complete sentences.

   ▶ Have students point to a paragraph in the book.

2. Point to the first line of Winnie's Paragraph.
   Say: Notice that the first line has some space in front of it. This shows the reader that you are starting a new paragraph. We call this indenting the paragraph. A paragraph indent is larger than the space between two words in a sentence.

   ▶ Have students point to the first line of a paragraph in the book.

3. Keep Winnie's Paragraph in a safe place so students can refer to it later.

Objectives
- Recognize what a paragraph is.

Learn

Sentences That Go Together

Introduce students to the structure and content of a paragraph. Gather Winnie's Paragraph, and turn to page WS 113 in *K¹² Language Arts Activity Book*.

1. Explain that a **paragraph** is a group of sentences that go together.

   ▶ The sentences go together because they are about the same idea or topic.
   ▶ A **topic** is the subject of a piece of writing.

   Remind students that a group of related sentences is similar to the body of a thank-you note. The sentences are all about the same topic.

Objectives
- Identify the topic of a paragraph.
- Identify details that support the topic of a paragraph.

2. Read the following paragraph to students:
Jared likes to ice skate. He laces his skates tightly. He has a green hat. He steps on the ice and glides away.

  ▸ What is the topic of the paragraph? ice skating
  ▸ Which sentence does not belong in the paragraph? He has a green hat.

3. If students have difficulty identify the sentence that doesn't belong, write out the paragraph for them on a sheet of paper or whiteboard. Ask them which sentence does not say something about the topic.

4. Read the rule on the Activity Book page. Then read Winnie's Paragraph with students. Use Winnie's Paragraph to complete the Guided Exercises with students.

5. Have students complete the rest of the Activity Book page. Provide support as necessary.

6. Keep Winnie's Paragraph in a safe place so students can refer to it later.

TIP Check that students have correctly identified the topic of the paragraph before they complete the activity.

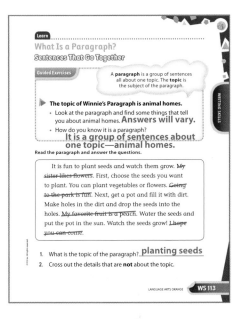

Try It

Topics and Details
Help students recognize that a paragraph consists of related sentences. Turn to page WS 114 in *K¹² Language Arts Activity Book*.

1. Read the directions to students. Read the paragraphs together.

2. Have students complete the Activity Book page. Provide support as necessary.

Online Alternative

This activity is OPTIONAL. It is intended for students who want extra practice or who would prefer to do online practice in place of the offline Try It. Feel free to skip this activity.

Objectives
- Recognize what a paragraph is.
- Identify the topic of a paragraph.
- Identify details that support the topic of a paragraph.

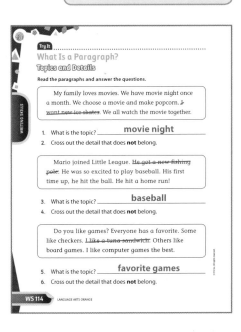

Choose a Topic

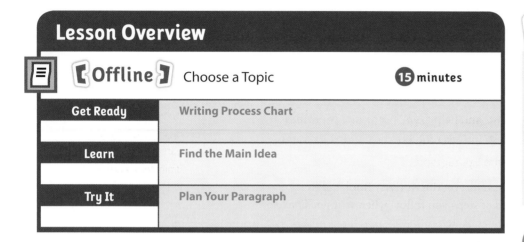

Lesson Overview

[Offline] Choose a Topic		**15** minutes
Get Ready	Writing Process Chart	
Learn	Find the Main Idea	
Try It	Plan Your Paragraph	

[Materials]

Supplied
- *K¹² Language Arts Activity Book*, pp. WS 111, 115–118

Also Needed
- whiteboard (optional)

Keywords

brainstorming – before writing, a way for the writer to come up with ideas

main idea – the most important point of the paragraph

prewriting – the stage or step of writing in which a writer chooses a topic, gathers ideas, and plans what to write

topic sentence – the sentence that expresses the main idea of the paragraph

writing process – a series of five steps (which can be repeated) followed during writing: prewriting, drafting, revising, proofreading, and publishing

Advance Preparation

Gather Winnie's Paragraph. If you have not already done so, remove page WS 111 in *K¹² Language Arts Activity Book*.

Content Background

Students frequently confuse main ideas with topics, but the two are not the same. A topic is the subject of the piece of writing. The main idea is the most important point about the topic. A paragraph usually contains a topic sentence. The topic sentence states the writer's main idea.

Big Ideas

- ▸ Writing requires thought and planning.
- ▸ Teaching the writing process encourages students to organize their ideas before they write and to revise their work after they write.

⟦Offline⟧ ⑮ minutes

Choose a Topic

You will work with students to complete Get Ready, Learn, and Try It activities.

Get Ready ···

Writing Process Chart

Introduce the writing process to students and help them brainstorm topic ideas.
Turn to page WS 115 in *K¹² Language Arts Activity Book*.

1. Tell students they are going to write a paragraph.

2. Show students the writing process chart on the Activity Book page.
   Say: The writing process is a series of steps you follow when writing. The five steps are prewriting, drafting, revising, proofreading, and publishing. Look at the arrows. Notice that you can do the steps in order, but you can also go back to a previous step if you have to do something over.

3. Point to the part of the chart labeled *Prewrite*.
   Say: Before they write, writers get ready. The things they do to get ready are called **prewriting**.

   ▸ What do you think you need to do before you start writing? Answers will vary. Possible answers: think of a topic, find a good place to write, get writing materials, know something about the topic

4. Describe some of the things writers do in prewriting.
   Say: Prewriting includes brainstorming, choosing a topic, and choosing a main idea. Sometimes prewriting includes finding information. Prewriting also includes creating a plan for the writing. Don't just start writing. You need a plan. You need to think about what you are going to write, and you need to think about the way you are going to write it. This is called prewriting. It's the work you do before you begin to write.

5. Keep the Writing Process Chart in a safe place so students can refer to it later.

6. Introduce brainstorming.
   Say: You are going to write a paragraph, but first, you need to choose a topic. Let's **brainstorm** some possible topics. Brainstorming is one way to choose a topic. Brainstorming means listing ideas to write about. When you are brainstorming, no idea is a bad idea. You want to get as many ideas as possible. Later on, you will choose one.

7. Have students write at least three ideas for possible topics on a sheet of paper. If they can come up with more than three ideas, encourage them to do so. If necessary, allow students to tell you their ideas while you write them down.

Objectives

- Recognize what a paragraph is.
- Brainstorm and develop possible topics.
- Generate ideas.

8. If students are struggling, use the following questions to guide them. Answers will vary.

   ► What do you want to write about?
   ► What is your hobby?
   ► Is there a famous person who interests you?
   ► What topic would you like to tell other people about?
   ► What do you like to do?
   ► Which animal is the most interesting?
   ► What hobby or sport would you like to learn more about?

9. Keep the list of topics students brainstormed in a safe place so they can use the list to plan their paragraph later.

Learn

Find the Main Idea

Introduce students to the main idea and topic sentence of a paragraph. Gather Winnie's Paragraph, and turn to page WS 117 in *K12 Language Arts Activity Book*.

1. Explain what the **main idea** of a paragraph is.
   Say: The main idea is the most important point in the paragraph. It is what the paragraph is mostly about. The main idea is what the writer wants to say about the topic. For example, if the topic of a paragraph is *cats*, the main idea could be *My favorite type of cat* or *How to take care of a cat*.

   ► If the topic is basketball, what might be a main idea? Answers will
   · vary. Possible answers: Basketball is a fun sport, How to play a game of basketball, My favorite basketball team

2. Introduce the idea of a **topic sentence**.
   Say: A topic sentence is the sentence that expresses the main idea. It is usually the first sentence in the paragraph. If your topic is *spring*, then your main idea might be why you like spring or what the weather is like in spring. The topic sentence of your paragraph will tell readers your main idea. Your topic sentence might be *Spring is my favorite season* or *Spring has the best weather*.

   ► What might be a good topic sentence if the topic is basketball?
   Answers will vary. Possible answers: Basketball is a fun sport. Basketball has a lot of rules but is easy to learn. My favorite basketball team is the Chicago Bulls.

3. Tell students that if they cannot state their main idea in a sentence, they might not have a clear main idea to write about.

4. **Say:** What is the most important point about animal homes that Winnie's Paragraph makes? This is the main idea of the paragraph.

Objectives

- Analyze ideas and select topic.
- Use organizational strategies to plan writing.
- Choose a main idea.
- Generate ideas.

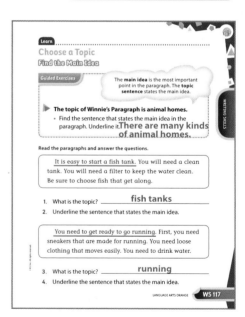

5. Read the rule on the Activity Book page. Use Winnie's Paragraph to complete the Guided Exercises with students.

6. Have students complete the rest of the Activity Book page. Provide support as necessary.

7. Keep Winnie's Paragraph in a safe place so students can refer to it later.

Try It

Plan Your Paragraph

Help students write a main idea and a topic sentence. Gather the brainstorming list of topics, and turn to page WS 118 in *K¹² Language Arts Activity Book*.

1. Have students transfer the topics they brainstormed to the Activity Book page.

2. Tell students to choose a topic to write about. They should pick a topic they know something about and are interested in.

3. Make sure students have settled on a topic they can write about. Topics should be broad areas of interest, like *basketball*, *cats*, or *spring*.

4. Remind students that the main idea is what they will say about their topic. For example, if they chose *soccer* as their topic, then the main idea might be *fun game* or *easy sport to learn*. The main idea does not need to be a complete sentence. Tell students they should be able to think of a topic sentence that states their main idea, but they don't need to write it down now.

5. Have students complete the Activity Book page. Provide support as necessary.

6. Keep the Plan Your Paragraph page in a safe place so students can refer to it later.

Objectives

- Analyze ideas and select topic.
- Use organizational strategies to plan writing.
- Choose a main idea.
- Generate ideas.

Try It

Choose a Topic
Plan Your Paragraph

Copy the ideas you brainstormed onto the lines provided. Choose one of the topics to write about and write it in the space below. Then, write the main idea that you will write about in your paragraph.

Brainstorming topics ___ Answers will vary.

My topic ___

My main idea ___

WS 118   LANGUAGE ARTS ORANGE

Create Supporting Details

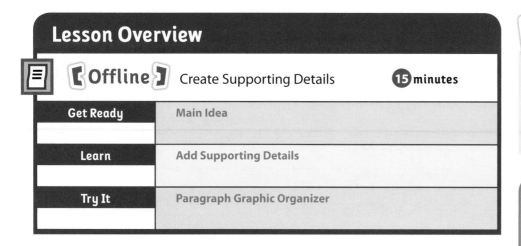

Lesson Overview

	Offline Create Supporting Details	**15** minutes
Get Ready	Main Idea	
Learn	Add Supporting Details	
Try It	Paragraph Graphic Organizer	

Materials

Supplied
- *K¹² Language Arts Activity Book*, pp. WS 111, 118–120

Keywords

supporting details – the sentences that give information about the main idea or topic sentence

purpose – the reason for writing

Advance Preparation

Gather Winnie's Paragraph and Plan Your Paragraph page. If you have not already done so, remove pages WS 111 and 118 in *K¹² Language Arts Activity Book.*

Big Ideas

- ▶ Writers must be able to articulate a main idea and support it with appropriate details.
- ▶ Writing requires thought and planning.
- ▶ Writers use various methods to plan, and novices should use what works for them: freewriting, listing, graphic organizers, or other methods.

Offline **15** minutes

Create Supporting Details

You will work with students to complete Get Ready, Learn, and Try It activities.

Get Ready ....

Main Idea

Review the differences among a topic, a main idea, and a topic sentence.

1. **Say:** The topic is the subject of a paragraph. For example, boats could be the topic of a paragraph.

Objectives
- Recognize that a topic sentence expresses the main idea of the paragraph.

2. **Say:** A paragraph needs to explain something, state an opinion, or give information about the topic. Any of these could be the **purpose** the paragraph.

   ▶ If the topic were *boats*, what could be a purpose for the paragraph? Answers will vary. Possible answers: to explain the parts of a boat, to list the kinds of boats

3. **Say:** A topic sentence states the main idea of a paragraph.

   ▶ What could be a topic sentence for a paragraph that states an opinion about boats? Answers will vary. Possible answer: I like boats because they can take you interesting places.

Learn

Add Supporting Details

Introduce supporting details to students. Gather Winnie's Paragraph, and turn to page WS 119 in *K¹² Language Arts Activity Book*.

1. Explain that every paragraph has a topic sentence. However, the topic sentence cannot stand on its own. There must be supporting details to explain it. **Say:** Paragraphs need details to support the main idea. For example, if your topic is *the sun* and your main idea is *The sun helps things grow*, you need to add supporting details. One detail might be *Sunlight helps plants grow straight.* Another detail might be *The sun helps plants make food.*

2. **Say: Supporting details** help explain the main idea. Details can be examples, descriptions, reasons, or feelings. Details tell about the main idea or add information.

   ▶ If the main idea is *May is a great month*, what details would support that statement? Answers will vary. Possible answers: Flowers bloom. Grass is green. The weather is warm.

   ▶ If the main idea is *Tigers are great animals*, what supporting details could you add? Answers will vary. Possible answers: They have beautiful markings. They are strong. They protect their young.

3. Read the rule on the Activity Book page. Complete the Guided Exercises with students.

4. Have students look at the graphic organizer on the Activity Book page. **Say:** First the writer chose a topic and main idea.

5. Point to the detail on the Activity Book page.
   Say: Next, the writer thought about what she knew about the main idea and added a supporting detail to the graphic organizer. For more information, the writer looked for facts in books, magazines, and on the Internet.
   Say: Writers can add more boxes to their graphic organizer if needed. Only one supporting detail should be written in each box.

Objectives
- Use organizational strategies to plan writing.
- Generate ideas.
- Use a graphic organizer to plan.
- Provide details to increase understanding.
- Use details that support the topic sentence, or given focus.

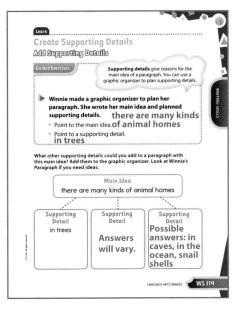

6. Have students complete the rest of the Activity Book page. Provide support as necessary. If students have trouble thinking of supporting details for the graphic organizer, allow them to look at Winnie's Paragraph for ideas.

7. Keep the Add Supporting Details page and Winnie's Paragraph in a safe place so students can refer to them later.

TIP If students are having difficulty locating the supporting details in Winnie's Paragraph, go through each sentence and ask how it is related to the main idea.

Try It

Paragraph Graphic Organizer

Help students add supporting details to their own paragraph. Gather the Plan Your Paragraph page, and turn to page WS 120 in *K¹² Language Arts Activity Book.*

1. Read the directions to students. Have students complete the Activity Book page.

2. Remind students that the details they add to the graphic organizer must support the main idea.

3. If students are unable to find three supporting details for their graphic organizer, suggest they switch topics or revise their main idea.

4. Remind students that they can add more details by adding boxes to the organizer.

5. Keep the Paragraph Graphic Organizer and the Plan Your Paragraph pages in a safe place so students can refer to them later.

TIP Help students think of supporting details by asking them questions such as *What do you need?* or *How many kinds are there?*

Objectives

- Use organizational strategies to plan writing.
- Generate ideas.
- Use a graphic organizer to plan.
- Provide details to increase understanding.
- Use details that support the topic sentence, or given focus.

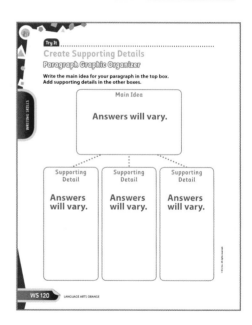

Draft a Paragraph

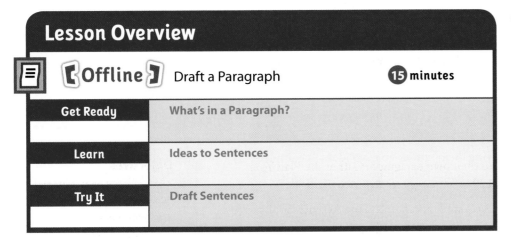

Lesson Overview

[Offline] Draft a Paragraph		**15** minutes
Get Ready	What's in a Paragraph?	
Learn	Ideas to Sentences	
Try It	Draft Sentences	

[Materials]

Supplied
- *K¹² Language Arts Activity Book*, pp. WS 115, 119–122

Keywords

drafting – of writing, the stage or step in which the writer first writes the piece

Advance Preparation

Gather the Writing Process Chart, Add Supporting Details page, and Paragraph Graphic Organizer. If you have not already done so, remove pages WS 115, 119, and 120 in *K¹² Language Arts Activity Book*.

Big Ideas

Written work is never perfect in its first version. First efforts are called drafts, and they are not meant to be final.

[Offline] **15** minutes

Draft a Paragraph
You will work with students to complete Get Ready, Learn, and Try It activities.

Get Ready ....

What's in a Paragraph?
Review what makes a good paragraph.

1. Ask students if they remember what goes into a paragraph.

   ▶ What part of the paragraph tells you the main idea? topic sentence
   ▶ What are some of the things you see in a paragraph? a topic sentence, details

Objectives
- Recognize the parts of a paragraph.

2. **Say:** Listen to this paragraph. Try to tell me the topic, main idea, and details. *My trip to the beach was fun. I got to swim in the ocean. The sun was warm. We saw dolphins jumping out of the water. At night we made a bonfire. I hated to leave.*

> ▶ What is the topic? my beach trip
> ▶ What is the main idea? My trip to the beach was fun.
> ▶ What are some of the details? swimming in the ocean, warm sun, dolphins jumping, bonfire

Learn

Ideas to Sentences

Introduce students to drafting by showing them how to go from ideas to complete sentences. Gather the Writing Process Chart and Add Supporting Details page, and turn to page WS 121 in *K¹² Language Arts Activity Book*.

1. Show students the section marked *Draft* on the Writing Process Chart.
   Say: Now we are going to look at the part of the writing process called **drafting**. After writers make a plan, they begin to draft. Drafting is when the writer first puts ideas into sentences, not just notes.

2. Describe a first draft to students.
   Say: In a first draft, ideas are written as complete sentences for the first time. The writing does not have to be perfect. The goal is to get ideas on paper.

3. Read the rule and examples on the Activity Book page. Complete the Guided Exercises with students.

4. Have students use the Add Supporting Details page to complete the rest of the Activity Book page. Provide support as necessary.

5. Keep the Writing Process Chart in a safe place so students can refer to it later.

Objectives

- Recognize the parts of a paragraph.
- Recognize details that support the topic sentence of a paragraph.
- Write sentences about the topic.

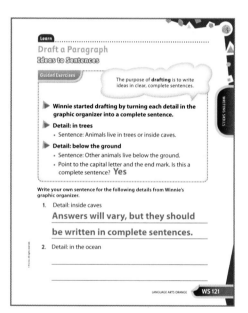

Try It

Draft Sentences

Help students write the ideas from their webs as sentences. Gather the Paragraph Graphic Organizer, and turn to page WS 122 in *K¹² Language Arts Activity Book*.

1. Read the directions to students.

2. Have students complete the Activity Book page. Provide support as necessary.

3. Remind students that the topic sentence and supporting details should relate to the main idea.

4. Have students check their sentences by answering the following questions:

   ▸ Is there one main idea?
   ▸ Do you have a topic sentence? Does the topic sentence express the main idea of the paragraph?
   ▸ Did you add at least three supporting details?
   ▸ Are there more ideas you can add?
   ▸ Are there any ideas that do not support your main idea?
   ▸ Are all the sentences complete sentences?

5. Have students read their sentences aloud to check them one more time. Students will use these sentences to write the first draft of their paragraph. They will keep working on their paragraphs to make them better.

6. Keep the Paragraph Graphic Organizer and Draft Sentences page in a safe place so students can refer to them later.

Objectives

- Write sentences and paragraphs that develop a central idea, consider purpose and audience, and use the writing process.
- Provide details to increase understanding.
- Use details that support the topic sentence, or given focus.
- Write a draft.
- Use planning ideas to produce a rough draft.

Try It

Draft a Paragraph

Draft Sentences

Use your Paragraph Graphic Organizer to write a topic sentence that expresses the main idea and at least three sentences with details that support the main idea.

Topic sentence _____ Answers will vary.

Detail sentences _____

WS 122   LANGUAGE ARTS ORANGE

Write a Paragraph

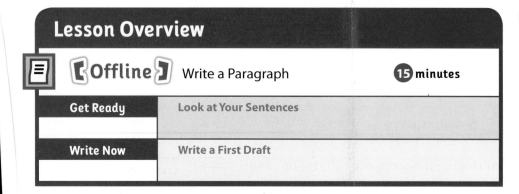

Lesson Overview

Offline	Write a Paragraph	**15** minutes
Get Ready	Look at Your Sentences	
Write Now	Write a First Draft	

Materials

Supplied

- *K¹² Language Arts Activity Book*, pp. WS 111, 120, 122–124

Advance Preparation

Gather Winnie's Paragraph, Paragraph Graphic Organizer, and Draft Sentences page. If you have not already done so, remove pages WS 111, 120, and 122 in *K¹² Language Arts Activity Book*.

 **Offline** **15** minutes

Write a Paragraph

You will work with students to complete Get Ready and Write Now activities.

Get Ready •••

Look at Your Sentences

Gather Winnie's Paragraph, Paragraph Graphic Organizer, and Draft Sentences page.

1. Have students read their Paragraph Graphic Organizer and their Draft Sentences sheet. Answers will vary.

   ▸ Did you turn your ideas into complete sentences?
   ▸ Are there any ideas that you need to add to your sentences?
   ▸ Are there any ideas that don't belong in the paragraph?
   ▸ Are there any ideas that don't belong together?
   ▸ Do you want to change any of the sentences?
   ▸ Do you want to change the order of any of the sentences?

 Objectives

- Recognize the parts of a paragraph.
- Use planning ideas to produce a rough draft.
- Recognize details that support the topic sentence of a paragraph.
- Use a graphic organizer to plan.
- Use details that support the topic sentence, or given focus.

2. Have students read Winnie's Paragraph aloud.
   Say: Notice that the writer indented the first line, started the paragraph with the topic sentence, and included several details that supported the main idea.

3. Keep Winnie's Paragraph and the Draft Sentences page in a safe place so students can refer to them later.

Write Now

 Write a First Draft

Help students write the first draft of their paragraph. Gather the Draft Sentences page, and turn to page WS 123 in *K¹² Language Arts Activity Book*.

Objectives
- Write sentences and paragraphs that develop a central idea, consider purpose and audience, and use the writing process.
- Write a draft.

1. Explain that students will use their Draft Sentences page to write the first draft of their paragraph.

   ‣ Remind students that the first line in each paragraph is indented.
   ‣ Remind students that the topic sentence should state the main idea.
   ‣ Have students include at least three details to support their main idea.
   ‣ Remind students that details should be written in complete sentences.

2. Explain that the sentences should be written in an order that makes sense. Let students know that details can be written in time order or in order of importance if that makes sense in the paragraph.

3. Encourage students to reorganize their sentences if it would improve the paragraph.
   Say: Think about the order of your sentences. If you want to change the order, you can use arrows or numbers to show the new order. Then write the sentences in the new order on your Write a First Draft page. Answers will vary.

   ‣ Do you want to move any of the sentences around to make the paragraph more interesting?
   ‣ Are there any ideas that belong together?
   ‣ Are there any ideas that are more important and should go first?
   ‣ Should you move any of the ideas around?

4. Remind students to write in complete sentences, use good handwriting, and leave spaces between words so that others can read what they wrote.

5. Use the materials and instructions in the online lesson to evaluate students' finished writing. You will be looking at students' writing to evaluate the following:

   ▸ Purpose and Content: The writing should be in the form of a paragraph. There should be a clear topic, main idea, and supporting details. The sentences should show variety in length and choice of words.
   ▸ Structure and Organization: The paragraph should begin with a topic sentence. The sentences should be in a logical order. The first line should be indented.
   ▸ Grammar and Mechanics: All sentences should be complete and punctuated correctly. There may be some grammatical errors.

6. Enter students' scores for each rubric category online.

7. If students' writing scored a 1 in any criteria, work with students to write better sentences for their paragraph.

8. Keep the Write a First Draft page in a safe place so students can use it later.

Reward: When students' writing is Level 2 or higher on the grading rubric, add a sticker to this unit on the My Accomplishments chart.

What Is a Pronoun?

Unit Overview

In this unit, students will
- ▸ Learn how to recognize pronouns.
- ▸ Learn how to use pronouns.

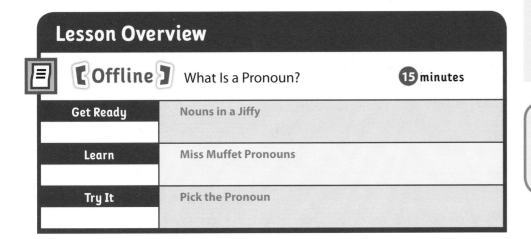

Lesson Overview

☰	**[Offline]** What Is a Pronoun?	**15** minutes
Get Ready	Nouns in a Jiffy	
Learn	Miss Muffet Pronouns	
Try It	Pick the Pronoun	

Content Background

Pronouns take the place of nouns in sentences. Singular pronouns include the following: *I, me, you, he, she, it, her,* and *him.*

Big Ideas

Using pronouns to take the place of some nouns helps writers avoid repetition.

[Materials]

Supplied
- *K¹² Language Arts Activity Book,* pp. WS 125–126

Also Needed
- household items – timer

Keywords

pronoun – a word that takes the place of one or more nouns

Offline · ⏱ 15 minutes

What Is a Pronoun?

You will work with students to complete Get Ready, Learn, and Try It activities.

Get Ready

Nouns in a Jiffy

Review what nouns are with this quick game.

1. Remind students that nouns are words that name people, places, or things.

2. Time students as they name as many people nouns as possible.
   Say: Some nouns name people, such as *girl* or *Mrs. Li.*

   ▶ In one minute, list as many nouns as you can that name people.
   Answers will vary. Possible answers: family, boys, lady, Dr. Tooth

   Say: Some nouns name places, such as *Lake Michigan* or *streets.*

   ▶ In one minute, list as many nouns as you can that name places.
   Answers will vary. Possible answers: zoo, parks, library, New York

   Say: Some nouns name things, such as *dogs* or *friendship.*

   ▶ In one minute, list as many nouns as you can that name things.
   Answers will vary. Possible answers: cow, toys, bugs, Sunday

Objectives
- Recall what a noun is.
- List nouns.

Learn

Miss Muffet Pronouns

Introduce how to identify and use singular pronouns. Turn to page WS 125 in *K¹² Language Arts Activity Book.*

1. Explain that a **pronoun** is a word that takes the place of a noun. Pronouns such as *I, me, you, he, she, it, him,* and *her* take the place of names for people and things.

2. Remind students that the pronoun *I* is always capitalized.

3. Tell students that pronouns help us avoid repeating the same noun over and over. Read the following rhyme, first with pronouns and then without.

With Pronouns	Without Pronouns
Little Miss Muffet	*Little Miss Muffet*
Sat on a tuffet,	*Sat on a tuffet,*
Eating her curds and whey;	*Eating Little Miss Muffet's curds and whey;*
Along came a spider,	*Along came a spider,*
Who sat down beside her	*Who sat down beside Little Miss Muffet*
And frightened Miss Muffet away.	*And frightened Miss Muffet away.*

Objectives
- Recognize pronouns.
- Use singular pronouns.

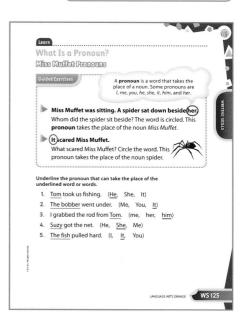

4. Read the third line in the original rhyme: *Eating her curds and whey.*
   Say: This line contains a pronoun. *Her* takes the place of someone's name.

   ▸ Whose name does the word *her* replace? Little Miss Muffet

5. Reread the sentence, replacing the word *her* with *Little Miss Muffet.*

6. Read the fifth line in the original rhyme: *Who sat down beside her.*

   ▸ What is the pronoun in that line? her
   ▸ Whose name does the word *her* replace? Little Miss Muffet

7. Read the rule on the Activity Book page. Complete the Guided Exercises with students.

8. Have students complete the rest of the Activity Book page. Provide support as necessary.

Try It •

Pick the Pronoun
Have students practice recognizing and using singular pronouns. Turn to page WS 126 in *K¹² Language Arts Activity Book.*

1. Read the directions to students.

2. Have students complete the Activity Book page. Provide support as necessary.

 If students replace the name in Exercise 8 with their own name, ask them the question "Did you play soccer?" Encourage them to write the answer beginning with the word *I.*

Objectives
• Recognize pronouns.
• Use singular pronouns.

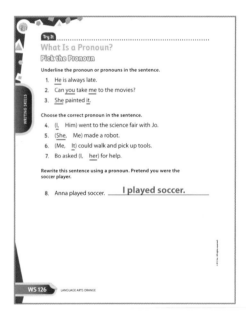

Plural Pronouns

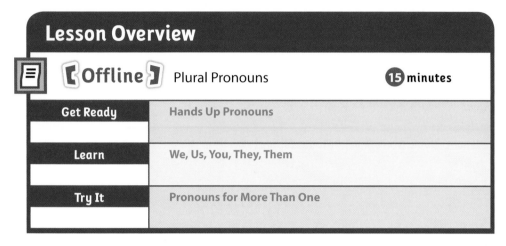

Lesson Overview

≡	**Offline** Plural Pronouns	**15** minutes
Get Ready	Hands Up Pronouns	
Learn	We, Us, You, They, Them	
Try It	Pronouns for More Than One	

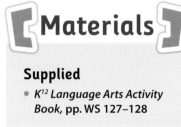

Materials

Supplied

- *K¹² Language Arts Activity Book*, pp. WS 127–128

Keywords

pronoun – a word that takes the place of one or more nouns

Content Background

▶ Pronouns may be singular or plural.
▶ The plural pronouns are *we, us, you, they,* and *them.* Note that the pronoun *you* may be either singular or plural.

Offline  **15** minutes

Plural Pronouns

You will work with students to complete Get Ready, Learn, and Try It activities.

Get Ready

Hands Up Pronouns
Review pronouns.

1. Remind students that pronouns are words that take the place of nouns. Examples of pronouns are *I, me, you, he, she, it, him,* and *her.*

Objectives
- Recognize pronouns.

2. Read the rhyme "There Was a Fine Lady Tossed Up in a Basket," and have students raise their hand each time they hear a pronoun.

> *There was a fine lady*
> *Tossed up in a basket,*
> *Seventeen times as high as the moon.*
> *Where* she *was going*
> I *couldn't but ask* it,
> *For under* her *arm* she *carried a broom.*
> *Fine lady, fine lady, fine lady, said* I,
> *Where are* you *going to up so high?*
> *To sweep the cobwebs out of the sky,*
> *Then* I *will be with* you *by and by.*

Learn

We, Us, You, They, Them

Introduce plural pronouns to students. Turn to page WS 127 in *K¹² Language Arts Activity Book.*

1. Explain that some nouns tell about more than one person, place, or thing. The pronouns that take their place are called **plural pronouns**. Plural pronouns include *we*, *us*, *you*, *they*, and *them*.

2. Read these two sentences to students: *Sandy has a game today. She is excited.*

   ► Whom are both of these sentences about? Sandy

3. Tell students that *Sandy* names one person, so it is a singular noun. The noun *Sandy* can be replaced with the singular pronoun *she*.

4. Now read these two sentences to students: *The girls have a game today. They are excited.*

   ► Whom are both of these sentences about? The girls
   Say: We replaced *The girls* with *They* in the second sentence because *girls* is a plural noun. It must be replaced with the plural pronoun *they*.

5. Read the rule on the Activity Book page. Complete the Guided Exercises with students.

6. Have students complete the rest of the Activity Book page. Provide support as necessary.

TIP To help students understand that the word *you* can be either singular or plural, have one student stand. Refer to the student as *you*. Then have another student or a pet join the first student and refer to both of them as *you*. You can also use the following examples. Singular: *Rex knows Sally and you.* Plural: *He likes both of you.*

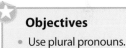

Objectives
• Use plural pronouns.

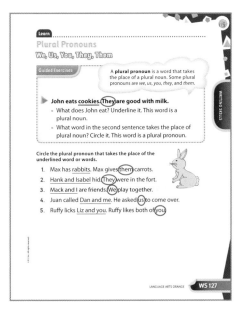

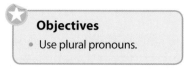

Try It

Pronouns for More Than One

Have students practice recognizing and using plural pronouns. Turn to page WS 128 in *K¹² Language Arts Activity Book*.

1. Read the directions to students. Read the sentences together.

2. Have students complete the Activity Book page. Provide support as necessary.

Objectives
- Use plural pronouns.

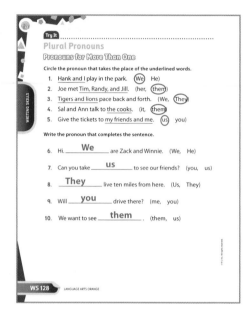

More Pronouns

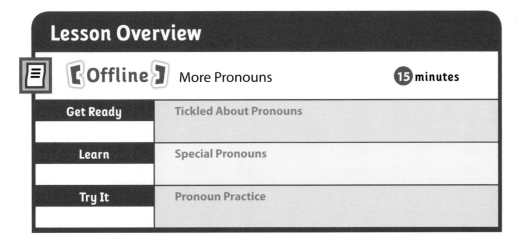

Lesson Overview

Offline	More Pronouns	**15** minutes
Get Ready	Tickled About Pronouns	
Learn	Special Pronouns	
Try It	Pronoun Practice	

Materials

Supplied

- *K¹² Language Arts Activity Book*, pp. WS 129–130

Keywords

possessive pronoun – the form of a pronoun that shows ownership

pronoun – a word that takes the place of one or more nouns

reflexive pronoun – a word that refers back to another noun or pronoun in the sentence and is necessary to the meaning of the sentence

Content Background

▶ Possessive pronouns show that someone owns or has something. The possessive pronouns are *my, mine, your, yours, her, hers, our, ours, their, theirs, his,* and *its.*

▶ Reflexive pronouns end in the suffix *–self.* Some examples of reflexive pronouns are *myself, yourself,* and *themselves.* Because it is a difficult term, this course will not use the word *reflexive pronoun* with students.

▶ Note that some grammar programs refer to possessive pronouns such as *my, your,* and *his* as possessive adjectives. This course refers to them as possessive pronouns.

 **15 minutes**

More Pronouns

You will work with students to complete Get Ready, Learn, and Try It activities.

Get Ready

Tickled About Pronouns

Review pronouns as you share these silly riddles with students.

1. Remind students that a pronoun is a word that takes the place of a noun.

   ▸ Name pronouns you know. Answers will vary. Possible answers: I, me, you, he, she, it, him, her, we, us, you, they, them

2. Read the riddles below and encourage students to answer each one. Then have students name the pronouns in each question and answer.

   ▸ *What did the pig say when the farmer picked him up by the tail?*
   (This is the end of me!) him; me
   ▸ *When can you catch water in a net?*
   (when it is an ice cube) you; it

TIP Challenge students to make up riddles that use pronouns in the question or in the answer. You might also wish to find books of riddles. Have students point out pronouns as they read the riddles.

 Objectives
- Recognize pronouns.
- List pronouns.

Learn

Special Pronouns

Introduce possessive pronouns and reflexive pronouns to students. Turn to page WS 129 in *K¹² Language Arts Activity Book*.

1. Have students listen as you read these sentences: *I have a crayon. It is my crayon. Remember that the crayon is mine.*

2. Explain that the words *my* and *mine* are pronouns. These pronouns tell who has or owns the crayon.

3. **Say:** Pronouns that talk about things that belong to you or to someone else are called **possessive pronouns**. The words *my, mine, your, yours, his, her,* and *hers* are some possessive pronouns. We use possessive pronouns so we don't keep repeating the same nouns.

 Objectives
- Recognize pronouns.
- Use reflexive pronouns.
- Use possessive pronouns.

4. **Say:** Another kind of pronoun is used to talk about you or someone else in the same sentence. Words such as *myself, yourself, himself, herself,* and *ourselves* are examples.

5. Read this sentence: *Dan drew a picture of himself.*

   ▸ What did Dan do? drew a picture of himself
   Say: *Himself* is a special pronoun that refers to Dan. It would be confusing to say *Dan drew a picture of Dan.*

6. Read the rule on the Activity Book page. Complete the Guided Exercises with students.

7. Have students complete the rest of the Activity Book page. Provide support as necessary.

TIP It is more important for students at this age to know how and when to use these special pronouns (reflexive pronouns) than what they are called.

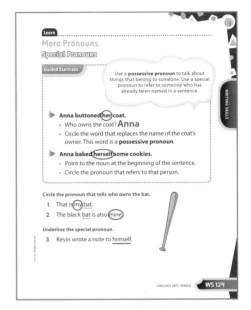

Try It

Pronoun Practice
Have students complete page WS 130 in *K¹² Language Arts Activity Book* for more practice recognizing and using possessive and reflexive pronouns.

1. Read the directions to students. Read the words in the word banks and the sentences together.

2. Have students complete the Activity Book page. Provide support as necessary.

Objectives
* Use reflexive pronouns.
* Use possessive pronouns.

Review Pronouns

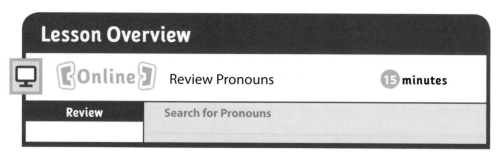

Lesson Overview

[Online] Review Pronouns		15 minutes
Review	Search for Pronouns	

[Online] 15 minutes

Review Pronouns

Students will work on their own to complete review and practice activities.
Help students locate the online activities and provide support as needed.

Review

Search for Pronouns

Students will practice recognizing and using singular and plural pronouns, possessive pronouns, and reflexive pronouns to review for the Unit Checkpoint.

Offline Alternative

No computer access? Review pronouns by gathering pages WS 125–130 in *K¹² Language Arts Activity Book* and reviewing the exercises students have completed in this unit. Then read sentences from books or newspapers to students and have them identify the pronouns. Finally read sentences, omitting the pronouns, and have students tell you an appropriate pronoun to complete the sentence.

Objectives
- Recognize pronouns.
- Use singular pronouns.
- Use plural pronouns.
- Use reflexive pronouns.
- Use possessive pronouns.

Unit Checkpoint

Lesson Overview

Offline	Unit Checkpoint	15 minutes
Unit Checkpoint	Pronouns	

[Offline] 15 minutes

Unit Checkpoint

You will work with students to complete the Unit Checkpoint.

Materials

Supplied
- *K¹² Language Arts Assessments*, pp. WS 29–31

Unit Checkpoint

Pronouns

Explain that students are going to show what they have learned about pronouns.

1. Give students the Unit Checkpoint pages.

2. Read the directions together. Have students complete the Checkpoint on their own.

3. Use the Answer Key to score the Checkpoint, and then enter the results online.

4. Review each exercise with students. Work with students to correct any exercise that they missed.

Objectives
- Recognize pronouns.
- Use singular pronouns.
- Use plural pronouns.
- Use possessive pronouns.

 Reward: When students score 80 percent or above on the Unit Checkpoint, add a sticker for this unit on the My Accomplishments chart.

Name _____ Date _____

○ Unit Checkpoint Learning Coach Instructions
Pronouns

Explain that students are going to show what they have learned about pronouns.

1. Give students the Unit Checkpoint pages.
2. Read the directions together. Have students complete the Checkpoint on their own.
3. Use the Answer Key to score the Checkpoint, and then enter the results online.
4. Review each exercise with students. Work with students to correct any exercise that they missed.

Name _____ Date _____

○ Unit Checkpoint Answer Key
Pronouns

Part 1. Choose the Pronoun
Choose the best pronoun to replace the underlined word or words.

1. <u>Evan</u> made an ant farm.
   - **(A)** He
   - B. Him
   - C. It

2. The ants ran from <u>Evan</u>.
   - A. his
   - **(B)** him
   - C. I

3. <u>Angela</u> is my sister.
   - A. You
   - **(B)** She
   - C. His

4. <u>The gerbil</u> has babies.
   - **(A)** It
   - B. You
   - C. Me

5. <u>The roses and daisies</u> smell good.
   - A. We
   - B. It
   - **(C)** They

6. The taxi stopped for <u>Paul and me</u>.
   - **(A)** us
   - B. them
   - C. I

Name _____ Date _____

7. We play <u>the Jets</u> tonight.
   - A. him
   - **(B)** them
   - C. it

8. <u>The Kings</u> play on Saturday.
   - **(A)** They
   - B. He
   - C. Us

9. <u>Chuck and I</u> ate pretzels.
   - A. You
   - **(B)** We
   - C. His

10. This magnet is <u>Bill's</u>.
    - A. mine
    - B. hers
    - **(C)** his

11. The hammers are <u>Sarah's</u>.
    - A. his
    - B. mine
    - **(C)** hers

12. This is <u>Janie's</u> dirty sock.
    - A. my
    - B. your
    - **(C)** her

Revise Your Draft: Introductions

Unit Overview

In this unit, students will
- ▸ Revise the first draft of their paragraph.
- ▸ Add transition words to their paragraph.
- ▸ Write a conclusion.

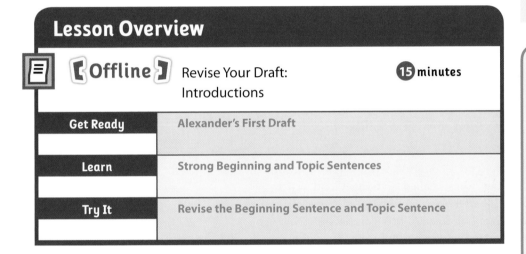

Lesson Overview

[Offline]	Revise Your Draft: Introductions	**15** minutes
Get Ready	Alexander's First Draft	
Learn	Strong Beginning and Topic Sentences	
Try It	Revise the Beginning Sentence and Topic Sentence	

Advance Preparation

Students need to have a completed first draft of a paragraph before they begin working on this unit. They should use the paragraph they drafted in the Write a Paragraph unit. Gather the Writing Process Chart and Write a First Draft page. If you have not already done so, remove pages WS 115 and 123 in *K¹² Language Arts Activity Book*. Pull out page WS 131 in *K¹² Language Arts Activity Book* (Alexander's First Draft). Keep the page in a safe place so you can refer to it throughout the unit.

Content Background

- ▸ The writing process is the series of steps writers take to transform ideas from their heads into words on paper.
- ▸ Writers begin with prewriting tasks such as brainstorming and organizing prior to writing complete sentences in an ordered form in their drafts. After drafting, writers revise and edit to restructure, reword, and add new ideas.
- ▸ The goals of revision are to have strong content, clarity, and coherence.
- ▸ The writing process is not linear. It is recursive. Writers may go back and perform steps again if they feel that their work needs more revision.
- ▸ A beginning sentence starts a paragraph. It could be a clever hook or introduction or it could be the topic sentence that tells the main idea of the paragraph.

Big Ideas

One of the most powerful ways to improve writing is to directly teach strategies for planning and revising until students can use these strategies on their own.

[Materials]

Supplied
- *K¹² Language Arts Activity Book*, pp. WS 115, 123, 131–134

Keywords

beginning sentence – the sentence that introduces a paragraph and tells what it is about

revising – the stage or step of the writing process in which the writer rereads and edits the draft, correcting errors and making changes in content or organization that improve the piece

topic sentence – the sentence that expresses the main idea of a paragraph

writing process – a series of five steps (which can be repeated) followed during writing: prewriting, drafting, revising, proofreading, and publishing

[Offline] (15) minutes

Revise Your Draft: Introductions

You will work with students to complete Get Ready, Learn, and Try It activities.

Get Ready •••

Alexander's First Draft

Introduce the idea of revising content to students. Gather the Writing Process Chart and Alexander's First Draft.

> **Objective**
> • Recognize the importance of revising written work.

1. Ask students to consider the first time they tried to do a cartwheel, rode a bicycle, jumped in a swimming pool, or climbed across the monkey bars. Ask them whether they accomplished their goal perfectly on the first try. Answers will vary.

2. Tell students that each time they sit down to write something, it is similar to trying a new skill. Writing, like any sport or physical skill, requires repeated practice in order to improve.

3. **Say:** The more you write, the better you become as a writer. Writing requires rewriting in order to get better. Rewriting is called **revising**. Good writers always revise their work to make it better. Even famous, published authors such as Dr. Seuss, Tommie DePaolo, Ezra Jack Keats, Chris Van Allsburg, and your favorite author all revised their writing before they published it.

4. Review the Writing Process Chart with students.

5. Explain that revising is the third step in the **writing process**. The writer goes back to the draft and makes changes to the ideas or the way the ideas are written.

   ▸ What other parts of the writing process do you remember? Answers will vary. Possible answers: brainstorming, drafting, proofreading, publishing

6. Remind students that they already completed the first two steps in the writing process when they drafted their paragraph.

7. Have students read Alexander's First Draft. Emphasize that it is not a finished piece of writing. Students will work on revising Alexander's paragraph as well as revising their own paragraph.

8. Remind students that a paragraph is written about one topic.

9. Keep Alexander's First Draft and the Writing Process Chart in a safe place so that students can refer to them as they work through the lessons on revising.

Learn •••

Strong Beginning and Topic Sentences

Explore the beginning sentence and topic sentence of a paragraph with students. Gather Alexander's First Draft, and turn to page WS 133 in *K¹² Language Arts Activity Book.*

1. Explain that the **beginning sentence** of a paragraph is an important sentence.

   ▸ The beginning sentence introduces the paragraph.
   ▸ It lets readers know what the paragraph will be about.
   ▸ The first sentence should be a strong, attention-grabbing sentence so the reader will be interested in what you have to say.

2. Remind students that the **topic sentence** is the sentence that tells the main idea of the paragraph.

3. Look at Alexander's First Draft with students.

   ▸ Does the paragraph begin with a sentence that introduces the topic? Yes
   ▸ Does the first sentence state the main idea of the paragraph? No
   ▸ What is the topic sentence of the paragraph? Parrots can be pets.
   ▸ Does the paragraph include details that support the main idea? Yes

4. **Say:** Often the beginning sentence is also the topic sentence, but it does not have to be. If the beginning sentence is not the topic sentence, a writer needs to include the topic sentence somewhere else in the paragraph.

   ▸ The topic sentence tells the main idea of the paragraph.
   ▸ The main idea is what the paragraph is mostly about.

5. Have students listen to these two topic sentences and choose the one that is stronger:

   ▸ *This is about pets.*
   ▸ *Pets can make you happy.* This is the stronger topic sentence.

   Explain that the first sentence tells you that the topic is *pets*. But it doesn't tell the main idea, and it is not very interesting. The second sentence tells you that the paragraph will be about how pets can make you happy. How pets can make you happy is something that may interest readers.

6. Tell students that a beginning sentence does not have to be a statement. It can be a question. Questions make good beginning sentences because they can involve the reader in the writing.

7. **Say:** Listen to this statement. How could you change it into a question that would still be a good beginning sentence?

   ▸ *Pets can make you happy.* Answers will vary. Possible answer: Do pets make you happy?

8. Read the rule on the Activity Book page. Complete the Guided Exercises with students.

Objectives

- Identify the topic sentence that expresses the main idea of a paragraph.
- Recognize the importance of the beginning sentence in a paragraph.
- Use beginning sentences.
- Write a topic sentence that expresses the main idea of a paragraph.

9. Have students use Alexander's First Draft to complete the Activity Book page. Provide support as necessary.

10. Keep Alexander's First Draft in a safe place so students can finish revising it later.

TIP Emphasize that Alexander's paragraph is a first draft and not a finished piece of writing. Students will work on revising Alexander's paragraph as well as their own paragraph.

Try It

Revise the Beginning Sentence and Topic Sentence

Help students write or revise the beginning sentence and topic sentence of their paragraph. Gather the Write a First Draft page (students' draft paragraph), and turn to page WS 134 in *K¹² Language Arts Activity Book*

1. Read the directions with students.

2. Have students read aloud the beginning sentence of their draft and complete Exercises 1 and 2. Provide support as necessary.

3. Tell students to find their topic sentence. Remind them that their topic sentence might be the beginning sentence, but it doesn't have to be.

4. Have students complete Exercises 3–5. Provide support as necessary.

5. When students have finished, help them mark their revisions on their draft paragraph.

6. Have students read their revised paragraph aloud.

   ▶ Did you think of any other way to revise the paragraph when you read it aloud? Answers will vary.

7. Keep the Write a First Draft page (students' draft paragraph) in a safe place so students can continue to revise it.

Objectives
- Use beginning sentences.
- Write a topic sentence that expresses the main idea of a paragraph.
- Revise using a checklist or rubric.
- Revise by adding or deleting text.

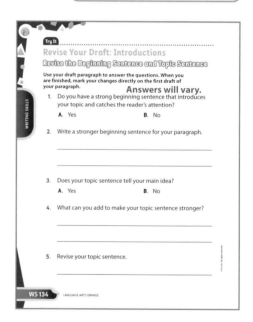

Get from Point to Point: Transitions

Materials

Supplied
- *K¹² Language Arts Activity Book*, pp. WS 123, 131, 135–138

Also Needed
- whiteboard (optional)

Lesson Overview

Offline	Get from Point to Point: Transitions	**15** minutes
Get Ready	Transition Words List	
Learn	Use Transitions	
Try It	Add Transitions to Your Draft	

Keywords
transition – a word or phrase that connect ideas

Advance Preparation

Gather the Write a First Draft page (students' draft paragraph) and Alexander's First Draft. If you have not already done so, remove pages WS 123 and 131 in *K¹² Language Arts Activity Book*.

Content Background

Transitions are words that help connect ideas within and between paragraphs by establishing the relationship among the ideas. Writing that lacks transitions frequently lacks coherence because readers are not able to understand the connection between the writer's thoughts and ideas. Using transitions not only makes the writing flow more smoothly, but also helps readers comprehend the writer's intent and meaning.

Big Ideas

Good writers use transitions to help create coherence in written text.

 **15 minutes**

Get from Point to Point: Transitions

You will work with students to complete Get Ready, Learn, and Try It activities.

Get Ready

Transition Words List

Introduce students to transitions and the way in which they connect sentences in paragraphs. Turn to page WS 135 in the *K¹² Language Arts Activity Book*.

Objectives
- Recognize the purpose of a paragraph.
- Recognize that transition words connect ideas.

1. Review the idea that a paragraph is a group of sentences that go together.

   ▸ The ideas in each sentence connect with each other.
   ▸ All the sentences in a paragraph are about the same main idea.

2. Explain that there are words or groups of words that help connect one sentence to another in a paragraph. These words are called **transitions**.

   ▸ Sentences in a paragraph should connect in an order that makes sense. If a paragraph is written in time order, words such as *first, next,* and *finally* help the writing make sense.
   ▸ Adding a transition word such as *also, too,* or *therefore* helps readers move from one sentence to the next.
   ▸ Transitions help readers understand the relationships among ideas. *If . . . then, because,* and *for example* are all transitions that connect ideas together.

3. Read the Activity Book page with students. Use the words in examples to show how the relationships work.

4. Have students look for transition words from the list in their favorite books.

5. Ask students to say what the transitions show. For example, in the sentence *She missed the bus, but she made it to her first period class,* the transition *but* shows a relationship. In the sentence *I missed school because I was sick,* the word *because* shows cause and effect.

6. Keep the Transition Words List in a safe place so students can continue to refer to it.

TIP Keep the Transition Words List in a visible place so students can refer to it as they write. You might want to hang it on the wall or put it with their writing materials.

Learn

Use Transitions

Explore how transitions connect ideas. Gather the Transition Words List and Alexander's First Draft, and turn to page WS 137 in *K¹² Language Arts Activity Book.*

Objective

- Use transitions to connect ideas.

1. Remind students that transitions are words and phrases that connect sentences. They used to show time, cause and effect, importance, relationships, or place. Show students examples of each kind of transition from the Transition Words List.

2. **Say:** These two sentences are related by cause and effect. One sentence makes the other sentence happen: *It is freezing. Wear a heavy coat.* A transition word can be added to connect the sentences: *It is freezing. Therefore, wear a heavy coat.*

3. Read these sentences to students: *Rosa went to see the Nutcracker Ballet. She liked the music. She liked the dancing best.*

   ▸ Where could you add a transition word? Answers will vary. Possible answer: She liked the music. However, she liked the dancing best.

   ▸ If students need assistance, write the sentences on a sheet of paper or white board.

4. Try a second example with students. Read the following sentences and ask what transition word students could use to connect them.

   ▸ *I am hungry. I will find a snack.* Answers will vary. Possible answers: so, therefore

   ▸ If students have difficulty, explain to them that the two sentences represent a cause-and-effect relationship. Suggest that they choose a cause-and-effect transition from the Transition Words List.

5. Read the rule on the Activity Book page. Complete the Guided Exercises with students.

6. Have students complete the rest of the Activity Book page. Provide support as necessary.

7. Keep the Transition Words List and Alexander's First Draft in a safe place so students can refer to them later.

TIP The word *and* can be used to combine two sentences into one sentence. It should not be used as a transition word at the beginning of a sentence.

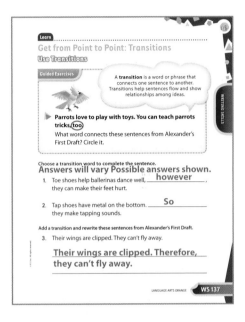

Try It

Add Transitions to Your Draft

Help students add transition words to their paragraph. Gather the Write a First Draft page (students' draft paragraph) and Transition Words List, and turn to page WS 138 in *K¹² Language Arts Activity Book*.

1. Tell students that they have had a little time since they wrote their first draft. It's good to return to a draft with fresh eyes and read it again to make sure it makes sense.

2. Read the directions to students. Have students complete the Activity Book page. Provide support as necessary.

3. Remind students to look at the Transition Words List to help them revise their paragraph.

4. When students have finished, review the revised paragraph with them. Make sure they added transition words to their paragraph.

5. Have students read their paragraph aloud.

6. Have students explain why they chose the transition words they did. Ask them what kinds of connections they were trying to make.

7. Keep the Write a First Draft page (students' draft paragraph) in a safe place so students can continue to revise it.

Objective

- Use transitions to connect ideas.

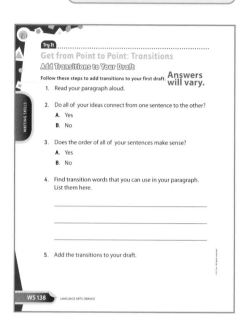

Write a Conclusion

Lesson Overview

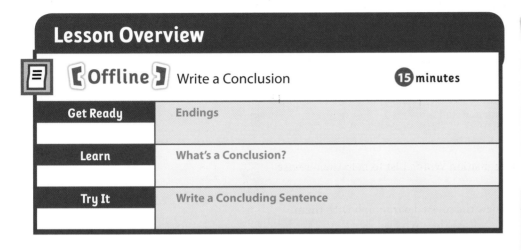

Offline	Write a Conclusion	**15** minutes
Get Ready	Endings	
Learn	What's a Conclusion?	
Try It	Write a Concluding Sentence	

Materials

Supplied

- *K¹² Language Arts Activity Book*, pp. WS 123, 131, 139–140

Keywords

concluding sentence – the last sentence of a paragraph that is not part of an essay; often summarizes the paragraph

Advance Preparation

Gather the Write a First Draft page (students' draft paragraph) and Alexander's First Draft. If you have not already done so, remove pages WS 123 and 131 in *K¹² Language Arts Activity Book*.

Big Ideas

▸ Writing requires rewriting or revision.
▸ Revision is best accomplished through discrete, focused tasks.

 **Offline** **15** minutes

Write a Conclusion

You will work with students to complete Get Ready, Learn, and Try It activities.

Get Ready ....

Endings

Explain to students why it is important for written work to have an ending or conclusion.

1. Ask students to name a favorite story or movie. Ask them to quickly summarize the story.

   ▸ How does the story end? Answers will vary.

2. If students have difficulty recalling the end, prompt them with *And then what happens?* until they are able to tell you the conclusion.

 Objectives

- Recognize the purpose of a conclusion.
- Recognize the purpose of a paragraph.
- Recognize that transition words connect ideas.
- Recognize the parts of a paragraph.

3. After students tell you the ending, explain that just as a good story has a good ending, or a **conclusion**, so must a paragraph have a conclusion. The conclusion tells readers it is the end of the paragraph.

4. Review the parts of a good paragraph.

   ▶ A paragraph has a strong topic sentence.
   ▶ A paragraph begins with an interesting beginning sentence.
   ▶ The sentences in the paragraph are all about the same main idea.
   ▶ Transition words help connect the sentences so that ideas can flow smoothly.
   ▶ A paragraph ends with a strong conclusion.

Learn

What's a Conclusion?

Introduce concluding sentences to students. Gather Alexander's First Draft, and turn to page WS 139 in *K¹² Language Arts Activity Book*.

1. Explain that a **concluding sentence** sums up the main idea of the paragraph.

   ▶ The conclusion is another way of stating the main idea of the paragraph.
   ▶ It is usually the last sentence of the paragraph.
   ▶ It is a chance to complete the paragraph, just like the ending of a story.

2. Read these sentences to students: *Our family likes to watch football. Last fall, we went to see a live football game. We sat near the top row. We could see the whole field.*

   ▶ Remind students that the conclusion should sum up the main idea of the paragraph.
   ▶ Have students suggest a concluding statement for the paragraph. Answers will vary. Possible answer: It was more fun seeing the game in person than watching it on TV.

3. Explain that although a conclusion is similar to the topic sentence, it shouldn't use the exact same words.

4. Read the rule on the Activity Book page. Use Alexander's First Draft to help students complete the Guided Exercises.

5. Have students complete the rest of the Activity Book page. Provide support as necessary.

6. Keep Alexander's First Draft in a safe place so students can continue to work on it.

TIP Tell students that concluding sentences are often statements, or telling sentences, but they don't have to be.

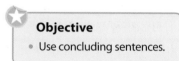

Objective
• Use concluding sentences.

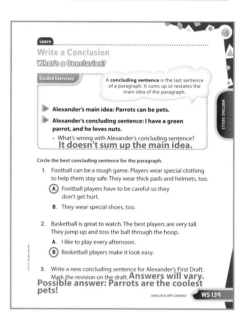

Try It

Write a Concluding Sentence

Help students write or revise the conclusion for their paragraph. Gather the Write a First Draft page (students' draft paragraph), and turn to page WS 138 in *K¹² Language Arts Activity Book.*

1. Read the directions to students.

2. Have students complete the Activity Book page. Provide support as necessary.

3. When students have finished, review the revised paragraph with them. Make sure students have written a revised concluding sentence that sums up the main topic of their paragraph.

4. Have students read their paragraph aloud. Ask them if they can think of any other ways to revise their paragraph.

5. Keep the Write a First Draft page (students' draft paragraph) in a safe place so students can continue to revise it.

TIP Although the concluding statement should sum up the main idea of the paragraph, it should use different words from the topic sentence. If students are having difficulty writing a concluding statement, help them reword the topic sentence in an interesting way.

Objective
- Use concluding sentences.

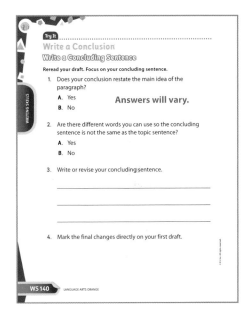

Try It

Write a Conclusion

Write a Concluding Sentence

Reread your draft. Focus on your concluding sentence.

1. Does your conclusion restate the main idea of the paragraph?
   A. Yes
   B. No
   Answers will vary.

2. Are there different words you can use so the concluding sentence is not the same as the topic sentence?
   A. Yes
   B. No

3. Write or revise your concluding sentence.
   _____
   _____
   _____

4. Mark the final changes directly on your first draft.

WS 140   LANGUAGE ARTS ORANGE

Revise for Content

Lesson Overview

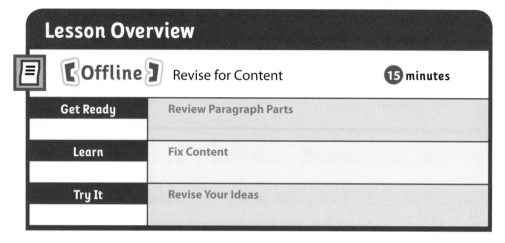

	Offline	Revise for Content	15 minutes
Get Ready	Review Paragraph Parts		
Learn	Fix Content		
Try It	Revise Your Ideas		

Materials

Supplied
- *K¹² Language Arts Activity Book*, pp. WS 123, 131, 141–142

Advance Preparation

Gather the Write a First Draft page (students' draft paragraph) and Alexander's First Draft. If you have not already done so, remove pages WS 123 and 131 in *K¹² Language Arts Activity Book*.

Big Ideas

▸ Revision is best accomplished through discrete, focused tasks.
▸ One of the most powerful ways to improve writing is to directly teach strategies for planning and revising until students can use these strategies on their own.

Offline · 15 minutes

Revise for Content

You will work with students to complete Get Ready, Learn, and Try It activities.

Get Ready

Review Paragraph Parts

Review the parts of a paragraph with students.

1. Ask students if they remember what goes into a paragraph.

   ▸ What part of the paragraph tells you the main idea? topic sentence
   ▸ What are some of the things you see in a paragraph? a topic sentence, details, a concluding sentence

Objectives
- Recognize the purpose of a paragraph.
- Recognize the parts of a paragraph.
- Use concluding sentences.

2. Read this paragraph to students and ask them to tell you the topic of the paragraph and which sentence does not belong.

   ▶ *Beth loves dogs. She has two that look like twins. When she sleeps, they snuggle with her. The blanket is warm, too. They wait at the door for her to come home.* The topic is Beth's dogs. The sentence that does not belong is *The blanket is warm, too.*

3. Read the paragraph again, and ask students to think of a concluding sentence. Answers will vary. Possible answer: Beth thinks that dogs are good pets and great friends.

Learn

Fix Content

Help students practice revising a paragraph. Gather Alexander's First Draft, and turn to page WS 141 in *K¹² Language Arts Activity Book.*

1. **Say:** One of the things writers do when they revise is to fix the content or the ideas in the paragraph.

2. Explain that students should ask themselves these questions when they revise a piece of writing:

   ▶ Do all the details support the main idea? Delete any that do not.
   ▶ Should you move any of your details to make better sense? Move them.
   ▶ Should you rewrite any of your ideas? Rewrite them.
   ▶ Are there more ideas that could be added? Add them.

3. Read the rule on the Activity Book page. Use Alexander's First Draft to complete the Guided Exercises with students.

4. Have students use Alexander's First Draft to complete the rest of the Activity Book page. Provide support as necessary.

Objectives
- Revise for clarity.
- Revise by adding or deleting text.

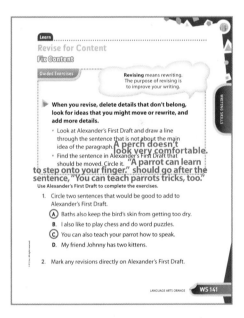

Try It ....

Revise Your Ideas

Help students revise the ideas in their paragraph. Gather the Write a First Draft page (students' draft paragraph), and turn to page WS 142 in *K¹² Language Arts Activity Book*.

1. Remind students that all writers, even real published authors, revise. Explain that students will revise their paragraph and look for ways to make their writing better.

2. **Say:** Revising means rewriting. As you revise you should

   ▸ Delete sentences that do not support the main idea.
   ▸ Add new sentences that contain details that support the main idea.
   ▸ Rewrite any ideas that could be written better.
   ▸ Move ideas if they make more sense somewhere else.

3. **Say:** Look at your paragraph to see if you can rewrite ideas, add details, or delete information that is not needed.

4. Read the directions to students.

5. Model for students how to draw a line through any text that has to be deleted and how to add a caret (^) to show where words or sentences are being added.

6. Have students revise their paragraph using the Activity Book page as a guide. Provide support as necessary.

7. Keep the Write a First Draft page (students' draft paragraph) in a safe place so students can continue to revise it.

TIP If students are comfortable making changes directly on their draft, they can do so instead of writing out changes on the Activity Book page.

Objectives

- Revise for clarity.
- Revise by adding or deleting text.
- Revise using a checklist.

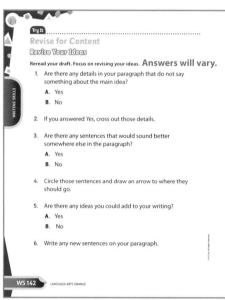

Revise a Paragraph

Lesson Overview

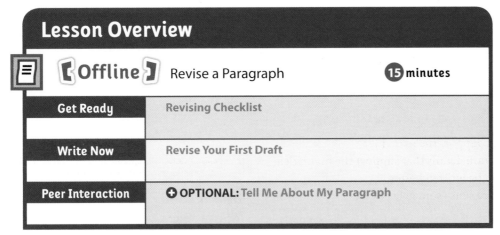

Offline	Revise a Paragraph	15 minutes
Get Ready	Revising Checklist	
Write Now	Revise Your First Draft	
Peer Interaction	⊕ OPTIONAL: Tell Me About My Paragraph	

Materials

Supplied

• *K¹² Language Arts Activity Book*, pp. WS 123, 143–148

Advance Preparation

Gather the Write a First Draft page (students' draft paragraph). If you have not already done so, remove page WS 123 in *K¹² Language Arts Activity Book*.

Big Ideas

▸ Revision is best accomplished through discrete, focused tasks.
▸ Working collaboratively with other students during various stages of the writing process can improve student writing.

Offline 15 minutes

Revise a Paragraph

You will work with students to complete Get Ready and Write Now activities.

Get Ready

Revising Checklist

Have students check the order of the ideas and the structure of their paragraph. Then help them use a checklist to make final revisions. Gather the Write a First Draft page, and turn to page WS 143 in *K¹² Language Arts Activity Book*.

1. Explain to students that they will use the Revising Checklist to help them revise their paragraph.

Objectives

• Recognize the purpose of a paragraph.
• Recognize the importance of revising written work.
• Make revisions based on audience and purpose.

2. Read the items on the checklist to students. Be sure students understand each question.

3. Review the revisions students made as they completed earlier lessons. Ask students if they are satisfied with those revisions. If they are, have students check those revisions off the list.

Write Now

 Revise Your First Draft

Have students revise the first draft of their paragraph. Gather the Write a First Draft page (students' draft paragraph), and turn to page WS 145 in *K¹² Language Arts Activity Book*.

1. Have students carefully read the instructions on the Activity Book page.

2. Tell students that they will create a complete and neat copy of their revised paragraph. Remind them to add any new or revised sentences to their paragraph, such as the beginning sentence, topic sentence, and concluding sentence.

3. Remind students to use complete sentences and indent the first line of the paragraph.

4. Have students write a complete and neat copy of their revised paragraph on the Activity Book page.

5. Use the rubric and the sample writing provided in the online lesson to check students' finished writing. You will be looking at students' writing to evaluate the following:

   ▸ Purpose and Content: The writing should be in the form of a paragraph. There should be a clear topic, main idea, and supporting details. The paragraph should show evidence of revision. The sentences should vary in length and choice of words.

   ▸ Structure and Organization: The paragraph should have a clear topic sentence that states the main idea. The paragraph should begin with a sentence that introduces the topic in an interesting way. The sentences should be in a logical order. The first line should be indented. Transitions should be used. There should be a concluding sentence.

   ▸ Grammar and Mechanics: All sentences should be complete and punctuated correctly. There may be some grammatical errors.

6. Enter students' scores for each rubric category online.

Objectives
- Use beginning sentences.
- Use concluding sentences.
- Use transitions to connect ideas.
- Revise for clarity.
- Revise using a checklist or rubric.
- Revise by adding or deleting text.
- Revise for logical order or sequence.
- Revise for sentence fluency.
- Revise for voice.
- Make revisions based on audience and purpose.
- Revise using feedback.

7. If students' writing scored a 1 in any category, work with them to revise their paragraph.

8. Keep the Write a First Draft page (students' revised paragraph) in a safe place so students can proofread, polish, and publish it later.

 TIP As you review the revision of students' paragraph, focus on the ideas and organization in the paragraph. Remember that this is not a completely polished paragraph. Students will work on editing, proofreading, and publishing it later. Be sure to provide feedback to students about their work.

Reward: When students' writing is Level 2 or higher on the grading rubric, add a sticker for this unit on the My Accomplishments chart.

Peer Interaction

⊕ OPTIONAL: Tell Me About My Paragraph

This activity is OPTIONAL. It is intended for students who have extra time and would benefit from extra practice. Feel free to skip this activity.

Students can benefit from exchanging paragraphs with someone they know or another student. To complete this optional activity, turn to page WS 147 in *K¹² Language Arts Activity Book*.

1. Have students exchange paragraphs with other students.

2. Have students use the Activity Book page to provide others with feedback about their writing.

3. Have students use the feedback to revise their own paragraphs.

 Objectives
- Use guidance from adults and peers to revise writing.
- Collaborate with peers on writing projects.

Semester Review

Unit Overview

In this unit, students will

► Review the grammar, usage, and mechanics skills that they have acquired this semester.
► Complete the two-part Checkpoint of those skills.

Materials

Supplied
● *K¹² Language Arts Activity Book*, pp. WS 1–4, 13–18, 31–34, 49–54, 65–72, 87–90, 105–110, 125–130

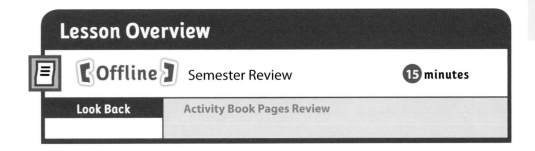

Lesson Overview

Offline	Semester Review	**15** minutes
Look Back	**Activity Book Pages Review**	

Advance Preparation

Gather the following pages in *K¹² Language Arts Activity Book*:

► WS 1–4 (Sentences, Sentences; Riddle Me; Begin and End It; Puddles of Sentences)
► WS 13–18 (State It; My Pet Wags; Do Your Ears Hang Low?; Ask a Question; Bumblebee Buzz; Two Kinds of Sentences)
► WS 31–34 (Jungle of Nouns; Noun Safari; Special Nouns; Puzzled About Nouns)
► WS 49–54 (Herb's Verbs; Fiddle-Dee-Dee Verbs; Interesting Verbs; Verb Crossword; Verb Play; Am, Is, Are, Was, Were)
► WS 65–72 (A Letter to Aunt Janie; Headings; Fix the Headings; Commas in Headings; Commas, Please; Capital Letters and Commas in Letters; Letter Fixes)
► WS 87–90 (One and More Than One; A Lot of Nouns; Tricky Nouns; Goose and Geese)
► WS 105–110 (Subjects and Verbs; Names and Actions; Making Subjects and Verbs Agree; I Agree!; Plural Subjects and Verbs; Plural Match Up)
► WS 125–130 (Miss Muffet Pronouns; Pick the Pronoun; We, Us, You, They, Them; Pronouns for More Than One; Special Pronouns; Pronoun Practice)

Offline ⏱ **15** minutes

Semester Review

You will work with students to complete the Look Back activity.

Look Back •••

 Activity Book Pages Review

Work with students to review pages they completed in *K12 Language Arts Activity Book*. Gather the Activity Book pages.

1. Focus on areas students struggled with during the semester.

2. Review the Guided Examples with students.

3. Ask students questions from the Activity Book pages.

4. Have students read the rules aloud and point out examples of the rules on the Activity Book pages.

Objectives

- Recognize word groups that are sentences.
- Use a capital letter to begin a sentence and an end mark to end it.
- Identify kinds of sentences.
- Identify and use proper and common nouns.
- Identify and use verbs in sentences.
- Use capital letters and commas correctly in the heading of a letter.
- Use capital letters and commas in the greeting and closing of a letter.
- Identify singular and plural nouns.
- Form and use plural nouns.
- Identify the subject and verb of a sentence.
- Use a verb that agrees with its subject.
- Recognize pronouns.
- Use singular and plural pronouns.
- Use possessive pronouns.

Semester Review:
Sentences, Nouns, and Verbs

Lesson Overview

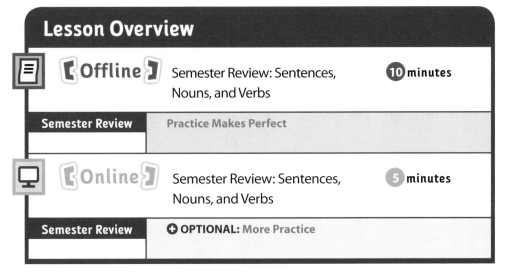

📄 [Offline]	Semester Review: Sentences, Nouns, and Verbs	**10** minutes
Semester Review	Practice Makes Perfect	
🖥 [Online]	Semester Review: Sentences, Nouns, and Verbs	**5** minutes
Semester Review	⊕ OPTIONAL: More Practice	

[Offline] **10** minutes

Semester Review: Sentences, Nouns, and Verbs
You will work with students to complete the Semester Review activity.

Semester Review •

Practice Makes Perfect
Help students review what they have learned this semester about sentences, nouns, and verbs. Turn to page WS 149 in *K¹² Language Arts Activity Book*.

1. Read the directions to students.

2. Have students complete the exercises. Provide support as necessary.

Objectives
- Recognize word groups that are sentences.
- Use a capital letter to begin a sentence and an end mark to end it.
- Identify kinds of sentences.
- Identify and use proper and common nouns.
- Identify and use verbs in sentences.

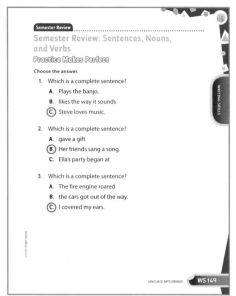

Semester Review

Semester Review: Sentences, Nouns, and Verbs

Practice Makes Perfect

Choose the answer.

1. Which is a complete sentence?
   - A. Plays the banjo.
   - B. likes the way it sounds
   - **C.** Steve loves music.

2. Which is a complete sentence?
   - A. gave a gift
   - **B.** Her friends sang a song.
   - C. Ella's party began at

3. Which is a complete sentence?
   - A. The fire engine roared
   - B. the cars got out of the way.
   - **C.** I covered my ears.

LANGUAGE ARTS ORANGE **WS 149**

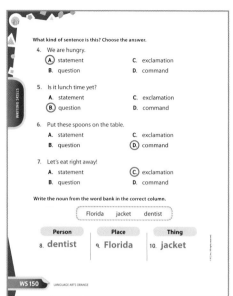

What kind of sentence is this? Choose the answer.

4. We are hungry.
   - **A.** statement
   - B. question
   - C. exclamation
   - D. command

5. Is it lunch time yet?
   - A. statement
   - **B.** question
   - C. exclamation
   - D. command

6. Put these spoons on the table.
   - A. statement
   - B. question
   - C. exclamation
   - **D.** command

7. Let's eat right away!
   - A. statement
   - B. question
   - **C.** exclamation
   - D. command

Write the noun from the word bank in the correct column.

Florida   jacket   dentist

Person	Place	Thing
8. dentist	9. Florida	10. jacket

WS 150 LANGUAGE ARTS ORANGE

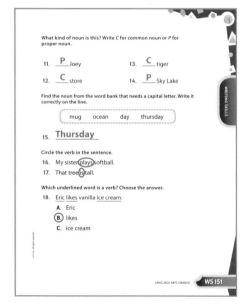

What kind of noun is this? Write *C* for common noun or *P* for proper noun.

11. __P__ Joey   13. __C__ tiger

12. __C__ store   14. __P__ Sky Lake

Find the noun from the word bank that needs a capital letter. Write it correctly on the line.

mug   ocean   day   thursday

15. __Thursday__

Circle the verb in the sentence.

16. My sister (plays) softball.

17. That tree (is) tall.

Which underlined word is a verb? Choose the answer.

18. Eric <u>likes</u> vanilla <u>ice cream</u>.
   - A. Eric
   - **B.** likes
   - C. ice cream

LANGUAGE ARTS ORANGE **WS 151**

 **5 minutes**

Semester Review: Sentences, Nouns, and Verbs

Students will work independently to complete the Semester Review activity. Help students locate the online activities and provide support as needed.

Semester Review ....

⊕ OPTIONAL: More Practice

This activity is OPTIONAL. This activity is intended for students who have extra time and would benefit from reviewing sentences, nouns, and verbs for the Semester Checkpoint. Feel free to skip this activity.

 Objectives
- Recognize word groups that are sentences.
- Use a capital letter to begin a sentence and an end mark to end it.
- Identify kinds of sentences.
- Identify and use proper and common nouns.
- Identify and use verbs in sentences.

Semester Checkpoint: Sentences, Nouns, and Verbs

Lesson Overview

[Offline]	Semester Checkpoint: Sentences, Nouns, and Verbs	**15** minutes
Semester Assessment	Semester Checkpoint	

[Materials]

Supplied
- *K¹² Language Arts Assessments,* pp. WS 33–37

[Offline] **15** minutes

Semester Checkpoint: Sentences, Nouns, and Verbs
Students will work independently to complete the Semester Checkpoint for sentences, nouns, and verbs.

Semester Assessment

Semester Checkpoint
Explain that students are going to show what they have learned about sentences, nouns, and verbs this semester.

1. Give students the Semester Checkpoint: Sentences, Nouns, and Verbs pages.

2. Read the directions together. Have students complete the Checkpoint on their own.

3. Use the Answer Key to score the Checkpoint, and enter the results online.

4. Review each exercise with students. Work with students to correct any exercise they missed.

Objectives
- Recognize word groups that are sentences.
- Use a capital letter to begin a sentence and an end mark to end it.
- Identify kinds of sentences.
- Identify and use proper and common nouns.
- Identify and use verbs in sentences.

Reward: When students score 80 percent or above on the Semester Checkpoint, add a sticker on the My Accomplishments chart.

Name _____ Date _____

Semester Checkpoint
Learning Coach Instructions
Sentences, Nouns, and Verbs

Explain that students are going to show what they have learned about sentences, nouns, and verbs this semester.

1. Give students the Semester Checkpoint: Sentences, Nouns, and Verbs pages.
2. Read the directions together. Have students complete the Checkpoint on their own.
3. Use the Answer Key to score the Checkpoint, and enter the results online.
4. Review each exercise with students. Work with students to correct any exercise they missed.

Name _____ Date _____

Semester Checkpoint Answer Key
Sentences, Nouns, and Verbs

Part 1. Complete Sentences
Which group of words is a complete sentence?

1.
   A. Wears a wool hat on winter days.
   B. Was cold and damp outside the tent.
   C. Snow fell all morning.

2.
   A. Lou heard a noise and ran away.
   B. Saw something scary in the bushes.
   C. The night that was dark.

Part 2. Sentence Beginnings and Endings
Which sentence begins and ends correctly?

3.
   A. Where is my glove!
   B. where is my glove.
   C. Where is my glove?

4.
   A. betty got a new bike.
   B. Betty got a new bike!
   C. betty got a new bike?

Name _____ Date _____

Part 3. Kinds of Sentences
Choose the sentence that is the kind of sentence listed.

5. Which sentence is a statement?
   A. Can we go to the circus?
   B. I'd love to see the elephants!
   C. We have a front row seat.

6. Which sentence is an exclamation?
   A. I saw your older brother today.
   B. Is he home for a visit?
   C. His hair is so long now!

7. Which sentence is a question?
   A. Why did the chicken cross the road?
   B. He did it to get to the other side.
   C. That's not a good joke!

8. Which sentence is a command?
   A. I'm sorry my room is messy.
   B. I've been so busy!
   C. Move those clothes and sit down.

Name _____ Date _____

Part 4. Nouns
Choose the noun or nouns in the sentence.

9. Kevin dances and sings really well.
   A. Kevin
   B. dances
   C. sings
   D. well

10. Come into the office and sit down.
   A. Come
   B. into
   C. office
   D. sit

11. Barry and Liz took the blue bus into town.
   A. Barry, Liz, bus, town
   B. took, bus, into, town
   C. Liz, took, bus, town

Name _____ Date _____

Part 5. Capital Letters
Which sentence uses capital letters correctly?

12.
   A. I opened the door for sue.
   B. i opened the door for Sue.
   C. I opened the door for Sue.

13.
   A. Mount Etna is actually a volcano.
   B. Mount Etna is actually a Volcano.
   C. Mount etna is actually a volcano.

Part 6. Verbs
Which word is the verb in the sentence?

14. Sasha runs five miles every day.
   A. Sasha
   B. runs
   C. miles
   D. day

15. That mirror is very large.
   A. mirror
   B. is
   C. very
   D. large

Semester Review: Letters, Nouns, Subjects & Verbs, and Pronouns

Lesson Overview

[Offline] Semester Review: Letters, Nouns, Subjects & Verbs, and Pronouns — **10** minutes

Semester Review	Practice Makes Perfect

[Online] Semester Review: Letters, Nouns, Subjects & Verbs, and Pronouns — **5** minutes

Semester Review	⊕ OPTIONAL: More Practice

Materials

Supplied
- *K¹² Language Arts Activity Book,* pp. WS 153–154

[Offline] **10** minutes

Semester Review: Letters, Nouns, Subjects, and Pronouns

You will work with students to complete the Semester Review activity.

Semester Review

Practice Makes Perfect

Help students review what they have learned this semester about capitalization and punctuation in letters, singular and plural nouns, subjects and verbs, and pronouns. Turn to page WS 153 in *K¹² Language Arts Activity Book.*

1. Read the directions to students.

2. Have students complete the exercises. Provide support as necessary.

Objectives

- Use capital letters and commas correctly in the heading of a letter.
- Use capital letters and commas in the greeting and closing of a letter.
- Identify singular and plural nouns.
- Form and use plural nouns.
- Identify the subject and verb of a sentence.
- Use a verb that agrees with its subject.
- Recognize pronouns.
- Use singular and plural pronouns.
- Use possessive pronouns.

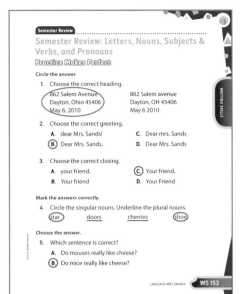

Semester Review
....

Semester Review: Letters, Nouns, Subjects & Verbs, and Pronouns

Practice Makes Perfect

Circle the answer.

1. Choose the correct heading.

   862 Salem Avenue
   Dayton, Ohio 45406
   May 6, 2010

   862 Salem avenue
   Dayton, OH 45406
   May 6 2010

2. Choose the correct greeting.

   A. dear Mrs. Sands!
   B. Dear Mrs. Sands,
   C. Dear mrs. Sands
   D. Dear Mrs. Sands

3. Choose the correct closing.

   A. your friend,
   B. Your friend
   C. Your friend,
   D. Your Friend

Mark the answers correctly.

4. Circle the singular nouns. Underline the plural nouns.

   star   doors   cherries   shoe

Choose the answer.

5. Which sentence is correct?

   A. Do mouses really like cheese?
   B. Do mice really like cheese?

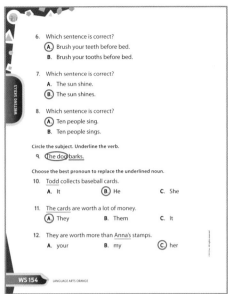

6. Which sentence is correct?

   A. Brush your teeth before bed.
   B. Brush your tooths before bed.

7. Which sentence is correct?

   A. The sun shine.
   B. The sun shines.

8. Which sentence is correct?

   A. Ten people sing.
   B. Ten people sings.

Circle the subject. Underline the verb.

9. The dog barks.

Choose the best pronoun to replace the underlined noun.

10. Todd collects baseball cards.

    A. It   B. He   C. She

11. The cards are worth a lot of money.

    A. They   B. Them   C. It

12. They are worth more than Anna's stamps.

    A. your   B. my   C. her

 **5** minutes

Semester Review: Letters, Nouns, Subjects, and Pronouns

Students will work independently to complete the Semester Review activity. Help students locate the online activities and provide support as needed.

Semester Review

⊕ OPTIONAL: More Practice

This activity is OPTIONAL. This activity is intended for students who have extra time and would benefit from reviewing capitalization and punctuation in letters, singular and plural nouns, subjects and verbs, and pronouns for the Semester Checkpoint. Feel free to skip this activity.

Objectives

- Use capital letters and commas correctly in the heading of a letter.
- Use capital letters and commas in the greeting and closing of a letter.
- Identify singular and plural nouns.
- Form and use plural nouns.
- Identify the subject and verb of a sentence.
- Use a verb that agrees with its subject.
- Recognize pronouns.
- Use singular and plural pronouns.
- Use possessive pronouns.

Semester Checkpoint: Letters, Nouns, Subjects & Verbs, and Pronouns

[Materials]

Supplied
- *K¹² Language Arts Assessments*, pp. WS 39–43

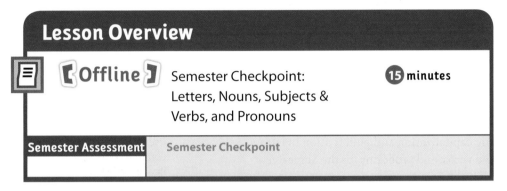

Lesson Overview

[Offline]	Semester Checkpoint: Letters, Nouns, Subjects & Verbs, and Pronouns	**15** minutes
Semester Assessment	Semester Checkpoint	

 **[Offline]** **15** minutes

Semester Checkpoint: Letters, Nouns, Subjects & Verbs, and Pronouns

Students will work independently to complete the Semester Checkpoint for letters, singular and plural nouns, subjects and verbs, and pronouns.

Semester Assessment ··

Semester Checkpoint

Explain that students are going to show what they have learned about capitalization and punctuation in letters, singular and plural nouns, subjects and verbs, and pronouns this semester.

1. Give students the Semester Checkpoint: Letters, Nouns, Subjects & Verbs, and Pronouns pages.

2. Read the directions together. Have students complete the Checkpoint on their own.

3. Use the Answer Key to score the Checkpoint, and enter the results online.

4. Review each exercise with students. Work with students to correct any exercise they missed.

 Reward: When students score 80 percent or above on the Semester Checkpoint, add a sticker on the My Accomplishments chart.

 Objectives
- Use capital letters and commas correctly in the heading of a letter.
- Use capital letters and commas in the greeting and closing of a letter.
- Identify singular and plural nouns.
- Form and use plural nouns.
- Identify the subject and verb of a sentence.
- Use a verb that agrees with its subject.
- Recognize pronouns.
- Use singular and plural pronouns.
- Use possessive pronouns.

Name _____ Date _____

Semester Checkpoint
Learning Coach Instructions
Letters, Nouns, Subjects & Verbs, and Pronouns

Explain that students are going to show what they have learned about capitalization and punctuation in letters, singular and plural nouns, subjects and verbs, and pronouns this semester.

1. Give students the Semester Checkpoint: Letters, Nouns, Subjects & Verbs, and Pronouns pages.
2. Read the directions together. Have students complete the Checkpoint on their own.
3. Use the Answer Key to score the Checkpoint, and enter the results online.
4. Review each exercise with students. Work with students to correct any exercise they missed.

Name _____ Date _____

Semester Checkpoint Answer Key
Letters, Nouns, Subjects & Verbs, and Pronouns

Part 1. Headings
Which heading is written correctly?

1. **(A)** 415 Bell Avenue
   Ames, Iowa 50010
   December 20, 2010

   B. 415 Bell avenue
   Ames, Iowa 50010
   December 20, 2010

2. A. 488 Briarhill Road
   Alta, Utah, 84092
   August, 19 2010

   (B) 488 Briarhill Road
   Alta, Utah 84092
   August 19, 2010

Part 2. Greetings and Closings
Which greeting or closing is written correctly?

3. A. Dear Jenny!
   B. Dear Jenny.
   (C) Dear Jenny,

4. A. Hello Mr. Richards
   B. Hello mr. Richards,
   (C) Hello Mr. Richards,

5. **(A)** Thank you,
   B. Thank you–
   C. Thank You.

Name _____ Date _____

Part 3. Singular and Plural Nouns
Choose the sentence with the kind of noun listed.

6. Which underlined word is a singular noun?
   A. The dog's feet are wet.
   B. Move the chairs away from the window.
   (C) I like the yellow and blue couch.
   D. Jack has a new set of beds.

7. Which underlined word is a plural noun?
   A. That rat is huge!
   B. The bus stops in front of the mall.
   (C) Did you see the cute puppies?
   D. I saw a black and white kitten.

8. Which underlined word is a plural noun?
   A. The white goose honked loudly.
   B. Kari is wearing a pretty lace dress.
   C. The circus is coming to town next week.
   (D) The mice made soft noises.

9. Which underlined word is correct in the sentence?
   A. Please hand me some hammer.
   (B) Please hand me some hammers.
   C. Please hand me some hammered.

Name _____ Date _____

Part 4. Identify Subjects and Verbs
Circle the subject and underline the verb in the sentence.

10. A fish swims.
11. The waves crash.
12. Tony and Maria dance.

Part 5. Match Subject to Verbs
Which verb goes with the subject?

13. Which sentence uses the correct verb?
    (A) One horse is brown and white.
    B. One horse are brown and white.

14. Which sentence uses the correct verb?
    A. The cowboys rides over the hill.
    (B) The cowboys ride over the hill.

Name _____ Date _____

Part 6. Pronouns
Which pronoun can replace the underlined word or words?

15. Bill gave a letter to Jeff.
    A. them
    (B) him
    C. her

16. Kelly wanted to read it, too.
    (A) She
    B. Her
    C. They

17. Then Sasha and Ellen asked to see it.
    A. we
    B. you
    (C) they

18. Can you give it to Will and me next?
    (A) us
    B. them
    C. they

19. It's not for George's sister.
    A. their
    B. him
    (C) his

20. The letter is Lisa's.
    A. ours
    (B) hers
    C. theirs

What Is Proofreading?

Unit Overview

In this unit, students will
- ▶ Use a dictionary and a thesaurus.
- ▶ Proofread their paragraph.
- ▶ Publish their paragraph.

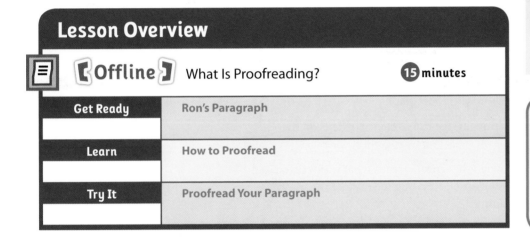

Lesson Overview

⟦ Offline ⟧	What Is Proofreading?	**15** minutes
Get Ready	Ron's Paragraph	
Learn	How to Proofread	
Try It	Proofread Your Paragraph	

⟦ Materials ⟧

Supplied
- *K¹² Language Arts Activity Book*, pp. WS 115, 145, 155–158

Also Needed
- whiteboard (optional)

Keywords
proofreading – the stage or step of the writing process in which the writer checks for errors in grammar, punctuation, capitalization, and spelling

Advance Preparation

Before you begin this unit, students need to have drafted and revised a paragraph. Students should use the paragraph that they drafted in the Write a Paragraph unit and revised in the Complete and Revise a Paragraph unit. Pull out page WS 155 in *K¹² Language Arts Activity Book* (Ron's Paragraph). Keep the page in a safe place so you can refer to it throughout the unit. Gather the Writing Process Chart and Revise Your First Draft page (students' revised paragraph). If you have not already done so, remove pages WS 115 and 145 in *K¹² Language Arts Activity Book*.

Content Background

- ▶ A complete sentence begins with a capital letter and ends with a mark of punctuation. For a group of words to be a complete sentence, it must also express a complete thought.
- ▶ There are two kinds of nouns: common nouns and proper nouns. A common noun names any person, place, or thing. A proper noun names a specific person, place, or thing. A proper noun is always capitalized.
- ▶ The subject and verb of a sentence must agree. A singular subject needs a singular verb, and a plural subject needs a plural verb. Common exceptions to the rule are the words *I* and *you*. Both words take the plural form of the verb.

Big Ideas

- ▶ Good writers carefully check their work for errors.

 **15** minutes

What Is Proofreading?

You will work with students to complete Get Ready, Learn, and Try It activities.

Get Ready

Ron's Paragraph

Review the steps in the writing process with students. Gather the Writing Process Chart and Ron's Paragraph, and turn to page WS 155 in *K¹² Language Arts Activity Book*.

1. Review the Writing Process Chart with students.

2. Remind students that they already completed the first steps in the writing process when they drafted and revised their paragraphs.

3. Have students point to the prewriting, drafting, and revising steps on the Writing Process Chart.

4. Remind students that revising is when the writer rereads what was written and makes changes to add ideas or fix the order. Revising means looking for ways to make your writing better, including

   ▶ Organizing your ideas better
   ▶ Rewriting to add or change ideas
   ▶ Adding or deleting details

5. Have students read Ron's Paragraph and think about ways to make it better.

6. Keep Ron's Paragraph and the Writing Process Chart in a safe place so that students can refer to them as they work through the lessons on proofreading.

> **Objectives**
> • Recognize the importance of revising written work.

Learn

How to Proofread

Explore proofreading with students. Gather Ron's Paragraph, and turn to page WS 157 in *K¹² Language Arts Activity Book*.

1. Explain that **proofreading** is a step in the writing process. To proofread, you look for and correct errors in grammar, punctuation, capitalization, and spelling. Fix errors by rereading each sentence, and look for these mistakes:

   ▶ Grammar errors such as subject-verb agreement and incomplete sentences
   ▶ Punctuation errors such as using the wrong end mark
   ▶ Capitalization errors in the first word in sentences and proper nouns
   ▶ Spelling errors in words you are not sure about

> **Objectives**
> • Proofread to improve grammar, spelling, punctuation, and capitalization.
> • Revise for clarity.
> • Revise for sentence fluency.

2. Write this sentence on a sheet of paper or a whiteboard:
   the dogs barks at the same tyme?
   Say: You can use **proofreading marks** to correct sentences. Draw a line or slash (/) through an error and write the correction above it. To add a word, draw a caret (^) and write the new word or words above it.

3. Explain that there are four errors in the sentence.

   ▸ What is the correct way to write this sentence? The dogs barked at the same time.
   ▸ Show students how to use slashes to fix the errors in the sentence.
   ▸ Show students how to use carets to add any new words or letters.

4. Explain that students will practice proofreading Ron's Paragraph before they proofread their own paragraph. Emphasize that both Ron's draft and the students' paragraph are not finished pieces of writing. They have to be checked for errors, and those errors have to be fixed.

5. Tell students that reading sentences aloud will help them find errors that they may miss when reading the sentences silently.

6. Read the rule on the Activity Book page. Complete the Guided Exercises with students.

7. Have students complete the rest of the Activity Book page. Provide support as necessary.

8. When students have completed the exercises on the Activity Book page, have them correct the errors on Ron's Paragraph. Some of the errors are on the Activity Book page, but students should look for others as well.

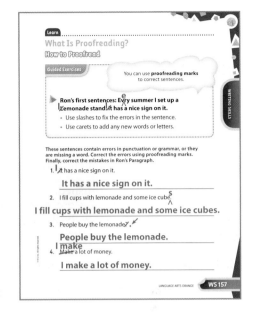

Try It

Proofread Your Paragraph

Help students proofread their sentences for errors. Gather the Revise Your First Draft page (students' revised paragraph), and turn to page WS 158 in *K*[12] *Language Arts Activity Book.*

1. Read the directions to students. Read the questions together.

2. Have students complete the activity. Provide support as necessary.

3. When students have finished, review the answers with them.

   ▸ Make sure that students made the proper edits to their paragraph.
   ▸ Have students read their edited sentences aloud.

4. Keep the Revise Your First Draft page (students' revised paragraph) in a safe place so students can finish proofreading it later.

Objectives

- Proofread to improve grammar, spelling, punctuation, and capitalization.
- Revise for clarity.
- Revise for sentence fluency.

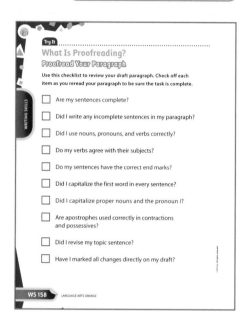

Try It

What Is Proofreading?

Proofread Your Paragraph

Use this checklist to review your draft paragraph. Check off each item as you reread your paragraph to be sure the task is complete.

☐ Are my sentences complete?

☐ Did I write any incomplete sentences in my paragraph?

☐ Did I use nouns, pronouns, and verbs correctly?

☐ Do my verbs agree with their subjects?

☐ Do my sentences have the correct end marks?

☐ Did I capitalize the first word in every sentence?

☐ Did I capitalize proper nouns and the pronoun *I*?

☐ Are apostrophes used correctly in contractions and possessives?

☐ Did I revise my topic sentence?

☐ Have I marked all changes directly on my draft?

WS 158   LANGUAGE ARTS ORANGE

Use a Dictionary

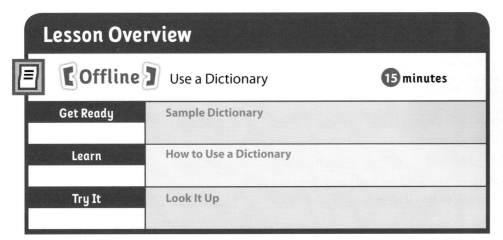

Lesson Overview

Offline	Use a Dictionary	**15** minutes
Get Ready	Sample Dictionary	
Learn	How to Use a Dictionary	
Try It	Look It Up	

Materials

Supplied
- *K¹² Language Arts Activity Book*, pp. WS 145, 159–162

Also Needed
- dictionary

Keywords

dictionary – a reference work made up of words with their definitions, in alphabetical order

guide words – two words at the top of a dictionary page that show the first and last words on the page

Advance Preparation

Gather the Revise Your First Draft page (students' revised paragraph) and Ron's Paragraph. If you have not already done so, remove pages WS 145 and 155 in *K¹² Language Arts Activity Book*.

Content Background

The writing process is fluid and recursive. Although we teach novice writers individual steps, good writers continually improve their work at various points until they are ready to publish. Help students understand that they can continue to make improvements even after the formal revision step of the process.

Big Ideas

It is important to know how to use reference materials such as dictionaries, thesauruses, atlases, almanacs, and others to find information.

 **Offline** ⏱ **15 minutes**

Use a Dictionary

You will work with students to complete Get Ready, Learn, and Try It activities.

Get Ready ●

Sample Dictionary

Introduce a dictionary and guide words to students. Turn to page WS 159 in *K¹² Language Arts Activity Book*.

1. **Say:** When you proofread, you improve your writing by correcting errors. You can use a **dictionary** to help you. A dictionary helps you check and fix the spelling of words. A dictionary also helps you use words correctly.

2. Tell students that they can use a dictionary at any point in the writing process. They don't need to wait until they proofread.

3. **Say:** Each word in a dictionary is called an *entry*. The entries are written in alphabetical (ABC) order.

4. **Say:** At the top of each dictionary page, there are two **guide words** that help you find the word you are looking for.

   ▶ Guide words show you which words can be found on that page.
   ▶ The words are written in ABC order.
   ▶ The word you are looking for will fall between the two guide words.
   ▶ The first guide word tells you the first word on the page. The second guide word tells you the last word on the page.

5. Tell students that if they do not know how a word is spelled, they can start with the letters that they do know, and then sound out the word and look it up.

6. Have students look at the Sample Dictionary page.

   ▶ What are the two guide words at the top of the page? pick, pin

7. Explain that the words on this page will come after the word *pick* in alphabetical order and before the word *pin*.

   ▶ What are some words that fall between *pick* and *pin* in alphabetical order?
   Answers will vary. Possible answers: pick, pie, piece, pig, pile, pin

8. Have students look at the Sample Dictionary page with you as you explain the parts of a dictionary entry. Explain that each entry shows the following:

   ▶ The correct spelling of the word
   ▶ The syllables in each word
   ▶ How to pronounce or say the word
   ▶ The part of speech (noun or verb)
   ▶ The meaning of the word
   ▶ An example of how the word is used in a sentence

Objectives

- Recognize the purpose of a dictionary.
- Use a dictionary.

9. Have students practice using the Sample Dictionary page.

   ▸ How do you spell the word *piece*? p i e c e
   ▸ How many syllables are in the word *pick*? one
   ▸ How do you pronounce the word *p-i-l-e*? pīl
   ▸ What part of speech is the word *pie*? noun
   ▸ What is the meaning of the word *pin*? a thin piece of metal with a sharp point
   ▸ Read the sentence that shows how to use the word *pig*. A pig loves to roll in the mud.

Learn

How to Use a Dictionary

Help students practice using a dictionary and guide words. Gather a dictionary and Ron's Paragraph, and turn to page WS 161 in *K¹² Language Arts Activity Book*.

1. Review with students what information can be found in a **dictionary**.

   ▸ What kinds of information can you find in a dictionary? the spelling of words, what words mean, how words are used in sentences, the syllables in words, how words are pronounced

2. Have students look at a dictionary. Have them point to the **guide words** on a page.

   ▸ What do guide words tell you? They tell you what words are on that page. All the words on the page are between the guide words in alphabetical order.

3. Have students pick a word they don't know from the dictionary. Answers will vary.

   ▸ How is the word pronounced?
   ▸ What is the definition of the word?
   ▸ How many syllables does it have?

4. Have students pick several other words and tell you their pronunciation, definition, and number of syllables.

5. Read the rule on the Activity Book page. Complete the Guided Exercises with students.

6. Have students complete the rest of the Activity Book page. Provide support as necessary.

7. Have students use a dictionary to correct the spelling of words in Ron's Paragraph. Have them mark changes on the page.

8. Keep Ron's Paragraph in a safe place so students can finish proofreading it later.

Objectives

- Recognize the purpose of a dictionary.
- Use a dictionary.

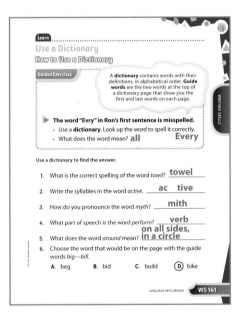

Try It

Look It Up

Help students use a dictionary. Gather the Revise Your First Draft page (students' revised paragraph), and turn to page WS 162 in *K¹² Language Arts Activity Book*.

1. Read the directions to students. Read the definitions and the words in the word bank together.

2. Have students complete the activity. Make sure that they write each word by putting its first letter in the box with the correct number. Words go across (left to right) or down (top to bottom). Provide support as necessary.

3. Have students use a dictionary to check the spelling of words in their own draft paragraph. Have them mark changes on the draft.

4. Keep the Revise Your First Draft page (students' revised paragraph) in a safe place so students can continue to proofread it.

(TIP) Remind students to use the guide words at the top of dictionary pages to help find words.

Objectives
- Recognize the purpose of a dictionary.
- Use a dictionary.

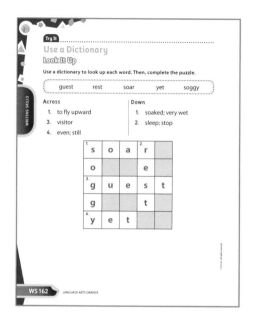

Use a Thesaurus

Lesson Overview

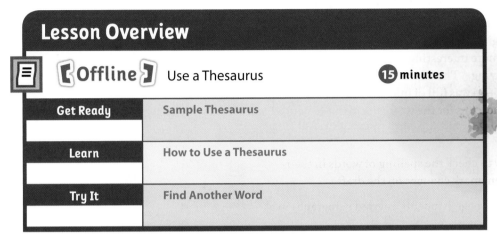

[Offline] Use a Thesaurus   🕐 15 minutes

Get Ready	Sample Thesaurus
Learn	How to Use a Thesaurus
Try It	Find Another Word

[Materials]

Supplied

- *K¹² Language Arts Activity Book*, pp. WS 145, 155, 163–166

Also Needed

- thesaurus

Keywords

thesaurus – a reference work that gives synonyms and antonyms for words

Advance Preparation

Gather the Revise Your First Draft page (students' revised paragraph) and Ron's Paragraph. If you have not already done so, remove pages WS 145 and 155 in *K¹² Language Arts Activity Book*.

Big Ideas

- ▶ The writing process is fluid and recursive. Writers make improvements to their drafts as needed.
- ▶ It is important to know how to use reference materials such as dictionaries, thesauruses, atlases, almanacs, and others to find information.

[Offline] 🕐 15 minutes

Use a Thesaurus

You will work with students to complete Get Ready, Learn, and Try It activities.

Get Ready ···

Sample Thesaurus

Introduce a thesaurus to students. Turn to page WS 163 in *K¹² Language Arts Activity Book*.

1. Ask students why they would use a dictionary when they are writing. to correct words that are spelled or used incorrectly, or to look up the meaning of a word

Objectives

- Recognize the purpose of a thesaurus.

2. **Say:** You can use the dictionary to make your writing better any time during the writing process. Another writer's tool is the **thesaurus**.

3. Explain that a **thesaurus** helps you find new words to replace the words you used in your writing.

   ▸ Some words are used too often. Words like "good" or "nice" are used over and over, but they do not give the reader a clear picture. It is better to replace these words with more interesting or descriptive words.

   ▸ For example, instead of saying, "The trip was good," you could say, "The trip was exciting" or "The trip was full of information."

   ▸ Have students suggest synonyms for the word *nice* in the sentence *I had a nice time*. Answers will vary. Possible answers: great, fun, exciting, terrific, wonderful

4. **Say:** A thesaurus is similar to a dictionary. The words are listed in alphabetical order.

   ▸ Some words have more than one meaning. Each meaning is listed separately. Make sure you are using the correct meaning when you look up each word. For example, the word *great* can mean "wonderful" or "large." In a sentence like *The boys had a great time*, only one of those meanings (wonderful) would make sense.

   ▸ A thesaurus can be used at any point during the writing process.

   ▸ A thesaurus gives you synonyms for each word. Synonyms are words that mean the same thing.

   ▸ A thesaurus also gives you antonyms for words. Antonyms are words that have the opposite meaning.

5. Have students look at the Sample Thesaurus page with you as you explain the parts of a thesaurus entry. Explain that each entry shows you

   ▸ The correct spelling of the word
   ▸ The part of speech (noun or verb)
   ▸ Words that have the same meaning (synonyms) and words that have the opposite meaning (antonyms) of the entry

6. Have students use the Sample Thesaurus page to answer these questions.

   ▸ How do you spell the word *repeat*? r e p e a t
   ▸ What part of speech is the word *return*? verb
   ▸ What are some synonyms for the word *reward*? prize, award, bonus, tip
   ▸ What are some antonyms for the word *return*? avoid, keep

Learn

How to Use a Thesaurus

Help students practice how to use a thesaurus. Gather a thesaurus and Ron's Paragraph, and turn to page WS 165 in *K¹² Language Arts Activity Book*.

1. Review with students what information can be found in a thesaurus.

   ▸ What kinds of information can be found in a thesaurus? synonyms and antonyms

2. Have students look at a thesaurus. Have them pick a word. Answers will vary.

   ▸ What are some synonyms for the word?
   ▸ What are some antonyms for the word?
   ▸ Are there different meanings for the word?

3. Have students pick several other words and give you their synonyms and antonyms.

4. Read the rule and example on the Activity Book page. Use Ron's Paragraph to complete the Guided Exercises with students. Have students mark changes directly on Ron's Paragraph.

5. Have students complete the rest of the Activity Book page. Provide support as necessary.

6. Keep Ron's Paragraph in a safe place so students can finish proofreading it later.

TIP Tell students to look up a verb in the present tense to find a synonym. For example, to find a synonym for the word *sat* you would have to look up *sit*.

Objectives
- Recognize the purpose of a thesaurus.
- Use a thesaurus.

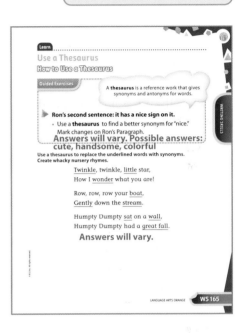

Try It

Find Another Word

Help students use a thesaurus. Gather the Revise Your First Draft page (students' revised paragraph), and turn to page WS 166 in *K¹² Language Arts Activity Book.*

1. Read the directions to students. Read the paragraph with students.

2. Have students complete the Activity Book page. Provide support as necessary.

3. Have students use a thesaurus to look up words they used in their revised paragraph.

4. Have students replace words if they find a better alternative in the paragraph. Have them mark changes on their revised paragraph.

5. Keep the Revise Your First Draft page (students' revised paragraph) in a safe place so students can continue to proofread it.

TIP Encourage students to replace words in their paragraph if they find a better one in the thesaurus. However, remind them that the original word they chose is often the best word. Synonyms often have slightly different meanings. Students should think carefully before they replace a familiar word with an unfamiliar one.

Objectives
- Recognize the purpose of a thesaurus.
- Use a thesaurus.

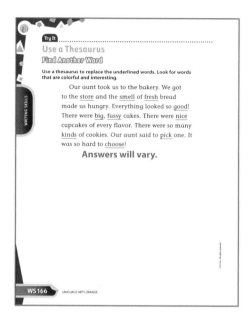

Try It

Use a Thesaurus
Find Another Word

Use a thesaurus to replace the underlined words. Look for words that are colorful and interesting.

Our aunt took us to the bakery. We got to the <u>store</u> and the <u>smell</u> of <u>fresh</u> bread made us hungry. Everything looked so <u>good</u>! There were <u>big</u>, <u>fussy</u> cakes. There were <u>nice</u> cupcakes of every flavor. There were so many <u>kinds</u> of cookies. Our aunt said to <u>pick</u> one. It was so hard to <u>choose</u>!

Answers will vary.

WS 166   LANGUAGE ARTS ORANGE

Use a Checklist

Lesson Overview

[Offline] Use a Checklist	**15** minutes

Get Ready	Writer's Checklist
Learn	Use the Checklist
Try It	Polish Your Paragraph

Materials

Supplied

- *K¹² Language Arts Activity Book*, pp. WS 145, 155, 167–170

Advance Preparation

Gather the Revise Your First Draft page (students' revised paragraph) and Ron's Paragraph. If you have not already done so, remove pages WS 145 and 155 in *K¹² Language Arts Activity Book*.

Big Ideas

- ▶ Good writers carefully check their work for errors.
- ▶ It is important to know how to use reference materials such as dictionaries, thesauruses, atlases, almanacs, and others to find information.

 **[Offline]** **15** minutes

Use a Checklist

You will work with students to complete Get Ready, Learn, and Try It activities.

Get Ready ....

Writer's Checklist

Introduce the writer's checklist to students. Turn to page WS 167 in *K¹² Language Arts Activity Book*.

1. Review what it means to revise and proofread writing.
   Say: When you revise and proofread your writing, you do several things:

   - ▶ Find and fix errors in grammar, punctuation, capitalization, and spelling.
   - ▶ Replace words with better or more interesting words.
   - ▶ Improve your writing for content or structure.

Objectives

- Recognize the importance of proofreading to improve grammar, spelling, punctuation, and capitalization.

2. Remind students that they can always go back and make fixes to their work. The writing process is not a strict process you have to follow in one direction from beginning to end. Good writers go back and forth among all the steps as they write.

3. Explain that a **checklist** is one way to revise your writing. The checklist reminds you what to look for as you reread your writing.

4. Have students read through the checklist.

   ▸ What are some of the things the checklist reminds you to do? look for errors in grammar, punctuation, capitalization, and spelling; use a thesaurus to look for better words; use a dictionary to check the spelling and meanings of words

5. Keep the Writer's Checklist in a safe place so students can continue to refer to it.

Learn

Use the Checklist

Help students practice using the Writer's Checklist. Gather Ron's Paragraph and the Writer's Checklist, and turn to page WS 169 in *K¹² Language Arts Activity Book*.

1. Remind students that proofreading means finding and fixing errors. Even while proofreading, you can still look for ways to improve your choice of words and make your writing more interesting or readable.

2. Read the rule and examples on the Activity Book page. Use the Writer's Checklist to complete the Guided Exercises with students.

3. Have students complete the rest of the Activity Book page. Provide support as necessary.

4. Remind students to mark their changes on the paragraph by crossing out words or using a caret and writing the correction above the error or word that has to be replaced.

5. Have students use the checklist to go over Ron's Paragraph.

   ▸ Ask students if they have checked all of the errors mentioned in the checklist.

   ▸ Have students mark any additional corrections directly on Ron's Paragraph.

Objectives
- Proofread to improve grammar, spelling, punctuation, and capitalization.
- Use a checklist for editing and proofreading.

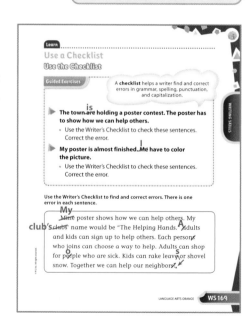

Try It

Polish Your Paragraph

Help students edit their paragraph. Gather the Revise Your First Draft page (students' revised paragraph) and Writer's Checklist, and turn to page WS 170 in *K¹² Language Arts Activity Book.*

1. Read the directions to students.

2. Have students edit their paragraph. Provide support as necessary.

3. Remind students to use the Writer's Checklist when checking their work.

4. Keep the Revise Your First Draft page (students' revised paragraph) and Writer's Checklist in a safe place.

TIP Model for students how to draw a line through any text that has to be changed. Add a caret (^) in the paragraph to show where words or punctuation are being added. Students can also rewrite their sentences on the Activity Book page.

Objectives

- Proofread to improve grammar, spelling, punctuation, and capitalization.
- Use a checklist for editing and proofreading.

Publish Your Work

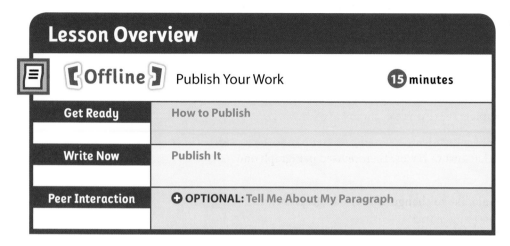

Lesson Overview

[Offline] Publish Your Work		15 minutes
Get Ready	**How to Publish**	
Write Now	**Publish It**	
Peer Interaction	⊕ OPTIONAL: **Tell Me About My Paragraph**	

[Materials]

Supplied
- *K¹² Language Arts Activity Book*, pp. WS 115, 145, 167, 171–174

Advance Preparation

Gather the Writing Process Chart, Revise Your First Draft page (students' revised paragraph), and Writer's Checklist. If you have not already done so, remove pages WS 115, 145, and 167 in *K¹² Language Arts Activity Book*.

Big Idea

Writers publish their final work by sharing it with others.

[Offline] 15 minutes

Publish Your Work

You will work with students to complete Get Ready and Write Now activities.

Get Ready ••

How to Publish

Introduce students to publishing. Gather the Writing Process Chart, Revise Your First Draft page (students' revised paragraph), and Writer's Checklist.

1. Have students look at the Writing Process Chart.

   ▸ What parts of the writing process have you done already? prewriting, drafting, revising, proofreading

2. Explain to students that they are ready for the last step in the writing process—publishing their work.

Objectives
- Write sentences and paragraphs that develop a central idea, consider purpose and audience, and use the writing process.
- Revise for clarity.
- Revise for sentence fluency.
- Use a checklist for editing and proofreading.

3. **Say: Publishing** your writing means making a clean and final copy that is ready for sharing.

   ▸ The final copy should not have any errors.
   ▸ All the revising and proofreading changes should have been made already.

4. Explain that the final copy should be written clearly and neatly on a clean sheet of paper.

   ▸ Why is it important to make a clear, neat copy of your writing before you share it with others? so your work is easy to read

5. Remind students to write in complete sentences and indent the first line of the paragraph.

6. Have students use the Writer's Checklist to review their revised paragraph one last time.

   ▸ Are there any things you would like to change in your paragraph before you make the final copy? Answers will vary.

Write Now

Publish It

Help students publish their paragraph. Gather the Revise Your First Draft page (students' revised paragraph), and turn to page WS 171 in *K¹² Language Arts Activity Book*.

1. Explain that students will publish a clean and neat copy of their paragraph.

2. Remind them to add any new or revised sentences to their paragraph, including the beginning sentence, topic sentence, and concluding sentence.

3. Have students make sure they have used complete sentences and indented the first line of the paragraph.

4. Tell students that they should use good handwriting and leave spaces between words so that others can read what they wrote.

5. Have students write a complete and neat copy of their paragraph on the Activity Book page.

6. Use the materials and instructions in the online lesson to evaluate students' finished writing. You will be evaluating their writing for the following:

   ▸ Purpose and Content: The writing should be in the form of a paragraph. There should be a clear topic, main idea, and supporting details. The paragraph should show evidence of revision. The sentences should show variety in length and choice of words. There should be some interesting or colorful word choices.
   ▸ Structure and Organization: The paragraph should begin with a topic sentence. The sentences should be in a logical order. The first line should be indented. Transitions should be used. There should be a concluding sentence.
   ▸ Grammar and Mechanics: All sentences should have been proofread and there should be few if any errors.

Objectives
• Write legibly following appropriate format.

7. Enter students' scores for each rubric category online.

8. If students' writing scored a 1 in any category, work with them to proofread and revise their work.

 When students complete their final draft, allow them to draw in the space provided on the Activity Book page. Encourage them to draw a picture that goes with their paragraph.

Reward: When students' writing is Level 2 or higher on the grading rubric, add a sticker for this unit on the My Accomplishments chart.

Peer Interaction

⊕ OPTIONAL: Tell Me About My Paragraph

This activity is OPTIONAL. This activity is intended for students who have extra time and would benefit from extra practice. Feel free to skip this activity.

Students can benefit from exchanging paragraphs with someone they know or another student. To complete this optional activity, turn to page WS 173 in the Activity Book.

Objectives

- Use guidance from adults and peers to revise writing.
- Collaborate with peers on writing projects.

1. Have students exchange paragraphs with other students.

2. Have students use the Activity Book page to provide others with feedback about their writing.

3. Have students use the feedback to revise their paragraph.